The Best Of

Popular science

Do-it-yourself

The Best Of

Popular Science

Do-it-yourself

Published by
Popular Science Books
Popular Science Books, New York, NY

Published by

Popular Science Books
Grolier Book Clubs Inc.
380 Madison Avenue
New York, NY 10017

Library of Congress Cataloging-in-Publication Data

The Best of Popular Science do-it-yourself.

  Includes index.
  1. Dwellings — Maintenance and repair — Amateurs'
manuals. 2. Dwellings — Remodeling — Amateurs'
manuals. 3. Woodwork — Amateurs' manuals. I. Popular
Science (New York, N.Y.)
TH4817.3.B475 1988 643'.7 88-2508
ISBN 1-55654-033-7

Manufactured in the United States of America

introduction

For many, *Popular Science* has been America's What's New magazine since 1872. Electric lights, refrigeration, and the telephone were just a few of the innovations worth writing about as the 19th century drew to a close. But for the fledgling magazine — and its readers of today — the automobile may have been the most significant invention because it gave rise to the suburbs. By the 1920s more and more families were experiencing the joys of home ownership, along with the fix-it hassles that go with it. And *Popular Science* was no longer just America's What's New Magazine; it had become America's How-to magazine as well. It remains so to this day, with over a third of each monthly issue devoted solely to home and workshop.

The Best of DIY

This volume comprises over 100 of the most informative, most rewarding *Popular Science* home-project articles of the past several years. The step-by-step advice and procedures you'll find inside take you through every part of your home, indoors and out.

You'll find projects conveniently arranged under five major headings. Some of them are the practical kind you'll want to have around for fast, everyday reference. Examples include Richard Day's "Kit for Emergency Plumbing Repairs," E. F. Lindsley's "Tuning Up Your Mower," and John Robinson's "Furniture Repairs" (yes, even seemingly hopeless breaks can usually be repaired with professional results right in your own living room). Other projects will spark your imagination with complete home remodeling and renovation ideas. The Home Remodeling section gives you a variety of ways to do exactly that — from creating a handsome basement entertainment area to raising your roof to gain needed living space without adding out. And if you don't believe a 1950s tract house could ever be a showplace, turn to page 32 and see how they did it in Boston.

The Most Popular Projects

Bathrooms, kitchens, decks, and storage spaces are America's most popular project areas, according to home-center industry experts. More than half of the 64 woodworking projects in Section III are concerned solely with bathrooms, kitchens, decks, and storage spaces. (These are also the projects that will put the most money in your bank account should you decide to sell your home.) And all of them are lavishly illustrated, often with full-color sequenced photos and detailed drawings by the most talented draftsmen-designers in the business.

Analysts also predict that America's DIY-related industry will grow from the $15 billion per year it accounted for just a few years ago to more than $60 billion by the turn of the century. Reasons for this growth include the increasing number of people entering the active do-it-yourself years — particularly women. But perhaps the best explanation of why more and more men and women are picking up hammer and saw is the money they save by helping design and build a new home (see pages 2 through 31) or rescuing a "handyman special" from oblivion.

Money-saving Techniques for Homeowners, Woodworkers — and More

Have you ever tried removing dried paint, candle wax, or cigarette burns from a wood floor? There *is* an easy way. How about installing a deadbolt lock or replacing a window frame? What should you look for when shopping for plastic plumbing — and look *out* for when wiring wall and ceiling fixtures? The answers to these questions can save you hundreds and even thousands of dollars, not to mention the needless risks uninformed homeowners take every year. You'll find those answers laid out for you under Home Repair and Maintenance.

If you love woodworking for the sheer pleasure of it, this book is for you, too. In fact it includes more in-depth advice on tool techniques, jigs, cuts, and choosing the right materials than you're likely to find in ordinary woodworking books. Then there are the projects themselves. The classic mahogany cupboard plans beginning on page 90, the Queen Anne table on page 132, and the colonial dollhouse on page 178 are but three examples of the heirloom-quality furniture projects included herein.

There's also an article from *Home* magazine, two from *Home Mechanix,* and five from *Practical Homeowner* to round out the contents. In all, it's a veritable smorgasbord for anyone who has ever enjoyed pointing to something and saying, "I made it myself." We know you'll learn from this book, save money with it, and enjoy the many projects it guides you through.

ROBERT A. MARKOVICH
Senior Editor
Popular Science Books

contents

Woodworking Techniques and Materials 274

Home Repair and Maintenance 310

post-and-beam kit homes

A precut woodland retreat needn't be dark and staid, as the owners of this vacation home well know. Built off a long unpaved road that runs through the heart of East Hampton's northwest woods, the cottage stands on one of the last expanses of forest left on Long Island. It's a surprising location in a resort area known primarily for its ocean beaches and potato fields.

The owners were drawn immediately to post-and-beam home kits. "We wanted a small, traditional-looking vacation home," said the owner, "and we liked the rugged look of exposed beams." After researching various companies, the clients settled on a Timberpeg kit. They were attracted by the package's high-quality components, design flexibility, and energy efficiency.

With the choice made, the clients hired Southampton-based designer Richard Lear. Lear, who had modified many Timberpeg house kits, showed them several Long Island houses he had designed; this gave his clients an idea of the different roofs and windows they could select. After these basic design decisions were made, Lear further developed his design around the bare bones of a 20-foot-wide Timberpeg barn kit.

Aware that the vacation home of their dreams would not spring complete from the Timberpeg kit alone, the owners and Lear embellished the package with additional features: A back-to-back brick fireplace was used to separate the dining area from the 16-square-foot living room; a 10-foot-wide shed dormer was added to the

The 10-foot-wide dormer (top) over the entry was added to the stock plan. The upstairs study (left) sits over openings to the entry and the kitchen. A corner post (above), helped by twin knee braces, holds up intersecting beams.

roof to highlight the main entrance below and provide space for a whirlpool tub in the upstairs bathroom; French doors open up the two-story dining area to southern light and give access to a brick patio; half-round windows at either end of the house were custom-made to match perfectly with the double-hung windows that came with the kit.

The posts, beams, shingles, clapboard and insulating material arrived on two 42-foot-long flatbed trucks from Claremont, New Hampshire, where the lumber is milled in the Timberpeg factory. Over 200 timber parts are marked to aid the builder in the assembly process. Letters and numbers on the timber correspond to letters and numbers on the set of blueprints the company supplies.

Bob Barmore, a builder who had once been a regional sales representative for Timberpeg, supervised the construction of the house. The project took less than six months to complete.

Both the designer and the owners wanted the house to harmonize with the natural, wooded setting of the two-acre site. Clear cedar clapboard, hand-split cedar shakes, and a brick chimney evoke a rustic woodland cottage, while the steep 90-degree pitch of the roof echoes the shapes of tall white pines surrounding the property.

In the same spirit, landscaping, by landscape designer David Seeler, was created to blend in with the surrounding forest. Small holly trees, a birch tree, some indigenous bushes and a wildflower garden were planted in keeping with the sylvan setting. A low-maintenance groundcover of bark chips was laid in place of a front lawn, and a classic white picket fence was used to enclose the backyard.

The country looks of the house's exterior were carried over into the interior spaces where the post-and-beam framing is exposed. The solid timber, ranging from 4x4s to hefty 8x12s, is joined together by real mortise and tenon joints that are pinned together with oak pegs the size of fat cigars.

Comlementing the airiness of the home's interior, the rooms project a simple, well-scrubbed brightness. Pine framing was pickled with a white stain, and the 1-by-6-inch pine floorboards were painted with a white epoxy deck paint. The pickling idea, which designer Lear had used in several of his other post-and-beam projects, "gave the house more of a modern feel," said the client. Consistent with the pale tones of the wood, buff-colored 12-square-inch ceramic tiles were laid in the entry and kitchen floors.

The custom touches and quality finish work brought the project's cost in at close to $120 per square foot, but greatly added to the home's charm. The personal elements reflected in the carefully chosen options make this vacation home well worth retreating to — by Alastair Gordeon. Photos by David Frazier.

The living room's Palladian windows (left) were added to bring daylight into the upper reaches of the cathedral ceiling. Track lighting mounted on the collar beam takes care of area lighting at night. A plank-floored area opposite the kitchen (above) is used for dining. French doors, which can be opened onto the deck, provide light, while the double-facing fireplace supplies warmth.

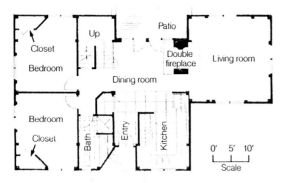

Clever additions to this post-and-beam package include a double fireplace, brick patio and shed dormer above entry.

LIST OF MANUFACTURERS

House by Timberpeg, Box 1500, Claremont, NH 03743; **Architectural Design** by Richard Lear, R. Lear Design, 30 Main St., Southampton, NY 11968; **Contracting** by Robert P. Barmore, Barmore Building Inc., P.O. Box 2037, Southampton, NY 11968; **Cabinetry** custom-made by John Nolan and Bruce McMann of R. Lear Design; **Palladian and Angled Windows** custom-made by Woodstone Co., Patch Rd., Box 223, Westminster, VT 04158; **All Other Windows** by Brosco Windows, 146 Dascomb Rd., Andover, MA 01810; **French Doors** by C-E Morgan Inc., 523 Oregon St., Oshkosh, WI 54901; **Tile** by American Olean Tile Co., 1000 Cannon Ave., P.O. Box 271, Lansdale, PA 19446-0271. Living room/Dining room: **Track Lighting** by Lightolier, 100 Lighting Way, Secaucus, NJ 07094-0508; **Ceiling Fan** by Hunter Fans, Robbins & Meyers Inc., Comfort Conditioning Div., 2500 Frisco Ave., Memphis, TN 38114.

The living-room side of the fireplace (left) offers a cozy niche with views across the 1,790-square-foot house. The U-shaped kitchen (top) is self-contained. Upstairs bedroom (above) provides ample storage with large wall closets. Roof dormer (next page) gives the upstairs bath extra room. Offset twin gables in the living room and main house allow more windows and offer a striking view.

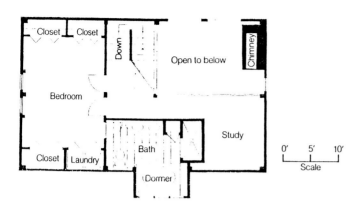

log homes aren't just cabins anymore

Impossible was the word my friend used. "I don't know a soul who is paying under $300 a month for the mortgage on a new house," he said. "Our fathers may have paid less than $300, but times have changed."

I admitted that house prices, mortgages, interest rates—everything—had been troublesome in recent years. But I explained that about $300 or less a month could conceivably be what he'd pay to live comfortably in a three-bedroom, one-bath, 960-square-foot log house. That figure represents about the monthly charge for principal and interest on a twenty-five-year mortgage required to put up the house.

Is there a catch? Not if the buyer is willing to put in his own labor, and assuming he already owns a small parcel of land. Here's how:

● Precut package (logs are precision-cut, predrilled, and numbered for walls. Package also includes posts for foundation, all other structural parts, spikes, sealant, caulking, trim, windows, and doors). Cost: about $20,000.

● All other materials and equipment (purchased locally) to complete the house. Cost: about $8,000.

● Foundation (logs for post foundation included in precut materials). Cost: $0.

● Labor (by owners, family, friends). Cost: $0. (This isn't quite true, because buyers do spend some money, even if family members pitch in; there are extra meals, for example, and perhaps a case of beer now and then. Trade-offs are another way to get "free" labor; an owner might, for example, trade the muscle-power to cut and deliver several cords of firewood for the services of a friend who just happens to be a licensed plumber.)

● Land (previously owned.) Cost: $0.

● Utilities (wiring and plumbing—enough to run house lines into the ground—are included in materials purchased locally). Cost: $0.

The only costs, then, are for the precut package and for the locally purchased materials you need. That brings the total to $28,000. After deducting a $7,000 down payment, a $21,000 mortgage is required, assumed here to be a twenty-five-year loan at about current rates.

The log house described is the AMP Econ-O-Plus, developed by Appalachian Log Structures. "AMP" stands for "Affordable Mortgage Payment." The company also offers a two-bedroom, one-bath, 720-square-foot model for a package price and estimated materials costs that are several thousand dollars less than the Econo-O-Plus.

While these prices may seem unusually modest, they are consistent with packages offered by most log-house manufacturers. The companies also produce many precut models containing between 1000 and 2500 square feet for package prices between $15,000 and $35,000 and finished costs in the 50s and 60s. Some log-house firms have been involved with homes costing over $500,000.

Once up and properly sealed, log houses deliver another saving—energy. "We were very pleasantly surprised," said Hal Dunham, an executive with Edison Electric Institute in Washington, D.C., referring to his utility bill. His log home is all-electric, and bills for December and January of one winter were only about $250 per month. "Owners of neighboring frame houses with less than our 3,500 square feet were paying that much just for the heating oil," he reported.

Wood is a natural insulator and thick wood is a heat bank, absorbing heat (solar or man-made) during the day and releasing it during cold winter nights. Most log walls are from 6 to 8 inches thick, and some are as much as 12 inches thick. None of these walls

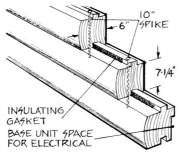

Most log houses are sold for use as year-round homes. Home below is from Ward; the one above is from Southern Structures. Indoors view, above right, model from Lincoln Logs, Ltd., Chesterton, NY, features flat-cut logs for easy furniture placement. Drawing and photo at right show log-joining techniques.

require additional insulation. In fact, log walls represent another saving—time. A frame wall begins on the outside with siding; then there's sheathing, framing, insulation, vapor barrier, plasterboard, taping, spackling, and either paint or wallpaper. A log wall, stacked once, is the finished exterior and interior, insulation and structural support, all in one.

Roy and Karen Ruddle of Hurricane, West Virginia, embarked on construction of their own log home last September, and it was ready for occupancy in mid-April. "Our log walls went up easily," says Karen. "Knowing they would help us make the decision to buy a log-house package. Finishing the inside, though, went more slowly than we expected, but then we had never done this before."

Was building their own log house worth the effort? "At first, we didn't think we could afford a loan for a house because the interest rates are so high," says Karen. "But then we discovered that log-house prices are more reasonable, and we both like the rough style (or maybe I talked Roy into it). Now that the house is com-

pleted, we know it was worth all our effort (and the labor of our parents, brothers and friends). We invested about $40,000 in house and land; we know we saved at least $20,000 and Roy is convinced we could get over $100,000 if we sold tomorrow.

Would they do it again? "Oh, yes," says Karen. "Staining shelves, pounding nails, and working on the yard are wonderful ways to take away the pressure of our careers. I teach mentally retarded high-schoolers, and Roy is working as a researcher for Union Carbide."

Like most companies, Lincoln Log Homes of Kannapolis, North Carolina, offers precut logs in a package, ready for do-it-yourself assembly. But Lincoln also offers a faster way to erect walls. Its logs are prebuilt into wall sections at the factory, fastened with lag bolts under high compression. Then sections are shipped to the site and put in place over a foundation with a crane. The shell of one such house was erected by a company crew in six hours, forty minutes.

Most manufacturers precision-cut their logs on huge power-driven saws.

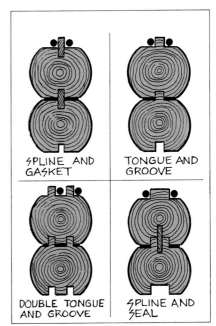

SPLINE AND GASKET

TONGUE AND GROOVE

DOUBLE TONGUE AND GROOVE

SPLINE AND SEAL

End views of log walls illustrate four typical methods for stacking log on log. Note that all the methods use some form of tongue or spline to assure an airtight fit. The joint usually has a foam gasket and is well caulked.

Spirits rise after the foundation is completed and the logs delivered. The forklift (left) is removing logs for an Appalachian Structures home for Roy and Karen Ruddle in West Virginia. The walls go up in a very short time. The crew (middle left) includes Roy and some relatives and friends. Photo (middle right) shows crane lifting logs from Lincoln Logs, Ltd., into place. Bottom photo is of Lincoln Logs ranch.

Most offer debarked logs left round outside, and many give you a choice of round or flat log walls inside. Others remove bark and shape the felled tree with a draw knife, straight hoe, and other hand tools. For example, Southern Rustics sells only hand-hewn whole logs, nearly always erected over a foundation by a professional crew using a boom or crane truck. Openings for doors and windows are cut later.

Eugene Davis, vice-president of Southern Rustics, points out that log houses lend themselves to do-it-yourself completion because there is much less to be done on the outer walls than must be done on a frame home. "But I see the real savings for a log house in reduced energy use year after year, low maintenance costs, and appreciation of one's investment. A log house does not deteriorate and lose value," he said.

Rick Steelman, president of Cedardale Homes, is even more enthusiastic. Says he, "Not only can you build a log house for 30 percent less than it would cost you to build a comparable home by conventional methods, but once you move in, it will cost about 30 percent less to heat and cool your house."

Doris Muir, editor of *Log Home Guide* and the moving force behind the newly formed North American Log Builders Association, lives in a log house she built on her own and is convinced that "log houses will last an average of 500 years . . . if built properly and foundation and roof are cared for (properly)."

Estimates of the number of buyers who complete their own log houses or act as their own general contractor (a potential saving of 20 percent over a contractor price) ranges from 50 to 75 percent of all log home buyers. Industry estimates put annual sales in past years at about 15,000 log houses. All companies contacted reported a rise in the number of do-it-yourselfers buying log house packages. "The buyers who completed our log houses on their own have represented 50 to 60 percent of our business for a number of years," said Wilbert Bossie, director of mar-

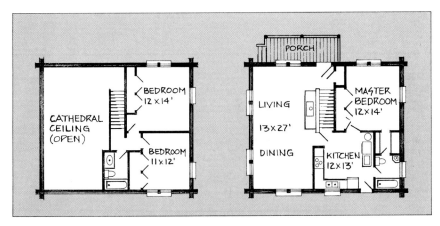

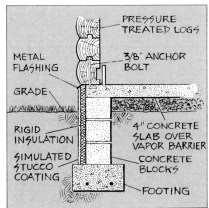

Styles are as numerous and flexible as those of conventional houses. Split level, from Appalachian Structures, has soaring cathedral ceiling on first level, as photo of customized model (left) shows. Plan demonstrates spaciousness within. Cross section (above) shows one method for tying logs to the foundation. Note the channel for wiring.

keting for Ward Cabin Co., oldest loghouse package company on the continent.

Most buyers opt to finish their log house interiors in the same rugged style, using hardwood flooring, cedar plank paneling for partitions, natural wood steps and railings, and pine or cedar kitchen cabinets. Others complete their houses as one would a conventionally framed home—all a matter of taste.

Just as we are relearning and applying passive solar techniques discovered centuries ago, perhaps we would do well to take a much closer look at log-house advantages our forefathers knew. After living in conventionally framed houses all their lives the Dunhams were asked how they liked their two-year-old log house. Hal Dunham put it simply: "We love it!"—*John H. Ingersoll.*

ADDITIONAL INFORMATION

Write to the manufacturers. Addresses of firms mentioned in this article are: Appalachian Log Structures, Burke-Parsons-Bowlby Corp., P.O. Box 86, Goshen, VA 24439; Cedardale Homes, Inc., 400 Friendship Center, Greensboro, NC 27409; Lincoln Log Homes, 1908 N. Main Street, Kannapolis, NC 28081; Lincoln Logs, Ltd., Riverside Drive, Chestertown, NY 12817; Southern Rustics, Inc., P.O. Box 296, Foley, AL 36536; Ward Cabin Co.,

double-shell houses

T his is a controversial house?" I thought, with something close to incredulity, as I entered an asphalt drive in Middletown, Rhode Island, a Newport suburb, and faced a gray-shingled Cape Cod cottage, a pleasant but ordinary rendering of a New England stereotype.

Once inside, though, it became apparent that this was no ordinary Cape Cod. The afternoon sun streamed in through skylights in a mostly glass solarium, spotlighting hanging plants and pots of white chrysanthemums. From inside it looked like a passive-solar house.

But it's not an ordinary passive-solar house, either. I got my first confirmation of its true thermal nature when I looked out a north window. Beyond the glass, a few inches away, was a second window. Wood slats, a fraction of an inch apart, bridged the gap between on all four sides. Looking closely between the slats I could see that the wall was hollow. And that's where the controversy begins.

The house, which belongs to Robert and Elizabeth Mastin, was one of the first double-shell houses built. The north wall is one part of a complete air plenum that envelops the house on four of its six sides. It includes the solarium, the attic, the space in the north wall, and a crawl space under the lower level. According to the original theory of double-shell houses, heated air from the solarium is supposed to flow by natural gravity convection around that plenum, distributing the heat evenly to the house and storing the excess in the crawl space and the earth below for use at night.

No sooner had one of these houses been built and publicized than the critics attacked. They started by disputing the basic theory, then went on to question performance claims, cost effectiveness, and even the safety of a house with a plenum through which fire might quickly spread. Just as vociferous were the proponents: owners who lived in the houses, architects who designed them, and others who just liked the idea of an energy-efficient house with no mechanical systems, no massive masonry walls, no jugs of water, and plenty of windows. About the only thing all agreed on was the need to monitor some of these houses and see: (1) if they work, and (2) how they work.

Now such studies have been done and the results analyzed. One of the most comprehensive used the Mastin house as its guinea pig. The conclusion: The house works— but for the wrong reasons.

Mastin house, a classic double-shell begun in 1978, was recently modified to improve performance. Roof glazing (photo above) was removed and replaced with much smaller area of operable skylights (photos left and right). Air plenum for convective air flow was blocked, and insulated ducts and a thermostatically controlled fan were installed to draw hot air from the top of the solarium and deliver it to crawl space below the lower level, to be stored for use at night, as shown in drawings, next page. Mastin (shown with author in photo left) also removed insulation from attic roof and beefed up ceiling insulation to R-60.

With that evidence in hand, Mastin, who has his own design firm (Natural Energy Design, Inc., 1355 Green End Avenue, Middletown, RI 02840), and a few others are modifying the basic double-shell concept in ways that may make it work even better.

The Brookhaven tests

To test the design, a team from the Department of Energy and the Environment of Brookhaven National Laboratory delivered a carload of instruments to the Mastin house. They installed thermistors to measure temperatures in nine locations, three recording hygrometers to measure relative humidity, and two recording pyranometers to measure solar insolation. To measure the exact amount of auxiliary heat used they installed a 1500-watt electric heater on each floor, each controlled by a thermostat set at 65 degrees F. (The Mastins were instructed to keep their fireplace and wood stove cold.) Monitoring took place in parts of January, February, and March. More tests were run in July. The following winter, thermocouples were installed to monitor the temperatures below the slab. "We collected data off and on for almost a year," says Mastin. "My wife got a little tired of all those instruments and wires hanging around."

It took Brookhaven months to analyze all the data. But finally the report was published. To begin with, it confirmed that the house needs very little auxiliary heat. "It used less than one-quarter the purchased energy of a recently built conventional house of comparable space," the report states.

But the tests didn't do much to confirm the theory. Stratification was an obvious problem. For a typical week in January, on sunny days the temperature in the attic always rose to 90 degrees, topping out at 106. In the crawl space, however, temperatures remained between 45 and 55 for the entire period. Temperatures on the three living levels reflected a corresponding stratification. "Auxiliary heat is needed on the lower level even when the upper level is overheated," the Brookhaven report notes. During

a typical two-day period in January, the heater on the top floor was on 5 percent of the time while the one on the lower level was on 82 percent. Clearly, gravity convection wasn't distributing heat evenly through the house.

Next, the Brookhaven team attempted to measure the convective flow directly. Actually, they instructed Mastin, who holds an engineering degree from the Naval Academy at Annapolis, Maryland, and he did the legwork. "They gave me a hand-held instrument called an ionized corona probe," he reports. "I did measurements at various times and all over the envelope."

What did he see? "In the heat-gain mode [a sunny day] I definitely saw air flow in the direction the theory predicts," he reports, "but it was fairly slow. At night, there wasn't any definite, consistent flow pattern. Most of the time it was just confused. But it was never static." Theory said it should reverse at night and flow in the direction opposite to daytime flow.

After analyzing the data Mastin turned in, the Brookhaven team concluded that the directions were too confused to be meaningful and the velocities definitely low. They pointed out, however, that since the volume of air is so large, a significant amount of heat could be moved even with the low velocities.

So Mastin devised a simple test to see how much the convective flow contributed to heating the house. He took building paper and a staple gun and covered the opening between the crawl space and the solarium, blocking the loop. The result: The blockage caused no performance degradation. In fact, the auxiliary heat needed was "lower by 5 to 20 percent (depending on insulation) with the loop blocked," Brookhaven reports.

Other tests indicated that there was little effective heat storage in the crawl space and the earth below. One way they checked this was by comparing the auxiliary heat requirements for two nights with similar outside temperatures. The first night followed a sunny day; the second, a cloudy day. If, indeed, solar heat is stored in the daytime and released to the loop at night, less auxiliary heat should have been required after the sunny day. In fact, slightly less was required after the cloudy day. Still, the warmth from the earth itself did keep the solarium above freezing at all times.

Having lived in the house for a year, Mastin had surmised that it had too much glazing in the solarium roof. To test that, he installed fiberglass batts over the upper half of the double row of windows, blocking both solar gain and heat loss. With the insulation in place, "the auxiliary heat required was reduced by 25 to 50 percent," Brookhaven's analysis revealed.

Limited tests done in July indicated that the house stays cool in summer as well as it stays warm in winter. For example, one July day when the temperature outside reached 87 degrees F and the solarium rose to equal that, the living areas of the house ranged from 71 to 74, without auxiliary cooling. Certainly the outer shell, which shades the living area from the sun, contributed to this. But the cooling tubes, a standard feature of double-shell houses in some climates, didn't seem to help much. In cooling mode, hot air is supposed to rise from the solarium and exit through attic vents, pulling fresh air that has been cooled and dehumidified by earth contact into the envelope through the cooling tubes. During part of the Mastin tests, air flow was in the wrong direction: It flowed from the house, through the cooling tubes, and out what was supposed to be the inlet.

(Actually, the Mastin house doesn't present much of a cooling challenge. It's about a mile from the Atlantic, and prevailing southwest winds bathe it in cool ocean air on most summer afternoons.)

After analyzing all the data collected, the Brookhaven team reached this conclusion: "The low energy needs of the Mastin house are attributable mainly to the excellent insulative value of its double shell." If cost were a simple overriding consideration, the report continues, "it would be difficult to rationalize the double envelope's use over the super-insulated house."

Christopher Shipp house (see drawing, right).

Super-insulated houses are exactly what the name implies. They are constructed to include an enormous amount of insulation. They conserve heat so well that internal heat gain—from people and appliances—is nearly enough to carry the house, even in a severely cold climate. They rely on solar heat very little, and hence have small windows, even on the south, since windows can be a large source of heat loss.

Hybridization

But, Mastin decided, why not have the best of both worlds? His current designs blend many aspects of a super-insulated house with some vestiges of the double-shell design. He calls the result a Hybrid Geotempered Envelope (HGE).

On a lovely wooded lot south of Boston, builder Robert Green completed an HGE house for Robert and Nina Heyd (see photo). Gary and Kathy Brennan and their five children recently moved into another near Little Compton, Rhode Island. Both have solariums, but there's no air plenum forming a loop around these houses. Instead, a

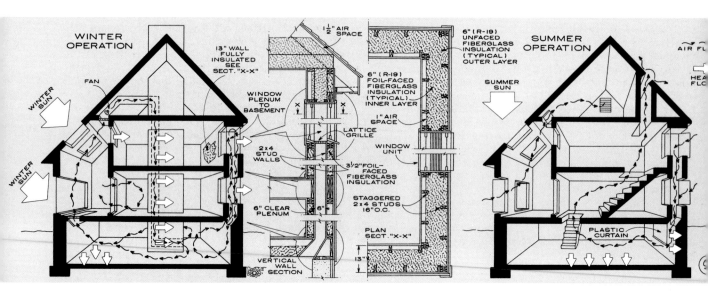

Mastin's Hybrid Geotempered Envelope design has super-insulated walls on north, east, and west: double-stud walls with 12-inch (R-38) insulation. Attic insulation is R-60; foundation, R-10. Double windows have plenums that open into basement. On a sunny winter day (left), 800-cfm fan draws hot air from top of solarium through insulated duct in attic and down a duct in masonry chimney. There it loses heat to the mass. Duct opens into basement, where warm air loses more heat to the mass there and to the earth below. Air is then drawn up through grates in solarium floor, and cycle repeats. In window plenums, air near outer glass cools and falls to basement, displacing warmer air, which rises into plenums. On winter nights, solarium is kept warm in similar way, and masonry chimney releases heat to house. In summer (right) attic vents draw solarium heat through opened trap door. Attic fan draws air through open outer windows, down plenums to basement, up stairwell, out attic.

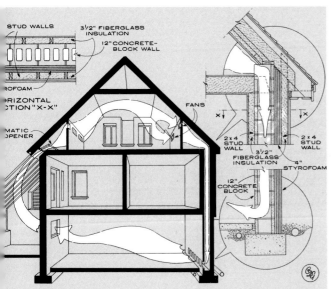

Air flow around loop in house designed by Christopher Shipp is fan-forced. On winter days, as sunspace warms, insulated doors at top open. Fans near north wall pull warm air across upper story and down plenum in super-insulated north wall (R-40). Plenum is formed by voids in concrete blocks (for fire resistance and heat storage). (Other walls are R-30, roof is R-45, foundation is R-20.) Air exits from north wall to lower level, where more heat is stored, then returns to sunspace, and cycle repeats. At night, insulated doors at top of sunspace close. In summer they are also closed. Then warm air from house is pulled down by fans through north wall and dumped in lower level, losing heat to mass. It returns up stairwell. Root cellar (not shown) doubles as heat exchanger.

thermostatically controlled fan takes hot air from the top of the solarium and delivers it through ducts to the basement.

The attic, foundation, and the north, east, and west walls of these houses are super-insulated (see diagram). The north, east, and west windows, however, look much like the north windows in Mastin's own house: two sets of double-glazed units. There is an air plenum at each window, but it's only as wide as the window and ends at the top (which tends to comfort fire inspectors). It does, however, run all the way down to the basement. "The true effectiveness of the double-shell design is in reducing heat loss through glass," Mastin says. "When the air between the windows is colder than the air in the basement, it's going to drop and displace the warmer air there, which will rise.

"The plenum also reduces infiltration," he points out. "Yet when you need ventilation, you can open an interior window and get it, without a blast of cold air." This mitigates the need for an air-to-air heat exchanger which super-insulated houses often require. And since the windows aren't horrible heat losers, HGE houses can have a good many, even on the north side.

Mastin is not alone in modifying the double-shell concept. In fact, a Pennsylvania designer, Christopher Shipp (R.D. 1, Box 331D, West Grove, PA 19390), has come up with an almost identical design, including both super-insulated walls and double windows with air plenums connected to the crawl space or basement. Shipp is also doing variations of the double-shell house that are closer to the original concept, but using fans to force the air flow (see diagram). At least, he intends that these houses use fans. So far the owners of the house in our photo haven't installed the fans.

"They only spent $60 on electricity to heat the house last winter, so spending $200 on fans seems needless," Shipp reports.

How do these hybrid designs compare in cost, performance, and livability with super-insulated houses?

"The best-performing houses anywhere are the super-insulated houses," Mastin admits. "They are also the most cost-effective to build. But their obvious shortcoming is lack of light, views, and natural ventilation."

If you count the solarium as an extra expense (about the same per square foot as the rest of the house), Mastin's HGE-type houses cost a good bit more to build than superinsulated houses. "But if you compare the cost with that of a super-insulated house with a sunspace," Mastin says, "the only cost increase is for the double windows and their plenums — about $250 or so per window. And you don't have the cost or nuisance of window insulation.

The auxiliary heat requirements for super-insulated houses generally come out to be even less than what the Brookhaven tests showed Mastin's house to need. Preliminary monitoring of one of Mastin's HGE houses, in South-

Ample window area on all sides of house is one advantage of HGE houses. This is southwest corner of the Heyd house.

ington, Connecticut, suggests that its heat needs are in the same ballpark, though somewhat more than the most efficient super-insulated houses. More such data will be forthcoming. Mastin spent one recent summer modifying his own house to make it more like the hybrid design (see opening page). Brookhaven subsequently brought back their instruments and remonitored the house.

Just what type of house is the most livable is a highly personal matter. "I didn't want a strictly solar house because I didn't want to cut down all my trees," says Robert Heyd, gesturing toward a stand of stately oaks to the south of his house. "And I didn't want a super-insulated house without much window space."

The Brennans are delighted with the choice they made. "I checked out everything," says Kathy. "I visited some passive-solar houses with whole south-facing glass walls. They turned into an oven during the day, then cooled off just as fast at night. I checked out others that had a basement full of rocks, and some with water drums in the living room—that really turned me off. With all the other designs I read about, it seemed we had to give up something. This was the only one with everything — *by V. Elaine Gilmore.*

For a free color brochure on Hybrid Geotempered Envelope (HGE) homes, write Natural Energy Design, Dept. PSB, 1355 Green End Avenue, Middletown, RI 02840.

foam homes

The large shell of what was rapidly becoming a house stood strangely white at the top of a gentle knoll. When we got to the construction site, it was apparent that the walls of the house were made of large white blocks, each labeled with a letter and number. Similar blocks formed the roof of the house, and a stack of them stood nearby, each with identical indentations in their edges. They were blocks of expanded-polystyrene (EPS) foam insulation. But in this house they were not *added* to the walls and roof; they *were* the walls and roof.

The house, on the outskirts of Madison, Wis., will soon be home to Don Peterson and his wife, Bonita. Peterson invented its unusual system of construction and is president of Cubic Structures, Inc., the company that he estab-

Chunky blocks of expanded-polystyrene foam (opposite page) are light enough for one worker to hoist two. Foam can be easily carved to form arches or other architectural features (top). Because the foam roof gives an R-value of 54, Cubic Structures houses usually do not have an attic; inside, cathedral ceilings soar to the 12-foot peak at the center. Cuts in foam blocks (left) are made at the factory. Note the slender slits where the PVC air stops will go. Cubic Structures model (above) near Madison, Wis., looks conventional.

lished to develop and market it.

Peterson's system is fundamentally this: The 12-inch-thick blocks of EPS-foam insulation board that form the walls of the house have channels in the edges to hold a special polymer-modified concrete called Insul/Crete and steel reinforcing bars, thus forming a post-and-beam skeleton. The roof is made of 14-inch-thick foam blocks laid between standard wood rafters. The foam is covered inside and out with a coating of Insul/Crete to give it strength, durability, and fire resistance. The result: a superinsulated house that is simpler to build than most and as energy efficient as anything available, says Peterson.

The customary way to build a superinsulated house is to erect, on site, double 2 × 4 stud walls, put eight to 12 inches of cellulose or fiberglass insulation between them, and perhaps add a sheathing of rigid insulation board. Then you wrap the house in a vapor barrier to keep moisture away from the insulation and to stop air infiltration. Finally, you finish the inside with wallboard and the outside with wood siding or the like.

Anatomy of a foam house

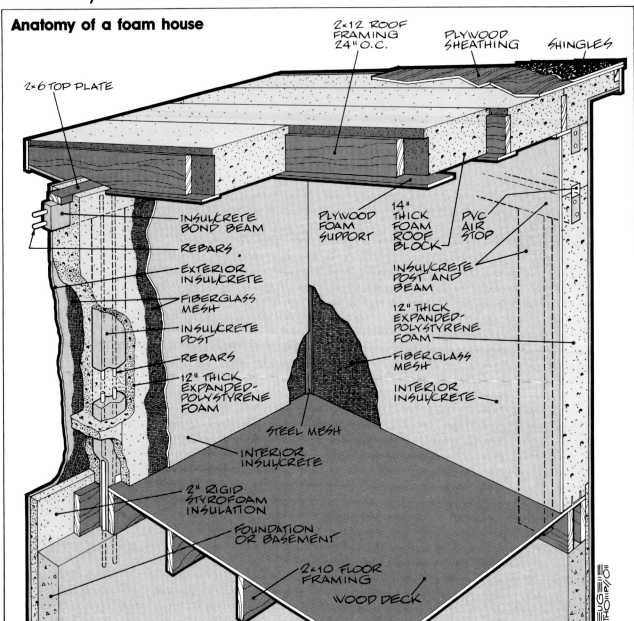

Anatomy of a foam house

A Cubic Structures house is essentially a post-and-beam structure. But the normal role of wood posts and beams instead is played by steel rebars and a specially modified concrete called Insul/Crete. Here's how it's done.

Twelve-inch-thick blocks of expanded-polystyrene foam have channels for the posts and beams. Rebars for the posts are tied conventionally into the foundation, slab, or basement, and the foam blocks are stacked around them to form the walls. Then Insul/Crete is poured into the channels to form the posts. Around the tops of the foam walls is a continuous horizontal channel. It, too, is fitted with rebars, and Insul/Crete is poured into the cavity to form the supporting beam. The Insul/Crete beam is topped with a 2 × 6, to which the rafters are attached.

The roof of the house is made of 14-inch-thick foam blocks,

cut to fit between 2 × 12 rafters (24 inches on center); the rafters are supported at the ridge by a steel I-beam, laminated wood beam, or interior bearing wall. The blocks rest on thin plywood strips below each rafter and overlap the rafters at the top.

Walls and roof, inside and out, are covered with Insul/Crete—a ¾-inch coating inside, and a ⅜- to ½-inch coating outside. First a fiberglass mesh is laid over the foam (wire mesh is employed as reinforcement around corners and openings). Inside, a base coat of Insul/Crete is troweled on, and this is followed by a top coat that looks like plaster. Outside, the Insul/Crete can be troweled over the mesh on the walls to look like stucco, aggregate can be laid in it, or other siding can be applied over it. Plywood sheathing goes on top of the roof, and shingles (or other roofing materials) are installed over the ply.

The result is a wall with an R-value (resistance to heat flow) between 32 and 46. (A conventional wall with 3½ inches of fiberglass insulation has a rating of R-11.) But for the house to perform up to specs, there must not be any gaps in the insulation or any holes in the vapor barrier. That means the house must be built with considerable care.

The Cubic Structures approach to superinsulation simplifies both the sandwich and the site work. The EPS-foam blocks are custom-formed at the foam factory following patterns supplied by Cubic Structures. The blocks are coded to indicate which goes where, then shipped to the building site. A standard four-by-eight-foot, 12-inch-thick block weighs about 32 pounds, so it's easy to carry. The wall blocks are joined by thin PVC air stops to block air infiltration. The EPS foam is not compromised by moisture, so no vapor barrier is required.

The week before I visited the Peterson house, the foam walls were propped in place and the rebars for the posts tied to the foundation reinforcement. Then the Insul/Crete team raised buckets of the stuff with a crane, and directed it into the cavities in the walls with a special funnel on the bottom of the bucket. "The spacing of the posts depends on the design of the house," said Peterson. "The maximum span is eight feet, but we often stand the blocks on end and place them every four feet."

At the tops of the walls, the builders used the same materials to form a continuous bond beam. Then they constructed the roof. Later, Insul/Crete will be troweled on inside and out to complete the walls and roof. "What we have," explained Peterson, "is a simple, unified system with R-46 walls, R-54 roof, minimum air infiltration, and no thermal bridging." The diagram (opposite page) illustrates the scheme.

Interior walls are standard stud walls; windows, too, are standard. The house will have double-glazed windows throughout. "No sense building a superinsulated house and putting in single windows," Peterson remarked.

A Cubic Structures house can use any type of heating system. Peterson's will have a sun room to collect solar heat, an energy-efficient fireplace, and a wood stove in the basement. Chopping wood is recreation to Peterson: "One of the few things I can do to forget business pressures is to run a chain saw."

The final backup heat source will be a heat pump. It could also provide air conditioning in summer, but Peterson does not expect to need it. A whole-house fan in the kitchen's dropped ceiling will help cool and ventilate the house. An air-to-air heat exchanger will keep the inside air fresh and the humidity comfortable.

Trial by fire

The idea for a foam home evolved, step by step, over many years. Peterson was working with the McFarland-based Insul/Crete Co., Inc., whose prime business was retrofitting commercial buildings by adding polystyrene board to the outside. Insul/Crete, a combination of portland cement, acrylic, and chopped fiberglass, was developed to coat the foam. It looks like stucco, but it's stronger, more resilient, and bonds better to polystyrene. Originally these retrofits were for looks, but since the 1973 oil embargo they've been done mostly for energy efficiency.

Noting how strong the foam boards became after Insul/Crete was applied, Peterson began to wonder if, with thicker foam, these panels could be used as the walls of a house. Paper studies and tests indicated that it would work, so a few years ago he built a small (500-square-foot) structure and launched a blitz to prove the concept.

Peterson then had about 13,000 pounds of stone evenly distributed across the center line of the structure's roof. Observers detected no deflection of the roof, no cracking of the Insul/Crete — indeed, no sign of stress. Next he replaced the stone with a 15,000-pound Mack truck. Still the little house showed no structural damage.

Then came the fire test. "We outfitted the house with kitchen cabinets, carpeting, and draperies," said John Lehman, spokesman for Cubic Structures. "We even bought furniture from Good Will. Then we called in local fire departments to supervise the torching."

The scheme was to start a fire simultaneously in the kitchen, living room, and bedroom. But in that tight house the fire wouldn't burn. Finally they left the doors and windows open to get the fire going. They let it rage 45 minutes before firefighters doused the flames.

All the furnishings were reduced to a char, and the foam did melt a bit in two spots—but there was no substantial damage. A fire marshal said that a conventional house would have burned to the ground in such a test. One reason the foam house didn't, Peterson maintains, is that the walls are solid, whereas stud walls have hollow cavities that act as a flue during a fire. "We went in a couple of days later with a pressure-washer and hosed everything down," said Peterson, "and patched the places where the foam had melted." Since then, the building has been used as a showroom and office.

These melodramatic tests got Peterson a great deal of publicity (as intended) and netted some 10,000 inquiries from around the world. Seven firms subsequently became distributors for Cubic Structures houses, and 15 houses have been built. Five are in the Madison area; others are in Texas, Minnesota, Georgia, and Florida. And the city of Milwaukee is building two to use for low-income housing.

The Wisconsin Electric Power Co. plans to monitor the energy use of the Milwaukee houses. But for now, no rigorous data are available to verify a foam home's heating and cooling efficiency. Based on blower-door tests for air infiltration and on computer simulations, Cubic Structures calculates that the houses use about 1.5 Btu per degree-day per square foot of floor space—right in the ballpark with other superinsulated houses. A conventional house with R-11 walls and an R-19 ceiling would require about 12 Btu/degree-day/sq. ft. A 1,500-square-foot foam house in Madison with electric baseboard heat was heated with $116 worth of electricity (at five cents per kilowatt-hour) one winter. Heating the same-size conventional house would have cost about seven times as much.

How much does a foam home cost? "We're competitive with other superinsulation systems that give equal R-values and equal airtightness," Peterson told me. Though these houses can be built faster than the double-stud-wall type, foam insulation is more expensive than fiberglass or cellulose, so the costs about balance out: in the $48-to-$60-per-square-foot range, according to Peterson. "That's about 12 percent higher than 2×6 stud walls with six-inch fiberglass batts, and about 15 percent higher than 2×4 stud walls with 3½-inch batts," he noted. Considering the savings on heating and cooling, the additional first-cost of a foam house should be a good investment in many cases. But the payback depends on the climate, the cost of heating and cooling fuel, and the interest you have to pay on the additional money.

Cubic Structures (4307 Triangle St., McFarland, Wis. 53558) offers several stock house plans or will adapt your own. A Homeowner's Portfolio, which includes floor plans, cost information, test data, and background on the company, is available – *by V. Elaine Gilmore. Illustration by Eugene Thompson.*

super-insulated houses

The conventional-looking house pictured here has very unconventional fuel bills. During an entire icy Saskatchewan winter, Peter and Judy Fretz's house used only as much fuel as a standard house would have needed in two weeks.

The secret is under the skin: 12 inches of insulation stuffed into double exterior walls; greatly increased insulation in the floors, ceilings, and foundation; a tightly sealed vapor barrier; and vestibule entries.

The Fretz house is one of a relative handful of homes in the United States and Canada that are pointing the way to a new trend in building. Super-insulated houses—also called low-energy or conservation houses—approach home heating by cutting energy demand instead of increasing supply. People who have built and lived in them believe that they perform better and cost less to build than houses with complicated active or passive solar systems.

In fact, super-insulation is a kind of passive solar design. Multiple-glazed windows are concentrated on the south side, and direct solar gain is an important source of heat. But, because heat travels both ways through windows, much less glass is used than in most passive homes. Also, no special attention is given to adding heat-storage mass.

Instead, dramatically increased insulation and decreased air leakage

seal in the modest solar gain and the internal heat given off by human bodies and electrical appliances. The result is an energy saving of at least 75 percent over a house with average insulation (see heat-loss drawing). A similar saving results in summer: By keeping hot air out, air-conditioning cost approaches zero.

Some super-insulated houses can even get by without a backup heating plant. "That's the quantum jump," says Harvard researcher William Shurcliff. That saving could make up the cost of other features.

So far, few builders have been

confident enough to eliminate the furnace, and most super-insulated houses have cost 3 to 8 percent more to build than homes with average insulation.

The slight capital-cost penalty does not dampen enthusiasm, though. "Within a few years, super-insulation will be the commonplace of building," says Wayne Shick, a retired University of Illinois architect whose Lo-Cal House design is credited with starting the super-insulation boom.

After Shick published his design, other academic and scientific groups took up the crusade. The Saskatche-

In the Fretz house walls, two sets of 2×4s separated by plywood plates and sheathing were constructed in sections, then raised into place. A continuous vapor barrier covers inside of plywood. Windows are concentrated on south; overhangs prevent overheating in summer. The Fretzes modified the Cape Cod design with help from Saskatchewan Research Council.

wan Research Council built and monitored a demonstration house that incorporated many of Shick's ideas. The same group is now sponsoring a "parade" of energy-efficient homes in Saskatoon.

But the breakthrough came when a number of independent owner-builders applied the concept in actual homes.

"I call those people the granola boys," says Harry Hart, a commercial builder in Lorton, Virginia. "Now it has gone beyond that stage." Hart has developed two subdivisions of houses based on the Lo-Cal design, and Enercon Builders, in Regina, Saskatchewan, has sold many super-insulated homes and licensed its design to other builders.

"Business is flying," says Enercon's Leland Lange. "In our area, all sectors of the industry—from the subtrades to the financial institutions—are getting involved."

Harry Hart is not so sanguine. He says that only about 20 percent of his buyers were sold by the energy efficiency of his houses. "The consumer is a funny cat. Many buyers say they are interested in energy, but they base their decisions on items like fancy bathroom fixtures."

"Energy awareness in building may have to work its way from the North down," comments Shick. "But as energy prices continue to soar, there will be a moment of awakening."

While super-insulation backers are universally excited about the concept, specific designs vary. Some favor double walls with 8½ inches of insulation, some 12 inches. Others get by with single 2×6 or 2×8 walls with exterior sheet insulation supplementing standard fiberglass batts. Some require an airtight seal, heat exchangers, and vestibule entries. Others say these aren't needed. There are many pieces to the super-insulation puzzle. How they go together makes a big difference.

Right now, many super-insulated houses are rather plain looking. But this is a result of builders and buyers trying to reduce cost, not of design limitations. Within certain constraints, such as the number of windows and overall size of the house, super-insulated houses could be architectural eyecatchers.

Will they replace other types of solar design? Shurcliff says there will still be a role in very sunny areas for passive houses with huge amounts of

glass and thermal storage. "But almost every kind of house has some sort of catch," he says. "With super-insulated houses, nobody has found an Achilles' heel"—*Daniel Ruby.*

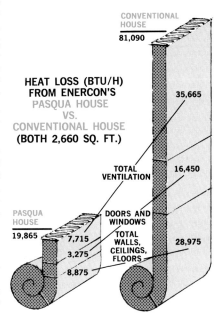

HEAT LOSS (BTU/H) FROM ENERCON'S PASQUA HOUSE VS. CONVENTIONAL HOUSE (BOTH 2,660 SQ. FT.)

Pieces of the puzzle

Typical insulation values and other features of a super-insulated house are shown in the drawing, but designs vary widely. "The key to a cost-effective design is striking a balance among the many elements," says David Robinson, a Honeywell development engineer who devised mathematical techniques to help designers. "If you are going to use only double glazing in the windows, for example, then it's a waste of money to put more than R-21 of insulation in the walls." The required R-values will determine what kind of wall construction is needed. Robinson's guidelines also indicate that you should spend the same amount of money on energy-saving installations as you'll spend on fuel over the life of the house. But his methods don't yield easy decisions on some other features. Airlock doors? The experts are split. They also dispute the importance of a perfectly sealed vapor barrier. Wayne Shick says a barrier is important mainly to protect insulation from humidity; perfect seal is less cost-effective than using superior windows. Leland Lange says sealing is crucial. "Upward of 40 percent of the energy load in an average house comes from heating infiltrated air." If sealing drops air-change rate to under 20 percent an hour, a fresh-air heat exchanger may be needed to combat indoor pollution.

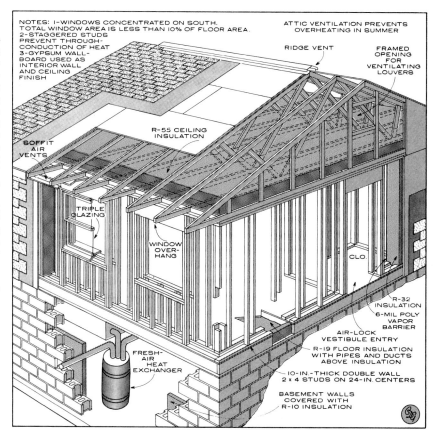

solar home for a sunless climate

Designing a solar home for the Sunbelt is no longer a major challenge. But what do you do in an area of the country that during one recent (and all too typical) winter had only one week of sun in three months? This was the question I faced when planning an alternate-energy home for my property in southeast Idaho, two hours from Yellowstone Park. In this area the winters are cold and unpredictable. And although a good solar heating system can be a great energy saver, you must have another efficient source of energy for those long periods when solar simply is not available.

My solution was to combine several alternate-energy systems and their controls. Some of the systems are quite familiar; some are very new. Basically, the house I designed is passive solar with a rock bed for heat storage. Wood heat is the primary backup, and an electric furnace backstops that. An advanced microprocessor controls heat distribution from all of the sources.

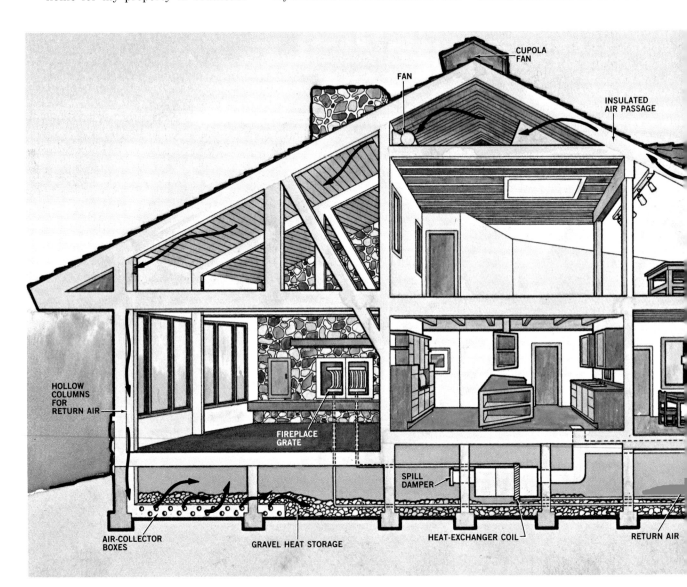

CUPOLA FAN

FAN

INSULATED AIR PASSAGE

HOLLOW COLUMNS FOR RETURN AIR

FIREPLACE GRATE

SPILL DAMPER

AIR-COLLECTOR BOXES

GRAVEL HEAT STORAGE

HEAT-EXCHANGER COIL

RETURN AIR

Together, the systems make my home energy-efficient regardless of the weather.

Here's how the systems work together. When the sun shines, a south-facing greenhouse captures the heat and a series of blowers generates an "envelope" of warm air. This surrounds the main living quarters, insulating them from the cold while at the same time providing heat. Simultaneously, two solar collectors heat the hot-water supply.

At night or when cloudy weather sets in, water flows through a hollow fireplace grating to a heat coil in the ducting. There, the heat extracted from the wood fire is distributed through the house's forced-air ducts. A small programmable controller and a series of automatic motorized dampers monitor temperatures throughout the house and direct the heat to where it's needed. If the fire isn't producing

enough heat to meet the demand, a small electric furnace kicks in.

Good weather or bad, night or day, this combination of energy systems and controls keeps the hot-water supply hot, the house warm, and the electric bills substantially reduced.

Despite the periodic lack of sun in southeast Idaho—or in any other sun-poor climate—the first task in designing an efficient alternate-energy home is still to use a system that capitalizes on solar energy when it is available. For my home, I decided on a passive solar collector and chose the classic south-facing greenhouse but with a somewhat unusual geometry.

The greenhouse has three sections of Thermopane glass surrounding three sides of a glassed-in, trapezoidal-shape dining room. The middle, and largest, section faces due south; the two remaining sections face southeast and southwest, respectively. These

three sections allow the capture of the sun's energy more effectively over a longer period of time than a greenhouse with only a south face. A tile floor combines with the generous air space to create a large heat-storage capacity.

Ceiling vents and attic fans circulate the warm air between the house walls and down to a gravel-filled under-floor plenum (see illustration). This modification of the classic envelope design creates a cocoon of warm insulating air that moves around the main living quarters of the house, transferring heat and storing excess heat in the rock bed for nighttime use.

The sunless solution

When the sun is cut off by clouds for extended periods of time, the envelope of warm air simply is not available. To provide heat during the long stretches of cloudy weather, I installed

Solar heating, Idaho style, starts with a three-sided, insulated greenhouse (above) designed to capture heat from the elusive winter sun. Three 400-cfm squirrel-cage blowers in the attic suck warmed greenhouse air up through ducts in the ceiling and into a six-inch, insulated passage below the rafters (left). The air exits into an insulated roof-peak chamber and is blown into the north side of the house, flowing along the vaulted ceilings until it's drawn down into a series of hollow columns along the north walls of the two rooms. The columns direct the air into a set of large, perforated wooden boxes buried in a rock bed in the insulated crawl space beneath the house. The migrating warm air exits the boxes and transfers its heat to the rock. Underneath the greenhouse, two variable-speed, 800-cfm fans blow the air back into the greenhouse for reheating. In summer, the same blowers force cool forest air up into the house. On cloudy days, pipes carry heated water from a fireplace coil to a heat exchanger in the crawl space (see detailed diagram).

CEILING VENTS

GREENHOUSE

FLOOR VENTS

FAN

Stuart Hall

COOL SUMMER AIR

DOMESTIC-HOT WATER TANK   PREHEATING WATER TANK   EXPANSION TANK

Water-heating system

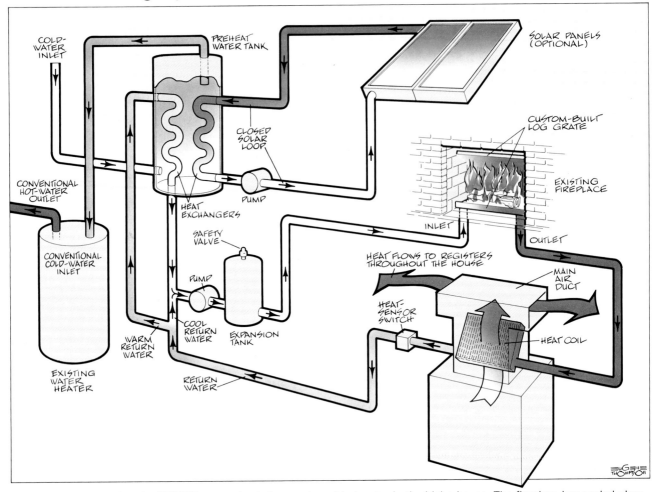

Linking wood and solar, the SWHIFT system heats house air and hot water in the Idaho house. The fireplace has sealed glass doors and a floor vent for outside combustion air. Water flows in a loop through the fireplace grate to a heat exchanger in the furnace ducting, then to the preheating water tank (also heated via solar panels) and through a safety-valve expansion tank back to the fireplace grate.

a heat-transfer system in two adjoining fireplaces.

Called SWHIFT (Solar and Wood Heat Inventions for Today), the system was developed by Lou Baribault (SWHIFT Fireplace Systems, 3170 Western Ave., Idaho Falls, Idaho 83401). The system differs from other fireplace heat exchangers in its versatility and built-in safety features (see diagram).

The system's basic component—a hollow, tubular grate filled with circulating water—is custom-built and so can be inserted into any existing fireplace or wood stove. In my house, the heated water is pumped to a heat coil that resembles an automobile radiator and fits into the main forced-air duct next to the furnace. But the hot water could just as easily be pumped directly into an existing hot-water baseboard heating system—or to a large, insulated storage tank.

When the thermostat calls for heat, the furnace fan switches on and blows cold air through the heat coil, extracting the heat and distributing it around the house through the existing heat registers. When the house is warm enough, a switching valve directs the hot water to a preheating tank coupled to the main domestic-hot-water tank.

In either case, the cooled water is pumped through an expansion tank equipped with a relief valve before returning to the log grate in the fireplace for reheating. The expansion tank ensures that if pressure builds up in the system, it will be released harmlessly through the valve instead of rupturing a pipe.

This versatile system is designed to use solar energy as well as wood heat. I chose one of the simpler options and connected two solar collectors to the preheating hot-water tank. As the tank was in place anyway, this allows

me to heat the hot-water supply during sunny days without building a fire.

Controlling the elements

With solar energy heating the house air on sunny days, solar collectors heating the hot-water supply, and the fireplaces heating both the house and the hot-water supply on cloudy days and at night, I needed an efficient way to control and distribute the energy. Because the house is large, approximately 5,000 square feet, getting maximum control was essential and not merely a case of fine-tuning the system.

I found the solution at a small local electronics firm. JBJ Controls, Inc. (P.O. Box 1256, Idaho Falls, Idaho 83402), had only recently developed the Thermatrol 6180, a unique, relatively inexpensive programmable controller. The modular unit can control almost any type of heating system.

The foundation for an energy-efficient house features a rock heat-storage chamber, shown here under construction. Foil-faced foam board insulates the plenum. The vertical concrete pipe transmits cool air to the greenhouse in summer.

It has six sensor inputs and up to six thermostat inputs. Temperature set points can be set at the factory or at the site, and changes in factory calibrations can be made at the site. There are 12 output connectors (either 115 or 24 VAC) for components such as fans, pumps, and dampers. The Thermatrol 6180 has one more advantage—because it's modular, you pay only for the complexity needed. You can add plug-in modules later if you want to expand your system. Some models can run well over $300.

For further control, I installed Trol-A-Temp (Trolex Corp., 740 Federal Ave., Kenilworth, N.J. 07033) automatic motorized dampers in the air ducts for each house zone. They ensure that whatever heat is available through the ducting is delivered only to that part of the house calling for heat.

How does the control system work? The 6180 controller monitors temperatures in five separate areas: the greenhouse, the rock storage area, and the east wing, center, and west wing of the house. If the greenhouse temperature rises above 70 degrees F on a winter day, the 6180 turns on three attic blowers and two floor blowers. The blowers move the envelope of warm air through the central portion of the house and through the rock storage chamber. When the greenhouse temperature drops to 67½ degrees F, the 6180 turns off the fans.

If the temperature in any of the house zones (but not in the rock storage area) drops below 68 degrees F, the 6180 controller opens the damper to that zone and checks for a source of heat.

First it checks the automatic spill damper in the main air duct near the furnace (see illustration). When the fireplace-heat-exchange system is operating, this damper "spills" excess warm air into the rock storage area. The controller shuts the spill damper and directs heat from the fireplace to the house zone where it's needed. When the temperature in that zone reaches 70 degrees F, the 6180 closes that zone's damper. If no other zone needs heat and the preheating hot-water tank is at the correct temperature, the controller reopens the spill damper so excess heat can once again be dumped into the rock bed for storage.

If the fireplace system isn't operating, however, the 6180 searches for a backup source. It first checks the rock heat-storage chamber. If there's heat available, the controller simply turns on the furnace fan, which draws its air from the chamber. If there's not enough heat stored in the rocks, the 6180 turns on the backup electric furnace.

In summer, when heat is not required during the day, the 6180 turns on a cupola fan to vent any excess heat in the greenhouse. Another fan sucks replacement cool air into the rock storage chamber through a one-foot-diameter concrete pipe. The pipe goes five feet down into the ground, where it turns 90 degrees and runs under house footings and 60 feet into the woods. Where it resurfaces, the air is relatively cool due to transpiration of the trees. Thus, the house is naturally air-conditioned during summer.

Comparing system components

The modified-envelope theory employed in this house is a particularly effective means of using warm air from a greenhouse, air that can reach temperatures as high as the mid-80s on a sunny winter's day. But the envelope is not easily retrofitted to an existing home.

The SWHIFT wood-heat and solar-panel system, however, can be integrated into new construction or installed in an existing home that uses either a hot-water baseboard heating system or an electric or gas forced-air furnace. This flexibility allowed me to install the system after I had already occupied the house and at a time when I was financially ready to make the purchase.

The Trol-A-Temp motorized dampers can also be retrofitted. Some type of heat-zone control, such as that provided by these dampers, is vital in a large house such as mine in which some rooms lose their warmth more rapidly than others. And when more-expensive electric heat must be used, the dampers prevent the furnace from heating areas of the house that are already adequately warm.

However, none of the above components, alone or in combination, would be quite as effective in my house if the JBJ programmable controller or some comparable unit were not used to monitor the house and control the system as required.

Before I installed the fireplace heat exchanger, when the house was heated by a combination of solar energy and electricity, my winter electric bills ran upwards of $425 per month. Afterward, with the JBJ controller operating the heat exchanger and the other system components at maximum efficiency, the average bill was well under $200 — and the comfort level was higher to boot — *by Ronald A. Cordes. Illustration by Stuart Hall. Drawing by Eugene Thompson.*

truss-framed construction

They may call it a revolution in home building, but it hails from a most unrevolutionary organization—the U.S. Forest Service. It's a new technique called truss-framed construction for building light-frame houses.

Unlike "stick-built" homes, the main structural elements of a truss-framed house are prefabricated. The truss frames, consisting of interconnected floor trusses, rafters, and wall studs, are tipped into position on site, much as you'd stand a deck of cards on end one at a time. The frames are then tied together with blocking at top and bottom.

Truss-framed construction could be a boon to a housing industry that is hard-pressed to keep costs down; the technique saves time and money by cutting down on the labor and material necessary to build a house.

The Forest Service's Forest Products Laboratory originally developed the technology to build rugged homes in disaster-prone areas. Engineers took a normal plate-frame roof truss, which is used in about 90 percent of new homes, and tied it directly to wall studs. The wall studs were in turn tied to a flat-floor truss. They found that the resulting house had, in effect, a strong, unitized frame.

The average house requires no more than 26 trusses, so an entire set of frames can be transported on a single truck. A do-it-yourselfer can easily handle construction—except for building the truss frames, which need the attention of a design engineer and the quality control of a truss fabricator. The job is too tedious and demanding for people without the proper equipment. Besides, by the time you pay retail prices for the materials, you'd save little, if anything, over purchasing the completed trusses from a professional supplier.

What about the price of the house? Because there are no floor beams, headers, or interior columns, the cost for lumber is significantly reduced. Construction costs (material and labor) average about 10 percent less than costs for a comparable house built conventionally. The saving can

Truss frame tips into position easily. Instead of trussed rafters, this end frame has vertical nailers for attaching gable sheathing. Frames go on 24-inch centers.

Truss frames can be made in a variety of designs, depending on size and shape of structure. In every design, upper end of each outside stud becomes part of roof truss to which it's attached. The bottom end of stud runs all the way to the lower edge of floor truss. The most important stipulation in designing trusses is that they must conform to standard design specifications, such as those outlined by the Truss Plate Institute. The guidelines give required lumber size and grade and identify the truss-plate requirements at joints. The frame members are typically 2 × 4s, but larger stock could be used—in fact, 2 × 6 frames *must* be used for long spans (greater than 30 feet). The 2 × 6 frames should be used, too, in earthquake zones or in areas where strong winds or heavy snow loads are prevalent.

go as high as 25 percent, however. Part of the saving comes from the open space left by the floor trusses, which makes for easy installation and lowered labor costs for heating and cooling ducts, electrical lines, and plumbing.

Putting the trusses up involves three main operations: getting the frames into the correct position, aligning them properly, and bracing them. The frames can be carried by hand, or a light crane or forklift can do the work.

First the end wall goes up: You square and anchor it to the foundation. Because it serves as the guide for the rest of the truss frames, it must be exactly vertical. The subsequent frames, remember, are spaced with blocks at the top and bottom of each stud. Check

Frames can be erected and braced in two hours. With standard methods, same-size house might take two days to frame.

each member for alignment with a level, and plumb every fourth one at the center and both walls to be sure alignment is maintained. If one frame member is out of alignment, the following ones will be, too; the cumulative effect can put the whole building out of whack.

Once the frames are up, brace them temporarily so that the house doesn't collapse like a row of dominoes. Ideally, you would install permanent wall

sheathing, which provides the real bracing strength, as soon as the first end wall and truss frame are aligned. You'd nail on the remaining sheathing as succeeding frames go up.

Windows, doors, fireplaces, and other wide openings can be a problem. However, you can put up the truss frames and then cut them, framing out the openings in a conventional way.

More than 1,200 homes have been built using truss-framed construction.

Many more are likely to be seen soon—*By Charles A. Miller. Drawings by Carl De Groote.*

Don't need a whole-house truss? Just truss-frame the floor

Trussed floors can by themselves be money savers. Trussed floor joists generally consist of parallel 2 × 4s (top and bottom) with lightweight galvanized-metal supports—called space joist webs—between. The metal webs attach directly to the top and bottom plates without nails; they range from 12 to 28 inches, depending on the strength required. Trussed joists can also be constructed using 2 × 4s between top and bottom plates with the sides covered by plywood, but this is usually a more expensive method.

What are the advantages of a trussed floor? Trussed joists are light and easy to install, reducing labor. They're anchored in place by nailing to the sill plate—no sawing required.

Trussed joists are also strong. The allowable spans are much greater than for conventional framing systems: For most homes, trussed joists can span the entire width of the house. This eliminates the need for supporting beams, bearing walls, and additional concrete footings in the foundation, saving both material and labor. And when used between floors in a two-story home, the clear span beneath allows flexibility in room design.

The open spaces within trussed joists can be used to pass air ducts, plumbing pipes, and wiring without having to saw or drill holes. This, too, not only saves time but eliminates the possible weakening of the floor structure.

Trussed joists save time and labor, too. They can be easily installed by the do-it-yourselfer and can be purchased from most truss fabricators. They should, however, be designed by an expert to ensure proper floor strength.

A truss-joist fabricator will need, at the very least, your foundation or floor plan. A full set of plans is preferable, however. The span of the truss is the critical factor in design—*Herb Hughes.*

prefab home with foam-core walls

"Building a dream house shouldn't be a nightmare," shout the advertisements for manufactured homes. But it's never an easy job to erect the house of your dreams. And another problem is that many prefab homes are not energy efficient.

A new kit home from Pre-Cut International Homes, however, is claimed to be both easy to build and energy efficient. It features an exterior wall—called a Thermo-Lam wall—with two inches of insulating foam glued between laminated 1×8 cedar boards.

The R-value of the wall is 17.9, though the company claims it performs as well as an R-23 wall because the insulation is continuous—there are no interruptions from studs as there are in conventionally insulated walls. Even if you discount that claim, the wall is likely to be a good performer, thanks to its solid profile: There's no way condensation can build up inside a stud cavity, and there are no interior air currents.

The lamination glue lines serve as moisture barriers, and because beads of adhesive are used in the constrution process (along interlocking seams), there's no infiltration.

Prices range from under $15,000 for a small leisure home to more than $90,000 for a big three-bedroom lodge—more if you want a larger custom house. The house is available in cedar only.

All the material necessary to make a weathertight shell comes with the kit: floor, roof, windows, doors—even nails and caulking. The price doesn't include foundation, finish, floor covering, cabinets, plumbing, heating, or wiring. Pre-Cut Intl. Homes, Inc., Box 886, Woodinville, Wash. 98072—*By Charles A. Miller.*

Foam core runs throughout exterior walls (right). Beads of adhesive are placed along shoulders of cedar laminations.

Cedar-and-foam home has interlocking walls made of laminated boards glued to two inches of expanded polystyrene.

thermally layered retreat

Whatever the temperature and wind conditions outdoors, thermosiphoning ensures comfort throughout this unique multilevel house. The rising of heated air generates currents that work to dissipate heat in summer or capture it for reuse in winter.

Award-winning architect Alfredo De Vido, who designed this passive solar house, describes it this way: "There are two basic heating modes and two for cooling.

"A. Cool weather: Shades to the greenhouse are opened; living spaces benefit from direct solar gain and nighttime radiation from thermal mass. Shades are pulled down over the greenhouse roof at night to conserve heat.

"B. Cold weather: In addition to the above, the 'double roof' between atrium and skylights collects a good deal of heat near the peak; a fan pulls this heat back down.

"C. Warm weather: The greenhouse shade is drawn against the sun, and the vent at the top of the air chimney is opened. As air here heats and rises through the vent, it pulls cool air into the house through underground vents.

"D. Hot weather: Atrium shades block the sun's penetration, and a fan in the plenum exhausts air through the house. The 'layering' of the house, plus all these controls, lets you fine-tune the thermosiphon system to match the season."

The key word in this design is *control*. The various options guard against overheating in summer and underheating in winter. The backup wood stoves that flank the open kitchen concentrate their heat in the activity areas. These are isolated from the three bedrooms, which are set halfway into the earth platform, below—*Al Lees*.

Stairs coil up through layered levels, rising from sunken solar greenhouse and bedroom hall to room under ridge. Another stair climbs from mid-level entry. Atrium offers sun-tempered area for winter work/play, wood storage; in summer it's a breezeway.

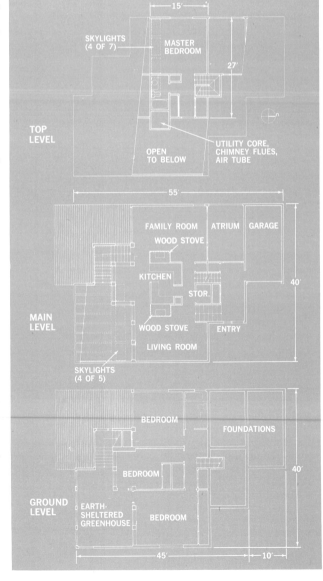

How to order your plans
For architect's working drawings of this house, write to Alfredo De Vido, 699 Madison Avenue, New York, NY 10021.

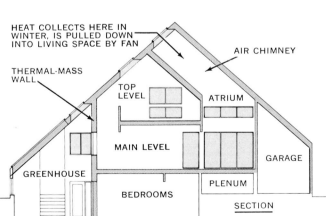

Front section of house nests into an earth pedestal: Greenhouse and three bedrooms are all earth-sheltered. Sun through inclined south glazing heats thermal masses of partition wall and tile floors of main level. Heat travels up air chimney at back. During summer, it's vented outside through openable skylights at peak, acting on thermosiphon principle for cooling.

little big house

It's just a little house in the woods in western Massachusetts. In fact, the house measures a mere 24 feet square. Inside, however, a sense of spaciousness belies its compact outside dimensions. The key is a soaring cathedral ceiling that opens up the ground floor.

"The idea," says architect John Fulop, "was to design a simple house that wasn't just a box, but one with an expansive use of space—a house that didn't give you the claustrophobic feeling you can get in 24-by-42-foot builder houses, for example, which would cost at least as much."

In fact, perhaps the most remarkable fact about Fulop's little house is that it was built just a few years ago for only $35,000. I'll describe Fulop's cost-cutting techniques later.

Aside from the cathedral ceiling, the house has several other space-expanding features:

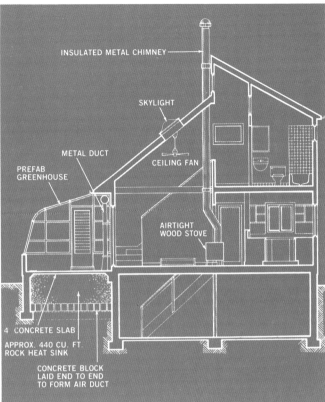

INSULATED METAL CHIMNEY

SKYLIGHT

METAL DUCT

CEILING FAN

PREFAB
GREENHOUSE

AIRTIGHT
WOOD STOVE

4 CONCRETE SLAB

APPROX. 440 CU. FT.
ROCK HEAT SINK

CONCRETE BLOCK
LAID END TO END
TO FORM AIR DUCT

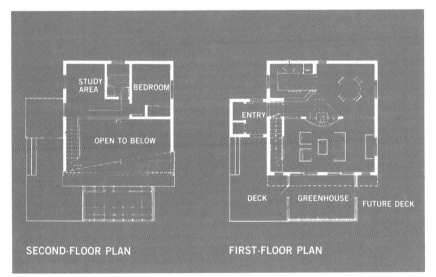

STUDY
AREA   BEDROOM

OPEN TO BELOW

ENTRY

DECK   GREENHOUSE   FUTURE DECK

SECOND-FLOOR PLAN   FIRST-FLOOR PLAN

● Double sliding glass doors give onto the deck, opening the interior to the outdoors.
● A clerestory admits light and solar heat to the upper-level bedrooms and bath.
● Small windows in the north wall provide a view and balance the light.
● An air-lock entry with storage closets shields the living area from blasts of wintry air.

As built for Fulop's client, the house is a direct-gain solar type: Sunlight enters the living space through south-facing windows.

Fulop's plans call for a greenhouse where the present deck is located. The greenhouse, with its integral rock-bed heat storage (see cross section), is sized to provide a substantial amount of the home's space-heating needs. A thermostatically controlled fan blows hot air from the greenhouse peak onto the rocks under the floor slab. Concrete blocks laid on their sides form the air plenums in the rock bed. At night, the process is reversed to maintain greenhouse temperatures. In this case, the home is an indirect-gain solar type.

An airtight wood stove in the living room handles most auxiliary-heat needs. Electric baseboard heaters are installed as backups but are rarely used. The owner reports that electric bills average below $40 a month.

How did Fulop design the house to keep building costs so low?
● Dimensions are based on multiples of standard building materials to minimize waste and cut labor costs.
● Kitchen and bath are stacked to minimize plumbing runs.
● The home's 24-by-24 foot size permits use of less-expensive 2×8 floor joists. (Going to 28 feet would have required 2×10s or 2×12s.)
● In side walls, 2×6s on two-foot centers cost less than 2×4s on 16-inch centers and permit extra insulation.

Unfortunately, one of Fulop's cost-saving features wasn't included. Because a local building inspector insisted on a masonry chimney, the double-wall prefab metal chimney specified in the plans had to be dropped—*By Richard Stepler. Architect: John Fulop.*

you can transform a tract house

Seldom has a remodeling job accomplished this much. When I first saw this house—and its before-and-after floor plans (right)—I knew it was a story POPULAR SCIENCE should tell. The transformation is far more than cosmetic: The entire character of the house has been changed from drably functional to excitingly spacious. As an important bonus, window-siting errors were corrected and additions made that greatly improve the home's energy efficiency.

Even if your present home isn't as uninspired as this one was, you can probably adapt many of the ideas detailed here. Some of them may look familiar: I first saw this project on the PBS television series "This Old House," hosted by Boston renovator Bob Vila. Normally, the show deals with the restoration of antique houses. But when I learned last year that Vila was tackling a 1950s ranch-style house familiar to thousands of our readers, I felt his many improvements were too shrewd to leave to the limited exposure of educational television.

First of all, note that the floor-plan orientation switches from *layered*

Most dramatic face lift is along north walls. "Decorative" shutter slats were scrapped and surfaces re-sided with same natural-finish vertical boards used as siding on breezeway. Garage-door entry was sealed into energy-saving solid wall. Home's canopied front door moved from dead center of wall to center of new breezeway, with privacy screen added.

zoning (with privacy areas—bedrooms and bath—at top, and public space—living, dining, kitchen—below) to *vertical* zoning (with private rooms to the left, public to the right). In a house this size, vertical floor-plan zoning is more practical for simultaneous dual function: Family members or house guests can retire for the evening while group activity continues in the other area.

As with so many quickly built, cheap mass-market houses of the postwar era, access to this home was through ill-planned doors that swung directly into living space. Not only was that awkward; it was energy-wasting since heated or cooled air was vented directly outside each time either the main entry or side door was opened. In the revised floor plan, that dead-center main entry was sealed (the top part of its opening became the bathroom window) and the main entry was moved to the new breezeway. The side door into the kitchen was retained, but since the kitchen was doubled in size (by absorbing an adjacent, undistinguished dining area), it was practical to tack on a mud room-pantry that serves as a kind of entry air lock. This side entry is totally restyled, with its stoop compressed and its stairs turned 90 degrees to climb along the wall. A new screen wall provides privacy from the street for both entries and deflects gusty winds from this entry patio.

One of Vila's shrewdest alterations was shifting that picture window from

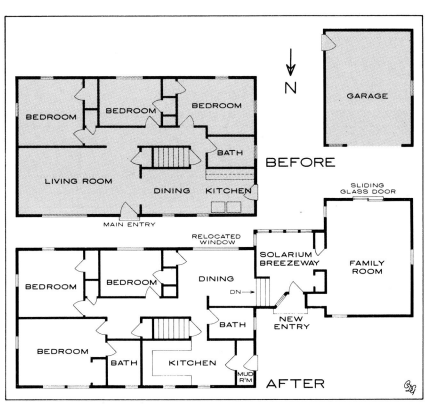

Compare floor plans above with photos on facing page. Only new structure is breezeway to connect house with unused garage. Converting garage to family room then creates new wing that wholly alters zoning of private and public areas.

Connecting structure changes character of entire house. Foundation of new solarium is concrete slab laid on grade, so it's at same level as garage floor. Old corner bedroom becomes dining area, with arched opening cut in outer wall through which stairs descend from original floor level. Note relocated picture window behind dining table. Solarium (right) has quarry-tile floor. This is now home's main entry—and first impression.

Old garage walls are finished off with drywall, pierced with new windows; rafters and tie beams are closed with wood strips.

Spacious new kitchen has room for breakfast table and improved triangular placement of the sink, range, and refrigerator.

Out goes the picture window from the front of the house. Simply removed as a unit and carried around to the opposite

corner, at back, it was installed in rough opening framed to take it (photo above; note corner of garage at left).

Concrete is dumped between new block footings connecting garage to house. Once slab cures, breezeway structure is

erected on it (right). Breezeway's ridge beam is tied into garage roof at far end and into cutaway wall in foreground.

The bridging breezeway is two-faced, providing new entry for front of house (left) and heat-capturing solarium for

south-facing back (above). New windows in former garage at left are same as seen in color interior at top of facing page.

the north wall—the street facade—where it not only got no sun but also compromised the privacy of the living room. As the top-right photos show, it was simply carted around back where

it contributed to the solar gain—and gave the new dining room a view of the wooded area out back. Its old opening was partially closed up (and, of course, insulated) for the installa-

tion of a new wide but shallow double-glazed window, to provide better privacy for the master bedroom that replaces the living room at the front corner. (A second window was added around the corner.)

The prize of Vila's remodeling, however, is the recreational suite added on the home's right end. By insulating and finishing off the detached garage and joining it to the house by means of a tile-floored solarium, he created not only a gracious entry but an activity area larger and more inviting than the discarded living room. The house is no longer a cramped box, and its architectural interest is greatly enhanced, both inside and out. To bridge the distance between existing structures without adding support posts, Vila created a massive ridge beam of four 2×12s. He also beefed up the vertical framing in the existing walls to handle the transfer of load from the new roof.

The alterations also increased the home's efficiency through better sitting of the windows for solar gain. The solarium, facing south, is an especially good passive collector. Its quarry-tile floor is laid over an eight-inch concrete slab atop a foot-deep bed of crushed stone. Rigid two-inch foam insulates the footings to a depth of two feet. This heat sink soaks up and later radiates heat from solar exposure. If insulating drapes were drawn across the panels of glass at night, the heat stored in the slab should keep the area cozy on all but the most severe winter evenings. For those, it might be best to close this area off from the family room—and draw an insulated drape across the sliding-glass door there, as well.

The entire remodeling project was budgeted at $25,000—including all new appliances for the kitchen and a wood-burning stove for the family room. The remodeling took longer than the original construction: This house was just one of 400 tract homes thrown up by a Boston developer in the mid-1950s. On average, he finished two a day, each house taking seven weeks from start to finish. What a contrast with today's homebuilding pace!

Projects like the one we've presented here in some detail offer just the type of inspiration homeowners today need to transform those less-than-ideal cookie cutter houses into homes worthy of pride and devotion — *by Al Lees.*

a room with a view

The front of my 100-year old house was falling down. The two-tiered porch pillars that were built of staves, like barrels, were coming apart. An overly dark attic and a glassed-in upper sleeping porch under an overhang were virtual breezeways. The roof was in an advanced stage of disrepair. It had got to the point where the town had given me an ultimatum: Remove the violations or face the consequences.

I already had given some thought to remodeling and,

prodded by the incentive supplied by the town, now launched into the project. Unfortunately, I quickly discovered that I lacked the skills of a professional, someone adept at designing and piecing together the details that would work with the existing structure. Help, as luck would have it, was not far away—I found the man for the job in my own town: John Hartwell Bennett, an architect and skilled building mechanic.

Our choices were pretty clear: We could build upward,

Two little-used dormers and a sleeping porch were eliminated on this house and replaced with a handsome shed dormer-studio.

expanding and finishing the attic to make a bright new room that conserved energy, or we could build out, enlarging the front rooms by eight feet (the depth of the porches). The latter, however, would mean expensive reconstruction, a new heating source, bigger fuel bills, and greater taxes. We could, of course, just restore what I had, but I would gain little and would have to live with the old discomforts and too-high fuel bills.

We raised the roof. Expanding the attic by adding an 18-foot-long shed dormer gave me a dramatic new studio room at the top of the house that measures 17 by 27 feet. Andersen casement windows in the dormer offer a spectacular view of the waterfront at the end of the street and vent the house effectively in summer (a big chimney effect) yet keep it snug in winter.

The old attic stairs had come up from a bedroom closet and allowed only a crouching entrance under the eaves. We gave this space back to the closet and brought new stairs, centrally located, through the ample-size, old-house bathroom. Entrance is now from the second-floor hall, and you come into the studio (standing erect) at the north end of the room. The new stair location gives the whole house better air circulation in both summer and winter.

By removing the glassed-in sleeping porch, we got rid of a white elephant—its sole function had become dark-ening all the front rooms. The old diamond panes on the porch had charm, but the frames were not reparable. The glazing caused my family to bake in summer and shiver from winter drafts.

After taking down the porch and pillars, we further improved the view by adding two windows on the facade upstairs. We also replaced the existing windows at the front with Andersen Perma-Shield Narroline double-hung units. Partly because they're carefully caulked, they closed dozens of heat leaks. All the new windows (both casements and double-hung) have Andersen's Perma-Clad vinyl cladding outside, relieving me of having to repaint the window trim in the years ahead. I bought the maker's storm-screen combinations, which give me triple glazing when necessary. It feels comfortable inside the house now.

The general renovation

We replaced the wood front door and aluminum storm door with a modern insulated steel door. The Pease Ever-Strait door we chose, with a 7.22 R-value and factory weatherstripping, effectively keeps all heat and cold away from the area of the entryway, which is located on the severe-weather side of the house. A thermometer tells me it's about six times more effective than the old double doors. The embossed door, with a Schlage drive-in latch and bolt

DETAIL OF ROOF AND DORMER FRAMING

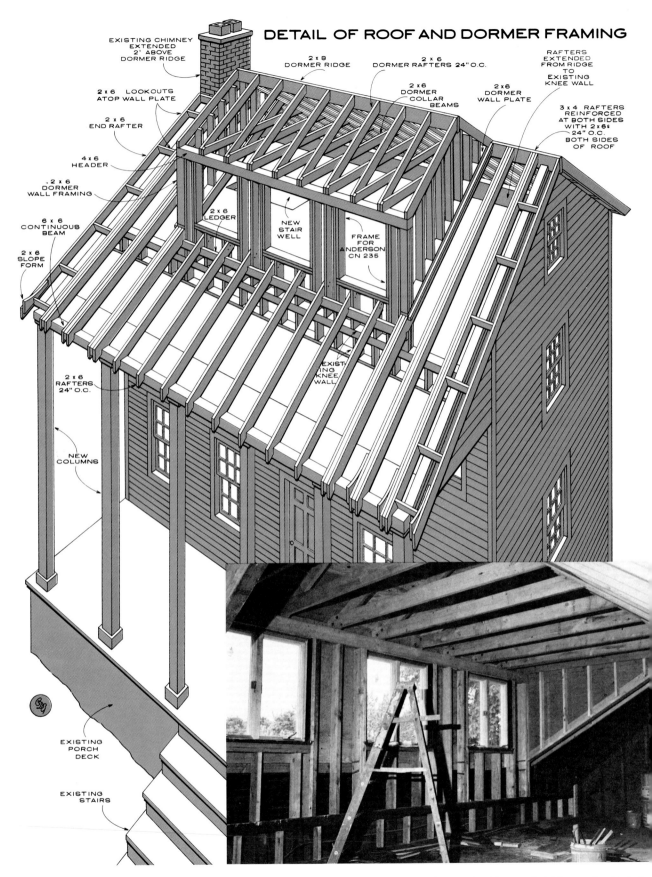

EXISTING CHIMNEY EXTENDED 2' ABOVE DORMER RIDGE

2 x 8 DORMER RIDGE

2 x 6 DORMER RAFTERS 24" O.C.

RAFTERS EXTENDED FROM RIDGE TO EXISTING KNEE WALL

2 x 6 LOOKOUTS ATOP WALL PLATE

2 x 6 DORMER COLLAR BEAMS

2 x 6 DORMER WALL PLATE

3 x 4 RAFTERS REINFORCED AT BOTH SIDES WITH 2 x 6s 24" O.C. BOTH SIDES OF ROOF

2 x 6 END RAFTER

4 x 6 HEADER

2 x 6 DORMER WALL FRAMING

2 x 6 LEDGER

NEW STAIR WELL

FRAME FOR ANDERSON CN 235

6 x 6 CONTINUOUS BEAM

2 x 6 SLOPE FORM

EXISTING KNEE WALL

2 x 6 RAFTERS 24" O.C.

NEW COLUMNS

EXISTING PORCH DECK

EXISTING STAIRS

The new upper room was part of a general renovation of the house. The house's roof was raised by sandwiching each affected 3×4 rear rafter with a pair of 2×6 rafters. That elevated the roof ridge four feet to create a cantilevered framework over the 18-foot middle section, which provides sufficient clearance overhead. The pitch of the rear of the new shed dormer matches that of the existing roof, and the front slope is parallel to the front roof. There is a series of 2×6 collar beams, which are through-bolted to the existing and new rafters to add strength. The taller front wall of the dormer; which resulted from the extension of the rafters, made space for larger casements. The height of the wall added space to the attic area, too. When it was built, the entire house had been framed with full-dimension long-grain fir. The original studs and rafters are 24 inches on center, and this spacing was maintained in the new construction. The new windows fit so that there are no heat leaks or tight pinches; they can be fitted with storm glazing.

The chimney had to be extended to accommodate the raised ridge. Johns-Manville shingles cover old roof contours. Bright and airy studio was formed by the renovation of the attic. Andersen casement windows seal room from weather.

lock and simple burnished-metal colonial-style plate, provides a handsome focus for the new facade.

All this work required re-siding the front, and I was lucky to find enough cedar drop siding to match the house.

I had previously tried to insulate the exterior walls with foam, but when I stripped the inside of the exterior walls, I found the foam had shrunk away from the studs and in some areas was nonexistent. These areas were packed with fiberglass insulation.

In the bath we added a linen cupboard under the new stair just inside the door and installed a five-foot Owens-Corning Fiberglas bath-shower unit. Because I no longer needed the long hallway leading to the sleeping porch, we turned the space it occupied into a walk-in closet for one of the front bedrooms.

For the new roof we selected Johns-Manville Woodlands Seal-O-Matic fiberglass shingles in Seadrift Grey to go with the stained cedar shingles on the dormer. This roofing casts an edge shadow that makes it look like wood shingles and handsomely masks irregularities in an old roof. Johns-Manville's Seal-O-Matic shingle stripe works with the sun's

heat to bond shingles together, and the new roof lies much tighter than did my previous asphalt roof. My house stands on the side of a hill just 300 feet from the water and takes punishment in winter storms. It's good to know that the new roof is warranted for 25 years and has a Class A fire-resistance rating (the highest) from Underwriters' Laboratory. The shingles also have a UL wind-resistance label, which means they should withstand the beating they take, even over an extended period.

When the building was done, I repainted the entire house with Olympic Stain paint (two coats), using Navajo red and Interlux semi-gloss white trim for the pillars and soffits. So far, the paint has weathered beautifully and shown no faults. Bennett, the architect, says it should be good for more than six years—*By David D. Vigren.*

SUPPLIERS OF MATERIALS

Andersen Corp., Bayport MN 55003; **Manville Corp.**, P.O. Box 5108, Denver CO 80217; **Olympic Stain** (Clorox, Inc.), 2233 112th Ave. N.E., Bellevue WA 98004; **Owens-Corning Fiberglas Corp.**, NMX Meeks, Fiberglas Tower, Toledo OH 43659; **Please Co.**, 900 Forest Ave., Hamilton OH 45023; **Schlage Lock Co.**, P.O. Drawer 3324, San Francisco CA 94119.

raising the roof to gain rooms

A typical A-shaped attic in a Cape Cod-style home built in 1942 offered an opportunity to create a dramatic new master bedroom and bath. However, to get the bright, airy bedroom and luxuriously sized bath shown on these pages, the owners had to work out design solutions to problems caused by the existing stairs, chimney, and plumbing. Their most significant decision, perhaps, was to raise the roof and build a dormer the full length of the house; in the end, this proved to be only slightly more expensive than the alternative of a much smaller dormer. The work progressed as follows:

1. The rear half of the roof was completely removed, rafters cut, crossties eliminated, and temporary bracing set under the front half of the roof.

2. Joists were extended for the dormer and balcony, new exterior walls framed, and a new roof and wall sheathing were applied.

3. New windows, sliding doors, and skylights were then installed.

4. The plumbing, wiring, and insulation were installed, the bath fixtures were set, and the balcony deck was completed.

5. The chimney was framed with a new wall and a closet was built on the north side of the chimney.

6. Next step was to drywall the interior.

7. New shingles were applied over the old roof and rolled roofing was installed over the dormer.

8. Finish work—painting, trim, gutters, tiling—was completed.

A special feature of the design is that all potentially lost space (the space between the studs, for example) was put to work. In the bathroom, it was used for a towel shelf; on the west wall, for plant shelving and a window seat; on the closet (chimney) wall, it became built-in bookshelves, and, in the area at the head of the stairs, two small storage closets were created.

The owners achieved the three goals they had set for themselves in this project: They created an inviting living/sleeping space and a luxurious bath. They created a room bathed in natural light and open to a beautiful view. And they maintained the integ-

Before-and-after photos show a pleasing transformation from Cape Cod peak to full-length dormer, which greatly increased living space at relatively reasonable cost. Note recommendations for roof circulation in drawing on next page.

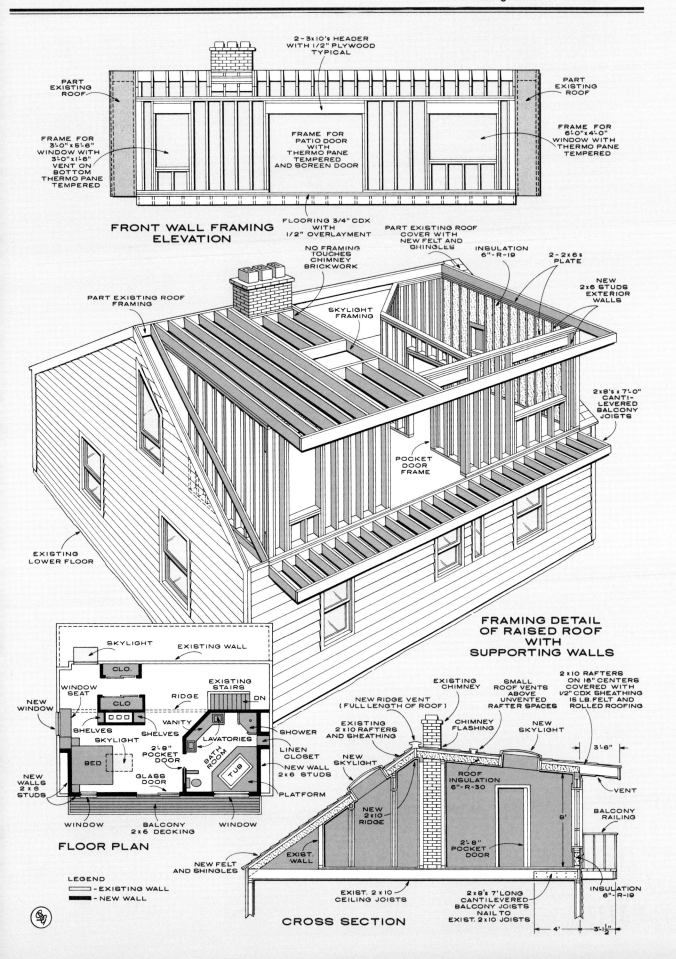

2-3x10's HEADER
WITH 1/2" PLYWOOD
TYPICAL

PART
EXISTING
ROOF

PART
EXISTING
ROOF

FRAME FOR
3'-0"x5'-6"
WINDOW WITH
3'-0"x1'-6"
VENT ON
BOTTOM
THERMO PANE
TEMPERED

FRAME FOR
PATIO DOOR
WITH
THERMO PANE
TEMPERED
AND SCREEN DOOR

FRAME FOR
6'-0"x4'-0"
WINDOW WITH
THERMO PANE
TEMPERED

FRONT WALL FRAMING
ELEVATION

FLOORING 3/4" CDX
WITH
1/2" OVERLAYMENT

PART EXISTING ROOF
COVER WITH
NEW FELT AND
SHINGLES

INSULATION
6"-R-19

2-2x6s
PLATE

NO FRAMING
TOUCHES
CHIMNEY
BRICKWORK

NEW
2x6 STUDS
EXTERIOR
WALLS

PART EXISTING ROOF
FRAMING

SKYLIGHT
FRAMING

2x8's x 7'-0"
CANTI-
LEVERED
BALCONY
JOISTS

POCKET
DOOR
FRAME

EXISTING
LOWER FLOOR

FRAMING DETAIL
OF RAISED ROOF
WITH
SUPPORTING WALLS

FLOOR PLAN

SKYLIGHT

EXISTING WALL

CLO.

WINDOW
SEAT

CLO

RIDGE

EXISTING
STAIRS

DN

NEW
WINDOW

SHELVES

SHELVES

VANITY

LAVATORIES

SHOWER

SKYLIGHT

2'-8"
POCKET
DOOR

BED

BATH
ROOM

TUB

LINEN
CLOSET

NEW WALL
2x6 STUDS

NEW
WALLS
2x6
STUDS

GLASS
DOOR

PLATFORM

WINDOW

BALCONY
2x6 DECKING

WINDOW

LEGEND
☐ - EXISTING WALL
■ - NEW WALL

CROSS SECTION

EXISTING
CHIMNEY

SMALL
ROOF VENTS
ABOVE
UNVENTED
RAFTER SPACES

2x10 RAFTERS
ON 16" CENTERS
COVERED WITH
1/2" CDX SHEATHING
15 LB. FELT AND
ROLLED ROOFING

NEW RIDGE VENT
(FULL LENGTH OF ROOF)

CHIMNEY
FLASHING

NEW
SKYLIGHT

EXISTING
2x10 RAFTERS
AND SHEATHING

3'-6"

NEW
SKYLIGHT

ROOF
INSULATION
6"-R-30

VENT

NEW
2x10
RIDGE

8'

2'-8"
POCKET
DOOR

BALCONY
RAILING

NEW FELT
AND SHINGLES

EXIST.
WALL

EXIST. 2x10
CEILING JOISTS

2x8's 7' LONG
CANTILEVERED
BALCONY JOISTS
NAIL TO
EXIST. 2x10 JOISTS

INSULATION
6"-R-19

4'   3'-1½"

rity of their home's architectural style, while adding contemporary living space. Equally satisfying, they kept the project within the budget they had set.

Finished in light tones and natural materials—light gray quarry tile, oak trim, white walls, and light gray carpeting—and with white furnishings, the room is a spectacular change from the old pink attic—*Cathy Howard. Photos by Karlis Grants.*

PRODUCTS USED IN THIS REMODELING

Fixtures: Steeping bath whirlpool, toilet (Wellworth), Castelle lavs (Country Gray), polished chrome faucets, Kohler Co., Kohler WI 53044. *Tile:* Rustic II (Graystone), U.S. Ceramic Tile Co., 1375 Raff Road, S.W., Canton, OH 44711. *Towels:* Dundee Mills, 111 W. 40th Street, N.Y., NY 10018. *Mirrors:* Hoyne Industries, East Tower, Suite 825, Golf Road, Rolling Meadows, IL 60008. *Heat/fan/ light,switch-plate accessories, concealed paper holder:* NuTone Division, Scovill, Madison and Red Bank Rds., Cincinnati, OH 45227. *Windows, sliding door:* Weather shield Mfg., Medford, WI 54451. *Blinds:* Shadow Gray (bedroom); Garnet Red (bath), Kirsch Co., 309 N. Prospect Street, Sturgis, MI 49091. *Roof window:* Model GGL, Velux-America, Inc., 74 Cummings Park, Woburn, MA 01801. *Track lighting:* Halo/Lighting Products Division, McGraw-Edison, 400 Busse Road, Elk Grove Village, IL 60007. *Furniture:* Techline, Marshall Erdman and Assoc., Madison, WI 53705. *Closet storage system:* Swedish Wire Products, Elfa Division, 1755 Wilwat Drive, Suite A, P.O. Box 861, Norcross, GA 30091.

The backside of the old roof is removed as far as the peak. Temporary braces are secured to front-roof rafters before removal of mating back-roof rafters.

Plumbing vent pipes (below left) will be rerouted horizontally between floor joists to outside wall. Balcony joists (below right) are secured to existing floor joists.

Above, entire back-wall frame is raised into place after assembly on new floor. Roof sheathing is applied, below left. Below right, sturdy scaffolding allows transport of heavy items to the second floor without need to enter the first floor.

Above, the concealed chimney serves as the hub of the new living area. A skylight brightens the bedroom, and a glass door opens onto the balcony. Below left, a trapezoidal window follows the slope of the ceiling. The window seat in front is tile-topped. Below, track lighting on a dimmer switch allows spotlighting effects.

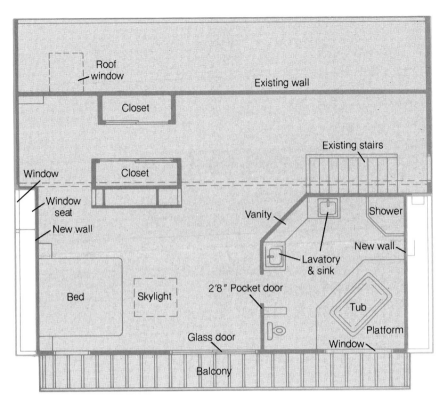

Floor plan, above, shows positions of closets, right, with wire basket storage. The luxurious master bath (below and below right) has dual lavatories. Tongue-and-groove cedar paneling highlights the end wall, tub platform, and light soffit.

four add-on sun spaces

1 **Sunny breezeway** forms a stylish connection between house and garage. All Pella glazing units have natural wood frames on the inside, ready for stain or paint. Vertical glazing units can be double or triple glazed, with fixed exterior glass and removable interior panels. Joint details B and C, labeled here, are constructed like those of the same letters in the dormer diagram (next page).

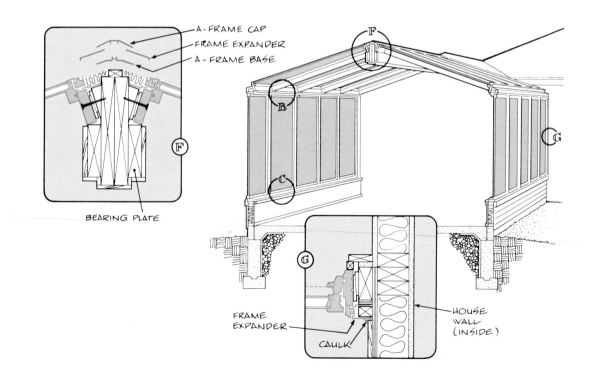

A - FRAME CAP
FRAME EXPANDER
A - FRAME BASE

F

BEARING PLATE

B

C

G

G

FRAME EXPANDER

CAULK

HOUSE WALL (INSIDE)

I t's called the Sloped Glazing System, and it's new from Pella: an integrated line of overhead, ⅞-inch tempered, insulated-glass units that you can combine in various ways and numbers with standard vertical windows and doors. Placement, size, and design of each sunspace is determined by your needs.

All glazing is framed in wood and clad on the outside with aluminum in a white or brown enamel finish. Aluminum flashing strips, in various configurations and finished to match the exterior of the glazing units, attach to the wood structure you build to give the whole sunspace a custom look and low-maintenance exterior. Anyone who'd tackle a standard room addition can easily build a sunspace with this system.

The four add-ons shown here—dormer, breezeway, air-lock entry, and daylight basement—are all from Pella Windows and Doors, 100 Main St., Pella, Iowa 50219—*By Al Lees and V. Elaine Smay. Drawings by Eugene Thompson.*

2

Dormer sun room can add warmth, light, ventilation, and headroom to an attic space. Pella's sloped and vertical glazing units fit together (with caulk and mullion covers) to form the dormer in the size and shape you want. Vertical glazing units can be fixed or operable. Pella also makes triangular (and trapezoidal) glazing units for the dormer sides. Or you can build and finish opaque sides to match the house.

FRAME EXPANDER

BEARING PLATE

BOTTOM FLASHING

FRAME EXPANDER AND RECEPTOR

SIDE FLASHING

90° CORNER MULLION COVER

3

Basic Pella sun room, shown in exploded diagram, is similar to air-lock entry and illustrates typical framing and construction methods of all such structures. Pella offers detailed plans for this sun room only. Where techniques vary for other structures, a Pella distributor can give guidance. Other Pella instructions tell how to assemble multiple-glazing units.

4

Sun-room walk-out can transform a dreary basement with both light and solar warmth. To preserve privacy and to control solar gain, Pella offers vertical glazing units with narrow-slat blinds between the panes and similar blinds that can be attached under the glass of the sloped glazing units. (Joint detail D here is illustrated in the dormer diagram, page 47.)

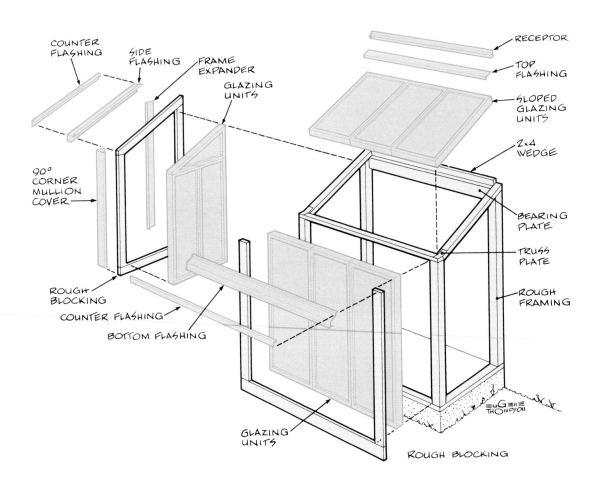

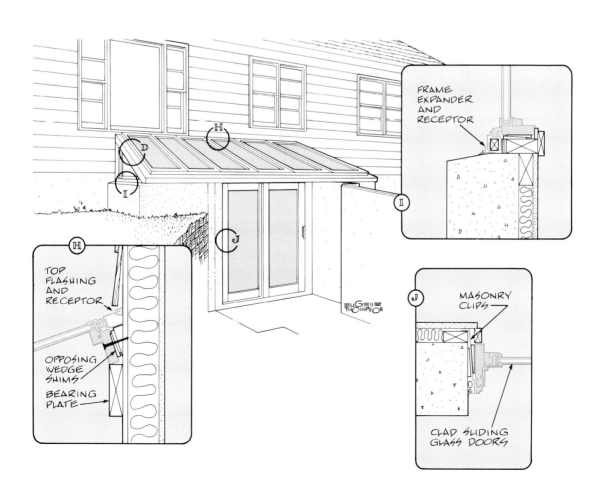

FRAME
EXPANDER
AND
RECEPTOR

TOP
FLASHING
AND
RECEPTOR

OPPOSING
WEDGE
SHIMS

BEARING
PLATE

MASONRY
CLIPS

CLAD SLIDING
GLASS DOORS

EUGENE
THOMPSON

skinny skylights speed sun room conversion

It was charming; it was unique; it was useless. The very details that made the fieldstone porch picturesque also made it unsuitable for summer relaxation. On three sides, elegant columned arches framed the view—and let in the bugs. And the steep roof, with its exposed-beam ceiling, created a dark and gloomy interior.

The owner's solution? Enclose the porch with glass to preserve the view, and insert skylights in the roof to bring in light. The result? A cozy, inviting sun room.

Such a conversion need not be a major construction job. By choosing materials that are relatively easy to install, a weekend carpenter can create a similar sunspace from a porch, breezeway, even a garage.

Here, the homeowner removed the arched trim, framed the openings with 2 × 4s, then inserted stock, double-glazed Caradco picture windows and doors between the columns.

To open up the roof without destroying the exposed beams, he used Dayliter Long-Lites skylights, made by the APC Corp. (Hawthorne, N.J.), to fit between rafters. No structural members needed to be cut, nor did the roof openings have to be framed to accept the 69½-inch skylights (see drawing). The skylights come in three other lengths and fit beams spaced either 16 or 24 inches on center—*By Susan Renner-Smith.*

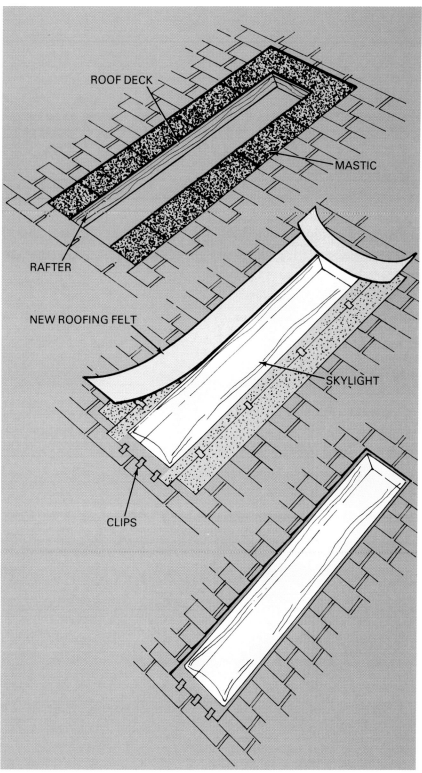

ROOF DECK

MASTIC

RAFTER

NEW ROOFING FELT

SKYLIGHT

CLIPS

Rustic, open fieldstone porch (below) was dark and uninviting. Slim skylights slotted into the roof of the now glassed-in porch (main photo, left) help transform it into an airy, year-round sun room. Double-glazed, bronze-tone skylights fit between roof rafters, allowing the 50-year-old exposed beams in the ceiling (top) to remain intact. Stock double-glazed windows and doors fill in the wall openings. Homeowner stripped roofing down to the decking (above) before installing skylight, but old roofing paper can be left on (see illustration at right).

To install skinny skylights, first measure the opening from inside and drive nails through to the outside at each corner. Remove the shingles from around the marked area, but leave the bottom course intact as shown (top). To avoid gumming up the saw, strip away roofing paper inside the cutout area. To ensure straight cuts, snap chalk lines between nails. Now cut through the roof deck with a circular or saber saw. Next, apply a bed of mastic over the existing roofing paper bordering the cutout. Set the skylight in place, snap on the special clips, then nail them to the roof. To prevent leaks, lay strips of roofing felt in a bed of mastic, arranging the strips to overlap the top and sides of skylight flange (see middle sketch). Replace the shingles, lapping them over the skylight flange then trimming them to fit against the dome. Note that bottom edge of skylight is left uncovered to promote drainage.

adding a solar room

Northeast winters tend to be cold and gray. But the sun-drenched room I designed and added to my home has changed that. It's a warm, bright add-on, suitable for use as a breakfast room, for simply relaxing with a book, or for hot-tubbing in a whirlpool tub I've installed. As I write this in midwinter, a small fan is quietly blowing 80-degree-F air from the sunspace into my house.

This project called for inexpensive, readily obtained materials and do-it-yourself building techniques, since I planned to do most of the construction. Also, I wanted to use the space both summer and winter, but with minimal shading or insulation.

A 60-degree sloped bank of windows is ideal for capturing the winter sun. However, combine that with a vertical knee wall (for ventilation) and a sloped roof (to shed water), and you have an unstable configuration. To solve this problem I designed a structural system of prefabricated plywood ribs. Located at the glazing joints, they provide both roof structure and window mullion.

An insulated roof helps keep the sunspace warm in winter and cool in

Snug interior of add-on sunspace during winter months is aided by fiberglass insulation for the floor and ceiling, plus moderate thermal storage mass to capture solar energy streaming through large, sloped windows during the day. The outdoor platform for a 195-gallon whirlpool spa (middle, far left) sits on a leveled gravel bed. During winter months, this portable Jacuzzi can be moved inside the sunspace (bottom, far left). Architect Milstein decided to glaze one end wall for a nice view (near left), leaving other wall solid except for a low awning to catch westerly summer breezes. Quarry-tile floor over concrete stores solar heat.

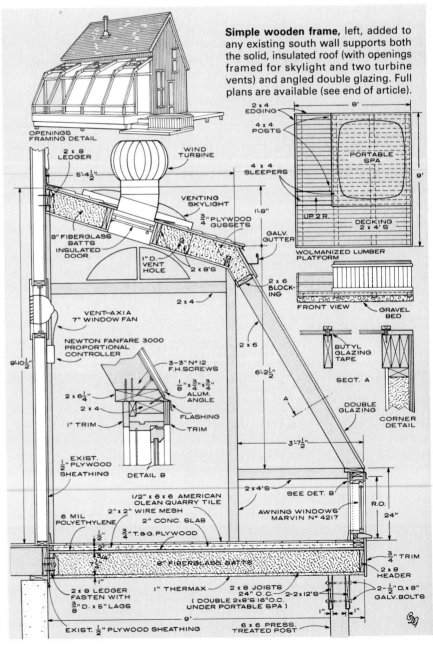

Simple wooden frame, left, added to any existing south wall supports both the solid, insulated roof (with openings framed for skylight and two turbine vents) and angled double glazing. Full plans are available (see end of article).

Pouring and smoothing cubic yard of concrete took an hour. After striking off excess flush with form, finish with bull float.

Half-inch quarry tiles atop 2-inch concrete slab create thermal storage mass. Bed them in a thin-set mortar.

Ribs are formed with plywood gussets glued and nailed across the joint on each face. Use waterproof glue such as resorcinol.

Inside finishes for the sunspace are ½-inch gypsum board on the wall and ceiling. A 6-foot-wide door opens into the house.

summer. A 2-inch-thick concrete floor slab covered with ½-inch quarry tile provides some thermal mass to store solar heat. To maximize solar heat for direct warming of adjacent areas of your house, you should keep thermal mass to this minimum. But to retain most heat *within* the sunspace—say, for growing plants—you may want a greater storage mass.

Natural ventilation for summer is important. Awning windows are installed along the floor perimeter, and two 14-inch-diameter wind turbines and a venting skylight are on the roof. Insulated, weatherstripped doors were built to seal off the turbine vents in the winter. On winter nights, I close the double French doors between the house and sunspace, allowing the outer temperature to drop into the forties.

To control the sunspace environment, I've installed a Vent-Axia window fan in the wall between the sunspace and the house. A special controller for the fan has a low setting

that protects plants from freezing by blowing heat from the house on unusually cold nights. Another setting blows warm air into the house on sunny days. A solid-state circuit automatically varies fan speed with demand.

A 10-foot × 10-foot × 8-inch concrete-block Trombe wall existed on the side of my house before I began the sunspace. After removing the glazing, this also became thermal storage mass. Unless you have a masonry house, a similar heat storage probably isn't available to you. But the equivalent thermal storage is possible with about twenty-five 20,000-Btu phase-change tubes placed in direct sun against the wall. Thirty cubic feet of water in containers against the wall can achieve the same mass.

Selecting the glazing material was easy: The 46 × 76-inch (or 34 × 76-inch) insulated, tempered, sliding patio-door replacements I used are the most economical double glazing I could find. I

bought them for less than $80 each by shopping around. Although low-iron glass would transmit more light into the sunspace, I found it was expensive and hard to find—*Jeff Milstein. Drawing by Carl De Groote.*

PROJECT SPONSORS—AND WHAT THEY SUPPLIED

American Olean Tile Co., Lansdale, PA 19446 (6 × 6-inch Canyon Red quarry tile); Celotex Corp., 1500 N. Dale Mabry Highway, Tampa, FL 33607 (Thermax insulation); Crown Vent, Dundee Park, Andover, MA 01810 (Vent-Axia fan); Jacuzzi Whirlpool Bath, P.O. Drawer J, Walnut Creek, CA 94596 (Cambio portable spa with redwood skirt); Koppers Co. Inc., Pittsburgh, PA 15219 (Wolmanized lumber for Jacuzzi platform); Marvin Windows, Warroad, MN 56763 (awning windows); Newton Electric, 2390 River Road, Selkirk, NY 12158 (proportional controller for fan); Olympic Stain, Box 1497, Bellevue, WA 98009 (exterior stain); Sears, Roebuck & Co., Sears Tower, Chicago, IL 60684 (14-inch-diameter wind-turbine vents; skylight; 5-foot sliding patio door with storm glazing).

converting attics to living space

Many attics offer enough head room to allow room additions without the added cost of raising the roof or extending outward from the existing foundation. Basically, roof construction is either by trusses or by conventional framing. A trussed roof consists of framing members, usually wood, constructed in a manner that leaves little extra space. Expansion into an attic with a trussed roof is almost always too expensive. Framing members can't be removed without weakening the roof structure, and nothing should be done without first consulting an architect or structural engineer.

A conventionally framed roof, on the other hand, can often be used to gain additional space. Normally this type of roof consists of no more than ceiling joists over the living space, rafters for the roof, and collar beams overhead every third or fourth rafter. Occasionally there are additional framing members—wood braces—used to cut down the span of rafters and, therefore, reduce their size. If your attic has these additional braces, design your expansion around them—they should not be removed without expert advice.

Is there enough space?

The generally accepted minimum headroom for any living space is 7 feet from floor to ceiling. A lower ceiling makes an area seem cramped and uncomfortable even to people under 6 feet tall. In fact, if your family members are exceptionally tall, you may even want to go to an 8-foot ceiling height.

Normally, an attic has 7 or 8 feet of headroom—and some have even more—near the roof ridge. The problem arises in the width of the area in which you can maintain the desired headroom. A 12-foot area can accommodate almost any use you might want to put it to, and the wider the area, the more versatile the design possibilities. If the usable width is less than 12 feet, you're severely restricted in how you can use the space and, if it is only a few feet wide, the attic is useful for little more than storage, unless you decide on the expensive approach of raising one or both sides of the roof.

To good advantage

There are four basic ways to take advantage of an attic space without disturbing the roof.

1. Build the side walls to standard room height and add a ceiling overhead. A ceiling will make the room feel like a standard room, since the sloping attic lines are lost, but this works only if the attic area is spacious.

2. Build the side walls to standard height and leave the top open to the rafters. This approach is suitable for attics that are not so wide—the openness overhead makes the space seem

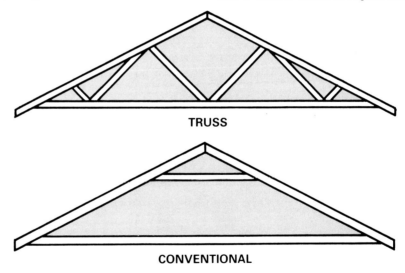

TRUSS

CONVENTIONAL

Trussed roof obstructs the use of an attic for living space. In most cases, a conventionally framed roof allows easy conversion of attic to living space.

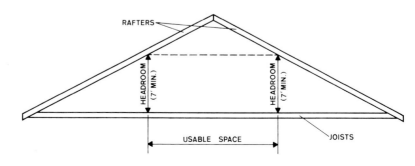

To determine how much of attic area is usable for living space, measure the width of the area in which you are able to maintain a minimum headroom of 7 feet.

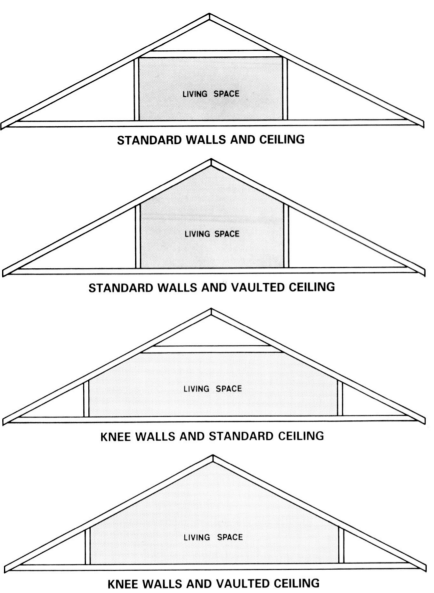

STANDARD WALLS AND CEILING

LIVING SPACE

STANDARD WALLS AND VAULTED CEILING

LIVING SPACE

KNEE WALLS AND STANDARD CEILING

LIVING SPACE

KNEE WALLS AND VAULTED CEILING

LIVING SPACE

The four ways to develop the shape of an attic: Side walls may be full height or shorter knee walls. And in either case, a standard flat ceiling can be used, or area can be left open to rafters for a more spacious feeling.

larger. Also, vaulted ceilings may have special design appeal.

3. Build shorter "knee walls" at the sides, instead of standard height walls, and add a ceiling. This will add to the size of the room, and the low ceiling space along the knee wall can be used for furniture, seating, and other uses that don't require full headroom.

4. Build knee walls and leave the top open to the rafters. Whether or not you install a ceiling is more a matter of taste than cost factor, but again, the room that's open above will seem larger than it is.

The generally accepted height for knee walls is 4 feet. But this standard was established when roof slopes tended to be steeper than they are today. A better way to determine the height is to locate the point at which

Before starting work in attic, put in temporary footing (plywood or similar material), securing it to joists. Place edges near a joist so you don't overstep and tip over the footing material.

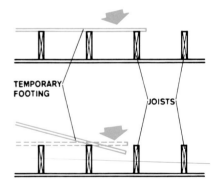

TEMPORARY FOOTING

JOISTS

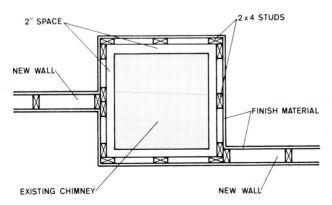

2" SPACE

2 x 4 STUDS

NEW WALL

FINISH MATERIAL

EXISTING CHIMNEY

NEW WALL

If chimney must be enclosed (above), maintain 2-inch spacing between it and framing materials. To reduce wasted space, try to combine it with a new wall system.

PANELED WALLS

EXISTING CHIMNEY

the headroom is 6 feet, or equal to the tallest member of the family over 6 feet, and then move 3 feet toward the outside wall. For a roof pitch of 8 in 12 (8 inches of rise per foot of width), the knee wall will be exactly 4 feet. A flatter roof will yield a taller knee wall. If, however, your roof is steeper, come back to the point where the knee wall will be 4 feet high. A shorter knee wall will make the area difficult to clean. Also, the 4-foot height makes installation of finish materials easier.

Which rooms?

An attic can be converted into almost any kind of facility, with a few notable exceptions. It's not a good idea, for example, to plan the area for use by elderly or handicapped persons who might find the stairs a problem. And don't plan the space as the main kitchen and family/great room. These are often-entered rooms and the location would create traffic problems and overburden the family with stair climbing. Also the outside access that is often an essential feature of a family/great room or kitchen is not available in an attic location.

Ideal uses for attic space include: standard bedrooms, master bedroom suite, guest bedroom, bath, recreation/ entertainment room, adult retreat, den, office/study, hobby/craft center,

Through-attic chimney is expensive to move, but it can be turned into the focal point of the new living area by using it as a room or space divider. A hearth can be added for cushions and seating, or to support a wood-burning stove or a free-standing fireplace.

library, stereo/music room, darkroom, artist's studio, playroom.

Plumbing in an attic

Since the attic is above the main level of the house, there is no problem getting the waste lines to drain by gravity flow, leaving you free to design any type of plumbing you wish. The only rule is that the attic walls containing the plumbing should be directly over the walls that contain plumbing in the floor below. This will greatly simplify and reduce the cost of plumbing hookups. If you want to install two baths, or a bath and kitchenette or wet bar, make the rooms back to back so you can use one connection to existing plumbing.

Adding natural light

Most attics are dark, having only a small gable window at each end—or no window at all. This is a relatively easy problem to solve; you can add skylights, gable windows, and/or dormers.

Skylights are the least expensive way of getting natural light into an attic room and can be installed with a minimum of labor. They can be installed at almost any location, making them the most versatile solution to the natural-light problem. Openable skylights have the further advantage of allowing room ventilation and a measure of temperature control. In warm weather, an openable skylight near the ridge will let hot air rise out

of the room, while cool air enters through a lower window.

Gable windows are more limited— they can only go in gable walls. If you have a hip roof, you can't install a gable window. If you already have a window in one or both of your gables, it's probably too small for your attic conversion. Remove it and install a new, larger window, or add extra windows on each side.

Dormers are a little more difficult to install; they require some roof removal, a lot more framing, and a new roof area. They do, however, give the attic area extra space, though usually not enough to make a real difference. They also affect the house's architectural appearance; for this reason, if dormers are part of your plan, you may want to add them to the rear of the house. If you add them on the front, put in at least two, equidistant from the house ends or otherwise balanced with the present design.

Chimneys, ducts, pipes

One or all of these are likely to be rising through your attic. Vent pipes and ducts can usually be enclosed as part of a new partition, or moved, if necessary, without too much difficulty. If the vent is a plumbing stack, it probably rises directly above the lower floor's plumbing wall, so it can be located within any new plumbing wall needed for the attic conversion.

A chimney is a tougher problem—

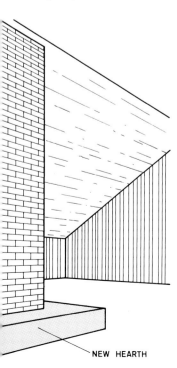

NEW HEARTH

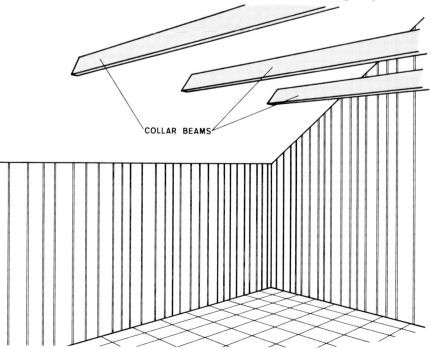

COLLAR BEAMS

Collar beams can be raised a few inches to gain room; but do not remove them without first consulting an expert. Instead, leave the collar beams exposed (above), and then, trim them out with finishing lumber for an interesting ceiling effect.

it costs a lot to move one. So, if possible, turn it into an asset by using it as a room divider (paint the brick, if you wish) or putting a wood stove or freestanding fireplace in front of it. If the chimney brickwork is too ragged to make it the focal point of a room, you can frame around it and cover the frame with finish materials. Keep the wood framework at least 2 inches away from the chimney and, if possible, work the enclosed chimney into any wall system you plan.

Adding a stairway

Another problem that must be considered when you plan an attic conversion is where to locate the stairs. Access to many attics is simply through a square hole in a hallway or closet ceiling, or up a folding staircase. Of course, neither of these is sufficient; if access to attic living space isn't reasonably convenient, the area will not be used. Try to install a standard staircase or, if space is very tight, a spiral staircase; nothing less will suffice.

The location of the stairs is usually dictated by the design of the main floor. Wherever the staircase can be placed on that level sets where it will enter the attic. But you should also consider the attic development. If the staircase enters in the middle of the attic, it makes a natural division for two rooms. If it must be located at one end of the attic, you may be limited to a single room, unless you have enough width for a hallway. The important thing is to plan your remodeling so the stairway does not begin or end in a private room—such as a bedroom—that family members must pass through in order to get to shared space.

Many municipalities require two exits for attics used for living space (especially bedrooms). Even if you're not required to, you may want to add an additional escape route for your family in case of fire. If you don't have room for two sets of stairs, get an emergency ladder and keep it near a window large enough to crawl through. An emergency ladder doesn't cost a lot, and it will add tremendously to your peace of mind. Just be sure every family member fully understands how the emergency escape is used.

Construction problems

Most attics are poorly ventilated and can become extremely hot. Before the area is insulated and a cooling system installed, temperatures can reach more than 140 degrees. That's why it's a good idea to avoid working in the heat of summer; even the young are susceptible to heat stroke. Also, it's easier to hire any subcontractors you may need in cooler weather—sometimes even at a better price than during their busy summer months. And make ventilation your first construction priority; skylights, windows, and vents should be installed as soon as you've laid temporary footing. Wear a breathing mask when doing any work, such as sawing, that creates dust. Don't take safety lightly, especially when working in a poorly ventilated and poorly lighted attic.

Getting large materials into the attic may also be a problem. If you can't hoist materials up from the outside through a window or other opening, you may have to cut them to size before transporting them to the attic.

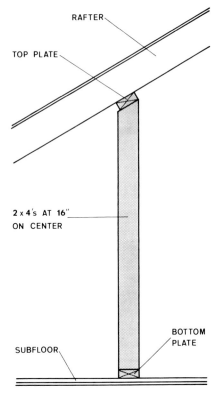

For walls perpendicular to rafters (above), studs should be cut on the same slope as the roof at the top, with the top plate secured to the rafters as shown in drawing.

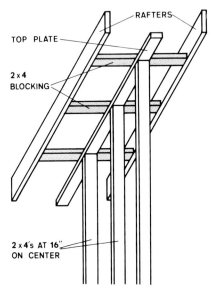

For walls that run parallel to the rafters (left), provide braces at the top, between the rafters, for added stability.

If flat ceiling is put in over attic rooms (below), it should be constructed in same way as a standard ceiling, with 40-pound live-load capability, full insulation, an access hole, and proper ventilation.

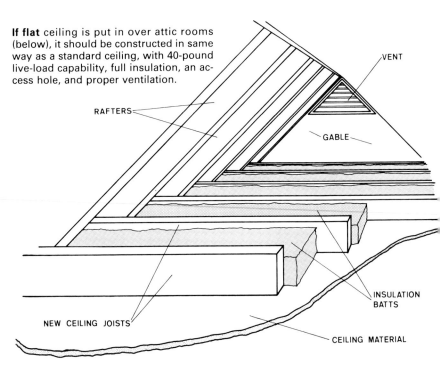

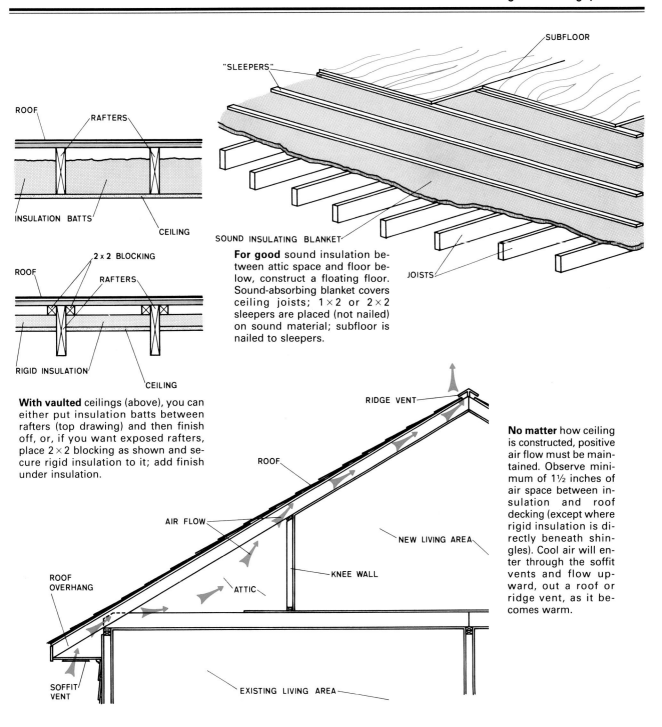

ROOF
RAFTERS
INSULATION BATTS
CEILING

2 x 2 BLOCKING
ROOF
RAFTERS
RIGID INSULATION
CEILING

"SLEEPERS"
SUBFLOOR
SOUND INSULATING BLANKET
JOISTS

For good sound insulation between attic space and floor below, construct a floating floor. Sound-absorbing blanket covers ceiling joists; 1 × 2 or 2 × 2 sleepers are placed (not nailed) on sound material; subfloor is nailed to sleepers.

With vaulted ceilings (above), you can either put insulation batts between rafters (top drawing) and then finish off, or, if you want exposed rafters, place 2 × 2 blocking as shown and secure rigid insulation to it; add finish under insulation.

RIDGE VENT
ROOF
AIR FLOW
NEW LIVING AREA
KNEE WALL
ROOF OVERHANG
ATTIC
SOFFIT VENT
EXISTING LIVING AREA

No matter how ceiling is constructed, positive air flow must be maintained. Observe minimum of 1½ inches of air space between insulation and roof decking (except where rigid insulation is directly beneath shingles). Cool air will enter through the soffit vents and flow upward, out a roof or ridge vent, as it becomes warm.

But carefully record any measurements needed for cutting so you don't waste expensive materials.

Although most ceiling joists are designed to support a minimum "live" load of 40 pounds per square foot, which is sufficient for furniture and normal activities, there is a possibility that your ceiling joists may need to be beefed up. If you are unsure, have an expert look at your attic and calculate the bearing capacity of the joists. Should they need additional support, he can advise you of the best approach to take.

The small cost of an hour or two of an expert's time could save you from an expensive disaster later.

Sound insulation

A thick carpet and pad installed in the attic will absorb most low-frequency sounds, such as footsteps. For additional sound insulation, construct a relatively inexpensive "floating floor." Lay a full covering of insulation or other sound absorbing material over the existing joists or decking. Then place 2 × 2 sleepers at 16 inches on center, perpendicular to the joists.

Don't nail the sleepers—just lay them in place. Then nail the subfloor to the sleepers. This will greatly reduce all frequency levels of noise traveling from one floor to another.

If carefully planned, an attic conversion can add a lot of living space at minimum cost. Look at your attic closely before you begin any work. Determine the problems you will encounter, then develop a strategy for solving those problems. When you do, the work will not only go more smoothly, but, in the long run it will cost a lot less—*Herb Hughes.*

creating a basement suite

A home is made for enjoyment, but if your family is typical, full enjoyment calls for more room than you've now got. If your house has a basement that's currently being used only for storage (or housing the family pet), additional living space is readily at hand.

The basement of the town house shown here was a combination laundry room–storage dump before being converted into this attractive family suite. It was created by Masonite Corp. as a showcase for prefinished hardboard paneling. The panels shown are called Woodfield, a narrow-groove textured board that comes in standard 4 × 8-foot sheets.

To achieve a similar transformation of your basement, start with a plan to scale (½ inch = 1 foot) that shows the location of all permanent objects such as the furnace or boiler, tanks, washtubs, support posts, and so forth. Try to isolate utility items from the living area by carefully plotting the location of partition walls. In our example (following), a stud wall of 2 × 4s on 16-inch centers was erected between the laundry area and the rest of the basement.

Next, in red pen, draw in the location of lights, vents, exhaust fans, and other obstacles that extend from the ceiling. Now draw a pattern of 1-inch squares (representing 2 × 2-foot ceiling tile) on a piece of tracing paper. Move the tracing paper over the plan so that the obstacles clear any of the seams in the tile. You may find that you'll have to reposition lights and other movable fixtures to ensure that support strips don't interfere (given the limitation of a reasonable starting point for the tile).

The Woodfield paneling from Masonite is designed to be butted together over stud framing. Use adhesive or color-coordinated finishing nails vertically spaced 12 inches apart to mount the panels directly to the studs. Paint the edge of all studs that stand behind panel joints black so that if the panels contract later because of weather, the gap won't be noticeable.

Use 2 × 2 stock to fur out along perimeter walls except where obstructions must be cleared. Where small pipes and conduit protrude, frame out the entire wall length with 2 × 4s.

Match these "before" shots with their color counterparts to appreciate what partitions, paneling, and furnishings can achieve. Study/entertainment area at left began as waste space in top photo. Recessed shelving in cozy dining nook is built into partition that hides old laundry area ("before" shot above). Open stairwell (below) was enclosed for storage.

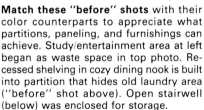

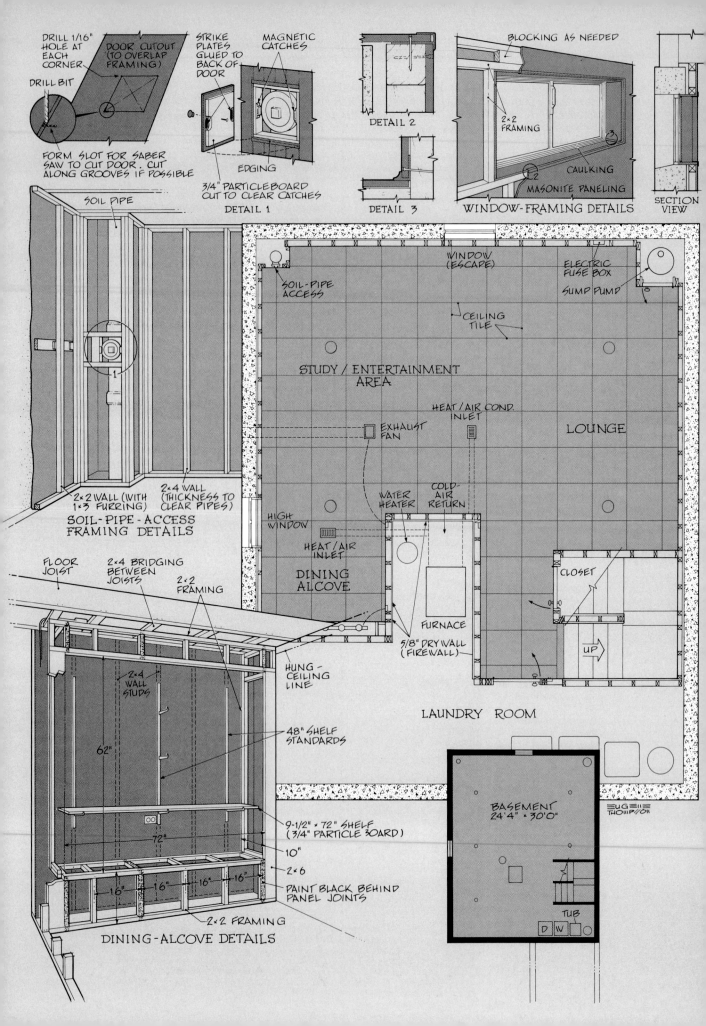

DRILL 1/16" HOLE AT EACH CORNER

DOOR CUTOUT (TO OVERLAP FRAMING)

STRIKE PLATES GLUED TO BACK OF DOOR

MAGNETIC CATCHES

DRILL BIT

FORM SLOT FOR SABER SAW TO CUT DOOR. CUT ALONG GROOVES IF POSSIBLE

EDGING

3/4" PARTICLEBOARD CUT TO CLEAR CATCHES

DETAIL 1

DETAIL 2

BLOCKING AS NEEDED

2×2 FRAMING

CAULKING

MASONITE PANELING

DETAIL 3

WINDOW-FRAMING DETAILS

SECTION VIEW

SOIL PIPE

2×2 WALL (WITH 1×3 FURRING)

2×4 WALL (THICKNESS TO CLEAR PIPES)

SOIL-PIPE-ACCESS FRAMING DETAILS

WINDOW (ESCAPE)

SOIL-PIPE ACCESS

ELECTRIC FUSE BOX

SUMP PUMP

CEILING TILE

STUDY / ENTERTAINMENT AREA

HEAT/AIR COND. INLET

LOUNGE

EXHAUST FAN

HIGH WINDOW

HEAT/AIR INLET

WATER HEATER

COLD-AIR RETURN

CLOSET

DINING ALCOVE

FURNACE

UP

5/8" DRYWALL (FIREWALL)

LAUNDRY ROOM

FLOOR JOIST

2×4 BRIDGING BETWEEN JOISTS

2×2 FRAMING

2×4 WALL STUDS

62"

HUNG-CEILING LINE

48" SHELF STANDARDS

BASEMENT 24'4" × 30'0"

9-1/2" × 72" SHELF (3/4" PARTICLE BOARD)

72"

10"

2×6

PAINT BLACK BEHIND PANEL JOINTS

16" 16" 16" 16"

2×2 FRAMING

DINING-ALCOVE DETAILS

TUB

D W

EUGE THOMPSON

OP PLATE NAILED TO JOISTS OR TRUSSES

PAINT STUDS
BLACK
BEHIND
PANEL
JOINTS

PLUMB WITH
LEVEL AND
SHIM BEFORE
NAILING TO
1×3 FURRING

SHIMS

1×3 FURRING
ATTACHED TO
FOUNDATION
OVER VAPOR
BARRIER

2×2
FRAMING

VAPOR
BARRIER

16"   16"

2×2 BASE
PLATE

VAPOR
BARRIER

DETAIL 4

2×2
FRAMING

2-1/2"   CHALK LINE

2 WALL-FRAMING DETAILS

ALIGN NEW PANELING FLUSH
WITH EXISTING DRYWALL

MASONITE
PANELING

EXISTING
POST

MASONITE
PANELING

EXISTING
WALL

DOOR

JAMB

STAIR
STRINGER

1/4
ROUND

NEW 2×4
FRAMING

CHALK
LINES

USE WOOD
SHINGLES
AS WEDGES
BETWEEN
FRAMING
AND JAMBS

CORNER
BEAD

DETAIL 5

CLOSET AND STAIRWELL DETAILS

Frame, too, around soil stacks, valves, electrical panels, and other fixtures that you'll have to get to from time to time so that access can be easily provided.

In our example, a small door was built in the framework around a soil pipe for access to the cleanout. A corner was built out and a full-length door added to maintain a passage to a sump pump.

To build small access ways, first measure the obstruction to determine the best location for an opening. Now, cut the framing for this opening to size. With a sheet of paneling lying face up on the floor, position your framing for the neatest effect with the panel grooves, letting the cut lines fall on the vertical grooves wherever possible.

Now drill $1/16$-inch holes at each corner of the opening. Mark a saw line between the holes. At two opposite corners drill several more holes close together along the saw line, forcing the drill back and forth to make a slot for the saber-saw blade.

Now turn the panel over and mark the cutting line of the opening between the corner holes, slip the saw blade into the drilled slots, and cut out the access door.

When you're finished, sand the edges of the opening smooth. If you put edging strips around the opening, any sawing imperfections will be concealed.

Glue a piece of particleboard or plywood to the back of the piece you've cut out to make a cover, and add a small handle and strike plates. Install the framework and add magnetic or other suitable catches to hold the cover in place.

Our stairwell closet was framed with 2×4s and covered with $1/2$-inch drywall before mounting the paneling. The door framing was positioned so that the door was centered on the short wall. Measure the distance from the edge of the panel to where the door opening is to be cut out, and adjust so that at least one cut line will fall along a panel groove.

Lay the door panel in position on the back of the paneling and trace its outline. Remove the door, put the panel on saw horses, and carefully cut the outline (from the panel's back) using a saber saw or trim saw, being sure to pad the front so as not to scar the finish.

Coat both the door and the back of the cutout paneling with contact cement and bring the coated surfaces together when the cement is tacky. (You'll want to use the slipsheet tech-

nique to ensure alignment, since you can't separate the pieces once you've started.) Roll the paneling with a rolling pin to be sure the bond is tight around all edges.

Now nail the wall paneling in place and hang the door. Add the stairwell paneling, including the corner beads. Note that the lower edge of the panel is cut on an angle to match the top of the stair stringer. Any imperfections along the cut edges of the paneling can be hidden by trim pieces.

The bookshelves are framed with 2×4 and 2×2 stock. After the main dividing wall is framed, install the back sheet of paneling before building the front section of the alcove. Install electrical outlets, switches, and overhead lights. The apron at the top is ideal for a 48-inch fluorescent fixture. Build the framework, then cut the rest of the paneling to size and install throughout, being sure to use inside and outside corner molding where panels meet at 90 degrees.

To install the ceiling, the lip of the perimeter support-angle pieces should be at least 3 inches below the lowest duct or pipe to allow enough room for you to insert the tile after the support grid is up. However, even if there are no projections, you should allow 6 inches of free space below the joists.

To show the position of the perimeter support-angle pieces, snap a chalk line (with the aid of a helper) around the room at a height that will allow inserting the tiles without interference. Use a level to be sure the line is perfectly horizontal all around.

Now install the support-angle pieces. Plan to run the main hangers of the system at right angles to the joists so as to avoid having to bridge between them. Install the hangers and tile.

In our example, the ductwork for the heating and cooling system of the house was extended and vented into the new family room. Air conditioning helps keep the new addition dry. In addition, an exhaust fan was installed to keep moisture and temperature-related expansion and contraction of the paneling to a minimum.

Once you've installed your flooring, you will be ready to move in your furnishings—and start living more spaciously—*Charles A. Miller.*

The materials for this project were supplied by these companies: *Paneling:* Woodfield Design paneling, Masonite Corp., 29 N. Wacker Drive, Chicago, IL 60606. *Furniture:* Marin County Collection upholstery and occasional tables, Composite Collection party table and chairs, desk, Riverside Furniture Corp., Fort Smith, AR 72902. *Ceiling:* Cumberland Pattern acoustical ceiling, Armstrong World Industries, Lancaster, PA 17604. *Carpeting:* Form III, North Vernon, IN 47265.

host's wine cellar

What was once a catchall for little-used items can become a place to get away to—a tasting room for sharing your prize wines with friends or for hosting intimate wine-and-cheese parties. Line the walls with bottle bins and you've got storage that lets you buy economically now, taking advantage of case discounts. At last you'll have space for "laying down" young wines to let them mature into the fine vintages you'd otherwise have to pay a fortune for in two to ten years.

This is what Syd Dunton, in cooperation with the California Redwood Association (591 Redwood Highway, Suite 3100, Mill Valley, CA 94941) created from a small basement that was previously the location of a gas furnace, water heater, and other household paraphernalia.

The basement was a designer's nightmare. It had exposed floor joists overhead, two ugly columns supporting a structural beam, a concrete floor,

and a 2-foot-high concrete abutment running around the perimeter, with open stud walls above it.

The job started with insulation: R-11 fiberglass in the stud cavities and a 3-mil polyvinyl moisture barrier stapled to the existing studs. That is covered with 1×12 redwood boards, applied at a 45-degree angle.

The abutment was turned into a bench in some areas, covered by 1×12 redwood planks. In the remaining area it's faced with redwood, to produce a wainscoting effect for the wine bins (seventy-two in all) built above it.

The furnace, along with the water heater and softener, is enclosed behind a partition wall insulated with fiberglass batts. Access to the utilities is through a hinged panel.

The concrete floor is covered with 12×12-inch unglazed terra-cotta tiles mortared in place. The floor joists overhead are covered with tar paper, over which strips of lath are nailed for a trellised effect. Lighting—aside from

candles—comes from incandescents in wall sconces. Lights are controlled by dimmer switches.

The only natural light reaching the cellar is through a stained-glass door, which filters the light for pleasant effect and better wine-storage conditions (the less ultraviolet light the better).

Perhaps the cleverest idea is the treatment of the support columns. One is built into a storage divider. The other becomes the support for a small round table where wine and cheese are served.

To add the look of age appropriate to a wine cellar, decorative corbels (cut from redwood) trim the beams, and the redwood throughout is distressed and mellowed with an oil stain.

The besement stays cool, a condition essential for proper storage of wine, thanks to the isolated heating devices. The utility enclosure also helps keep vibrations away from the wine bottles, which store better in peace and quiet—*Charles A. Miller.*

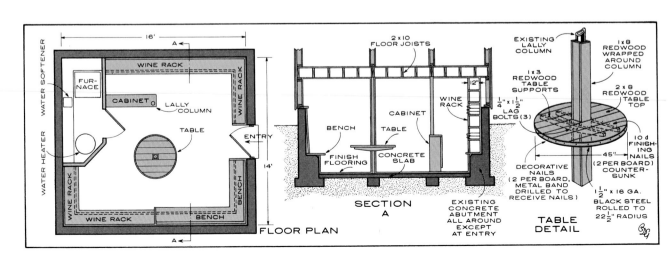

daylighting your basement

A sun-bathed basement wall is what prompted this homeowner to install a bay window to create a cheery bedroom for two small girls. Even if your house sits a lot lower in the ground, you can do the same by regrading or digging a window-well.

Breaking through the wall takes a cold chisel and hammer for block; a power chisel or rented jackhammer for poured concrete. (Wear safety goggles.) Smooth the opening's edges and butter them with a stiff mortar mix. Then set in a three-sided frame of nominal 2-inch-thick lumber as wide as the concrete is thick. The existing house plate serves as the top of the frame. Plumb and level the frame while the mortar is still wet—this is the rough opening for the window you will install.

The bay window should be built in advance (see illustration), so you can make the frame and opening to match. The stock window need not be double-hung, of course; a casement window would be easier to open at arm's length, for example. Assembled ready-to-install bay and bow windows are available in standard sizes. You may want to consider these before making the rough opening.

Double-hung window, flanked by fixed sash, forms bay unit (left). Set into opening cut through foundation wall, it's shingled on top. Roof could also be copper-covered plywood. Besides light and air, deep-set window provides wide shelf or seat (below). Narrow cedar trim frames window, matches wood ceiling. Valance hides the window shade; heat register is above it.

Photos: Western Wood Products Assn.

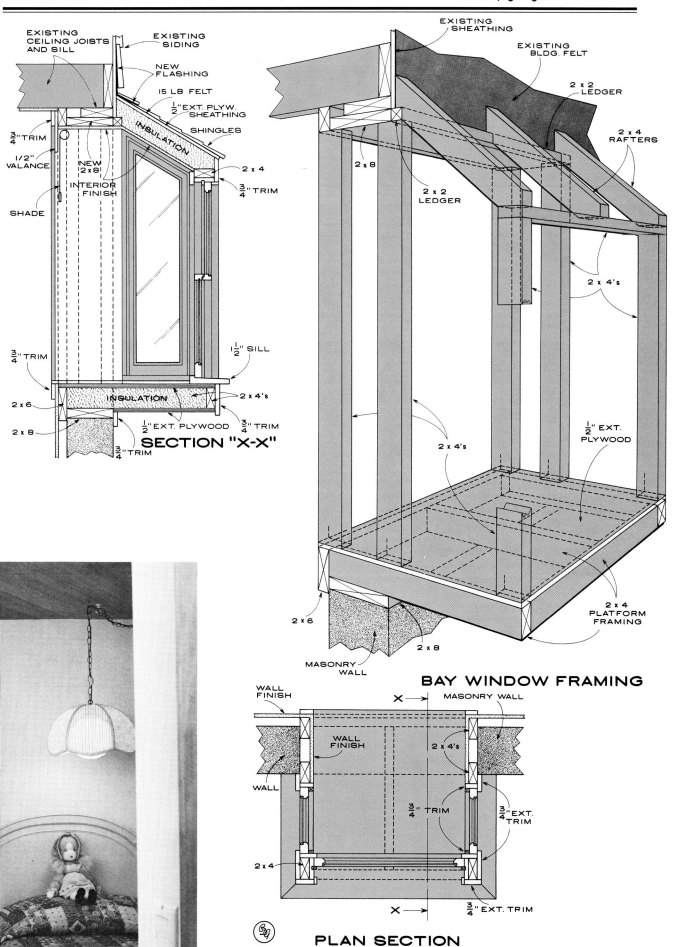

EXISTING
CEILING JOISTS
AND SILL

EXISTING
SIDING

NEW
FLASHING

15 LB FELT

½" EXT. PLYW.
SHEATHING

SHINGLES

INSULATION

¾" TRIM

½" VALANCE

NEW
2 x 8

INTERIOR
FINISH

SHADE

2 x 4

¾" TRIM

¾" TRIM

1½" SILL

INSULATION

2 x 6

2 x 8

2 x 4's

½" EXT. PLYWOOD

¾" TRIM

¾" TRIM

SECTION "X-X"

EXISTING
SHEATHING

EXISTING
BLDG. FELT

2 x 2
LEDGER

2 x 4
RAFTERS

2 x 8

2 x 2
LEDGER

2 x 4's

2 x 4's

2 x 4's

½" EXT.
PLYWOOD

2 x 4
PLATFORM
FRAMING

2 x 6

2 x 8

MASONRY
WALL

BAY WINDOW FRAMING

WALL
FINISH

MASONRY WALL

WALL
FINISH

2 x 4's

WALL

¾" TRIM

¾" EXT.
TRIM

2 x 4

¾" EXT. TRIM

X

X

PLAN SECTION

how to handle condensation problems

Condensation, a nagging problem for most homeowners, is simply the result of water in the air changing from a vapor to a liquid. Condensation occurs whenever warm, moist air meets a cooler, drier surface—a wall, window, whatever.

Condensation problems run the gamut from minor to serious, such as decayed framing. Among the most common complaints: (1) Windows that drip condensed water onto sills, where paint peels and wood rots. (2) Damp basement walls that foster mildew and erode the joint between the wall and floor. (3) Sweating fixtures, particularly toilet tanks.

A home may also have hidden condensation problems that can cause structural decay and decrease the energy-saving effectiveness of wall insulation. Ironically, it is the tight, heavily insulated, newer house that is most susceptible to these hidden problems. In fact, severe condensation inside tight construction can produce so much water that the homeowner mistakes the sweating for a leaky roof.

Here's how a typical, hidden condensation cycle develops. First, the air inside the house accumulates moisture from cooking, washing, bathing, and other sources (estimates run from 7 to 10 gallons a day). This airborne moisture behaves like water—that is, it seeks its own level. Moisture-laden air doesn't bunch up in a corner; it distributes itself throughout the house and always moves toward drier air—particularly the cold, winter air outside.

During this equalizing process, the vaporized moisture penetrates interior surfaces, including wood, paint, and most wallpapers. This can contribute to such surface problems as bad paint adhesion and cracked wallboard joints, but the real trouble is inside the wall. There, the warm, moist air contacts studs, rafters, joists, pipes, and other surfaces that are absorbing cold from outdoors. The result? Seven to ten gallons of condensation, soaking and compressing fiberglass insulation and coating framing members, pipes, and sheathing with water. The dark, unventilated, thoroughly soaked cavity is a near perfect environment for the production of odors, mildew, and rot.

Even after the wall cavity surfaces are soaked, there may be enough moisture left to continue the equalizing path toward drier, outside air. When this happens, the moisture cracks and peels the exterior paint film as it passes through the siding. In other words, the moisture is going to get out one way or another—it's just a question of how much damage it does along the way.

In modern, tight, heavily insulated houses, it's not uncommon to have an extra duct to bring in enough outside air to support furnace combustion. If a duct is needed to bring in air, a duct is needed to move moisture-laden air out.

This leads to **Step 1** in the whole-house solution to condensation: *Duct out moisture from the source.* This means installing a bathroom vent fan; a kitchen vent fan or, better yet, a range hood; clothes-dryer vents.

Step 2 is an extension of the venting operation: *Ventilate attic and crawl spaces.* There are formulas for determining whether existing ventilation needs to be increased.

For attics, the overall rule is one square foot of vent for 300 square feet of attic floor. For greatest efficiency, continuous-strip or plug-type vents should be used in roof soffits in addition to conventional, gable-end, grill vents. If there is a vapor barrier, you should have 1 square foot of inlet (soffit type) and 1 square foot of outlet (gable type) per 600 square feet of attic floor. At least half the total vent area should be at the gable ends. Without a vapor barrier, about twice as much vent space is needed.

For crawl spaces, the rule is one square foot of vent per 150 square feet of bare ground. A complete vapor barrier (4-mil or thicker polyethylene or

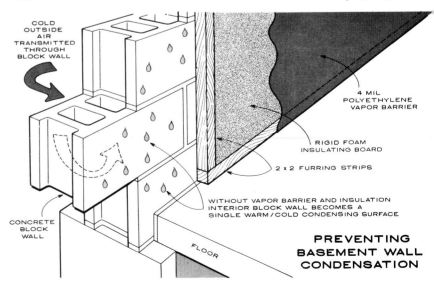

COLD OUTSIDE AIR TRANSMITTED THROUGH BLOCK WALL

4 MIL POLYETHYLENE VAPOR BARRIER

RIGID FOAM INSULATING BOARD

2 x 2 FURRING STRIPS

WITHOUT VAPOR BARRIER AND INSULATION INTERIOR BLOCK WALL BECOMES A SINGLE WARM/COLD CONDENSING SURFACE

CONCRETE BLOCK WALL

FLOOR

PREVENTING BASEMENT WALL CONDENSATION

Perm ratings for common materials

Brick, 4-inch-thick	0.80 – 1.10
Concrete block, 8-inch-thick	2.40
Plaster on gypsum lath	20.00
Gypsum wallboard, ⅜-inch	50.00
Hardboard, ⅛-inch	1.10
Fir sheathing, ¾-inch	2.90
Fir plywood, ¼-inch exterior	0.70
Mineral wool	29.00
Expanded polystyrene bead	2.00 – 5.80
Aluminum foil	0.00
Polyethylene, 4-mil	0.08
Polyethylene, 8-mil	0.04
Asphalt felt paper, 15-pound	5.60
Enamel, two coats on plaster	0.50 – 1.50

55-pound asphalt-impregnated paper, lapped at least 3 inches at the seams) reduces vent requirements to one foot per 1,500 square feet of crawl space.

Step 3 is as crucial as it is unknown to most homeowners: *Balance your perms.* What's a perm? It's the rating unit used to indicate the amount of moisture that can pass through building materials (permeability) at a given temperature and pressure. The lower the number, the greater the material's resistance to water-vapor transmission. Aluminum foil, for instance, is rated at 0.00; porous gypsum drywall, at 50.00. Every material in a wall has a perm rating, and the placement of materials, each with a different perm rating, determines whether or not moisture transmission will cause damage.

For example, consider how interior moisture would pass through a brick veneer exterior wall with these characteristics: The interior paint (primer and finish coat) has a perm rating of 4.00. Underneath it is drywall, rated at 50.00. These materials allow moisture to penetrate up to the 4-mil, polyethylene vapor barrier, which is rated at 0.08.

This nearly impervious barrier stops most of the moisture and, because the paint and drywall transmit the warm room temperature to the barrier surface, the moisture does not condense at this point. The low perm rating for polyethylene allows only small amounts of moisture through the barrier into the wall cavity—amounts that pass right through the kraft-backed insulation, rated at 29.00 for the insulation, 42.00 for the paper backing.

With the wall's insulation still dry and intact, the moisture, in very modest amounts, would then pass through the structural insulating board, rated at about 50.00, until it meets the cold, brick veneer (rated at about 1.00), where it would condense. An air space

between the sheathing and the brick is provided to ventilate this area. Similarly, aluminum siding has small vent holes placed to let air in, or, in severe conditions where no vapor barrier is used, to let condensation out.

The message is simple: A continuous vapor barrier (perm rating from 0.00 to 0.50) must be installed on the warm side of the wall to prevent interior moisture from entering the wall cavity, where it can cause structural damage and destroy the thermal resistance of insulation. Foil-backed insulation, sold as combined insulator/vapor barrier, works effectively only if the foil skin is continuous (lapped and securely stapled over studs).

Here's how to deal with some of the common condensation trouble spots.

First, let's take windows, where condensation blocks the view, rusts metal fittings, peels paint, and rots sills. The best solution: Storm windows. Single-thickness glass has a U-factor (heat-transmission rate) of 1.13 and loses heat ten times faster than an insulated wall. The high temperature variation from side to side makes it an ideal condensing surface. A second pane of glass cuts the U-factor to .50, gives you 40 to 50 percent more thermal resistance, and eliminates the single, warm/cold condensing sur-

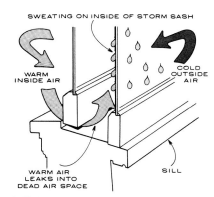

INTERIOR WINDOW SASH LEAKING

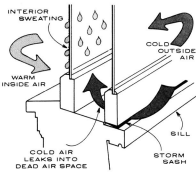

EXTERIOR STORM SASH LEAKING

face. Extra protection for wood components can be derived from coats of glossy, oil-based paints and, if necessary, a finish coat of marine-grade spar varnish.

The second common complaint is wet basement walls. In this case, you must distinguish between seepage and condensation. One test involves gluing a small pocket mirror or aluminum foil patch to the wall overnight. If the back is wet and the surface is clear, you've got a leak. If the surface is fogged and damp, you have condensation.

Combat condensation on masonry basement walls with insulation (eliminating the single, warm/cold condensing surface) and a vapor barrier (preventing moisture from getting to the masonry surface). This can be a complicated and costly process, although you will wind up with finished walls—an obvious and valuable improvement. The work involves (1) furring out the walls, (2) adding fiberglass batts or, to save space, rigid foam panels, (3) covering with a vapor barrier, and (4) finishing with drywall, over which you may panel.

Before you undertake the insulation and vapor barrier solution, there are two steps you should try. First, eliminate or duct out sources of moisture. This step should include a check of your clothes dryer's vent pipe, which can become clogged with lint. Second, check into the cost of a dehumidifier. They are rated by the pints of water they can remove from 80-degree air at 60 percent relative humidity in a twenty-four hour period. A serviceable unit should include a humidistat control, which you can adjust to maintain the relative humidity of basement air just below "wall-sweating" conditions. This moderate investment may be more than enough to control a variable and seasonal problem.

The third common condensation complaint, sweating toilet tanks, is more of a problem in summer. In this case, the porcelain tank acts as the single, warm/cold condensing surface. The inside is chilled by the cold water, while the outside is warmed by moist bathroom air. Two solutions are possible. First, if condensation is minor, improving ventilation may solve the problem. Second, where condensation is persistent, empty the tank, let it dry thoroughly, then apply a ½-inch-thick foam rubber lining with waterproof resin glue. This insulating layer (on the tank walls only) should last indefinitely—*Mike McClintock.*

floating stairs

Louise Rigg's stairs are a flight of fancy. The dramatic steps, which hang from the soaring ceiling of Rigg's modern Berkeley, California, home, give one a sensation of floating, the interior designer says. "It's an unattached feeling, not like climbing at all. But people who are nervous about heights must be careful."

The steps are not Rigg's first floating staircase. Most of the thirteen homes she has built and lived in over the years have included a variation on the theme, but her collaboration with architect Alex Achimore may be the most successful. The design is not just a thing of beauty; it also opens more usable floor space in the redwood-paneled living room—which Rigg uses to striking effect as the setting for her grand piano.

The steps, laminated assemblies of 2-inch-thick planks, are supported on both ends: They are tied into the adjacent wall with hidden steel-plate angle brackets, and they hang from the ceiling on threaded steel rods. Achimore said that the support rods could have been eliminated and the steps fully cantilevered, but a stronger wall would have been necessary. In fact, Rigg did just that with her previous stair design, but then the supports ran through the wall into an adjoining garage. In this case the wall faced an outdoor patio, so the structure had to be entirely contained within the wall. Besides, the support rods serve a second purpose as hand grips. Copper sleeves around them blend visually with the redwood theme.

The wall is a double-stud frame with a 3 × 12 stringer running from the lower to the upper level. Support

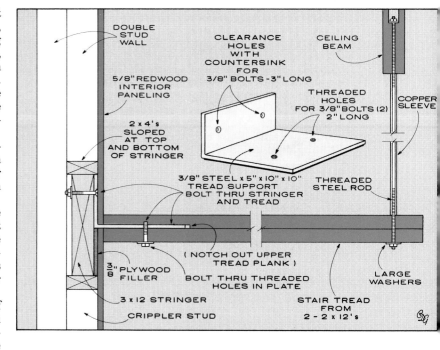

brackets fabricated from ⅜-inch-thick steel plate are bolted through the stringer and into a groove notched in the stair treads. The stringer is sandwiched by parallel 2 × 4s that hold the space needed for the brackets, and additional studs run to ceiling and floor as backing for panel treatment.

The vertical supports are anchored with nuts and washers into a beefed-up roof beam. Since that beam had to be drilled and installed before the roof went on (long before the stairs were installed), it created some interesting problems for the builder. According to Achimore, the contractor laid out the holes in the beam by placing the stairs on the floor and shining a vertical light from a homemade laser onto the

overhead support. Then he drilled holes and secured the steel rods before proceeding with the roof. The rods dangled there for more than a month until finish work was begun and the stairs were hung.

The entire house—inside and out—is covered with redwood, partly because of its resistance to fire and termites and its good acoustical properties, but mainly because its warm texture complements the owner's taste for unusual shapes and angles. The material is not strong enough to support great weight, however, so both the stair treads and ceiling beam are made from Douglas fir, stained to match the vertical-grain paneling—*Daniel Ruby. Photos by Jeff Weissman.*

extra living space within your walls

It started out simple, as home-improvement projects often do. We wanted to divide a studio/work area from our dining area with a partition. But we soon realized that, unless we created additional rooms, we'd soon outgrow our home. We commissioned architect Jeff Milstein to develop a complete interior redesign. Our requirements were:
● A master bedroom with closets and dressing area.
● A guest or child's bedroom.

● Two work areas, one for a graphic designer, a second for a writer-editor.
● Built-in shelves for a large collection of books.
● A walk-in storage closet.

In addition, since most of the space we were working with had no direct access to windows, daylighting and ventilation had to be carefully considered.

Along with his preliminary drawings, Jeff prepared a scale model of the project. This helped us visualize the new rooms and make changes before we actually started building. As you can see from the final floor plans, Jeff created a multi-level set of interlocking rooms, all contained in an interior area that measures about 12½ by 24 feet.

While our project was designed for

When you're carving a new room out of an existing one, a curved wall lessens the impact of the intrusion. Hallway with entrance to dressing room is at left, walk-in closet is at right. Master bedroom (inset) is on upper level, behind curve. Half walls are topped with cherry wood.

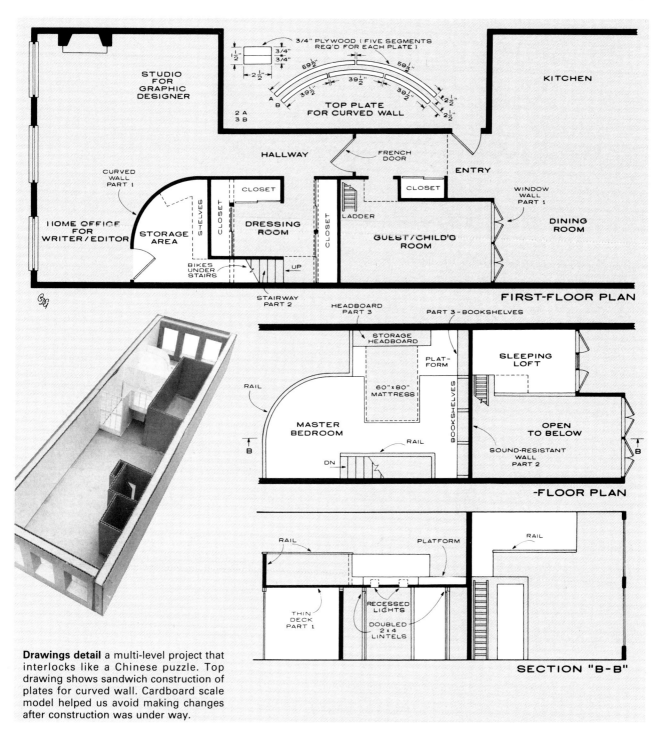

First-floor plan labels:

STUDIO FOR GRAPHIC DESIGNER

KITCHEN

3/4" PLYWOOD (FIVE SEGMENTS REQ'D FOR EACH PLATE)

1/2" · 3/4" · 3/4"

2 1/2"

59 1/2" · 59 1/2"

39 1/2" · 39 1/2" · 39 1/2"

2 1/2" · 2 1/2" · 2 1/2"

A · B

2 A
3 B

TOP PLATE FOR CURVED WALL

HALLWAY

FRENCH DOOR

ENTRY

CURVED WALL PART 1

CLOSET

CLOSET

WINDOW WALL PART 1

HOME OFFICE FOR WRITER/EDITOR

STORAGE AREA

SHELVES

CLOSET

DRESSING ROOM

CLOSET

LADDER

GUEST/CHILD'S ROOM

DINING ROOM

BIKES UNDER STAIRS

UP

STAIRWAY PART 2

FIRST-FLOOR PLAN

Floor plan labels:

HEADBOARD PART 3

PART 3 - BOOKSHELVES

STORAGE HEADBOARD

PLATFORM

SLEEPING LOFT

RAIL

60" x 80" MATTRESS

BOOKSHELVES

MASTER BEDROOM

RAIL

OPEN TO BELOW

DN

B

SOUND-RESISTANT WALL PART 2

B

-FLOOR PLAN

Section B-B labels:

RAIL

PLATFORM

RAIL

THIN DECK PART 1

RECESSED LIGHTS

DOUBLED 2 x 4 LINTELS

SECTION "B-B"

Drawings detail a multi-level project that interlocks like a Chinese puzzle. Top drawing shows sandwich construction of plates for curved wall. Cardboard scale model helped us avoid making changes after construction was under way.

a full floor with 12½-foot ceilings in a 100-year-old cast-iron loft building-turned-residential-condominium, many of the ideas and construction techniques we used could be adapted to your own home-remodeling projects. This article shows you tricks for faster framing; how to construct a curved wall; and how to install an ultrathin deck that might just make a second level practical—for storage or as a sleep loft—in a room with a lower ceiling than ours. There are ways to

build stairways and sound-resistant walls, lighting tips for low ceilings, and detailed plans of built-ins for the master bedroom.

We began by drawing chalk lines to mark the location of first-floor walls. A fast way to frame partitions is to use metal channels as bottom plates. Screw the channel to the floor and then pop studs in one at a time, fastening each with two screws, one driven from each lip of the channel. (A screw gun is an essential tool.) We

used wood studs and top plates—doubled in most walls—for the strength needed to support the deck. To save space, we used 2 × 3 studs throughout most of the project.

We used a six-foot-long string to mark the location of the curved wall's bottom plate. Then we temporarily tacked strips of ¾-in. plywood to the floor and scribed the same curve on them. These were removed, cut, and assembled for top plates (see drawing and photo for details). We cut the

Curved plates are sandwiches of five segments cut from ¾-in. plywood (see drawing, page 73). Skil's Sand Cat belt sander smooths edges once segments have been glued and screwed.

Framing for the curve: 2×3 studs are oriented radially. Decking is nailed to curved top plate. Note higher hallway headroom with conventional 2×6 joists to support the ceiling.

Studs were screwed to metal channel plates. Skil's cordless Boar Gun makes working on a large project easier (no snaking extension cords). Note doubled top plate and t&g decking.

How to build stairways

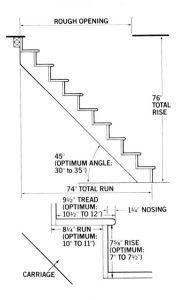

ROUGH OPENING

76" TOTAL RISE

45°
(OPTIMUM ANGLE:
30° to 35°)

74" TOTAL RUN

9½" TREAD
(OPTIMUM:
10½" TO 12")

1¼" NOSING

8¼" RUN
(OPTIMUM:
10" TO 11")

7⅝" RISE
(OPTIMUM:
7" TO 7½")

CARRIAGE

The most comfortable angle for a stairway is 30 to 35 degrees, but any angle between 20 and 50 degrees is possible. Minimum width for a stair is 24 in.; for two-way traffic, width should be at least 36 in. If you follow these rules, the stairway will be safe and comfortable to use: 1 run + 1 riser = 17 to 18 in.; 1 run + 2 risers = 24 to 25 in.; 1 run × 1 riser = 70 to 75 in. Generally 30- to 35-degree stairs are designed with a rise of 7 to 7½ in. and a run of 10 to 11 in. The run plus the nosing give the tread width. It's essential that all risers be equal and all treads be equal, or you'll trip on uneven steps.

One of the industrial shielded light fixtures we used inside closets (see text).

How to build sound-resistant walls

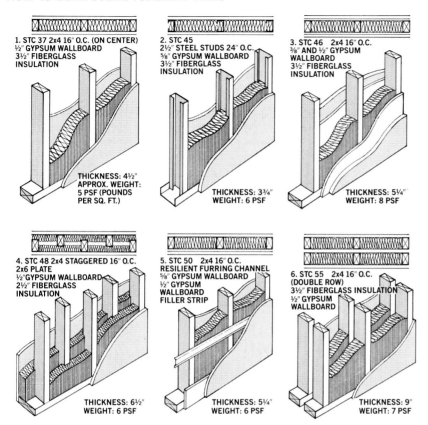

1. STC 37 2x4 16" O.C. (ON CENTER)
½" GYPSUM WALLBOARD
3½" FIBERGLASS
INSULATION

THICKNESS: 4½"
APPROX. WEIGHT:
5 PSF (POUNDS
PER SQ. FT.)

2. STC 45
2½" STEEL STUDS 24" O.C.
⅝" GYPSUM WALLBOARD
3½" FIBERGLASS
INSULATION

THICKNESS: 3¾"
WEIGHT: 6 PSF

3. STC 46   2x4 16" O.C.
⅜" AND ½" GYPSUM
WALLBOARD
3½" FIBERGLASS
INSULATION

THICKNESS: 5¼"
WEIGHT: 8 PSF

4. STC 48 2x4 STAGGERED 16" O.C.
2x6 PLATE
½"GYPSUM WALLBOARD
2½" FIBERGLASS
INSULATION

THICKNESS: 6½"
WEIGHT: 6 PSF

5. STC 50   2x4 16" O.C.
RESILIENT FURRING CHANNEL
⅝" GYPSUM WALLBOARD
½" GYPSUM
WALLBOARD
FILLER STRIP

THICKNESS: 5¼"
WEIGHT: 6 PSF

6. STC 55   2x4 16" O.C.
(DOUBLE ROW)
3½" FIBERGLASS INSULATION
½" GYPSUM
WALLBOARD

THICKNESS: 9"
WEIGHT: 7 PSF

For typical sound walls shown, STC ratings indicate how well a wall stops noise. Here's what they mean in terms of blocking loud speech, according to Certainteed: STC 30—loud speech audible and understandable; STC 35—loud speech audible but not understandable; STC 40—loud speech barely audible; STC 45—you must strain to hear loud speech; STC 50-loud speech not audible. There are three ways to reduce sound transmission; added mass, with extra layers of gypsum board; discontinuous construction to minimize direct connection of wall materials; and fiberglass batts to absorb sound in the wall.

channel almost through with a carbide saw blade every five inches and then screwed it to the floor along the chalk line. Studs for the curve are 12 inches on center; we determined where gypsum-board joints would fall and used doubled studs at those points. Finally, we nailed on the top plate.

We used ⅜-in. gypsum board horizontally, and applied it dry—without first wetting or dampening it. We first nailed one end firmly to the starting stud. Then we *slowly* bent the sheet around the curve, nailing it at each stud as we went. We lapped two ⅜-in. layers on the outside of the curve for strength. Tips: You'll need two people—one to bend, the other to nail. Be sure to use lots of nails. And finally, when it comes to spackling and finishing the joints, use lots of compound.

To preserve headroom, Jeff devised a tongue-and-groove deck that takes up only 1½ inches of space. For a 12-foot-six-inch ceiling, that leaves six feet two inches-plus for each level.

"The 2×6 t&g decking will just support the loads if no span exceeds seven feet," Jeff advised. Besides the doubled top plates of first-floor walls, two doubled 2 × 4 lintels support the decking. The lintels keep maximum spans within specs.

We installed the decking one piece at a time, snugging each joint as tightly as possible. Hammering blocks of scrap decking are essential to avoid damaging the t&g joints. We face-nailed the boards with two 16-penny nails at each support. The "finish" side of the decking faces down; it's the ceiling for the first floor. Gray industrial carpeting covers the top.

When the deck was finished, the project began to look as though we were building a small house inside our home.

The architect's plans called for a stairway for access to the master bedroom. (For the guest bedroom's smaller and higher sleeping loft, we opted for a simple ladder.) Because of our

tight space limitations, the stairway is only 24 inches wide, just adequate for one-way traffic. It also rises at a 45-degree angle. That's about as steep a stair as you'd want to use in residential construction, according to Humanscale, a design guide published by MIT Press. Humanscale specifies a 45-degree stair with eight-inch risers and nine-inch treads, including the nosing (see "How to Build Stairways," above.) In our case we had a total rise of 76 inches and a total run of 74 inches. That allowed 10 risers at 7⅝ inches and nine treads at 9½ inches, including a 1¼-inch nosing. While it's not intended for continuous use, the stairway is more than adequate for access to a single room. It's also reasonably comfortable to climb and descend, keeping in mind that it is a short flight of stairs. For most general-purpose stairs, however, follow the guidelines outlined in the box above.

For privacy between the adjoining bedrooms, plans called for a sound-resistant wall. We decided on a wall that provides an STC (sound-transmission class) rating of 50. At 5¼ inches thick (see example 5), the wall takes up almost no more space than a normal partition. It uses metal channels applied horizontally on 24-inch centers to studs to minimize the direct connection of drywall on one side. Fiberglass batts fill stud cavities to further reduce sound transmission. In sound-wall construction, it's important to seal all joints carefully; we caulked around all edges—and all electrical outlets, as well.

When framing is complete, electrical work can be done. While electricians installed the wiring (required by code in my locality), we started the drywall, taking care not to enclose *both* sides of any one wall before it had been wired.

Low-ceiling lighting

Lighting our new rooms presented special problems. In closets the low (six ft. two in.) ceiling precluded, for obvious safety reasons, the bare bulbs normally used. We chose industrial-type steel-and-glass safety lamps, commonly called "vaportights," (see photo). Vaportight fixtures are available from electrical-supply houses, or the manufacturer listed at the end of this article can provide a list of local dealers.

The dressing room demanded adequate lighting, yet it, too, had only a six-ft.-two-in. ceiling. We used two recessed lights—Progress P 7's—equipped with Fresnel-lens trims that are flush with the finished ceiling. The

7¾-in.-deep recessed fixtures are housed inside the platform bed in the master bedroom above.

The hallway also has a relatively low (seven foot) ceiling, which prevented us from using track lights or hanging fixtures. This ceiling is framed with 2 × 6s that provide a cavity adequate for three Progress P 6 recessed lights. These shallow housings are only five inches deep. They're fitted with step baffle trims and reflector floods to light artwork on the hallway walls.

The master bedroom occupies the new second story we added above the dressing room and closets, and is reached via its own staircase (at lower right in the photo below). It's a generous room, measuring 12½ by 18 feet at its longest point (see floor plan). The built-ins contribute to the efficient use of space in the master bedroom:
• The peninsula position of the carpeted platform bed eats less floor space.
• The bed's storage headboard gets maximum use from normally wasted space.
• The wall of bookshelves holds a 750-volume library and cuts only 9¼ inches from the room.

Carpet bed

The platform bed, made for a queen-size mattress, takes up less space than a conventional bed. And since it's covered with the same carpet as the floor, it also looks smaller than it really is. Construction is simple:

Atop the bedroom's tongue-and-groove 2 × 6 floor, we built a 12-inch-high box of ¾-inch-thick plywood. (Inside the box: recessed lights for the first-floor dressing room.) The box is

Wall of shelves holds a sizable book collection with ease. A pair of clip-on spotlights on headboard illuminates artwork gives reading light, too.

Dressing room has walls of closets. Birch-veneer sliding doors hang on Stanley's extruded-aluminum tracks and adjustable nylon rollers.

Shaker-style pegboard mounted on one wall of dressing room is handy for hanging clothes. Behind wall: stair to master bedroom.

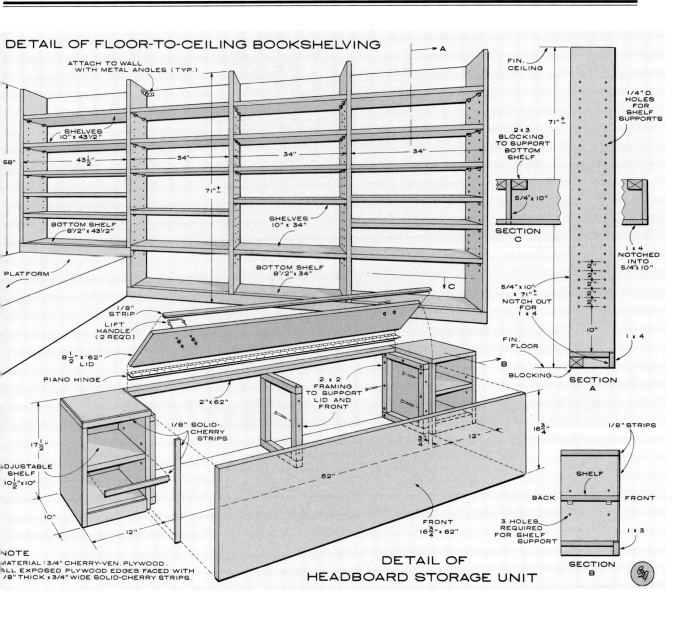

DETAIL OF FLOOR-TO-CEILING BOOKSHELVING

ATTACH TO WALL
WITH METAL ANGLES (TYP.)

SHELVES
10" x 43½"

58"

43½"   34"   34"   34"

71"±

BOTTOM SHELF
8½" x 43½"

PLATFORM

SHELVES
10" x 34"

BOTTOM SHELF
8½" x 34"

FIN.
CEILING

1/4" D.
HOLES
FOR
SHELF
SUPPORTS

2 x 3
BLOCKING
TO SUPPORT
BOTTOM
SHELF

5/4" x 10"

SECTION
C

5/4" x 10"
x 71"±
NOTCH OUT
FOR
1 x 4

71"±

1 x 4
NOTCHED
INTO
5/4" x 10"

FIN.
FLOOR

BLOCKING

SECTION
A

1/8"
STRIP

LIFT
HANDLE
(2 REQ'D)

8½" x 62"
LID

PIANO HINGE

2" x 62"

1/8" SOLID-
CHERRY
STRIPS

2 x 2
FRAMING
TO SUPPORT
LID AND
FRONT

16¾"

3/4"   12"

17½"

ADJUSTABLE
SHELF
10½" x 10"

10"

12"

62"

FRONT
16¾" x 62"

3 HOLES
REQUIRED
FOR SHELF
SUPPORT

1/8" STRIPS

SHELF

BACK   FRONT

1 x 3

SECTION
B

NOTE
MATERIAL: 3/4" CHERRY-VEN. PLYWOOD.
ALL EXPOSED PLYWOOD EDGES FACED WITH
1/8" THICK x 3/4" WIDE SOLID-CHERRY STRIPS.

DETAIL OF
HEADBOARD STORAGE UNIT

reinforced by a 2×3 knee wall in the middle. The entire platform and bedroom floor are covered with well-padded carpeting.

The headboard has handy shelves for reading material, and a generous storage bin for bedding. This 62-inch-long-by-17-inch-deep-by-9½-inch-wide compartment is accessible through the hinged lid on top.

Using a table saw, I first cut out all pieces needed for the unit, as shown in the drawing above. All parts came easily out of a four-by-eight-foot sheet of ¾-inch-thick cherry-veneer plywood. Next I assembled the two mini bookcase units for each end of the headboard. They're glued and screwed together. I countersank all exposed screws and filled the holes with plugs cut from solid cherrywood. All exposed plywood edges are faced with ¾-inch-

wide-by-⅛-inch-thick strips, ripped from solid cherry.

The center bin's components—the headboard and top—are screwed from the inside to 2×2 bracing. The bracing is screwed to the end units and to the plywood platform. A piano hinge and brushed-aluminum-wire pulls complete the sleek, high-tech look of the unit. As finish for the cherry, I rubbed on tung oil.

What better location for a wall of books than against a sound-resistant wall? The bookshelves line the entire sound wall from floor to ceiling. For a unified look, I used ⅝-by-10-inch lumber for both uprights and shelves. This stock is a full 1¼ inches thick, which allows the shelves in the left-hand bay to span its 43½-inch width unsupported.

All shelves except the bottom-most

are adjustable, resting on steel pins inserted into ¼-inch holes in the uprights. Four pins support each shelf. I bored the rows of ¼-inch holes on a drill press, clamping several uprights together and drilling them simultaneously. The center uprights have holes bored through them; I set the drill-press depth adjustment so that the bit stopped halfway through the end uprights.

The uprights are attached to the floor with 2×3 blocking (see drawing). Steel angles secure them to the wall. A coat of clear sealer helps preserve the wood's light tone—*Richard Stepler. Design by Jeff Milstein. Drawings by Carl De Groote.*

MATERIAL SOURCES
Recessed lights: **Progress Lighting**, Erie Ave. & G St., Philadelphia PA 19134. Sliding-door hardware: **Stanley**, New Britain CT 06050. Vaportight fixtures: **Rab Electric Mfg. Co.**, 321 Rider Ave., Bronx NY 10451.

cut the cost of adding on

When you are adding on to your home, you have a constant enemy: the budget. It's not uncommon for square footage to shrink and accessories to be scratched from the list between initial planning and the completed project.

But there is a way to cut your costs and save a lot of time, without sacrificing what you want. By using a modular system to design and build your addition, you can minimize material and labor waste.

Planning. Planning on a modular basis means that your addition is designed to accommodate standard size construction materials. The result is that the work requires fewer cuts and less seaming, and there is less waste for both framing and finishing materials. Most of the material you purchase then goes into your home—it's not hauled to the dump as scrap—and that means you get maximum square footage with a minimum of building materials.

Also, the labor saved makes the job go much more quickly. And, if you are using a contractor, the time saved can substantially lower the price you have to pay.

Overall dimensions. Although construction materials are available in a wide variety of sizes, there is a system of commonality throughout. With few exceptions, building materials work best on a module of 4 feet.

The message here is that you should plan your addition so the length and width are in multiples of 4 feet. If you do, the work will go more smoothly and materials will go farther. Some additional savings are possible if the length of your room addition is planned in multiples of 8 feet; however, depending upon circumstances, the savings may not amount to much.

Floor framing. Generally, joists are designed to span the short dimension (width) of a house. In order to avoid using extremely large joists, one or more beams may be run the length of the house to reduce the span.

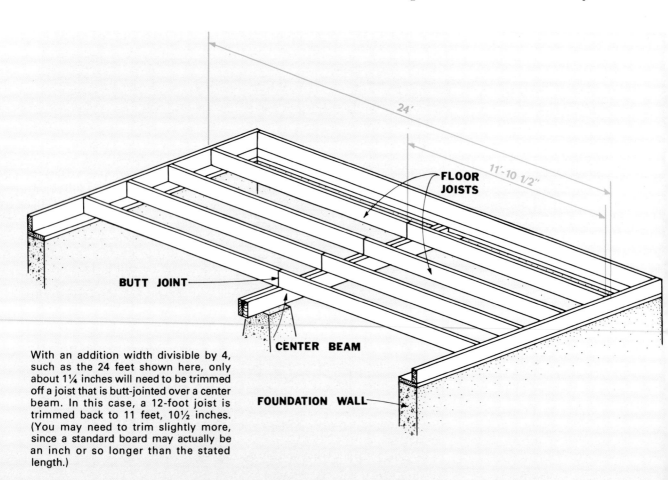

With an addition width divisible by 4, such as the 24 feet shown here, only about 1¼ inches will need to be trimmed off a joist that is butt-jointed over a center beam. In this case, a 12-foot joist is trimmed back to 11 feet, 10½ inches. (You may need to trim slightly more, since a standard board may actually be an inch or so longer than the stated length.)

BUTT JOINT

CENTER BEAM

FOUNDATION WALL

FLOOR JOISTS

24'

11'-10 1/2"

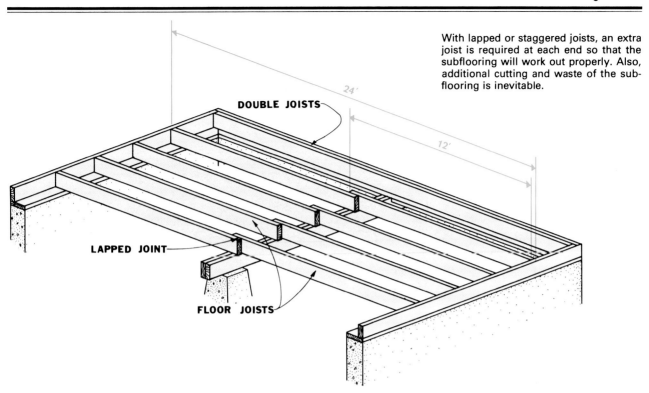

DOUBLE JOISTS

LAPPED JOINT

FLOOR JOISTS

24'

12'

With lapped or staggered joists, an extra joist is required at each end so that the subflooring will work out properly. Also, additional cutting and waste of the subflooring is inevitable.

Most additions will have either one center beam or none at all, depending upon the actual dimension. A 4-foot module works well for each. Since framing lumber is furnished in multiples of 2 feet, only a small piece must be trimmed from the end, as shown in an accompanying illustration.

Lapped or staggered joists may eliminate the need for cutting joists, but it requires double joists at the ends of the addition and additional work on the subfloor. "Butting" the joists is a better choice—it makes the overall job easier.

Framing system

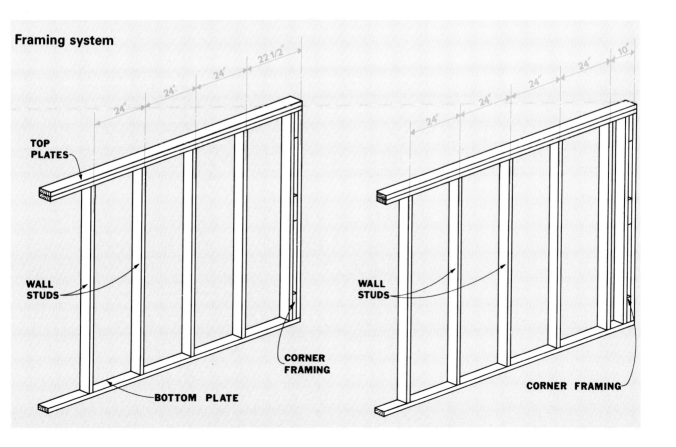

TOP PLATES

WALL STUDS

CORNER FRAMING

BOTTOM PLATE

24" 24" 24" 22 1/2"

WALL STUDS

CORNER FRAMING

24" 24" 24" 24" 10"

With a width in multiples of 4 feet and length in multiples of 8 feet, as shown, subfloor can be applied without any cutting or waste by allowing the seams to align along a single joist. Recent field tests have shown results of this technique to be equal in strength to a staggered subfloor.

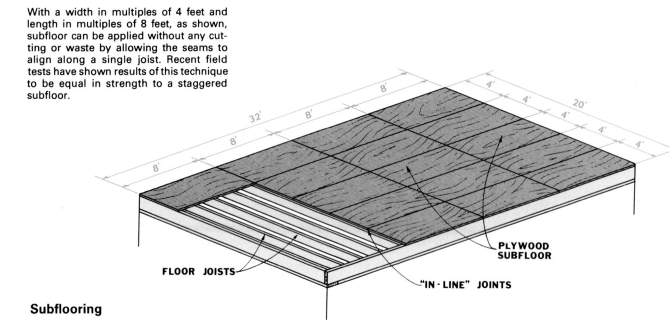

FLOOR JOISTS

PLYWOOD SUBFLOOR

"IN-LINE" JOINTS

Subflooring

The 4-foot module also works well for the length of the addition. Both 16-inch and 24-inch on center framing systems work out evenly in 4 feet. This helps maximize material usage by eliminating the need for an extra joist just a few odd inches from the end of the addition.

Subflooring. Most of the subflooring materials used today are manufactured in 4 × 8-foot sheets. The 8-foot dimension is placed at 90 degrees to the joists. When an addition's width is in multiples of 4 feet, and length is in multiples of 8 feet, the subfloor can be applied without any cutting or waste. This is accomplished by allowing the sheets to butt along the same joist. Field tests performed in recent years have shown that the common method of staggering plywood on subfloors and roof decking is no stronger than allowing the sheets to butt "in-line," along a single joist or rafter (check local codes).

Even if the length cannot be on an 8-foot module, adhere to a 4-foot module. The cutting will be at a minimum and waste may be eliminated or, at least, reduced.

Wall framing. As in floor framing, both 16-inch and

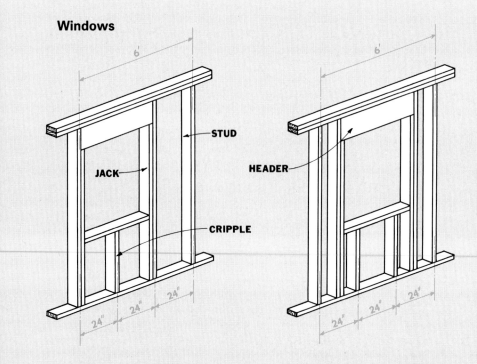

Windows

STUD

JACK

HEADER

CRIPPLE

WINDOW ON MODULE

WINDOW OFF MODULE

One advantage of modular construction can be seen in the accompanying drawings. When you use a 4-foot module, either the 16-inch or 24-inch (shown) framing system can be used with good results, and this applies to floor and roof framing as well as wall framing. Without a modular system, you can run into problems that cost time and extra material—you may, for example, be forced to place an extra stud or joist just inches from the end of your addition, as shown at the bottom of page 79. This page: Window at far left works with the framing system and will save one stud and cripple, compared to a window that works against the system, like the one near left. If, because of a window's width, only one side aligns, you still save cutting and placing one cripple.

24-inch stud framing work out evenly in a 4-foot module, eliminating odd sized stud spacing at the end of a wall. Today's sheathing materials and finish plywood and fiberboard panel siding all come in 4-foot widths. The only cutting for these materials, when using a modular system, will be for windows and doors.

There are many types of lapped siding, but most come in 8-, 12-, and 16-foot lengths. On a 4-foot module, there will also be less waste for this type of exterior or finish.

For masonry or masonry-faced walls, both the standard 8-inch brick and 16-inch block course out evenly in 4 feet. This reduces the need for breakage and the over- or under-sized mortar joists sometimes required to fit odd wall lengths.

Design your windows and doors to work *with* the wall framing, instead of against it. By aligning at least one side of a window or door on the stud spacing pattern you will cut down on the number of studs you need to frame the opening.

Corners. If your plans call for your new addition to be something other than rectangularly shaped, continue the 4-foot module through the wall corners. Design the width of a corner and the distance from corner to corner in multiples of 4 feet, as is shown in the illustration below. This will allow the framing and finishing materials to continue working out evenly, and so reduce the additional labor and extra materials usually associated with projects involving more than four corners.

Roofs. Both 16-inch and 24-inch framing and roof trusses work well in a 4-foot module. By observing a 2-foot overhang on both ends, the module will remain 4 feet in length for roof decking, though the width will vary because of the pitch of the roof. For flat (built-up) roofs, it will work out well in length and width.

As in floor framing, plywood decking may be seamed along a single rafter or truss, rather than staggered. If you use plywood clips on the roof decking, you eliminate the need for wood blocking underneath.

Roof trusses work particularly well with modular design. They provide strength equivalent to a conventionally framed roof, but at a much lower cost. Trusses are readily available from manufacturers in most areas, but can also be easily constructed on site.

Interior finish materials. The ideal room to finish is 12 × 12 feet, with a standard 8-foot ceiling. This allows walls to be covered evenly with two 4 × 12 sheets of gypsum board laid horizontally, or three sheets of 4 × 8 gypsum board or paneling laid vertically. The only cutting required would be for windows and doors. The floor could be covered with 12-foot-wide sheet vinyl or carpet, without seaming, and the ceiling would require three uncut 4 × 12 sheets of gypsum board. Such a room would waste virtually no materials and labor would be minimal.

But all rooms can't and shouldn't be 12 × 12 feet. Because of wall thickness, a home on a 4-foot module will have to have an odd-sized room.

Of course, you will want some rooms larger than 12 feet wide. Most carpets and sheet flooring also come in 15-foot widths. By observing 12 feet or 15 feet for one room dimension, the other dimension can be varied to make a larger or smaller room, but keep standard wall and ceiling material sizes in mind when setting the other dimensions. For a very large room, such as a recreation room, keep the width near, but not over, 24 feet. This allows laying two 12-foot widths of finish flooring side by side, requiring only one seam with little or no waste. The 24-foot width also works out well on walls and ceilings.

Interior finishing

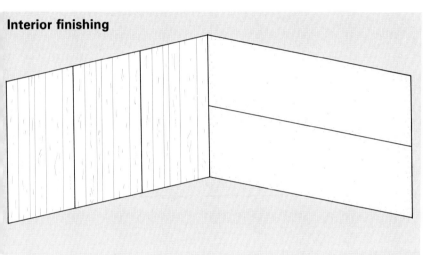

A 12-foot-wide interior wall with standard 8-foot ceiling can be conveniently covered with two 4 × 12-foot sheets of gypsum board laid horizontally (right) or three 4 × 8-foot sheets of gypsum board or paneling laid vertically (left). Only cutting required will be for windows and doors.

Areas that jut out

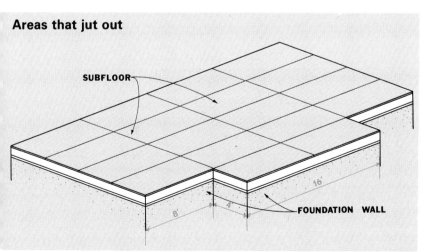

Are you planning an addition that is something other than rectangularly shaped? Even, for example, if your addition is to jut out from a main area, it's possible — and worthwhile — to keep everything on a modular system. To do that, make the jut width and length in multiples of 4 feet as shown.

In-line framing

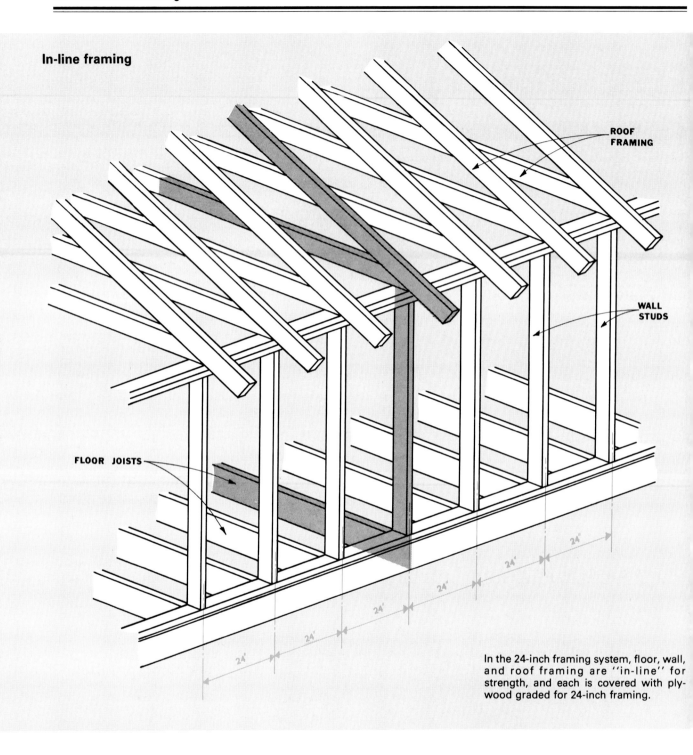

ROOF FRAMING

WALL STUDS

FLOOR JOISTS

24" 24" 24" 24" 24" 24"

In the 24-inch framing system, floor, wall, and roof framing are ''in-line'' for strength, and each is covered with plywood graded for 24-inch framing.

Construction: 24-inch framing. Floors, walls, and conventionally framed roofs have been customarily built on a 16-inch framing system. But with the present day popularity of the money- and labor-saving roof truss, normally placed on 24-inch centers, many homes being built today are based on the 24-inch framing system throughout, with floor joist, wall stud, and roof truss in line for strength. Plywood sheathing is required for the 24-inch system, but this works nicely if you plan to use plywood siding as a finish material for walls.

The 24-inch framing system could save a lot of material and labor, but be careful. While accepted by national agencies and commissions, the system has not been approved by all municipalities. Check your local building department first. Also, the floor joists will need to be larger and the plywood subfloor thicker. The additional cost of these could offset other savings, so check material prices and compare.

Whether you use the 24-inch framing system or not, modular design can save substantially in material and labor. So before you pound the first nail, be sure you've planned carefully for a minimum-waste, low-labor addition—*Herb Hughes.*

remove a supporting wall

If your house is conventionally built, the walls that run parallel to the roof ridge are usually supporting walls. Typically, these include the outer walls, supported by the foundation, and a central interior wall above the basement girder, which is supported by posts or Lally columns along its length.

The outside supporting walls carry the outer ends of the second floor or attic joists. The central interior wall carries the inner ends of the same joists. Thus, as it carries the inner ends of the joists on both sides, the interior wall supports approximately double the load of the outside walls, which carry only the outer ends of the joists on *one* side of the house.

If you want to remove a portion of a supporting wall, you must, of course, provide a means of support for the load the removed portion of wall originally carried.

First steps

However, before you even begin to remove the wall, you had better check it for plumbing that may be inside. This is usually easy to see in the basement. While wiring in a wall is fairly easy to relocate, major plumbing isn't so easy to shift. Be sure you know how you'll do it before removing any portion of the wall.

The first step in the actual removal job is opening the wall by removing the wallboard or other covering to expose the framing. Before you start removing the framing, it is necessary to place temporary supports at intervals (typically about 3 feet apart) between the studs. The supports should be long enough to jam at a *slight* angle between the 2 × 4 plate above the

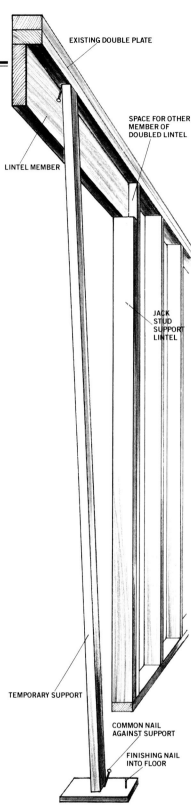

EXISTING DOUBLE PLATE

SPACE FOR OTHER MEMBER OF DOUBLED LINTEL

LINTEL MEMBER

JACK STUD SUPPORT LINTEL

TEMPORARY SUPPORT

COMMON NAIL AGAINST SUPPORT

FINISHING NAIL INTO FLOOR

After removing wallboard, remove studs by cutting near bottom after temporary supports have been put in place between floor and existing plate. Cut studs long enough so two can be used as jack studs at sides of wall opening.

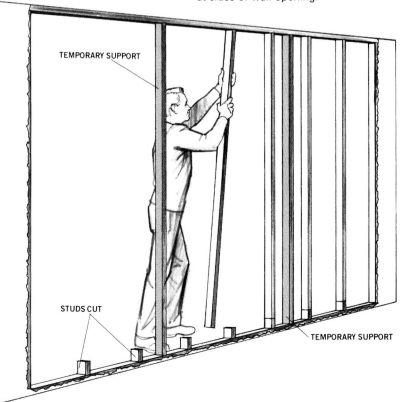

TEMPORARY SUPPORT

STUDS CUT

TEMPORARY SUPPORT

Temporary support here bears against existing plate, allowing one member of doubled lintel to be set in place. This supports plate while temporary supports are removed, so second member of lintel and spacer can be placed. A nail part way into underside of plate keeps upper end of support from slipping. At lower end, a wood pad keeps the temporary support from skidding on the floor. A common nail keeps support in place on pad, and a finishing nail into floor prevents skidding. The holding nails are removed with the support.

studs and the floor. A wood pad with a finishing nail driven part way into the floor at the base of each support will keep the lower end from skidding.

With the supports in place, you can remove the studs. This can be done by cutting through them near the bottom, so that the remaining upper pieces will be long enough to serve as the lintel-supporting member of the doubled stud at each side of the wall opening. (You need only two of these, but you might as well use the existing pieces of studding.) Hacksaw off any protruding nails left by stud removal.

The sole (2 × 4 at the base of the studs) is removed at this stage, allowing space for the doubled studs at each side of the wall opening. Since the sole is nailed to the subfloor, there will be a gap in the finished flooring where it is removed. The gap should be filled in with matching flooring, or covered with a shallow sill, depending on the finished appearance required by the individual job.

Extra studs

Nail the extra stud in place at each side of the opening, allowing just enough space to fit one of the lintel members snugly between the stud's upper end and the underside of the

JOISTS OVERLAP

JOIST

SUPPORTING WALL

OUTER SUPPORTING WALL

JOISTS OVERLAP ON GIRDER

JOIST

GIRDER

FOUNDATION WALL

GIRDER SUPPORT POST

FOUNDATION FOOTING   POST FOOTING

GABLE END

JOIST

END WALL

PARTITION WALL

PARTITION WALL

SUPPORTING WALL

SUPPORTING WALL

JOIST

POST

GIRDER

In typical house, supporting walls run parallel to roof ridge. Walls at right angles to ridge (partitions) usually are nonsupporting. End walls, though nonsupporting, are essential to rigidity of the structure.

Because girder, usually under centerline of house, supports ends of joists from both sides of house, it carries double the load of outer foundation walls, which support ends of joists from only one side.

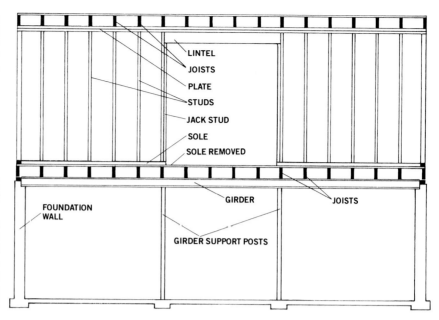

If removed wall section matches span between two girder support posts, the posts still carry the same load, because lintel above wall opening supports joists above it, and carries the load down doubled studs to the structure below.

plate. This calls for care. A small piece of the lumber size being used for the lintel can be helpful as a guide.

The temporary supports are left in place while the first member of the doubled lintel is set in place and nailed. After that, with the temporary supports removed, the first member of the doubled lintel provides support while you install the second member.

Spacers

As the doubled lintel doesn't add up to the same thickness as the 2 × 4 plate, spacer pieces must be used between the lintel members to avoid wall finishing complications. How thick the spacers must be depends on the age of the original lumber.

Today's 2 × 4 lumber is 1½ × 3½ inches. Older 2 ×4s were 1⅝ × 3⅝ inches. If the existing plate is the old size, and the doubled lintel is the modern size, you can use ⅝-inch plywood for the spacer. This can add a little strength if it's in fairly long strips the same width as the lintels.

If plate and lintel members are both modern size, you can use a strip of ½-inch lumber for a spacer.

Lintel width

As to lintel width, follow your local code if there is one. Otherwise, figure on doubled lintels of 2 × 4 lumber for spans less than 4 feet (like a doorway), doubled 2 × 6 for spans from 4 to 6 feet, doubled 2 × 8 for spans of 6 to 8 feet, and doubled 2 × 10 for spans of 8 to 10 feet. These are minimums.

If the opening is in the central supporting wall (above the basement girder), you can use the next larger lumber size for the spans, from 6 feet up if there's a second floor or occupied attic above. Beyond 10 feet, it's wise to use a truss with advice from your building inspector or an architect or professional builder. You can order the truss made to your required span through your lumberyard, but be exact in your dimensions and in describing the purpose of the truss—*George Daniels.*

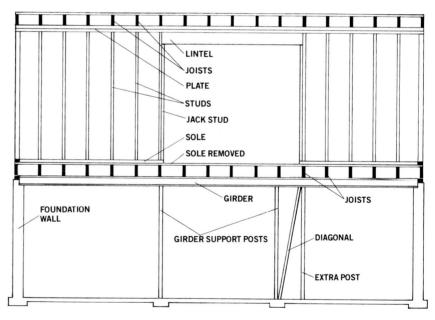

If wall opening exceeds span between posts below, extra post can be used to prevent sag beyond post. Diagonal may also be used. These extra posts—boxed or in partitions—may be needed in house of more than one story.

cutting a roof truss

You expect to see waves at the seashore, not on a living-room ceiling. But incredibly, they were there. I was standing in a house in New Jersey, and the ceiling above my head dipped up and down like a roller coaster. It was not a new decorating effect, but a small disaster.

A contractor had cut several of the ceiling joists to make a stair opening to the attic. But those weren't merely ceiling joists that he'd cut; they were the bottom chords of roof trusses. When the chords were cut, the ends pulled apart and sagged.

The strength and balance of a truss are dependent on each structural member. Most of us know not to violate the framing of a truss. Yet almost all tract-built homes are now constructed with trussed roofs, and many of these houses—like the one I just described—are built on slab-on-grade foundations. So people often turn to their attics to find extra storage or living space. Installing a skylight window in a trussed roof involves the same problem of altering trusses (see drawings, opposite page).

Does truss construction mean that the attic is unusable, entirely off limits? The answer is no—not if the truss is redesigned in the right way and carefully reconstructed. The secret to cutting a truss successfully is to build a box around the cutout piece. The box will bridge around the gap, rejoining the cut member. But the box must be designed so it reacts to roof forces in the same way as the missing truss piece. The box must transfer the forces to keep the truss in balance.

Basically the top chords of trusses are in compression from roof loads (roof weight, snow, and wind), and they push out on the bottom chord, putting it in tension (see drawing). Most trusses in new homes are complex in design, and have short internal members. Plywood or metal gussets secure the joints between truss members.

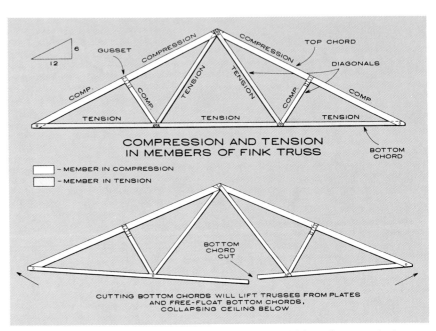

COMPRESSION AND TENSION IN MEMBERS OF FINK TRUSS

☐ – MEMBER IN COMPRESSION

☐ – MEMBER IN TENSION

CUTTING BOTTOM CHORDS WILL LIFT TRUSSES FROM PLATES AND FREE-FLOAT BOTTOM CHORDS, COLLAPSING CEILING BELOW

Forces on trusses from the roof compress top chords, which push out on the bottom chord, holding it in tension (top drawing). If bottom chord is cut, it will sag or drop, depending on interior partitioning and extension of the truss over outside walls. Most trusses today are 2×4s in complex designs, such as Fink trusses shown here. Short internal members of these trusses are in compression or tension themselves, so should not be cut either.

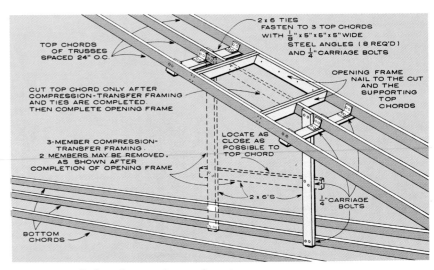

Skylight installation often requires cutting a top chord. Short vertical member can be used in a knee wall. Additional braces increase strength.

There is an appropriate box design for cutting either a top chord, bottom chord, or both (see drawings). Before any truss is cut, the truss members and gussets should be inspected. If they are sound, the truss must be thoroughly braced—both internally as well as to several adjacent trusses on both sides of the cutout.

After bracing and cutting the truss, the box can be built. Particular care must be taken at joints on a bottom chord, because that chord (in tension) will be pulling away from the box. Lumber and truss members are double-bolted, not just nailed, at all box joints. The braces can be removed only after the box is completed.

Complex-shaped lightweight trusses divide attic space awkwardly, and they can bear only limited amounts of weight. If you have some usable area between truss members, it doesn't mean that the 2 × 4s or 2 × 6s of the bottom chord will permit heavy storage or use as a living area. How much weight a bottom chord can bear depends on the dimensions of the lumber, spacing of trusses, and many other factors. Before starting a truss project, check with an architect or engineer to determine the limits of attic use, and work from professionally approved, detailed drawings—*By Paul Bolon. Concepts and sketches by Carl De Groote.*

Bottom chords of several trusses can be cut to install a staircase (photo above). Vertical and horizontal box members (drawing, left) were used to continue tension across the bottom chord of Fink trusses. Only Douglas fir or other dense, select structural lumber should be used as framing for any of the box configurations.

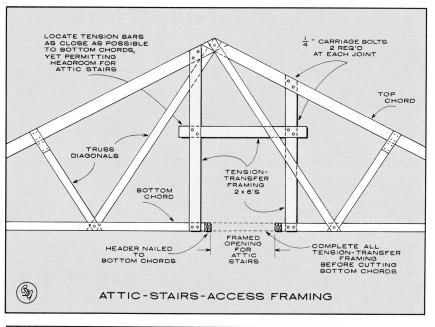

LOCATE TENSION BARS AS CLOSE AS POSSIBLE TO BOTTOM CHORDS, YET PERMITTING HEADROOM FOR ATTIC STAIRS

¼ " CARRIAGE BOLTS 2 REQ'D AT EACH JOINT

TOP CHORD

TRUSS DIAGONALS

TENSION-TRANSFER FRAMING 2 x 6'S

BOTTOM CHORD

HEADER NAILED TO BOTTOM CHORDS

FRAMED OPENING FOR ATTIC STAIRS

COMPLETE ALL TENSION-TRANSFER FRAMING BEFORE CUTTING BOTTOM CHORDS

ATTIC-STAIRS-ACCESS FRAMING

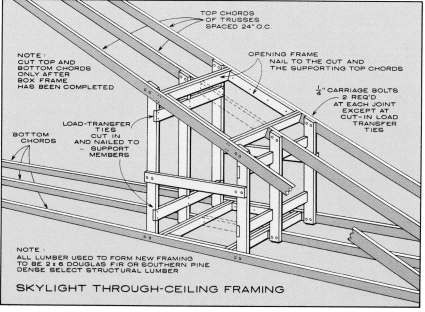

TOP CHORDS OF TRUSSES SPACED 24" O.C.

NOTE : CUT TOP AND BOTTOM CHORDS ONLY AFTER BOX FRAME HAS BEEN COMPLETED

OPENING FRAME NAIL TO THE CUT AND THE SUPPORTING TOP CHORDS

¼" CARRIAGE BOLTS 2 REQ'D AT EACH JOINT EXCEPT AT CUT-IN LOAD TRANSFER TIES

LOAD-TRANSFER TIES CUT IN AND NAILED TO SUPPORT MEMBERS

BOTTOM CHORDS

NOTE : ALL LUMBER USED TO FORM NEW FRAMING TO BE 2 x 6 DOUGLAS FIR OR SOUTHERN PINE DENSE SELECT STRUCTURAL LUMBER

SKYLIGHT THROUGH-CEILING FRAMING

Cutting both top and bottom chords requires building the most complicated type of box (drawing at left). Such a box would serve when adding a through-the-attic skylight in a shallow-sloped roof. In new construction, it would be simpler just to double the adjacent trusses. Lining the box walls with plywood will strengthen it.

adding three feet to a garage

What do you do when you buy a second car and your garage is meant for only one?

When I faced the problem, my friends offered ideas galore. One advised separating the garage at the peak and moving the walls over. Another suggested tearing the whole thing down and starting from scratch.

My own solution was cheaper and more practical. Since a mere 3 feet more space would accommodate the new car, I decided to detach one wall and move it out.

I started by taking off the old siding—but very carefully; I wanted to reuse it, both to cut down on costs and because it matches the house. I also reused as much other material as possible—insulation board, 2 × 4s, 2 × 6s. The old garage door, which I couldn't reuse, I sold for $70. Since I didn't like the existing window, I purchased a new one.

I poured the foundation for the new wall 3 feet deep and 12 inches wide.

Extending the roof 3 feet was simply a matter of splicing a piece to the ridge board and adding plates, studs, and three rafters on each side. I was able to find shingles to match the original

Front of the garage is shown above during the construction period. Two 2 × 8s were used over the door opening to support the new double doors. Old siding was reused to save money.

Rear view of the garage extension can be seen in photo above as portion of the roof that is not yet shingled. Shown at right is the garage interior, with side wall finished off and new window in place.

ones. I hired a commercial firm to hang the door.

While measuring the floor, I discovered that one corner was a good 4 inches below level, creating a small water basin. I knew that just applying another thin layer of concrete would be impractical—sooner or later, it would break up—and I didn't want to pour a whole new floor. Instead, I had the floor blacktopped and then painted it light gray.

Outside, I built a small brick wall to the left of the garage entrance and installed a wrought iron post similar to one at the entrance of the house. The result: A two-car garage that looks like it was always there—*Richard C. Redmond.*

Finished two-car garage, with decorative wall and post to match house.

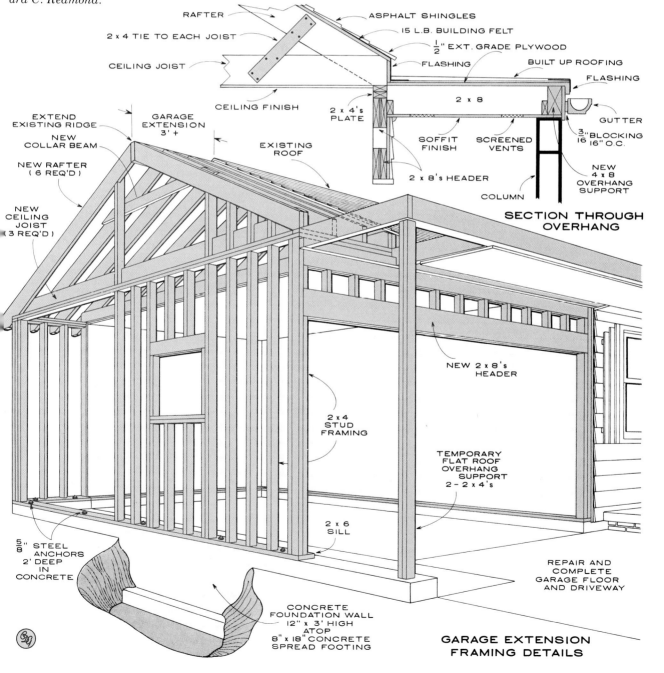

RAFTER
ASPHALT SHINGLES
2 x 4 TIE TO EACH JOIST
15 L.B. BUILDING FELT
½" EXT. GRADE PLYWOOD
CEILING JOIST
FLASHING
BUILT UP ROOFING
FLASHING
CEILING FINISH
2 x 8
2 x 4's PLATE
GUTTER
SOFFIT FINISH
SCREENED VENTS
3/16" BLOCKING 16" O.C.
2 x 8's HEADER
NEW 4 x 8 OVERHANG SUPPORT
COLUMN

SECTION THROUGH OVERHANG

EXTEND EXISTING RIDGE
GARAGE EXTENSION 3' +
NEW COLLAR BEAM
EXISTING ROOF
NEW RAFTER (6 REQ'D)
NEW CEILING JOIST (3 REQ'D)
NEW 2 x 8's HEADER
2 x 4 STUD FRAMING
TEMPORARY FLAT ROOF OVERHANG SUPPORT 2 - 2 x 4's
2 x 6 SILL
⅝" STEEL ANCHORS 2' DEEP IN CONCRETE
CONCRETE FOUNDATION WALL 12" x 3' HIGH ATOP 8" x 18" CONCRETE SPREAD FOOTING
REPAIR AND COMPLETE GARAGE FLOOR AND DRIVEWAY

GARAGE EXTENSION FRAMING DETAILS

traditional american cupboard

Some furniture pieces, more than others, speak truly to that which is home. A cupboard of plain board lumber worn to satin with use is one of them.

Originally a small, utilitarian closet with a cabinet for food storage and open shelves for dishes, cupboards saw timeless service in Early American kitchens. Later, cupboards got fancier and moved into the dining room or hallway. Now, regardless of any particular stamp a cupboard is a distinguished piece—always popular and still useful for display and storage.

Our Traditional American Cupboard is a personal design that follows general cupboard lines but also includes some nice richness of detail through raised panels, moldings, a simple curved embellishment near the top, and small articles of hardware. The cupboard also is designed for basic construction in the home workshop with standard power tools. You can have this edition in two or three weekends of sizing, cutting, assembling, and finishing.

We went for mahogany throughout. The construction plan itself actually is two pieces—the base cabinet and the top network of open shelves.

We began by first gluing up ¾ × 5½-inch mahogany stock to form the cupboard's top, sides, and two shelves. Edge the boards square on a jointer-planer and then cut ⅜ × ⅜-inch rabbets along the sides of each board for a better glue joint. The boards are then edge-glued and bar-clamped together to dry.

Across each end and across the middle, we C-clamped 2 × 3-inch boards to keep the glued-up stock flat while under the pressure of the bar clamps. After the glue has dried for twenty-four hours, the glue beads between each joint must be removed and any raised lips between the joints planed smooth.

We then used a belt sander to quickly smooth the large glued-up

Inside edges of door frames are routed to accept raised-panel inserts. The rounded corners are chiseled out square by hand.

panels. When making furniture, it is easier to sand the individual pieces than to try to sand the complete piece after it has been put together.

The door-and-drawer frame comes next. We first rip-cut the ¾-inch stock to size and then put the frame together with ⅜ × 2-inch wood dowels and glue. Before applying glue, however, put the frame together dry and bar clamp in place to be sure all parts fit together correctly. This may seem like extra work, but one incorrect board throws the entire frame out of square.

The center door divider is ½-inch stock glued in place. Across the top and bottom of this divider

Raised panels are cut on radial-arm saw with the blade set in the bevel-rip position. Bevel angle should be 74 degrees.

¼ × 2¼ × 5½-inch strips of mahogany are then glued in place—with the grain running horizontally. The center raised panel, which is cut later, is then glued and C-clamped onto the ½-inch center board.

The door frames that hold the two raised panels in each door are made of 2½-inch wide stock put together with 2-inch dowels and glue and bar-clamped to dry. When making doors, it is essential that all boards be free of warpage. Warp causes any door to fit incorrectly when hinged.

When the glued frame has dried, ¼-

Center door-divider goes into door-and-drawer frame (backside shown) and is secured with strips glued top, bottom.

inch deep-by-⅜-inch wide rabbets are cut with a rabbeting bit-and-guide around the inside front edges—these to accept each raised-panel insert. After routing, the rounded corners must then be chiseled square before the raised panels fit.

We cut the five raised panels next. Each panel is cut from ¾ × 5½ × 17½-inch stock, using a radial arm saw. We first constructed a jig to secure the panel while pushing it through the blade. A new guide fence also must be made to accommodate the blade in the bevel-rip position; the back fence pieces must be removed for the tilted blade.

To cut the panels, secure the boards Reprinted from *HOME MECHANIX magazine, copyright by Times Mirror Magazines, Inc.*

in the jig and set the saw in the bevel-rip position at a 74-degree angle. Then lower the saw until the outside edge of the beveled panel measures ¼-inch and the panel bevel is 1½-inches wide.

By using a carbide-tip blade, the bevels can be cut in one pass. The ⅛-inch thickness of the blade tips form the upper edges of the panel at a 74-degree angle—which you then sand to a 90-degree angle. This eliminates the need for making four additional cuts at 90 degrees.

Before cutting, be sure the blade moves freely, as the cut of the blade is lower than the table surface. Make the first cut with the grain, then remove the jig arm and make the next cut across the grain. Replace the arm and make the next cut across the grain.

Reposition the arm and make the third cut with the grain; then make the last cut across the grain. The panel is then sanded to remove any saw marks. Each of the five panels is now glued in place.

While you have the saw set up for cutting raised panels, cut the panel for the drawer front. At the same time, you also can cut the beveled edge that forms the shelf top. When cutting this 74-degree angle, raise the saw blade ⅛ inch so that you have a flat bevel without a ⅛-inch lip.

Next, cut ⅜ × ¾-inch dadoes across the insides of the cupboard's two sides for the two shelves. The bottom dado also is cut across the back of the door frame for the bottom shelf. Do not cut dadoes across the front frame for the center shelf.

Cut ⅜ × ⅜-inch rabbets along the inside edges of the front frame and the two sides. A ¼ × ⅜-inch rabbet also is cut along the inside back edge of the two sides for the ¼-inch plywood back. We used a T-guide clamped to the sides to cut the dadoes and a router guide to cut the dado across the bottom back edge of the door frame.

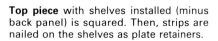
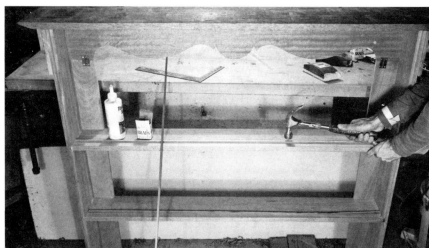

Top piece with shelves installed (minus back panel) is squared. Then, strips are nailed on the shelves as plate retainers.

Glue along the dadoes and rabbets and connect the two shelves and the front frame to the sides. The five pieces must then be bar-clamped together to dry. Metal corner braces can be screwed to the undersides of the two shelves for added support.

While the cabinet dried, we fashioned the drawer guides. They are made of ¾-inch stock and put together with glue and wood screws.

Each guide is then secured to the cabinet sides and front with glue and 1¼-inch wood screws. The top drawer guide is secured to the cabinet top with glue and screws after the top has been connected to the cabinet base with 1-inch metal corner braces and screws.

The drawer for the cabinet is made of ½-inch mahogany and ¼-inch lauan mahogany plywood for the bottom. The raised panel drawer front is glued and nailed to the ½ × 4⅜ × 38¾-inch board—allowing ½-inch on each end and ¼-inch across the bottom edge for drawer sides and bottom. The drawer sides, bottom, and center divider are glued and nailed in place after squaring the pieces.

The cupboard display shelves are made of ¾-inch and ½-inch mahogany. We first cut the two scrolled top pieces with a saber saw. The sides and shelves were cut next—with ⅜ × ¾-inch dadoes in the sides for insertion of the shelves.

To make the shelves' front edges fit flush with the front side rails, ½ × 3⅝-inch notches were cut in the three shelves. Before gluing the shelves in place, cut a ⅜ × ½-inch rabbet along the inside back edge of the two sides for the ½-inch stock that forms the back. Glue and bar-clamp the shelves in place.

The ½ × 4-inch front side rails are glued and nailed in place, as is the 5½-inch scrolled section. The smaller scrolled piece is then glued and C-clamped on top of it, as are the side pieces. The top, made earlier, is now nailed in place.

The shelf back is made of ½ × 9¼-inch boards that are nailed in place. To keep plates from falling over, ¼ × ¼-inch strips are glued and nailed 1-inch from the back of each shelf.

To finish the shelves, we cut a ¼-inch bead-and-cove edge, with the router and guide, along the underside of each shelf. Countersink all nail holes and cover with putty.

We gave the cupboard a finish coat of Watco Dark Walnut Danish Oil and went over this with two coats of tung oil. When the finish dried, the hinges and handles were attached—*Bruce Murphy. Photos by Bruce Blank.*

Back of top piece is not sheet material. Instead, ½-inch mahogany boards, each 9¼ inches wide, are used for their butt-grain effect.

colonial cabinets

The colonial-style family room wall shown consists of a main cabinet, with two smaller units on each side. The size of your room will determine whether you build one or more modules. The main cabinet accommodates a TV and video recorder and provides ample space for books, games, and a display of your favorite keepsakes.

Earth-tone colors and the black, hammered hinges and locks on the raised-panel doors give the cabinets an authentic touch of early American charm. Despite its size, the project isn't difficult, and it requires only commonly available materials.

Four shelves are joined to the sides by dadoes, while the two remaining shelves are adjustable, supported by clips that mount into holes drilled into the sides. Face frames are assembled with mortise and tenon joints, but dowels may be used instead. The backs nest in rabbets machined into the rear inner edges of the sides, and nails lock them to all fixed shelves, integrating the construction. While you'd never guess it from the appearance, a simplified construction technique makes building the raised-panel doors easy.

First steps

Before starting, measure the length of your room wall exactly. Then, figure the width of the center cabinet—the one that will accommodate your TV set—and still allow an even number of 28-inch-wide cabinet modules on each side of it. Provide ½ inch for trimming and fitting the entire line of cabinets into the room length by using extra-wide, overhanging stiles on the end cabinets for scribing to the walls.

As the side cabinets are all the same, it's smart to cut out all the parts at one time, and then make up the center cabinet while the assemblies using these parts are drying. Begin by cutting out sides and shelves. Note that shelf No. 5, without edging, will be flush with the face frame when in-

stalled, while all others, except Nos. 1 and 6, include a pine edge in the overall dimensions for appearance. Shelves 1 and 6 don't require edging, as they'll be glued to the back of the face frame.

Glue the edges on shelves that require them, and sand them flush when dry. Rout the rabbets in the rear inner edges of all sides and lay out the shelf dadoes on the inner surfaces. You can make these dadoes several ways: (1) With a radial saw, set up dado blades to a width that's a touch over ¾ inch and cut the dadoes using table stops both for speed and accurate location. (2) Use a clamp guide and machine them with your router. (3) Score the dado outlines with a utility knife guided by a rafter square; then use your backsaw or portable saw with a veneer blade, guided by a fence to remove the waste.

Presand all exposed surfaces, test-fit the shelves in the dadoes, and, if all is well, glue and clamp or nail the basic cabinet carcasses together. Remove any excess glue immediately— while it's easy. Now, cut the backs and fasten them to the rabbets and shelves with glue and box nails.

Face frames are the next order of business. Each cabinet really has two—a top section with arches and a lower section into which the doors are inset. The top sections are made up of 1½-inch-wide stiles (vertical members) plus the arch pieces cut from plywood, while the lower section uses 1½-inch- and 2½-inch-wide stiles, a 2½-inch top rail, and a 3½-inch bottom rail. If you're not set up for ripping the stiles with a table saw, you can buy them from lumberyard stock as 1 × 2, 1 × 3, and 1 × 4.

Face frames

Before cutting face frames, decide whether you'll assemble them with mortise and tenon joints or dowels. Tenoned pieces require an additional ¾ inch on each end for machining.

Tenons can be cut on a table saw, with a router, or by hand. Mortises can be done on a drill press equipped with a mortising attachment; they can also be made by drilling a row of holes and chiseling away the waste, or completely by hand with a mortising chisel (available from Garret Wade Co., 161 Avenue of the Americas, New York, NY 10003, or Woodcraft Supply, 313 Montvale Avenue, Woburn, MA 01801). To make the arched pieces, set up your router with its trammel point and a straight-sided ½-inch diameter bit adjusted to swing a 4½-inch radius

arc. Lay out the arches on plywood, including the trammel point location. Then, starting with a minimal cut, swing the router back and forth, gradually increasing the plunge of the bit on each successive pass. When the arches are completely cut through, trim the sides, top and bottom to size. If you have no router, cut the arches with a jig or saber saw and sand.

If you're using dowels instead of mortises and tenons, dry-assemble the frames and clamp them together before drilling. Then, drill from the outside in, going completely through the outer member. In either case, glue and clamp the frames together after fitting, and let them dry thoroughly.

Lay the cabinet carcasses on their backs and assemble the face frames to them with glue and nails. Line up the center stile of the upper section and nail it to the upper surface of shelf No. 5, making sure the face frames are flush against both its top and bottom surfaces. Then finish the carcass by setting the nails, filling, and sanding.

Cut the door stiles and rails, making the rails ¼-inch longer on each end to provide for the short tenons, unless you're going to use dowels. Next, rout or saw out ¼ × ¼-inch grooves on all inner edges of the stiles and rails to receive the raised panels. Cut panel blanks from pine, allowing an extra ¼ inch all around to fit into the grooves you just made. Then, to prevent panel swelling from splitting door frames, shave ¹⁄₁₆ inch from all panel edges, so the panels "float" in their grooves.

Since these are bevel-raised panels, they can easily be machined on a radial saw with a Safe-T-Planer attachment (Wagner Co., Gilmore Pattern

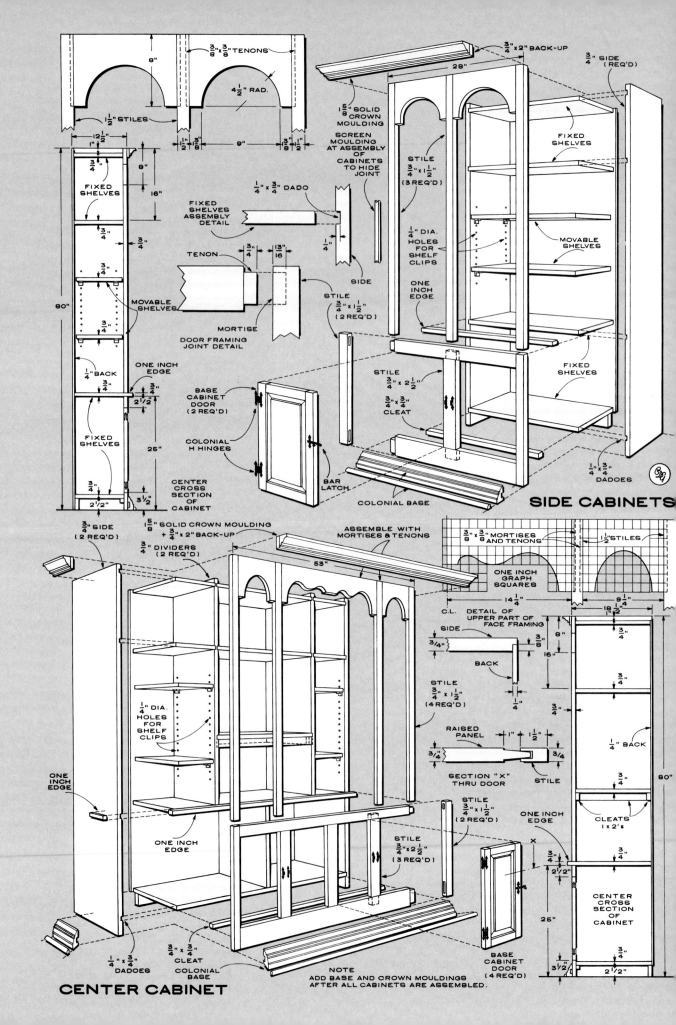

8"

$\frac{3}{8}$" x $\frac{3}{8}$" TENONS

4 $\frac{1}{2}$" RAD.

1 $\frac{1}{2}$" STILES

12 $\frac{1}{2}$"

$\frac{1}{2}$" $\frac{3}{8}$" 9" $\frac{3}{8}$" $\frac{1}{2}$"

1" $\frac{3}{4}$"

8"

16"

FIXED SHELVES

$\frac{3}{4}$" $\frac{3}{4}$"

$\frac{3}{4}$"

MOVABLE SHELVES

$\frac{3}{4}$"

80"

$\frac{1}{4}$" BACK $\frac{3}{4}$"

ONE INCH EDGE

$\frac{3}{4}$"
2 $\frac{1}{2}$"

FIXED SHELVES

25"

$\frac{3}{4}$"

2 $\frac{1}{2}$" 3 $\frac{1}{2}$"

FIXED SHELVES ASSEMBLY DETAIL

$\frac{1}{4}$" x $\frac{3}{4}$" DADO

$\frac{1}{4}$"

TENON

$\frac{3}{4}$" 1 $\frac{3}{16}$"

SIDE

MORTISE

DOOR FRAMING JOINT DETAIL

STILE $\frac{3}{4}$" x 1 $\frac{1}{2}$" (2 REQ'D)

BASE CABINET DOOR (2 REQ'D)

COLONIAL H HINGES

BAR LATCH

COLONIAL BASE

CENTER CROSS SECTION OF CABINET

1 $\frac{5}{8}$" SOLID CROWN MOULDING

SCREEN MOULDING AT ASSEMBLY OF CABINETS TO HIDE JOINT

$\frac{3}{4}$" x 2" BACK-UP

28"

$\frac{3}{4}$" SIDE (REQ'D)

FIXED SHELVES

STILE $\frac{3}{4}$" x 1 $\frac{1}{2}$" (3 REQ'D)

$\frac{1}{4}$" DIA. HOLES FOR SHELF CLIPS

ONE INCH EDGE

MOVABLE SHELVES

FIXED SHELVES

STILE $\frac{3}{4}$" x 2 $\frac{1}{2}$"

$\frac{3}{4}$" x $\frac{3}{4}$" CLEAT

$\frac{1}{4}$" $\frac{3}{4}$" DADOES

SIDE CABINETS

$\frac{3}{4}$" SIDE (2 REQ'D)

$\frac{3}{4}$" DIVIDERS (2 REQ'D)

1 $\frac{5}{8}$" SOLID CROWN MOULDING + $\frac{3}{4}$" x 2" BACK-UP

ASSEMBLE WITH MORTISES & TENONS

53"

$\frac{1}{4}$" DIA. HOLES FOR SHELF CLIPS

ONE INCH EDGE

ONE INCH EDGE

$\frac{1}{4}$" x $\frac{3}{4}$" DADOES

$\frac{3}{4}$" x $\frac{3}{4}$" CLEAT

COLONIAL BASE

STILE $\frac{3}{4}$" x 1 $\frac{1}{2}$" (2 REQ'D)

STILE $\frac{3}{4}$" x 2 $\frac{1}{2}$" (3 REQ'D)

$\frac{3}{8}$" x $\frac{3}{8}$" MORTISES AND TENONS

1 $\frac{1}{2}$" STILES

ONE INCH GRAPH SQUARES

14 $\frac{1}{4}$"

9 $\frac{1}{4}$" 18 $\frac{1}{2}$"

C.L. DETAIL OF UPPER PART OF FACE FRAMING

SIDE

$\frac{3}{4}$"

BACK

$\frac{3}{8}$"

8"

16"

$\frac{3}{4}$"

$\frac{3}{4}$"

$\frac{1}{4}$" BACK

$\frac{3}{4}$"

80"

CLEATS 1 x 2's

$\frac{3}{4}$"

2 $\frac{1}{2}$"

25"

STILE $\frac{3}{4}$" x 1 $\frac{1}{2}$" (4 REQ'D)

$\frac{1}{4}$"

RAISED PANEL

1" 1 $\frac{1}{2}$"

$\frac{3}{4}$" $\frac{3}{4}$"

SECTION "X" THRU DOOR

STILE

STILE $\frac{3}{4}$" x 1 $\frac{1}{2}$" (3 REQ'D)

BASE CABINET DOOR (4 REQ'D)

CENTER CROSS SECTION OF CABINET

$\frac{3}{4}$"

$\frac{3}{4}$"

3 $\frac{1}{2}$"

2 $\frac{1}{2}$"

NOTE
ADD BASE AND CROWN MOULDINGS
AFTER ALL CABINETS ARE ASSEMBLED.

CENTER CABINET

The easiest way to handle making of the cabinet arches is with a router and trammel point. The trick is to keep increasing the plunge with each pass.

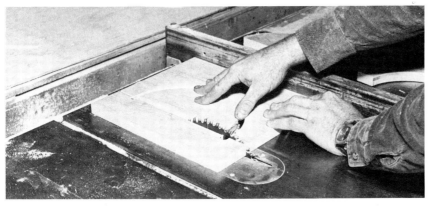

After you have machined out the arches, trim the tops, sides, and bottoms with the table saw and then fine-sand all of the edges.

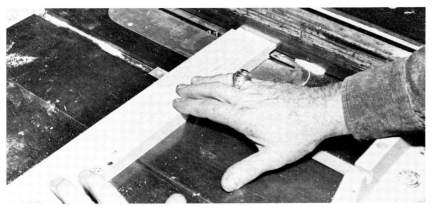

The quickest way to make the tenons in the home workshop is on the table saw. First step is to cut the shoulder lines. After that, you are ready to crossfeed.

Works, 1164-R North Utica, Tulsa, OK 74110), or on a table saw by angling the blade.

When you assemble the doors, use no glue between the panel edges and the rail and stile grooves, only at the corner joints. Make sure the doors are square when you clamp them up. Fit the inset doors into the frame openings using a block plane (which can be operated with one hand) and identify

Materials
Paint: Martin Senour, Williamsburg, John Greenhow Green, and Coachhouse Green.
Hardware: Latches—Amerock No. 8572; Mc-Kinney No. 537. Hinges—Amerock No. 1616; McKinney No. 520. Shelf clips—Amerock No. 3828.

both doors and openings. It's best to provide at least ¹⁄₁₆-inch gaps all around between the door and the frame to avoid sticking later. Now, mount the hinges and latches and make any final corrections.

Make a drill template from scrap ¹⁄₄-inch plywood and use it to drill all the shelf-support clip holes (¹⁄₄-inch diameter) on the inner faces of the sides.

Construction of the center cabinet is quite similar to the smaller ones, except the shelf that holds the TV is cleated and reinforced, and the arch shapes must be cut with a pattern or by hand.

Final steps
Take off the hardware and check that all surfaces are filled and sanded. Re-

move all dust, first by vacuuming, and then by wiping with a tack cloth. Apply a couple of coats of enamel underbody, sanding after each coat. Remove all dust and give everything a finish coat of paint. When dry, reinstall all H hinges, bar latches, and shelf clips.

To install the cabinets, first locate the wall studs and fit the cabinets temporarily in place. Scribe the outer stiles to the walls as necessary, and mark the stud locations on the cabinets. Line the cabinets up horizontally by placing shims under any low spot, and vertically, by placing shims between the wall and the cabinets at the stud locations. Add base, crown, and screen moldings (to hide joints between cabinets), and paint them—*Bernard Price.*

cherry paneling with mantel and cabinetry

Cherry frame-and-panel wall paneling and fireplace mantel (right) were created by layering frames and moldings atop a base of cherry plywood. Built-in cabinets (left) flow out of the paneling and provide storage for books and hi-fi equipment, plus a display area for pressed wildflowers in frames.

There's just no better way to give a room a rich, dramatic look of luxury than with built-in cabinetry surrounded by cherry frame-and-panel. Even so, you don't see many rooms done that way these days. One reason is that there aren't many craftsmen around who know how to do the work. Another is that few people could afford to pay for all the man-hours such a job requires.

In the next few pages, we'll show you how to simulate the custom-carved look of frame-and-panel and build those cabinets, without the skills of an Old World craftsman. Then, once you know how to do the job yourself, you won't have to come up with all that money to pay for all those man hours.

We'll be using simple techniques throughout: glue and nails, butt and miter joints. Although these techniques do not require a tremendous amount of skill, they do require time, and lots of it. I'd estimate my brother and I put in well over 550 hours paneling my living room and building in the matching cherry cabinetry. If the results are worth it to you, then let's get started.

Where to begin

Your first step is to make simple sketches, to scale, of every wall you intend to panel. Then plan your panel layouts. You'll be working with 4 × 8 sheets of plywood, so your maximum panel width will be 4 feet. If you have a wall 12 feet long, you can cover it perfectly with three panels. If, however, a wall is 15 feet long, you'll have to use four panels and juggle panel widths so that they're all the same. In this case, divide 15 by 4 to find the width of each panel (3 feet, 9 inches), and then draw your panel layout to scale.

You may also have to juggle your layout to cope with windows and doors, as I did. If so, it's easiest to plan your layouts so panel frames run alongside the openings and double as window or door trim (fig. 1). I also had a pair of windows so small they would fit into the center of my panels, so I paneled around them and then made special casings to trim them out (fig. 2).

After you lay out your panels, draw in the frames and baseboard. Then plan the moldings that line the frames, plus the details of your crown molding along the ceiling. The sketches show the moldings I used. Many of these are quite complicated and were created with custom molding cutters I ground myself. Please feel free to use simpler moldings. We'll talk more about making your own moldings in a little while.

For the plywood that makes up the panels, get ¼-inch veneer grade plywood. I used cherry, but other woods will work as well. If possible, get "flitch-cut" plywood sheets that have been cut in sequence from the same log. This will allow you to create matched panels because the grain patterns in each sheet will be nearly identical.

For your trim, get ¾-inch solid hardwood to match your plywood. Ordinary lumber yards usually don't carry veneer grade plywoods or hardwoods. Your lumber yard may be able to order the plywood for you, but you will probably get a better deal on the solid stock if you hunt up a local mill or hardwood dealer. *Get at least 20 percent more hardwood than you think you will need.*

Putting up the paneling

Begin by removing all your existing trim. Then, draw your panel layout right on the wall with a heavy pencil. This will help you visualize your layout full-size and point out any mistakes before you start cutting up valuable wood.

If you are happy with your layout, put up the plywood. Cut the sheets to size, if necessary. Pay attention to the grain patterns to achieve a grain match from one panel to the next. To install the plywood, use panel adhesive and finishing nails. You can put the nails along the edges of the panels, to be hidden by your trim, and behind where the center rail in your frames will go.

Panels up? Now rip out your stock for the baseboards and top rail. Install the baseboards with finishing nails, then snap a chalk line marking the lower edge of the top rail. If you follow my layout exactly, this should be 4½ inches down from the ceiling. Then fasten in the top rail, using finishing nails near the top edge of the rail.

Next, cut out and install the full-length stiles that cover the panel edges. Glue and nail these in place, centering them over the seams between panels. Then put up your center rails, and then your short center stiles. Each frame piece should be custom-cut to fit its space snugly.

Now it's time for your moldings. Best way to get the moldings you need is to make your own. You can use a router, a shaper, a molding head, or (for big coves) a table saw with crosscut blade. I used a router for some of my moldings, the molding head for some of the more intricate moldings, and the saw for my coves (fig. 3).

The router is fast and easy for small, simple moldings. That's why I'd advise most people to stick with router-made moldings for every part of the job except the big ceiling cove. To make router moldings, select one or two bits you like. My favorites are the "classical" and ogee with fillet. The classical combines a bead and cove with some square fillets to produce a nice intricate design with lots of lines and detail. The ogee is more open and flowing, but still creates plenty of interest.

Just rout the edge of a nice straight board, then rip off the edge to the desired width. Then rout and rip again. Keep up this rout-and-rip operation until you have all the molding you will need—again, *plus about 20 percent.* Cutting to length will create some waste, and there is always the chance you will make a mistake.

Putting up the moldings

Before you install your moldings, go over your frames with a sander. Smooth them out and pay special attention to all joints, making sure they are all even. If they aren't, I like to hit them with a belt sander and 120 grit belt to "plane" all members down to the same level. Then touch up with an orbital sander to remove any crossgrain sanding scratches.

Now put up your moldings. Use miters at all joints and aim for perfection. The best way to cut the miters is with a power miter box, right at hand in the room you are

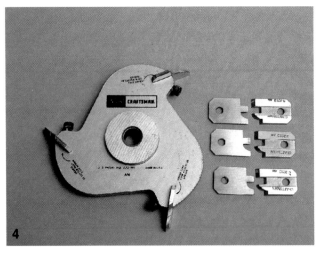

4

5

6

paneling so you can cut and fit until your joints are just right. Put moldings up with small finishing nails and a bit of glue. Keep nails to a minimum. Every one you drive will have to be set and filled over later on.

Built-in cabinets

These are built in two sections. The upper cabinets are built separately from the base cabinets, and simply fasten in place atop the base unit countertop. A boxlike soffit connects the upper cabinets and houses eyeball fixtures to light the center display area. The soffit is finished off with the same ceiling moldings used with the paneling.

The plans show you what you need to know, and all construction is pretty simple. One part that might be new

to you is the door construction, so let's take a look at that in detail.

Like the paneling, the doors are a frame-and-panel design. The frames are made on the table saw, with a molding head and a special double set of cutters sold by Sears. You need set 9-3210 and set 9-3213 (fig. 4). Set 9-3210, at left in photo, cuts the dado for the door panels and, at the same time, cuts a bead molding. You use this cutter along the inside edges of all frame parts.

Set 9-3213, shown at right in photo, is the exact opposite of the first. You use it to cut both ends of all the horizontal frame parts, or rails. When you do so, you profile (or cope) the ends of these so they fit perfectly into the cuts along the inner edges of the vertical frame parts (the stiles). This creates a strong, interlocking glue joint.

There are a few tricks to using this cutter set:
● Cut a few "dummy" frame parts at the start to get things right. These needn't be the right width or length, but they must be the same thickness as your frame parts.
● Be sure to cut your rails ½ inch longer than the frame opening of your doors. This allows for the part of the rails that sticks into the stiles.
● Alignment is critical. Make all your dado/bead cuts on all parts first, using the fence protector and hold-downs shown in figure 5. Then switch over to the 9-3213 set of cutters. You use these with the special end-milling jig shown in the sketch and photos. This jig fastens to an extension screwed to your miter gauge.

Jig position is also critical. To set it, take one of your dummy parts and clamp it in the jig. Unplug your saw and rotate the molding head so one of the cutters is up. Slide the jig left or right until the groove in the cutter that forms the "tongue" on your stock aligns perfectly with the dado already cut in your stock. Clamp the jig to your miter gauge extension (fig. 6) and check again to see that it hasn't moved. If alignment is right, fasten the jig permanently in place with two screws into the miter gauge extension.

Make a test cut and check it for depth. It should make a complete cut across the end of the stock, but shouldn't cut so deeply that it reduces the length of the stock. Adjust depth if necessary and make another test cut.

When you get the right degth, check the part for fit in one of your frame parts. If you have good alignment, the faces of both pieces should be flush. If they aren't you'll have to adjust the jig slightly left or right. One you get your jig set up properly, put a fresh stop on the jig. The "kerf" in this stop created by the cutter head must align perfectly with the cutters. If it doesn't, the stop won't back up the stock adequately, and the cutter will tear chips off the trailing edge of your rails.

Once you have the jig set right, cut all your rail ends using a smooth, steady pass. You can then cut the plywood door panels (aim for grain matches whenever possible), and glue the doors up.

Door edge moldings

Cabinet doors are of the ⅜-inch overlay type. In other words, a ⅜-by-⅜-inch rabbet around the door edges forms a lip that overlaps the door openings. Normally, you would cut this rabbet out of the door with a router, or a door-edge cutter in a molding head. We created the rabbet by adding on a special molding instead (fig. 7).

Why? Because we goofed and made the doors too small. The moldings brought the doors out to the proper size, gave us the rabbet we needed, and actually enhanced the look of the doors in the process. The point is, all woodwork-

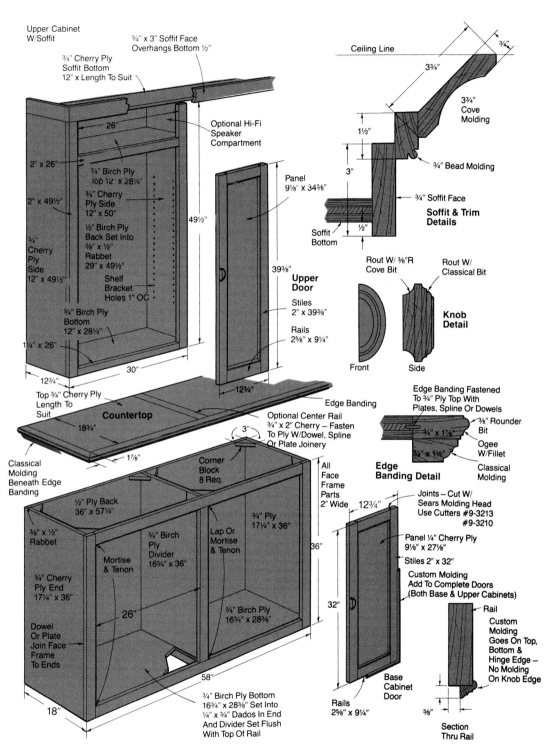

Upper Cabinet
W/Soffit

¾" x 3" Soffit Face
Overhangs Bottom ½"

¾" Cherry Ply
Soffit Bottom
12" x Length To Suit

Optional Hi-Fi
Speaker
Compartment

26"

2" x 26"

¾" Birch Ply
Top 12" x 28¼"

¾" Cherry
Ply Side
12" x 50"

Panel
9⅛" x 34⅜"

2" x 49½"

½" Birch Ply
Back Set Into
⅜" x ½"
Rabbet
29" x 49½"

¾"
Cherry
Ply
Side
12" x 49½"

49½"

Shelf
Bracket
Holes 1" OC

39⅜"

Upper
Door

¾" Birch Ply
Bottom
12" x 28¼"

Stiles
2" x 39⅜"

1¼" x 26"

Rails
2⅝" x 9¼"

12¾"

30"

Top ¾" Cherry Ply
Length To
Suit

12¾"

Countertop

18¾"

Edge Banding

Optional Center Rail
¾" x 2" Cherry — Fasten
To Ply W/Dowel, Spline
Or Plate Joinery

1⅞"

Classical
Molding
Beneath Edge
Banding

½" Ply Back
36" x 57¼"

Corner
Block
8 Req.

3"

All
Face
Frame
Parts
2" Wide

12¾"

¾" Ply
17¼" x 36"

⅜" x ½"
Rabbet

¾" Birch
Ply
Divider
16¾" x 36"

Lap Or
Mortise
& Tenon

36"

¾" Cherry
Ply End
17¼" x 36"

Mortise
& Tenon

32"

26"

¾" Birch Ply
16¾" x 28⅜"

Dowel
Or Plate
Join Face
Frame
To Ends

58"

Rails
2⅝" x 9¼"

18"

¾" Birch Ply Bottom
16¾" x 28⅜" Set Into
¼" x ¾" Dados In End
And Divider Set Flush
With Top Of Rail

Base Cabinet Door

Base Cabinet Carcase

Ceiling Line

¾"

3¾"

3¾"
Cove
Molding

1½"

¾" Bead Molding

3"

¾" Soffit Face

**Soffit & Trim
Details**

Soffit
Bottom

½"

Rout W/ ⅜"R
Cove Bit

Rout W/
Classical Bit

**Knob
Detail**

Front   Side

Edge Banding Fastened
To ¾" Ply Top With
Plates, Spline Or Dowels

⅜" Rounder
Bit

¾" x 1⅞"

Ogee
W/Fillet

¾" x 1½"

Classical
Molding

**Edge
Banding Detail**

Joints — Cut W/
Sears Molding Head
Use Cutters #9-3213
#9-3210

Panel ¼" Cherry Ply
9⅛" x 27⅛"

Stiles 2" x 32"

Custom Molding
Add To Complete Doors
(Both Base & Upper Cabinets)

Rail

Custom
Molding
Goes On Top,
Bottom &
Hinge Edge —
No Molding
On Knob Edge

⅜"

**Section
Thru Rail**

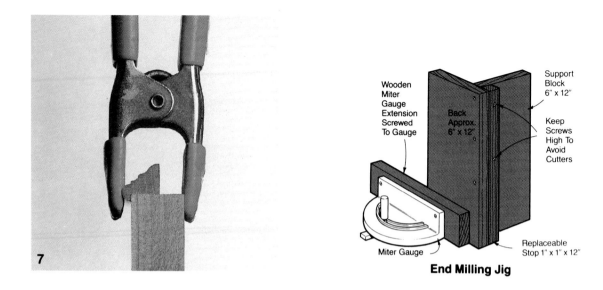

7

Wooden Miter Gauge Extension Screwed To Gauge

Back Approx. 6" x 12"

Support Block 6" x 12"

Keep Screws High To Avoid Cutters

Miter Gauge

Replaceable Stop 1" x 1" x 12"

End Milling Jig

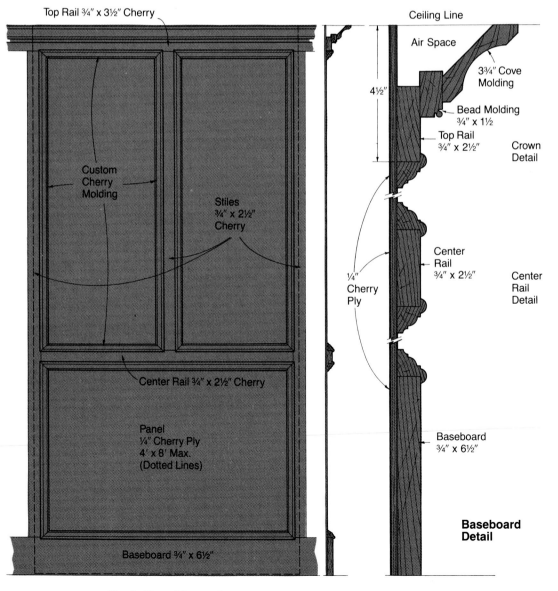

Top Rail ¾" x 3½" Cherry

Custom Cherry Molding

Stiles ¾" x 2½" Cherry

Center Rail ¾" x 2½" Cherry

Panel
¼" Cherry Ply
4' x 8' Max.
(Dotted Lines)

Baseboard ¾" x 6½"

Basic Panel Layout

Ceiling Line

Air Space

4½"

3¾" Cove Molding

Bead Molding ¾" x 1½

Top Rail ¾" x 2½"

Crown Detail

¼" Cherry Ply

Center Rail ¾" x 2½"

Center Rail Detail

Baseboard ¾" x 6½"

Baseboard Detail

ers make mistakes. What separates the men from the boys is the ability to correct those mistakes.

The mantel

The mantel itself is just a sandwich of plywood, built up to create the required thickness. The edge is then finished off with three different moldings, stacked to look like a single big one (fig. 8).

The mantel rests on columns that are equally straight-forward. At heart, they are nothing but channels of cherry plywood standing on end. The base, capital, and frame are appliqued on top, and a few moldings are thrown in to give everything a smooth, carved look.

Finishing

The cherry, especially the plywood, began as a lifeless grayish, pinkish brown. Rather than stain it, I gave it all a coat of Watco Danish Oil, brushed on and wiped off after 20 minutes.

As soon as oil hit wood, the cherry took on a deep, warm tone. I left it that way for several months, allowing oxygen and light to age the wood even more. As time passed, the cherry got even mellower. Finally I gave everything three coats of alkyd varnish, sanding between coats (see my Frame-and-Panel Oak Cabinet chapter on page 65 for details). The lustrous patina made all that work worthwhile —*by A.J. Hand. Drawings by Richard Meyer.*

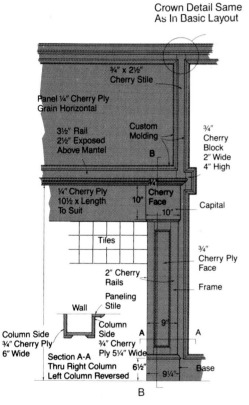

Fireplace Layout

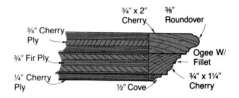

Section of Built-Up Mantel

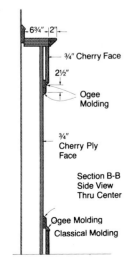

Section B-B Side View Thru Center

modular storage units

T hese modular cabinets are smartly styled, allow quick room-design changes, and are easy to make. They are laminated inside and out with Wilsonart Union Maple pattern, and separated by spacers finished in Wilsonart black suede.

Cabinets are in three heights, but all are the same width and depth. Upper units have smoked Lucite doors; base units, laminated ones—all with invisible hinges. Center cabinets have movable shelves.

The cabinets can be set up as single, double, or triple stacks (3×3 array with nine spacers) to cover 7 feet

Standard 3½-inch-high spacers nest ¾ inch into adjoining units, securely interlock cabinet stacks.

of wall space. Other options: Combine two base cabinets, four spacers, and a slab top for a telephone nook with plenty of storage space. Or set up cabinet columns in varying heights by stacking three mid-size cabinets next to three base ones. Or separate two full-height stacks with a cabinet-width space and hang the third top cabinet between them. Or fit mid-size cabinets with flap doors to create a counter-height desk complex for household papers and bills.

Detailed instructions for applying the plastic laminate are given in an accompanying box. While you're making the cabinets, keep in mind that, until the laminate is applied to the core (Novoply or an equivalent high-density particleboard), it's brittle and subject to cracking—so handle it carefully. Also, leave the protective paper on Lucite doors until you drill the hinge holes and sand edges. To avoid scratches, rest these doors on a soft, nonabrasive surface when drilling pull holes. Finally, follow the game plan closely to take advantage of the assembly and finishing method.

First, laminate the *edges* of all core pieces. Then, laminate inside surfaces of the sides, the movable shelves on both sides, and the fixed shelves on one side. Laminate only inner surfaces of the large doors until the hinge bores are drilled, or the spade bit pilot will go through to the outer surface.

Now make the rabbets on the rear inner edge of each side piece—yes, right through the laminate. Cut the backs to size and prime and paint them. While the backs are drying, make up the shelf-stiffener assemblies and laminate stiffener fronts. Screw sides to the fixed shelves and nail in the backs with small brads. This squares up the cabinet.

Next, laminate outer surfaces of the sides this way: Set a straight cut laminate edge flush with the rear edge of the side and file or sand the edge (you can't use the laminate trimmer properly in this situation). This completes the cabinet boxes.

Saw the Lucite doors to size, sand the edges, and drill the hinge holes. Drill the bores for the hinges in the large plastic laminate doors ½-inch deep and apply laminate to the front surfaces of the doors.

Mount the hinges (self-closing) on all doors now (remove protective paper from Lucite ones first). All hinges screw into plates (wing-type for large hinges, straight-type for smaller

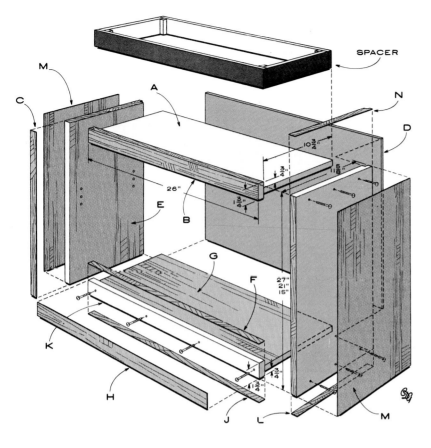

SPACER

LAMINATE SCHEDULE

	INSIDE	OUTSIDE	TOP	BOTTOM	FRONT	BACK	LEFT	RIGHT
SIDES	✓	✓	✓	✓	✓	-	-	-
TOP FIXED SHELF	-	-	-	✓	-	-	-	-
MOV. SHELF	-	-	✓	✓	✓	-	-	-
STIFFENER	-	-	✓	✓	✓	-	-	-
BACK	-	-	-	-	-	-	-	-
LAM. DOOR	-	-	✓	✓	✓	✓	✓	✓
BOT. FIXED SHELF	-	-	✓	-	-	-	-	-

A - TOP FIXED SHELF WITH LAMINATE ON BOTTOM SURFACE
B - TOP SHELF STIFFENER
C - SIDE LAMINATE FRONT EDGE
D - MASONITE BACK (1/8")
E - SIDE PLUS SURFACE LAMINATE ON BOTH SIDES
F - STIFFENER LAMINATE TOP EDGE
G - BOTTOM FIXED SHELF WITH LAMINATE ON TOP SURFACE
H - STIFFENER LAMINATE FRONT EDGE
J - STIFFENER LAMINATE BOTTOM EDGE
K - STIFFENER
L - SIDE LAMINATE BOTTOM EDGE
M - SIDE LAMINATE SURFACE
N - SIDE LAMINATE TOP EDGE

ALL SUBSTRATES 3/4" NOVAPLY (R) OR EQUIVALENT
ALL PLASTIC LAMINATES 1/32"

To make cabinets. *Top row, below:* Combination bit as shown (left) will make pilot hole, shank clearance hole, and countersink in one drilling pass. Line up stiffener and fixed shelf by resting shelf on ¾-inch-thick spacer (center). Guide line locates assembly screw holes. Use soap or other lubricant to make driving screws easy (right). Drive four or five to lock pieces firmly. *Center row:* Run cabinet sides through the saw (left), face down, then at 90 degrees to machine rabbet that will hold the back. To assemble sides and fixed shelf (center), rest shelf, laminate side up, on a ¾-inch-thick spacer; then drill holes. Pump assembly screws in to lock sides to shelves (right). Make sure the screwheads are below the surface. *Bottom row:* Drill the 26mm (1-inch) holes for the Lucite door hinges slowly (left), using a spade bit to avoid chipping and cracking. Smooth saw edges of doors by going from No. 120 to No. 400 grit with wet-or-dry paper used wet. Remove protective paper from doors and install hinges and cover plates. Mount hinges and make horizontal adjustment. Test for door-edge and door-to-door clearance and adjust gap. Tighten lock screw. Right: Make large hinge bores (35 mm), using 1⅜-inch diameter spade bit from door back (front laminate *off*).

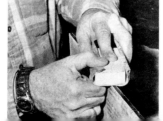

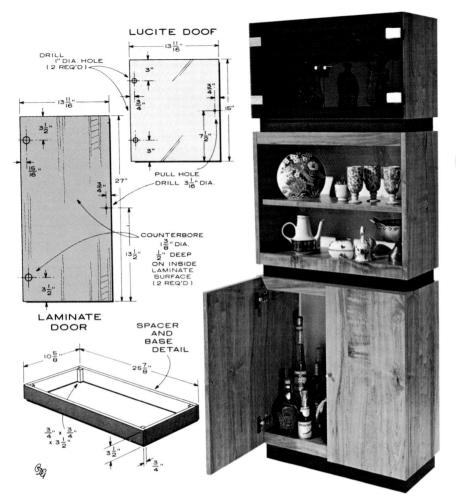

LUCITE DOOF

DRILL 1" DIA. HOLE (2 REQ'D)

13 11/16"

3"

3/4"

3/4"

3"

15"

7 1/2"

PULL HOLE
DRILL 3 1/16" DIA.

13 11/16"

3 1/2"

15/16"

27"

3/4"

13 1/2"

3 1/2"

COUNTERBORE
1 3/8" DIA.
1/2" DEEP
ON INSIDE
LAMINATE
SURFACE
(2 REQ'D)

LAMINATE
DOOR

SPACER
AND
BASE
DETAIL

10 5/8"

25 7/8"

3/4" x 3/4"
x 3 1/2"

3 1/2"

3/4"

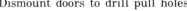

ones), which, in turn, mount to the inner surfaces of the sides.

To hang the doors, snap all hinges out to the "door open" position. (You'll feel the detent action of the self-closing hinges.) Screw the inner parts of the hinges to the plates, so the outer plate ends are as close as possible to the hinge fulcrums. Holding each door at the correct vertical position,

with the inner door edge just touching the front, mark the plate location.

Plates for large door hinges have slotted screw holes to allow vertical adjustment, but plates for smaller hinges can't be adjusted after mounting. Separate plates and hinges. Then, punch-mark plate-mount holes, screw plates in place, and remount hinges. All hinges will adjust the doors both horizontally and out from the cabinets, so provide inner-door-edge and door-to-door clearance before locking hinges to plates.

Dismount doors to drill pull holes

1. Upper units are 15 inches high, have smoked Lucite doors, and self-closing hinges.

2. Inter-cabinet spacers nest ¾ inch into each adjoining unit.

3. Back is ⅛-inch painted Masonite panel.

4. Mid-size unit is 21 inches high and has adjustable shelves.

5. Base, 27 inches high, has wood-grain plastic laminate over Novoply door, with hidden self-closing hinge.

Several stacking arrangements are shown on these pages. Two 27-inch-high base cabinets and a slab top make a desk, shown at bottom, far left, which complements the rich wood grain of the wall units. Single stack of wall units and construction details are at the top, far left, and, near left, a combination setup. Many variations are possible.

Materials
Plastic laminates: Wilsonart Union Maple (No. 7901 13), ¹⁄₃₂ inch, 4x8 feet; Black (No. 1595, 6 Vel), ¹⁄₃₂ inch, 4x8 feet. **Hardware** (available at Albert Constantine & Co.): hinges, full overlay wood door (HC8V2X/OB); wing mounting plates (HBOV3Z/2); pull, satin brass, with ½-inch screws for Lucite doors and with 1-inch screws for laminate doors (T-7050 R); hinges, full overlay glass (HC10533/OW); cover plate, satin brass for glass-door hinges (HB80102 R); flathead screws to mount plates and large hinges (No. 8x⅝ or ¾ inch).

and, in mid-size cabinet sides, drill ¼-inch diameter holes for shelf-support clips. Assemble and laminate black spacers, and laminate a flush door (1 foot by 6 feet, 8 inches) for a slab-top telephone table.

Any slight tilt discrepancy in spacer-to-cabinet fit is easily shimmed with a dry laminate scrap. If you're using cabinets full height against a wall, fasten the back of the top cabinet with a screw, nails, or Molly—*Bernard Price*.

Steps in lamination process: (1) Apply water-base latex contact cement to back side of laminate and edge of the substrate (core). After drying for thirty minutes, it will appear "flat." Place laminate on edge and lock it down with scrap and hammer. (2) Roller guide on special router base can be adjusted to control depth of cut made by combination carbide tipped bit. (3) First, test cut on scrap. Then hold router flat on surface to trim laminate. Move router counterclockwise. (4) To prepare edge surface for adjacent pieces, smooth slight laminate overhang with #120 grit sanding belt. (5) With all edges trimmed, hand file all corners to a smooth bevel. Expose only minimum "dark inner" laminate. (6) Before laminating main surface, belt sand all edges on both sides, working from outer edge inward on surface. Apply cement to backside of surface and main core surface. Go for a thin, but complete, coat. (7) Place the laminate down accurately, using waxed paper or dowels to prevent it from sticking in the wrong places. Then lock it down. (8) Trim surface edge in two steps—first, make a straight cut; then, a bevel cut. Be very careful not to cut too deeply. (9) Finishing the edge is also done in two stages—first, with a plastic file; then make it perfectly smooth with a fine scraper or sanding block.

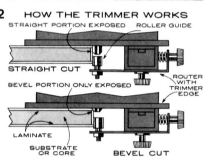

HOW THE TRIMMER WORKS
STRAIGHT PORTION EXPOSED   ROLLER GUIDE
STRAIGHT CUT
BEVEL PORTION ONLY EXPOSED
ROUTER WITH TRIMMER EDGE
LAMINATE
SUBSTRATE OR CORE   BEVEL CUT

Tips on applying plastic lamination

For vertical applications and cabinet work, $1/32$-inch-thick laminate is best. Laminates come in various patterns and surface finishes. Grain patterns must be carefully planned to insure economical use of material. A dimensional pattern, such as solid black, may be applied in any direction, so you have more latitude.

For efficiency, cut all substrates (cores) and laminate edges and surfaces at one session. Make sure your saw cuts at 90 degrees relative to the surface—even slightly bevel core cuts will cause trouble in trimming the laminate. Various methods are used to cut laminate. Table or radial saws, jigsaws, snips, or special shingle cutters (available at laminate suppliers) will do the job. Take care to avoid chipping or cracking.

The laminate is bonded to the core with water-base latex contact cement and the edges are finished. To do this, you'll need one or more tools to cut the laminate, a roller with a low-nap cover, a small natural bristle brush, a hammer and scrap block or a pressure roller, a router with a laminate trimming guide base, a combination straight cut plus bevel carbide bit, and a plastic file and some sandpaper or a fine scraper.

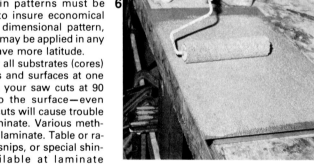

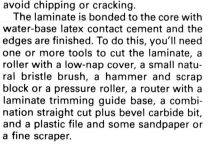

fold-up stool

I deal for sitting on at a fireworks display or marshmallow roast and sturdy enough to stand on while searching the upper closet shelf, this collapsible stool folds up for compact storage or travel.

A table saw, jointer, and drill press speed things up, but hand tools will do. No special hinges or fittings are needed. Wood may be either clear pine or hardwood. To prevent pivot nuts from loosening, use ¼-20 self-locking nuts with a plastic or fiber insert. I used full 1⅛-inch stock for the seat halves, but if you use 1-inch stock, you'll have a stool that folds flush and easily slides under a car seat.

Construction tips
● Rip, plane, and sand 1×1¼-inch stock and cut to length.
● Pivot holes are for ¼×1¼-inch stove or hex-head bolts. A ⁵⁄₁₆-inch counterbore will drop bolt head below surface, but doesn't allow extension above surface on opposite side. Nuts must be self-locking type. A ⅜-inch deep counterbore will permit nut to clear surface, so folding parts slide past.
● Don't try to predrill counterbores. Start assembly and counterbore to screwhead or nut depth as you go. Best tool is piloted ¼ inch to align in ¼-inch bolt holes. Alternate way is to counterbore first with spade bit and follow with ¼-inch drill.
● Install seats and leg braces last. Pilot drill ⁹⁄₆₄ inch or ⅛ inch (depending on wood hardness) for 1¾-inch #8 screws. During assembly, space pass-

ing surfaces of legs with thin cardboard (calling card or matchbook) while drilling seat and brace pilot holes. Otherwise stool will be too snug to open and close easily.
● Chamfer or round seat edges and ends. Oil or wax finish is recommended—*E. F. Lindsley.*

Stool makes a good gift. Little people, and big ones, love a handy little seat that collapses for lugging around or for storage. Folded stool will slide under car seat or slip into closet. Seat can be made of 1-inch stock.

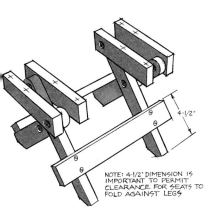

NOTE: 4-1/2" DIMENSION IS IMPORTANT TO PERMIT CLEARANCE FOR SEATS TO FOLD AGAINST LEGS

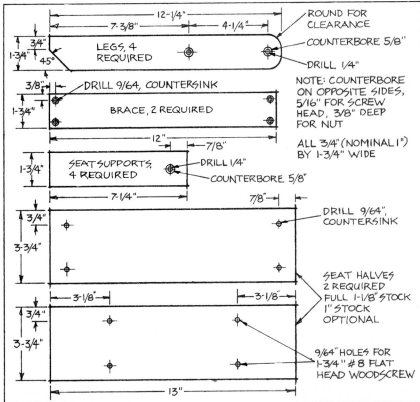

appliance and wine rack

Those Mondrianlike doors on that colorful kitchen closet (see below) aren't what you think. Only the two skinny ones are conventional hinged panels; the other two are spring-roller window shades—and one of them is mounted upside down (see drawing for installation tips).

My kitchen needed utility storage in a hurry, and because it's all very crisp and white I designed the simplest shelf unit I could, keeping the lines clean, but introducing panels of bold color. A honeycomb sheet-metal wine rack set the dimensions for the lower-left compartment—but posed a problem: This wall faces a sunny window, so the stored wine would have to be protected from the light and heat of direct exposure. Rigid panel doors on compartments of this size are clumsy—and cut off cooling air flow.

Besides, racked wine makes a fine display when solar protection isn't required, so I wanted a cover I could quickly dispense with. A colorful shade, mounted backwards to minimize the roller, proved ideal.

It then seemed logical to give the upper compartment the same treatment—except that my shelf unit stands 8 feet tall, lifting a top-mounted roller out of reach. I contacted Joanna Western Mills (a manufacturer of quality window shades) for advice, and learned of its special kit that would let me mount this shade low and raise it with cords and pulleys, as I'm shown doing in the second color photo. So the two Joanna shades you see are: for the wine rack, a translucent custom shade called Viking (the color is "tan"); the Bottom Up shade is also Viking cloth in light gold.

The problem with most built-in compartmentalized storage is complexity of construction. Here, I've kept the shelf assembly so simple you can do the whole job with hand tools. I used ¾-inch panels (particleboard for the uprights, plywood for the shelves), assembled with glued-and-screwed butt joints—no rabbets or grooves; and the structure is tied into the end wall by means of metal L-brackets anchored with expansion fasteners (Molly bolts).

The ⅝-inch-plywood doors for the two skinny compartments shouldn't be cut until the shelving unit is in place—you want a neat fit against that end wall. To avoid cutting hinge gains, I surface-mounted with brass flathead screws—1½-inch No. 6 for attaching the leaves to the edge of the particleboard upright. Note that the broom-closet door has no stop strip. It simply closes against two wall-mounted magnetic catches—*Al Lees*.

Closetless kitchen offered ample cabinet space but no place to store mops and brooms, bulky appliances, cookbooks—or author's growing wine collection. Tucking super-simple rack in wall niche solved all problems. Note window-shade doors.

Butt joints, fastened with glue and screws, simplified assembly of rack's ten panels. Note that when shelves and uprights were painted, joint lines and edges to be glued were skipped (left). Plywood doors for right-hand sections use magnetic catches.

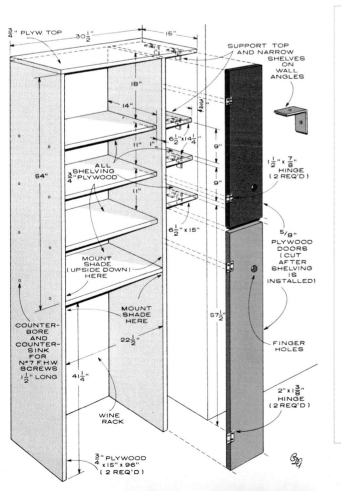

Mounting an upside-down shade

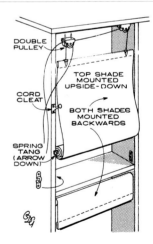

The appliance rack calls for a special shade since you can't mount a regular one upside down. The shade must be under constant tension, since it has only two positions—all the way up or down. Constant-tension rollers are available in custom lines, such as Joanna Western Mills Viking; Joanna calls this mounting a Bottom Up shade and offers a kit with brackets, pulleys, cord, cord cleat, and instructions. (If you can't find a local dealer, write Joanna at 2141 S. Jefferson Street, Chicago, IL 60616.) Two metal clips snap onto the shade slat for attaching the cords. Cords pass up over their respective pulleys, screwed under the top shelf. One cord is long enough to pass across to the second pulley, to join the first on its way down to the cord cleat where they're both secured.

kitchen island

This island is my kitchen's centerpiece. Topped by a massive 3×7-foot chunk of butcher block, it holds a lot of cooking gear in two standard kitchen base cabinets; one has slide-out shelves (lower photo, facing page) for handy storage of pots and pans next to the island's drop-in range. (We used custom-built cabinets; you could substitute knock-down versions, sized to fit.)

The range is positioned slightly off-center to provide generous space for food preparation to one side. There's a 6-inch overhang on one side of the island; with bar stools it doubles as an eating area. The island's sleek, off-white enameled sides face the dining area, screening the unfinished sides and backs of the cabinets within.

Since the island divides the kitchen from our dining area, the chef isn't left out when dinner guests arrive. In keeping with the "stage center" aspect of the island, the work top is lighted by three track-mounted flood-lights, controlled by a dimmer.

Putting it together

Construction begins with the 2×4 framing: We built it in three sections, shimmed and nailed *square* to the floor (see drawing). Next, we attached the butcher-block top; our supplier cut the range opening for us—highly recommended since rock-hard maple is no joy to saw. Shim and level the top if necessary; this is especially important when you're installing a range that hangs from the counter top (you don't want your omelets to slip to one side of the pan!). Predrill holes for screws and attach the butcher-block

top from the underside of the upper framing members. A power screw-driver such as Skil's Boar Gun makes this task a lot easier.

We faced both sides of the 2×4 framing with ½-inch-thick drywall. We reinforced outside corners with metal beading before we taped the drywall. (Tip: If you're not an experienced taper, a damp sponge helps to even the joint compound.)

Next we pulled up old flooring and ran gas and electric service between floor joists. The two base cabinets and filler strips needed for the range go in next; we placed an electric outlet in one filler strip, convenient to the work area. The drop-in range really does—once it's hooked up to the gas line and plugged into a second electric outlet inside the island—*Richard Stepler.*

Photos by John Keating

closet-door pantry

In today's compact homes, the old-time pantry has been eliminated. So canned and packaged goods must be stored in deep cabinets below and above counters and appliances, often forcing the hapless cook to crouch uncomfortably or climb a precarious step stool to reach needed items.

Yet if you have a closet near the kitchen—or even a basement stair—you can convert the door into a serviceable mini-pantry by adding this shelf unit to the back surface.

Mine has seven shelves spaced 6¼ inches apart and is simply attached to the door with four wood screws through the back panel of ¼-inch plywood. Narrow plywood strips, nailed across the front edges of the shelves, create a lip that keeps stored items from being jostled off when the door is opened and closed.

For easy cleaning with a damp cloth or sponge, you'll want to seal all surfaces with varnish or a quality enamel before the unit is mounted.

A major advantage of this type of shallow-shelf storage is that your supplies can be inventoried at a glance. Since everything shows, you can tell at once exactly what needs replenishing.

You might even want to add smaller units to the backs of some of your cabinet doors. And because the shelf is detachable, you can take it with you should you move—*Louis Hochman.*

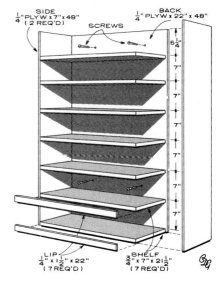

Sleek sides of this island face a dining area (left photo); the business side (below) shows off its generous and handy storage. Drawing at right shows construction.

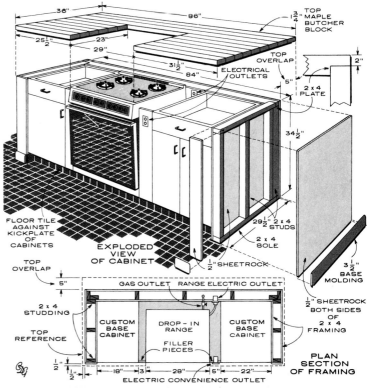

build an add-on kitchen-island rack

I was running out of space. I urgently needed some sort of space-saving unit in which to store my growing collection of cookware—something that wouldn't get in the way. Happily, I solved the problem with a combination kitchen rack and wine-glass hanger. With it, I store my cooking utensils (including lids, thanks to shelving at the top of the rack) and safely stow long- and short-stem wine glasses.

I used custom-milled oak for the project, cut to full dimensions. There is no reason why nominal lumber wouldn't work, though it should be a quality hardwood. A radial-arm saw is best for all the cuts and dadoes, but

Kitchen island didn't have enough space for heavy, bulky pans. Rather than cutting into island top, author notched uprights with a dado blade on a radial-arm saw.

Holes for carriage bolts and nuts are countersunk with a ⅞-in. Forstener bit then drilled on center with a ⅜-in. bit. On the inside of the cabinet are large washers (1½ in.) against the cabinet wall, then a lock washer and nut. The carriage bolts at the top use standard washers. The detail at top right shows the profile of the top rack. The shelf holds lids, and the molding provides a rest for the long-stem wine glasses. J-hook attaches to oak slider with round-head wood screws.

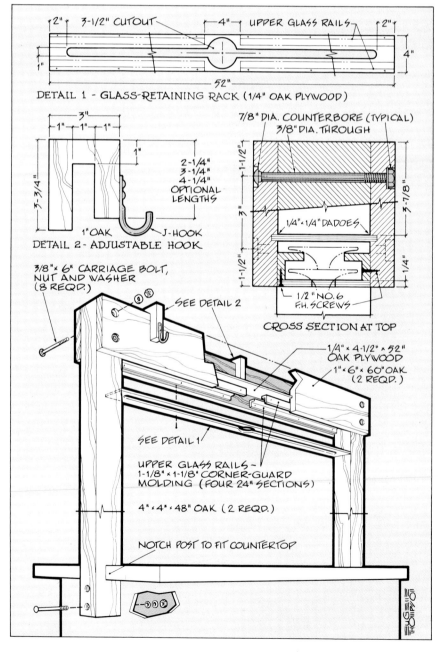

DETAIL 1 - GLASS-RETAINING RACK (1/4" OAK PLYWOOD)

2" 3-1/2" CUTOUT 4" UPPER GLASS RAILS 2"

52"

3"
1" 1" 1"
1"
3-3/4"
1" OAK   J-HOOK
2-1/4"
3-1/4"
4-1/4"
OPTIONAL LENGTHS

DETAIL 2 - ADJUSTABLE HOOK

3/8" x 6" CARRIAGE BOLT, NUT AND WASHER (8 REQD.)

7/8" DIA. COUNTERBORE (TYPICAL)
3/8" DIA. THROUGH
1-1/2"
3"
3-7/8"
1/4" x 1/4" DADOES
1/4"
1-1/2"
1/2" NO. 6 F.H. SCREWS

CROSS SECTION AT TOP

SEE DETAIL 2

1/4" x 4-1/2" x 52" OAK PLYWOOD
1" x 6" x 60" OAK (2 REQD.)

SEE DETAIL 1

UPPER GLASS RAILS - 1-1/8" x 1-1/8" CORNER-GUARD MOLDING (FOUR 24" SECTIONS)

4" x 4" x 48" OAK (2 REQD.)

NOTCH POST TO FIT COUNTERTOP

a table saw (with dado blades) would do just as well. The uprights are 48 inches long, which provides ample counter space below the rack; the rack causes no interference at the counter level, even when fully loaded.

To build the rack: Before assembling the pieces, drill and countersink the bolt holes, then dado the grooves on the inner face of each horizontal 1 × 6 to accept the ¼-inch-plywood upper shelf. After that, fasten 1¼-inch corner molding on the inner face of both

1 × 6s. Use flathead wood screws. The molding runs from the faces of the 4 × 4 uprights to within two inches of the center cutout. If you're using glue, apply it to the shelf edges and clamp the assembly together.

To make the cutout in the hanger for the wine glasses, first mount a ¼-inch piece of oak plywood (cut to width and length) on a length of 1 × 6 pine, making sure it's square; this is a backup piece to add working stability. Rip parallel cuts as shown. Now, with

a coping saw, fashion the two semi-circular finish cuts on either end and the large insertion cutout in the center. Fit the finished piece onto the bottom of the rack, and (with the lid shelf in place) attach it with ½-inch brass screws to the corner molding.

Finish to suit, assemble the rack and uprights, then fasten the uprights to the island. The utensils hang from chrome hooks on sliding wooden hangers, which are finished to match—*By W. David Houser. Photos by the author.*

How far should glasses extend? You can choose by placing them in the rack—the long-stem glasses go on the inner molding, and the short-stem glasses hang from the cutout at the bottom of the horizontal assembly. The hooks fit on either side of the rack. Each hook is a different length to accommodate different-size pots and pans.

two kitchen dividers

Want the airy feel of a large, open kitchen in limited floor space? Room dividers are a good way to define separate areas while maintaining overall spaciousness. They can also provide useful storage and display space.

Both kitchens shown here feature dividers that offer a wine rack as the centerpiece of their designs. The country kitchen uses a floor-to-ceiling divider whose open-grid wine rack, shelving, and rough-texture wood lend a rustic tone to the home. The modern kitchen (below) has a floor island whose counter height permits access and conversation between dining and working areas while providing elegant storage for an ample collection of wines.

Both dividers are easy to build with pine and plywood (see captions). Sheet-vinyl flooring from Congoleum completes the decorating schemes of the two kitchens—*By Daniel Ruby. Designs From Congoleum Corp.*

Floor-island divider features storage for standard-size wine bottles and cabinets for pots and dishes (not shown in drawing) on both sides. Build wine rack to desired size by cutting ½-by-6¾-in. slots at four-in. intervals in ½-in. boards with bevel-cut ends. After painting, slip pieces together in eggcrate fashion. Now assemble storage unit with four-in. base, vertical divider, and shelving. Slip rack into place, then add moldings, doors, and counter top. Fill all nail holes, and paint as desired.

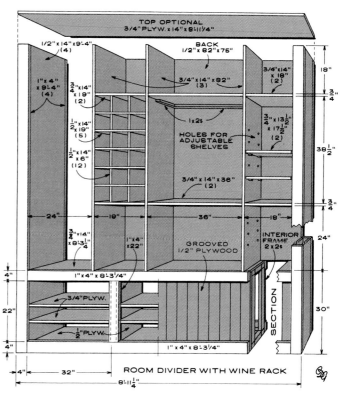

ROOM DIVIDER WITH WINE RACK

Floor-to-ceiling divider provides open shelving for laundry room in base section and storage and display space for dining-room side above the counter. Build interior frame of counter first, then add bottom board, shelving, and face paneling. Add a plastic-laminate counter top, then erect the upper divider frame. On left side, a vertical box beam bulks up the design. Wine rack is made by nailing two six-in. vertical pieces to each horizontal board, then stacking and toe-nailing. Finish with satin polyurethane.

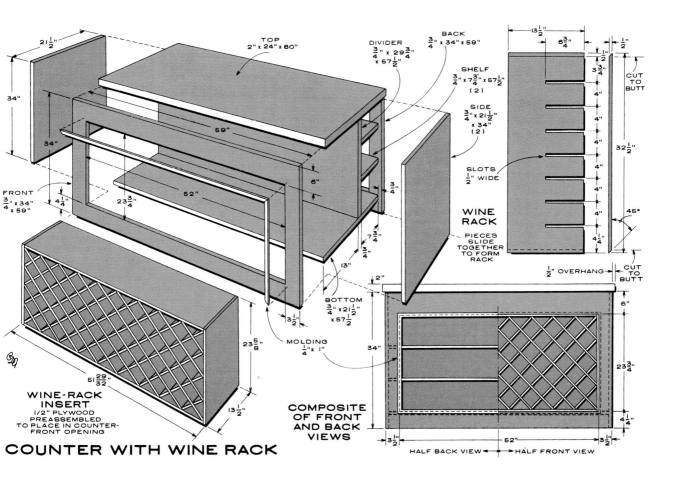

COUNTER WITH WINE RACK

WINE-RACK INSERT
1/2" PLYWOOD PREASSEMBLED TO PLACE IN COUNTER-FRONT OPENING

WINE RACK

COMPOSITE OF FRONT AND BACK VIEWS

breakfast table

Not much free time on your hands? Here's a project as quick and easy to make as the three-minute egg you'll be eating on it. The size of the table can be adjusted to your needs. Just be sure to increase or decrease the width of the base in proportion to the diameter of the tabletop. The tabletop is plastic laminate, so you can select the right color for your decor. Design by Jim Eldon.

Construction
Illustration A
1. Cut the horizontal base members to size.
2. Lay out and cut two 3/8" deep × 2"-wide dadoes in each horizontal member.
3. Face-glue the horizontal members together in pairs, forming four horizontal units. The dadoes on each pair of horizontal members should match to form two mortises in each unit.

Illustration B
4. Lay out and cut a 2½" radius on the corners of each horizontal unit.
5. Lay out and cut a 1½"-wide × 1¼"-deep edge half-lap joint at the center of each horizontal unit. Join the horizontal units to form two "X" units.
6. Drill and countersink two holes at the intersection of each "X" unit to accept #10 × 1½" flathead wood screws. Fasten each "X" unit together with glue and #10 × 1½" flathead wood screws.
7. Machine a ¼" radius on all edges of the "X" units.

Illustration C
8. Cut the vertical base members to size.

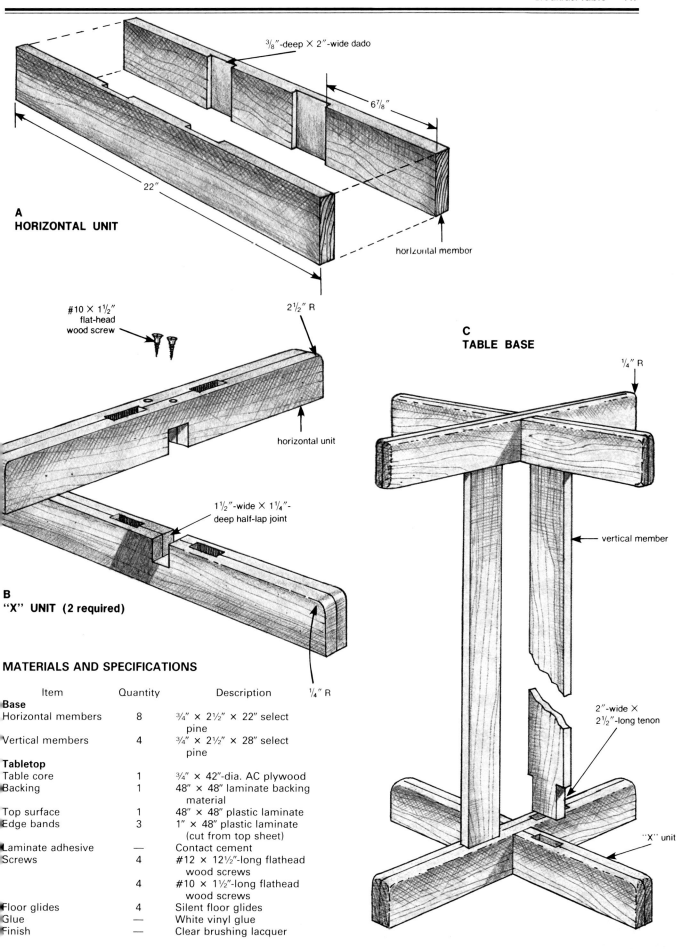

A
HORIZONTAL UNIT

³⁄₈"-deep × 2"-wide dado

6⁷⁄₈"

22"

horizontal member

#10 × 1¹⁄₂"
flat-head
wood screw

2¹⁄₂" R

horizontal unit

C
TABLE BASE

¹⁄₄" R

vertical member

1¹⁄₂"-wide × 1¹⁄₄"-
deep half-lap joint

B
"X" UNIT (2 required)

¹⁄₄" R

2"-wide ×
2¹⁄₂"-long tenon

"X" unit

MATERIALS AND SPECIFICATIONS

Item	Quantity	Description
Base		
Horizontal members	8	³⁄₄" × 2¹⁄₂" × 22" select pine
Vertical members	4	³⁄₄" × 2¹⁄₂" × 28" select pine
Tabletop		
Table core	1	³⁄₄" × 42"-dia. AC plywood
Backing	1	48" × 48" laminate backing material
Top surface	1	48" × 48" plastic laminate
Edge bands	3	1" × 48" plastic laminate (cut from top sheet)
Laminate adhesive	—	Contact cement
Screws	4	#12 × 12¹⁄₂"-long flathead wood screws
	4	#10 × 1¹⁄₂"-long flathead wood screws
Floor glides	4	Silent floor glides
Glue	—	White vinyl glue
Finish	—	Clear brushing lacquer

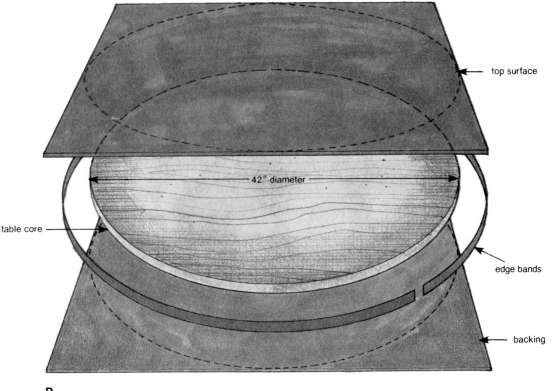

D
TABLETOP

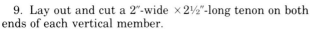

E
TABLE ASSEMBLY

9. Lay out and cut a 2″-wide ×2½″-long tenon on both ends of each vertical member.

10. Machine a ¼″ radius on the exposed edges of each vertical member.

11. Glue and clamp the vertical members into the "X" units to form the table base.

12. Apply a clear finish to the table base.

Illustration D

13. Cut the table core and backing to size.

14. Fasten the backing to the underside of the table core using contact cement.

15. Machine the backing flush with the edge of the table core using a laminate trimmer.

16. Cut the edge bands to size.

17. Fasten the edge bands to the table core with contact cement. Trim the edges flush.

18. Cut the top surface to size.

19. Attach the top surface to the top side of the table core with contact cement.

20. Machine the top surface flush with the edge of the tabletop.

Illustration E

21. Drill and counterbore the top horizontal members of the base to accept #12 × 2½″ flathead wood screws.

22. Attach the assembed tabletop to the table base using #12 × 2½″ flathead wood screws.

23. Attach the floor glides to the bottom of the table base.

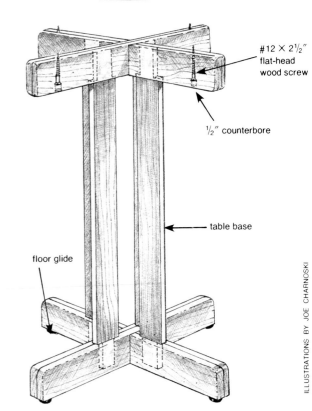

Reprinted by permission of Rodale's *PRACTICAL HOMEOWNER* magazine.

ILLUSTRATIONS BY JOE CHARNOSKI

davenport desk

A Davenport desk is small, with the prototype believed to have been a shipboard desk ordered by a Captain Davenport in the early 19th century in England. It was a very popular style in the early and middle Victorian years.

Although there was considerable variety of design, all Davenport desks had drawers in the side (one or both sides), rather than in the front. The writing surface was usually a hinged compartment-lid, but some desks had pull-out writing surfaces. Many early Davenport desks had secret compartments, swing out drawers, and compartments with small drawers and pigeon holes that rose above the desk top when a catch was released. The desks tended to be elaborately decorated. Ours is made of cherry, with Carpathian elm burl veneered panels. The panel trim is walnut.

The dimensioning of this desk started with a modern hanging file. The lower double drawers will each accommodate these useful files. You could quite properly have drawers on one side only, with dummy drawer fronts on the other side, or a combination of drawers that ran the full width of the desk with some that didn't. Dummy drawer fronts can be made up that are attached to the drawer rails so you could easily reverse the side with the drawers when the desk is moved to a different location.

Opportunities are endless for tailoring this desk to your exact needs. Plans are given for an interior compartment with drawers and pigeon holes if you want them in your desk; materials for the compartment, however, have not been included in the cutting list.

You will need about 35 board feet of ¾" cherry lumber for the desk. Begin by planning how to get all the parts out of your lumber. When you plank the parts, leave some extra al-lowance on lengths for squaring and fitting. (Dimensions are given assuming nominally ¾" thick wood; when you surface sand the wood, it usually ends up less than ¾" thick.)

Begin construction with the front and back frames of the drawer case. Rabbet top rails, bottom rails, and stiles to receive the veneered plywood panels. Assemble the frames with dowels. Four drawer frame assemblies are required. They are identical except that the top one does not have drawer guides. Rails and guides can be doweled, rather than mortise and tenoned as shown. The back drawer rail is doweled in place after the rails and guides are assembled.

When laying out dowel hole locations note that the bottom drawer frame assembly is spaced up ¼" from the bottom of the case and the space is to be filled with a filler block. This was done to keep the face of the bottom drawer rails clear of the base cove molding.

The center drawer guides are positioned with a gap between them for inserting a piece of plywood to serve as a drawer stop. Shims can be added

to the face of the plywood for exact drawer positioning.

The ends of the parts for the base frame and the sides, and the ends of the front and back of the box should all be formed at one time. Both the base and the box use identical lock miter joints. I prefer this joint to a splined miter (a plain miter would not be strong enough for the desk) as it is far easier to clamp. Alignment of the joint is positive and you only have to clamp from one side. Follow the steps shown to make the joints, and start with several pieces of scrap the same thickness as your stock for test cuts.

After forming the lock miter joints, cut the grooves in the inside of the box sides, front, and back for the bottom panel, and in the base frame parts for glue blocks and cleats.

Rabbet and dado the base frame parts and do a trial assembly, then glue. Do not assemble the box at this time.

All of the moldings for the base and box should be formed at one time with one setup. For safety in handling, I glued the box trim strips and the base back and front strips back-to-back to waste pine. Follow the sequence shown to form the molding.

Miter the base top parts and assemble them with reinforcing dowels. Use the base frame as a jig to get the parts cut correctly. When glued, drill all screw holes for attachment to the base frame cleats. Next, position the base top on the inverted drawer case and drill for screws.

Before the box is assembled make jigs and rout out the recesses in the sides, front, and back for the veneered panels. These recesses should be 5/16″ deep. The bottom panel is made narrower than the front to back opening and glued only at the front to allow expansion and contraction with changes in humidity. With normal humidity change, the top can be doweled to the sides and back.

To assemble the box, glue the bottom panel to the box front, then glue up all corner joints immediately. After the box is glued, rabbet around all sides to receive the molding, which can be mitered and glued to the box. The rabbet provides a better looking joint, and allows more thickness to be left on the molding for safer ripping from the blank.

Turn the two columns following the pattern. The top of the column is fitted with a short hanger bolt that threads into a steel threaded insert in the bottom of the box. A longer hanger bolt in the bottom of the column passes through clearance holes in the base

Base Frame

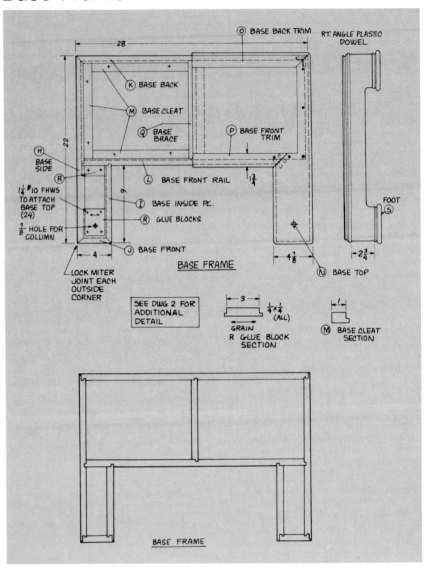

Lock Miter Joint Detail

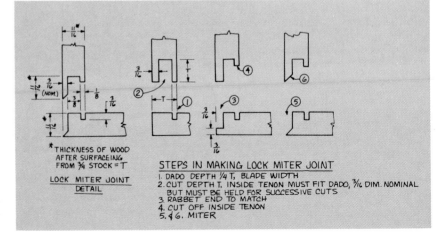

Molding Detail

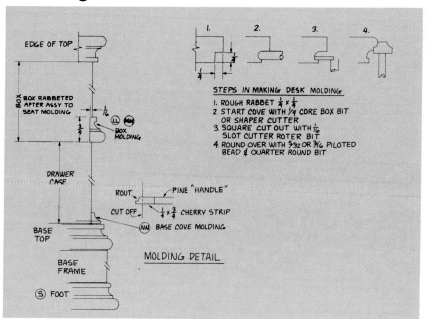

EDGE OF TOP

BOX RABBETED AFTER ASSY TO SEAT MOLDING

BOX

BOX MOLDING

DRAWER CASE

BASE TOP

BASE FRAME

S FOOT

STEPS IN MAKING DESK MOLDING
1. ROUGH RABBET $\frac{1}{4}$ x $\frac{1}{4}$
2. START COVE WITH $\frac{1}{4}$ CORE BOX BIT OR SHAPER CUTTER
3. SQUARE CUT OUT WITH $\frac{1}{16}$ SLOT CUTTER ROTER BIT
4. ROUND OVER WITH $\frac{5}{32}$ OR $\frac{3}{16}$ PILOTED BEAD & QUARTER ROUND BIT

ROUT

CUT OFF

PINE "HANDLE"

$\frac{1}{4}$ x $\frac{3}{4}$ CHERRY STRIP

NN BASE COVE MOLDING

MOLDING DETAIL

Drilling dowel holes requires accuracy. The best way to do it is in a horizontal boring setup, such as can be done on a Shopsmith. No matter how you jig up to drill dowel holes, always work with only one side of the stock as the reference surface. This way, when you are slightly off the centerline, the parts won't be twisted when you dowel them together.

Assembling the drawer case. Before doing any gluing, completely assemble the case dry. When gluing, it is absolutely essential that the first joint is true. The top drawer frame is being glued and aligned to one side with a pair of shop-made right angle gluing jigs, and double-checked with a carpenter's square. As each successive frame is added, it will be aligned by having the free side (top) dry-dowelled to the other side of the case.

CUTTING LIST
All dimensions in inches

Key	Part Name	Qty.	Material	Dimensions
A	Top rail	2	¾ Cherry	3⅜ × 19
B	Bottom rail	2	¾ Cherry	3⅝ × 19
C	Stile	4	¾ Cherry	4⅜ × 21¼
D	Drawer rail	8	¾ Cherry	2 × 10½
E	Drawer support	8	¾ Hardwood	1¼ × 23½
F	Drawer back rail	4	¾ Hardwood	3 × 8
G	Drawer guide	6	¾ Hardwood	1⅛ × 12½
H	Base side	2	¾ Cherry	2¾ × 22
I	Base inside piece	2	¾ Cherry	2¾ × 9¼
J	Base front	2	¾ Cherry	2¾ × 4
K	Base back	1	¾ Cherry	2¾ × 28
L	Base cross brace	1	¾ Cherry	1⅞ × 27
M	Base cleat	6	¾ Hardwood	1¼ × 12
N	Base top	2	¾ Cherry	4⅞ × 23
O	Base back trim	1	¾ Cherry	1¾ × 29
P	Base front trim	1	¾ Cherry	1¾ × 24
Q	Base brace	1	¾ Hardwood	1⅞ × 12
R	Base glue blocks	3	¾ Hardwood	3 × 3 (split one)
S	Foot	4	¾ Cherry	4⅞ × 4⅞
T	Box side	2	¾ Cherry	7½ × 21
U	Box front	1	¾ Cherry	4 × 27
V	Box back	1	¾ Cherry	7½ × 27
W	Box top	1	¾ Cherry	6⁷⁄₁₆ × 27⅞
X	Box lid	1	¾ Cherry	16⅝ × 27⅞
Y	Box bottom	1	¾ Cherry	20 × 26
Z	Panel	2	¼ Plywood	15 × 19
AA	Drawer front	6	¾ Cherry	5³⁄₁₆ × 10⅜
BB	Lower drawer side	4	½ Oak	11 × 13
CC	Lower drawer back	2	½ Oak	11 × 10⅜
DD	False rail	2	¾ Cherry	¾ × 10⅜
EE	Middle drawer side	4	½ Oak	5³⁄₁₆ × 13
FF	Middle drawer back	2	½ Oak	5³⁄₁₆ × 10⅜
GG	Top drawer front	2	¾ Cherry	1¾ × 10⅜
HH	Top drawer side	4	½ Oak	2 × 13
II	Top drawer back	2	½ Oak	2 × 10⅜
JJ	Drawer bottom	6	¼ Birch Ply	9⅞ × 12¾
KK	Drawer runner	6	½ Hardwood	2¼ × 13
LL	Box side molding	2	¾ Cherry	½ × 23
MM	Box front, Back molding	2	¾ Cherry	½ × 29
NN	Base cove molding	3	¼ Cherry	⁵⁄₁₆ × 28
OO	Column	2	Cherry	3 × 3 × 24

The drawer case completely assembled. Gluing the second side to all of the frames involved 16 dowels—assistance is a good idea for this gluing. The frame-to-side joints are reinforced with screws.

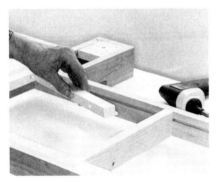

Gluing up the base frame. Lock miter joints are easy to assemble; alignment is positive, and clamping is required in one direction only.

Cleats are tenoned into the base frame after being drilled for attaching the base top.

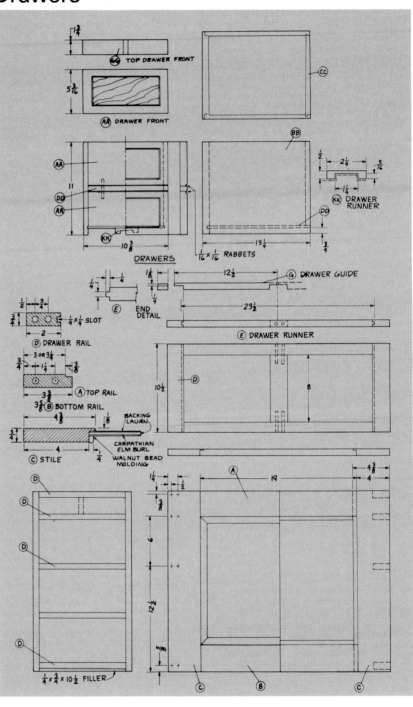

Fingerboards help hold the box top against the fence for making the first rabbet (see drawings, step 1 in forming the molding).

Drawers

top and glue block and is secured with a washer and nut.

The two large drawer fronts are given the appearance of being two drawers. The fronts and dummy rails are glued up with dowels. Before gluing, rout a 1/16" by 1/16" rabbet in the drawer fronts as shown to enhance the two-drawer appearance. If either of the big drawers is going to contain a hanging file, notch the sides for the

support rails before you assemble the drawers. The drawer fronts are routed out a depth of 5/16" to receive the Carpathian elm burl panel. The panel should be glued into the drawer after routing the dovetails and before drawer assembly. I used a thin walnut bead molding strip ripped from scrap wood.

The drawers otherwise are built conventionally. Sides, front, and back

are joined with router-jig dovetails. The drawer bottom is slotted into the sides and front, but passes under the back. The runner is doweled or mortised into the drawer front and nailed to the drawer back.

The Carpathian elm burl veneer was a real problem to handle: It would not lay flat and was extremely brittle. It was difficult to cut without breaking, and impossible to clamp flat to

Box Frame Corner Joints

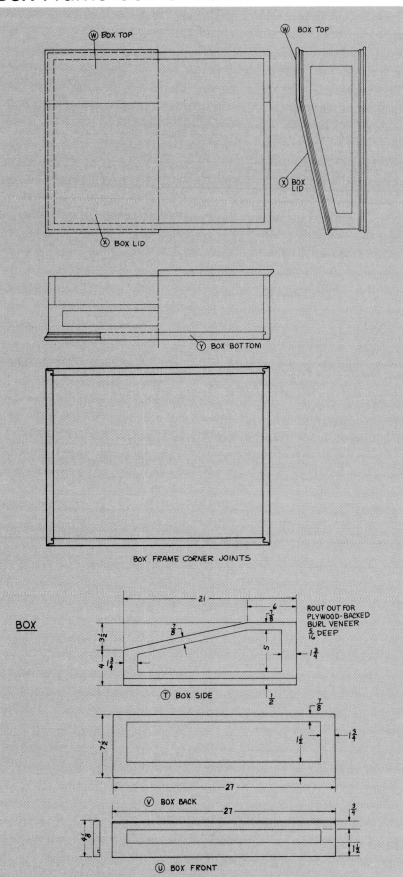

BOX FRAME CORNER JOINTS

BOX

T BOX SIDE

ROUT OUT FOR
PLYWOOD-BACKED
BURL VENEER
$\frac{5}{16}$ DEEP

V BOX BACK

U BOX FRONT

A Rockwell tenoning jig is invaluable for holding workpieces while forming the lock miter joint tenon on a table saw (see drawings, step 2 in making lock miter joint).

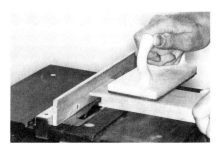

The Dremel table saw is hard to beat for precise cuts on small workpieces, such as cutting off the inside stub tenon while forming a lock miter joint (drawings, step 4). I also used the Dremel to make the miters.

true the edges for book-matching the large drawer case panels.

To get the veneer to lie flat, it had to be treated with the following mixture: 3 parts plastic (urea) resin glue (powder), 4 parts cold water, 2 parts glycerine (drug store), 1 part denatured alcohol.

Measurements are by volume. The plastic resin glue must be fresh; the powder goes bad in the can. Mix the powder and water, add the other two ingredients. The dilute glue sizes the veneer to add strength, the glycerine provides flexibility. The alcohol speeds drying. Soak the veneer in the solution for two minutes, drain dry, wipe the surfaces and put the veneer between sheets of aluminum foil, stack between boards and weight the pile to flatten. Drying will take several days. The veneer will come out flat, flexible and able to be easily cut.

Quarter-inch lauan plywood was used for the large drawer case panels, and the backside was veneered with low-cost veneer to balance out any warp. Veneer for the small panels inset in the drawers and box were glued to $\frac{1}{8}''$ plywood. No veneer was added to the backs as these panels will be glued into the drawers. All of the veneered panels were trimmed with walnut bead molding.

Typical Drawers and Pigeon Holes

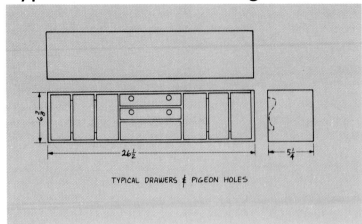

TYPICAL DRAWERS & PIGEON HOLES

Gallery

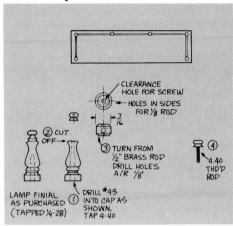

Base Frame

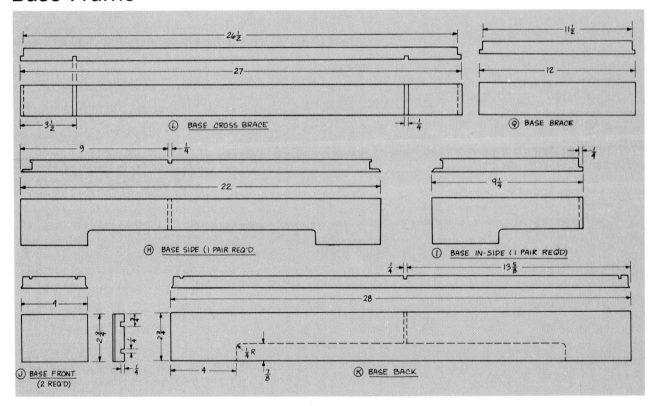

Column

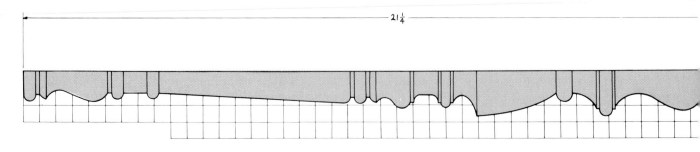

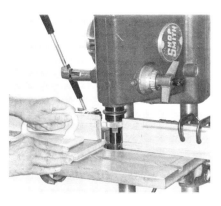

The undercut cove part of the desk molding was formed on a Shopsmith set up for shaping as I did not have the correct bit for routing.

The squared edge of the cove part of the molding was cleaned out with a slotting cutter with the router set up in a shaping table.

Carpathian elm burl veneer is not normally flat and easy to cut. The selection purchased for the desk was especially curled and brittle. Before use, it was treated (see text) to add strength and flexibility. After

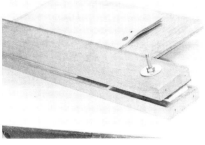

the veneer was pressed flat and dried, the greater ease of use was amazing.

To dress veneer edges for butt joint, I clamp the stacked veneer between boards and sand it on a bench disc sander.

The box is attached to the drawer case with brass screws through the box bottom into the top drawer rails.

The gallery was made using inexpensive brass table lamp finials for posts. Drill the finials from the bottom to $\frac{1}{16}''$ from the top with a #43 drill, then tap the hole for 4-40 threads. Cut off the tops of the finials as shown and dress the cut edges. Turn the rail post sections from $\frac{1}{2}''$ brass rod, and drill for $\frac{1}{8}''$ diameter brass rod rails, and a clearance hole for a 4-40 threaded rod. Attach the posts to the desk top by threading $\frac{1}{4}$-28 threaded rod into the wood. Thread the finial onto the rod. Cut $\frac{1}{8}''$ rod for the rails and insert in post rail sections. Secure these sections to the finials with the finial tips and 4-40 threaded rod.

The wood can either be stained, or allowed to naturally darken with age. I stained, using fruitwood stain on the cherry, walnut stain on the walnut, and a light-colored oak stain on the Carpathian elm burl. All the parts can be stained and varnished completely before assembly, which makes the task a lot easier. The top coat consisted of two coats of UGL's ZAR Quick Dry polyurethane coating lightly sanded between coats to knock off any dust particles, etc., followed by three coats of their Gloss ZAR with more thorough sanding between coats. All coats were applied with foam brushes which inherently lay on a thinner and smoother coat than you will get with a brush—*By Thomas H. Jones.*

The desk was built in modules—base frame, base top, drawer case, and box.

Attaching the box to the drawer case with brass screws—brass, because the ones at the front of the sides will show.

After the box top and lid have been mortised for hinges, the top is attached to the box with dowels.

cane-bottomed chair

This classic country-style chair is very popular today for use in kitchen or dining room. Almost any hardwood can be used; however, oak has become the typical choice for these chairs.

Construction

Although the chair looks fairly simple to build, the bending required for legs and other parts makes it somewhat complicated.

Legs. The first step in construction is to turn the back (B) and front (A) legs. Then bend them into the shape shown in the squared drawings. Bending wood works most easily if the wood to be used is green and unseasoned. It should be straight grained and without any knots or weak spots. The usual method of bending wood uses steam to make the wood more pliant. Steamed wood pieces are then bent and fastened over a form.

There are several homemade shop steamers that can be constructed for steaming wood pieces. Or, you can steam in the old-fashioned way with a simple outdoor fire and boiling water to create the steam. You can even make up a smaller unit to use on your kitchen stove (for steaming small parts).

Regardless of which method you use, the wood should be steamed for at least one hour for each inch of thickness. Then remove it from the steam using heavy rubber gloves, being careful not to burn yourself, and clamp it to the form as quickly as possible. Note that the bend in the form must be a bit more pronounced than the final curve you want in the bending stock.

Dry wood as fast as possible with a heat lamp, but do not expose it to direct sunlight. It will take a bit of experimentation to get the form curved properly for each individual piece, type of wood, and size of stock.

Once the legs are bent and dried, locate and bore the counterbored holes in the sides of the back legs for countersunk screws to hold the seat board to the legs.

Back splats. Cut the top back splat (L) to shape. Enlarge the squared drawing and carve to the proper pattern. Then bend it to shape as well. Cut the lower back splat (K) to size and shape and bend it to fit.

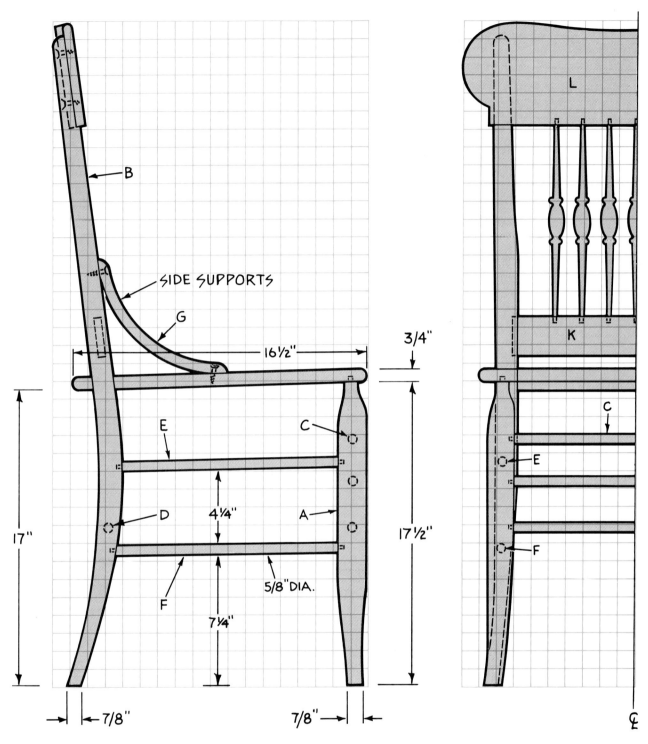

B

SIDE SUPPORTS

G

16½"

3/4"

L

K

E

C

C

E

A

17½"

D

4¼"

F

5/8" DIA.

F

7¼"

17"

7/8"

7/8"

¢L

Side supports. Turn these supports (G) to size and shape on a lathe, then bend them into the required shapes. It will take a great deal of work to get both of these in the exact shape and bend needed to match them up. But this must be done correctly or they can force the chair out of square during assembly.

Bore holes for the back spindles (M) in the bottom edge of the top splat (L) and the upper edge of the bottom splat (K).

Rungs. Turn all the rungs (C-F) to shape and size. Be sure to make tenons on each end of each rung.

Seat Board. The seat board (H-J) is made by first mak-ing up a framework of ¾"-thick pieces, held together with dowels and glue (see detail drawing). Then rout a recess in the top inside edge of the framework for the cane and spline. Using a saber saw or coping saw, round the corners of the seat board and cut the back recesses for the back legs (see detail drawing). Then sand the edges round on both top and bottom of the seat board. Bore the holes for the front legs (A) in the bottom of the seat to the angle shown.

Assembly

Proper sizing of the tenons, dowel ends, and the holes in

MATERIALS LIST

A. Front Legs: 1¾ × 1¾ × 17⅛", 2 req'd.
B. Back Legs: 1¾ × 1¾ × 36", 2 req'd.
C. Front Rungs: ⅝ × ⅝ × 14½", 3 req'd.
D. Back Rung: ⅝ × ⅝ × 14½", 1 req'd.
E. Top Side Rungs: ⅝ × ⅝ × 12¾", 2 req'd.
F. Bottom Side Rungs: ⅝ × ⅝ × 13¼", 2 req'd.
G. Side Supports: ⅝ × ⅝ × 11½", 2 req'd.
H. Seat Board, Front: ¾ × 3½ × 18", 1 req'd.
I. Seat Board, Back: ¾ × 3 × 15", 1 req'd.
J. Seat Board, Sides: ¾ × 3½ × 9½", 2 req'd.
K. Lower Back Splat: ¾ × 2¼ × 15", 1 req'd.
L. Top Back Splat: ¾ × 5½ × 21½", 1 req'd.
M. Back Spindles: ¾ × ¾ × 11¼", 7 req'd.
   Cane to fit

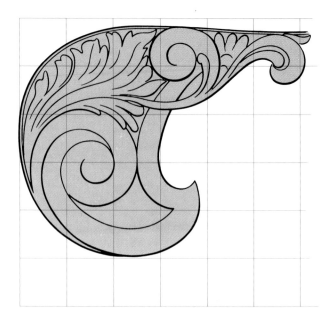

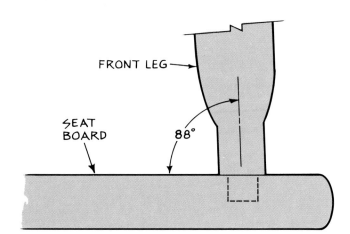

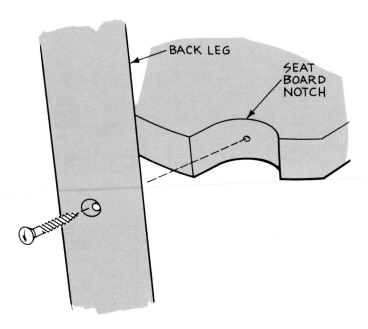

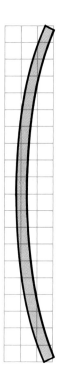

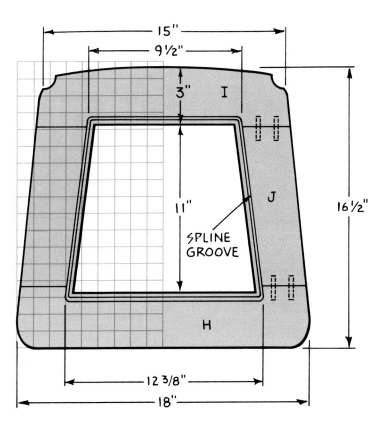

15"

9½"

3"   I

11"

J

SPLINE
GROOVE

16½"

H

12 3/8"

18"

Assembly starts with the front legs (A). Insert their doweled ends up into holes bored in the seat bottom. Then place the front rungs (C) between them and temporarily clamp together. Put this assembly aside for a few moments and assemble the lower back leg assembly. Put the lower back splat (K) and the back lower rung (D) between the back legs (B), and clamp this assembly together. Fit the side rungs (E, F) in the back leg assembly. Then put the front leg assembly in place, with side rungs in their correct holes. Locate the correct position for the back edges of the seat board and fasten in place with countersunk wood screws inserted through the counterbored holes in the back legs.

Stand the leg assembly on a smooth, flat surface and make sure it doesn't rock on its legs. Clamp the entire assembly together with band clamps. Install the side support pieces (G) with screws into the seat board and back legs.

Upper back assembly. To assemble the upper back, insert the back spindles (M) into the holes in the lower splat and then slide the top back splat (L) down over their ends. Anchor it to the back legs with countersunk ovalhead wood screws driven through the back legs. Make sure none of the screws break through.

Stain and finish after a thorough sanding, then install cane. To do this, buy cane pre-woven (many do-it-yourself stores and catalogs supply it), cut larger around than the seat opening. Soak according to directions supplied with cane. Place the cane into the groove routed in the seatboard, and hammer the spline in place. Make sure to stretch the cane tightly. Finish the cane seat according to the instructions supplied with the pre-woven cane—*Monte Burch. Drawings by Gerhard Richter.*

which they fit is very important for a properly constructed, long-lasting chair. Tenons and dowels should be snug, but they should not have a hard "drive-on" fit or there will be no room for the glue that holds the parts securely. Place glue on each tenon or dowel end before insertion, but not so much that it squeezes onto the surrounding wood surface.

queen anne table

Reprinted with permission from *Workbench* magazine

Modeled after the fine pieces made in eighteenth-century England, this Queen Anne tea table is assembled with a simplified, modern technique using ready-made cabriole ("Queen Anne") legs. For the craftsman who would rather make his own, we show a pattern in a squared drawing. The pattern can be modified, of course, by the more experienced craftsman who enjoys creating an individual design.

No matter how you change the design of the leg, remember the axiom that a vertical centerline through the top of the leg should intersect the center of the foot.

Cut the four aprons to size and shape, miter the ends, then glue and clamp them together on a flat surface. Be sure to let the glue set completely, as it will be the only thing holding the corners together until they are reinforced with the legs.

Cut the legtops as indicated, unless you use the optional legs that attach with plates, and glue and screw them inside each corner of the apron assembly as shown. Reinforce them with the glue blocks as indicated.

Make the two frames, one of picture-frame molding (purchased or made as detailed) and one of ½-inch stock. Glass is fitted in the rabbet of the molding—this should be plate glass at least ¼-inch thick—then the molding

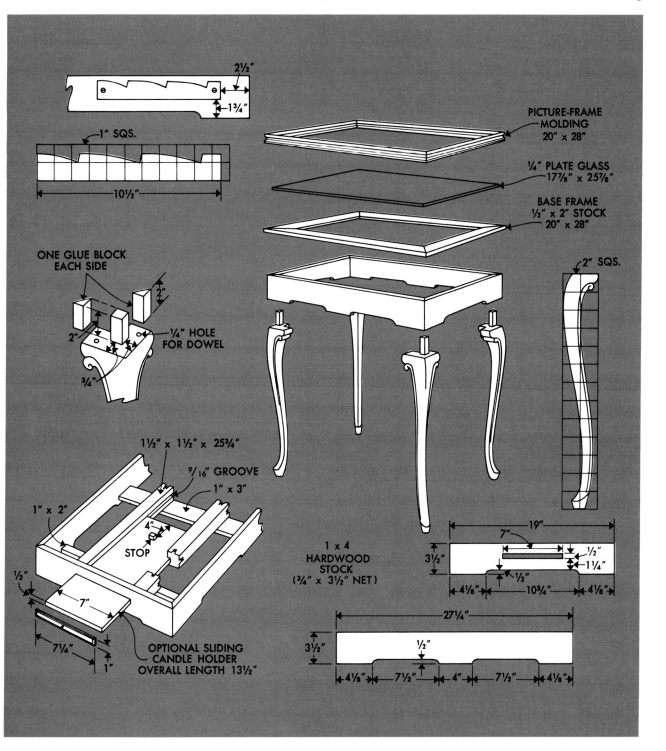

Top can be tilted up to display reference materials.

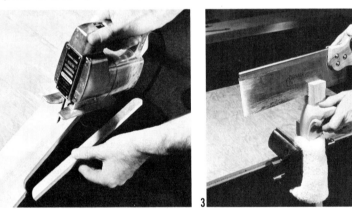

Profiles on lower edges of aprons are cut with portable jig saw, pieces saved. Jig saw or band saw can be used instead.

Ends of aprons are mitered, glue applied, then assembled and held with strap clamp. Check for square corners.

If ready-made legs are used, tops are cut to provide "shelf" ¾ inch wide on which adjacent aprons rest.

Holes for ¼- or ⁵⁄₁₆-inch dowels are drilled in lower edges of aprons. Thumb tack makes dowel-center tool to mark holes.

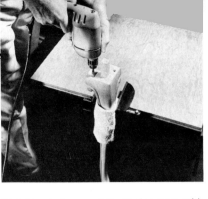

Matching holes are drilled in leg tops, with legs held in vise. Legs are padded to prevent vise damaging them.

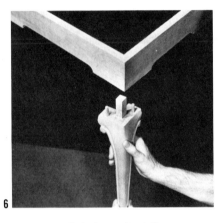

Place dowels in legs, check fit to aprons. Make any necessary adjustments to assure perfect fit between legs and aprons.

Projections on leg tops are cross-drilled for No. 8 × 1-inch brass screws. Glue is applied, screws driven into aprons.

Triangular blocks are glued to each side of each leg top to reinforce the attachment to the apron.

13

Pressed-wood ornament is located at center of each long apron ¼ inch above lower edge. Use glue and small brads.

Optional leg attached with metal plate is attractive and functional; not quite as graceful as leg used on original.

14

Picture-frame molding (made or purchased) is attached to frame of ½-inch stock with screws driven into molding.

Three of the screws that hold metal leg plate are driven into lower edges of adjacent aprons. Predrill holes.

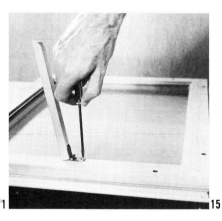

15

If you wish top to tilt up for display or for convenient reading or study, attach brace with ¾-inch brass butt hinge.

Optional leg is ready-made type that fastens by means of metal plate. In this case, glue and screw triangular pieces.

Notched hardwood bracket is screwed to inside of one or both side aprons to accept end of brace that holds up top.

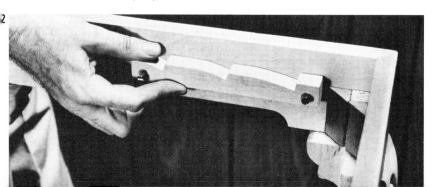

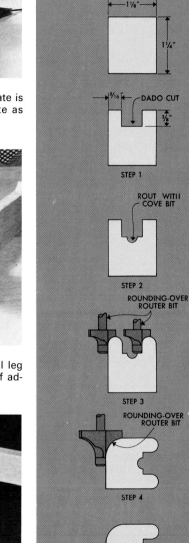

is screwed to the frame of ½-inch stock.

If the top is to be tilted so you can use it for display or easy reading, install two hinges inside one long apron and on the long side of the frame assembly as indicated. Also install the prop and notched bracket. Position the prop to hold the top at the three angles you wish.

If the optional candle trays are installed, replace the glass with a piece of ¼-inch hardwood paneling so the "mechanism" is hidden.

Stain and finish to suit your decor. Apply a number of coats of varnish or lacquer for a deep, rich finish—*John W. Sill.*

double-duty room

Like a lot of homes, mine isn't so big that I can devote a whole room to activities that occur just a few times a year. And it certainly isn't so big that I can waste two rooms that way. If I had a dining room, I'd use it less than once a month. A guest room? Maybe half that often.

Still, there are times when we do need such rooms. My solution? Combine them both. Now, what used to be a little-used guest room is a dining room—with built-in buffets and cabinets for china, tablecloths, silver, and so on—that also contains a disappear-

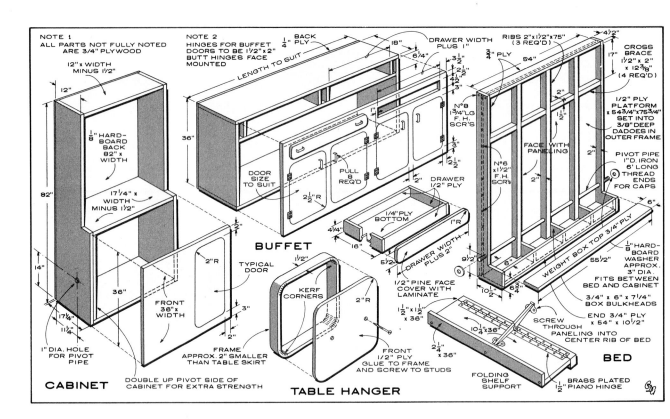

Cabinets (A) flanking fold-up bed are made with cabinet-grade ³/₄-inch particleboard. This material is heavier, stronger, and smoother than underlayment grades. Glue and screw cabinets using white or yellow glue and 1³/₄-inch screws. Fasten back to cabinet with glue and 1-inch screws. All screw-heads are countersunk and capped with polyester auto-body filler, belt-sanded smooth and flush. Apply laminate, then cut out doors (see photo caption). Cover door backs with laminate, too, to prevent warping. Add shelves as desired using standard pin or spade-type supports in ¹/₄-inch holes. Fasten cabinets in place by driving screws through bottom into floor. Buffet (B) is built much the same as cabinets. Drawers are simple butt-joined plywood with bottoms glued and nailed to frame. They ride on Knape and Vogt ball-bearing slides. Mount drawers—without pine faces—on sliding hardware. Then close them and temporarily tack pine faces in position using hot-metal glue, carefully aligning them before the glue cools. Hold them in place by hand until the glue sets. Bolt-through drawer pulls—when

added—will hold drawer faces firmly in place. The plywood platform for bed (C) is made of two identical pieces 27³/₈ inches wide. The bed's outer frame captures the platform in a dado. After frame and platform are assembled, glue and screw the three ribs to the platform, running the center rib directly over the seam in the platform. Next add cross-brace parts and counterweight box bulkheads. Both the bed frame and the counterweight box are covered with laminate and mounted on a pivot made from pipe. Paneling is glued and nailed to bottom of bed, and folding leg is screwed in place over the paneling. To make table hanger (D), cut frame to size, and kerf at corners to facilitate bending. Cut out plywood front, and glue frame to back of front. Let glue dry, then apply laminate to edges of the hanger. To do this, use a torch or heat gun to warm laminate, and prebend it around curves in frame. Then cement in place as usual. Use flathead screws through front and into wall studs to secure the hanger to wall. Apply laminate to its front, and trim the excess laminate with a router.

In the dining-room mode circular table in the center of the room provides seating space for up to eight. Bed is folded against the wall between the two cabinets in the background, its underside covered with prefinished oak paneling. Table hangs out of the way, and bed folds down (below), turning room into cozy sleeping space.

Door openings (above left) for buffet and cabinets are cut after laminate is applied, using a super-fine blade such as a Trojan X-FS to prevent chipping. To cut the openings accurately, draw their outlines on laminate, and drill starting hole for jigsaw behind where one hinge will mount. Tilt saw shoe 5 degrees to bevel door edges for clearance. First, saw only hinge edge of door, then face-mount hinges and finish cut. Door will be perfectly hung with kerf-wide clearances all around. Laminate for both the buffet top and the left-hand cabinet top (above) is applied in one piece to eliminate need for tricky joint. Carefully cut and dry-fit the piece as shown here before cementing in place. Use slip sheets to ensure proper positioning. The counterweight box beneath pivot pipe (left) makes the pivoting bed easier to raise and lower. Box is filled with rocks "buttered" in place with concrete so they don't rattle.

ing bed. Most of the time we leave it set up as a dining room, using the table year-round for sewing, crafts projects, or updating household accounts.

But if we have overnight guests, the table top goes up on the wall, and the bed pops down from between two cabinets. Pillows and blankets come out of the closet, and we have a comfortable and cozy place for friends and relatives to sleep.

All this fits neatly into a 12-by-12-foot room, with space left over to store a sewing machine, ironing board, crafts, and games, plus eight folding chairs to go with the dining table.

Best of all, the room was inexpensive and easy to convert. Although the drawings and photos on these pages may make the project look complicated at first, nothing could be simpler. With the exception of cutting a dado in the bed frame, everything else is basic butt-joint, glue-and-screw construction. Even the cabinet doors hang themselves automatically and fit perfectly. If you can cut particleboard accurately, you can build a room like this.

Despite the simplicity, everything looks good. The reason? All those basic butt joints and screw heads are covered with a plastic laminate. If you have never worked with these laminates, I suggest you give them a try. They are by far the fastest, easiest way to put a professional finish on a project. With a little practice, you can cover a piece like one of these cabinets in an hour or two. A first-class paint job could take four or five days and might not look as good or last as long as laminate does.

So if you have a room in your home that's not earning its keep, consider giving it a double life—by A.J. Hand. Drawing by Carl De Groote.

three-shelf bookcase

Construction Notes

This attractive bookcase is fairly simple to build and can be used in a living room, bedroom, or study.

The boards are ripped to size, with the shelves cut ¼ inch narrower than the sides to allow for the rabbet. The dadoes in the side pieces are made with the router or on the table saw. If a router is used, cut both sections at one time to ensure that the dadoes will be perfectly aligned. Fasten the pieces firmly to a flat surface, lay out the position of the dadoes, and clamp a straightedge to the work, allowing the proper clearance for the router base. Unless a hardwood is being used, the ¼-inch deep cut may be made in one pass. The tool should be fed slowly, and the base kept solidly against the straightedge.

After the dadoes are cut, the back edges of the side pieces are rabbeted. Then the curved sections are laid out and cut with a saber saw. After the sides are completed, rip the subtop to size. The widths of subtop and sides must match.

Before assembling the parts, a router with a rounding bit is used to round all exposed edges. The router must not be run through the dadoes, but should be stopped just short of them. Likewise, the rounding of the shelves should stop ¼ inch from the ends. Failure to do so will leave a gap at these points when the parts are later assembled.

Bore the screw and button holes as required, and then assemble the parts with glue and screws. The shelf ends should be glue-sized beforehand. The screws in the base piece are angled slightly into the end pieces, as shown in Detail E. The ends and front base piece are fastened with 1¼-inch FH screws driven from the inside. The base should be installed so that its upper edge is ¹⁄₁₆ inch above the bottom edge of the bottom shelf.

The subtop is fastened to the sides using two-inch finishing nails, driven from the topside into the rabbet.

Bore four ³⁄₁₆-inch screw clearance holes in the subtop one inch from the edges and two inches from each end. Fasten the top to the subtop with screws driven through these holes. Use 1¼" FH screws. The top is centered from side to side, but it should project ¼ inch past the rear edge of the subtop. See Detail F.

Install the back panel with one-inch brads. Finish with stain and several topcoats of clear lacquer or varnish—*By John Capotosto.*

BILL OF MATERIALS

Except as noted, all lumber is pine.
All measurements are in inches.

Part	Description	Size	Qty.
1	Side	¾ × 9 × 42¼	2
2	Back, plywood	¼ × 33¾ × 40¼	1
3	Top	¾ × 8½ × 36¼	1
4	Subtop	¾ × 7 × 33¾	1
5	Skirt	¾ × 2¾ × 35½	1
6	Shelf	¾ × 8¾ × 33¾	3
7	Base	¾ × 4 × 36¼	1
8	Apron	¾ × 2 × 33¼	1
9	End	¾ × 4 × 9	2
10	Base, rear	¾ × 3¹⁵⁄₁₆ × 33¼	1
A	Screw	1½—8 FH	16
B	Screw	1¼—8 FH	4
C	Button	½ × ⅝	16
D	Finishing nail	2	4
E	Brad	1	18

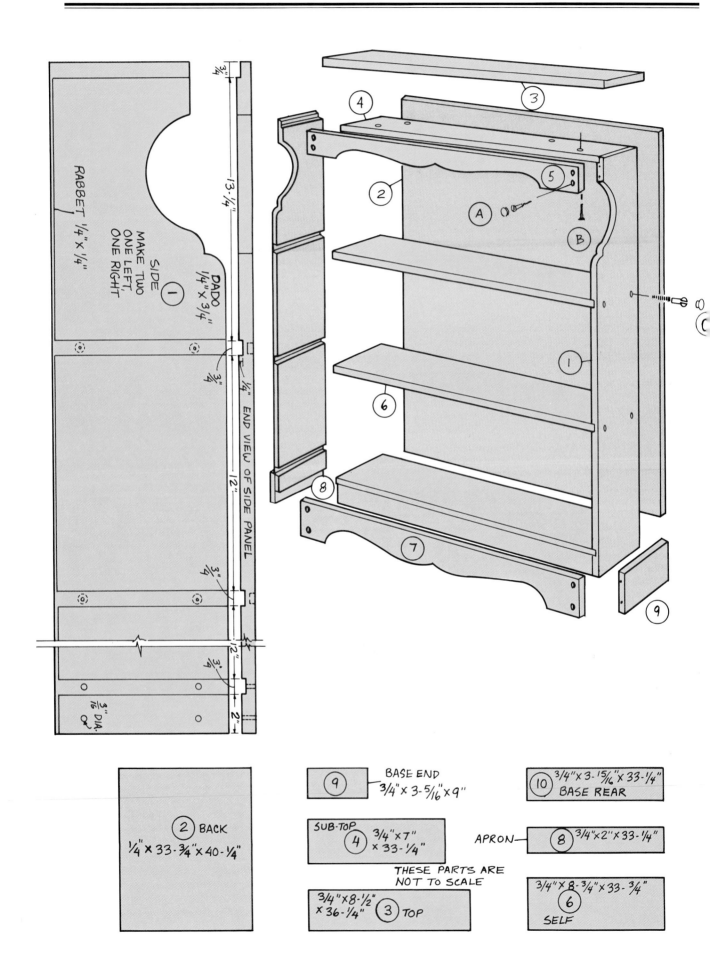

RABBET 1/4" X 1/4"

SIDE
MAKE TWO
ONE LEFT,
ONE RIGHT

DADO
1/4" X 3/4"

①

3/4"

13-1/4"

3/4"

1/4" END VIEW OF SIDE PANEL

12"

3/4"

12"

3/4"

3/16"
3" DIA.

2"

④

②

⑤

A

B

③

①

⑥

⑧

⑦

C

⑨

② BACK
1/4" X 33-3/4" X 40-1/4"

⑨ BASE END
3/4" X 3-5/16" X 9"

SUB-TOP
④ 3/4" X 7"
X 33-1/4"

THESE PARTS ARE
NOT TO SCALE

3/4" X 8-1/2"
X 36-1/4" ③ TOP

⑩ 3/4" X 3-15/16" X 33-1/4"
BASE REAR

APRON — ⑧ 3/4" X 2" X 33-1/4"

3/4" X 8-3/4" X 33-3/4"
⑥
SELF

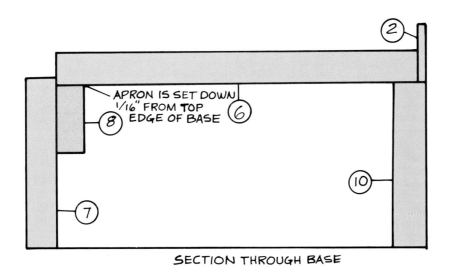

SECTION THROUGH BASE

APRON IS SET DOWN 1/16" FROM TOP EDGE OF BASE

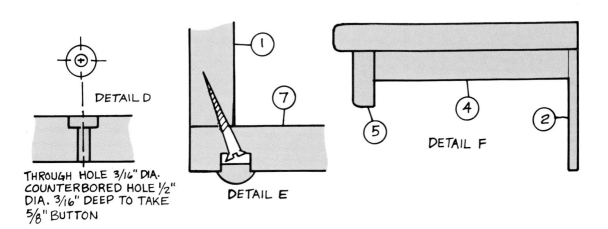

DETAIL D

THROUGH HOLE 3/16" DIA. COUNTERBORED HOLE 1/2" DIA. 3/16" DEEP TO TAKE 5/8" BUTTON

DETAIL E

DETAIL F

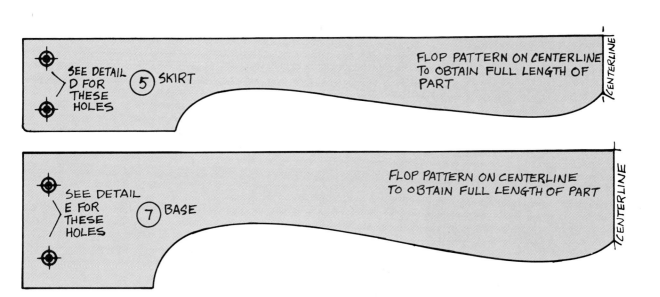

SEE DETAIL D FOR THESE HOLES

⑤ SKIRT

FLOP PATTERN ON CENTERLINE TO OBTAIN FULL LENGTH OF PART

SEE DETAIL E FOR THESE HOLES

⑦ BASE

FLOP PATTERN ON CENTERLINE TO OBTAIN FULL LENGTH OF PART

three elegant carts

Americans are famous for eating on the run. And we often find ourselves moving around in our homes to eat: barbecues and breakfasts outdoors in warm weather, snacks around the television, or a meal out on the deck as a break from the table routine. When we do change scenes, something is usually left behind—the knives, the coffee, or the ketchup—and we jump up and trot back to the kitchen fetching the missing item.

An answer to that problem is one of these handy cart designs from Georgia Pacific (see photos and drawings). You can either load a cart in the kitchen and roll it to where you're eating, or you can plant a well-stocked cart where you often prepare food or entertain. The appliance cart brings cooking tools back to the kitchen, too.

Best of all, the three carts are planned for construction with common sizes of lumber: 1×2s, 2×2s, and so on. You don't need a shopful of power tools to recut and dress the wood. (A portable circular saw will be a big labor saver when cutting large plywood sections, and a sabre saw is a must for the free-form cutouts on the serving-cart frames. Otherwise, hand tools are all you'll need.)

A two-tone paint job brightens up the carts' appearance, or you may want to finish boards with a clear, exterior sealer.

More detailed plans and patterns for the serving cart and appliance center are available in a booklet that includes eight other projects. Write to Redi-Cuts, PS, Georgia Pacific, 900 S.W. Fifth Avenue, Portland, OR 97204. For more details on the barbecue cart, write to Housekit, Georgia Pacific, same address—*Paul Bolon.*

Serving Cart

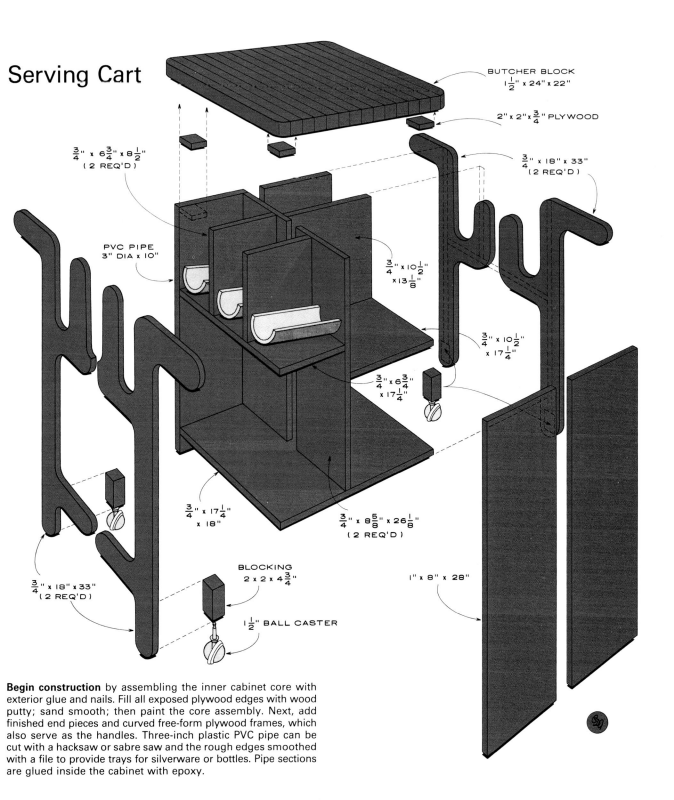

Begin construction by assembling the inner cabinet core with exterior glue and nails. Fill all exposed plywood edges with wood putty; sand smooth; then paint the core assembly. Next, add finished end pieces and curved free-form plywood frames, which also serve as the handles. Three-inch plastic PVC pipe can be cut with a hacksaw or sabre saw and the rough edges smoothed with a file to provide trays for silverware or bottles. Pipe sections are glued inside the cabinet with epoxy.

Barbecue Cart

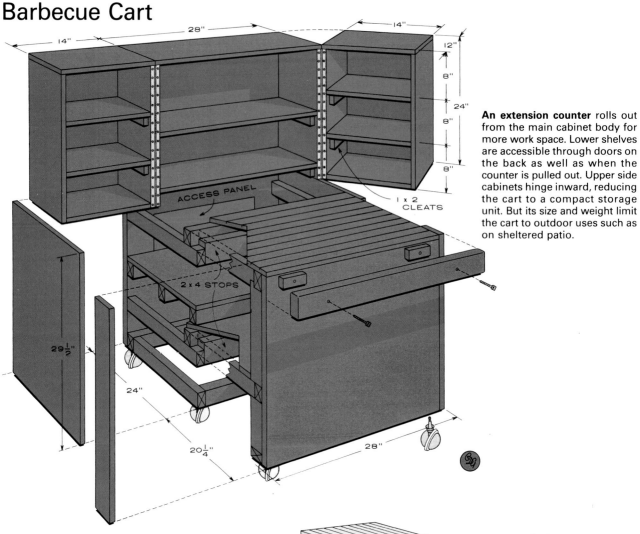

ACCESS PANEL

2 x 4 STOPS

1 x 2 CLEATS

An extension counter rolls out from the main cabinet body for more work space. Lower shelves are accessible through doors on the back as well as when the counter is pulled out. Upper side cabinets hinge inward, reducing the cart to a compact storage unit. But its size and weight limit the cart to outdoor uses such as on sheltered patio.

Appliance Center

This setup is designed as a work area to accommodate all the portable appliances in a kitchen. Cutout on the back panel is for the cord of a 10-inch power strip with continuous outlets. For the best finish, the cart should have two or three coats of exterior paint or sealer. Ideal paint job is one coat of an oil-base paint followed by two coats of enamel. The plan here is modified from a detailed plan in the Redi-Cuts booklet.

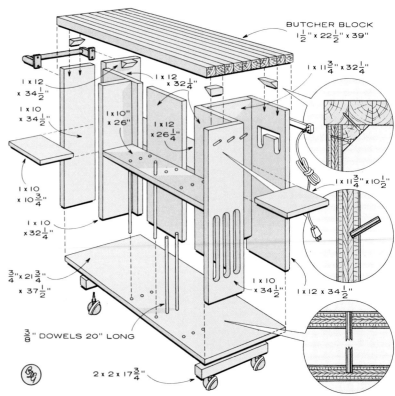

BUTCHER BLOCK
$1\frac{1}{2}$" x $22\frac{1}{2}$" x 39"

$\frac{3}{8}$" DOWELS 20" LONG

2 x 2 x $17\frac{3}{4}$"

inside shutters that save energy

If your house is well insulated, you can double-glaze, triple-glaze, and weatherstrip your windows until you are sick of the whole business, and the windows will still be your biggest source of heat loss. The ad of a leading window company humorously suggests that the only cure is to board up the windows.

A less drastic solution is well-fitted, weatherstripped, wood shutters, mounted inside the windows. While insulated wood shutters are more effective than plain wood ones, either is more effective than triple-glazing. Triple-glazing in the sash can reduce heat loss over double-glazing by 18 percent; well-fitted, weatherstripped, wood shutters will save 48 percent, and insulated shutters 61 percent over double-glazing.

Heat is lost through a window two ways. Heat passing through the glass is called *transmission loss*. It can be reduced by trapping a layer of dead air between two layers of glass. It can be further reduced by trapping a second layer of dead air by triple-glazing, or by adding a shutter. A shutter is better than glass, as the wood itself blocks the flow of heat.

Infiltration is the second form of window heat loss. It is air passing through the cracks between the sashes and the window frame. Weatherstripping and tight-fitting window sashes reduce infiltration. A well-fitted shutter with weatherstripping can cut this loss by providing an additional barrier.

Energy-saving capability is just one advantage that wooden, interior shutters have over triple-glazing. Privacy is another—shutters effectively seal off a room from the outside. Shut-ters may even contribute to your home's security; if a potential intruder can't see in, and there's obviously more there than a window shade or draperies, he's likely to play it safe and go elsewhere.

On the following pages are three approaches to building interior shutters. But these designs are only a starting point.

For one thing, the shutters shown are not likely to fit your windows, so you'll have to modify the plans to suit your needs. Here are other things to consider in designing your own energy-saving shutters:

● You may want to substitute ⅛-inch hardboard for plywood in insulated shutters. This will reduce the thickness to 1 inch, with little reduction in the desired thermal insulation.

● Allow 1/16-inch clearance all around, and between shutters to avoid sticking. Also, do not leave more than 1/16 inch between the back of the shutter and the wood doorstop.

● While you would expect closed-cell foam weatherstripping to be more effective than the lower-priced, open cell type, we found that the open-cell foam stayed in place better (though neither will last forever).

● For a tight fit, shutters must be latched to the window frame, not to each other.

You'll find that you can build energy-saving shutters for less than you would have to pay for light-weight interior shutters. Your biggest outlay will be for hinges and latches.

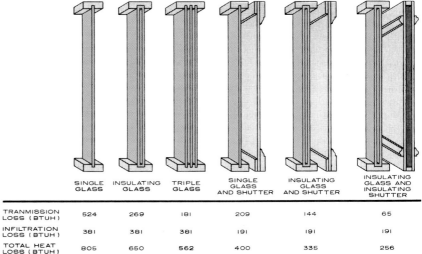

	SINGLE GLASS	INSULATING GLASS	TRIPLE GLASS	SINGLE GLASS AND SHUTTER	INSULATING GLASS AND SHUTTER	INSULATING GLASS AND INSULATING SHUTTER
TRANMISSION LOSS (BTUH)	524	269	181	209	144	65
INFILTRATION LOSS (BTUH)	381	381	381	191	191	191
TOTAL HEAT LOSS (BTUH)	805	650	562	400	335	256

INFILTRATION LOSS CALCULATED FOR ALUMINUM OR WOOD DOUBLE-HUNG WINDOWS

Effectiveness of shutters as energy-savers is shown above, BTUH losses are given for 8-square-foot windows, 58-degree inside-outside temperature difference, 15 mph wind. Window sashes are average fit, and like shutters, weatherstripped.

Design 1

These shutters were designed for a basement powder room, facing north, that was always colder in the winter than other rooms. Both sides of the shutters are decorated, making them equally attractive open or closed. The shutters are lapped for an air-tight fit.

Construction: Cut plywood panels to slightly oversize dimension, cut interior frame parts to size, miter decorative molding. Assemble mitered moldings and nail and glue to plywood, running the nails through the plywood, into the molding. Assemble the frame with glue only, then glue and nail to one face panel. Keep the nails out of hinge, lapped edge, and latch areas. Cut polyfoam insulation to fit, insert, glue, and nail second panel. Rout the mating edges to form the overlap. No-mortise hinges were used.

Shutters fashioned for basement powder room are shown at top, right. You can miter decorative molding for just one, or both sides of the shutters (above). Although moldings can be glued and nailed to shutter face panel one by one, it is easier and faster to assemble the decorative frame in a frame clamp, or set of corner clamps (center). Before applying glue, position decorative frame on plywood panel as shown above, right, clamp, turn over, and pin into position with partially driven nails. After gluing, drive nails all the way and clamp. Once an internal frame has been glued to a shutter panel, cut polyfoam insulation to fit and glue it to the second side, as shown in the photo below, right.

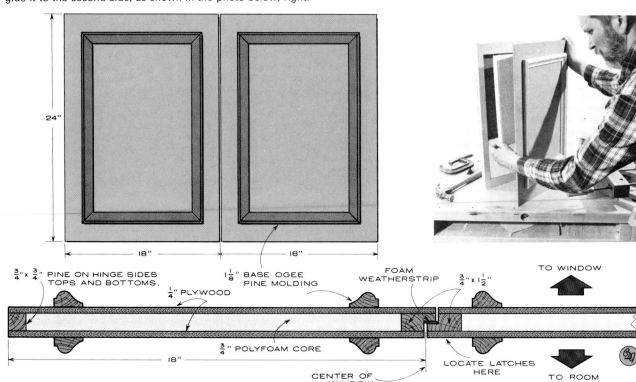

24"

18"   18"

18"

¾" x ¾" PINE ON HINGE SIDES TOPS AND BOTTOMS.

1⅛" BASE OGEE PINE MOLDING

¼" PLYWOOD

FOAM WEATHERSTRIP

¾" x 1½"

TO WINDOW

¾" POLYFOAM CORE

CENTER OF WINDOW

LOCATE LATCHES HERE

TO ROOM

Design 2

These uninsulated wood shutters are mounted on loose-pin hinges so they can be taken down during the warm part of the year. When up, they are kept closed most of the time, so only one side of the shutters was decorated.

Construction: Blank rails, lay out curved edge, saber-saw to outline, and sand smooth. Cut posts overlength for ease of clamping when routing. Glue frames together, clamp to bench (spaced up with ¾-inch scrap), and rout opening with ball-bearing piloted Roman ogee bit. Glue ¼-inch plywood panels to frame backs and trim panel backs with lattice. Mortise for hinges and rout slots for tongue-and-groove closure. Glue foam weatherstrip in groove for snug fit when closed.

(Continued)

These shutters are intended for easy removal. Surface bolts secure them to window frame and hold them tightly against weatherstripped molding. Above: Curved side of rails are cut with saber saw. Below: After cutting, rough edge is smoothed with drum sander.

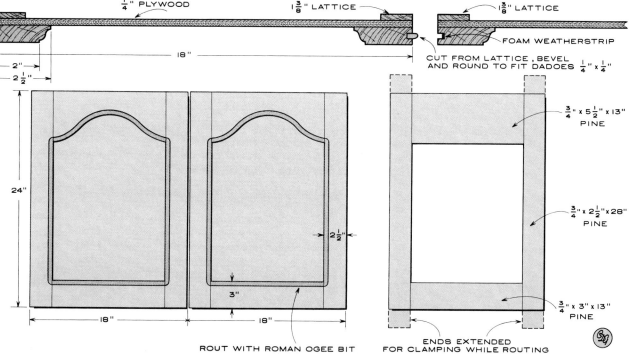

¼" PLYWOOD   1⅜" LATTICE   1⅜" LATTICE

FOAM WEATHERSTRIP

CUT FROM LATTICE, BEVEL AND ROUND TO FIT DADOES ¼" x ¼"

18"

2"
2½"

24"

2½"

3"

18"   18"

ROUT WITH ROMAN OGEE BIT

¾" x 5½" x 13" PINE

¾" x 2½" x 28" PINE

¾" x 3" x 13" PINE

ENDS EXTENDED FOR CLAMPING WHILE ROUTING

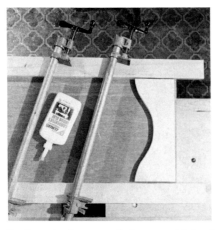

Posts and rails are ready for assembly in photo at left. Glued butt joints were reinforced when the panel was glued on. Projections are for clamping while routing. Center: After gluing plywood panel and lattice backside trim to frames, slots are routed in mating edges for tongue-and-groove closure. Bottom of groove is lined with foam weatherstrip. Tongue is ripped from lattice; profile requires additional rounding for smooth closing. Right: As hinge mortises extend across full thickness of shutters, both shutters are clamped and routed back to back. Simple clamp-on jig guides router.

Design 3

Poorly weatherstripped tracks allowed cold air to get through our 6-foot wide, sliding aluminum windows, even with storms. To cover the windows, we made shutters in folding pairs. The shutters are oak (it was cheaper than available select pine). Eight surface bolts hold them tightly against the weatherstripped doorstop, which minimizes infiltration.

Construction: Cut frames to dimension, allowing for rail tenons. Rout slots for plywood panels; then rout post ends to form mortises. Saw tenons to fit mortises. Glue three sides of each frame; then insert panel and glue fourth side. Trim shutters to fit window and rout hinge mortises. We hinged our shutters to the window frame with 3×3 butts; between pairs, we used invisible hinges, but ordinary butts would do. Facing sides of shutters have shallow tongue and grooves. The round-bottom groove is routed with a ½-inch core bit; the mating tongue is ½-inch, half-round molding, set in a ¹/₁₆-inch-deep dado. As with other shutters, foam weatherstrip was glued in mating groove for airtight fit. Rout mortises for hinges, and slots for tongue and groove—*Thomas H. Jones.*

Shutters designed for 6-foot-wide windows. In summer, they help keep room cool.

Sawing tenons on shutter rails can be done accurately in miter box (top), if stop-block is clamped to box and bench to keep tenon lengths identical. Tenon is finished with chisel. Shutter frames and panels are assembled with glue (bottom).

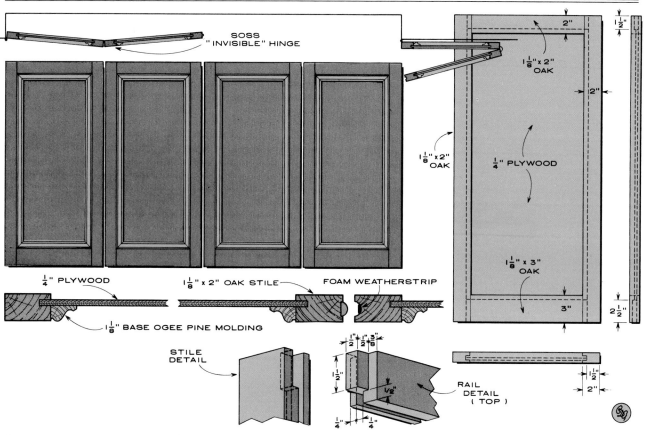

SOSS "INVISIBLE" HINGE

2"

1½"

1⅛" x 2" OAK

2"

1⅛" x 2" OAK

¼" PLYWOOD

1⅛" x 3" OAK

3"

2½"

¼" PLYWOOD

1⅛" x 2" OAK STILE

FOAM WEATHERSTRIP

1⅛" BASE OGEE PINE MOLDING

STILE DETAIL

½" ⅜" ¾"

1½"

½"

¼" ¼"

RAIL DETAIL (TOP)

½"

2"

Construction details for Shutter 3. Top row: Left—Hinges are 3×3, loose-pin butts, set in mortises. Right—Soss invisible hinges join shutter pairs. Middle row: Left—Doorstop molding is positioned about ¹⁄₁₆ inch behind shutter. Center— Adhesive-backed, foam weatherstrip on doorstop is tightly compressed when shutter is latched. Right—Surface bolts latch shutters to sill. Bottom row: Left— Brass-plated, steel-type surface bolts (left in photo) are available at Sears; solid-brass type (right), at hardwares. Center— Strike plate for bolt is mortised into sill. Right—Frames were stained.

swing-out partition shelves

If your house has a pair of Lally columns supporting an upper floor, you can use them to anchor a shelved storage cabinet with a set of swing-out doors. The doors—with adjustable shelves—give you an easy-access, roomy partition unit. Face it with perforated hardboard, and you can use Peg-Board hooks and brackets to hang small items from front and back.

To secure the unit, fasten 2×8s to the support columns with U-bolts. I made mine by heating threaded ⅜-inch-diameter rods with a propane torch to bend them to shape, using the columns as a form. Mark the supports, drill two holes for each rod, then fasten with flat washers and nuts. Use three rods for each side.

Cut the shelving for the stationary section to length. Support each shelf at both ends with uprights of the same stock cut to the desired height. Starting at the bottom, wedge in the shelving supports and shelves successively, supporting the shelves in the center with pieces of the same height nailed through each shelf as it is positioned. On the back, attach sheets of ⅛-inch Peg-Board.

To make the doors, use ¾-inch plywood cut into 12-inch strips for each unit's sides, top, and bottom. Back this frame with Peg-Board and mount a 3-inch-diameter wheel on the bottom of each unit. Shelves in the doors can be made fixed or adjustable using any suitable hardware.

Attach the door units with 6-inch strap hinges attached at three points as shown—*W. David Houser.*

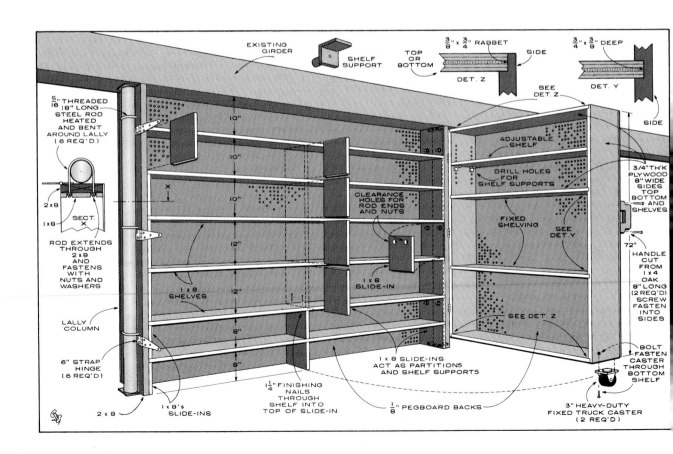

Doors open easily (above) on wheels secured to bottom shelf. Below, Peg-Board on back of the unit is for hanging tools.

free-standing closet

Think *your* home is short of closets? Pity the poor buyer of loft space in any major city: He gets *no* storage because what he's buying is open space. At best, kitchen and bath have been partitioned off, as in my loft pictured below. But the rest of the floor is as naked as a basketball court—not even a place to hang a hat.

Solving that problem was the first task I set for myself, designing a sturdy closet that's a spacious wardrobe. (Line it with cedar and it would be an ideal out-of-season storage-partition for family room or den.)

My structure makes economic use of its 4×8 plywood and particleboard panels. Two uncut ¾-inch panels are butted edge-to-edge to form the back, with the joint glued and screwed along a 2×4. Another ¾-inch sheet is cut down the center to form two end panels—each framed in 2×2s, which, with the grooved 4×4 base, create a structural trim.

I used particleboard for the back panel and two end doors. The center door is ⅝-inch plywood; since each door is 33 inches wide, you'll have scrap strips for shelving. I used a 5-inch strip of the ⅝-inch panel for the cornice that hides the door track.

The doors were hung with an 8-foot sliding-door set (Stanley 2850) that features dial-alignment hangers. Since the outer edges of two doors complete the frame around the end panels, alignment is critical—the hangers simplify adjustment.

Three different colors of enamel complete the project. The end panels are MDO plywood for a smooth face to contrast with the particleboard textures on back and outer doors—*Al Lees.*

Ratchet driver with extension socket will sink bolt heads below groove bottom.

Compartmentalizing helps in meeting special storage needs.

Also handy to exit: grocery cart. Extra leaves for dining table go in slot, right.

Storage from scratch: an innovative built-in that can be adapted to any home that's short on closet space.

In the unpartitioned loft above we designed an island closet (tucked under a structural beam here, though it's designed to stand free); it masks the entry door from the living space, screens off the bathroom door to the right, and provides ample storage for outerwear and bulky items that must be handy to the exit.

The plywood-particleboard case is assembled on a simple frame, most of which is external and treated as a design element. Hung within the recessed end panel shown are vulnerable artworks: a silver plaque and a Jon Baugh glass assemblage.

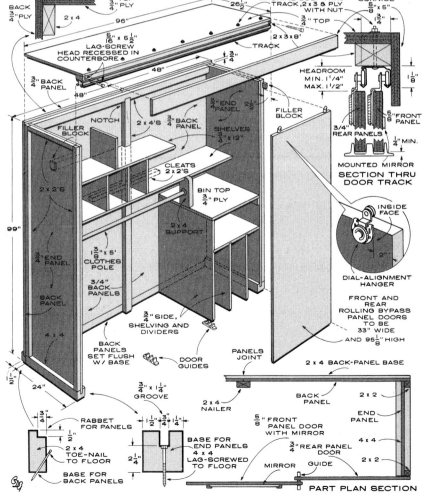

darkroom work cabinet

A darkroom area must, above all, be functional. This means it must serve as a storage area for most, if not all, your photographic equipment. The compact worktable-storage area shown here will adequately store such items as chemical bottles, mixing bucket, contact printer, print dryer, film washer, trays, developing tanks, filters, enlarging lenses, paper-mounting press, and timers, as well as provide a comfortable work area—*Claudia* and *John Caruana*.

Above right, measurements, for components. They are coded (A, B, etc.) to drawing. In parentheses: how many of same size pieces are needed.

Measurements in inches

A = ½ × 60 × 17	(1)	**L** = ¾ × 1½ × 13 (1)
B = ½ × 59 × 16¾	(1)	**M** = ¾ × 1½ × 12½ (3)
C = ½ × 38 × 17	(2)	**N** = ½ × 13½ × 7½ (2)
D = ½ × 34½ × 16¾	(3)	**O** = ½ × 11⁷/₁₆ × 6⁷/₁₆ (2)
E = ½ × 14 × 16¾	(3)	**P** = ½ × 17¼ × 6⁷/₁₆ (4)
F = ¼ × 35¾ × 59		**Q** = ½ × 11⁷/₁₆ × 6⁷/₁₆ (2)
	Masonite (1)	**R** = ¼ × 11⁷/₁₆ × 16¼ (1)
G = ½ × 3 × 59	(1)	
Ha = ½ × 13½ × 15	(1)	Masonite (2)
Hb = ½ × 14 × 15	(1)	**S** = ½ × 2 × 59 (1)
Ia = ½ × 13½ × 18	(2)	**T** = ½ × 2 × 17¾ (2)
Ib = ½ × 14 × 18	(1)	**U** = ½ × 8 × 16¾ (1)
J = ¾ × 1½ × 32½	(4)	**V** = ½ × ¾ × 16¾ (16)
K = ¾ × 1½ × 60	(2)	**W** = ½ × ¾ × 14¼ (2)

It takes about thirty hours, including cutting the pieces, to make this darkroom cabinet (twenty hours, if the pieces are precut). Equipment needed: tablesaw, handsaws (rip, crosscut), sandpaper (medium, fine), hammer, plane, 6-foot ruler, pencil, level, angle, miter box and saw, chisel, files (medium, fine, coarse), router, screwdriver, 6d finishing nails, brush (medium size), and glue.

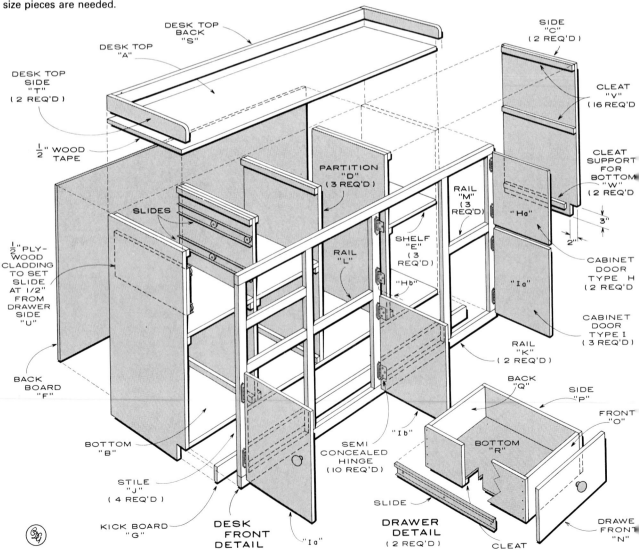

magazine cradle

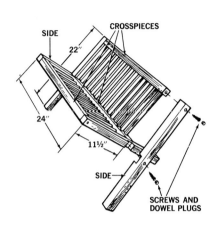

This dowel-and-redwood rack displays a selection of magazines of varying size for easy access. And it's quickly made with hand tools and a power drill.

Begin by gathering all materials and cutting pieces to length (see table). Next, cut the lap joints in the side pieces (the width of the redwood and halfway through each piece). Mark the crosspieces for the dowel holes: Place the first mark 1⅛ inch from the end and the rest 1¼ inch on center. Use a ½-inch drill; make holes slightly deeper than ¼ inch. Sand all pieces.

Drill and counterbore holes in the four sides for screws and ½-inch plugs. Tap one row of dowels into the center crosspiece, then set the dowel tops into a top crosspiece. Tap lightly on the crosspiece to secure the dowels. Repeat for the other row of dowels. Glue and screw the sides to the crosspieces. Glue the dowel plugs in place and sand them flush when the glue is dry. Apply a clear finish—*V. E. Smay.*

LUMBER	CUT TO	FOR
Redwood		
2 6' 2×2's	4 22" lengths	Sides
	3 21" lengths	Crosspieces
DOWELS		
8 4' ½" dia.	32 10½" lengths	Supports
HARDWARE AND MISCELLANEOUS		
6 2¼" #10 flat-head wood screws		
Wood glue		

wine rack

This redwood rack survives damp storage. The design calls for two sturdy 2×8s, half-lapped to the base of the uprights and reinforced with glued-in dowels for extra strength. But if the joists in your basement ceiling are exposed, just make the rack's sides tall enough to tie into them for greater stability—*Paul Bolon.*

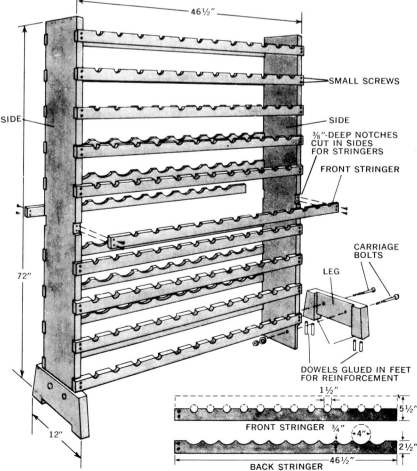

Front stringers of rack are fashioned by boring holes in 1×6s, then rip-sawing the boards in half. Scallops for the back stringers must be cut individually.

home computer center

If you're like me, you probably have a space set aside somewhere that you call your home office. And if your home office is anything like mine was until recently, it may be a table containing heaps of papers, stapling machines, calculators, miscellaneous supplies, tools, and work in progress.

I've been meaning to build in a really efficient home office for years. And when I brought my new computer home recently, I decided the time had come. I wanted something handsome and useful. A place that would be pleasant to work in. A place in which everything I need—from the computer keyboard to a postage stamp—would be instantly available and convenient. It was a simple project; a few weekends of work and it was completed. You can see the result on the opposite page.

The main features are evident. The computer console sits on a typing wing where it is easy to operate. Most standard typing tables are 26 or 27 inches tall. That's slightly higher than I like, so I built this computer surface 25 inches from the floor. The main desk surface is at 28 inches—again 1 to 2 inches below standard. Adjust these figures to whatever you find most comfortable.

Just to the left of the computer console is the printer. My Epsom MX-80 sits on top of a box open at front and back. A 3-inch-thick supply of paper sits on the shelf below the printer. The box is mounted on standard nylon-roller drawer hardware, so the printer pulls out easily when needed, and disappears beneath the desk at other times.

The disc-drive mounting is straightforward. Disc drives are usually allowed to take up valuable desktop space. But mounted under the table the unit is even more convenient.

Construction is simple throughout. The horizontal desk-top surfaces are butt-joined to the vertical supports at the ends. I didn't want to drive screws through the visible surfaces, so I installed a 1×1 where the two panels came together and used 1¼-inch flathead screws and glue to make the joint secure. A 1×1 also serves as the shelf support at the right end of the typing wing. A ¾-inch plywood desk top always looks skimpy to me,

so I used screws and glue to attach a 1×3 to the underside of the front of each of the two desktop elements. Then I veneered the front edges, with 1-inch veneer on the vertical elements and 2-inch on horizontal exposed edges. It doesn't show in the drawings, but I used ¼-inch plywood gussets at the rear to stabilize the vertical members. The entire structure goes together easily and quickly with glue and screws.

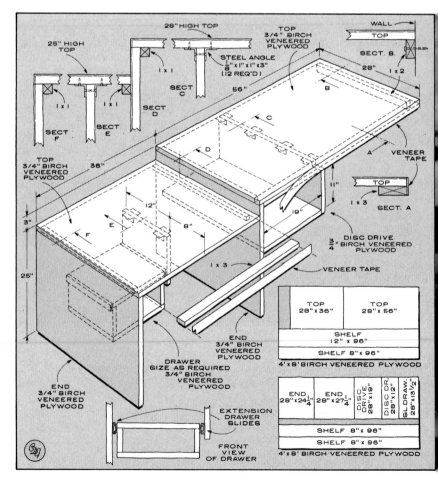

Several problems remain unsolved. The principal one is disc storage. I was unprepared for the fact that I would generate a lot of discs as I put my computer to work as a word processor, bookkeeper, and list retriever. But the discs are piling up. I now keep them in boxes on the shelf just above the computer. But this means that I am always shuffling through boxes of discs. I hope to build a filing system of some sort, although I don't have the design worked out as yet. I suspect that it may be built of Plexiglas, a versatile material that comes in many nice colors. And I think I'll design it to hang under the shelf behind or just to the left of the computer. It should let the discs slide out easily, and it should have some kind of tab identification system so that the de-

sired disc can be located quickly and easily.

My other storage problems have been solved in a conventional manner. While I was building the desk/computer stand, I also put four shelves on the wall above and behind it. The bottom one is 12 inches wide, convenient for holding the stationery cabinet you see in the picture, large books, and other outsized items. The three top shelves are 8 inches wide, suitable for all but the largest books. All shelves are mounted on conventional brackets and standards. Since I expected a heavy load of books, I mounted the standards on 20-inch centers and used heavy-duty brackets. The two plastic six-drawer units you see on the desk surface to the right of the computer hold bills that

need paying, stamps, address labels, letter openers, and a wide variety of other supplies.

I chose birch veneer with a tung-oil finish for the project because I like the color; the entire structure has a light, airy feeling. You can pick any material and finish, of course. Other furniture-grade plywood veneers would be handsome, as would a unit made of MDO plywood and painted.

My computer wing is 36 inches long, fine for most home computers. If your printer is larger, you may want to make this surface longer to leave room for the printer and your legs underneath. My main desk top is 56 inches—again a convenient length. Adjust dimensions to your equipment and to the wall you want to fit—*C. P. Gilmore.*

home finance center

The design of this home finance center is based on the dimensions of a legal-size envelope (4¼ by 9½ inches). These envelopes containing receipts, statements, canceled checks, etc., can be filed in the top compartments. Movable dividers are provided for flexible organization. At the end of each year, all of the envelopes can be banded together and placed in the long-term storage compartment in the bottom of the cabinet. The shelves are movable to suit your storage needs.

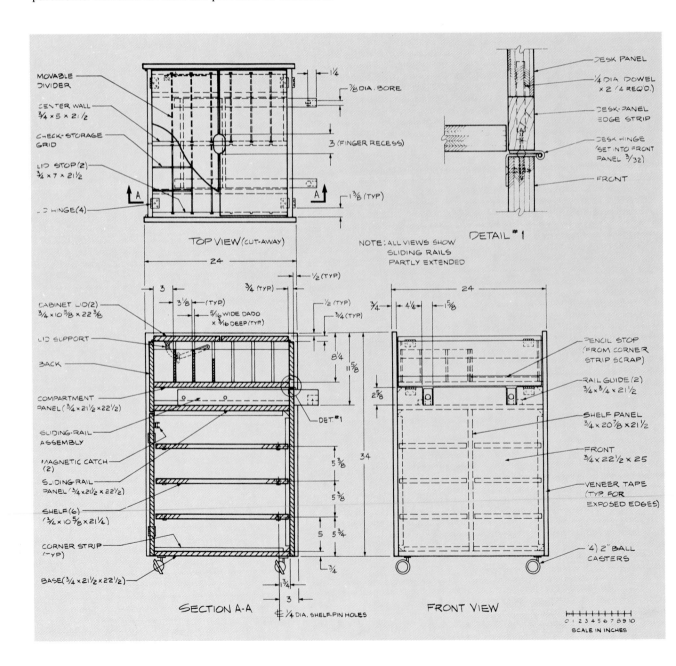

Reprinted by permission of Rodale's
PRACTICAL   HOMEOWNER
magazine.

MATERIALS AND SPECIFICATIONS

Item	Quantity	Description
Sides	2	¾″ × 24″ × 34″ birch plywood
Front	1	¾″ × 22½″ × 25″ birch plywood
Back	1	¾″ × 11⅛″ × 22½″ birch plywood
Compartment panel	1	¾″ × 21½″ × 22½″ birch plywood
Lid stops	2	¾″ × 7″ × 21½″ birch plywood
Center wall	1	¾″ × 5″ × 21½″ birch plywood
Cabinet lids	2	¾″ × 10⅝″ × 22⅜″ birch plywood
Desk panel	1	¾″ × 6¼″ × 22⅜″ birch plywood
Storage doors	2	¾″ × 11⅛″ × 21½″ birch plywood
Base	1	¾″ × 21½″ × 22½″ A-C plywood
Sliding-rail panel	1	¾″ × 21½″ × 22½″ A-C plywood
Shelf panel	1	¾″ × 20⅞″ × 21½″ A-C plywood
Shelves	6	¾″ × 10⅝″ × 21¼″ A-C plywood
Rail guides	2	¾″ × ¾″ × 21½″ pine
Corner stripping	—	⅝″ × ⅝″ × 45° chamfer strip (200 linear inches)
Sliding rails	2	1½″ × 2½″ × 22¼″ pine
Cross ties	2	½″ dia. × 13¾″ wood dowel
Desk-panel edge strip	1	¾″ × 1½″ × 22⅜″ pine
Edge-strip dowels	4	¼″ dia. × 2″ wood dowel
Movable dividers	7	¼″ × 3½″ × 10⁷⁄₁₆″ hardboard

CHECK-STORAGE GRID

Long walls	2	¼″ × 5″ × 10⁷⁄₁₆″ hardboard
Short walls	2	¼″ × 5″ × 6⅜″ hardboard
Lid hinges	4	1½″ × 2″ (open) brass hinges
Desk hinges (storage-door hinges)	6	1½″ wide offset cabinet hinge for ¾″ thick doors (brass plated)
Lid support	1	Right-hand brass-plated lid support
Door catches	2	Standard magnetic cabinet-door catches
Casters	4	2″ plate mounting brass-colored ball casters
Shelf supports	24	Plastic shelf pins
Veneer tape	—	¾″ wide birch veneer tape
Glue	—	Wood glue
Nails	—	3d finishing nails
	4	6d finishing nails
	—	1″ wire brads
Paint	—	Latex paint
Filler	—	Latex wood filler

Construction

1. Cut the sides to size.

2. On the sides, lay out the locations of the compartment panel, the base, the sliding-rail panel, the front and back, and the shelf-pin holes.

3. Drill ¼-inch-diameter holes ½ inch deep for the shelf pins.

4. Cut the front to size. Lay out and cut two 2⅝-inch-deep-by-1⅝-inch-wide notches in the top edge of the front to allow a passageway for the sliding rails.

5. Install two desk hinges on the top edge of the front, setting the hinges ³⁄₃₂ inch into the top edge.

12. Glue and nail the center wall to the compartment panel.

13. Cut the shelf panel to size.

14. Drill shelf-pin holes in the shelf panel.

15. Glue and nail the shelf panel between the sliding-rail panel and the base.

16. Cut the corner stripping (used to strengthen butt joints between panels) to size.

17. Glue and nail the compartment panel, the sliding-rail panel, the base, and the front to one of the sides. Do not attach the back. (You may find it easiest to attach corner stripping to the sides at this time, before assembly.)

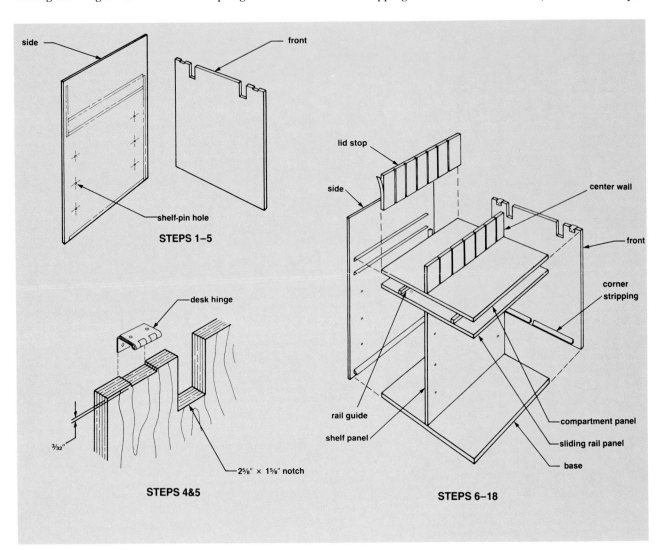

6. Cut the back, the base, the sliding-rail panel, and the rail guides to size.

7. Attach the rail guides to the "C" side of the sliding-rail panel with glue and nails.

8. Cut the compartment panel, the lid stops, and the center wall of the top compartment to size.

9. Using an electric iron, apply veneer tape to the top and front edges of the center wall and the lid stops.

10. Machine six dadoes, ³⁄₁₆ inch deep and ⁵⁄₁₆ inch wide, on the inside face of each lid stop.

11. Machine six dadoes on both faces of the center wall. Make sure that the spacing of the dadoes from back to front is identical to that of the lid stops.

18. Glue and nail the other side in place. Glue and nail the lid stops in place.

19. Cut the sliding rails to size.

20. Drill two ½-inch-diameter holes through each sliding rail.

21. Cut the cross ties for the sliding rails to size.

22. Drill a ⅞-inch-diameter fingerhole 1¾ inches deep into the end of each sliding rail.

23. Drill a ⅞-inch-diameter hole into the bottom of each sliding rail intersecting the hole from Step 22.

24. Glue and nail the sliding rails onto the cross ties.

25. Insert the sliding-rail assembly between the compartment panel and the sliding-rail panel.

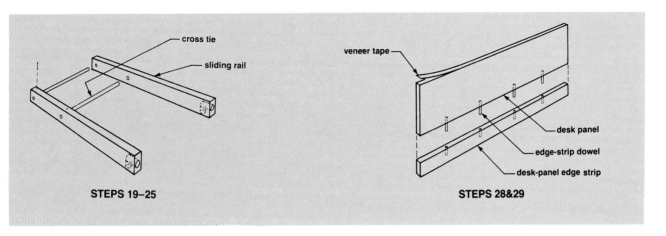

STEPS 19–25

STEPS 28&29

26. Cut the cabinet lids to size.

27. Cut a finger recess into one edge of each lid.

28. Cut the desk panel and the desk-panel edge strip to size.

29. Attach the edge strip to the desk panel by drilling four ¼-inch-diameter holes into each and attaching with the edge-strip dowels.

30. Apply veneer tape to cover all end grain of lids and desk panel and the top edge of the back panel.

31. Hinge together the back panel and one of the lid panels. Set the hinges in ³⁄₃₂ inch, or until the crack between the panels is minimal.

32. Hinge together the desk panel with the second lid, setting the hinges as in Step 31. (All lid hinges will be removed for painting.)

33. Glue and nail the back panel in place.

34. Apply veneer tape to the exposed edges of the sides.

35. Cut the shelves to size. Trim one corner of each shelf as needed to clear the corner strips adjoining the front and side panels.

36. Cut the storage doors to size. Drill a ⅞-inch-diameter fingerhole in each door.

37. Cut the pencil stop to size. Glue and nail the pencil stop in the top compartment.

38. Cut the movable dividers of the top compartment and the long and short walls of the check-storage grid to size.

39. Cut two ¼-inch-wide-by-2½-inch-long notches across each long wall of the check-storage grid. Cut notches, also ¼ inch wide and 2½ inches long at the center and at one end of the short walls of the grid.

40. Assemble the check-storage grid by gluing the long and short walls at the notches to form cross-lap joints.

41. Apply wood filler where needed, and sand all surfaces until smooth. Paint all parts the color of your choice.

42. Reinstall all lid hinges. Hinge the storage doors to the sides. Install a magnetic catch for each storage door and a lid support.

43. Install the shelf pins and shelves.

44. Install the casters on the base.

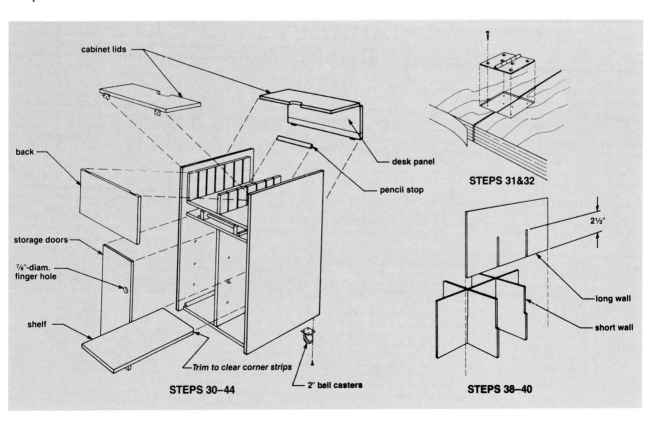

STEPS 30–44

STEPS 31&32

STEPS 38–40

built-ins for a window bay

Hidden beneath the cracked plaster, rotted moldings, and layer upon layer of paint in the old San Francisco townhouse were some charming features. In Marshall Roath's all-redwood renovation, the three-foot-deep window bay became the living room's visual centerpiece with the addition of a built-in bench and adjacent cabinet. And they provide what almost every living room, new or old, lacks: concealed storage space.

While the entire room is surfaced in redwood, a wide range of grades, textures, and board sizes are used for variety. The windows themselves are framed with smooth redwood 1 × 4s to contrast with the rough-textured resawed paneling that covers the walls and front faces of the cabinets. Simi-

larly, top-quality clear-all-heart boards are varied with sapwood-streaked clear-grade for greater interest. (For complete information on the types and uses of redwood, write to the California Redwood Assn., 591 Redwood Hwy., Mill Valley, Calif. 94941, for a literature list.)

The seat and cabinet are framed with lumber as shown, then faced with tongue-and-groove paneling applied directly over the framing in some places and glued to plywood sheathing in others. Both storage units have a hinged center panel for access (a lid or a door) featuring unobtrusive hardware. Three long 2×12 shelves over the cabinet give space for display—*By Daniel Ruby.*

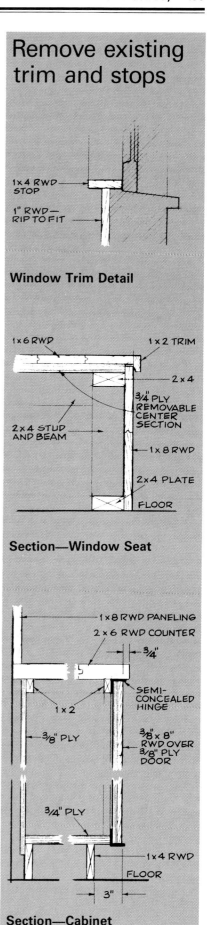

Remove existing trim and stops

Window Trim Detail

1×4 RWD STOP

1" RWD RIP TO FIT

1×6 RWD

1×2 TRIM

2×4

3/4" PLY REMOVABLE CENTER SECTION

2×4 STUD AND BEAM

1×8 RWD

2×4 PLATE

FLOOR

Section—Window Seat

1×8 RWD PANELING

2×6 RWD COUNTER

3/4"

1×2

SEMI-CONCEALED HINGE

3/8" PLY

3/8"×8" RWD OVER 3/8" PLY DOOR

3/4" PLY

1×4 RWD

FLOOR

3"

Section—Cabinet

Run-down interior offered several niches for built-in storage—notably a window bay.

Window seat's lid lifts to give access to 15 cu. ft. of easy-to-reach storage. T&G planks are used for all cabinet surfaces.

Windows get the redwood treatment after existing casings are stripped. Original curved top sashes were retained.

wraparound counter for attic built-ins

A room of one's own is a prize for any teen-ager—even if the "room" is little more than a broad landing at the top of the attic stairs. But converting a pocket of attic space into the welcoming aerie shown at right required both creative design and careful selection of materials. By combining the classic simplicity of natural pine with the clean lines of multi-level built-ins, the architect created a room that looks—and is—more spacious than seems possible in such a small area.

The bed, a simple platform of ¾-inch plywood, is sized to accept the teen-ager's existing box spring and mattress. But a more conventional foam mattress could also rest on the platform.

The built-ins establish the open look of the room while providing essential work and storage space. The desk, for example, is tucked into a corner where the ceiling slants low. But the desk-top position allows the student to be far enough away from the knee wall so there's ample headroom when rising. The storage cabinet at the end of the wall unit also puts an otherwise awkward space to good use.

Extending the desk-counter around the wall not only adds extra shelf space: It also carries the eye around the room, making the space seem larger. The counter's mate, on the other side of the bed, can serve as a conventional bedside table or as a stand for whatever artifacts the teen-ager wants to display.

Even the 1 × 6 pine trim that finishes the plank headboard has several functions. Extended to sweep around the wall, the board not only repeats the room-expanding lines of the counter below but also serves as a mounting surface for pegs and lights. In this installation, the trim conceals the track-light wiring. Light fixtures could, of course, be clipped directly to the board, and it could be studded with as many peg hangers as needed.

A bookshelf suspended between the eaves expands the natural-pine motif beyond the built-ins. Both the eave window and the skylight are trimmed in polyurethane-finished pine, and the stairwell is framed in it. Even a support column has been clad in the wood. These finishing touches erase any look of attic rawness about the room.

Congoleum's Contempora sheet-vinyl flooring (in the "Royal Court" design) does more than add pattern to the room. The flexible, tear-resistant flooring cuts easily with scissors and can be fitted around obstacles with minimal difficulty. In a room such as this, where it may be impractical to construct the furniture elsewhere, the Contempora flooring can be neatly laid after the built-ins are in place—*By Susan Renner-Smith. Drawing by Eugene Thompson.*

The multilevel shelf looks like a continuous unit; however, the units are mounted separately on cleats nailed to wall studs (usually 16 in. on center). First assemble the bed platform and mount the headboard; then construct the flanking shelf and table. Next, assemble and install the cabinet and counter top. Finally, install the natural-pine headrail.

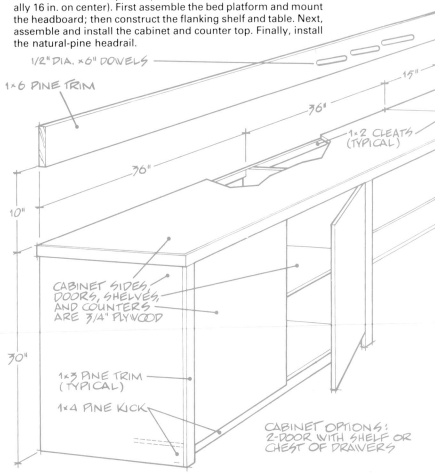

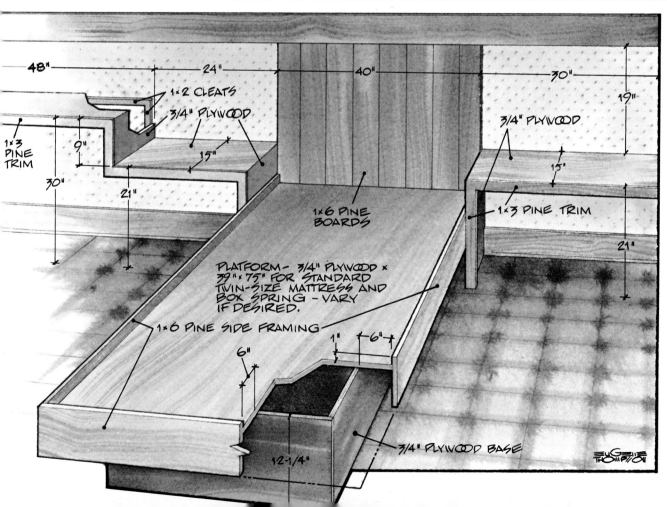

48"

24"

40"

30"

1×2 CLEATS

3/4" PLYWOOD

3/4" PLYWOOD

19"

1×3
PINE
TRIM

9"

15"

15"

30"

21"

1×3 PINE TRIM

1×6 PINE
BOARDS

21"

PLATFORM- 3/4" PLYWOOD ×
39"× 75" FOR STANDARD
TWIN-SIZE MATTRESS AND
BOX SPRING - VARY
IF DESIRED.

1×6 PINE SIDE FRAMING

1"   6"

6"

3/4" PLYWOOD BASE

12-1/4"

sewing center

Here's a convenient and efficient sewing center you can build. Even though the unit is better than most of the expensive commercial models, it was built a few years ago at far less cost.

The main section of the unit holds a fold-down table to which a portable sewing head is bolted; four storage compartments; a sixty-spool thread rack; a recessed fluorescent lighting fixture; and a triple-slot electrical outlet for the machine, light, and electric scissors. There are large top and bottom storage compartments.

The unit is constructed of ½-inch particleboard. Dimensions of the unit—81 inches high, 31 inches wide, and 19 inches deep—allowed most efficient use of available material, but you can vary them. The basic cabinet, including doors, is cut from two 4×8-foot sheets. Sections cut out as door openings are used for doors themselves; to compensate for size difference, ½-inch half-round is used on inside edges of door openings and all door edges. This allows for a strong, attractive, one-piece cabinet front.

After drawing the sections on par-

Materials

Two 4×8 sheets particleboard
Ten 10-foot lengths ½-inch half-round
Four 10-foot 1×2 pine
One 5-foot 1⅜-inch dowel
2 feet ½-inch dowel
12 feet ³⁄₁₆-inch dowel
One 30×78-inch ⅛-inch hardboard
One 7½×31-inch Peg-Board (³⁄₁₆-inch holes)
6 feet decorative molding
29-inch piece 2×4 (table mount)
5 feet particleboard shelving (8-inch)
Two pair 2-inch strap hinges
Six pair 2-inch self-closing hinges
Six door pulls
Four 1¼-inch flathead screws
18-inch fluorescent fixture
12-foot electrical cord
Three-slot receptacle
As required: eighteen ⅝-inch brads, seventeen 1-inch brads, 4d and 6d finishing nails, carpenter's glue, spackling paste, paint, and/or stain.

ticleboard sheets as shown in diagrams 1 and 2, drill ½-inch holes in diagonal corners of each door opening and use them as starter holes for your saber saw to cut out doors. Cut remaining parts as shown.

To assemble the cabinet:

1. Using 4d finishing nails and carpenter's glue, assemble so each compartment bottom is flush with lower edge of its door opening. Top piece should be flush with top edge of front and sides.
2. Cut 1×2-inch stock to length for vertical corner supports (twelve required) and fasten in place.
3. For small shelves, cut 1×2-inch stock in 6-inch lengths (six required).

Fasten three to inside of left side of cabinet, spaced to suit needs, and the others to one side of small-shelf vertical support in corresponding positions.
4. Install small-shelf vertical support flush with back edge of compartment bottoms. Glue in shelves.
5. Using a little glue, install the 7½×7½-inch shelf supports in upper and lower compartments.
6. Put 4½×29-inch base front in place.
7. Place table mount (29-inch 2×4) flat on main compartment bottom, snug against small-shelf vertical support. Nail through cabinet sides into ends with 6d finishing nails.
8. Close cabinet back using tempered

hardboard and eighteen ⅝-inch brads.
9. Cut and install ⅝-inch shelving in top and bottom compartments.
10. Install molding around top. With ½-inch half-round and eighteen 1-inch brads, add decorative touch to each side (see photo).
11. Using ½-inch half-round and seventeen 1-inch brads, cover exposed particleboard edges, including inside of door openings and six doors.
12. Spackle as required and sand.

To construct the spool rack:

1. Fasten the 3×30-inch triangular supports to a 7½×31-inch piece of Peg-Board (³/₁₆-inch holes) using eighteen ⅝-inch brads.

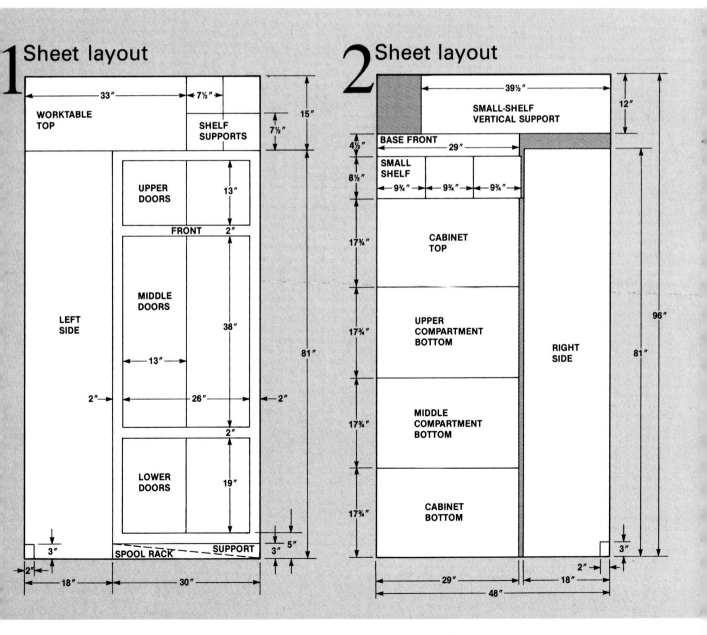

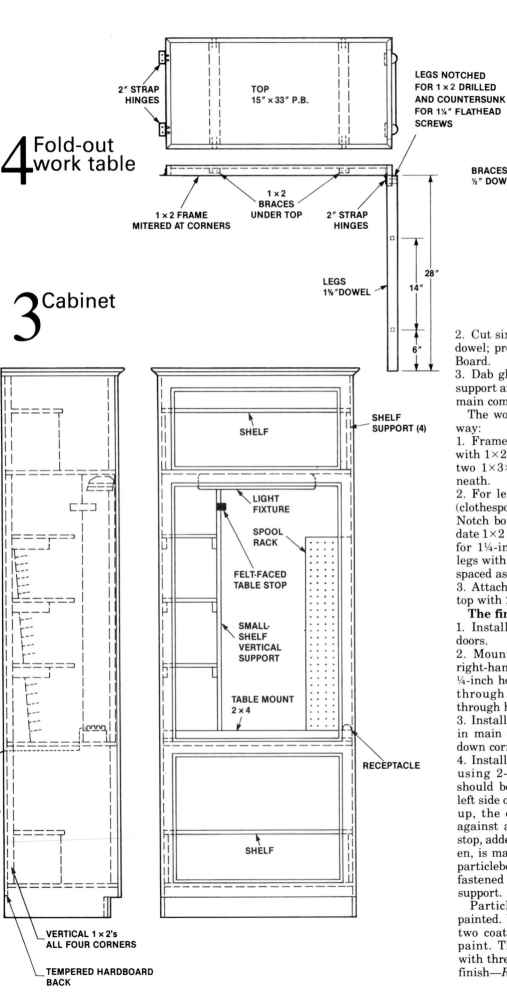

4 Fold-out work table

2" STRAP HINGES

TOP 15" × 33" P.B.

LEGS NOTCHED FOR 1 × 2 DRILLED AND COUNTERSUNK FOR 1¼" FLATHEAD SCREWS

1 × 2 FRAME MITERED AT CORNERS

1 × 2 BRACES UNDER TOP

2" STRAP HINGES

LEGS 1⅜" DOWEL

28"

14"

6"

BRACES ½" DOWEL

5½" **5½"**

7¼"

8¼"

3 Cabinet

SHELF

SHELF SUPPORT (4)

LIGHT FIXTURE

SPOOL RACK

FELT-FACED TABLE STOP

SMALL-SHELF VERTICAL SUPPORT

TABLE MOUNT 2 × 4

RECEPTACLE

SHELF

VERTICAL 1 × 2's ALL FOUR CORNERS

TEMPERED HARDBOARD BACK

2. Cut sixty 2-inch pieces of 3/16-inch dowel; press into every hole in Peg-Board.

3. Dab glue on bottom of spool-rack support and set in right rear corner of main compartment.

The work table goes together this way:

1. Frame 15×33-inch particleboard with 1×2, mitered at corners. Fasten two 1×3×15-inch braces flat underneath.

2. For legs, cut one 1⅜-inch dowel (clothespole) into two 28-inch lengths. Notch both on one end to accommodate 1×2 brace. Drill and countersink for 1¼-inch flathead screws. Brace legs with two pieces of ½-inch dowel, spaced as shown in diagram 4.

3. Attach leg assembly to worktable top with 2-inch strap hinges.

The final steps:

1. Install hardware, fit and mount doors.

2. Mount three-slot receptacle on right-hand end of table mount. Drill ¼-inch hole behind table mount and through back for cord. Run cord through holes and install plug.

3. Install 18-inch fluorescent fixture in main compartment and run cord down corner to receptacle.

4. Install work table to table mount using 2-inch strap hinges. Table should be positioned 6 inches from left side on table mount. When folded up, the outside end of table rests against a felt-faced table stop. The stop, added after photograph was taken, is made from two pieces of scrap particleboard (a 1×2 glued to a 2×4) fastened to the small-shelf vertical support.

Particleboard can be stained or painted. We used a good primer and two coats of semigloss white latex paint. The worktable was stained with three coats of an oil-based resin finish—*Robert Chase.*

yarn box

Here's an attractive, useful gift you can make—at almost no cost. The base and center frame of the box are made of wood salvaged from wine crates; the trays, from fruit boxes. The hinges are made of ¼-inch shock cord. Other supplies needed are: elastic strips (used across the trays to keep yarn from falling out), scrap wood for thumb grips and handle, white glue, Duco cement, ½-inch brads, plastic wood, and a finish of your choice.

If you live in a city you can probably obtain boxes discarded by wine merchants, supermarkets, or grocers. Ask your local merchant to save them for you. Select crates ³/₁₆ to ⅜ inch thick; under ⅛ inch will not be strong enough.

The wood should be stored in a dry place for two or three months before use, since it will probably be green. After the crates are broken apart, the seasoned wood should be planed to a uniform thickness. Measure and cut your pieces; dado the edges for gluing. Sand all inside surfaces before assembly.

Use white glue for assembly and wipe carefully if a natural finish is to be applied. Use thin, ½-inch brads; set and fill holes with plastic wood to match the finish you plan to use. (I chose a dull gloss varnish and used two coats, sanding lightly between. When second coat was dry, I rubbed with 0000 steel wool and polished with terry cloth.)

The toggle action of the shock cord hinges locks the two trays open or closed. Allow about 12 inches of shock cord (available at camping equipment stores) for each hinge. Ends can be single knotted, trimmed, and coated with Duco cement to prevent raveling. But *don't trim knots until you're sure the tension is correct.* If it's too tight, the trays will bind; if too loose, they will sag open.

Hand carve the handle from pine, or use a commercial handle for easy carrying—*Earl Chapin.*

Box dimensions can be varied to suit needs. Best way to tie hinges is with trays out of frame, placed flat with bottom sides together. Experiment to get right tension; it should require a rather firm pull to separate trays enough to slip over and down frame to position. Elastic strips are held in place by two ½-inch brads (see drawing). Don't stretch elastic tight and predrill ¼-inch pilot holes for brads.

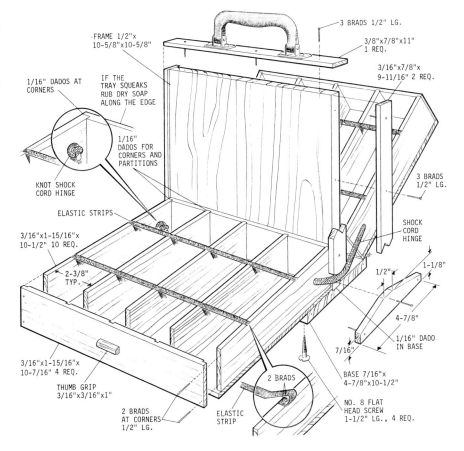

easy-to-build home design center

Design center holds matte boards and architectural-style drawings conveniently. Supplies go on shelves and in drawers.

I f you or someone in your family constantly clutters the house with large matte boards and rolls of working drawings, this home design center can help eliminate the mess. It provides ample work space along with a place to store art supplies of all sizes conveniently.

The project was designed by Clell Boyce for Louisiana-Pacific Corp. (111 S.W. Fifth Ave., Portland, Ore. 97201) to show the versatility of Waferwood, L-P's brand of waferboard.

The design center consists of three basic cubes—small, medium, and large. Its base is made of waferboard, which is braced to support the weight of the drawers and cabinetry. Included are rolled-paper holders and a board holder tucked out of the way below the counter top. For this project, the counter top is covered with plastic laminate for a smooth writing surface, but the rest of the unit is coated with clear polyurethane.

Waferboard sands to a clean edge with fine-grain sand-paper, but where an especially smooth edge is desired, apply wood-filler paste, sand lightly, and finish. For variety, you can use standard wood molding nailed and glued in place; corner-guard molding wraps around an edge and half-round molding covers it, adding a softer look.

Most of the joints in the design center are butt joints held with small nails or screws and glue. There should be no problem with these simple joints, as long as they are not overly stressed.

Cut out the pieces carefully. Glue and nail together with 4d finishing nails to form the basic boxes. When assembling the boxes, match diagonal measurements (measure from corner to corner) to be sure each box is square. Attach backs with glue and ¾-inch brads.

The rolled-paper storage rack is made of a series of mailing tubes glued together. The door below is made of waferboard with a piece of plastic laminate cemented to it—*By Charles A. Miller.*

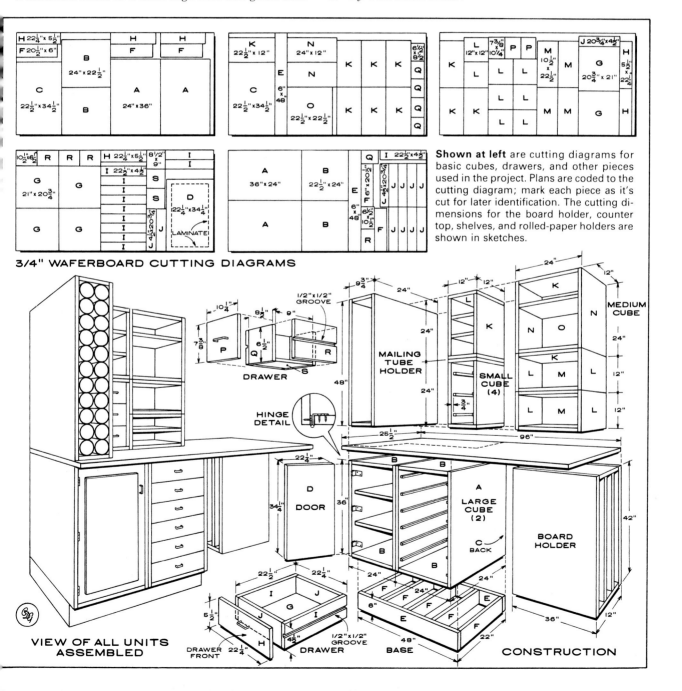

Shown at left are cutting diagrams for basic cubes, drawers, and other pieces used in the project. Plans are coded to the cutting diagram; mark each piece as it's cut for later identification. The cutting dimensions for the board holder, counter top, shelves, and rolled-paper holders are shown in sketches.

3/4" WAFERBOARD CUTTING DIAGRAMS

VIEW OF ALL UNITS ASSEMBLED

DRAWER FRONT   DRAWER   BASE   CONSTRUCTION

bed shelving

Here's a bedroom where a bed/shelf unit becomes the focal point, encompassing an entire wall and using otherwise wasted space.

The bed underframing is a rectangular box (think sandbox) made of mitre-cut, kiln-dried 2 × 10-inch lumber. The mattress foundation consists of two slabs of 1⅛-inch plywood. Two 4 × 8-foot sheets of top-grade, tongue-and-groove flooring will do for this. For a queen-size mattress, cut two 40 × 60-inch slabs; for a standard, double mattress, two 37½ × 54-inch slabs; for a king size, 40 × 77-inch slabs. Sand rough edges and slightly round corners of the slabs with medium-grit paper. Edges can be trimmed with 1⅛-inch bull nose stop, and the slabs then painted to match

the frame and should be painted if bedding will be tucked. Or you can do as I did and leave this step for a later date, since the slabs will be concealed by bedding.

The shelves that span the wall above the bed head are built of 2 × 10-inch kiln-dried lumber. Avoid green lumber—it may warp, split, and shrink as it dries, and moisture sealed into the wood by paint could cause the paint to crack and chip. The shelf unit is assembled without glue, nails, screws, or any other fasteners. Vertical uprights are held fast to the ceiling with adjustable tension devices, and horizontal shelves merely slip into dado grooves.

Start by trimming the four vertical uprights for shelving. If your bedroom has a standard 8-foot ceiling and is

carpeted, the boards will be 94 or 94½ inches, depending on floor-covering thickness; with uncarpeted floors, they'll be 95 inches.

Now lay out all four uprights and, starting at the bottom, scribe lines across them at 4, 5½, 17½, 19, 34, 35½, 47½, 49, 64, 65½, 77½, and 79 inches. You will notice that these are pairs of lines 1½ inches apart that are separated alternately, by 12 and 15 inches.

If you don't own a router and can't borrow one, you might rent one. (A word of caution: If you've never used a router, be sure to practice on scraps, and always clamp any material you rout to a solid work surface.) Use the router to make ½-inch-deep, 1½-inch-wide dado grooves between the paired lines. To assure accuracy, make a router guide from wood scraps, or

clamp a straightedge across the board in front of the router to keep the tool on a true, left-to-right track. Check each dado with a piece of 2×10 to see that shelves will fit snugly into the grooves. Use a narrow rasp and coarse sandpaper to remove just enough wood in the grooves for a proper fit.

Once all dadoes are routed, two uprights—they will be the extreme left and right vertical ones—are finished. The other two, the center uprights, will need two dado grooves to accommodate the center shelves. Lay these uprights out, grooved sides down, and scribe lines across at 57, 58½, 72½, and 74 inches from the bottom. Rout grooves between the paired lines as before.

Use a drill guide and ½-inch bit to make a starter hole 2 inches inside the front and rear edges of each vertical upright. Then use a wood bit to drill holes to size for the tension devices. Push female portions of the devices into holes and gently tap them in with a hammer.

Shelves are cut shorter for the sides of the unit, longer for the center. Two variables determine the cutting measurements: length of the wall the unit will span and bed width. There should be 4-inch clearance on each side of the bed from the center vertical uprights. For a queen-size bed, center shelves should be about 69 inches long; for a double bed, about 63 inches, and for a king, 86 inches. But wait to cut these shelves; lengths might vary by a fraction of an inch and they must be cut precisely to fit.

First, cut the twelve side shelves. Our bed, a queen size, called for 30-inch side shelves. Had it been a

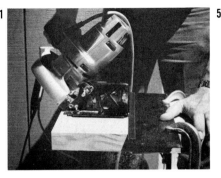

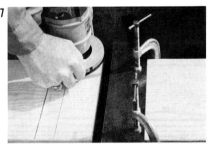

Start (1) by miter-cutting two 2×10 bed-frame panels to 60 inches, two to 40 inches (queen-size). Apply glue to ends, join to form box. **(2)** Using miter clamp to hold frame joint, secure with four 8d finishing nails—two from each direction. With #120 paper, sand edges. **(3)** From scrap 2×4, make four 4-inch stop-blocks. Drill and countersink two ¼-inch holes in each. **(4)** Center frame on plywood slabs, set face down. **(5)** With glue and 2-inch #12 flathead wood screws, attach stop-blocks to slab undersides at each inside corner of frame. Start wall unit by **(6)** clamping 2×10 vertical upright to solid surface and **(7)** carefully measuring, marking, and routing grooves for shelves. **(8)** Use drill guide and ¼-inch bit for starter hole at top of each upright.

What you need

Materials: Two 4×8-foot sheets of 1⅛-inch plywood; thirteen 8-foot kiln-dried 2×10s; 4 feet of 1⁵⁄₁₆-inch corner molding; scrap of 2×4 (at least 16 inches long); sixteen 8d finishing nails; eight 2-inch #12 flathead wood screws; small container of 1-inch brads; wood filler; small bottle of white glue; several sheets coarse-grit (#60), medium-grit (#120), and fine-grit (#220) sandpaper; eight tension devices; ½-inch thick household sponge; 4 feet of 1×2 (optional); 1 gallon flat or semigloss latex paint.

Tools: Circular saw; electric drill; router; combination or carpenter's square; steel tape measure; pencil; hammer; center punch; mitre clamp; pair of C-clamps; screwdriver; narrow groove rasp; drill guide; sanding block (optional); backsaw and mitre box (optional); adjustable wrench; paintbrush.

standard double, shelves would have been 33 inches to compensate for a 6-inch narrower bed; had the wall been 14 instead of 11 feet, with a queen-size bed, the side shelves would have measured 48 inches—you get the idea. Once the side shelves are cut, sand

them and the uprights lightly, wipe them clean, and paint to suit the room decor.

Start shelf assembly by standing the extreme left and right uprights in position at the corners of the room. Protect the ceiling from marks by placing

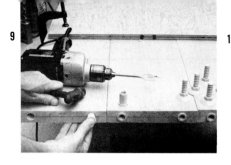

Alternate Shelf Construction Methods

Design of this bedroom shelf unit can be modified to fit needs. The distance between shelves can be altered, and the assembly method can be changed entirely.

If the idea of dadoed grooves doesn't appeal to you, you might wish to butt the shelves to the uprights and attach them with wood screws. For this method use 3½-inch #12 wood screws in each end of the side shelves. The center shelves should have the added support of a shelf bracket attached to the wall on the underside of the lower shelf.

A simpler modification calls for using cabinet-type metal shelf supports. These are small, L-shaped fixtures that fit into holes drilled into the vertical uprights. If you want adjustable shelves, drill two lines of holes, spaced 3 to 6 inches, in each vertical upright. Then insert the metal shelf supports. Or, instead of cabinet-type shelf supports, you can make your own out of ½-inch dowel rod. If you decide against the dadoed shelf joints, remember to cut your shelves an inch shorter than those in my original design.

Perhaps you want a more permanent unit. Then you can forget the tension devices. Instead, affix the extreme left and right verticals to the walls with screws. Center uprights can then be attached to the top and bottom side shelves with wood screws. The center shelves and remaining side shelves can be slipped in place as in the original design. Now you have a semipermanent unit that, with only slight effort, can be dismantled for moving, redecorating, painting.

To continue work on wall section: **(9)** Use wood bit to drill holes for tension devices. Insert female section into holes and tap in gently. **(10)** Cut twelve side shelves from 2×10 stock. (Note the homemade saw and router guide used to assure accuracy.) **(11)** Begin assembly by standing vertical uprights against wall and securing to ceiling with tension devices. **(12)** Measure for two center shelves; then cut, sand, and paint them. Slide the shelves into place. **(13)** The space under the plywood slabs, inside the bed frame, provides storage space for bedding and other items. **(14)** The fluorescent lights under the center wall cabinet make good reading lamps and are simple to install.

circles cut from a new household sponge between it and the tension devices. Tighten the devices with a wrench.

Stand the center uprights in place so the end uprights brace the side shelves. Slide the shelves into the dado grooves, adjusting the center uprights as required. When all shelves are in place, make final adjustments and tighten the tension devices on the center uprights.

Now is the time to measure for those center shelves mentioned earlier. Stretch a steel tape measure from the inside of one dado groove to the other, and double check the distance. Cut two shelves to length, paint them, and slide them into their grooves to finish the wall unit.

Customizing

There are several ways to modify the shelf unit to fit your own needs and tastes. For example, although the center shelves need no additional

support, a small vertical upright can be cut to 15 inches and inserted into dado grooves that have been routed into the center of these shelves, dividing them into separate shelves. I added two such vertical uprights and created 11½-inch-wide cubbyholes on each end of the center shelves, where we keep our nightcaps—not the cranial variety, but a decanter of brandy and two snifters on one side, a decanter of sherry and glasses on the other.

Another improvement I made later was the addition of four 9½-inch pieces of 1×2 that I inserted between the tension devices and the ceiling. This simple modification helped give the unit a permanent, built-in appearance.

Lighting fixtures can be attached to the wall above the bed, to the sides of the center uprights, or to the bottom of the lower center shelf. We decided on the latter and used inexpensive, fluorescent under-cabinet lights that are easy to install.

The design of this unit is flexible enough to accommodate just about any size bedroom. Its mobility is particularly suited to the renter who will want to take it with him when he moves or to the family that might wish to put a child's bedroom to some other use when the youngster grows up and moves out.

The shelf unit goes well in any room where shelves are needed. A desk work table, sewing machine, or love seat would fit nicely between the center uprights. So if the shelves outlive their usefulness in the bedroom, you can move them to another room—*Kenn Oberrecht.*

bed under floor

Remove a bed and the "found" space in a room amounts to what you see in this boy's room. A trundle bed is an old space-making trick useful for storing a guest bed anywhere. And this bi-level arrangement, covered with Congoleum sheet vinyl, is a good way to make use of the space over it. Base molding is removed for platform construction, replaced around top.

Materials: 2 × 4 plates—one 10 feet long, two 2 feet long; 2 × 10 beams—four 6 feet long; 2 × 4 joists—seven 10 feet long; 2 × 4 bed framing—two 75 inches long, two 42 inches long, two 39 inches long; ½-inch plywood flooring (sub) and ½-inch plywood bed board—three 4 × 8-foot sheets; ¾-inch plywood—16 inches × 10 feet; blocking (bed) 2 × 6—1 foot long; ¼ × 1½-inch molding—10 feet long; heavy-duty casters—four 2- or 2½-inch; finish flooring of your preference, with the appropriate cement for application; three drawer pulls in any style you choose; a good supply of nails.

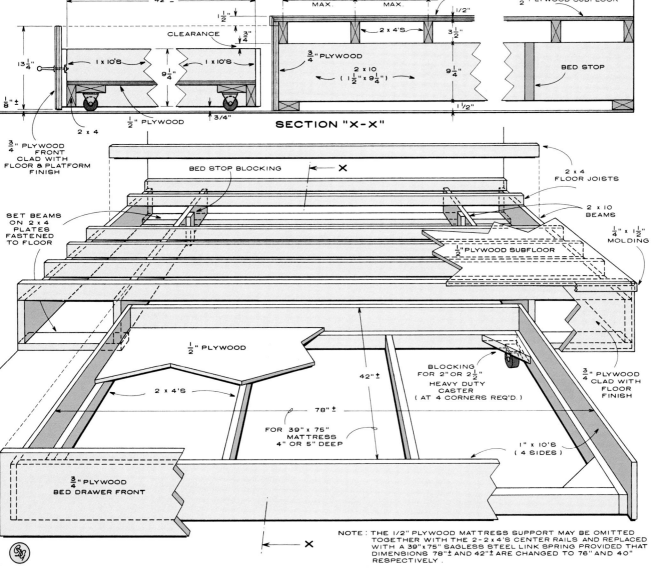

SECTION "X–X"

¾" PLYWOOD FRONT CLAD WITH FLOOR & PLATFORM FINISH

42"±

CLEARANCE

1½"

¾"

13¼"

1 x 10'S

1 x 10'S

9¼"

⅛"±

2 x 4

½" PLYWOOD

¾"

12" MAX.

12" MAX.

FINISHED FLOOR

½"

2 x 4'S

3½"

¾" PLYWOOD

2 x 10 (1½" x 9¼")

9¼"

1½"

½" PLYWOOD SUBFLOOR

BED STOP

BED STOP BLOCKING

X

2 x 4 FLOOR JOISTS

SET BEAMS ON 2 x 4 PLATES FASTENED TO FLOOR

2 x 10 BEAMS

½" PLYWOOD SUBFLOOR

¼" x 1½" MOLDING

½" PLYWOOD

2 x 4'S

42"±

BLOCKING FOR 2" OR 2½" HEAVY DUTY CASTER (AT 4 CORNERS REQ'D.)

¾" PLYWOOD CLAD WITH FLOOR FINISH

78"±

FOR 39" x 75" MATTRESS 4" OR 5" DEEP

1" x 10'S (4 SIDES)

¾" PLYWOOD BED DRAWER FRONT

X

NOTE : THE 1/2" PLYWOOD MATTRESS SUPPORT MAY BE OMITTED TOGETHER WITH THE 2-2 x 4'S CENTER RAILS AND REPLACED WITH A 39"x 75" SAGLESS STEEL LINK SPRING PROVIDED THAT DIMENSIONS 78"± AND 42"± ARE CHANGED TO 76" AND 40" RESPECTIVELY .

child's desk

Everyone needs a special place to get away from it all—children, too. With just a little shopwork and imagination, you can create a child's hideaway in the most cramped of homes. The cabinet, desk, and bulletin board I built for my daughter Carrie are designed around the theme of trees and flowers. They give her a quiet, cheerful place to play, study, and store her treasures.

I began with a basic plywood box for the cabinet (most dimensions are unspecified so you can adapt the design). The top, bottom, and sides meet in tongue-and-dado joints; the thinner back fits into grooves in each piece. The box is raised a few inches off the floor on a black-painted square base.

The front face and door of the cabinet were made using some richly textured butternut wood that I had available. First I made and permanently attached a mitered frame to match the outside front dimension of the box. The door itself is a multilayered assembly: Its frame of butternut strips is mortise-and-tenoned to stand up to the strain it will get in use. The inside back of the frame is rabbeted (before assembly) to receive the door panel. I made the panel from tongue-and-groove stock glued up at a 45-degree angle and cut off square. The front edges of the panel were rabbeted back 3/16 inch more than the frame rabbet to allow for expansion. For the same reason, I didn't glue the panel in but secured it with battens. Assembled, the slightly recessed panel makes an ideal setting for an applied design.

Next came the work surface: particleboard cut to fit the corner, covered with vibrant-green Wilson Art laminate, and finished with a molding strip on the visible edge. It is supported at a height of 28 inches by wood strips screwed to the cabinet top and walls. An inch of space between the cabinet and work surface allows for storage of artwork. For more storage I hung particleboard shelves.

No child's room is complete without a bulletin board. I covered the entire wall over the desk with 1/4-inch cork mounted with countersunk nails and trimmed around the edges with butternut strips. The flower is made from the same cork. I cut about 100 identical petals and arranged them in five rings on the floor. Then I painted them, using solid yellow for the inside ring and adding more and more blue as I moved outward. To mount the blossom, I ran concentric circular beads of adhesive and positioned each petal with a finishing nail—*Paul Levine. Drawing by Carl De Groote.*

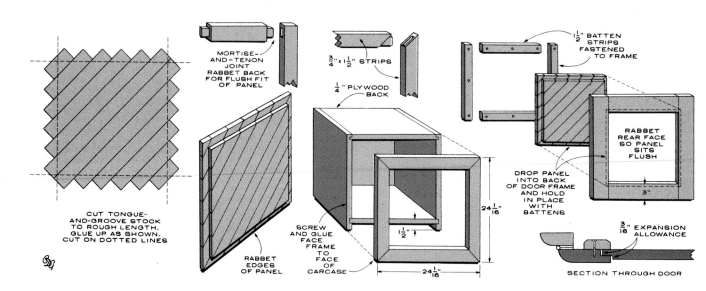

CUT TONGUE-AND-GROOVE STOCK TO ROUGH LENGTH. GLUE UP AS SHOWN. CUT ON DOTTED LINES

MORTISE-AND-TENON JOINT RABBET BACK FOR FLUSH FIT OF PANEL

RABBET EDGES OF PANEL

3/4" x 1 1/2" STRIPS

1/4" PLYWOOD BACK

SCREW AND GLUE FACE FRAME TO FACE OF CARCASE

1 1/2"

24 1/16"

24 1/16"

1 1/2" BATTEN STRIPS FASTENED TO FRAME

RABBET REAR FACE SO PANEL SITS FLUSH

DROP PANEL INTO BACK OF DOOR FRAME AND HOLD IN PLACE WITH BATTENS

3"

3/16" EXPANSION ALLOWANCE

SECTION THROUGH DOOR

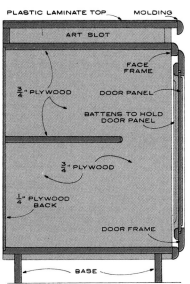

PLASTIC LAMINATE TOP — MOLDING

ART SLOT

FACE FRAME

$\frac{3}{4}$" PLYWOOD

DOOR PANEL

BATTENS TO HOLD DOOR PANEL

$\frac{3}{4}$" PLYWOOD

$\frac{1}{4}$" PLYWOOD BACK

DOOR FRAME

BASE

Carrie's inner sanctum combines practical storage with appealing design. Warm butternut, plus such decorative features as the free-form tree and cork flower, disguise this project's humble origins—a plywood box and particleboard shelves.

three classic toys
colonial dollhouse

The Stanley Colonial Dollhouse is based on an actual house built in the "1776" period in New England. This house is still in use today and is an excellent example of a most attractive, sturdy, functional and lasting form of domestic architecture.

Families were big, so there were many bedrooms. People didn't have many clothes, so there were no bedroom closets. And of course, there were no bathrooms since indoor plumbing did not come into general use until late in the nineteenth century.

There were fireplaces in almost every room since there was no such thing as central heating. All cooking was done over the open fire in the kitchen-keeping room. It became the most important room in the house, the place where the entire family would gather for meals, warmth, and companionship.

On the third floor or attic there was often a smoke oven for smoking hams, sides of bacon, and game. Hickory bark or corncobs were burned in the oven to provide the smoke.

We have adapted the room arrangements of the original house so the plan functions well as a dollhouse. We have also changed certain materials so the dollhouse can be built with supplies that are readily available. For example, door hinges in Colonial houses were generally wrought iron strap, H, or H-L hinges made by a local blacksmith. But because miniature versions of these are not commonly available, we have used butt hinges instead.

These plans provide detailed instructions for making an authentic replica, like the realistic model in the photograph. You can also make a simpler version. Just build the basic structure out of plywood, paint it, and add shadows to give the appearance of real shingles and siding. For an easy window substitute, use clear plastic with painted white divider strips stapled to the inside of the window opening.

General Construction:

Exploded view shows method of construction. First, build base and then add the two end panels. Next, install the first floor partition, then add the second floor along with its partitions and stairs from first to second floor. Install third floor and partitions and stairs. Add front and rear panels. Add fixed section of roof, then movable sections of roof and, finally, the chim-

MATERIALS FOR BASIC HOUSE:

3 sheets—4′ × 8′ × ³⁄₈″ plywood—two sides good
18′—1 × 2 for base and blocking
7′—1 × 1 for corner posts, front and back steps
6 flathead screws—1¼″ No. 10 for end panels
1 box No. 18 brads 1″ long
1 box No. 18 brads ¾″ long
1 box No. 18 brads ½″ long—for trim
Carpenter's white wood glue
Hinges*: 6—¾″ × ⁵⁄₈″ for roof
　　　　4—¾″ × ⁵⁄₈″ for front and back door
　　　　8—1½″ × ⁷⁄₈″ for front and rear panels

Note: Balsa and basswood required if you install trim, paneling, stairs, windows, etc., are available at hobby shops.
*Stanley Classic Brassware solid brass hinges.

Please note that the overall dimensions of the Colonial Dollhouse are 38″ long, 30″ wide and 30″ high. If you plan to move the dollhouse from the area in which it is built, measure doorways, etc., to make sure the dollhouse can be moved through easily.

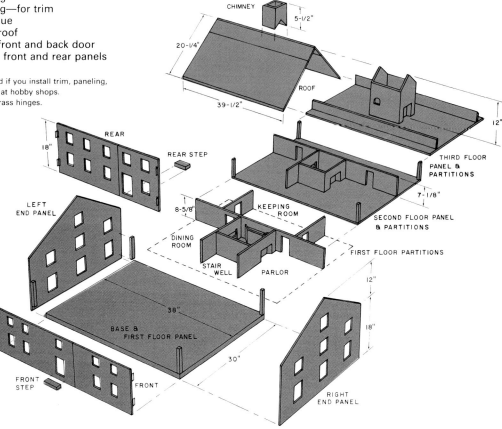

ney. Siding and roofing go on last.

To insure a perfect match of identical elements—base panels, floor panels, end panels, front and rear panels and movable section of roof—clamp the pieces together and cut both at the same time. If you are going to install the wood windows, openings for them must be cut very accurately to insure a perfect fit.

Because of restricted access, complete each floor—painting, staining, paneling, trim, wallpaper, etc., before proceeding with next floor. Apply wallpaper before installing interior trim, chair rails, and corner posts. Paint all interior and exterior trim and elements for windows before cutting to size. Use glue and ½-inch brads to apply all trim.

Detailed dimensions on drawings show measurements to fractional parts of an inch, but variations are bound to occur as the work progresses, so measure for each element and make necessary adjustments as needed—*Courtesy of The Stanley Works.*

Build base

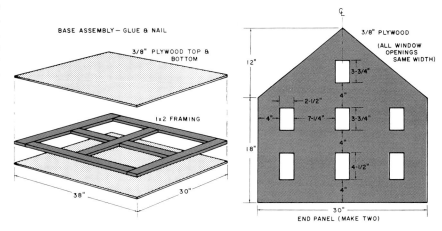

1. Use glue and one-in. brads to assemble 1 × 2 frame and plywood panels. Stain or paint top of upper panel that serves as first floor. Make up the two end panels, and cut openings for windows with brace and bit and keyhole saw. Note the first-floor windows are taller than those on second and third floors. Secure panels to base with glue and three 1¼-in. screws per panel.

Install first floor partitions

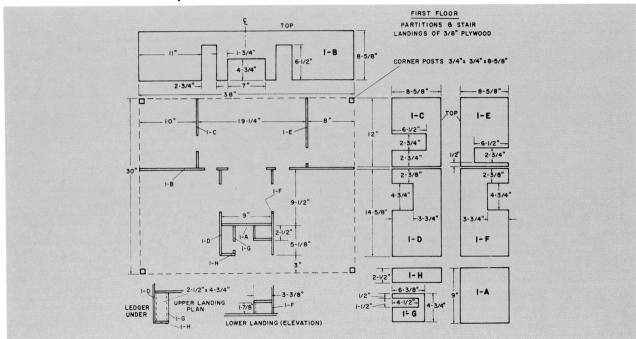

2. Start with center partition B. Temporarily tack this into place and then C and E. Add panel A—the chimney enclosure. Add partitions D, F, H, and G. Note height of G is only 6⅜ in. The upper landing of stairs will rest on top of G. You can indicate the understairs closet door on G with trim rather than installing a hinged door.

Remove partitions and install paneling if desired. Details of paneling are given in Fig. 11.

Before final installation of partitions, apply wallpaper, if desired, to exterior walls in dining room and parlor. Seal the plywood first with latex paint. Coat back of paper with wallpaper paste or dilute white glue and allow to remain until paper is damp before applying paper. Install trim around windows, corner posts and chair rails (Fig. 12). On all non-paneled walls ³⁄₃₂-by-⅛-in. chair rails can be set 2½ in. above floor. Install partitions with glue and ¾-in. brads toe-nailed into floor.

You'll need nine pieces of ³⁄₃₂-by-⅜-in.-by-36-in. long balsa for all the interior trim and paneling for a room. You will also need four pieces of ⅛-by-4-in. basswood 22 in. long for panels for all the paneled walls. For fireplace details, see Fig. 13.

Add second floor

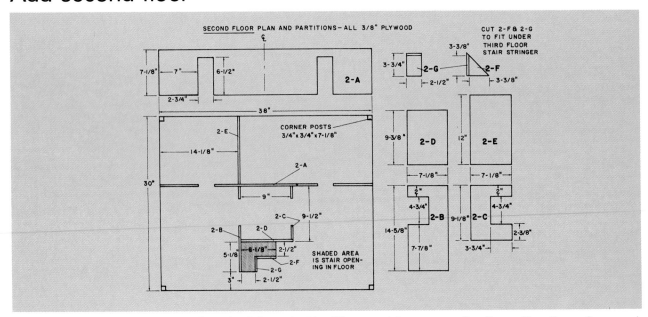

3. Cut L-shaped opening in floor panel for stairs. Paint underside of floor panel that serves as first-floor ceiling. Secure floor panel to end panels with glue and one-in. brads. Add support to first floor partitions by driving ¾-in. brads through second floor into top edge of first floor partitions. Make up second floor partitions, and install in same manner as first floor partitions. You'll need five pieces of 36-in. long ³⁄₃₂-by-⅜-in. balsa for trim around second-floor windows and door and for chair rails.

Install first floor stairs

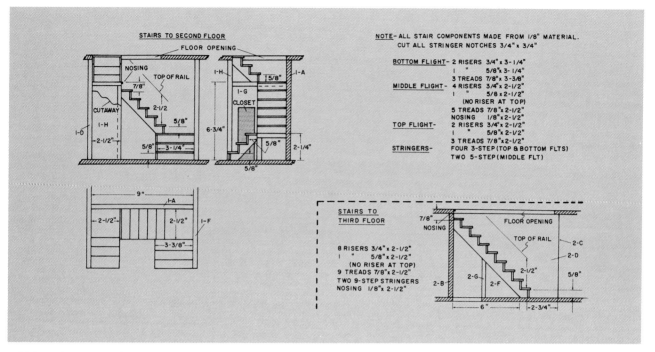

4. Make stringers out of ⅛-in. basswood. Glue inside stringers to wall. Outside stringers are glued at top and bottom to floor and landing. Install lower short stringer to wall. Construct lower landing with L-shaped support to hold it in place (Fig. 2). Add second short stringer, and glue to floor and lower landing. Install upper landing on top of partition G (Fig. 2). Glue inside stringer to wall, and fasten outside stringer with glue to lower and upper landing. Install upper short stringer. Attach risers first, then treads to stringers with glue. Drill ⅛-in. hole near end of each tread for balusters. Make balusters 2⅝ in. long from ⅛-in. dowel, and glue them into holes so they extend 2½ in. above treads. Make handrail out of ¼-by-¼ in. basswood. Round off top with sandpaper, and glue to balusters.

You'll need two pieces of ⅛-by-4-in. basswood 22 in. long and two 36-in. lengths of ⅛-in. dowels for both flights of stairs. Pattern for stair stringers is Fig. 15.

Add third-floor panel

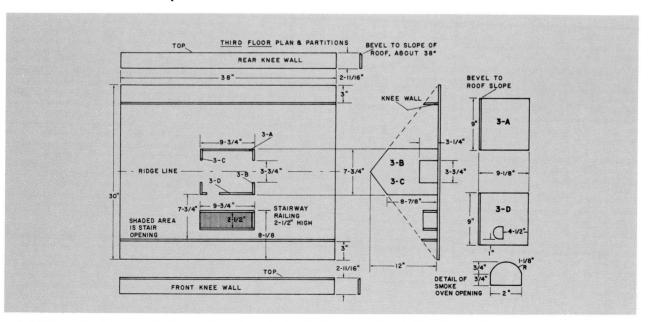

5. Cut opening for stairs, and attach panel to end panels. Install chimney enclosure. The pitch for the side pieces of this unit must match the pitch of the roof. Cut the two side pieces to correct width, then set them against end panel and use end panel as guide to mark correct angle for cut. Make openings for fireplace and smoke oven. Install knee walls. Bevel top edge of walls to about 38 degrees to match pitch of roof. Install stairs (Fig. 4). Use ⅛-in. dowels and ¼-by-¼-in. basswood for railing around stair opening.

Make front and rear hinged panels

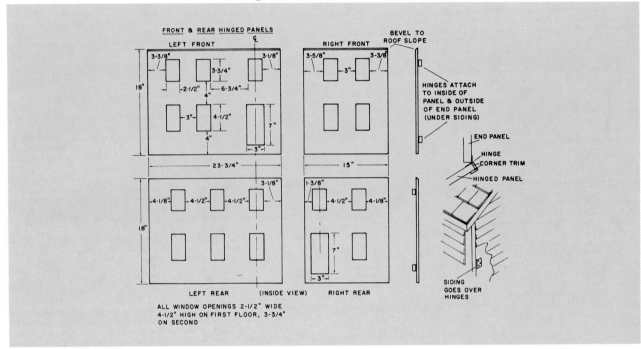

6. Cut both at same time, then cut each into two sections as shown in Fig. 6. Bevel top edge to about 38-degree angle to conform with roof angle. Cut opening for windows and doors. Center door openings on windows directly above. Attach panels to corners with two hinges per panel. Make up front and back doors (Fig. 14). Add outside steps made of 1 × 1.

Add roof and chimney

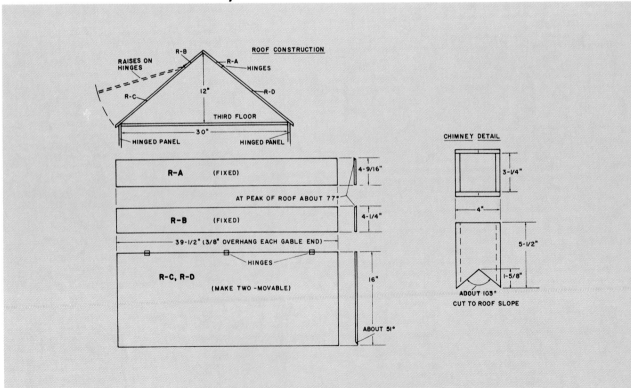

7. Install fixed section of roof, then attach movable sections of roof to fixed sections with three hinges per section. Install chimney (Fig. 7). If you cover it with chimney paper, apply before securing chimney to roof with glue and brads.

Make windows

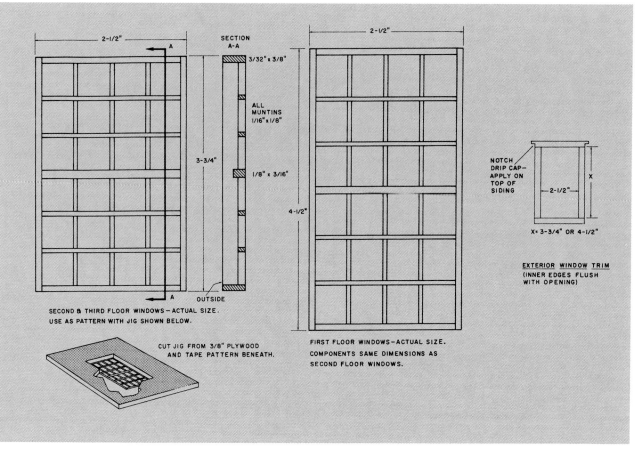

SECTION A-A

3/32" x 3/8"

ALL MUNTINS 1/16" x 1/8"

1/8" x 3/16"

2-1/2"

3-3/4"

4-1/2"

SECOND & THIRD FLOOR WINDOWS—ACTUAL SIZE.
USE AS PATTERN WITH JIG SHOWN BELOW.

CUT JIG FROM 3/8" PLYWOOD
AND TAPE PATTERN BENEATH.

2-1/2"

OUTSIDE

FIRST FLOOR WINDOWS—ACTUAL SIZE.
COMPONENTS SAME DIMENSIONS AS
SECOND FLOOR WINDOWS.

NOTCH DRIP CAP—
APPLY ON
TOP OF
SIDING

2-1/2"

X

X= 3-3/4" OR 4-1/2"

EXTERIOR WINDOW TRIM
(INNER EDGES FLUSH
WITH OPENING)

8. These are made of three sizes of balsa—3/32-by-3/8-in., 1/16-by-1/8-in., and 1/8-by-3/16-in. An easy way to assemble the windows is to build a jig as shown in Fig. 8 out of 3/8-in. plywood. Two jigs are required because the first-floor windows are higher than those on the second and third floors. Cut them out and lay them on the jig, and then cover with plastic so glue won't stick to the paper. Assemble all elements with glue. Install the windows and outside trim around them. If you are going to install clapboard siding, do not install the drip cap at top until after the siding is on. For each window and outside trim you will need one piece of 3/32-by-3/8-in. balsa 36 in. long, 1/16-by-1/8-in. balsa 25 in. long and 1/8-by-3/16-in. balsa 2½ in. long.

Apply the siding and roofing

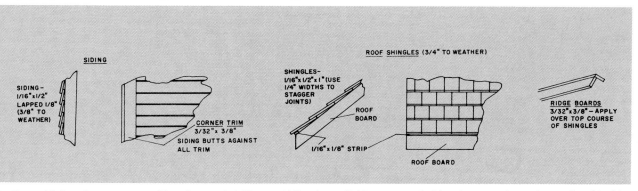

SIDING

SIDING—
1/16"x1/2"
LAPPED 1/8"
(3/8" TO
WEATHER)

CORNER TRIM
3/32" x 3/8"
SIDING BUTTS AGAINST
ALL TRIM

ROOF SHINGLES (3/4" TO WEATHER)

SHINGLES—
1/16"x1/2"x1" (USE
1/4" WIDTHS TO
STAGGER
JOINTS)

ROOF
BOARD

1/16"x1/8" STRIP

ROOF BOARD

RIDGE BOARDS
3/32"x3/8"—APPLY
OVER TOP COURSE
OF SHINGLES

9. First add the trim at corners. Manufactured dollhouse siding is available at many hobby shops, or it can be made with thin strips of balsa or thin cardboard cut from large sheets with paper cutter or utility knife. Paint siding before installing. Siding is easier to apply with staples than with glue. Install drip cap around windows after siding is on. You'll need four pieces of 3/32-by-3/8-in. balsa 36 in. long for corner trim.

10. Apply 1/16-by-1/8-in. eave board along edge of roof. Roof shingles should be ½ in. wide and one-in. long laid ¾-in. to the weather. If table saw is available, cut 1/16-in. strips out of ¾-in. cedar or pine and then cut to one-in. length with paper cutter. Shingles can also be made out of thin strips of cardboard. Dollhouse shingles are also available at many hobby shops.
Apply shingles with staples or with glue. Install ridge boards and roof boards made of 3/32-by-3/8-in. balsa.

Paneling

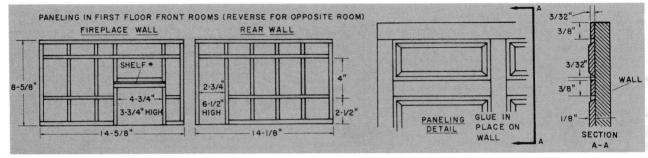

PANELING IN FIRST FLOOR FRONT ROOMS (REVERSE FOR OPPOSITE ROOM)

FIREPLACE WALL   REAR WALL

SHELF *

8-5/8"   4-3/4"   2-3/4"   4"
3-3/4" HIGH   6-1/2" HIGH   2-1/2"
14-5/8"   14-1/8"

PANELING DETAIL   GLUE IN PLACE ON WALL

3/32"   3/8"   3/32"   3/8"   1/8"

WALL

SECTION A-A

11. For paneling, install stiles and rails, then fit panels into place. Use utility knife to bevel edges of panels.

Fireplace

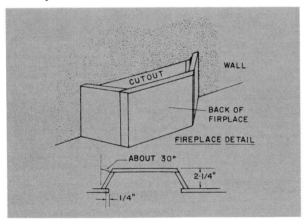

CUTOUT   WALL

BACK OF FIRPLACE

FIREPLACE DETAIL

ABOUT 30°

2-1/4"   1/4"

13. Fireplaces are made of three pieces of ⅜-in. plywood. Cut the edges of each piece at a slight angle so the sides will slant inward. Tack a piece of scrap to the floor inside the fireplace enclosure to hold the plywood pieces in place until glue has set. Paint inside of fireplaces black.

Front and back doors

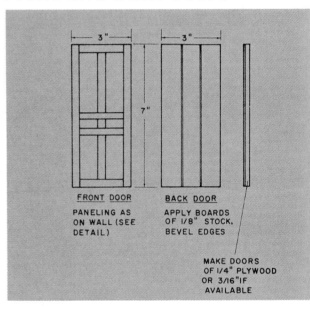

3"   3"   7"

FRONT DOOR   BACK DOOR
PANELING AS ON WALL (SEE DETAIL)   APPLY BOARDS OF 1/8" STOCK, BEVEL EDGES

MAKE DOORS OF 1/4" PLYWOOD OR 3/16"IF AVAILABLE

Molding and window molding

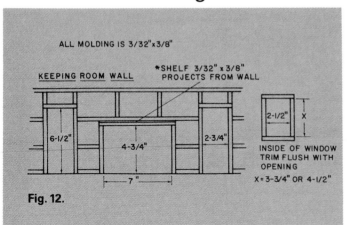

ALL MOLDING IS 3/32"x3/8"

KEEPING ROOM WALL   *SHELF 3/32" x 3/8" PROJECTS FROM WALL

6-1/2"   4-3/4"   2-3/4"   7"

2-1/2"   X

INSIDE OF WINDOW TRIM FLUSH WITH OPENING
X = 3-3/4" OR 4-1/2"

Fig. 12.

Pattern for stair stringers

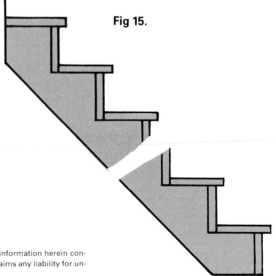

Fig 15.

revolving crane

Construction Notes

This Revolving Jib Crane will bring many hours of joy to your young engineer. Made like the real ones, the crane rotates in a full circle on a ball-bearing swivel. The ratchet and pawl controls the angle of the boom. The handwheel raises and lowers the load, which hangs from the ball and hook.

All part numbers correspond to those in the materials list. Cut the lumber to size as per the list, then shape and work each piece as per the drawings. Assemble the parts as indicated in the exploded view. Note that the spacers are tapered slightly. Use a sander to make the taper after the pieces have been cut to size.

The ratchet was cut from a 2½-inch faced wheel the same as used elsewhere on the crane. If you do use such a wheel, be sure to make the notches for left- or right-hand use. See the note on the drawing.

The swivel can be mounted two ways—as shown or as suggested by the manufacturer. I think the method shown is the most practical. Proceed as follows: Locate the bearing on the platform (part 1) using the four inner holes, which are spaced $3\frac{3}{16}$ inches apart. For ease of installation, make screw starter holes using an awl then a small drill. Likewise, make similar holes on the underside of the base piece (part 3) using the four holes spaced $3\frac{3}{16}$ inches apart. Fasten the bearing to the top side of the platform, then, holding the superstructure upside down, place the platform (also upside down) in position over the base. Rotate as necessary to align the holes in the bearing with those in the base piece. Do this through the $\frac{5}{8}$-inch clearance hole in the platform. As each screw is driven home, rotate to the next quadrant and repeat until the four screws are installed.

The wheels and axles are assembled with glue. Glue the hubs to the wheels first, then fasten the wheels to the axles. To mount the ball, drill a $\frac{1}{16}$-inch hole through its center then counterbore the hole with a $\frac{3}{64}$-inch drill $\frac{3}{4}$ inch deep. Insert the twine, knot then pull through until the knot stops at the narrowed hole. Apply a little glue to the walls of the $\frac{3}{64}$-inch hole, then attach the screw hook. Run the twine over the pins as shown then through the hole in the shaft. Tie a small knot, then secure with a drop of glue.

Finish as desired. The unit shown was given two coats of clear lacquer then rubbed—*By John Capotosto.*

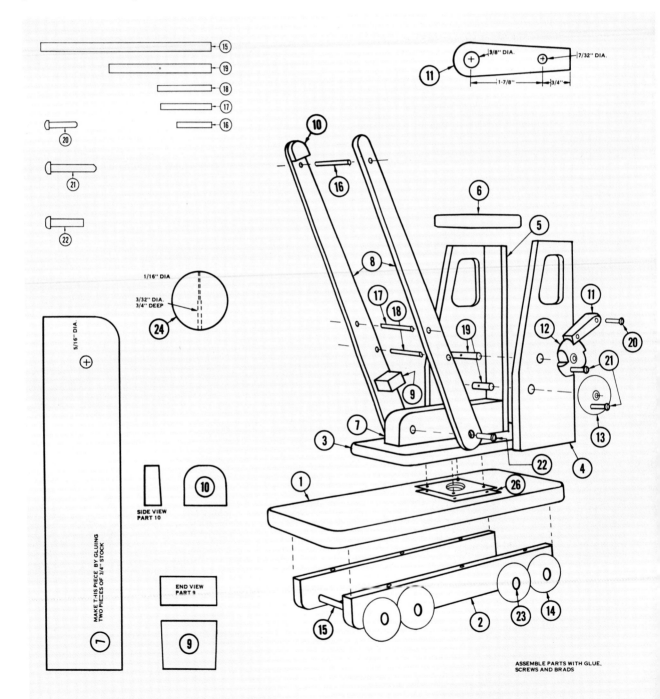

ASSEMBLE PARTS WITH GLUE, SCREWS AND BRADS

Note: Exploded view shows the controls installed for a left-handed child. If child is right-handed, place the controls on opposite side, as shown on page 187.

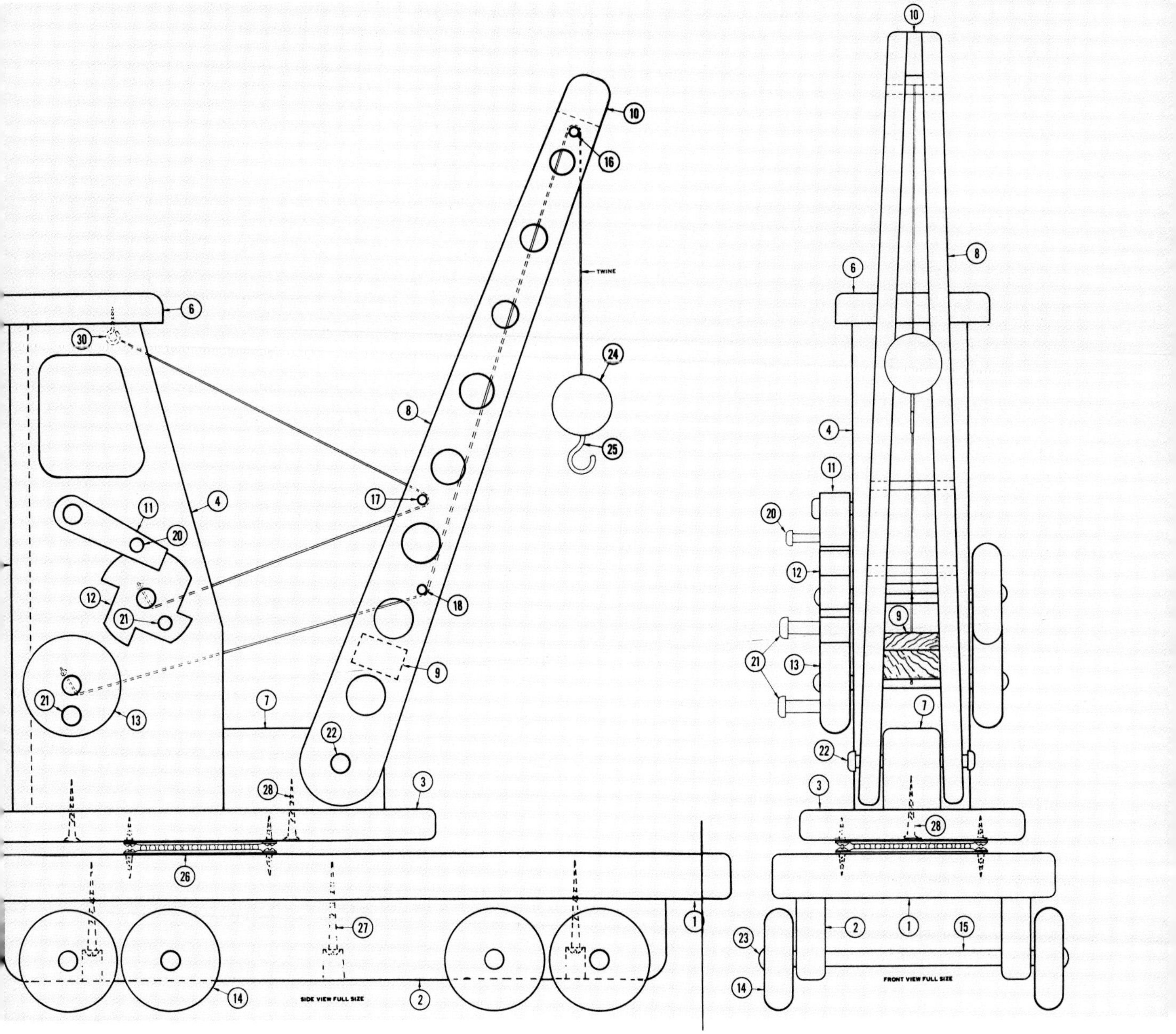

BILL OF MATERIALS

All measurements are in inches.

Part	Description	Size	Qty.
1	Platform	1⅛ × 7¼ × 20	1
2	Axle support	¾ × 2 × 17	2
3	Base	¾ × 5¾ × 12	1
4	Side	¾ × 5⅜ × 12	2
5	Rear	½ × 1½ × 12	1
6	Top	4 × 4½	1
7	Boom support	1½ × 2 × 9	1
8	Boom	½ × 2 × 19	2
9	Spacer, lower	¾ × 1¼ × 1½	1
10	Spacer, upper	7/16 × 1 × 1⅛	1
11	Pawl	¾ × ⅞ × 3	1
12	Ratchet wheel	¾ × 2½ dia.	1
13	Hand wheel	¾ × 2½ dia.	3
14	Wheel	¾ × 2½ dia.	8
15	Axle	⅜ × 7¼ dowel	4
16	Pin	¼ × 1½ dowel	1
17	Pin	¼ × 2 3/16 dowel	1
18	Pin	¼ × 2 5/16 dowel	1
19	Shaft	⅜ × 4⅜ dowel	2
20	Handle	7/32 × 1⅛ (AP-1)	1
21	Handle	5/16 × 2 (AP-2)	2
22	Boom pin	5/16 × 1⅜ (AP-2)	2
23	Hub	⅜ × ½ head (MWP)	13
24	Ball	1½ dia. (BA-1½)	1
25	Screw Hook	⅝ dia.	1
26	Lazy Susan bearing	4 (SWB-1)	1
27	Screw	2—8 RH	6
28	Screw	1½—8 FH	2
29	Nail	1½ finishing	14
30	Screw Eye	⅜	1

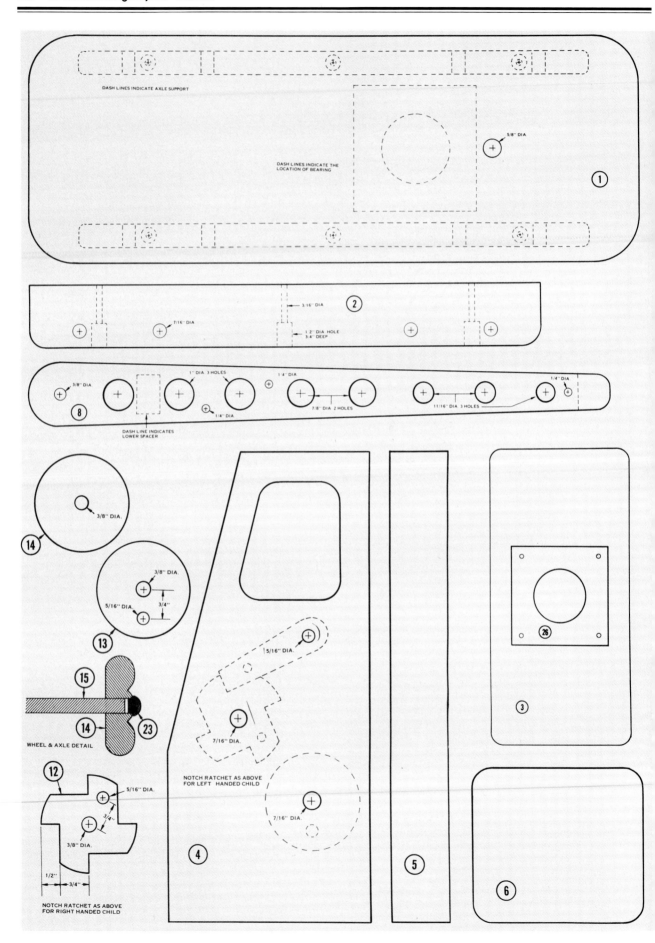

DASH LINES INDICATE AXLE SUPPORT

DASH LINES INDICATE THE
LOCATION OF BEARING

5/8" DIA

①

3/16" DIA

②

7/16" DIA

1.2" DIA HOLE
3.4" DEEP

3/8" DIA

1" DIA 3 HOLES

1/4" DIA

1/4" DIA

1/4" DIA

⑧

1/4" DIA

7/8" DIA 2 HOLES

11/16" DIA 3 HOLES

DASH LINE INDICATES
LOWER SPACER

3/8" DIA.

⑭

3/8" DIA.

3/4"

5/16" DIA

⑬

⑮

⑭   ㉓

WHEEL & AXLE DETAIL

5/16" DIA.

7/16" DIA.

NOTCH RATCHET AS ABOVE
FOR LEFT HANDED CHILD

⑫

5/16" DIA.

3/4"

3/8" DIA.

1/2"

3/4"

NOTCH RATCHET AS ABOVE
FOR RIGHT HANDED CHILD

7/16" DIA.

④

⑤

⑥

㉖

③

log hauler

This 14-wheeler Log Hauling Truck will provide hours of enjoyment for the young lumberjacks of the family. Designed like a real one, the tractor features a realistic exhaust pipe and an air deflector above the cab. One-inch dowels are glued together and form an integral part of the truck frame. Lumber used is pine, but other species may be substituted. Size: seven by 25 inches.

Construction Notes

This 14-wheeler Log Hauler is made of pine and is easy to build. The "logs" are an integral part of the truck and serve to connect the tractor to the hitch at the rear. The logs, which are one-by-12-inch dowels, are glued to each other and to the log brackets, thus preventing them from constantly falling off and getting underfoot, which could be dangerous.

Before assembly drill the necessary holes as indicated. Join the parts with white glue and brads. The brads serve to hold the parts in place while the glue sets.

The exhaust pipe is made in three pieces: inner, outer, and cap. The inner pipe is a straight dowel with an axle peg inserted into one end. The outer pipe is drilled with numerous holes to give it a realistic appearance. Make it as follows: Draw four equally spaced lines along the length of the ¾-inch dowel. Since accuracy is not important, you can gauge the lines by eye. The ¼ inch holes are spaced and staggered as shown. Drill each hole about ¼ inch deep. Do not go through the dowel, as the exit hole will tear and splinter the wood. When all the ¼-inch holes are drilled, bore the 9/16-inch center hole through the length of the dowel. Do this in steps starting with a ⅛-inch hole, then ¼ inch, ⅜ inch, and finally 9/16 inch. If you use a lathe to bore the holes, you can drill straight through from one end. If you use a portable drill or drill press, it would be best to drill from both ends, meeting at the center—otherwise the drill may walk or wander off course.

The wheels are glued to the ⅜ axles (dowels) and the one-inch dowels are glued to each other and to the brackets. Stagger the logs lengthwise to add realism. The "ropes" consist of heavy shoelaces wrapped around the logs twice and glued in place. Make the knot for the laces on the underside. Add a drop of glue to the knots to keep them from loosening.

Paint or finish clear as desired. Use non-toxic materials. The little people can be painted as shown. If you paint them, be sure to seal the wood first with shellac or other suitable sealer. The features are added with a felt marker—*by John Capotosto.*

MATERIALS LIST

Except for dowels and wheels, lumber is pine. Wheels and dowels are maple. Measurements are in inches.

TRUCK

Part	Description	Size	Qty.
1	Side	¾ × 3½ × 9¾	2
2	Chassis	¾ × 2½ × 9¾	1
3	Hood	¾ × 2½ × 3	1
4	Roof	½ × 3 × 4½	1
5	Fender	¾ × 1½ × 6¼	2
6	Bumper	¼ × ¾ × 4½	1
7	Cab, rear	½ × 2¼ × 2½	1
8	Bracket	¾ × 1¼ × 4	1
9	Pin	⅜ × 1½ dowel	1
10	Axle	⅜ × 5⅝ dowel	1
11	Axle	⅜ × 7 dowel	1
12	Exhaust outer	¾ × 3 dowel	1
13	Exhaust inner	½ × 4¼ dowel	1
14	Exhaust cap	Axle peg, 5/16 tenon	1
15	Deflector	¼ × 1 9/16 × 3	1
16	Bracket	¾ × ⅝ × 1	2
17	People	¾ × 2 5/16	2
18	Log	1 × 12 dowel	6

TRAILER

Part	Description	Size	Qty.
19	Side	¾ × 2 × 5⅜	2
20	Top	¾ × 1⅞ × 5⅜	1
21	Bracket	¾ × 1¼ × 4	1
22	Wheel	2¼ dia.	14
23	Axle	⅜ × 6⅝ dowel	2
24	Rope	Shoelace	2

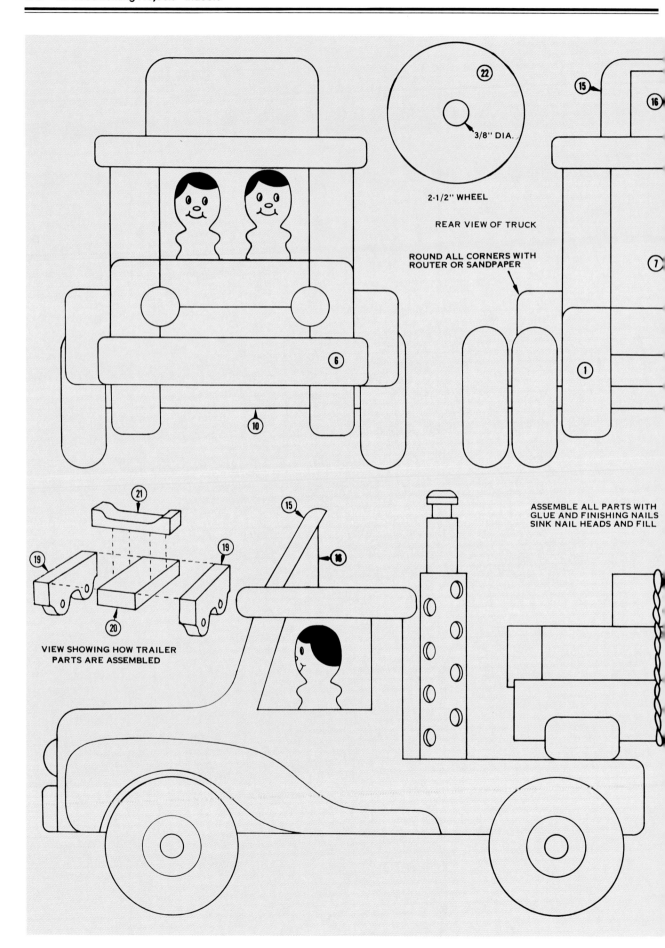

22

3/8" DIA.

2-1/2" WHEEL

REAR VIEW OF TRUCK

ROUND ALL CORNERS WITH
ROUTER OR SANDPAPER

15

16

7

1

6

10

21

15

19   19

16

20

VIEW SHOWING HOW TRAILER
PARTS ARE ASSEMBLED

ASSEMBLE ALL PARTS WITH
GLUE AND FINISHING NAILS
SINK NAIL HEADS AND FILL

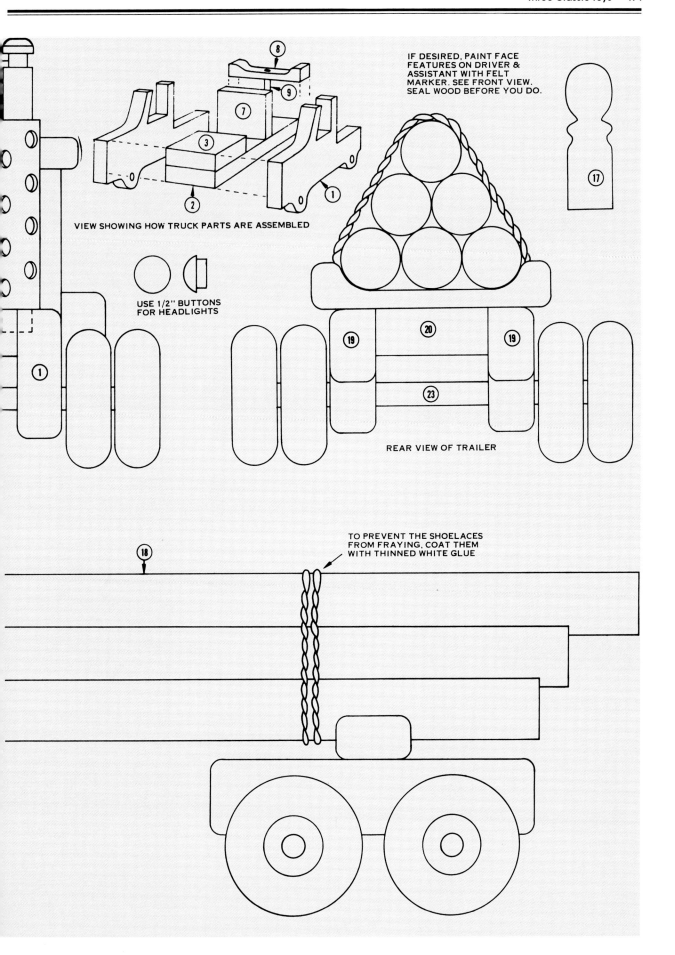

VIEW SHOWING HOW TRUCK PARTS ARE ASSEMBLED

IF DESIRED, PAINT FACE
FEATURES ON DRIVER &
ASSISTANT WITH FELT
MARKER. SEE FRONT VIEW.
SEAL WOOD BEFORE YOU DO.

USE 1/2" BUTTONS
FOR HEADLIGHTS

REAR VIEW OF TRAILER

TO PREVENT THE SHOELACES
FROM FRAYING, COAT THEM
WITH THINNED WHITE GLUE

Truck parts

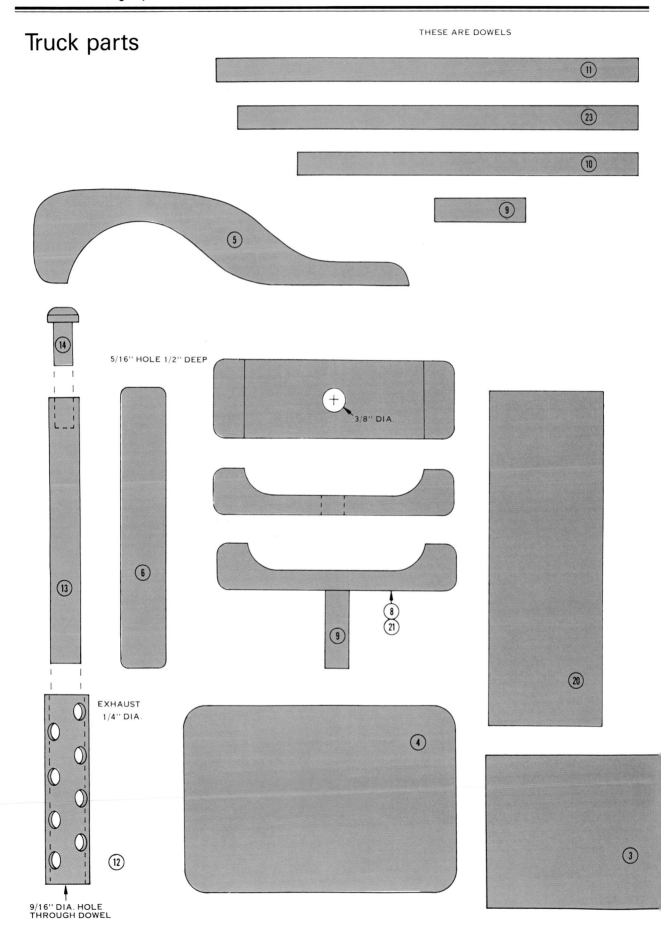

THESE ARE DOWELS

⑪

㉓

⑩

⑨

⑤

⑭

5/16" HOLE 1/2" DEEP

3/8" DIA.

⑬

⑥

⑨

⑧
㉑

⑳

EXHAUST
1/4" DIA.

④

⑫

③

9/16" DIA. HOLE
THROUGH DOWEL

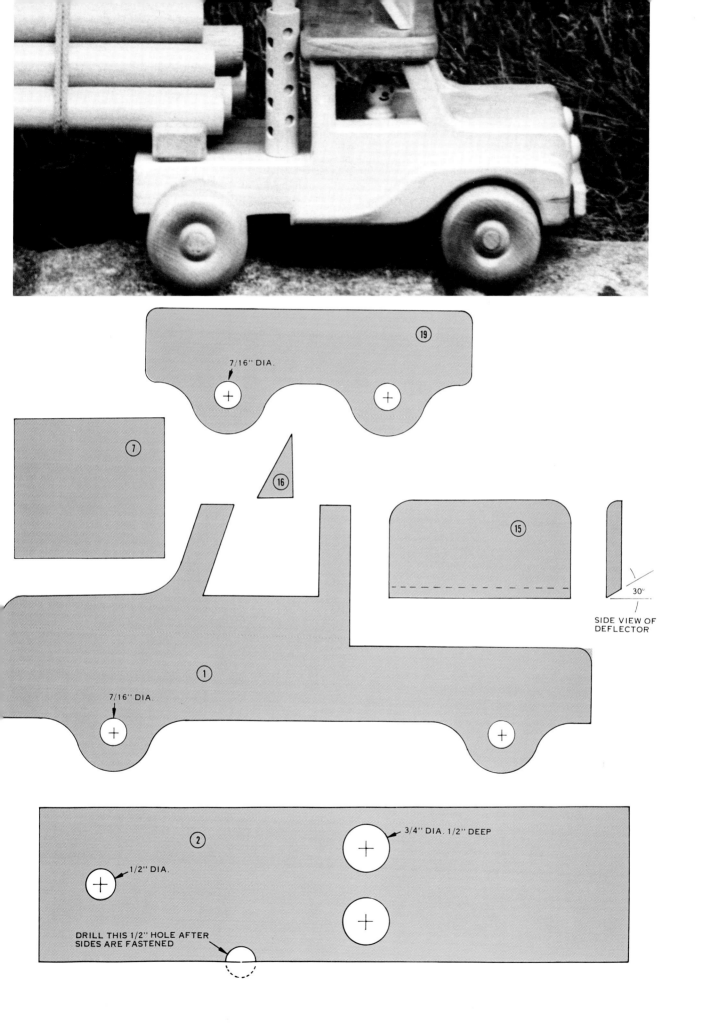

19

7/16" DIA.

7

16

15

30°

SIDE VIEW OF
DEFLECTOR

1

7/16" DIA.

2

3/4" DIA. 1/2" DEEP

1/2" DIA.

DRILL THIS 1/2" HOLE AFTER
SIDES ARE FASTENED

one-wall vanitory

There's a lot more than the plumbing in a bathroom. In addition, there usually are a vanitory cabinet, medicine chest, mirror, some electrical convenience outlets, and lighting. Knowing how to build, finish, and install such items can be a real money-saver in the remodeling of what amounts to the most expensive area of your home (on cost per square foot basis).

We took a partly finished bath and finished it, continuing with the same materials and colors. Since the floor and some walls already were tiled, the same American Olean Siena putty shade was used for the vanitory top. The vanitory base, the medicine chests, and the light enclosures we laminated with Wilsonart's Natural Almond, a color that matched existing fixtures.

The work began with building the vanitory cabinet and top, medicine chests, and light enclosure. These pieces are of simple, but strong construction. For the chest and light enclosure, butt-joining was used only in developing the box structure, while the vanitory was butt-joined everywhere except the face-frame, which requires mortises and tenons. All doors are slab overlays and all drawers, simple boxes with separate laminated faces. The mirror arrangement lets the user see the back of his head. (There is one mirror on the back of each medicine chest door, and another, larger one mounted between the chests.)

All the cabinet work, assembly, lamination, and tiling procedures are covered in accompanying photos and drawings, but here are some suggestions that could be helpful:

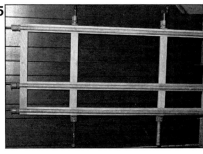

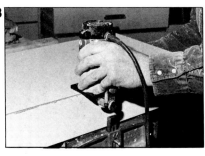

- Mount medicine chest doors with Stanley No. 131 pin hinges. The hinges allow the door at the internal corner to open properly.
- Silicone caulking—for example, Phenoseal—can be used to mount the mirrors on the backs of doors.
- A GFCI (Ground Fault Circuit Interrupter) outlet should be used in the area of the vanitory or lavatory.
- Use only noncombustible, water-base latex contact cement.
- Once the drawers have been assembled, they should be mounted on the three-point suspensions and adjusted. Then the prelaminated fronts should be aligned and marked for mounting. The screw hole for the drawer pull should be drilled completely through front and slightly into the drawer as a pilot. The pilot hole may be countersunk or enlarged for screwhead clearance.

1. Location for the new vanitory cabinet, with the old medicine chest cut out and the plumbing stubs showing.
2. Mortise is made with drill press and hollow chisel adapter. With workpiece in a clamp or vise, bore a continuous row of overlapping square holes.
3. Tenon is made on a table saw. The shoulders are first cut to the correct depth with aid of miter head and rip fence.
4. Second step in making tenon is the cutting away of waste. Blade height and fence adjustment are left as before. Flanks of tenon are cut away by rapid back and forth motion across the blade, gradually advancing toward output end.
5. The components are glued and then bar-clamped together as shown here.
6. After assembly has dried and been sanded, it's glued to cabinet sides.
7. The drawer members are butt-joined with glue and nails. Quarter-inch dadoes support bottom shelf.
8. Contact cement is brushed on the front surface of the piece to be covered with laminate and on the back surface of the matching piece of laminate.

9. After the cement dries, laminate is positioned and pressure is applied—here, by means of a wood block scrap and a hammer—in order to lock the laminate down in the proper position.
10. Laminate edges are trimmed with a small router/trimmer and solid carbide bit. Use the flat cutting edge as opposed to the bevel part. Setup shown uses the guide on the router itself.
11. The trimmed edges are belt-sanded with #120 grit; the motion of belt is from outer to inner part of the panel. This motion helps you avoid chipping or otherwise damaging the laminate.
12. Edge corners—and wherever two laminated surfaces join at 90-degree angles—are carefully worked with file.
13. Whenever two laminate edges meet, the overlap is trimmed with the router.
14. Here, the front face of chest is being jigsawed as a "picture frame."
15. Feed direction for the router when trimming the inside and outside edges.
16. With completed cabinet in position and level, drill the holes for screws through face-frame and into wall studs.

(Steps continued on page 197.)

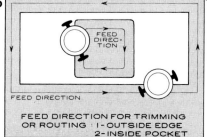

FEED DIRECTION

FEED DIRECTION FOR TRIMMING OR ROUTING : 1-OUTSIDE EDGE 2-INSIDE POCKET

● When you begin to mount the medicine chests and the large mirror and its retainers, exercise care to keep everything square. Otherwise gaps are likely to develop between the components.

● The baseboard bullnose tile—it probably would prevent the vanitory cabinet from seating flush against the wall—should be removed as necessary. Later, the tile can be retrimmed at the ends—*Bernard Price*.

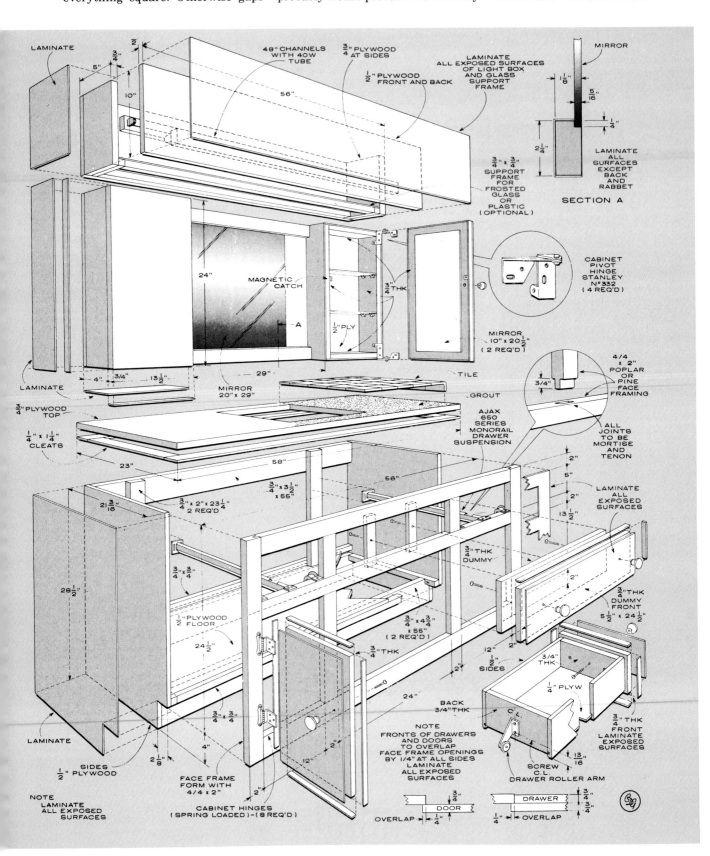

17. The cabinet top is scribed in order to ensure proper fit against the wall.

18. A template and star-wheel tracer are used for marking the location of the cutout for installation of the lavatory.

19. Jigsaw is used to make the cutout.

20. Dry-fit all the tiles before applying any mortar to the vanity top. Tiles are then removed and placed close at hand in the order of application.

21. The trowel used to apply the mortar has ¼-inch-square notches.

22. Border tiles are set first and spaced,

as they generally lack spacing projections found on most flat tiles.

23. The tiles are locked in mortar by striking over them in several directions with a hammer and scrap of plywood.

24. The grout is applied with a rubber-bottomed float to fill all cracks.

25. While grout is still wet, excess is removed with a squeegee pulled over the tiles in a dragging motion.

26. As the grout dries, a dry haze will form over the tiles. This should be removed by polishing with burlap.

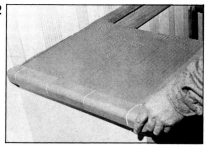

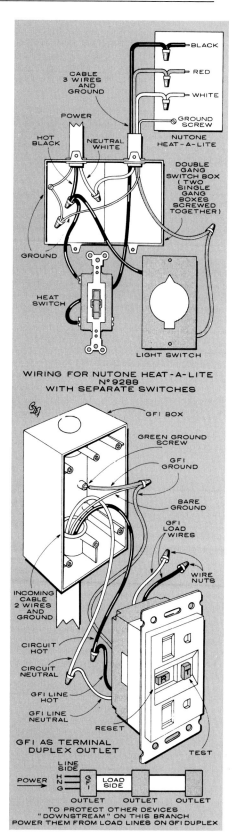

WIRING FOR NUTONE HEAT-A-LITE N° 9288 WITH SEPARATE SWITCHES

GFI AS TERMINAL DUPLEX OUTLET

TO PROTECT OTHER DEVICES "DOWNSTREAM" ON THIS BRANCH POWER THEM FROM LOAD LINES ON GFI DUPLEX

Project participants

Laminate (Natural Almond D30-6): Wilsonart, 600 General Bruce Drive, Temple, TX 76501. Tile (Siena): American Olean, 2743 Cannon Avenue, Lansdale, PA 19446. Wallcovering: Reed Wall Covering, Atlanta, GA 30349. Ceiling fixture (Model 9288 Heat-A-Lite): Nutone, Madison and Red Bank Rds., Cincinnati, OH 45227. Faucet (FA 102 washerless): Nibco, Inc., 500 Simpson Street, Elkhart, IN 46515. Epoxy, grout: L and M Surco Mfg., Inc., Whitehead Avenue, South River, NJ 08882.

bathroom built-ins

If you have a bathroom the size of a gym, remodeling it is no problem. All the home magazines are full of ideas on where to put your his-and-hers sinks and toilets, hot tub, and steeping bath. Fine, but what can you do with a real-world bathroom like mine—one that measures just 5×6 feet?

I soon discovered that if I wanted a good-looking vanity that wasn't so large that it blocked the door to the room, I'd have to make it myself. And as long as I was going to make the vanity, I decided to make the rest of the furnishings as well. That way they would all match and I could use a few ideas to make the room look and function like a larger one.

Medicine chest is sized to fit the narrow wall at the left end of the vanity. This frees the area over the counter for the large mirror, which gives the room a feeling of depth. Chest construction is simple: Make an oak frame with a hardboard back, sized to fit between studs. Fasten on the oak trim and secure the unit in place. The back edge of the door is rabbeted to give a thinner look. Be sure to rout the front of the door with a rounding-over bit *before* cutting the rabbet, or the bit pilot will have no surface to follow.

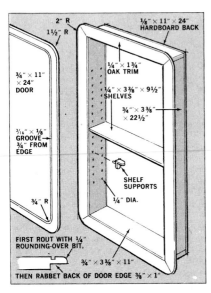

The photos and sketches show what was done using $120 worth of solid oak and $100 worth of stock oak butcher block. Other materials and fixtures used are as follows:

The walls and floor are finished with American Olean's Tanbark Siena ceramic tile and Tuscany Malt grout. The tub is Kohler's Villager; the toilet, Kohler's Wellworth Water Guard—both in Mexican Sand finish. The sink is a tiny 12-inch-round bowl from Mayfair China, hand paint-ed at the factory with trim bands to match the wallpaper. With Kohler's Antique brushed-chrome faucets, it creates an old-fashioned dry-sink look.

My remodeling raised one practical problem: The position of the vanity blocked the bath's hot-air register. Solution: I fed the duct in under the bottom of the vanity and cut louver slits in the front of the toe board to let the hot air out—*A. J. Hand.*

Photos by the author
Drawings by Gerhard Richter

Vanity, made from solid oak, is designed to fit into a corner of the room. The counter and leaf were cut from a single piece of 16×60-inch oak butcher block. The leaf section makes good use of the normally wasted space over the toilet, but can be removed to allow access to the tank. The rounded corner of the vanity looks difficult to make but is really quite simple. Start by making an ordinary butt joint, backed up by a 1×1 oak cleat. Trace an arc with a 2-inch radius on the top and bottom edges of the joint. (I just traced around a coffee can.) Then plane the corner down to match the curve. The back-splash is made from resawn oak: Using thin oak provided clearance for the faucet handles. Even so, the position of the faucets pushed the sink out slightly, so the rear surface of the vanity's top rail had to be routed to clear it. The vanity, counter, and back-splash were sealed with Watco oil, then given three coats of satin varnish. The mirror is also framed in oak. Its floral design was etched into the rear surface of the mirror, then hand painted.

Towel-and-magazine rack is built in between wall studs to create extra space. In the original bathroom a conventional double-hung window occupied this position. I removed it and placed a Pella awning window up high, making space for the rack. To build the rack, you cement foam insulation to the sheathing between studs. Then cement hardboard over the foam. Paint or paper the hardboard, then cut oak frame and trim parts to fit. Thin oak for the trim and face of the magazine rack was made by resawing ¾-inch oak.

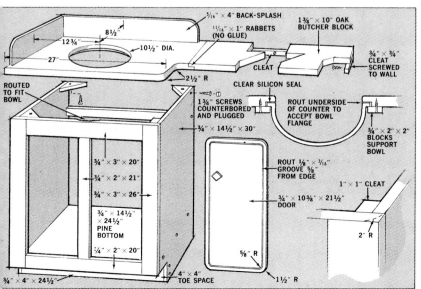

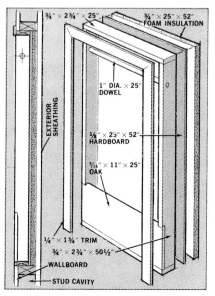

early american medicine chest

Your bath or powder room doesn't have to be all chromium plate and porcelain enamel. Take, for example, the medicine cabinet shown here. It's made entirely of lumberyard pine and styled Early American. It does everything today's cabinet does, but with a lot more warmth. You can build it at little cost (most expensive element is the mirror), and with only a small investment of your time.

This cabinet is made entirely of ½-inch pine, with brads and glue joinery. Cut and shape pieces as illustrated. Then follow these steps.

• Spread glue along a side edge and drive brads through the back into the edge. Keep the back and side edges flush. Do the same with the other side.

• Measure the distance between the sides and cut the top and bottom to fit. Glue and nail these two pieces in place. Sink brads that go through the sides and fill holes, preferably with slivers of wood that you sand smooth, although any wood filler will work.

• Cut shelves ¹⁄₁₆ inch shorter than the top and bottom pieces, but do not rip them to width yet. (Our cabinet has two shelves; you may want three, depending on what you'll keep on them.)

• Measure the opening between top and bottom of the two sides. Put the mirror-frame door together as shown, making it barely smaller than the opening. The corners are mitered, and the mirror and backing are held in place with thin strips ripped off the edge of ½-inch pine.

• Rip the shelves to proper width by removing an edge exactly equal to the thickness of the door, including the strips that hold the mirror in place. Thus, the shelves become the stops that let the door close properly.

• Determine shelf positions and fasten cleats in place with ½-inch brads and glue. Cleats can be "off-fall" from the strips on the back of the door.

All that's left now is finishing and hinging. Choose an Early American pine stain in the color you want for the outside. Give the interior two

Drawing below, right, shows how cabinet goes together after pieces are cut to shape and size. Shelf width is determined by door thickness. Rip ½-inch stock 1½ inches wide and cut rabbet from back as shown below, left; miter corners for good fit. Buy mirror to fit frame; back it up with hardboard and fasten in place with a thin strip fastened to frame with brads.

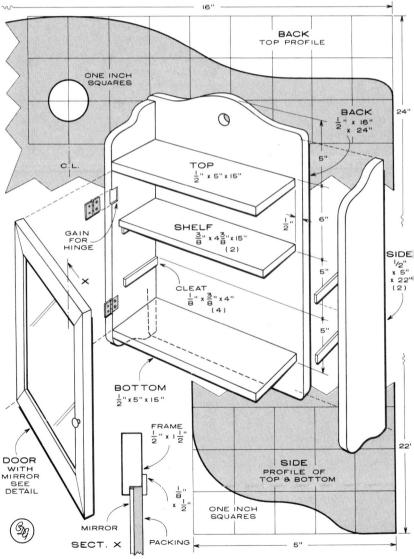

The back is 16 inches wide—two ½×10s edge-glued and ripped to size. To cut the shape at the top, draw 1-inch squares on the back as shown in the drawing above, or draw the shape on cardboard and trace it on both top corners. Follow the same technique for cutting the sides to shape (drawing at right). The top and bottom curves are identical. After cutting the sides, sand the cut edges.

coats of glossy enamel to make cleaning easy.

Your hardware store carries small brass butt hinges and brass knobs. Buy the ½-inch size. Mount them about 2 inches from the top and bottom of the door. Mortising the edge of the door deep enough to accept the entire hinge is easier than mortising both the edge and the cabinet side.

In keeping with Early American style, the cabinet back has a hole at the top. It provides you with an easy mounting method—*if there is a stud* behind the hole. If not, mount the cabinet with two toggle bolts through the back into the wall—*Jackson Hand.*

airtight attic door

A pull-down staircase makes it easy to get things up into an attic, but it also lets cold air spill down into the living areas of the home. When all the weatherstripping and sealants I tried didn't keep the cold wind from cascading down my hallway, I devised the "airlock"—an airtight double door that permits easy access to the attic, but keeps cold drafts out.

No more than a bottomless box with a hinged lid, the airlock is easily built with under $30 worth of materials and installs in minutes without altering the ceiling. The parts can be cut from plywood, particleboard, or 1-inch lumber. I made mine with 1×12 sides and a scrap of underlayment for the door. Also needed: a pair of 2-inch strap hinges; a roll of adhesive foam insulating tape; a screen-door handle; a hook-and-eye latch; a few nails, screws, and stove bolts.

Cut the sides of your airlock to form a box with outside dimensions a half-inch smaller in length and width than the opening in the ceiling. Make certain the box depth will accommodate the folded stairway. Butt join the sides, using glue, screws, or nails. Use 2×2 corner cleats for an easier and stronger assembly, but make sure the hardware doesn't interfere with the ladder or folding mechanism. Attach the door with strap hinges secured with wood screws or stove bolts and washers. Seal door edge with foam tape or felt weatherstripping.

A helper stationed in the attic simplifies installation. Slide the box up to him, then lower it into place. Fasten it to a header with nails or screws, square it with shims, and secure the remaining sides. Fill any gaps between the box and ceiling frame with insulation and pull the fiberglass batts snugly against the sides. Mound shredded cellulose fill around the airlock to eliminate cold spots and gaps. Staple a batt to the top of the door for an added R-value or two, and screw on the door handle. Bumps on the head can be avoided by supporting the trap door with a friction lid prop or pneumatic door closer. Letting the door swing open to rest on the joists will, however, create a firm landing and loading platform.

To prevent attic winds from lifting the door and vacuuming warm air from the house, install a hook-and-eye latch to help hold the weatherseal—*Joel Hamm.*

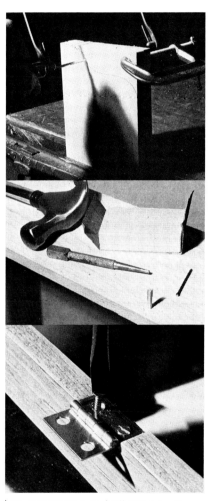

Lay out curves as indicated in the drawings; then clamp two pieces of pine together (top) and saw them both at once for perfect uniformity. Construction is entirely brad-and-glue (center). Sink brads, then insert wooden plug in hole; break it off at surface and sand smooth. Cut into door edge with a mortise deep enough to accept both wings of hinges—simpler than mortising both cabinet edge and side—as shown (bottom).

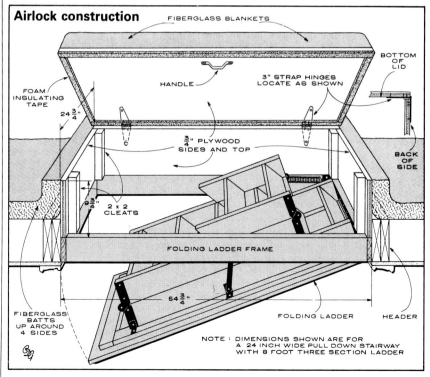

Airlock construction

FIBERGLASS BLANKETS

FOAM INSULATING TAPE

HANDLE

3" STRAP HINGES LOCATE AS SHOWN

BOTTOM OF LID

24¾"

¾" PLYWOOD SIDES AND TOP

BACK OF SIDE

9¾"

2 x 2 CLEATS

FOLDING LADDER FRAME

54¾"

FIBERGLASS BATTS UP AROUND 4 SIDES

FOLDING LADDER

HEADER

NOTE : DIMENSIONS SHOWN ARE FOR A 24 INCH WIDE PULL DOWN STAIRWAY WITH 8 FOOT THREE SECTION LADDER

laundry storage center

Even at best, a homemaker's close encounters with the basement laundry room are not likely to be the high point in home fun. If the room happens to be dismal and inefficient, those encounters can be awful. The solution: Make your laundry set up as attractive and efficient as possible.

The conversion shown here provides cabinet storage for all cleaning necessities, a folding area for finished laundry, and a rolling hamper cabinet. Rich oak panels have been installed over a drywall-reinforced stud wall, and electrical outlets, vents, and service lines have been neatly positioned for accessibility and appearance.

All cabinets and appliances fit flush against the wall and the room has a suspended ceiling and vinyl tile floor. This project, well within the ability of the average do-it-yourselfer, takes only about a week to complete, but will provide years of satisfaction.

Before starting, decide on the exact location and gather up all the required materials. Begin the job by erecting the stud wall(s); do it right and the rest is downhill.

The wall structure (studs, top and bottom plates) must be plumb when checked at the stud edges. And they must be plumb when checked at the stud faces with all studs parallel. The bottom plate may be concrete-nailed to the floor and the top plate to either the bottom edges of the first floor joists or to inter-joist blocking (should the joists run parallel with your proposed wall).

Mark out both top and bottom plates together for accuracy, on 16-inch centers. Now, locate and nail up the top plate. Drop plumb lines from both ends of this plate to locate the bottom plate, but don't nail it down just yet. Instead, fit and toenail the studs to the marked centers of both plates and then adjust the final position of the bottom plate with the aid of a level before nailing.

Mount the electrical box(es) for the outlets and make sure that the vent tube, hoses, and any gas connections will clear all studs when the appliances are brought up to the wall. Staple up the insulation (foil side facing inwards), and nail on the drywall. Finish up the wall by installing the panels with the appropriate color panel nails, cutting out for boxes and tubes as you go. Close up the electricals after inspection.

Suspended ceiling

We found it easiest to install the suspended ceiling framework at this time—no reaching behind cabinets or climbing over appliances. In addition to the 2×4-foot panels, a suspended ceiling requires wall angle, main runners, crosspieces, and suspension wires. Try to leave about a 4-inch space between the joists and the ceiling framework so you'll be able to insert the panels easily.

Begin the ceiling by mounting the wall angle, using box or drywall nails. A stretched string and line level will help you to get a straight, horizontal installation. Continue this procedure around the perimeter of the room. Wall angle (runners and crosspieces as well) can easily be trimmed to length with a metal snips.

In order to center the panels in the room, follow the method described in an accompanying box; then trim the ends of the main runners and locate them the appropriate distances from the walls parallel to them. Now, suspend the main runners with wires every 4 feet of their length and fill in

Before conversion, the laundry center was nothing more than a washer and the dryer dumped near the necessary outlets in the basement. No counters, no storage cabinets, no amenities. Page opposite—the same center after the conversion. Now appliances are flanked by utility cabinets. There's space for sorting and folding clothes and even a rolling hamper.

the structure with 4-foot crosspieces, making a grid of 2×4-foot openings, except as calculated at the borders. Then, adjust the structure with the wires to eliminate any sags or bulges, making sure that the openings are square. Drop in the panels, and you're done with this major job.

Cabinet construction

The appliances in our laundry have a combined width of 55 inches; if your washer and dryer have the same combined width, use the dimensions given on the drawing for the right-side cabinet. If the combined width of your appliances is other than 55 inches, make the calculation given in an accompanying box to determine the actual width of the cabinet; then modify the widths of the top, bottom, back, divider, front, and shelf to accommodate the change.

The cabinet construction uses plywood surfaces and pine trim, assembled with white glue and nails. Cut out all cabinets and assemble them, except for the face frames. Fill and sand all exposed edges, or—even better—edge them with pine. Paint the cabinets, then hook up the appliances. Install the lower cabinets next to the appliances, allowing ¼-inch spacing between the appliances and between the appliances and the cabinets. Place the upper cabinet in position and clamp it to the outer sides of both left- and right-hand cabinets with the front edges flush (to receive the face frame). Screw or nail all cabinets to the wall. Screw or nail the upper cabinet to the outer side extensions and, for additional support, install a prepainted cleat under it. Trim the face frame pieces to fit and install them with glue and nails. Set all nails, fill all holes and sand them smooth before touching up the paint.

Hang the prepainted doors covering the end compartments of the upper cabinets with self-closing hinges designed for overlay doors and add the door pulls. Install a pull grip to the front face of the roller cabinet and check the cabinet's alignment with the left-side, lower cabinet. Minor discrepancies can be corrected by shimming between the roller cabinet bottom and the castor mounting pads.

Upper Cabinet Dimensions

TOP SHELF	¾ × 12 × 94½	PLYWOOD
BOTTOM SHELF	¾ × 12 × 94½	PLYWOOD
DIVIDERS	¾ × 12 × 18	PLYWOOD
SIDES	¾ × 12 × 20¼	PLYWOOD
BACK	¼ × 21 × 96	PLYWOOD
NAILERS	¾ × ¾ × 12	PINE
FACE FRAME	¾ × 21 × 96*	PINE
DOORS	¾ (L & W TO SUIT)	PLYWOOD

*FACE-FRAME DIMENSIONS NOT INCLUDING LEFT AND RIGHT SIDE VERTICAL STILE EXTENSIONS TO LOWER CABINETS

Left-Side Cabinet Dimensions

OUTSIDE	¾ × 28 × 76	PLYWOOD
INSIDE	¾ × 28 × 35¼	PLYWOOD
TOP	¾ × 21 × 28	PLYWOOD
BOTTOM	¼ × 19½ × 27¼	PLYWOOD
BACK	¾ × 19½ × 35¼	PLYWOOD
NAILERS	¾ × ¾	PINE

Roller Dimensions

BACK	¾ × 18 × 27	PLYWOOD
FRONT	¾ × 18 × 27	PLYWOOD
SIDES	¾ × 24 × 27	PLYWOOD
FRONT FACE	¾ × 21 × 35¾	PLYWOOD
BOTTOM	¾ × 16½ × 24	PLYWOOD

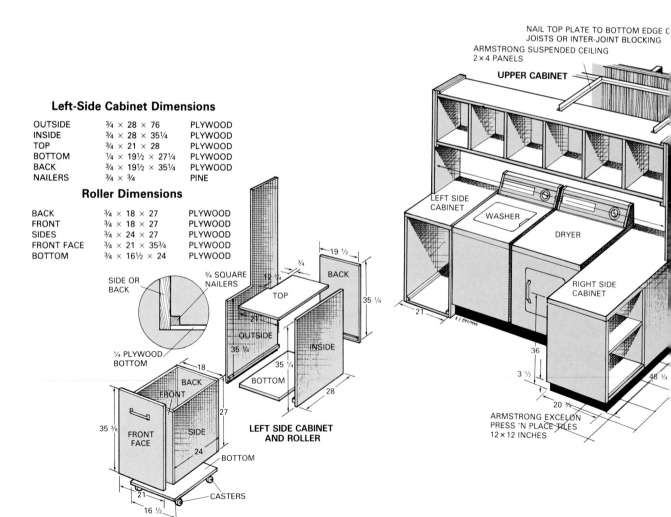

The floor

Center the floor tiles using the same method as with the ceiling. Before laying them, make sure the surface is smooth and free of dust. Minor bulges can be hammered down and hollows may be filled with cement patch (no aggregate).

Snap a chalk line on the floor at a convenient location according to your centering calculation, then simply peel off the protective papers and press the tiles in place. Butt them tightly to avoid any gapping. A scissors or shears will handle any trimming to an edge or around obstacles. Apply some compatible colored molding where applicable—*Bernard Price*.

Calculations

Panels to center ceiling. Measure the length of the room in inches. Divide this number by the width of the panel you're using in that direction. You'll get a number and a remainder. The whole number represents full-size panels. Add the remainder to the width of the panel you're using in that direction and divide the sum by two. The result is the width of the border panels. Do the same type of calculation for the adjacent wall. Example: The panel width is 48 inches and the wall dimension is 136 inches. Divide 136 inches by 48 inches and get two full panels, plus 40 inches. Add 40 inches to 48 inches to get 88 inches. Divide by two and get 44 inches for the width of border panels.

Width of the right-side cabinet. Add the combined width of your washer and dryer to ¾-inch spacing requirement. Add this sum to 20¼ inches (left-side cabinet minus the thickness of the outer side). Subtract this from 96 inches (width of upper cabinet) and then add ¾ inch (thickness of right-side outer piece) to the result. Example: Combined width of washer and dryer is 56 inches. Add ¾ inch and get 56¾ inches. Add 20¼ and get 77 inches. Subtract 77 inches from 96 inches and get 19 inches. Add ¾ inch to 19 and get 19¾ inches for the actual width of the right-side cabinet.

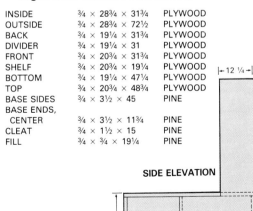

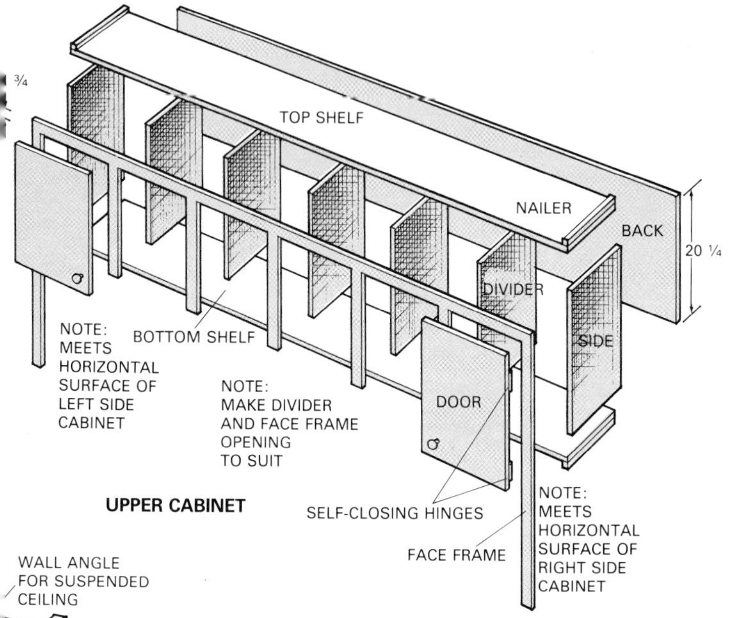

Right-Side Cabinet Dimensions

INSIDE	¾ × 28¾ × 31¾	PLYWOOD
OUTSIDE	¾ × 28¾ × 72½	PLYWOOD
BACK	¾ × 19¼ × 31¾	PLYWOOD
DIVIDER	¾ × 19¼ × 31	PLYWOOD
FRONT	¾ × 20¾ × 31¾	PLYWOOD
SHELF	¾ × 20¾ × 19¼	PLYWOOD
BOTTOM	¾ × 19¼ × 47¼	PLYWOOD
TOP	¾ × 20¾ × 48¾	PLYWOOD
BASE SIDES	¾ × 3½ × 45	PINE
BASE ENDS, CENTER	¾ × 3½ × 11¾	PINE
CLEAT	¾ × 1½ × 15	PINE
FILL	¾ × ¾ × 19¼	PINE

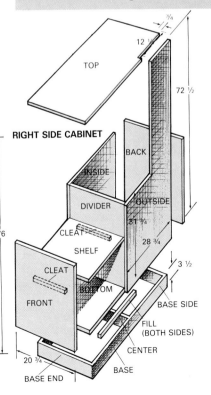

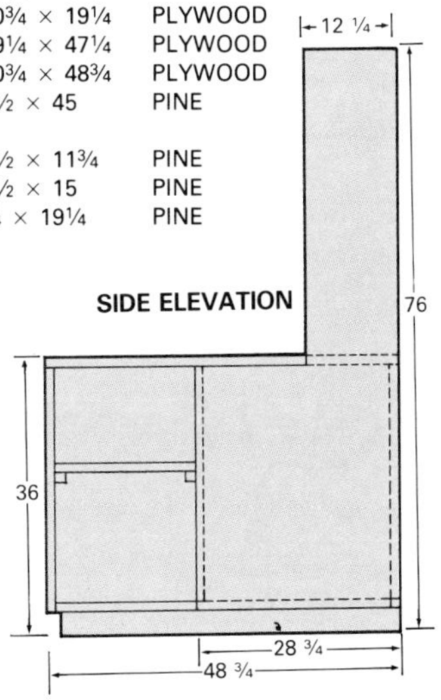

utility storage

Utility storage areas eliminate clutter and let you find items fast. Those spare windshield-wiper blades, for example, should be stowed with other car accessories, not buried behind paint cans. Storage centers can also keep dangerous items—poisons, caustic cleaners, power tools—away from curious children and pets.

These two clever storage centers, built for us by the American Plywood Association, are easy to construct, and will help in organizing your shop, basement, or garage.

One storage center, illustrated at right, is a freestanding shelf unit. This design uses the shelving's own weight and load to hold the unit firmly against a wall. Follow the plans pro-

vided to cut three 6½-foot-long shelves from a single sheet of plywood.

The second design, shown below, is a childproof storage center on wheels that can double as a mini-workbench. Shallow shelves on one side keep small cans and bottles readily accessible. The perforated-hardboard insert has hooks for paintbrushes or small garden tools. The opposite side of this mobile center has four divided shelves, each almost a foot deep, that provide plenty of room for buckets, air filters, paint trays, and rollers.

Open or closed, the storage center will roll into a corner or push against a wall. The top has more than 4 feet of work surface for quick paint jobs or potting plants. Remove the lock and the unit becomes a toybox. Assembly?

Just build the two boxes and hinge them together—*Bob Wilson*.

MATERIALS LIST

Freestanding shelves
A-C exterior or A-D interior APA grade-trademarked plywood—one 4 × 8 × ¾-inch sheet
Standards and brackets—four 8-foot 2 × 4s
Nails and white glue

Rolling chest
A-C APA grade-trademarked plywood—two 4 × 8 × ½-inch sheets
Perforated hardboard—2 × 4 × ½-inches
36-inch continuous hinge, five industrial rubber-wheel casters, padlock hasp and turnknob, nails, and glue

Rolling Chest

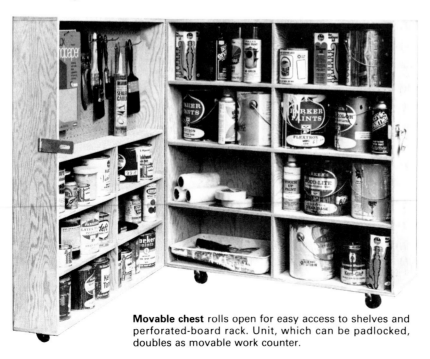

Movable chest rolls open for easy access to shelves and perforated-board rack. Unit, which can be padlocked, doubles as movable work counter.

Freestanding Shelves

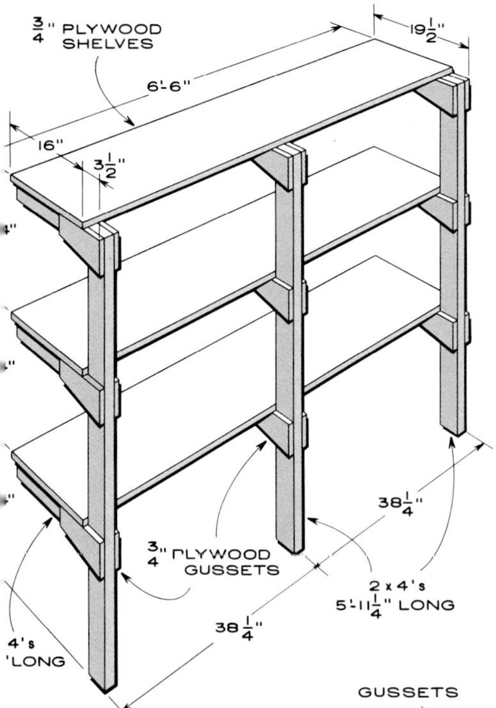

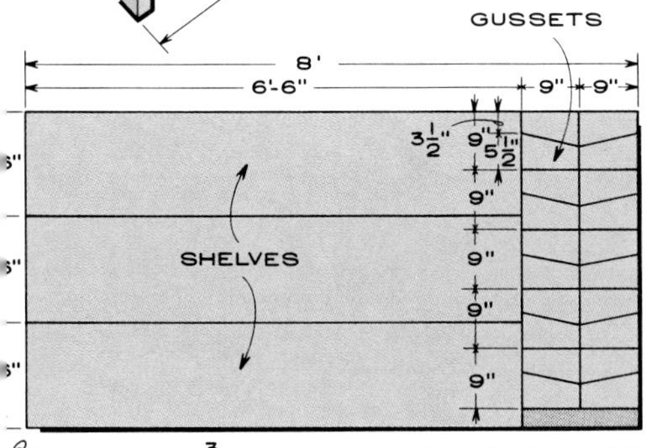

Labels (upper left diagram):
- ¾" PLYWOOD SHELVES
- 6'-6"
- 19½"
- 16"
- 3½"
- 38¼"
- 38¼"
- ¾" PLYWOOD GUSSETS
- 2 x 4's 5'-11¼" LONG
- 4's LONG

Cutting diagram:
- GUSSETS
- 8'
- 6'-6"
- 9" 9"
- 3½"
- 9"
- 5½"
- 9"
- SHELVES
- 9"
- 9"
- 9"
- ¾" PLYWOOD CUTTING DIAGRAM

Instant storage on nearly 20 feet of shelves makes this unit especially handy for a masonry wall. Even when empty, shelves do not need anchoring.

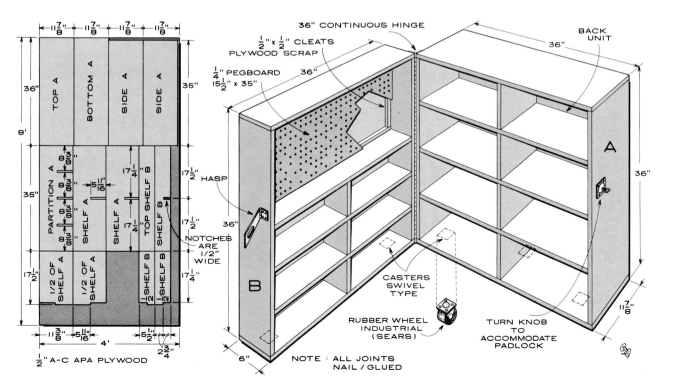

Labels (lower left cutting diagram):
- 11⅞" 11⅞" 11⅞" 11⅞"
- TOP A
- BOTTOM A
- SIDE A
- SIDE A
- 36"
- 8'
- 35"
- 35"
- PARTITION A
- SHELF A
- SHELF A
- TOP SHELF B
- SHELF B
- 8⅜" 8⅜" 8⅜" 8⅜"
- 5 11/16"
- 17¼"
- 17¼"
- 17½"
- 17½"
- ½ OF SHELF A
- ½ OF SHELF A
- ½ SHELF B
- ½ SHELF B
- 17½"
- 17¼"
- 11⅜"
- 5 11/16"
- 4'
- 5½"
- ¾"
- ½" A-C APA PLYWOOD

Labels (right assembly diagram):
- 36" CONTINUOUS HINGE
- BACK UNIT
- ½" x ½" CLEATS PLYWOOD SCRAP
- ¼" PEGBOARD 15½" x 35"
- 36"
- 36"
- 36"
- A
- 36"
- 36"
- B
- HASP
- NOTCHES ARE ½" WIDE
- CASTERS SWIVEL TYPE
- 11⅞"
- RUBBER WHEEL INDUSTRIAL (SEARS)
- TURN KNOB TO ACCOMMODATE PADLOCK
- 6"
- NOTE: ALL JOINTS NAIL / GLUED

modern slat chair

Curved lines fit the contours of your body and sleek design fits any room of your home. A chair like this is so versatile, even the size can be adapted to fit any nook or lined up to make a sofa-like unit for any wall. However, a single chair should be no more than 24 inches wide.

If the chair will be viewed from the side, you may want to select a high-quality plywood, such as oak, or plan to cover it with a fabric that matches or coordinates with draperies. If several chairs will be lined up from wall to wall, a less costly material, such as a lower grade of plywood or a particleboard, would be a good option that would take paint well.

Drawing and Cutting

To start, carefully draw the first side-panel shape on the face side of a sheet of plywood or other building material, using a compass to make the curve of the seat.

Make a rough cut around this piece. It will later be trimmed to the lines you just drew. Now, tightly clamp the rough-cut piece to another part of the plywood sheet so reverse sides are together. Cut both sides of the chair at the same time using a circular saw for the straight sides. Be sure to use a good plywood blade. A saber saw will be needed for the curves. (You'll have the best luck using a saber saw with a splinter guard.)

Each time you move the clamps, make sure the cut sides and grain still match up.

Next, draw the radius for the corner pieces on the 2 × 2 and 2 × 4 material and use a table saw to rough cut the radius of the corner pieces as close to the dimensions on the drawing as possible. Sand the ridges off to make a smooth curve on the corner pieces.

Use the sanded corner pieces to draw the corners on the side pieces and make those curves with the saber saw.

Sand the side-panel edges, then band them with plywood edging. Roll

the tape as you go. Then sand so the edge of the tape is flush with the side of the plywood.

Make the cleats from 1 × 2 and 1 × 4 material. Mark the notches on the cleats with the corner pieces. On the side panels, measure in the width of a 1 × 2 on edge. Precision here is important because the chair slats will fit on top of the cleats. The bottom and back are measured in the width of a 1 × 2 laid flat.

Joining the Parts

Glue and screw or nail the cleats into place. Now connect the rounded 2 × 2 and 2 × 4 corner pieces to one side panel and then the other. Measure between the side panels for the back and bottom pieces. Glue and nail or screw these pieces on.

Cut chair slats, and sand them on one side. Starting at the bottom of the chair, glue and nail them on (sanded side out), working your way to the top

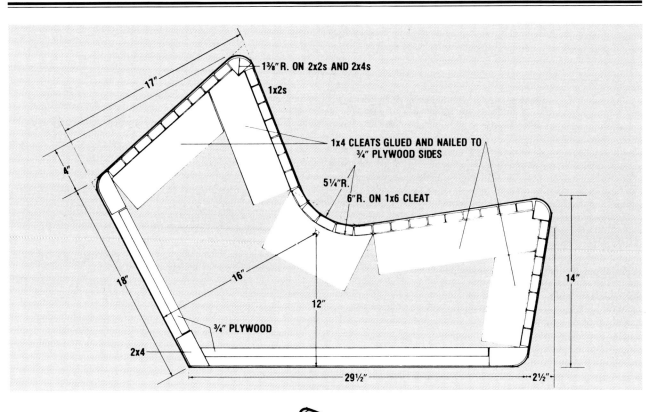

of the chair. As you near the top of the chair, measure carefully so you can trim a little off of several slats if the remaining space doesn't divide precisely. Put slats on the top of chair, working from the back. Again, measure carefully as you near the placement of the final slats.

Adding the Finishing Touches

Fill nail holes. Paint or stain. Add large pillows or a cushion that will be comfortable for sitting.

Add an Ottoman for Real Relaxation

Lean back, relax and put your feet up on the classy ottoman that matches your new chairs. Directions for the ottoman are the same as for the chair—only easier. The cleats and the slats will go on top, bottom, front, and back of the ottoman. For design coordination (and added comfort), top the ottoman with a cushion that matches the chair's pillows—*Courtesy of Georgia-Pacific Corporation.*

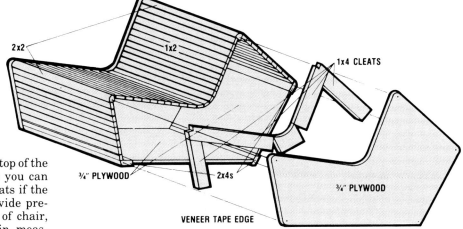

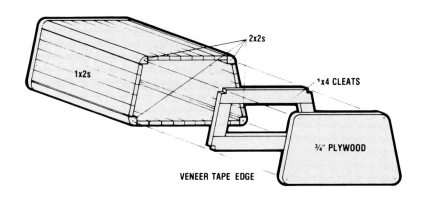

an affordable sauna

Do you drag home from work each evening, not an ounce of energy left in you? Does winter's cold seep so deeply in your bones you forget what it's like to be delightfully warm? This project offers the perfect panacea for these problems: A do-it-yourself indoor sauna.

The design costs over 85 percent less than comparable commercial units, yet can perform every bit as well. Instead of the many thousands you might expect to pay for a stripped-down sauna kit (one with no lights, benches, or bucket and ladle), the total cost to build your sauna, *including* the heater and all the luxuries that make it an efficient and comfortable room, is under $2000.

The sauna is framed with 2 × 4s, then insulated, drywalled, and paneled inside with tongue-and-groove cedar. (You can substitute redwood if it's more readily available or less expensive in your area.) This sauna is carefully designed to be tight enough so very little heat escapes through unseen cracks or crevices, but not so tight that the air quality inside will suffer. Also, careful use of materials helps to hold down costs. The door pulls, for example, are really trowel handles picked up at a local hardware store.

On these pages are listed materials needed, overall dimensions, and the basic construction steps for building the sauna. Blueprints, step-by-step illustrations, and instructions are available from: Project File #500, Box 155, Emmaus, PA 18049.

Construction

1. Frame the sauna's walls and ceiling with kiln-dried spruce 2 × 4s and 12d common nails.

2. CAUTION: All wiring must meet code specifications. Install the light fixture and switch box flush with the plane of the finished wall. Complete all rough wiring for the light, its switch, and the sauna heater. (All finish wiring will be completed after the drywall and paneling are installed.) Instructions for mounting the sauna heater are included in the owner's manual.

3. Install 3½"-thick × 15"-wide foil-faced insulation with the foil facing the inside of the sauna in the wall and ceiling frames. Staple the insulation in place.

4. Fasten ½"-thick drywall to the interior and exterior of the walls and ceiling. Apply tape and joint compound to all joints.

5. Panel the sauna's interior walls and ceiling with kiln-dried, V-joint, tongue-and-groove, clear cedar 1 × 6s. Lay out and cut an opening for the electrical box. Install filler pieces along the door's frame.

6. The following sauna accessories are built from kiln-dried redwood 1 × 4s and 2 × 4s:
Benches: Cut and assemble the frame of the upper bench (18" × 77¾") and the lower bench (24" × 77¾"). Fasten 1" × 3" slats to the top of each frame for the seat surface. Fasten supports to the walls at each end of the sauna with ⅜" × 4" lag bolts to hold the benches in place.
Backrest: Assemble the backrest using two triangular 4" × 18½" sides, one 2¼" × 12¾" back and seven 2½" × 15" top slats.
Duck board: Assemble the duck board by fastening nine 2¼" × 44" slats to the tops of three 4½" × 23½" bottom support members.

7. A sauna door can be purchased ready to install. To cut costs, we built our own 2' × 6' insulated door. Frame the door with cedar 1 × 2s. Install rigid polystyrene insulation in the frame.

Safety Tips

1. We recommend that elderly persons, pregnant women, and people with heart conditions or high blood pressure consult a physician before using a sauna.

2. The sauna's door should swing out from the sauna. The door handle must be made of wood and no locking device should be used. Allow a ¾" airspace at the base of the door for ventilation.

3. Use only galvanized nails in the sauna, and be sure each is countersunk and filled.

4. Do not apply any finish to the wood surfaces in the sauna's interior.

5. Use only tempered insulating glass or clear sheet polycarbonate for the sauna's window.

6. Do not use carpeting on the sauna's floor.

7. Use only a vaporproof light fixture.

8. Avoid using any sapwood; the sap can heat up and cause burns.

9. Unless you're a skilled do-it-your-selfer, leave the electrical installations to a qualified electrician.

10. Most building codes insist that the sauna heater have a thermostat and 60-minute timer.

Fasten ³⁄₁₆" lauan plywood to both sides of the door frame. Cover the door's interior plywood surface with tongue-and-groove interior siding. Finish the exterior plywood door surface with filler and paint. Attach hinges (including one spring hinge) and door pulls. Construct the jamb, stop, and trim of the door of ¾" inch clear cedar.

8. The window's jamb, stop, and trim are also constructed from ¾"-inch clear cedar. Install a 10½" × 52½"

Thermopane window and ⅛" × 1" blocks to hold the glazing securely in place.

9. Install interior and exterior clear cedar trim as needed.

10. Install the sauna heater. Construct a heater guard of clear cedar 1 × 3s to protect bathers from accidental contact with the heater.

Reprinted by permission of Rodale's *PRACTICAL HOMEOWNER* magazine.

MATERIALS LIST

Insulation	
Door	One 1½" × 24" × 96" sheet extruded polystyrene
Ceiling and walls	Two 75'-long rolls 3½" × 15" foil-faced insulation
Walls	Six ½" × 48" × 96"-drywall panels
Door	One ³⁄₁₆" × 48" × 96" sheet lauan plywood
Window	10½" × 52½"-tempered Thermopane
Framing	Forty-three 8'-long spruce 2 × 4s
Benches and posts	Seven 8'-long redwood 2 × 4s
Jambs	Four 8'-long clear cedar 1 × 6s
Paneling and door siding	Sixty 8'-long T & G clear cedar 1 × 6s
Benches, backrest, duck board, heater guard, stops, and trim	Forty 8'-long clear cedar 1 × 3s

Sauna heater available from many sources, including Sears, Roebuck, & Co.

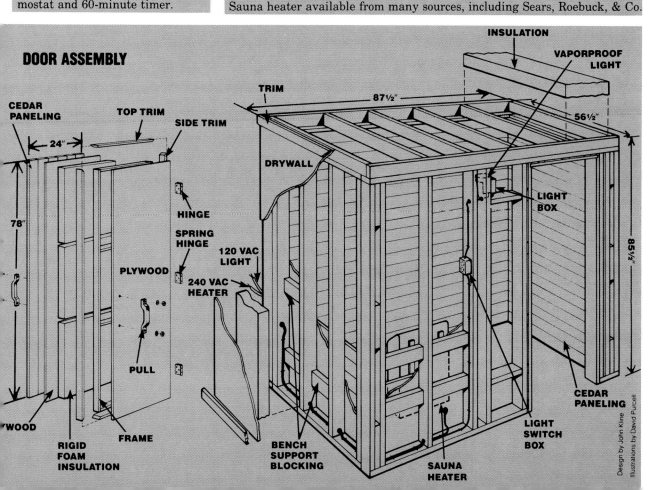

DOOR ASSEMBLY

CEDAR PANELING — TOP TRIM — SIDE TRIM — 24" — HINGE — SPRING HINGE — PLYWOOD — PULL — 78" — WOOD — RIGID FOAM INSULATION — FRAME

INSULATION — VAPORPROOF LIGHT — TRIM — 87½" — 56½" — DRYWALL — LIGHT BOX — 85½" — 120 VAC LIGHT — 240 VAC HEATER — CEDAR PANELING — BENCH SUPPORT BLOCKING — SAUNA HEATER — LIGHT SWITCH BOX

Design by John Kline
Illustrations by David Purcell

shop tool storage units

H ere's a complete tool organizer for your home shop. The system consists of a 30 × 60-inch, wall-mounted cabinet above a cabinet with drawers. Some of its advantages:

1. The drawer section can be constructed small enough so it takes up no more room than a modest-sized workbench. But, if you have room, it can be made much larger.

2. Although, when it is closed, the box cabinet, uses only 10 square feet of wall space, when it is open, it provides 40 square feet of storage—and that's not even counting the front faces.

3. Either unit may be mounted separately.

4. Fold-out doors of the box cabinet (it is a modification of a tall kitchen cabinet) can be used to group tools according to the type of work for which they will be used. For example, I devote one entire section to router bits and accessories and another to woodwork measurement.

5. When the cabinet is open, tools are both visible and accessible. When it is closed, the tools are kept clean and dust-free.

6. Somewhat larger tools and bulkier supplies can be stored in the slide-mounted drawers of the lower section.

7. Neither piece is difficult to construct, and both use standard plywood as the basic material.

8. You may build both units at one time, or either unit at any time, depending upon your storage requirements and the time you have to devote to the project.

Drawer cabinets

The drawer sections may be built any length down to a minimum of two drawer widths. The 16-foot-long drawer unit shown—it was decided upon because enough space was available for it—took two full lengths of plywood.

Start by building the platform from 1 × 4 stock to provide a toe space and a level base for the cabinet. Assemble the box-frame platform, and level. You can do this either by scribing and trimming down the high spots, or by wedging up the low ones with undercourse shakes (these do the job as well as finish shake siding, and they cost a lot less).

Next, cut out the drawer section dividers, top and bot-

When top cabinet is open, tools are visible and easily accessible. Slide-mounted drawers of lower section are used for large tools. Both units are easy to construct and are primarily made of plywood. See the exploded view of cabinet.

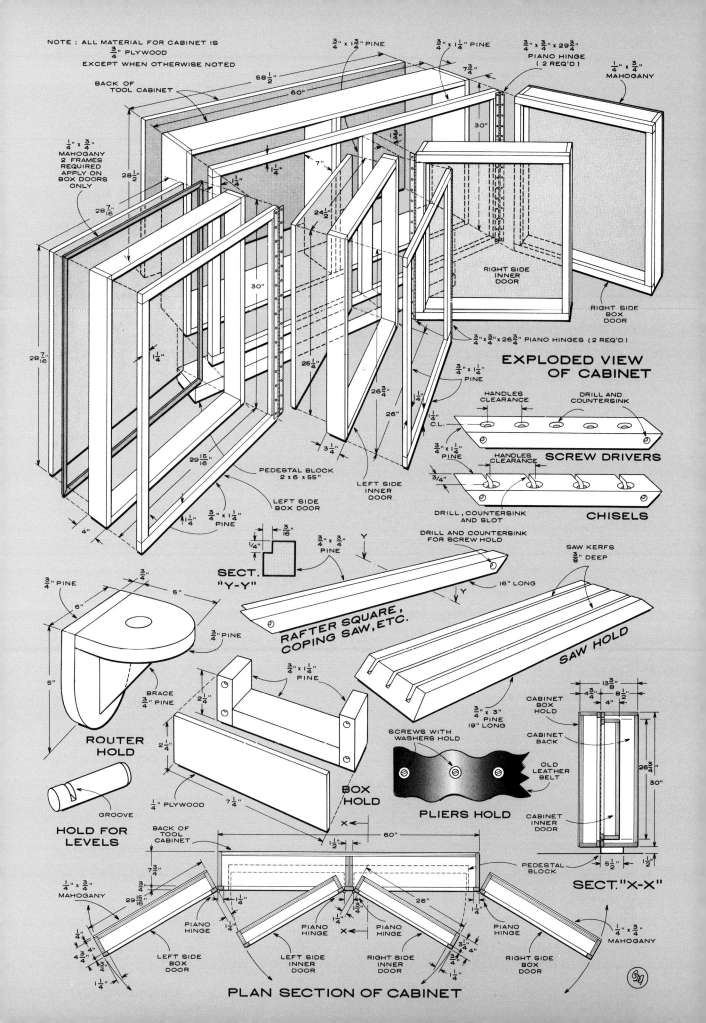

NOTE : ALL MATERIAL FOR CABINET IS $\frac{3}{4}$" PLYWOOD
EXCEPT WHEN OTHERWISE NOTED

$\frac{3}{4}$" x 1$\frac{3}{4}$" PINE

$\frac{3}{4}$" x 1$\frac{1}{4}$" PINE

$\frac{3}{4}$" x $\frac{3}{4}$" x 29$\frac{3}{4}$"
PIANO HINGE
(2 REQ'D)

$\frac{1}{4}$" x $\frac{3}{4}$"
MAHOGANY

BACK OF
TOOL CABINET

58$\frac{1}{2}$"

60"

7$\frac{3}{4}$"

30"

$\frac{1}{4}$" x $\frac{3}{4}$"
MAHOGANY
2 FRAMES
REQUIRED
APPLY ON
BOX DOORS
ONLY

28$\frac{1}{2}$"

28$\frac{7}{16}$"

1$\frac{1}{4}$"

1$\frac{1}{4}$"

7"

24$\frac{1}{2}$"

RIGHT SIDE
INNER
DOOR

RIGHT SIDE
BOX
DOOR

28$\frac{7}{16}$"

30"

1$\frac{1}{4}$"

25$\frac{1}{4}$"

26$\frac{3}{4}$"

26"

$\frac{3}{4}$" x $\frac{3}{4}$" x 26$\frac{3}{4}$" PIANO HINGES (2 REQ'D)

$\frac{3}{4}$" x 1$\frac{1}{4}$"
PINE

EXPLODED VIEW
OF CABINET

HANDLES
CLEARANCE

DRILL AND
COUNTERSINK

29$\frac{15}{16}$"

4"

3$\frac{1}{4}$"

1$\frac{1}{4}$"

1$\frac{1}{4}$"

$\frac{3}{4}$" x 1$\frac{1}{4}$"
PINE

C.L.

SCREW DRIVERS

$\frac{3}{4}$" x 1$\frac{1}{4}$"
PINE

HANDLES
CLEARANCE

$\frac{3}{4}$"

PEDESTAL BLOCK
2 x 6 x 55"

LEFT SIDE
INNER
DOOR

DRILL, COUNTERSINK
AND SLOT

CHISELS

LEFT SIDE
BOX DOOR

$\frac{3}{16}$"

$\frac{1}{4}$"

$\frac{3}{4}$

$\frac{3}{4}$" x $\frac{3}{4}$"
PINE

Y

DRILL AND COUNTERSINK
FOR SCREW HOLD

DRILL AND COUNTERSINK
FOR SCREW HOLD

SAW KERFS
$\frac{3}{8}$" DEEP

$\frac{3}{4}$" PINE

$\frac{3}{4}$

5"

6"

$\frac{3}{4}$" PINE

SECT.
"Y-Y"

16" LONG

13$\frac{3}{8}$"

4$\frac{3}{4}$"

8$\frac{1}{2}$"

5"

RAFTER SQUARE,
COPING SAW, ETC.

Y

CABINET
BOX
HOLD

4"

BRACE
$\frac{3}{4}$" PINE

$\frac{3}{4}$" x 1$\frac{1}{4}$"
PINE

SAW HOLD

CABINET
BACK

26$\frac{3}{4}$"

ROUTER
HOLD

2$\frac{1}{4}$"

2$\frac{1}{4}$"

$\frac{3}{4}$" x 3"
PINE
19" LONG

SCREWS WITH
WASHERS HOLD

OLD
LEATHER
BELT

30"

GROOVE

$\frac{1}{4}$" PLYWOOD

7$\frac{1}{4}$"

BOX
HOLD

PLIERS HOLD

CABINET
INNER
DOOR

HOLD FOR
LEVELS

BACK OF
TOOL
CABINET

X

60"

$\frac{1}{2}$"

PEDESTAL
BLOCK

5$\frac{1}{2}$"

$\frac{1}{2}$"

SECT."X-X"

7$\frac{3}{4}$"

$\frac{1}{4}$" x $\frac{3}{4}$"
MAHOGANY

$\frac{3}{4}$

29$\frac{15}{16}$"

$\frac{3}{4}$

1$\frac{1}{4}$"

1$\frac{1}{4}$"

26"

$\frac{1}{4}$" x $\frac{3}{4}$"
MAHOGANY

$\frac{1}{4}$"

$\frac{1}{4}$"

$\frac{3}{4}$

$\frac{3}{4}$

$\frac{1}{4}$"

1$\frac{1}{4}$"

PIANO
HINGE

PIANO
HINGE

X

PIANO
HINGE

PIANO
HINGE

PIANO
HINGE

$\frac{3}{4}$

$\frac{3}{4}$

1$\frac{1}{4}$"

LEFT SIDE
BOX
DOOR

LEFT SIDE
INNER
DOOR

RIGHT SIDE
INNER
DOOR

RIGHT SIDE
BOX
DOOR

PLAN SECTION OF CABINET

tom. Then notch the dividers for the 1 × 3 and 1 × 4 horizontal stiffeners, but note that the front stiffeners are joined to the dividers with half laps (half the notch in the divider and half in the stiffener).

With a rafter square, carefully lay out the tops and bottoms to receive the dividers—when the drawers are installed with their slides, you should have a ½-inch space between each drawer side and its respective divider. This will ensure proper sliding action.

Mark off the half lap notches on the front stiffeners, using the top or bottom layout as a pattern. After cutting all notches, assemble the complete drawer sections and mount them to the platform. Apply border trim to the top to hide all raw edges.

Cut out all drawer parts and machine in the rabbets and grooves with a table saw or router. Assemble the box drawers, except for the face fronts, being careful to keep everything square. Next, lay out the drawer-pull screw holes and drill the large screw clearance holes in the front members. These will provide room for the screwheads, which mount the drawer pulls to the face fronts that will be installed shortly.

Now install the drawer sides according to the manufacturer's instructions. Then line up the face fronts on the drawers, mark their locations on the rear, and screw them in place. Mark and drill the face fronts for the No. 10 pull-mounting screws. Remove all hardware, identify the drawers and their respective openings, and apply your favorite finish. When the finish is dry, install all the hardware and the drawers in their proper places.

Wall-mounted cabinet

The wall-mounted cabinet is basically a divided box frame with both external and internal doors, continu-

Each fold-out door can be used to group tools according to work they're used for.

Wall-mounted box cabinet requires only 10 square feet when it is closed; open, it provides 40 square feet of storage.

ously hinged. The entire structure is made of ¾-inch plywood, with pine edging to cover the raw edges and provide solid screw-mounting surfaces for the doors. There's a little mahogany trim on the outer door edges for cosmetic purposes.

Cut out the pieces, assemble them, and add the pine edging. Sand these assemblies and apply your finish. Mount the divided box frame to the wall, using a bottom cleat if no drawer section is to be fitted beneath, or with a 2 × 4 or 2 × 6 to raise it off the top if a drawer cabinet is used.

Hinge all doors and mount magnetic latches for the outer doors only. Note that the inner doors can fold out to cover the opposite half of the divided box. Add the mahogany trim to the outer door edges.

Some of the devices shown for stor-

ing various tools may suit your purposes, but if not, here's a great chance to let your imagination run freely. Plan the tool panels according to the type of work you do most frequently. Just be careful to place the "thicker" tools where they won't conflict with anything else on the opposing surface when the doors are closed. Spring clips, leather pieces, dowels, slotted wood, ledges, and door sides and bottoms themselves can hold tools. For greatest efficiency, place the cabinet under an existing light or, if necessary, add one—*Bernard Price*.

Manufacturers

Cabinet material: Georgia Pacific plywood, ¾-inch AD Interior
Tools: Sears, Roebuck & Co.
Drawer slides: Grant Hardware
Drawer pulls, backing plates: Amerock Corp.

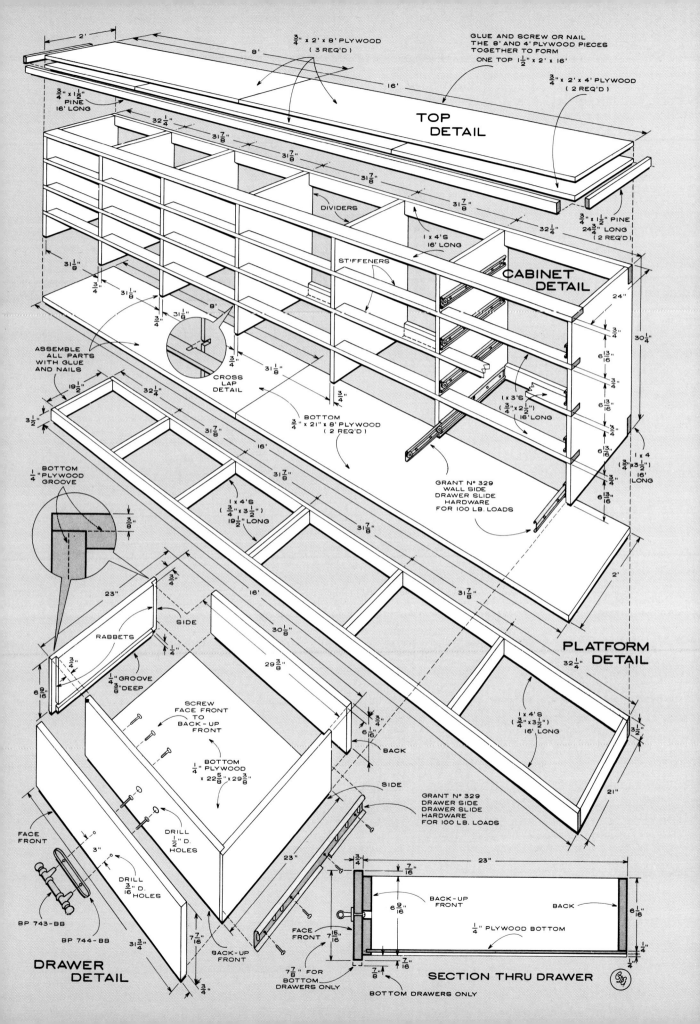

three redwood gazebos

Whether you use it as a place to entertain, as a garden shed or poolside cabana, or merely as a shady retreat from the summer sun, a backyard shelter makes an enticing addition to any home. An octagonal gazebo with latticework painted white is an American tradition, but these variations—designed and built by Homecrafters of California for homes in Fresno—show how tradition can be updated.

That customary white treatment must be renewed every few seasons to prevent decay. Today's chemically treated woods will stand up to outdoor conditions for many years. But garden-grade redwood is naturally resistant to insects and decay—and dimensionally stable. These qualities, combined with its warm and rustic visual appeal, make redwood a natural choice for garden and poolside shelters.

The California Redwood Assn. lists four garden grades of redwood; these are less expensive than the architectural grades but have knots and are not kiln-dried. Construction heart and merchantable heart grades contain no

Curved Pool Pavilion

sapwood, and thus are recommended for structural members and for use in or near the ground. Construction common and merchantable grades, which do have sapwood streaks, are good choices for decking, fencing, trellises, and similar uses. Merchantable grades contain larger knots than construction grades. The wood will weather differently depending on the finish. Unfinished, it will gradually turn gray; with a water repellent applied, the wood will stabilize at tan; to keep its red tone, you'd have to apply a deck stain—*By Daniel Ruby. Photos by Karl Riek. Drawings by Eugene Thompson*

Three inviting shelters are variations of basic post-and-beam design. Curved pool pavilion (left) has a flat slatted roof and airy crisscross latticework. A side door opens into the house. Classic garden gazebo (right) takes on a rustic look when built with garden-grade, knot-patterned redwood. Its shingled pyramid roof keeps out rain; lattice walls screen the sun. Angular pool shelter (below) has a shed-type slat roof that leaves part of the diagonal deck exposed to sun, part shaded.

Garden Gazebo

Angular Pool Shelter

CURVED POOL PAVILION

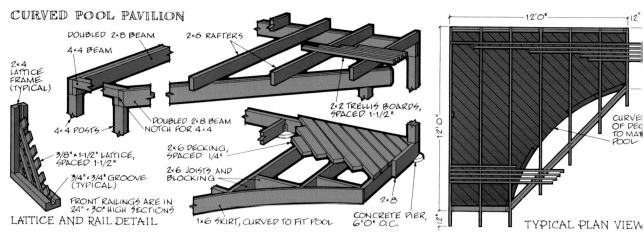

2×4 LATTICE FRAME (TYPICAL)

DOUBLED 2×8 BEAM

4×4 BEAM

2×6 RAFTERS

4×4 POSTS

DOUBLED 2×8 BEAM NOTCH FOR 4×4

3/8" × 1-1/2" LATTICE, SPACED 1-1/2"

3/4" × 3/4" GROOVE (TYPICAL)

FRONT RAILINGS ARE IN 24" × 30" HIGH SECTIONS

2×2 TRELLIS BOARDS, SPACED 1-1/2"

2×6 DECKING, SPACED 1/4"

2×6 JOISTS AND BLOCKING

2×8

LATTICE AND RAIL DETAIL

1×6 SKIRT, CURVED TO FIT POOL

CONCRETE PIER, 6'0" O.C.

12'0"   12"

12'0"

CURVE OF DEC TO MA POOL

TYPICAL PLAN VIEW

GARDEN GAZEBO

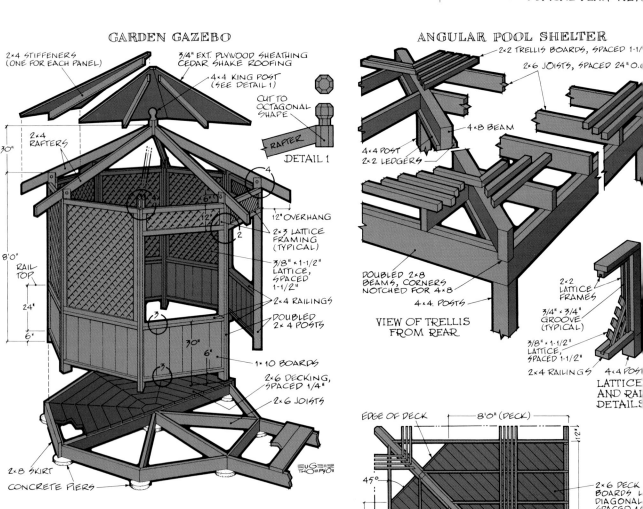

2×4 STIFFENERS (ONE FOR EACH PANEL)

3/4" EXT. PLYWOOD SHEATHING CEDAR SHAKE ROOFING

4×4 KING POST (SEE DETAIL 1)

CUT TO OCTAGONAL SHAPE

RAFTER

DETAIL 1

2×4 RAFTERS

30"

8'0"

RAIL TOP

24"

6"

12" OVERHANG

2×3 LATTICE FRAMING (TYPICAL)

3/8" × 1-1/2" LATTICE, SPACED 1-1/2"

2×4 RAILINGS

DOUBLED 2×4 POSTS

30"

6"

1×10 BOARDS

2×6 DECKING, SPACED 1/4"

2×6 JOISTS

2×8 SKIRT

CONCRETE PIERS

EUGENE THOMPSON

ANGULAR POOL SHELTER

2×2 TRELLIS BOARDS, SPACED 1-1/

2×6 JOISTS, SPACED 24" O.

4×8 BEAM

4×4 POST
2×2 LEDGERS

DOUBLED 2×8 BEAMS, CORNERS NOTCHED FOR 4×8

4×4 POSTS

VIEW OF TRELLIS FROM REAR

2×2 LATTICE FRAMES

3/4" × 3/4" GROOVE (TYPICAL)

3/8" × 1-1/2" LATTICE, SPACED 1-1/2"

2×4 RAILINGS   4×4 POST

LATTICE AND RAIL DETAILS

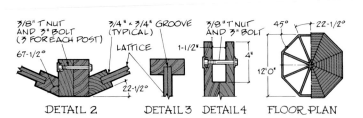

3/8" T NUT AND 3" BOLT (3 FOR EACH POST)

67-1/2°

3/4" × 3/4" GROOVE (TYPICAL)

LATTICE

22-1/2°

1-1/2"

3/8" T NUT AND 3" BOLT

4"

45°   22-1/2°

12'0"

DETAIL 2   DETAIL 3   DETAIL 4   FLOOR PLAN

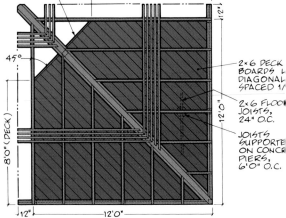

EDGE OF DECK

8'0" (DECK)

12"

45°

8'0" (DECK)

12'0"

2×6 DECK BOARDS L DIAGONAL SPACED 1/

2×6 FLOO JOISTS, 24" O.C.

JOISTS SUPPORTE ON CONCR PIERS, 6'0" O.C.

12"   12'0"

TYPICAL PLAN VIEW

latticework bench

The arresting, striped-and-slatted look of this corner bench is achieved by spacing the redwood structural members with thinner stock. The idea is practical, too, since it allows fast drainage and drying after a rain. (The same technique can be applied to a straight version as shown in the first sketch. For a materials list, write California Redwood Assn., 591 Redwood Hwy., Mill Valley, Calif. 94941.)

For the latticework top, first rough-cut to length six 2 × 4s for each "wing" of the bench (note how they lap at the corner). Next, cut all spacers from 1 × 4 stock in the two lengths shown. To assemble the herringbone corner, nail up a 90-degree work frame of two long, straight 2 × 4s with a cross brace. Working on the outside of this frame, butt-join the shortest 2 × 4s and the six-inch corner spacers as shown. Nail from the face of both corner spacers into the end of the lapping 2 × 4, using 16-penny nails. Next, nail the three 12 inch spacers to the faces of the 2 × 4s, using 10-penny nails. Proceed with the next pair of 2 × 4s and their spacers, using 16-penny nails throughout, but alternating the triangular nailing pattern through the spacers. Repeat this procedure with four more pairs of 2 × 4s.

At the outer bench corner, trim down one spacer as shown so the projecting leg insert will snug under it after this spacer is nailed flush with the top edge of the last 2 × 4s.

When assembly is complete, trim the open ends of the 2 × 4s even and proceed with the outer frame. For the butt-joined version shown at the left end of the assembly sketch (and in the sketch of the straight version), cut the end 2 × 4s the width of the latticework, including outer spacers. Attach these to each 2 × 4 end with one 16-penny nail, in a zigzag pattern. Next, trim four side-frame members to lap the end frame, and attach with three nails per bench spacer plus two nails into each frame end.

For legs, assemble pairs of 14½-inch 2 × 6s with spacers as shown. Place the four-inch spacer flush with the foot and the six-inch spacer projecting two inches above the top. Clamp the assembly, and drill one center hole per spacer. Insert a ¼-by-four inch carriage bolt, snugging it up with a washer and nut on the inside face. Now, fit the leg projection into an end slot so that the leg's 2 × 6s are flush with the ends of the bench. Join the leg to the bench top with right-angle brackets. (There's no projection at the top of the inside corner leg; attach with six corner angles, as shown.)

Finish with two coats of water repellent, two weeks apart.

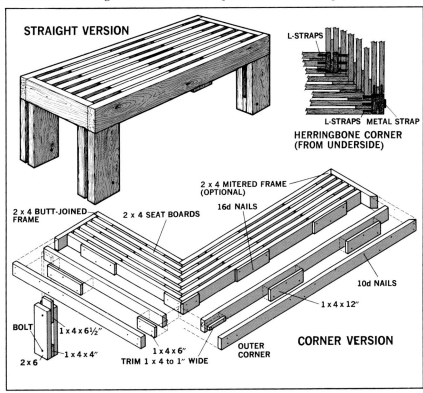

Expensive-looking bench is actually crafted from garden-grade redwood. This has more knots and sap streaks than top grades but is nearly as durable.

bi-level outdoor living

This deck, designed to add convenient outdoor living space to a bi-level home, offers direct access to its 40-foot length from the kitchen, family room, and master bedroom. Cantilevered 8½ feet above a garden patio, the deck is a lofty vantage point with a splendid view of neighboring gardens. Yet the alternating boards forming the balustrade of the deck afford the owners complete privacy.

Supported on a wood girder by five Lally columns, the deck shades a pleasant underdeck recreation area for garden living and dining. Tables and flower shelves attached to the columns and "look-outs" (supports for hanging plants) are practical, beautiful design features.

An aluminum spiral staircase preserves the light, suspended-in-air feeling created by cantilevering: a conventional staircase would have spoiled this with a space-consuming assembly of 4 × 4 posts.

The plans shown here include all details and specifications for erecting the deck. Construction Heart grade redwood was used. Here is the construction schedule:
● Install the Lally columns approximately 12 inches deep in concrete footing. Allow three or four weeks for concrete to cure.
● Fasten girder to top plates of Lallys with ¼-inch galvanized lag screws, 3 inches long.
● Place and fasten the *bottom* of the 2 × 8½-inch higher than the *top* of the girder ledger to give the deck a slight pitch for run-off.
● Assemble joists and joist blocking with 2 × 8 joist hangers at the ledger and 10d hot-dipped galvanized nails at the girder. (Joists were cut from 10-foot lengths to 9 feet, 1½ inches to provide blocking of 10½ inches between joists.)
● After placing the 2 × 8 header and 2 × 4 railing posts, cut 1 × 6 bracing

into the tops of joists where shown on plan.
● Lay 2 × 6 decking with 10d button-head galvanized nails and assemble railing as shown.
● Assembly and erection of spiral staircase requires three or four hours, including fastening to patio and deck. The staircase is made by Columns Inc., Pearland, TX 77581.
● "Look-outs" used to support hanging plants are 18-to-25-inch long 2 × 4s capped with half-round waste from Lally column tables. They are fastened between the railing posts with wedges

under the lower 3½-inch blocking so they can be easily relocated.
● For a proper deck finish, write California Redwood Association, 1 Lombard Street, San Francisco, CA 94111 and request data sheets (4B1-4) on redwood deck finishes.

Engineering your deck

For the benefit of readers who would like to know the methods and formulas for determining the safe loading of joists, girders, and Lally columns, we include architect Carl De Groote's

*computations for this unique canti-
levered deck.*

The deck is entirely built of redwood, the specific gravity of which is
.374 to .387. The weight of a cubic foot
of water is 62.425 pounds. Therefore,
redwood weighs 62.425 pounds × .387
= 24.158475 pounds per cubic foot, or
2.04 pounds per board foot. (A board
foot is 144 cubic inches.)

A total of 1837 board feet of redwood
was used on this deck. Therefore: 1837
× 2.04 pounds = 3747.481 pounds.
The size of the deck is 40 × 9½ feet
= 380 square feet. Weight per square
foot is 3748 ÷ 380 = 9.9 pounds or 10
pounds.

Thus the dead load (weight of the
structure itself) is 10 pounds per
square foot. This is a weight advantage. If fir were used (weight: 34

pounds per cubic foot), the dead load
per square foot would be 14 pounds—
for a total dead load of 5320 pounds.
Being light in weight and high in resistance to decay and insect attack,
redwood qualifies as a most desirable
material for outdoor construction,
such as a deck.

The cantilevered area of the deck is
4½ feet wide. A deck should be designed for a live load of 40 pounds per
square foot—in addition to the 10
pounds per square foot dead load.
Therefore, the load per running foot
on the cantilevered section will be 4½
× 50 pounds = 225 pounds. As the
floor joists are to be spaced 1 foot, center to center, this will also be the load
to be supported by an overhanging
joist. This load could be considered to
be uniformly distributed over the 4½-

foot length of unsupported joist or
could be concentrated at the free end
of the deck. One man standing at the
railing could equal that load.

For a 2 × 8 joist, fixed at one end
and loaded at the other, the safe load
in pounds is equal to the width of the
joist multiplied by the square of the
depth of the joist times 55.6. This total
is then divided by four times the
length of feet cantilevered. The 55.6
is a structural quality value. For
Douglas Fir and S. L. Yellow Pine it
is 66.7. For West Coast Hemlock common it is also 55.6. However, for East-
ern Hemlock common it is only 44.

Thus the safe load in pounds =

$$\frac{1.5 \times 7.25 \times 55.6}{4 \times 4.5} = 243.54 \text{ pounds}$$

243.54 pounds being larger than the 225 pounds required at the free end of joist, indicates that the 2 × 8 joist will suffice to support the 4½-foot cantilevered section of the deck, provided the joists are spaced 12 inches, center to center.

The girder is supported by Lally columns spaced 9 feet, center to center. One half of the area on the deck between the ledger and the girder will be supported by the ledger. But because the loading could occur to a maximum at the center and front

railing of the deck, I prefer to design the girder to be qualified to support the entire deck. Therefore, the segment of deck area to be considered is 9 feet × 9.5 = 85½ square feet and 85½ square feet × 50 pounds = 4275 pounds. This is the load to be carried by the girder between Lally columns. In considering the use of a girder composed of three 2 × 10s, the safe load in pounds is equal to two times the width of the girder multiplied by the square of the length of the girder times 55.6. This total is then to be divided

by the span in feet, or

$$\frac{2 \times 4.5 \times 9.25 \times 55.6}{9}$$

$$= 4757 \text{ pounds}$$

Since 4757 pounds is larger than the 4275 pounds design requirement it is evident that three 2 × 10s will suffice. A 3½-inch Lally column with a maximum unbraced length of 8 feet can

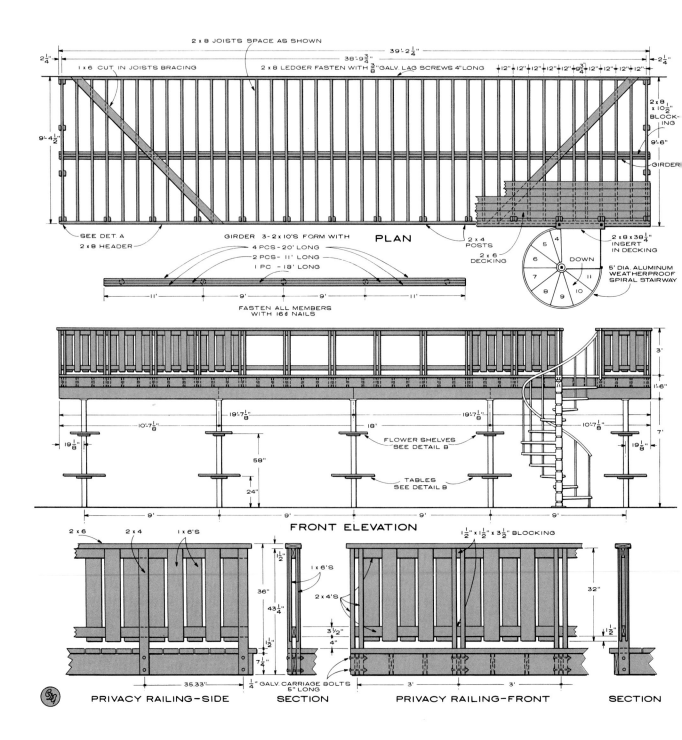

support 32,300 pounds—well in excess of what is needed. The size of the foundation and footing for each Lally column is based on the load in tons per square foot on foundation beds allowed by building codes. In New York City, for example, a load of 1 ton per square foot is allowed on soft or wet clay. A ton being 2000 pounds, an 18×18-inch footing will provide a bearing for 4500 pounds and a 2×2-foot footing will provide a bearing for 8000 pounds—*Carl De Groote*
Photos: Richard Hochman

Raised deck is cantilevered on main girder resting on five Lally columns. This makes possible an open, under-deck patio shaded from midday sun. Redwood tables, attached directly to columns (see plan detail), are convenient for entertaining large groups. The spiral staircase comes knocked-down, can be assembled in a few hours, is attached to deck and concrete. Alternating boards of balustrade provide ventilation and ensure privacy. The deck is cantilevered at midpoint on girder made of three 2×10s. Joists are 2×8s, 12 inches on center. They are connected to 2×8 ledger on house with joist hangers. The railing posts are secured to the joists with carriage bolts.

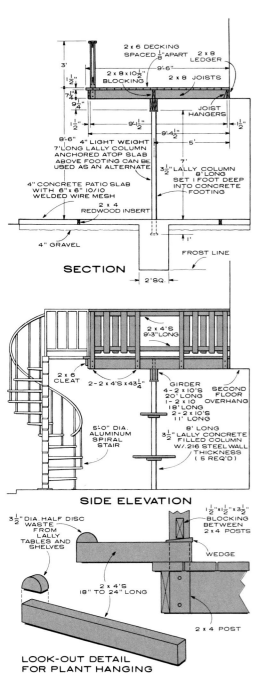

SECTION

SIDE ELEVATION

LOOK-OUT DETAIL FOR PLANT HANGING

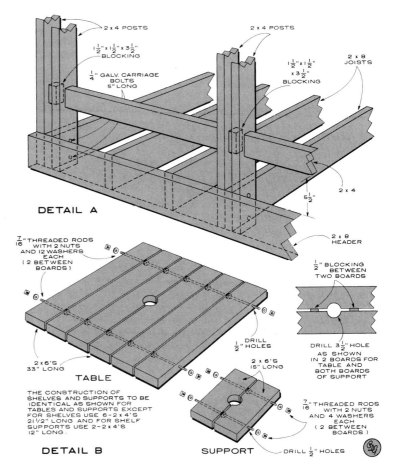

DETAIL A

DETAIL B

TABLE

SUPPORT

modular deck in stages

I s the best-size deck the one you don't have time to build? Or the one you can't afford at the moment? The answer may be to start one that's modular. The design shown here is versatile enough to be built in stages or with parts of it omitted completely, the sum of any of the parts making a useful whole. Among the options are a central barbecue area with storage bins and counter tops, a sun deck, a trellis deck, and a children's play area that allows kids to play within sight of the house. All of the sections are connected by walkways or steps.

The plans were created by Duo-Fast Corp. (3702 River Road, Franklin Park, IL 60131) to demonstrate the feasibility of using its pneumatic nailer and stapler to cut assembly

Barbecue and play decks (right and below) are at extreme left and right in top view above; construction details, next page. Turn page for planter, bench, and dry-sink plans and for assembly sketch of trellis deck. Sun deck and connecting walkway are simple flat platforms.

time of large-scale projects. (Write to the company directly for information on the air-powered tools, or look into local rental.)

You can customize the modules to your house and lot: If you already have a sliding glass door to the back yard, position the modules so this access catches the barbecue deck. The plan, even if built in its entirety, still leaves enough open space for a garden, volleyball net, or small expanse of lawn—*Charles A. Miller.*

BARBECUE DECK

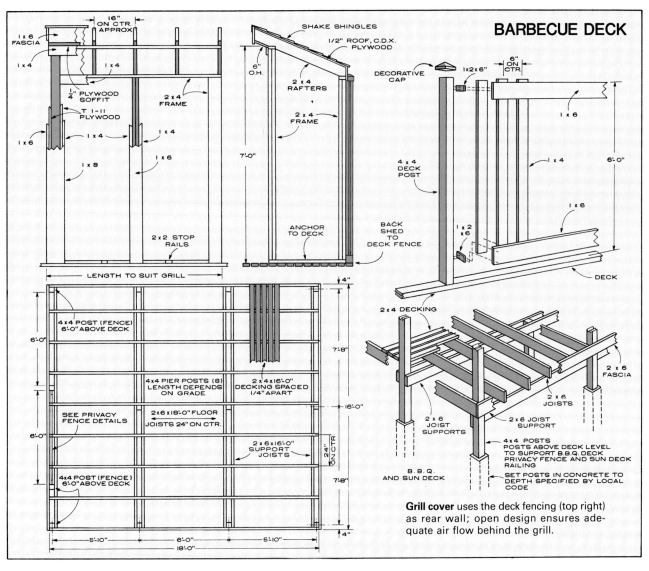

Grill cover uses the deck fencing (top right) as rear wall; open design ensures adequate air flow behind the grill.

KID'S DECK

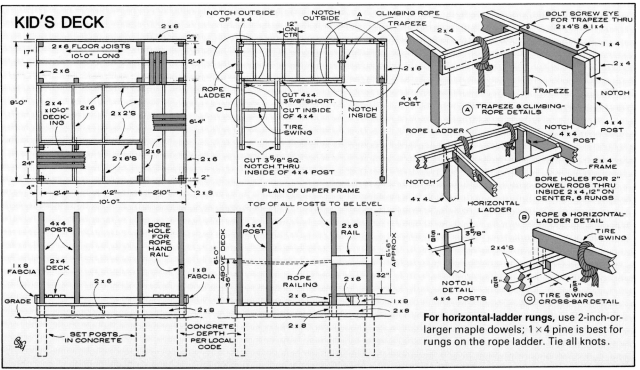

For horizontal-ladder rungs, use 2-inch-or-larger maple dowels; 1 × 4 pine is best for rungs on the rope ladder. Tie all knots.

TRELLIS DECK

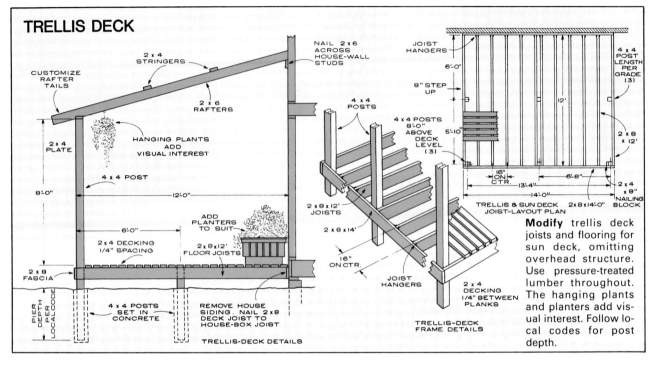

Modify trellis deck joists and flooring for sun deck, omitting overhead structure. Use pressure-treated lumber throughout. The hanging plants and planters add visual interest. Follow local codes for post depth.

PLANTER

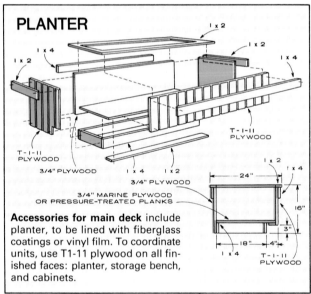

Accessories for main deck include planter, to be lined with fiberglass coatings or vinyl film. To coordinate units, use T1-11 plywood on all finished faces: planter, storage bench, and cabinets.

DRY-SINK STORAGE

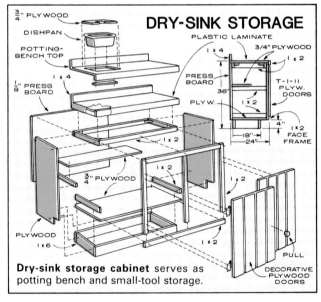

Dry-sink storage cabinet serves as potting bench and small-tool storage.

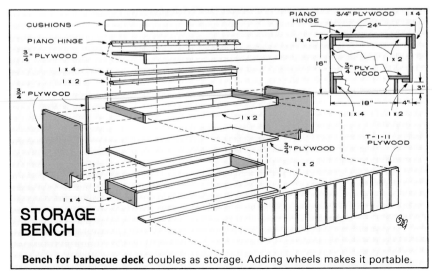

STORAGE BENCH

Bench for barbecue deck doubles as storage. Adding wheels makes it portable.

outdoor seating ideas

Does your landscaping include a place to sit? A convenient and pleasant spot to rest a bit after spading the flower bed? Extra permanent seating for outdoor entertaining? A quiet place to read a book?

Don't overlook using elements of your landscape design as a way to add seating. Put a surface on a retaining wall, for example, or if the wall is too high, divide it into two steps that can be used for sitting. Or surround a tree with a seat. Or make a seat wall of bricks or concrete blocks with caps. Garden seats can be anything from picturesque sections of log or well-placed rocks to sophisticated accessories, perhaps with colorful cushions.

Professional landscape architects almost always include seating in their plans. If you want to add outdoor seating on your property, this portfolio offers a wide range of ideas, some elaborate and some simple—*John Robinson*.

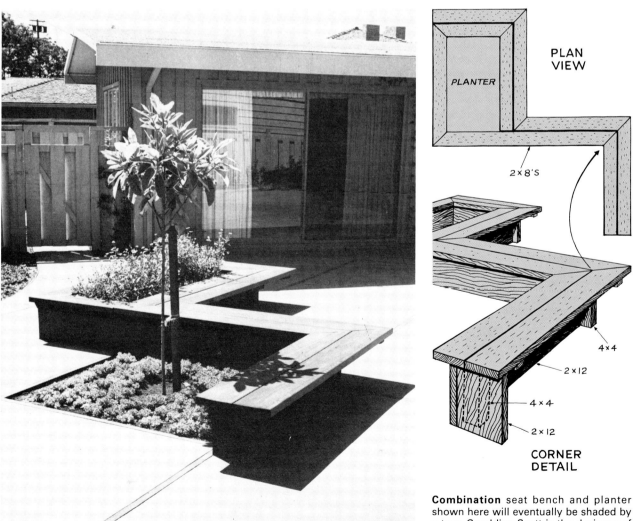

PLAN VIEW

PLANTER

2 × 8'S

4 × 4

2 × 12

4 × 4

2 × 12

CORNER DETAIL

Combination seat bench and planter shown here will eventually be shaded by a tree. Geraldine Scott is the designer of this handsome garden furniture.

The bench shown at left is light, handsome, and strong. It is relatively easy to make with a table saw. The materials (see inset) are 1-inch unsurfaced stock. The legs are sawed all on the same pattern from 1×4s, and a single 1×2 cross brace holds alignment at the bottom (see drawing). A long bolt goes all the way through to hold the legs in place. The bolt can be loosened to fold the legs for storage.

This way for good seats

- Outdoor seating should be located where it will be used. A fancy wrought-iron chair, placed to show it off to best advantage, is likely to be treated like garden sculpture and seldom sat on. And don't locate seats too close to a busy pathway. A seated person should be able to stretch his legs safely, without interfering with someone trying to serve drinks or food.
- Outdoor seating should be sturdy. No one can relax on an unsteady seat. Most pieces shown in this portfolio are made with 2-inch lumber.
- Outdoor seating should be weather-safe. Pads are fine for adding comfort and a touch of color, but they should be waterproof, or easily removed for storage in bad weather.
- Make seats 16 inches off the surface—certainly not less than 14 inches. Too high, and they press painfully across the bottom of the legs; too low, and the sitter's knees stick up in front—particularly awkward when one is juggling a plate of food.
- Make the seating surface wide enough—at least a foot, preferably wider— to be comfortable for even a large person.
- Use lumber surfaced on at least one side to eliminate danger of splinters. Or do some sanding or planing on the seating side.

16"

16 PIECES

BOLT THROUGH,
COUNTER SINK
WASHER

On the opposite page: Far left—This seat, planter, and trellis were designed as a unit by Ned Rucker. Construction around the curve is tangential. Top, near left—At the owner's request the designer, Henry Van Siegman, fashioned this seat to extend back into the planting bed. The homeowner had coil springs and pads made to fit the seat. Bottom, near left—Rustic log seat is made from large utility poles that were carefully ripped down center. The back supports are the same material, fastened from behind before the shrubs were planted. This page: Top—Seat around the tree is made of 2 × 12s, and it requires careful mitering. The seat surface is 2 × 8s with supports hidden. The paving extends under the seat. The designer is Thomas Church. Bottom left— Cantilevered seat is anchored to 4 × 6 timbers, which are fastened down at other end. A part of the load is taken up by the 2 × 4s at the bottom, which thrust against the wall. The design makes it easy to clean under the seat. Bottom right—Attractive low wall creates a raised bed for planting, although it is too low and too narrow for any lengthy sitting. For brick seat walls, figure common brick as 2¼ inches thick, about ½ inch for mortar, so five or six bricks high is right.

The Thomas Church design at top of this page is made of 2 × 12s (including seat surface). Supports are 4 × 4 posts that hold vertical pieces. In addition to providing casual seating, the low walls separate paved area from raw earth around tree. Pictured at bottom of page is a bench that provides auxiliary seating around swimming pool. Bench is a simple, box-type construction of 2 × 6s and 2 × 4s, with lid that lifts up to provide storage for items needed in maintaining the pool. Bench to fit within a curved wall (top, page opposite) is built in sections. Seat surface is 2 × 2s with pieces of 1 × 2 as dividers. Supports are 2 × 8s. Sections are slightly tangential to fit around curve (see construction details). The designer: Robert Babcock. The simple, easily portable bench shown at center of page opposite is made somewhat like a sawhorse; it can provide seating at a picnic table, can be moved out of sun or rain. Robert Babcock also designed the yard furniture shown at the bottom of the page opposite. The landscape architect added the built-in seat and planter to the railing that was required at the edge of the terrace.

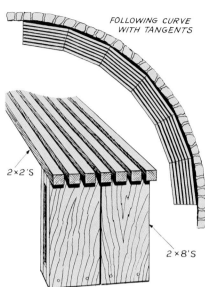

FOLLOWING CURVE
WITH TANGENTS

2×2'S

2×8'S

2×12

1×2

2×4

weatherproof chairs

This simple, clean-lined chair of select heart redwood is used both indoors and at an outdoor dining table at the William L. Russell residence in San Diego, California. It has a framework of 2×2s with 2×2-inch slats for the seat and a 2×6-inch backrest. The seat is 18×21 inches. Height to top of backrest is 28½ inches. Seat support members are routed ½ inch to accept slats. The backrest is slightly canted for comfort. The chair is finished with polyurethane sealer. Mortise and tenon joints are used for all main structural members, and all edges are beveled and sanded. Proper joinery is one evidence of fine cabinet work, and the mortise (rectangular broach) and tenon (tongue that fits mortise) used here is one of the strongest and most popular. Four of the many ways to make this joint are shown here—*George Lyons* and *Bernard Price.*

Design by Designplace, El Cajon, Cal.
Photo by George Lyons

1 Hand Method

After laying out the four-shouldered tenon with a square and marking gauge (near right), cut shoulder stop lines with a back or other fine-toothed saw. Finish tenon by removing waste wood stock from all four sides, down to the shoulder cut (far right), again using a fine-toothed saw. Make square cuts.

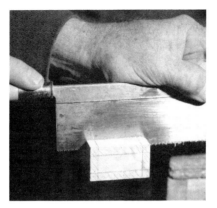

2 Table Saw Method

If you own a table saw, make shoulder stop cuts with blade raised to correct height (near right). Keep piece square with miter head and shoulder cut at the correct depth against the rip fence. To remove waste stock from all four sides (far right), remove miter head and pass stock over blade transversely very rapidly in a reciprocating motion (left and right). Keep blade at same height and the fence acts as a stop.

3 Hand Chisel Method

To make the mortise by hand, lay it out first and, using a mortising chisel (near right), break rectangle into segments. Strike down on the chisel with a wooden mallet and pop out waste in the middle. Let the ends go until last; clean these by striking down on chisel, but with flat side facing end. Mortise should fit tenon with reasonable pressure (far right), but not so tight as to squeeze out assembly glue and leave dry joint.

4 Drilling and Shearing Method

First lay out mortise. Then drill a series of holes along centerline of the rectangle to required depth (near right). This method may be done with bit and brace or a drill guided by Portalign jig. With most waste removed by drilling (far right), clean ends of mortise with a chisel, flat face to end. Clean mortise by shearing long walls down with a broader chisel, flat face toward walls.

easy-to-build outdoor furniture

1. Deck Chair

This easy-to-make chair has a reclining canvas seat; the frame is Simpson clear-grade redwood.

For the frame, you need 2×2 wood as follows: Front legs—four 24-inch lengths. Back legs—four 22½-inch. Arms—four 24-inch. Back—three 23-inch. Front crosspieces—two 23-inch. Leg blocks—two 6-inch.

Materials for the seat: 1½ yards of heavy-duty, 36-inch canvas; #10×2½-inch galvanized wood screws (flathead).

The basic construction method:
• Cut all wood to length.
• Assemble front two legs and crosspieces. Join with waterproof glue, reinforced with countersunk screws. For best appearance, fill all screw holes with wood putty.
• Attach arm pieces to inside of front legs using glue and screw. Make sure all angles are square.
• Glue and screw back pieces to arms, keeping angles square. Attach back legs in same manner. Level legs with front adjuster blocks.

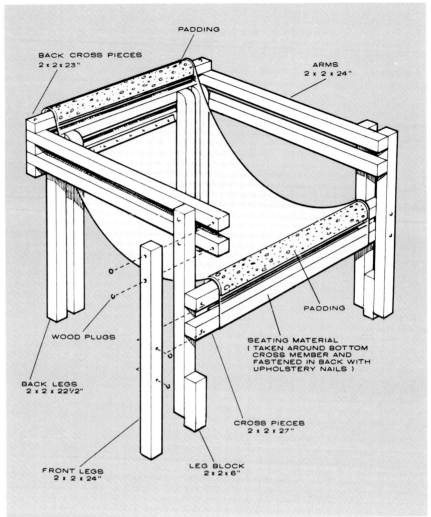

2. Patio Lantern

This unique candleholder can be made of scrap redwood. Upright members are 1⅛ inches square and about 14 inches high. Blocks at the base are 2¾×4 inches and are nailed to a 4-inch-square base, to which a brass candleholder base is bolted. Upper blocks are also nailed to a 4-inch-square block—it has a circular hole that fits the circumference of the chimney. The upper portion, including the glass chimney, lifts out of the uprights for ease in lighting the candle. To make the holder a hanging lantern, attach small chains to the uprights with screweyes—*Designed by William L. Russell, San Diego, Calif.*

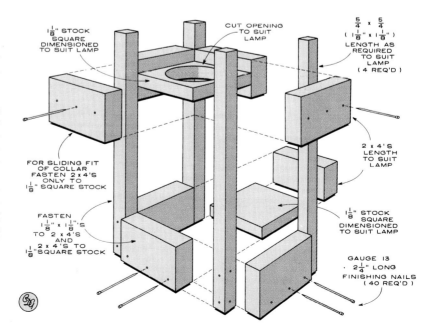

(Continued)

3. Picnic Table

This handsome family-size picnic table, with the unusual, decorative top, was designed by a person who "wanted something different." He was glad to share this design with other readers "because it's easier than it looks."

The table and benches are made of cedar and finished with polyurethane. To prevent rust marks, use only hot-dipped galvanized, stainless steel or aluminum alloy nails.

The top frame, which fits snugly

into the lap joints of the leg supports, is secured to them with four hooks and eyes for easy removal for storage—*Designed by Norman Johnston, Ypsilanti, Mich.*

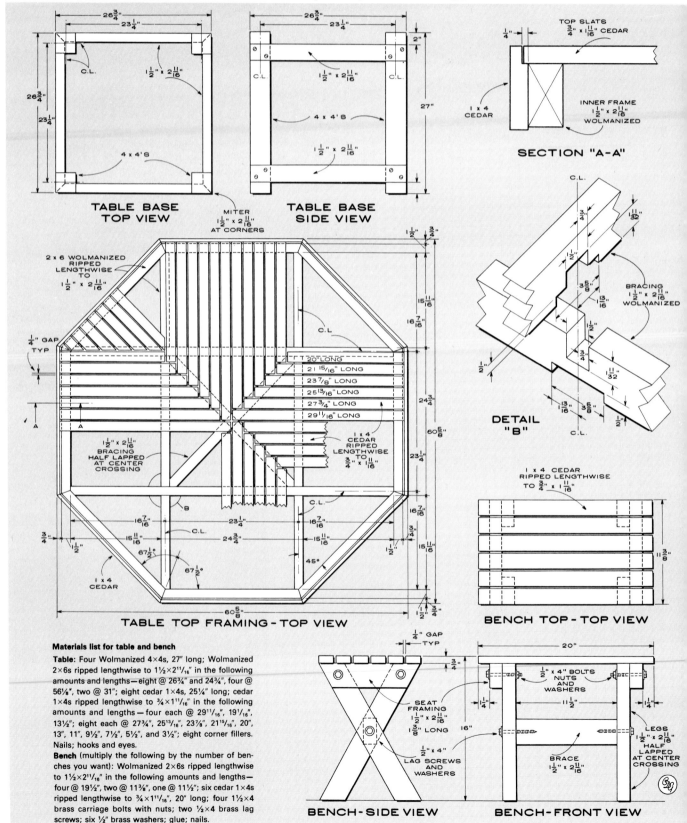

TABLE BASE TOP VIEW

TABLE BASE SIDE VIEW

SECTION "A-A"

DETAIL "B"

TABLE TOP FRAMING - TOP VIEW

BENCH TOP - TOP VIEW

BENCH - SIDE VIEW

BENCH - FRONT VIEW

Materials list for table and bench

Table: Four Wolmanized 4×4s, 27" long; Wolmanized 2×6s ripped lengthwise to 1½×2¹¹⁄₁₆" in the following amounts and lengths—eight @ 26¾ and 24¾", four @ 56⅛", two @ 31"; eight cedar 1×4s, 25¼" long; cedar 1×4s ripped lengthwise to ¾×1¹¹⁄₁₆" in the following amounts and lengths — four each @ 29¹¹⁄₁₆", 19¹⁄₁₆", 13½"; eight each @ 27¾", 25¹³⁄₁₆", 23⅞", 21¹⁵⁄₁₆", 20", 13", 11", 9½", 7½", 5½", and 3½"; eight corner fillers. Nails; hooks and eyes.

Bench (multiply the following by the number of benches you want): Wolmanized 2×6s ripped lengthwise to 1½×2¹¹⁄₁₆" in the following amounts and lengths— four @ 19½", two @ 11⅜", one @ 11½"; six cedar 1×4s ripped lengthwise to ¾×1¹¹⁄₁₆", 20" long; four 1½×4 brass carriage bolts with nuts; two ½×4 brass lag screws; six ½" brass washers; glue; nails.

framework for a modular garden

The traditional vegetable garden, with neat rows of vegetables stretching on and on, is a poor strategy for people with limited space. What's more, the pathways between the rows end up compacted, leaving the soil less able to absorb as much moisture as it needs. Raised bed planting is a far better way to utilize your garden space, and it's better for the plants in many ways.

The biggest problem in any garden is getting the full advantage of the local growing season. By enclosing your raised beds, you gain extra weeks of growing and precious protection against wind and rain damage. Most gardeners I know prefer to frame their beds with wood. Wood-framed beds are easier to care for and look much neater. Cheap, construction grade pine is sufficient, provided you treat it with a wood preservative such as Cuprinol. Avoid creosote as a preservative: It's toxic to plants and isn't very good for humans, either.

To give your bed plenty of height, 2×8 or 2×10 lumber is best. One-inch boards tend to warp quickly, and the edges aren't particularly comfortable to kneel on. You can make the beds as narrow as you like, but they shouldn't be much wider than 4 feet, or you risk falling in when trying to reach the vegetables in the middle of the bed. 4′ × 4′ beds are nearly ideal, being an easy size to maintain.

These plans incorporate a basic raised-bed frame with a removable cold frame and trellis. Both accessories fit into the sides of the bed frame that are made from two 1×10s with spacers in between. The cold frame can be used early in the season, to protect young plants from the cold; as the

The grow frame with glazing flaps down and doors off. Inside, the crop (lettuce here) gets a little breather.

Framework for a Modular Garden

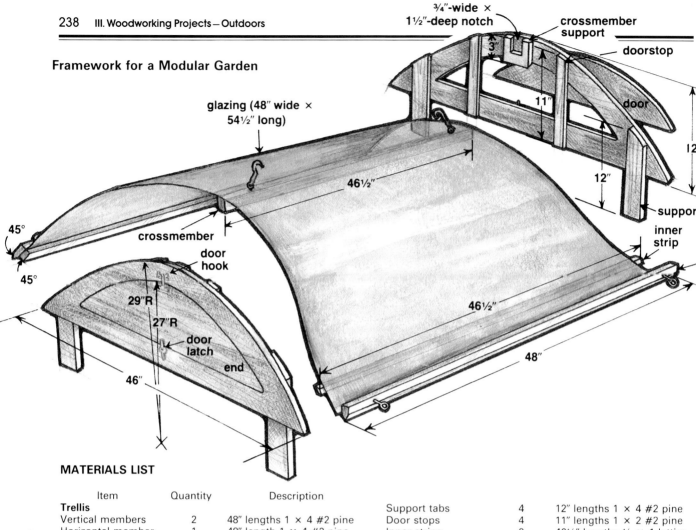

¾"-wide × 1½"-deep notch

crossmember support

doorstop

3"

door

11"

12"

12"

support

inner strip

glazing (48" wide × 54½" long)

46½"

crossmember

45°

45°

door hook

29"R

27"R

door latch

end

46"

46½"

48"

MATERIALS LIST

Item	Quantity	Description
Trellis		
Vertical members	2	48" lengths 1 × 4 #2 pine
Horizontal member	1	48" length 1 × 4 #2 pine
Pins	6	2½" lengths wooden dowel, ⁵⁄₁₆"-dia.
Raised-Bed Frame		
Sides	2	48" lengths 2 × 10 construction grade pine
End members	4	45" lengths 1 × 10 #2 pine
Spacers	20	9¼" lengths 1 × 2 #2 pine
End fasteners	12	#18 ⁵⁄₁₆ T-nuts (barbed)
Side-to-end fasteners	12	#18 ⁵⁄₁₆ hex-head bolts, 3" long
Washers	12	⁵⁄₁₆" flat washers
Nails	½ lb.	6d cement-coated box nails
Cold Frame		
Ends	2	12 × 46½" pieces ¾" Exterior plywood

Item	Quantity	Description
Support tabs	4	12" lengths 1 × 4 #2 pine
Door stops	4	11" lengths 1 × 2 #2 pine
Inner strips	2	46½" lengths ¼ × 1 lattice
Outer strips	2	48" lengths 1 × 2 #2 pine
Door hook	2	Screen hangers
Door latches	2	2" turn buttons
Glazing	1	48" × 54½" piece of fiberglass glazing
Hooks	6	2" hook latches
Screws	28	#8 × 1¼" flathead wood screws
Screws	10	#6 × ¾" flathead wood screws
Washers	2	#6 finishing
Ridge support	2	3" lengths of 1 × 4 #2 pine
Crossmember	1	46½" length of 1 × 2 #2 pine
Preservative for *all* pieces		Copper naphthenate

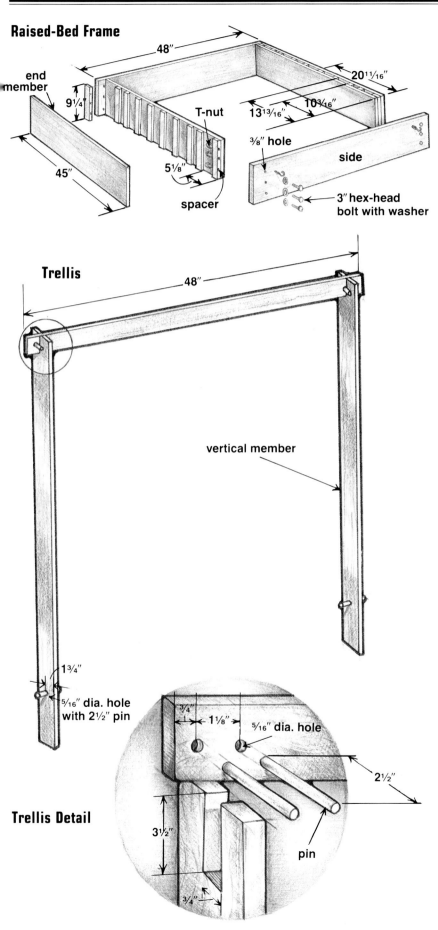

Raised-Bed Frame

48"

end member

9¼"

45"

T-nut

20¹¹⁄₁₆"

10³⁄₁₆"

13¹³⁄₁₆"

⅜" hole

side

5⅛"

spacer

3" hex-head bolt with washer

Trellis

48"

vertical member

1¾"

⁵⁄₁₆" dia. hole with 2½" pin

Trellis Detail

¾"

1⅛"

⁵⁄₁₆" dia. hole

2½"

3½"

pin

¾"

season progresses, to protect new plants of later crops; and even in the fall, to extend the season for a late planting of salad greens or to keep the chill off a bed of cold-sensitive crops. It also features removable side doors which act as vents to help regulate the temperature within the frame. In summer, the glazing can be replaced with netting to shade plants and fend off hungry birds.

The trellis allows you to plant more intensively by utilizing the space above the garden to grow climbing plants. It can be as high as you'd like, but 6 feet is probably as much as you'll need. This one is made from three lengths of 1 × 4: Two risers, and a crosspiece that fits into slots at the top. You can staple string, wire, or netting in the middle to give the plants something to grab on to.

Construction

To build this 4′ × 4′ raised-bed frame, simply gather all that's specified in the materials list and assemble it as shown in the accompanying diagram. After you cut all pieces to size and drill ⅜" holes for the T-nuts, paint all lumber with a copper naphthenate wood preservative (such as Cuprinol). Then hammer T-nuts into the holes of the end spacer sandwiches with nails. Bolt them to the 2 × 10 sides, and you're finished.

The cold frame is trickier. Start by cutting the plywood ends. Lay out the 29″ radius first and cut it with your saber saw to give a half-moon shape to the ends. Then cut out a door along a 27″-radius. Cut the pine members as specified on the materials list: You'll need to further modify the support tabs and door stops by cutting a radius on top to match the plywood ends. Also, you'll need to rip two 45-degree angles along the outer glazing strips, so that the bottom edge of each strip comes to a point. (A table saw is almost essential for these cuts.) When the glazing top is in place, one of the 45-degree edges will lie flat on the raised-bed frame's top edge; the other will be parallel with the raised bed side. Paint all lumber with copper naphthenate before assembly. For the glazing, use any flexible, thin plastic sheet, such as Filon's Solar Plate or Solar Components Corporation's Sun-Lite Premium II.

The trellis is very straightforward (see illustrations)—*Michael Lafavore*

Reprinted by permission of Rodale's *PRACTICAL HOMEOWNER* magazine.

adjustable trellis/sun shade

Don Weber, a Colorado builder, wanted a deck outside his sun room. The room doubles as a passive solar collector, so Weber didn't want to screen out winter sun. Yet he needed summer shade for both the deck and the room.

His solution was an adjustable trellis. This structure has removable slats, which slip in or out of the frame easily, so you can adjust the amount of shade to the season.

"When the sun starts getting strong in the spring, you start by slipping every third board into the frame," Weber told me. "As the sun gets stronger, you go to every other board. By summer, you have them all in."

The adjustable trellis also lets you vary the amount of shade that falls on the deck and where it falls. "If you want full shade close to the house—say, for shade-loving plants—you put all the boards in at the beginning of the season and leave them there," Weber said.

But if you want direct sun on one part of the deck for sunbathing, it's a simple matter to slip out some slats. "It takes probably 10 seconds per slat," Weber said, "and about 20 minutes to take them all down."

In fact, Weber dismantles the whole trellis for the winter. "Only the support posts stay up," he said. "I do it that way to get maximum solar gain. I don't want even the shadow from a 1 × 8 falling on the glass."

Building the deck and trellis was a fairly straightforward task, Weber says, once he determined the correct angle for the slat slots. After studying insolation tables, he decided that slanting the boards at 40 degrees would provide the best midsummer shade.

"I first erected the corner support posts," explained Weber. "Next I lag-screwed a nailer to the house, then nailed galvanized joist hangers on it for deck joists. After laying the decking, I attached an upper nailer to the house for the trellis framework."

The two inner supports have slat blocks and 1 × 2 stops nailed to *both* faces, as shown in the diagram below. These angle-cut blocks hold the slats at the correct pitch.

For the joists, decking, and support posts, Weber found it sensible to use construction heart redwood, a textured "garden grade" that is rot resistant and dimensionally stable yet costs less than the architectural redwood grade.

For the trellis slats, he used clear all-heart redwood. "It's better-look-ing," he explained, "and these boards are the most visible."

Weber made the slats four feet long. "Any longer and they might have too much sag," he warned. He added that the slats may sag anyway as they dry. In that case, "all you do is take them out, turn them around, and put them back in," he said. "They'll straighten right out."

Weber says the adjustable trellis has worked well for him—and for the many homeowners who have since commissioned him to build similar trellised decks. "I must have built 50 of them since I did mine," he said, "and I haven't changed the design at all—just altered the deck to fit the space available"—*By Susan Renner-Smith.*

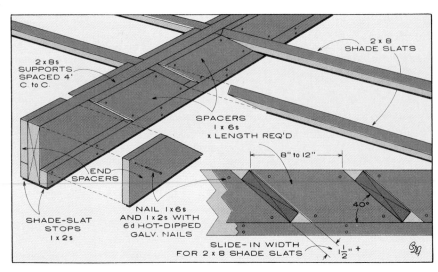

Trellis slats slip into grooves formed by spacer blocks nailed inside the support frame. Cut blocks to identical angles and nail them to the 2 × 8s, flush with their top edges. Trellis slats fit snugly in gaps between spacer blocks and are held in place by a 1 × 2 stop nailed below. Galvanized hardware was used throughout.

Lifting out a louver (above) adds a sunny spot to the well-shaded deck (right). Removable slats allow winter sun to heat the sky-lighted sun room (top). Designer Weber estimates that it takes only about 10 seconds to remove or replace each board.

outdoor swing

T his outdoor swing exemplifies passive cooling at its rudimentary best. After a grueling day at the office or a few hours of gardening and lawn work, nothing is more soothing than rocking to and fro.

Our outdoor swing offers tradition with a modern twist. Every edge of the swing is rounded and sanded smooth, providing added comfort and visual appeal. The swing is constructed with clear cedar, but redwood, oak, maple, or any other available hardwood that is free from knots can also be used. To protect the swing from the weather and decay, be sure to finish all parts with an exterior polyurethane or paint.

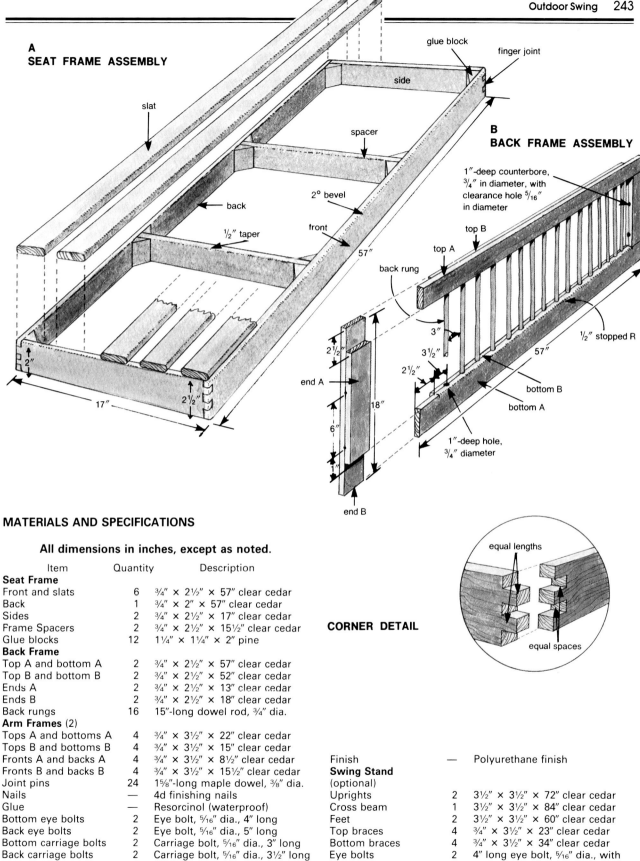

A
SEAT FRAME ASSEMBLY

slat

glue block

finger joint

side

spacer

B
BACK FRAME ASSEMBLY

back

2° bevel

1"-deep counterbore, 3/4" in diameter, with clearance hole 5/16" in diameter

½" taper

front

top B

57"

top A

back rung

3"

½" stopped R

2½"

3½"

57"

2½"

18"

bottom B

6"

bottom A

end A

1"

1"-deep hole, 3/4" diameter

end B

2"

17"

2½"

MATERIALS AND SPECIFICATIONS

All dimensions in inches, except as noted.

Item	Quantity	Description
Seat Frame		
Front and slats	6	3/4" × 2½" × 57" clear cedar
Back	1	3/4" × 2" × 57" clear cedar
Sides	2	3/4" × 2½" × 17" clear cedar
Frame Spacers	2	3/4" × 2½" × 15½" clear cedar
Glue blocks	12	1¼" × 1¼" × 2" pine
Back Frame		
Top A and bottom A	2	3/4" × 2½" × 57" clear cedar
Top B and bottom B	2	3/4" × 2½" × 52" clear cedar
Ends A	2	3/4" × 2½" × 13" clear cedar
Ends B	2	3/4" × 2½" × 18" clear cedar
Back rungs	16	15"-long dowel rod, 3/4" dia.
Arm Frames (2)		
Tops A and bottoms A	4	3/4" × 3½" × 22" clear cedar
Tops B and bottoms B	4	3/4" × 3½" × 15" clear cedar
Fronts A and backs A	4	3/4" × 3½" × 8½" clear cedar
Fronts B and backs B	4	3/4" × 3½" × 15½" clear cedar
Joint pins	24	1⅝"-long maple dowel, 3/8" dia.
Nails	—	4d finishing nails
Glue	—	Resorcinol (waterproof)
Bottom eye bolts	2	Eye bolt, 5/16" dia., 4" long
Back eye bolts	2	Eye bolt, 5/16" dia., 5" long
Bottom carriage bolts	2	Carriage bolt, 5/16" dia., 3" long
Back carriage bolts	2	Carriage bolt, 5/16" dia., 3½" long
Back washers	4	¼" flat washer
Washers	8	5/16" flat washer
Nuts	8	5/16" nut
"S" hook	2	#2½" "S" hook
Screw hooks	2	Large screw hook (2½" long)
Chain	20 ft.	Welded link chain
	(or as required)	

CORNER DETAIL

equal lengths

equal spaces

Finish	—	Polyurethane finish
Swing Stand		
(optional)		
Uprights	2	3½" × 3½" × 72" clear cedar
Cross beam	1	3½" × 3½" × 84" clear cedar
Feet	2	3½" × 3½" × 60" clear cedar
Top braces	4	3/4" × 3½" × 23" clear cedar
Bottom braces	4	3/4" × 3½" × 34" clear cedar
Eye bolts	2	4" long eye bolt, 5/16" dia., with washer and nut
"S" hooks	2	#2½" "S" hook
Fasteners	18	4"-long carriage bolt, 5/16" dia., with washer and nut
Cross beam fasteners	2	5"-long carriage bolt, 5/16" dia., with washer and nut
Finish	—	Clear polyurethane finish

Construction
Illustration A
1. Cut the seat-frame front, back, and slats to size.
2. Cut or plane a 2° bevel along the top edges of the seat-frame front and back.
3. Cut the seat-frame sides to size.
4. Lay out and cut a ½" taper on the top edge of each side.
5. Lay out and cut a finger joint at each corner of the seat frame (see Corner Detail).
6. Glue and clamp the seat frame.
7. Cut the seat-frame spacers to size.
8. Lay out and cut a ½" taper (to match the sides' taper) along the top edge of each spacer. Fasten the spacers in place, using glue and 4d finishing nails.
9. Cut the glue blocks to size. Fasten the blocks in the corners of the seat frame and in the spacer corners with glue.
10. Machine a ¼" radius along all edges of the seat frame, spacers, and slats.
11. Fasten the slats to the seat frame, using glue and 4d finishing nails.

Illustration B
12. Cut the back-frame tops (A and B) and bottoms (A and B) to size.
13. Face-glue top A to top B and bottom A to bottom B, leaving a 2½" step at each end of top and bottom A for a half-lap joint. These assembled pieces are the top and bottom of the back frame.
14. Machine a ½" stopped radius along the inside edges of the top and bottom.
15. Lay out and drill 16 holes, ¾" diameter, 1" deep, in the inside edge of the top and bottom to accept the back rungs.
16. Cut the back-frame ends A and B to size.
17. Face-glue an end A to an end B, leaving a 2½" step at the top and bottom of the end B for a half-lap joint. Repeat the procedure for the other end of the back frame.
18. Locate and drill two counterbores, ¾" diameter and 1" deep, with clearance holes, ⁵⁄₁₆" diameter, in each of the end pieces to accept 3"-long carriage bolts.
19. Cut the back rungs to size. Glue the back rungs into the ¾" holes drilled in Step 15.
20. Glue and clamp the ends to the top and bottom, forming half-lap joints at each corner of the back frame.

Illustration C
21. Cut eight joint pins to size. Lay out and drill two holes, ⅜" diameter, through each of the four corner joints of the back frame to accept the joint pins. Glue the joint pins in place.
22. Lay out and cut a 2" radius along the four corners of the back frame.
23. Finish machining the ½" radius along all edges of the back frame.

Illustration D
24. Cut the arm-frame tops (A and B) and bottoms (A and B) to size.
25. Face-glue top A to top B and bottom A to bottom B for each arm frame, leaving a 3½" at each end of top and bottom A for a half-lap joint. These assembled pieces are the tops and bottoms of the arm frames.
26. Cut the arm frame's fronts (A and B) and backs (A and B) to size.
27. Face-glue front A to front B and back A to back B for each arm frame leaving a 3½" step at the top and bottom

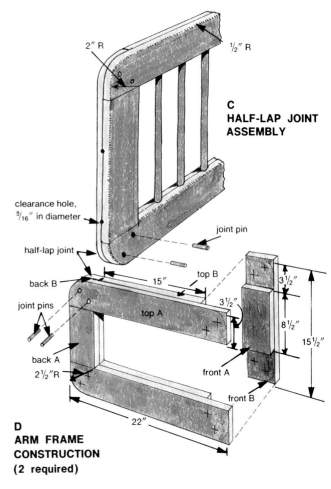

C
HALF-LAP JOINT ASSEMBLY

2" R

½" R

clearance hole, ⁵⁄₁₆" in diameter

joint pin

half-lap joint

back B

joint pins

top B

15"

top A

3½"

3½"

8½"

15½"

back A

2½"R

front A

front B

22"

D
ARM FRAME CONSTRUCTION
(2 required)

of front and back B for a half-lap joint. These assembled pieces are the fronts and backs of the arm frames.
28. Glue and clamp the front and back to the top and bottom, forming half-lap joints at each corner.
29. Cut sixteen joint pins to size. Lay out and drill two holes, ⅜" diameter, through the corner joints of both arm frames. Glue the joint pins in place.
30. Lay out and cut a 2½" radius at the four corners of each arm frame.
31. Machine a ½" radius along all edges of the arm frames.

Illustration E
32. Clamp an arm frame to each end of the seat frame.
33. Drill two holes, ⁵⁄₁₆" diameter, at the base of the arm frame and through the seat frame, one at the back to accept a carriage bolt, and one at the front to accept an eye bolt.
34. Lay out and drill a hole, ⁵⁄₁₆" diameter, through the upper back corner of each arm frame aligned with the top hole already located at each end of the back frame to accept an eye bolt. Drill a second hole through the back of each arm frame aligned with the lower hole on each end of the back frame to accept a carriage bolt.
35. Sand the seat, back, and arm frames, and apply a polyurethane finish.
36. Open the eye in four eye bolts.
37. Cut two pieces of chain, 40" long, and two pieces of chain, 32" long. (The amount of chain required may vary depending on the location of the swing.) Fasten the ends

of each piece of chain to an eye bolt by closing the eye around the chain.

38. Assemble the swing using the eye bolts and carriage bolts with washers.

39. Fasten two large screw hooks (at least 2½″ long) into overhead joists. (If the swing stand is going to be used, two ⁵⁄₁₆″ × 4″ eye bolts with an "S" hook will be used instead of the screw hooks.)

40. Hang the swing and adjust the height and balance to a comfortable position using additional chain and an "S" hook.

Illustration F (Swing Stand (optional)

1. Cut the uprights to size.

2. Lay out and cut a 1¾″ notch for a half-lap joint on the bottom of each upright. Cut a 2¾″-deep shoulder at the top of each upright.

3. Cut the cross beam to size.

4. Position the cross beam in the shoulders of the uprights. Counterbore and drill a clearance hole at an angle through the cross beam and each upright to accept a ⁵⁄₁₆″ × 5″ carriage bolt.

E
PORCH SWING ASSEMBLY

F
SWING STAND ASSEMBLY

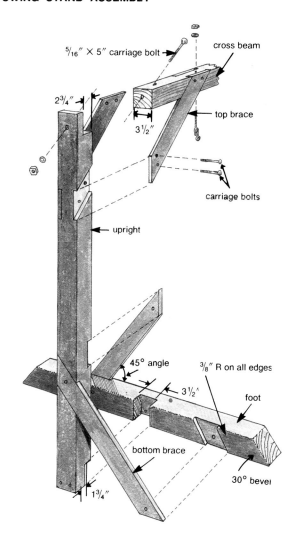

5. Cut the feet to size. Lay out and cut a 30° bevel on both ends of each foot.

6. Lay out and cut a 1¾″ × 1¾″ half-lap on each foot to accept the uprights.

7. Connect the feet to the uprights forming a half-lap joint, using two carriage bolts for each foot.

8. Cut the top and bottom braces to size.

9. Position the braces from the uprights to the feet and cross beam at 45° angles. Scribe lines on both sides of each brace indicating the proper cutting lines on the uprights, feet, and cross beam.

10. Hollow out the appropriate notches in the feet and uprights to accept the bottom braces, and in the cross beam and uprights to accept the top braces.

11. Mark and cut each brace to its finished shape.

12. Drill holes for carriage bolts and fasten braces to uprights, cross beam, and feet.

13. Machine a ⅜″ radius on all edges of the stand. Some of the fasteners may have to be removed for this step.

14. Sand the assembled stand and apply a polyurethane finish.

Reprinted by permission of Rodale's
PRACTICAL HOMEOWNER
magazine.

wraparound tree bench

Encircle your favorite tree with this hexagonal bench, and you create a cool, convenient resting place. The handsome bench is also maintenance free. It's constructed of Wolmanized, pressure-preservative-treated lumber that's totally resistant to fungus, damp rot, bacteria, and all insects, including termites. Though the bench shown here rests on a decorative stone base, the treated lumber could rest on the ground. And since Wolmanized lumber weathers to an attractive natural gray, you don't even have to paint the bench (though I did for color contrast).

The bench has two half sections, each containing three seat segments. The halves are joined at the tree. This procedure lets you work in your shop or on a level surface outside.

Each segment of the hexagon has four seat boards, two seat supports, and a pair of cross-lapped legs. That adds up to a lot of miter cuts. Such angular cutting is normally best done with a table or radial-arm saw. But for those readers who don't own such equipment, I developed a couple of simple but effective jigs. Using these special jigs, you can mass-produce the miter cuts with a portable circular saw and basic hand tools.

The dimensions shown are for a tree trunk about 12 inches in diameter, with an extra 4 inches allowed for growth. Alter the dimensions to suit your own tree taking into account its growth patterns. For a rapid grower you might want to stretch the inside diameter of the bench. And remember: Trees are wider at ground level than at seat level. I forgot this until I assembled the two bench halves around the tree and found that the rear legs were too close to the bottom of the trunk. Sawing a small triangle off the rear of each leg solved the problem.

To make mitering jig for seat boards (right), use a 2 × 4 as shown above to set exact spacing between the parallel strips. Next, measure the distance between saw blade and base edge (top right) to determine how far away from the cut line you should put the saw guide. It will be supported by lengths of 2 × 3 scrap nailed beyond the first and last spacer strips. The cut line is pencil-drawn at a 60-degree angle across the near end of the boards inserted between the spacer strips. The four seat boards were previously cut to working length.

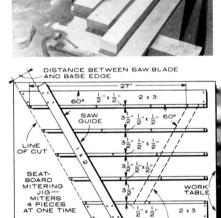

Miter-cut seat boards after attaching the saw-guide strip to the two outer support boards. The angled guide bridges the work pieces, extending about 8 inches beyond each end so the saw base is accurately guided as it enters and leaves the work. Adjust saw-blade depth so it cuts about $\frac{1}{16}$ inch into the work board. Using this jig, cut one end of all six sets of boards before doing next step.

Nail a stop strip at a 60-degree angle across the rear end of the spacer strips. Reinsert the seat boards so the mitered ends butt up against the stop. Again using the saw guide, miter the opposite ends of the boards. If the guide is accurately set, all six sets of seat boards will assemble into a perfect hexagon.

Inviting-looking bench above is as useful as it is handsome. For precise cutting of its many parts, the author devised special jigs.

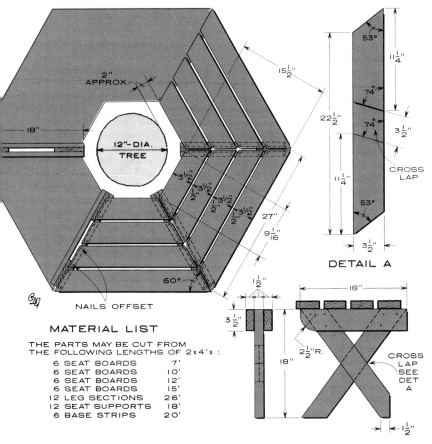

2" APPROX.

18"

12"-DIA. TREE

15½"

22½"

27"

9 1/16"

60°

3½"

1½"

1½"

3½"

3½"

3½"

3½"

NAILS OFFSET

DETAIL A

53°

11¼"

74°

74°

3½"

CROSS LAP

11¼"

53°

3½"

1½"

18"

3½"

2½"R.

18"

CROSS LAP SEE DET A

1½"

MATERIAL LIST

THE PARTS MAY BE CUT FROM
THE FOLLOWING LENGTHS OF 2x4's :

6	SEAT BOARDS	7'
6	SEAT BOARDS	10'
6	SEAT BOARDS	12'
6	SEAT BOARDS	15'
12	LEG SECTIONS	26'
12	SEAT SUPPORTS	18'
6	BASE STRIPS	20'

The plans indicate this revision, even though it doesn't show up until the last photo in the construction sequence.

To make the decorative base, first prepare border strips. Rip six lengths of 2 × 4 down to 2¾-inch width and miter the ends to 60 degrees. Next, use a pointed mason's trowel and an ice chopper to dig a 2-inch-deep, 1½-inch-wide hexagonal trench around the bench.

To do an accurate job of it, first drive a 3-inch finishing nail into the bottom of each border strip at either end. Push these spikes into the soil to hold the strips in place, then use the strips as a guide to marking trench position. Run the trowel along the edge of the strips with a sawing motion to mark and cut the turf. Remove the strips, deepen the cuts if necessary with the ice chopper, then lift out the pieces of sod. Reinsert the strips. They should project about ¾-inch above the surface of the lawn to allow neat mowing and contain the stones at the base. Varied colors and sizes of small stones are available at masonry supply houses. The stones will highlight the bench and help keep weeds down—*Ro Capotosto.*

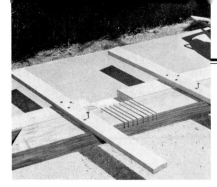

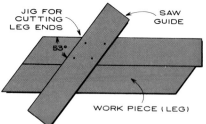

JIG FOR CUTTING LEG ENDS — SAW GUIDE

53°

WORK PIECE (LEG)

Make a third jig (bottom left) to form cross-lap joints in the legs. On an extra 2 × 4, nail two scraps parallel to each other, spaced so that both the saw and a 2 × 4 can fit between them. Make a rectangular notch in the 2 × 4 by cutting about eight kerfs. Clear out the waste with a chisel. To use the jig, first slide a leg piece under the guide strips, centering it against the notch in the jig. Prevent slipping by partly driving two nails through the strips and into the work. Then adjust the saw blade so it penetrates only half the leg thickness, and cut a series of kerfs through the center of the leg (top). For the end kerf cuts, run the saw against each guide. Make the inner cuts freehand about ⅜ inch apart. Note that the twelve leg pieces are identical, so there's no problem with left or right miters. Finally, use a broad chisel to knock out waste between kerfs (center). Also use the chisel to shave off high spots.

Run a block plane over top front and rear edges of each seat piece (top) to give them a slight round. Lightly sand ends, then arrange boards in a hexagon shape (partially done here). Mark nail locations on each board, aligning marks with neighboring boards for uniformity. Nails should be slightly offset to avoid splitting seat supports. Next, make a leg-mitering jig (above) by nailing a 2 × 4 scrap to another scrap at a 53-degree angle. With this jig cut twelve pieces of 26-inch stock down to 22½-inch legs with parallel miters.

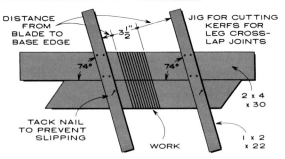

DISTANCE FROM BLADE TO BASE EDGE

3½"

JIG FOR CUTTING KERFS FOR LEG CROSS-LAP JOINTS

74°   74°

2 × 4 x 30

TACK NAIL TO PREVENT SLIPPING

WORK

1 x 2 x 22

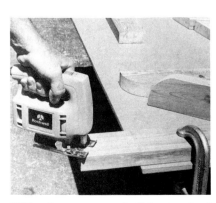

With saber saw, round off front ends of seat supports (see diagram, preceding page, for dimensions). Dense wood such as this requires coarse-set tooth blade.

Assemble bench legs first, cross-lapping pieces, then nailing a seat support to either side. Use galvanized nails and drill pilot holes to prevent splitting.

Nail seat boards to legs, aligning miters so that boards are ½ inch apart. A temporary cleat tacked to seat support helps center seat boards over legs.

Hold unfinished bench half (foreground) steady by temporary tack-nailing to the completed three-segment section. Use smooth finishing nails for this job—rough-surfaced galvanized nails are difficult to withdraw. After the final segment is inserted in place, pull out the nails to separate the two half sections.

With a level, check how evenly the bench section rests. Lawn surfaces are rarely even, so you'll have to dig away soil under some legs to obtain solid footing. If desired, put down a layer of small stones (see text). Then nail the last two sets of seat boards to the seat supports to fit the bench around the tree.

rustic planter

To the wood enthusiast who likes to garden, the container is as important as what it holds. It takes time to construct the project shown here, but unlike a purely practical box, the result is attractive and shows its contents to best advantage.

Quite often, pieces like this can be made from leftover odds and ends of wood. But buying wood for the planter is justified, since the project should show thought and craftsmanship. We chose kiln-dried, heart-grade redwood. Oak or ash would do, but if you choose either, it would be wise to paint the inside surfaces with a liquid asphaltum before filling with soil.

Start the project by cutting the two bottom boards, holding them together with corrugated nails. Drill the drainage holes. Cut the two side pieces, beveling the bottom edges 30 degrees and shaping the top edges in curves similar to those shown in the drawing. Nail these to the bottom and then add the ends. Note that the ends are

cut at an angle to conform to the slope of the sides. Add the two bottom risers with nails long enough to penetrate the end pieces.

We distressed the top edges of ends and sides by working them over with a rasp and then smoothing them with sandpaper. Also, we banged the outside surfaces a bit with a short length of chain. You don't have to do this, but a little rough treatment seems to

make the project more compatible with its function.

We used a tile as the center piece. You can find substitutes such as a length of rectangular or square flue tile. Whatever you use, just set it in place; it does not have to be secured.

Our container holds sedum and Monterey pine. The soil is a fifty-fifty mix of potting soil and clean sand— *R. J. De Cristoforo.*

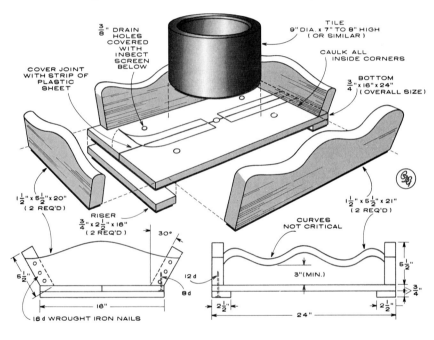

Clear heart redwood was used for this planter, and the edges were rough cut and distressed. Round or square building tile can serve as centerpiece.

cold-frame hot bed

Some call it a poor man's greenhouse. In fact, the modest cold-frame hot bed shown here serves almost as a greenhouse—and for far less effort and money.

Cold frames alone can be very simple. My neighbor lashes old storm windows together and uses the box so created to "harden off" annuals grown indoors. If that's the only use you have in mind, a simple, portable frame, with a polyethylene cover, will do. But a well-built cold-frame hot-bed combination can extend your gardening season at both ends. With a heating cable in half of mine, I get four-season use of it. Here's a sampling:

Spring: Harden annuals started indoors; start early crops of hardy annuals (radishes, lettuce, pansies, etc.); start tender annuals (tomatoes, peppers, etc.) weeks before they can be planted in the garden.

Summer: Start biennial and perennial flowers (covers can be put on in heavy rain); give house plants a "summer vacation" (lathing or cheese cloth can be used to cut intense summer sun).

Fall: Plant hardy crops (carrots, radishes, lettuce, etc.) for harvesting long after frost kills garden; "heel in" garden surplus, such as onions and carrots, before ground freezes; shelter young perennials and biennials from the worst winter weather.

Winter: Sink in pots of hardy bulbs for root development, then bring inside for earliest spring bloom; give hardy bonsai plants necessary winter rest period.

The frame shown takes a couple of weekends to build. It's meant to be a permanent, rugged addition to the garden. Locate it where its sloping roof faces south, and where it gets full exposure to winter sun. (If it can also be sheltered from cold north winds, that's a bonus.) An excellent choice is the south wall of a house. Size is easily adjusted to needs. However, if a frame is too big, the "garden" is awkward to tend; if it's too small, it heats and cools too quickly.

The foundation is the most critical part of construction. First, dig a rough, 5⅓ × 9⅓-foot hole to a 16-inch depth. Set the sod and top soil aside. Use the rest of the soil to build a protective hill along the north wall and cover this with sod. Top soil, lightened with compost or peat moss, will go back into the frame.

I used 15⅝ × 7⅝-inch concrete blocks, setting them in dry and filling in holes with dirt. I left about ⅛-inch between blocks. If your blocks are a different size, build the foundation as shown; check inside measurements; and adjust frame dimensions accordingly. Extra care in leveling and squaring the first row of blocks helps ensure true construction throughout.

I treated my wood with a brush-on preservative. (Even more protection is achieved with pressure-treated wood.) The preservative should be of the water-borne salt type; oil-borne preservatives, such as creosote, give off fumes that are toxic to plants and humans.

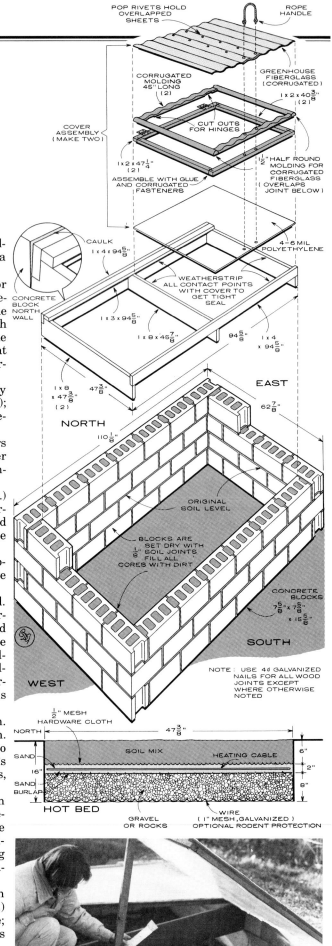

If blocks in first row are level and straight, the rest is easy.

As each row is set, fill block holes with dirt.

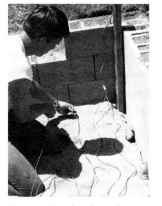

Wet sand makes it easier to get heating cable to stay put.

Assemble the wood frame outside the foundation.

Fill in foundation with rocks or gravel, burlap, sand, hardware cloth (to keep an errant trowel from hitting heating cable), and soil as diagrammed. Construct the frame and secure in place with masonry nails (one every 1½ feet is plenty).

I chose corrugated fiberglass for the outside cover. It's strong—takes a heavier snow load than flat fiberglass. And it's safe—glass covers make me nervous; I'm afraid a child might fall through. The material must be designed for greenhouse use; others deteriorate with exposure to sunlight. I put polyethylene inside the cover to create a dead air space. This is inexpensive, but it has to be replaced every few years.

The special half-round and ripple "filler strips" for attaching the fiberglass should be available from your fiberglass dealer. You should also be able to get clear sealant and appropriate nails. I used aluminum nails with a deformed shank to help grip the fiberglass better and a neoprene washer at the head.

While the frame is designed to provide warmth and protection, it can do its job too well and overheat. All that's necessary, then, is to prop the top open with a stick. (I use clamps on the top, the kind sold for hanging tools. One end of the stick is secured in a clamp, and the other is poked into the dirt in the frame. The top then remains lifted to the desired height.)

However, automatic ventilation is the answer for frame tenders who can't be home to catch a sudden sunny spell that sends temperatures soaring and threatens to bake a crop of young plants. I prefer the simple vents that use a temperature-sensitive chemical in a cylinder over electricity. "SolarVent" is one such device. It's available from Dalen Products, Inc., 201 Sherlake Drive, Knoxville, TN 37922. This type of vent is easy to install and can be disengaged for manual operation. I put one on the hotbed side of my frame – GREG STONE.

The frame should fit tightly inside the prepared foundation. Caulk any gaps to prevent cold air from getting in.

Drive in nails where they line up with big hole in block.

Lay sealant; overlap panels; use "POP" rivets with washers.

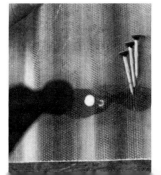

Attach cover with aluminum nails, washers every 4 inches.

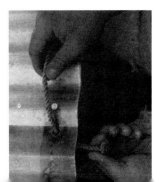

Handle is ½-inch rope, with a figure-eight knot on inside.

Fold polyethylene at edges, pull tight, and staple.

Materials

Wood: One 14-foot 1×8; two 8-foot 1×4s; one 8-foot 1×3; four 8-foot 1×2s; two 8-foot half-round filler strips; two 8-foot ripple filler strips.

Hardware: ¼ lb. 2-inch masonry nails; ¼ lb. 1½-inch aluminum nails (for fiberglass); ½ lb. 4d common nails (galvanized); two 2-inch loose pin hinges; corrugated or Skotch fasteners (small box).

Other: Two 26-inch×8-foot corrugated fiberglass panels (4–5 ounce); one 4×8-foot sheet polyethylene; 20 inches ¼-inch rope; 30 feet weather stripping; 69 concrete blocks; waterproof glue; ¼-inch staples; 4×8-foot sheet burlap; 5 cubic feet builders' sand; 15 "POP" rivets with washers.

post lamp and mail center

Architects are often dissatisfied with ordinary fixtures around their homes—inside or out. Julia Sturdevant, a landscape architect in Portland, Ore., is no exception. She saw no reason to stick a traditional mailbox—a 4 × 4 with a galvanized metal box on top—out in front of her contemporary home.

Her solution was an elegant design that combines a mailbox, an outdoor light, and a newspaper box in one project. The lamp and mail center was built of Douglas fir that was stained and sealed. Underground wiring for a low curb light was already in place, so it was only necessary to set a concrete footing and extend the wire and conduit up between the posts to the fixture (see drawing on facing page for construction details). Then the posts and wood parts were assembled around the conduit and secured to the footing.

Note that custom-built mailboxes require prior approval from your local postmaster before you can substitute them for existing types. Boxes are generally 3½ to four feet above the roadway (not the top of the curb), but it's a good idea to check with your postmaster for an exact height and what, if any, street or box numbers need to be inscribed on the side of the box—*By Paul Bolon. Julia Lundy Sturdevant and Ralph Cereghino, designers.*

The appearance is striking, yet lamp and mail center blends with surroundings because of all-wood construction.

Major frame pieces are shown at left before assembly, except for decorative chamfers to be cut on posts. Wiring for light comes from house via underground conduit; switch is in house. Light bulb is changed by removing peaked cap. Photos by Western Wood Products Assn.

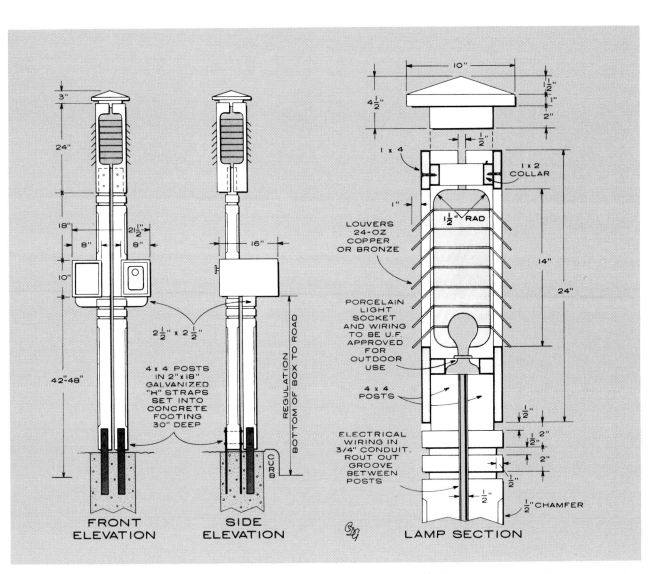

Backbone of lamp post is two full-length 4×4s secured by galvanized straps embedded in concrete footing. Dadoes for conduit are routed in post's mating faces; decorative chamfer is also routed. Boxes fit in notches in tall posts and are supported by crossmember atop third, short post. Light socket is special porcelain model for outdoor applications. Copper or bronze louvers are cemented in slots with small amount of exterior-type epoxy. Box sides and back are rabbeted together and screwed to posts and crossarm support. Check with local postmaster for height from road to box bottom.

upgrade your walkways

The walk in front of my house had been getting shabby, to put it mildly. The undergrowth was taking over, and the stepping stones of precast concrete on a bed of marble chips made walking difficult for visitors at night.

My solution was a new duckboard walk, which I designed in removable modules so I could get to a septic cleanout in front of my house. Also, by making the walk in sections, it was easy to build modules away from where they were to be placed—where I had access to power tools—and then move them to their final position.

You can adapt this design to suit your home, but use weather-resistant materials throughout. I used unpainted pressure-treated lumber (I'll allow it to weather) and heavily creosoted railroad ties, which bound the walk on either side.

My walk goes down to the bottom of a rise at the side of my house, where the boundary ties meet with others to form a wall on a 90-degree turn down to the driveway.

At the 90-degree turn there's a step down to a lower walk. It's actually a four-foot-square module placed on top

Completed modules are ready to be moved. Each board is secured with two galvanized nails at lifters to prevent distortion.

Ground beneath the walk is sloped slightly for runoff. The photo shows railroad ties in position, anchored by rebar.

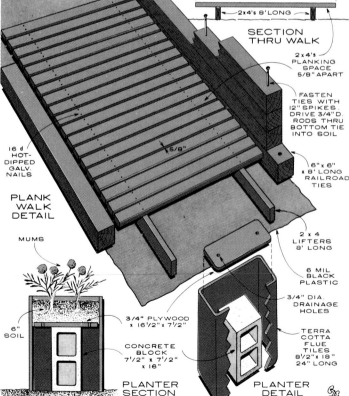

SECTION THRU WALK

48"

2 x 4's 8' LONG

2 x 4's PLANKING SPACE 5/8" APART

FASTEN TIES WITH 12" SPIKES. DRIVE 3/4"D. RODS THRU BOTTOM TIE INTO SOIL

6" x 6" x 8' LONG RAILROAD TIES

16 d HOT-DIPPED GALV. NAILS

5/8"

PLANK WALK DETAIL

2 x 4 LIFTERS 8' LONG

6 MIL BLACK PLASTIC

3/4" DIA. DRAINAGE HOLES

TERRA COTTA FLUE TILES 8 1/2" x 18" 24" LONG

MUMS

6" SOIL

3/4" PLYWOOD x 16 1/2" x 7 1/2"

CONCRETE BLOCK 7 1/2" x 7 1/2" x 16"

PLANTER SECTION

PLANTER DETAIL

Entry walk from driveway to front of house is shown above. The half step is created by a smaller, four-foot-square module. Photo at left shows finished walk with landscaping of evergreen bushes and pine-bark chips. Below the duckboard is a sheet of six-mil-thick black plastic. Septic cleanout is in the center of the walk under a removable duckboard module.

of an eight-foot one. A fascia board covers the end of the smaller unit. In effect, there's a half step down to the lower level of the walk.

I nailed all the ties together with 12-inch spikes and anchored the boundary ties (and the bottom course of ties in the wall) with three-foot-long ¾-inch rebars.

The modular duckboard fits snugly between the firmly anchored railroad ties, so there's little danger of the walk upending if someone steps on the edges.

I used planters made of sections of chimney-flue tile to border the railroad ties, positioning them so that if a modular unit must be removed, the planters won't get in the way. This is a good feature, particularly with my house: If I ever needed to get to my septic system for extensive repairs, a large hole in the front would obliterate a concrete walk and planter.

The flue tile shouldn't be filled all the way to the bottom with dirt; otherwise, in a prolonged spell of freezing weather, moisture in the soil might expand and cause the tile to crack. I used a false bottom of plywood (see diagram).

A helpful hint: The best way to ensure that the duckboard doesn't curl or warp is to place the wood so that the end grains arch upward—that way water can drain instead of pooling in the middle of the board.

Thus far, I've enjoyed the walk. Future plans include low-voltage lighting to highlight the planters and front of the house, and a trellis at the front door.—*By W. David Houser. Photos by the author.*

berming your yard

The flaws in our circa 1950 home included minimal prefab construction, a crushed rock driveway that ended in nothing at one end of the house, sandy soil devoid of vegetation, and a topography as flat as the new, uncarpeted floors.

Some of these conditions gradually yielded to our efforts at improvement, but not the lay of the land. After years of labor, top soil, grass seed, shrubs, flowers, and trees, the terrain—however lush—was still flat and uninteresting.

The good earth

When we excavated for a small addition, that flatness inspired us to have the earth from the hole set aside in our own yard. Our intention was to use it to break up the topographic monotony.

Such an excavation is a direct source of mounding or fill earth. If you're not digging up your own yard, you might be lucky enough to spot a neighbor who is and offer your place as a convenient dumping site for his diggings. But, if you don't plan to ex-

A mound of earth left from the excavation for a new addition to your home can be the makings of a berm. Later, top soil, sod, and other plantings will cover it.

Materials

Ties: I used 15.
Wood preservative: One quart.
Dry-mix concrete: One bag.
Mound or fill earth: It took about 50 cubic yards for this hill, covering about 600 square feet of ground. Your costs will be lower if a large truck can reach the dump point (smaller trucks require more trips).
Top soil: Check local recommendations for finishing over your subsoil. I used a 6-yard load of pulverized, screened black dirt.
Sod: Covering my berm required 130 rolls.

Method for marking contour posts

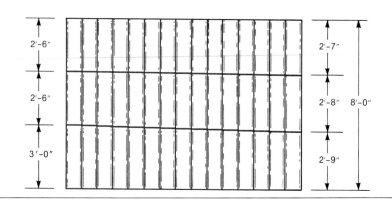

cavate and aren't lucky, turn to your local supplier of topsoil. Most can either provide, or help you find a source of less expensive mound or fill earth.

In the case of our excavation, the operator of the scoop inadvertently imposed a lot of extra earth-moving on us. He failed to see the mind's-eye vision we had of our proposed berm, so he spread the earth too far and in the wrong place. It's a much better idea to have the earth dumped as close as possible to where you will be using it.

Retaining wall

Researching materials for a retaining wall led me to give up on those that required mortar, for which I felt I did not have the required expertise. Of the treated timbers readily available in my locality, I chose from a pile of old creosoted railroad ties that I located through the Yellow Pages. The ties are strong and rustic looking, and they were cheaper than anything else I could find.

Old ties, slabbed on two sides, are about 6 inches thick, from 9 to 11

Railroad ties cut to follow contour of mound, make an effective retaining wall for a berm, as shown at top, left. Berm is shaped with a high crown and an easy grade for mowing, as shown in bottom photo. It can be planted with shrubs and trees as a sound deadener between your home and the street. In any case, a berm is sure to enhance the appearance—and value—of a flat piece of property.

Cut ties with care. Get help if possible. Keep toes clear.

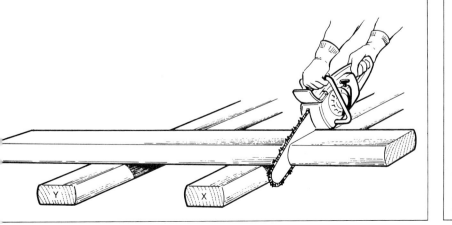

Tools

Shovel: long-handled.
Tamping rod or bar: You can use shovel handle, a 2×4, or any other device that will pack the earth around the posts.
Log saw: large bucksaw, bow saw, or one-man log saw will do, if it's sharp and you want exercise, or a two-man log saw, if you can get help. Easiest of all is a chain saw. If you don't own, and can't borrow one, try a tool rental company.
Rake: for smoothing hill.

inches wide to the rounded sides, and 8 feet long. They may be less than straight in the rounded silhouette. The ties are heavy—you know you've been working after wrestling with a few. So calculate each lift and wear gloves.

Here is the procedure for building your berm:

1. An average of five tie widths, flat surface out, makes 4 lineal feet of wall. I got three segments from each of fifteen ties; creating forty-five widths to achieve about 36 feet of low, curved wall. The ties were laid out, marked, and cut as shown in the drawing. Before sawing, inspect ties for metal and remove any you find.

2. Do the layout—in a curve, angle, or straight pattern, depending on your circumstances. Trench to a depth at least half the exposed wall height and wide enough for post insertion, filling, and tamping.

3. Insert tallest posts at highest point of your wall and work toward lower ends. Control diminishing post-top contour by digging or filling under each post. Use plumb or level to check wall and post vertical. Set each post as true as possible; once you move on, it's impractical to adjust those that came before. Tamp each post with loose soil, using shovel handle end, a rod, or pole. Unless ties are slabbed on all sides, they may not make smooth contacts; if you wish, join rounded sides as I did. Bottom of post to ground line should be one-third to one-half of post length.

4. After posts are set, some contour trimming may be needed. Use concrete to fill any exposed hollow centers and cracks in fresh-cut post tops before painting with preservative.

5. Shovel mounded earth against hill side of posts. Move high crown down into retaining wall and, with long-handled shovel, shape rest into a pleasing contour. Keep slope under 30 degrees for ease in lawn trimming.

6. Condition soil for seeding or sodding and other plantings.

Results

When it's over, you'll be glad you're through and happy with the results. Your property value will increase, and that new slope, a joy to see— *Fergus Retrum.*

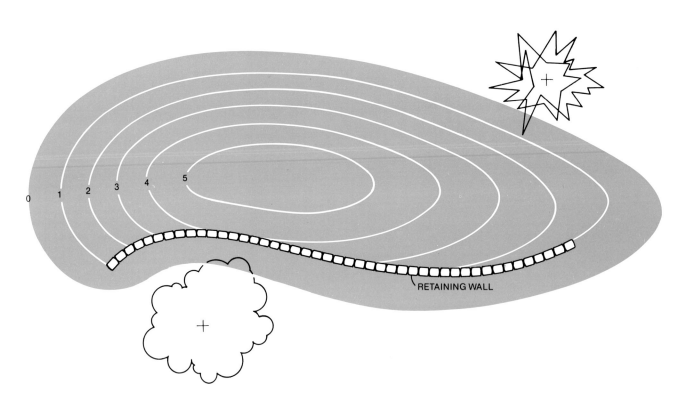

RETAINING WALL

Elevation: Wall side, showing post-setting depths

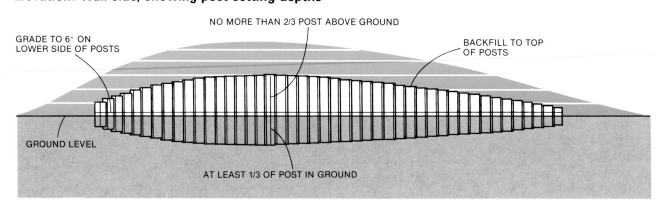

GRADE TO 6″ ON LOWER SIDE OF POSTS

NO MORE THAN 2/3 POST ABOVE GROUND

BACKFILL TO TOP OF POSTS

GROUND LEVEL

AT LEAST 1/3 OF POST IN GROUND

how to deck out an above-ground pool

When we decided to install an above-ground pool in our yard, we were determined to make it look as much like an in-ground pool as possible. With the help of Kirk Olson, a twenty-two-year-old telephone repairman with no formal design training, we were able to do all the planning and construction—without calling in the pros.

To minimize the raised look, we established the first level of our deck flush with the bottom of sliding doors from the kitchen. The second, or pool level, would be 7 inches below this. With the levels determined, we could get started.

Artfully designed two-level deck gives above-ground pool the look of a built-in. Top deck level is flush with house entry, making it convenient for outdoor dining and entertaining. Main deck area is 7 inches lower, so swimmers can step from deck into pool. Board-on-board fence screens pool from the street. Safety railing is of simple construction.

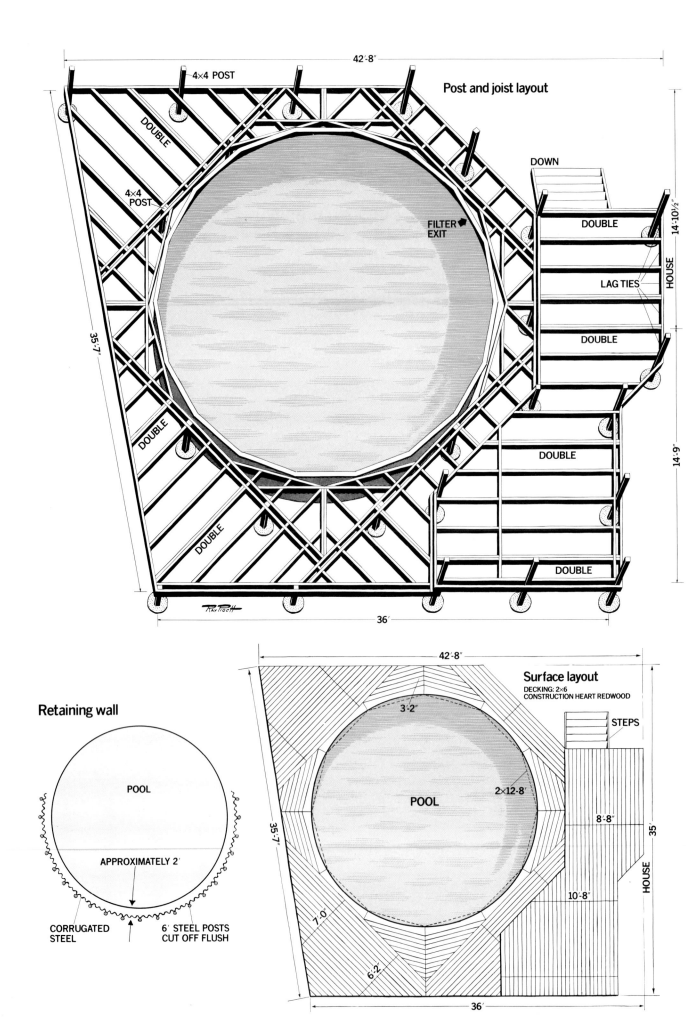

Post and joist layout

42'-8"

4×4 POST

DOUBLE

4×4 POST

DOUBLE

DOUBLE

DOUBLE

35'-7"

FILTER EXIT

DOWN

DOUBLE

LAG TIES

DOUBLE

DOUBLE

DOUBLE

HOUSE

14'-10½"

14'-9"

36'

Retaining wall

POOL

APPROXIMATELY 2'

CORRUGATED STEEL

6' STEEL POSTS CUT OFF FLUSH

Surface layout

DECKING: 2×6 CONSTRUCTION HEART REDWOOD

42'-8"

3'-2"

POOL

2×12-8'

STEPS

35'-7"

7'-0"

6'-2"

8'-8"

10'-8"

35'

HOUSE

36'

Doors that provide access to all sides of the pool and to the filter and pump, also conceal a storage area used for pool supplies and garden tools.

Construction details

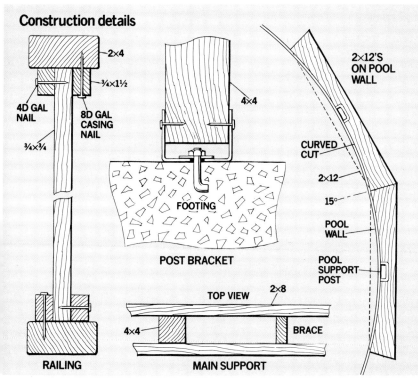

We began by leveling the ground for the 4 × 24-foot circular pool. We had to excavate 3 feet deep where our lot sloped up to the back fence.

We dug a 28-foot-diameter hole to provide working room around the pool wall. Wherever the dirt bank was more than a foot high, we built a retaining wall with corrugated steel roofing set on edge and supported by 6-foot steel stakes that were driven into the ground.

Footings. We attached the back ledger board to our 4 × 4 fence posts, which are in 30-inch concrete footings. For the corners, we used a two-man, 12-inch power auger to drill twenty-one holes 48 inches deep. (Our frost line in Nebraska is approximately 42 inches.) We filled the footings with a total of 2¼ yards of concrete and placed a ½-inch bolt in the center of each. The brackets we used to hold the 4 × 4 posts—they are known as "AB" Adjustable Port Braces and are manufactured by the Simpson Company—worked well and, in fact, saved us a lot of trouble.

These brackets served two important functions:

1. They held the posts 1 inch above the ground. That protects the posts from absorbing moisture.

2. They allowed us to move the posts about 1½ inches in any direction to line them up and make them plumb during construction.

Support structure. All the 4 × 4 posts that were to be extended above the deck for railing were made of redwood to match the deck surface. The rest of the posts, and all of the 2 × 8s underneath, are cedar.

The main support joists were built with paired 2 × 8s, which were secured to the posts with 30d galvanized nails. Joist hangers and six-way corner brackets were used wherever possible to provide additional strength. The frame required approximately 1700 board feet of lumber.

Decking. All the exposed decking wood is Construction Heart redwood. The decking boards are 2 × 6s, which were spaced apart with a 16d nail. We nailed the top down with 10d galvanized casing nails (we used 35 pounds of them). As you can see in the accompanying illustrations, the pattern of the deck boards at pool level gave us a chance to learn how to make some difficult angle cuts.

One puzzle was how to cut the pool wall itself. Kirk Olsen solved this in his design, by using 2 × 12s and cutting one side to curve with the pool. We used a reciprocating saw for these cuts. The larger size board allowed us to make a curved cut on a piece and still leave plenty of board for support. The deck top required approximately 2300 board feet of Construction Heart redwood, including the railing and sides.

The railing looks complicated, but was really quite simple to build. We used 2 × 4s. For use on the side pieces and the spokes, we ripped the 2 × 4s to ¾ inch.

Sides. Since we didn't want the pool to show, we enclosed the sides. For this, we framed in 2 × 4s and covered with 1 × 8s. There are three doors for access underneath to the filter and pump. We can also use the doors for access to storage, although the area gets quite wet at times. We built a 12 × 12-inch trap door right above our filter and mounted it on a piano hinge (the filter is cleaned through top).

In addition to the underdeck storage, we built a cabinet by extending the overhang on the house down to the deck. This cabinet holds all the tools and materials needed for pool maintenance, including chemicals, which means they can't create an odor problem in the house or garage—*Gordon Muirhead.*

hot-tub deck

O n most patio decks you have a choice between sitting and standing. This one, you can jump into.

It has a built-in hot tub. After a summer soak, your dip into the pool will be that much more refreshing. And at the end of the season—when it's too cool for the pool—the tub extends your outdoor fun.

The L-shaped all-redwood deck, designed by Larry and Florence Regular, is approximately 150 square feet supplemented by an adjoining 50-square-foot deck containing a gas-fed

brick-lined firepit. The built-in butcher-block benches and steps were adapted from the Design-a-Deck plans kit. The Design-a-Deck plans kit is available from the California Redwood Association, 591 Redwood Highway, Suite 3100, Mill Valley, CA 94941.

All decking, stairs, and benches are made with knot-textured construction-heart redwood. Deck boards are 2×6s; the understructure is made from 4×4s anchored to concrete footings and flanked by 2×6s, forming the main structural beams at the deck's perimeter; joists are 2×6s; and

benches and stairs are made from 2×4s and 2×6s.

The main deck encircles a 6-foot-wide, 4-foot-deep tub made of kiln-dried, vertical-grain, clear all-heart-grade redwood. The tub shown comes as a kit, but tubs are available preassembled as well. The tub is recessed 18 inches into the ground, resting on a 1-foot layer of gravel to dampen any ground shifts. Blocking supports the deck boards, which are trimmed to match the tub's contour (see drawing). No ledgers should be attached to the tub itself, and you'll want to leave

breathing space between tub and deck boards.

A variety of tub sizes and shapes are available from manufacturers. A list of sources is available from the California Redwood Association. The tub you choose should meet or exceed the standards set by the International Association of Plumbing and Mechanical Officials. Also, before installation check all local plumbing and electrical codes. In most cases electrical and gas hookups must be done by a licensed electrician and plumber—*William J. Hawkins.*

Drawings by Gene Thompson

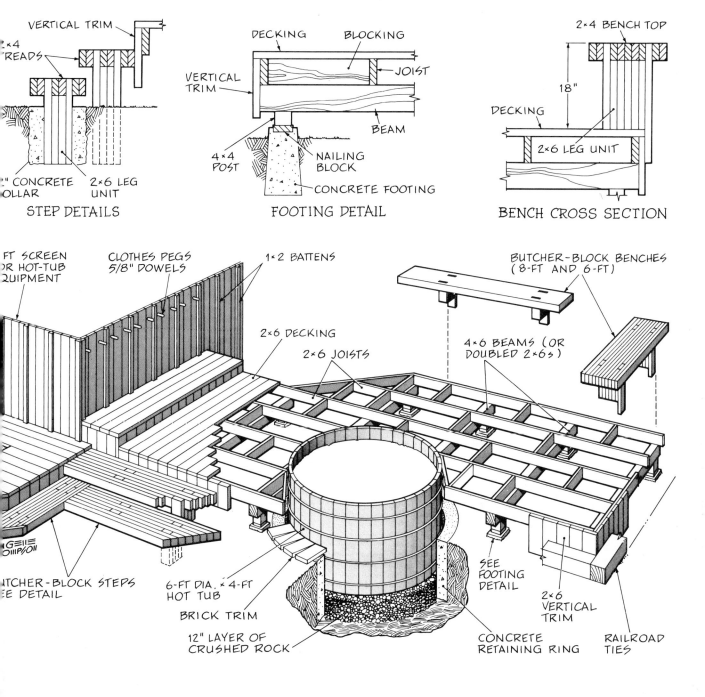

VERTICAL TRIM

2×4 TREADS

CONCRETE COLLAR   2×6 LEG UNIT

STEP DETAILS

DECKING   BLOCKING

VERTICAL TRIM   JOIST

BEAM

4×4 POST   NAILING BLOCK

CONCRETE FOOTING

FOOTING DETAIL

2×4 BENCH TOP

18"

DECKING

2×6 LEG UNIT

BENCH CROSS SECTION

FT SCREEN OR HOT-TUB QUIPMENT

CLOTHES PEGS 5/8" DOWELS

1×2 BATTENS

BUTCHER-BLOCK BENCHES (8-FT AND 6-FT)

2×6 DECKING

2×6 JOISTS

4×6 BEAMS (OR DOUBLED 2×6s)

TCHER-BLOCK STEPS E DETAIL

6-FT DIA. × 4-FT HOT TUB

BRICK TRIM

12" LAYER OF CRUSHED ROCK

SEE FOOTING DETAIL

2×6 VERTICAL TRIM

CONCRETE RETAINING RING

RAILROAD TIES

kids' backyard play centers

1. Swing Set with Playhouse

My son and his buddies spend much of their time in a geodesic-dome playhouse (perched 6½ feet above the ground) or sliding, swinging, and climbing on the play equipment below. I designed and built the structure rather than settling for a standard bolt-together set of steel tubes, swings, and slides. My main objection to those: They tend to rust after a few years and become a maintenance problem. And commercial wooden swing sets are rather expensive. I built this wooden play center for less than $400.

Except for the playhouse siding, all the wood is Wolmanized for easy upkeep and durability. The geodesic-dome playhouse is easily assembled with the help of Starplate connectors (see drawing, following page). Its frame is of 2 × 4s; its siding is ½-inch exterior-grade chipboard. A coat of preservative helps protect the walls.

I began the construction by sinking the 4 × 4 posts in the ground to below the frost line. I used a full bag of ready-mix cement to stabilize each one. Then I built the frame for the deck by attaching four 2 × 8s to the posts (see diagrams, following page) with four-inch lag screws. Next, I put joists of 2 × 6s on 24-inch centers between the 2 × 8s and planked the deck with 2 × 6s, trimming the edges after the dome was in place.

Dome construction was simple. The instruction booklet that comes with the Starplate connectors tells how to

make any size dome. I built the dome on the ground, then, with helpers, lifted it to the deck and attached it securely with nails and lag screws.

The swings hang from a 2 × 6 beam, which I fastened to the tops of two base posts using eight-inch galvanized spiral spikes. The swing is a piece of 2 × 8 hung by galvanized chain from large screw eyes. I also made a glider-type swing for adults.

I made the slide of 18-inch-wide galvanized metal (the kind used for ductwork). It's nailed to a base made

of two 2 × 8s assembled edge-to-edge with bracing. The sides of the slide are also made of 2 × 8s, rabbeted to cover the nailheads. I left extra metal on the top of the slide and attached it to the playhouse deck with decking nails. I notched the edges of the slide to fit tight against the deck at the appropriate angle. Two scrap 4 × 4s, set about 18 inches deep in cement, anchor the bottom of the slide.

The ladder is made completely of 2 × 4s. Its legs are mounted in cement. I made the steps 13 inches apart to

keep toddlers from climbing up.

To make the railing, I ripped 2 × 4s in half for the uprights and placed them about every seven inches. A 2 × 4 nailed along the top and another along the side just below complete it.

After I had finished the construction, I took a router and rounded all edges. This wasn't just for looks. Even treated lumber will crack and split slightly as it ages. With the edges rounded, I'm less likely to have to pluck splinters from small fingers and toes—*By Bryan P. Shumaker.*

2. Swing Set for a Slope

Like many backyards, ours isn't exactly pool-table flat. In fact, it's a ravine with a 25 percent slope—that is, one foot of drop for every four horizontal feet. A further complication: Even that space is of limited size. When we set out to buy outdoor play equipment for our young son, it quickly became apparent that off-the-shelf swing sets, jungle gyms, slides, and so-called customized play equip-

ment just couldn't be used.

So I decided to apply my architectural training to the problem. The result is a unique play structure (next page) that uses its hillside location to advantage. It provides opportunity for many activities, and it cost me much less than a comparable manufactured play set. Materials will come to about $200 or so.

The entire structure is cantilevered from five 4 × 4 wood posts. These are

set in a concrete slurry in holes dug about 24 inches deep into the sloping ground. I assembled the structural elements with carriage bolts and a few joist hangers. I used pressure-treated lumber for durability. Its natural wood tone blends with the wooded site.

The plan and elevation on the following page show the design in detail. All materials used are readily available, and you can adapt the design to your site—*By James Calhoun.*

1. Swing set with playhouse

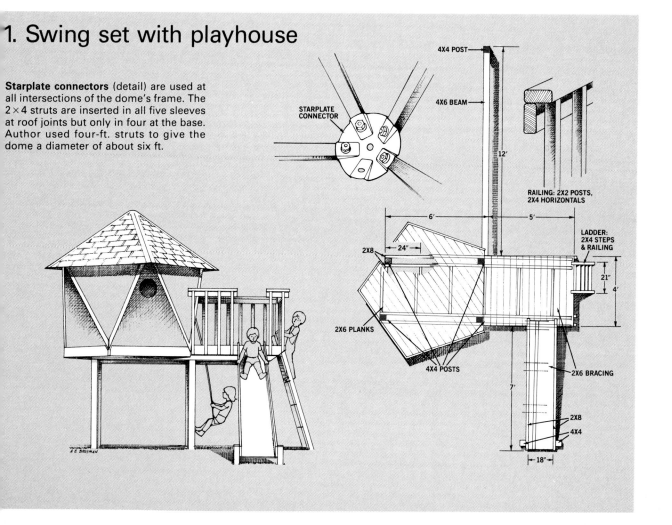

Starplate connectors (detail) are used at all intersections of the dome's frame. The 2 × 4 struts are inserted in all five sleeves at roof joints but only in four at the base. Author used four-ft. struts to give the dome a diameter of about six ft.

STARPLATE CONNECTOR

4X4 POST

4X6 BEAM

12'

RAILING: 2X2 POSTS, 2X4 HORIZONTALS

6'

5'

LADDER: 2X4 STEPS & RAILING

2X8

24"

21"

4'

2X6 PLANKS

4X4 POSTS

2X6 BRACING

7'

2X8

4X4

18"

2. Swing set for a slope

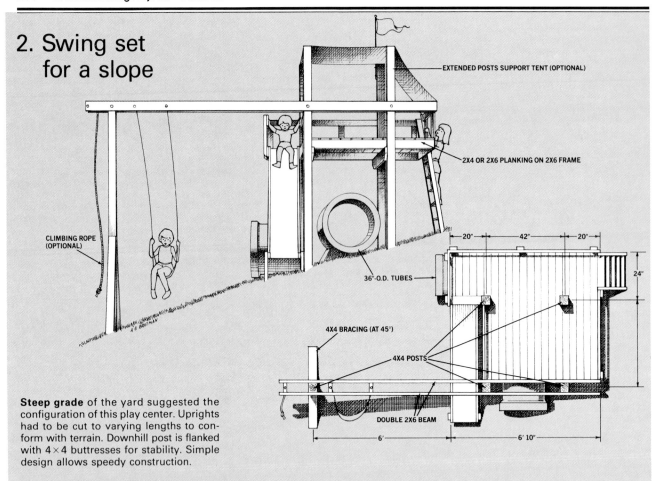

EXTENDED POSTS SUPPORT TENT (OPTIONAL)

2X4 OR 2X6 PLANKING ON 2X6 FRAME

CLIMBING ROPE (OPTIONAL)

36"-O.D. TUBES

20"   42"   20"

24"

4X4 BRACING (AT 45°)

4X4 POSTS

DOUBLE 2X6 BEAM

6'   6' 10"

Steep grade of the yard suggested the configuration of this play center. Uprights had to be cut to varying lengths to conform with terrain. Downhill post is flanked with 4 × 4 buttresses for stability. Simple design allows speedy construction.

drop-leaf swim deck

Out on a lake, swimming from a runabout results in a lot of rocking and sloshing as bathers climb back aboard—even with a ladder slung over the side. My solution is a wooden swim deck hinged to the transom. The deck swings up and out of the way when the boat is moving. Materials for the deck (see drawing) cost about $60 or so.

The deck makes swimming more enjoyable and, I think, a little safer. And faced with ever-higher fuel prices, boat owners will be indulging in a lot more "at-anchor" activities such as swimming—*J. R. Holt.*

Position the swim deck at or just above the waterline on the boat's transom. The size of the cutout for the motor depends on whether you have an outboard or stern-drive unit—in any case you'll have to adapt this basic design to your own rig. One-inch hardwood boards can be substituted for the 2-inch pine deck lumber shown here. The deck's depth should be less than the distance from the hinge to the top of the transom. Offset or hatch-style hinges allow ample clearance between the deck and transom.

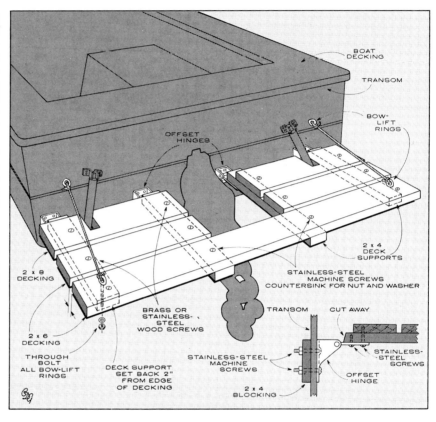

firewood shelter-fence and kindling bin

A proper place for wood and kindling adds to the pleasure of putting wood by. With this shelter-fence and kindling bin, you can forget the hassles that accompany makeshift wood covers. Here are some of the features:

● The 12-foot shelter-fence shown here will protect nearly three cords of wood—or shelter both wood and yard implements. You can increase capacity by extending the fence and increasing the number of hinged roof panels.

● The fence screens off your work area, giving privacy while sparing neighbors the temporary clutter of your cutting and splitting.

● The kindling bin will hold 2 cubic yards of bark or other kindling while it seasons.

By recycling some scrap timber and hardware, I was able to keep costs for

For access under the shelter fence or for stacking wood, you raise and prop middle panel before side panels (above). When the shelter is full of wood, simply reach through the framing to fetch it (below). Kindling bin is smaller structure at right.

the two shelters for under $100. I made my own fence posts by halving the trunk of a cedar tree that a neighbor was removing. Cedar is one of the most decay-resistant woods, and it splits easily down the center with a sledge and a few wedges. The posts should be treated with preservative to about one foot above ground level. Or you can purchase posts specially impregnated for subsoil use.

Construction

The fence posts should be sunk a minimum of 2½-feet—at least below the frost line. A horizontal notch, or dado, for 2×4 rails should be made with a bow saw and hatchet after the posts are erected. If you make notches on both posts before setting, it will probably mean extra digging, tamping, and hauling posts in and out repeatedly to line up the notches. Since the wood would otherwise weather rapidly, it's best to use a 2×4 rail that has been treated for outdoor use.

Fencing is inexpensive 1×2 pine mitered on one end and nailed up back-to-back to look like a picket fence. Each pair of pickets is nailed on alternate sides of the rails. By staggering the vertical pickets, you achieve an ideal compromise of screening and air circulation. And the more air circulated within the woodpile, the faster the wood will dry. Be sure to use galvanized nails for the pickets—5d or 6d should be long enough.

The covering panels are exterior-grade ¼-inch Aspenite (flakeboard) on frames of 1×3 pine. The middle panel overlaps the side panels to keep rain out. One 4×8-foot panel will shelter about a cord of wood. I trimmed mine to 7-foot lengths, anticipating heavy snow loads on the light-duty pine framing. The V-frame supporting the panels is 1×3 pine bolted to the frame

A sawing jig or miter box allows uniform cutting of four or five stacked slats. Here, 8-foot furring is cut to 6-foot lengths, leaving 2-footers for slatting of bin.

and joined to each other with a carriage bolt. (Were I to build another shelter-fence, I'd make the Vs narrower so that I could scoot underneath easier as the firewood is depleted.)

Shelter hinges consist of large eye screws in the frame of the panels. They rotate on a steel rod supported by eye bolts through the rail. I wrapped baling wire around the frame member holding the eye screw to prevent end-splitting. Hinges for the kindling box are just a length of pipe or a bolt through both the roof frame and the support posts (see illustration).

The kindling bin was made from scraps of odd sizes, scrap timber, and 1×2 furring left over from the fence construction. Vertical slats nailed inside the framing withstand the outward pressure of the kindling. The bottom of the bin is left open but is covered with masonry rubble to raise the kindling pieces off the soil. The lid is aluminum sheeting, but a flakeboard panel painted with a good weatherproof enamel would serve well too—*Neil Soderstrom.*

Use a level to keep slats true (top). Staggered slats provide good air circulation. Finished fence has birdhouses atop posts (above); they handily shed snow and rain.

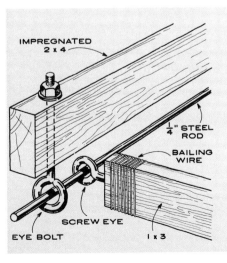

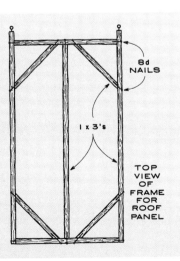

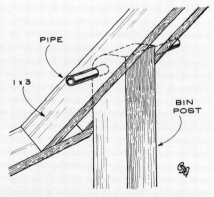

Simple hinge pin supports the roof of the kindling bin. Pins can be salvaged lengths of either pipe or just spikes.

cedar-sided shed

The long, slender yard shed in these color photos is both visually and physically a cluster of three enclosures that have separate functions:

● Facing front, an open-topped pen with hinged doors for trash cans. They're out of sight, and secure from neighborhood animals.

● Sandwiched in the middle, an open-sided section that holds more than a cord of firewood. It's built to hold heavy loads (see photo) and roofed to keep wood dry.

● At rear, there's enclosed storage for bicycles, lawn mower, and other garden tools and equipment. It's lockable for security.

This diverse assemblage is particularly striking because it's sided in western red cedar, nailed up at 45-degree angles. Cedar shingles roof the covered sections.

Stapling chicken wire to the inside edges of the trash-can enclosure's framing lets this section double as a compost bin. The chicken wire keeps the compost away from the sides of the enclosure and allows air to circulate. It you opt for this use, you'd be wise to select pressure-treated wood for the framing. In any case, it's advisable to use preservative-treated wood for ground-contact outdoor projects such as this yard shed.

The overall dimensions of the shed were dictated by site requirements; local zoning forbade any structure within 5 feet of the property line, and the clients wanted it placed in a narrow side yard so the shed could double as a privacy fence. You could alter the overall size or add or delete sections to fit your own needs. For example, if you need both storage for trash cans and a compost bin, add a second pen at the rear of the structure, next to the shed. Its doors could face toward the rear or open to the side—*Richard Stepler. Design by Julia Lundy Sturdevant. Photos by Western Wood Products Association.*

Framing for wood storage and shed is complete. Note that units are separated by exterior-grade plywood panels; trash-can enclosure will be attached at left.

Upper shelf, for split wood and kindling, is built of closely spaced 2 × 4s, wide side up. Heavy logs go on the lower shelf—here the 2 × 4s are narrow side up.

Alternating panels of western red cedar applied at a 45-degree angle add visual interest to long, skinny yard shed (bottom). On the house side, there's plenty of clearance for access to wood storage (left) and the enclosed shed (below).

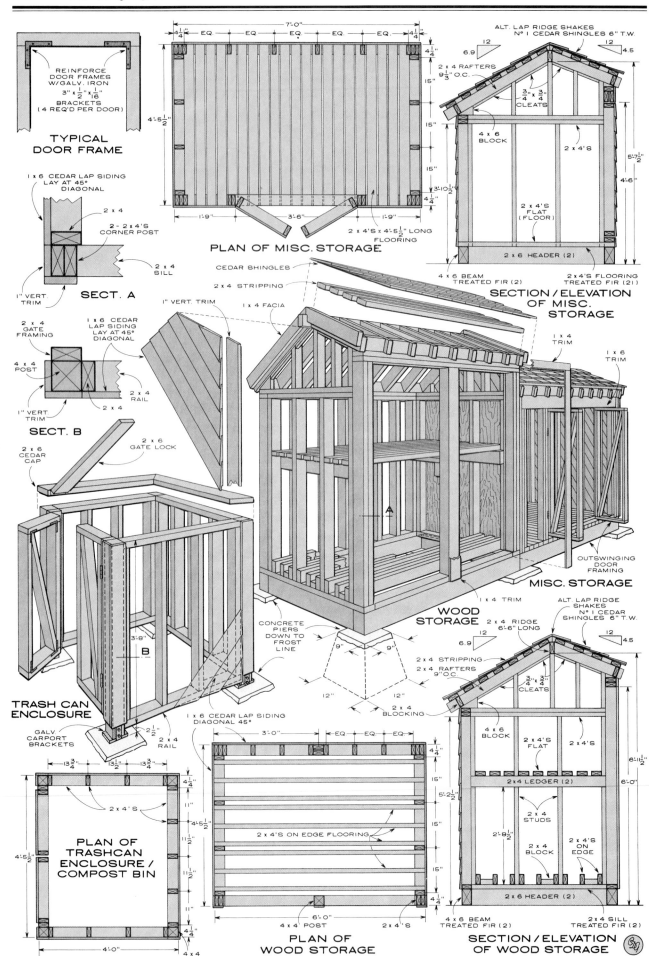

REINFORCE DOOR FRAMES W/GALV. IRON 3" x $\frac{1}{2}$" x $\frac{1}{16}$" BRACKETS (4 REQ'D PER DOOR)

TYPICAL DOOR FRAME

1 x 6 CEDAR LAP SIDING LAY AT 45° DIAGONAL

2 x 4

2 - 2 x 4'S CORNER POST

1" VERT. TRIM

2 x 4 SILL

SECT. A

2 x 4 GATE FRAMING

1 x 6 CEDAR LAP SIDING LAY AT 45° DIAGONAL

4 x 4 POST

2 x 4 RAIL

1" VERT. TRIM

2 x 4

SECT. B

2 x 6 CEDAR CAP

2 x 6 GATE LOCK

TRASH CAN ENCLOSURE

GALV. CARPORT BRACKETS

2$\frac{1}{2}$"

2 x 4 RAIL

3'-8"

B

7'-0"

4$\frac{1}{4}$" EQ. EQ EQ EQ. EQ. 4$\frac{1}{4}$"

4$\frac{1}{4}$"

15"

15"

15"

3'-10$\frac{1}{2}$"

4$\frac{1}{4}$"

4'-5$\frac{1}{2}$"

1'-9"   3'-6"   1'-9"

2 x 4'S x 4'-5$\frac{1}{2}$" LONG FLOORING

PLAN OF MISC. STORAGE

CEDAR SHINGLES

2 x 4 STRIPPING

1" VERT. TRIM

1 x 4 FACIA

1 x 4 TRIM

1 x 6 TRIM

WOOD STORAGE

MISC. STORAGE

1 x 4 TRIM

CONCRETE PIERS DOWN TO FROST LINE

9"   9"

12"   12"

2 x 4 BLOCKING

OUTSWINGING DOOR FRAMING

ALT. LAP RIDGE SHAKES N° 1 CEDAR SHINGLES 6" T.W.

12   6.9   4.5

2 x 4 RAFTERS 9$\frac{1}{3}$" O.C.

$\frac{3}{4}$" x $\frac{3}{4}$" CLEATS

4 x 6 BLOCK

2 x 4'S

2 x 4'S FLAT (FLOOR)

2 x 6 HEADER (2)

5'-7$\frac{1}{2}$"

4'-6"

4 x 6 BEAM TREATED FIR (2)

2 x 4'S FLOORING TREATED FIR (21)

SECTION / ELEVATION OF MISC. STORAGE

2 x 4 RIDGE 6'-6" LONG

ALT. LAP RIDGE SHAKES N° 1 CEDAR SHINGLES 6" T.W.

12   6.9   4.5

2 x 4 STRIPPING

2 x 4 RAFTERS 9" O.C.

$\frac{3}{4}$" x $\frac{3}{4}$" CLEATS

4 x 6 BLOCK

2 x 4'S FLAT

2 x 4'S

2 x 4 LEDGER (2)

2 x 4 STUDS

2 x 4 BLOCK

2 x 4'S ON EDGE

2 x 6 HEADER (2)

6'-11$\frac{1}{2}$"

6'-0"

2'-8$\frac{1}{2}$"

4 x 6 BEAM TREATED FIR (2)

2 x 4 SILL TREATED FIR (2)

PLAN OF TRASHCAN ENCLOSURE / COMPOST BIN

13$\frac{3}{4}$" 13$\frac{1}{2}$" 13$\frac{3}{4}$"

4$\frac{1}{4}$"

2 x 4'S

11"

4'-5$\frac{1}{2}$"

11$\frac{1}{2}$"

11$\frac{1}{2}$"

11"

4$\frac{1}{4}$"

4'-5$\frac{1}{2}$"

4$\frac{1}{4}$"

4 x 4

4'-0"

1 x 6 CEDAR LAP SIDING DIAGONAL 45°

3'-0"   EQ   EQ   EQ

4$\frac{1}{4}$"

15"

15"

5'-2$\frac{1}{2}$"

15"

15"

4$\frac{1}{4}$"

2 x 4'S ON EDGE FLOORING

6'-0"

4 x 4 POST   2 x 4'S

PLAN OF WOOD STORAGE

SECTION / ELEVATION OF WOOD STORAGE

folding sawbuck with limb vise

Ever try to buck a small log or tree limb with your chain saw? The log chatters, or bounces up, halting the chain and causing the clutch to slip. You can eliminate the problem by building this sawbuck, which holds lightweight wood in a vise. It's sturdy enough to handle larger logs, too. The rule of thumb: If you can lift it, the buck can hold it. It also folds flat for easy storage.

Buck parts can be fashioned from scrap 2 × 4s and 1 × 6s, three short dowels cut from an old broom handle, and forty-two 2½-inch No. 10 galvanized flathead screws. If you expect to leave the buck out in wet weather, treat the raw lumber with preservative or invest in pressure-treated lumber.

Vise parts consist of scrap 1 × 3s, a 3-inch long carriage bolt, two washers with a nut, two 3-foot lengths of nylon cord, and a few logs from your woodpile, to make up the lever apparatus.

Although it's okay to use a carriage bolt in the vise (because the saw won't come close to it if you cut the log to stove-wood length), don't use bolts in place of the wooden dowels as pins for crossing the sawbuck's 2 × 4s. Such bolts would lie in the path of a misguided saw chain. A bolt could damage the chain and perhaps even break it.

This little sawbuck doesn't take long to build. Once you're finished, you've got a buck that will not only support larger logs but also keep that lighter wood from being such a hassle and a hazard—*Neil Soderstrom.*

Sawbuck operates simply: Left foot pressing down on lever closes vise on small log, holding it firmly in place; once foot is removed, weight on other end of lever causes rig to release its grip. To open sawbuck (inset photo), set one pair of legs on ground, swing other pair outward. Center unit over lever. Note: Placement of 1 × 6s *A* and *B* here allows left-handed hand sawyer to place right foot inside buck under *A*. For right-handed sawyer, switch *A* and *B* heights.

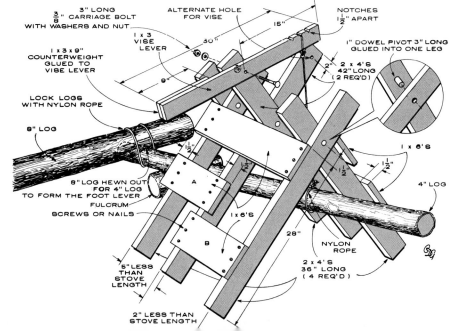

how to buy lumber

The buying of lumber and plywood can be a confusing experience. Here's what you should know about the way wood is classified and graded so you can buy the right materials for your projects and get the most for your money.

What's called *rough lumber* has been sawed, edged, and trimmed at a sawmill; it shows marks on all sides. *Surfaced* or *dressed lumber* that you buy in a lumberyard has also been through a planing machine to smooth the sides, but not always all sides.

Softwood lumber grading standards have been set by the government. The actual grading is done by inspectors of such associations as the Western Wood Products Association (WWPA), Northeastern Lumber Manufacturers Association (NELMA), and Redwood Inspection Service (RIS).

For grading purposes, all softwood lumber is divided into two groups: green lumber and dry lumber (moisture content is 19 percent or less). All softwood lumber is further divided into three use classes: (1) yard lumber for ordinary construction and building purposes; (2) structural lumber for use where high stress will be encountered; (3) factory and shop lumber for manufacturing into molding, siding, and furniture.

Lumberyard stock is almost exclusively dry yard lumber, and classified as board, dimension, and timber.

Boards

Board means a thin piece of lumber that, considering its thinness, is both long and wide. Softwood lumber boards are made in eleven standard thicknesses, but most of those sold in lumberyards are ¾ inch thick. Widths are standard, too.

Softwood boards are sorted into select or finish grades (good stuff) and common grades (knotty). They are graded after being surface-planed, and looking at the good side. A board is graded as a whole, not in sections. In the common grades, it is not the

number of knots that determines the grade, but their size, and whether they are sound, loose, or missing, plus such things as warp, wane, splits, rot, and other defects. In select grades, both number and size of knots are limited.

What each board grade is called depends on where the tree grew. Western woods are graded mostly under WWPA rules. Lumber from the northeast comes under NELMA grading rules. Idaho white pine, although graded under WWPA rules, carries its own grade designations.

Each board grade describes the type, size, and number of defects per-

mitted in the worst board in that particular grade. Most boards in a grade surpass requirements. However, these gradings are made when the board is just out of the planer; if a board is improperly stored, it may develop a lot more warp than that allowable at inspection.

Dimension lumber

Dimension lumber is 2-by, 3-by, and 4-by softwood used for framing—joists, studs, rafters, planks, light posts, etc. The lumber is divided into several classes, such as Light Framing, Utility, Studs, Joists and Planks, Appearance, Structural Light Fram-

STANDARD

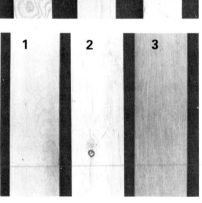

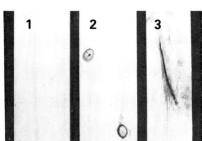

ECONOMY

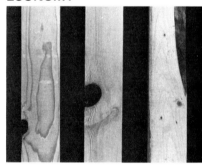

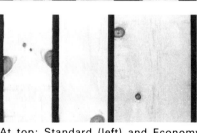

At top: Standard (left) and Economy (right) 2×4 dimension lumber. Center, left: Select boards—1 is B & BTR pine; 2 is C & CTR pine (there's only one knot in this 8-foot 1×6); 3 is Clear All Heart redwood. Center, right: Except for knots, these boards, bought as knotty pine, would meet C & BTR Select. Bottom: Common lumber—1 and 2 are second-best quality (No. 2 Common, Sterling, etc.) normally found in yards; 9-inch pocket puts 3 in No. 3 Common grade (several scattered pockets allowed).

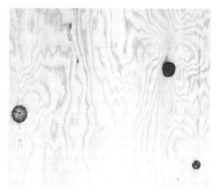

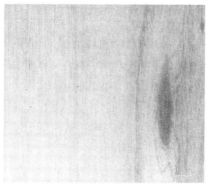

Top: Fir plywood A grade veneer, left, with five boat patches visible in this about 4-square-foot panel, and, right, C grade veneer (knots and knotholes up to 1½-inch diameter allowed). Center: Fir plywood, D grade veneer (knotholes up to 3 inches allowable) at left, and right, Lauan (Philippine mahogany) underlayment surface veneer (good side has few, if any, defects; backside may be another story, with wide splits possible, though much of panel will be usable on both sides). Bottom: Birch veneer plywood. Most "veneer" in yards is not graded, much is imported. You can buy it good-one-side (G1S) or good-two-sides (G2S).

ing, and Machine Stress-Rated. Only dimension lumber in the first three of the classes is usually available in retail lumberyards.

Light Framing. Light framing dimension lumber is sorted into several grades. Construction, the top grade, is for general framing; although it has good appearance, it is graded primarily for strength and serviceability. Standard, also for general framing, is almost as good, but bigger knots, knotholes, and other defects are permitted.

Utility. For noncritical framing, such as studding, blocking, plates, bracing, and rafters. Allowable knots and knotholes are bigger still, and more warp and other defects are permitted. Economy—in this grade almost anything goes except that the ends can't be broken or slabby.

Studs. There is only one stud grade and it's called *Stud*. It is suitable for all stud use including load-bearing walls. In Economy Stud, as in Economy Light Framing, almost any defect is allowed.

Joists and Planks. This class of dimension lumber is intended for use full length to support floors, roofs, etc. Grades are Select Structural, No. 1, No. 2, and No. 3, and Economy, with grade quality requirements similar to those for Light Framing, except for allowable knots.

Appearance Framing. This class has only one grade—Appearance. This dimension lumber is for exposed use in housing and light construction. In strength, it is equivalent to No. 1 Structural Light Framing with no unsound knots allowed. There are also tight limits on defects affecting the appearance of the lumber.

Structural Light Framing. Grades of dimension lumber in this class have strength and stiffness that

are specified percentages of those of clear straight-grained wood. Grades are Select Structural (67 percent), No. 1 (55 percent), No. 2 (45 percent), No. 3 (26 percent), and Economy, for which there is no specified fiber stress in bending value.

Other classes of dimension lumber include Machine Stress-Rated lumber, in which class each piece is non-destructively tested; Foundation lumber (red cedar and incense cedar heartwood only); Decking; and Scaffold Plank.

Timbers

Timbers have a minimum thickness of 5 inches and are produced in several classes and grades.

Beams and stringers are 5 inches or more in thickness, and more than 2 inches wider than they are thick, making the minimum dimensions in this class 5×8. There are four grades.

Select Structural is graded primarily for strength, but most pieces can be used exposed where good appearance is important. Other grades, in descending order of strength and appearance are No. 1, No. 2 (No. 1 Mining), and No. 3 (No. 2 Mining).

Posts and timbers are 5×5 and

TABLE I. Typical grading softwood lumber

	USE	Grading based on 1"x8"x12' piece. Defects in other size pieces proportional. Grading based primarily on WWPA rules. Rules for other lumber may vary, particularly on allowable knots.	Northeastern Lumber NELMA	Western Lumber WWPA	Idaho White Pine IWP	West Coast Lumber WCLB	Redwood RLB	Western Red Cedar WCLB & WWPA	Southern Pine SPIB
SELECT & FINISH	Lumber of exceptional quality and appearance. Many pieces absolutely clear.	Two sound, tight pin knots (½" max.) or slight traces of pitch, or a very small pocket, or equivalent combination. Very light torn grain, skip and cup. Wane on reverse side on an occasional piece.	—	B & BTR 1 & 2 Clear Superior Finish	Supreme	—	Clear All Heart Clear	Clear Heart	B & B Finish
	Lumber of fine appearance for high quality interior trim and cabinet work.	Two small, sound tight knots (¾" max.) or light pitch, or a small pitch streak, or two very small pockets, or equivalent combination. Very light torn grain, cup and crook. Light skip. Wane on reverse side on an occasional piece.	C & BTR Select C Select	C Select	Choice	C & BTR Finish	—	A	C Finish
		Four small fixed knots (¾" max.) or four small pockets, or medium pitch, or equivalent combination. Medium stain, scattered light torn grain, light crook, short split on end, wane on reverse side.	D Select	D Select	Quality	D Finish	—	B	D Finish
COMMON	Best quality knotty lumber with all sound tight knots	Sound tight knots and smooth red knots 2¼" max. Very light torn grain and cup. Very short splits, one each end. Light crook and pitch. Two small dry pockets. Wane on reverse side on an occasional piece.	Finish and 1 Common	1 Common	Colonial	Select Merchantable	Select Heart Select	Select Merchantable	No. 2 Board
	Knotty lumber for exposed paneling and shelving and exterior house trim.	Sound and tight red knots 3" max., sound and tight black knots 1⅜" max. Light torn grain, cup, shake. Medium-light crook, short splits (one each end), three small dry pockets, medium wane, some firm hearth pith, 12 scattered pinholes.	Premium and No. 2 Common	2 Common	Sterling	Construction	—	Construction	No. 2 Board
	Knotty lumber for use where appearance and strength are important in shelving, paneling, siding and fencing.	Sound and tight red knots 3½" max., unsound knots, loose knots, knot holes 1½" max. Medium torn grain and crook, cup. Light-to-medium shake. Some unsound wood, heavy pitch, split up to ⅙ of length. Only one knot in a board can be the maximum size.	Standard No. 3 Common	3 Common	Standard	Standard	Construction Heart Construction Common	Standard	No. 3 Board
	Knotty lumber for general construction—subfloors, roof and wall sheathing, concrete forms and crates.	Fixed, firm and tight knots up to ⅔ width 3" loose knots and knotholes. Heavy torn grain, cup, wane. Large pockets. heavy streaks and patches of massed pitch over ½ area. Medium to heavy shake full length, split ⅓ length. Pinholes and small holes unlimited.	No. 4 Common	4 Common	Utility	Utility	Merchantable	Utility	No. 4 Board
	Lowest grade knotty lumber.	Large knots, very large holes, unsound wood, massed pitch, heavy splits, shake, wane in any degree or combination. But some pieces may be only slightly below No. 4.	No. 5 Common	5 Common	Industrial	Economy	Economy	Economy	—

larger, but the width cannot be more than 2 inches greater than the thickness.

These are graded Select Structural (good appearance), No. 1 and No. 2.

Plywood

Plywood is made of an odd number of thin layers of wood (called veneers) that are glued up and sandwiched together, with the grain of the veneers alternating at right angles. Softwood plywood—usually called *fir plywood*—is manufactured in this country under U.S. Product Standard PS 1. Most plywood you find in a lumber yard is marked with a grade-trademark of the American Plywood Association (APA). This mark tells you everything you need to know about the plywood.

Fir plywood is not exactly the right name, because many woods be-

sides fir are used. But fir plywood, to use the common term, is what you get when you go to the lumberyard and ask for plywood. The plywood is made in two types and many grades.

The two types are exterior and interior. One difference is the glue. Exterior is always made with waterproof glue, while water-resistant glue may be used on the interior type, though waterproof glue is sometimes used here, too.

Each type is made in many grades. The grades are based on surface veneer quality and the plywood's intended use. The face veneer grades are N, A, B, C, C-plugged, and D, running from best to worst.

N: Smooth surface, natural finish veneer. No open defects, and not more than six repairs (with wood) allowed per 4×8 panel, made with the grain and well-matched for grain and color.

A: Smooth, paintable. Not more than eighteen neatly made repairs per 4×8 panel.

B: Solid surface veneer. Shims, circular repair plugs, and tight knots up to 1 inch across permitted.

C: Knotholes up to 1 inch across permitted, plus occasional 1½-inch knotholes within specified limits. Splits permitted.

C-plugged: Improved C-grade veneer with splits limited to ⅛ inch in width and knotholes and borer holes limited to ¼×½ inch. Synthetic compound repairs permitted.

D: Knots and knotholes up to 2½ inches across the grain permitted, with some up to 4 inches permitted within specified limits.

These grades spell out veneer quality. Plywood is also divided into Appearance and Engineered grades. The common A/D Interior and A/C Exterior are appearance grades.

Engineered grades are used for sheathing, subflooring, underlayment, and decking, where strength and solid integrity is of more importance than the appearance and the surface finish.

Other plywood

Lauan plywood is imported from Korea, Japan, and elsewhere, mostly as ¼-inch underlayment. Lauan actually can be any of several wood species, all of which look like mahogany. Besides using it as underlayment, it is the best all-around choice for anything needing ¼-inch plywood, such as drawer bottoms and cabinet backs.

All plywood is made of veneer, but *veneer plywood* means plywood of something better than the fir used for the face veneers and, usually, for the inside veneers, too. This is the plywood to use for furniture or anything you plan to put a clear finish on. Choice of veneers includes pine, birch and most other domestic hardwoods, redwood, mahogany, and even exotic imported woods.

Not all plywood has veneer cores like fir plywood. *Lumber-core plywood* contains a thick center core made up of strips of lumber, glued up and faced with cross-banding veneer and face veneer. Lumber-core plywood costs more than veneer-core plywood, but is better for furniture work

---

Typical grade marks for dimension lumber

Western Wood Products Association (WWPA) Lumber was produced and graded at mill 12 (name of brand could substitute for number). The lumber had moisture content of more than 19 percent (S-GRN) at time of grading. Wood species is Mountain Hemlock (M HEM). Grade: Standard.

Western Wood Products Association (WWPA). Wood had moisture content of 19 percent or less when graded (S-DRY), and Utility grade shipment is a mixture of Mountain Hemlock, Hemlock and Fir (M-H HEM FIR).

S-DRY   001
STUD
ASPEN

Northeastern Lumber Manufacturers Association (NELMA). Wood had a moisture content of 19 percent or less (S-DRY) at grading time. Species: Aspen (ASPEN). Grade: Stud.

Typical grade marks for plywood

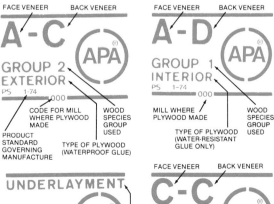

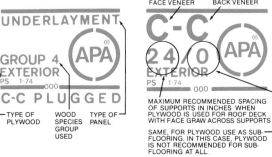

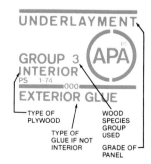

At top: Left, A-C Exterior plywood; center, A-D Interior plywood; right, underlayment—face veneer is Plugged-C; inner plywood construction resists surface indentation. Bottom: Left, A-D Interior plywood. Right, numbers indicate maximum recommended spacing for roof decking and subflooring in inches.

Wood characteristics

WANE

CUP

BOW

CROOK

TWIST

SPLIT

SHAKE

KNOTS

A   B   C

D   E   F

While manufacturing defects are also a factor, lumber grades are determined primarily by natural characteristics of a log that appear in the lumber. These include. . .

Wane. Presence of bark or lack of wood on edge or corner of board.

Cup. Curvature of wide face of board, edge to edge.

Bow. Curvature of wide face, end to end.

Crook. Curvature of narrow face of board, measured end to end.

Twist. Deviation from flat plane of all four faces.

Split. Separation of wood, usually at end of the lumber, due to tearing apart of wood cells.

Shake. Lengthwise separation of the wood. Shakes usually occur between or through the annual growth rings.

Knots. Varieties include: **A.** Knothole through two wide faces. **B.** Sound, encased, fixed round knot through two wide faces. **C.** Sound, watertight, intergrown through two wide faces. **D.** Sound, watertight, tight intergrown spike through two faces; **E.** Intergrown round knot through four faces; **F.** Edge knot.

that calls for doweling, splines, or dovetail joints.

"Plywood" is also made with a *flakeboard* core. Face veneers are applied directly to the flakeboard.

Veneer, lumber-core, and flakeboard plywoods all have advantages and disadvantages. Here's a rundown of what you can expect from each:

Veneer (all inner plies of wood veneers). General thickness: ¼ to ¾ inch. Remarks: Best screwholding power from face or back of panel. Core imperfections and grain may "print" through face veneer. Exposed edge difficult to stain; shows core voids and imperfections. Most susceptible to warpage. Most difficult to work.

TABLE II. Dimension lumber and timber grades (Requirements

		LIGHT FRAMING 2" TO 4" THICK 2" TO 4" WIDE 6' AND LONGER			ECONOMY	STUDS 2" TO 4" THICK 2" TO 6" WIDE 10' AND SHORTER	
		CONSTRUCTION	STANDARD	UTILITY		STUD	ECONOMY STUD
TYPE OF KNOT PERMITTED		Sound, firm, encased, and pith. Must be tight.	Any kind	Any kind		Any kind, well spaced	Any kind
SOUND KNOTS, SIZE PERMITTED — WIDTH OF PIECE	2"	3/4"	1"	1 1/4"		3/4"	Knots up to 3/4 of cross section permitted
	3"	1 1/4"	1 1/2"	2"		1 1/4"	
	4"	1 1/2"	2"	2 1/2"		1 3/4"	
	5"	—	—	—		2 1/4"-3"	
	6"	—	—	—		2 3/4"-3 3/4"	—
	8"	—	—	—		—	—
	10"	—	—	—		—	—
	12"	—	—	—		—	—
	14"	—	—	—		—	—
SPIKE KNOTS ACROSS WIDE FACE		1/4 of cross section	1/3 of cross section	1/2 of cross section		N.A.	N.A.
LOOSE KNOTS & KNOTHOLES, SIZE PERMITTED — WIDTH OF PIECE	2"	5/8"	3/4"	1"		3/4"	Knotholes up to 3/4 of cross section permitted
	3"	3/4"	1"	1 1/4"		1 1/4"	
	4"	1"	1 1/4"	1 1/2"		1 1/2"	
	5"	—	—	—		1 3/4"	
	6"	—	—	—		2"	
	8"	—	—	—		—	
	10"	—	—	—		—	
	12"	—	—	—		—	
	14"	—	—	—		—	
KNOTHOLE SPACING		1 per 3 lin. ft.	1 per 2 lin. ft.	1 per lin. ft.		1 per lin. ft.	
SLOPE OF GRAIN		1 in 6	1 in 4	1 in 4		1 in 4	
SHAKE		Several heart shakes up to 2' long, none through	1/2 of thickness at ends. elsewhere longer, some through	Surface shakes at ends, same as split through; 1/3 length		At end, same as split if through; elsewhere 1/3 of length	Not limited
SPLITS (MAX.)		Length equal to width of piece	Length equal to 1 1/2 times width of piece	1/6 of length of piece		Length equal to twice width of piece	1/4 of length of piece
WANE Typical, many exceptions		1/4 of thickness 1/4 of width	1/3 of thickness 1/3 of width	1/2 of thickness 1/2 of length		1/3 of thickness 1/2 of width length unlimited	1/4 of thickness 3/4 of face length unlimited
WARP Includes bow, crook, cup, twist or any combination		1/2 of medium	Light	Medium		1/2 of medium	Crook and twist 1" max in 8' stud
UNSOUND WOOD • Spots and streaks only • Must not destroy nailing edge		Not permitted		1/3 of cross section		1/3 of cross section	

ALL LUMBER CHARACTERISTICS ALLOWED EXCEPT BROKEN OR SLABBY ENDS LARGE KNOTS AND KNOTHOLES, UNSOUND WOOD, HEAVY SHAKE, SPLITS AND WANE OR ANY COMBINATION PERMITTED. PIECES 9' AND SHORTER MUST BE USABLE FULL LENGTH

DIMENSIO

NOTE: AT EDGE OF WIDE FACE—AT CENTERLINE OF WIDE FACE, WHEN TWO SIZES GIVEN FOR STUDS AND JOISTS AND PLANKS; ON NARROW FACE—WIDE FACE FOR BEAMS AND STRINGERS

Flakeboard. General thickness: ¾ inch. Remarks: Most stable. No core printing. Poor edge screwholding. Heaviest panel. Exposed edge difficult to stain (but can be finished).

Lumber-core (lumber strips 1 to 4 inches wide, edge-glued together). General thickness: ¾ inch. Remarks: Easiest worked. Solid exposed edges

(for stain). Stable construction. Good holding for screws into edge, for example, for installing hinges.

Hardwood

Unlike softwood, which is graded looking at a piece as a whole, hardwood is graded assuming it will be cut up to make furniture parts. Softwood

is inspected after the piece has been planed smooth; hardwood is graded in the rough, and the inspector doesn't care about the defects—just the amount of clear wood between them.

The top grade is *Firsts and Seconds* (FAS). FAS is graded from the poorer side to allow good cuttings all the way through. *Select,* the next grade, is

shown are simplified; additional factors enter into grading)

LUMBER					APPEAR-ANCE 2" TO 4" THICK 2" AND WIDER 6' AND LONGER	TIMBERS			
JOISTS AND PLANKS 2" TO 4" THICK 5" AND WIDER 6' AND LONGER						BEAMS AND STRINGERS 5" AND THICKER WIDTH MORE THAN 2" GREATER THAN THICKNESS 6' AND LONGER		POSTS AND TIMBERS 5" × 5" AND LARGER WIDTH NOT MORE THAN 2" GREATER THAN THICKNESS 6' AND LONGER	
SELECT STRUCTURAL	NO. 1	NO. 2	NO. 3	ECONOMY	APPEARANCE	SELECT STRUCTURAL	NO. 1	SELECT STRUCTURAL	NO. 1
Sound, firm, encased, and pith; tight and well-spaced	Sound, firm, encased, and pith; tight and well-spaced	Any kind, well-spaced	Any kind, well-spaced		Sound, tight, well-spaced	Sound, tight, well-spaced	Sound, tight, well-spaced	Sound, tight, well-spaced	Sound, tight, well-spaced
— 1"–1 1/2" 1 1/8"–1 7/8" 1 1/2"–2 1/4" 1 7/8"–2 5/8" 2 1/4"–3" 2 3/8"–3 1/4"	— 1 1/4"–1 7/8" 1 1/2"–2 1/4" 2"–2 3/4" 2 1/2"–3 1/4" 3"–3 3/4" 3 1/8"–4"	— — 1 5/8"–2 3/8" 1 7/8"–2 7/8" 2 1/2"–3 1/2" 3 1/4"–4 1/4" 3 3/4"–4 3/4" 4 1/8"–5 1/4"	— — 2 1/4"–3" 2 3/4"–3 3/4" 3 1/2"–4 1/2" 4 1/2"–5 1/2" 5 1/2"–6 1/2" 6"–7"		1/2" 3/4" 1" 1 1/4" 1 1/2" 2" 2 1/2" 3" 3 1/8"	— — — 1 1/4"–2" 1 1/2"–2 1/2" 1 3/4"–3" 2"–3 1/4" 2 1/4"–3 1/2" 2 3/8"–3 3/4"	— — — 1 7/8"–3" 2 1/4"–3 3/4" 2 1/2"–4 1/2" 3"–4 3/4" 3 1/4"–5" 3 1/2"–5 1/2"	— — — 1" 1 1/4" 1 5/8" 2" 2 3/8" 2 1/2"	— — — 1 1/2" 1 7/8" 2 1/2" 3 1/8" 3 3/4" 4"
N.A.	N.A.	N.A.	N.A.		N.A.	N.A.	N.A.	N.A.	N.A.
— — 7/8" 1" 1 1/4" 1 1/4" 1 1/4" 1 per 4 lin. ft.	— — 1 1/8" 1 1/4" 1 1/2" 1 1/2" 1 1/2" 1 per 3 lin. ft.	— — 1 3/8" 1 1/2" 2" 2 1/2" 3" 3 1/2" 1 per 2 lin. ft.	— — 1 7/8" 2" 2 1/2" 3" 3 1/2" 4" 1 per lin. ft.		None permitted	None permitted	None permitted	None permitted	None permitted
1 in 12	1 in 10	1 in 8	1 in 4		1 in 10	1 in 15	1 in 11	1 in 12	1 in 10
1/2 of thickness at ends; else-where 2' long, none through	1/2 of thickness at ends; else-where 2' long, none through	1/2 of thickness at ends; else-where 3' or longer, some through	Surface shakes permitted		Not specified	1/6 of thickness	1/6 of thickness	1/3 of thickness on one end	1/3 of thickness on one end
Length equal to width of piece	Length equal to width of piece	Length equal to 1 1/2 times width of piece	1/6 of length		Length equal to width of piece	Length equal to 1/2 of width of piece	Length equal to width of piece	Length equal to 3/4 of thickness	Length equal to width of piece
1/4 of thickness 1/4 of width up to 1/2 of length	1/4 of thickness 1/4 of width up to 1/2 of length	1/3 of thickness 1/3 of width up to 2/3 of length	1/2 of thickness 1/2 of width up to 7/8 of length		1/12 of thickness 1/12 of width 1/6 of length	1/8 of any face	1/4 of any face	1/8 of any face	1/4 of any face
1/2 of medium	1/2 of medium	Light	Medium		Very light	—	—	—	—
Not permitted	Not permitted	Not permitted in thicknesses over 2"	1/3 of cross section		Not permitted	—	—	—	—

ALL LUMBER CHARACTERISTICS ALLOWED EXCEPT BROKEN OR SLABBY ENDS, LARGE KNOTS AND KNOTHOLES, UNSOUND WOOD, HEAVY SHAKE, SPLITS, WANE OR ANY COMBINATION PERMITTED. PIECES 9' AND SHORTER MUST BE USABLE FULL LENGTH

TABLE III. Readily available APA grade-trademarked "Fir" plywood

	Grade	Use	Veneer Grade			Commonly Available Thickness
			Face	Core	Back	
APPEARANCE GRADES	A-D Interior	For painted built-ins, shelving, projects where only one side will show. Do not use where edges will be exposed or where voids in core ply under face will be objectionable.	A	D	D	¼", ⅜", ½", ¾"
	B-D Interior	Same uses as A-D Interior.	B	D	D	¾"
	A-C Exterior	For painted outdoor projects where only one side will show. Also used for indoor projects requiring a more solid plywood than A-D Interior or where edges will be veneered or finished.	A	C	C	¼", ⅜", ½", ⅝", ¾"
ENGINEERED GRADES	C-C Exterior	Unsanded plywood for roof decking, subflooring and sheathing.	C	C	C	5/16", ⅜", ½", ⅝", ¾"
	C-D Interior	Wall and roof sheathing, subflooring. Usually available with waterproof glue as CDX.	C	D	C	⅜", ½", ⅝", ¾"
	C-Plugged D Interior	Touch sanded. For backing wall and ceiling. Not waterproof. Not for underlayment because does not have indentation resistance. Available with waterproof glue.	Plugged-C	D	D	¼"
	Underlayment Interior	Touch sanded. Use over structural subfloor. Available with exterior glue. Provides smooth surface for resilient flooring.	Plugged-C	C&D	C	¼"
	Underlayment C-C Plugged Exterior	Touch sanded. Use over structural subfloor. Provides smooth surface for resilient flooring where severe moisture conditions may be present.	Plugged-C	C	C	¼", ⅜"

graded from the good side to allow cuttings that are good on one side. *No. 1 Common grade,* next, is graded from the poorer side and yields cuttings good on two sides, but only smaller cuttings with a lot of waste. Grades go downhill from there.

Tips on buying

• When working on a big home-improvement project where you can't estimate materials to the last foot, buy 80 to 90 percent of what you think you need. By the time you get near the end and have changed the design a few times, you'll be able to figure up exactly what additional material you need.

• Avoid economy grades of dimension lumber. If the wood is any good, it wouldn't be in that grade.

• Figure board and dimension lumber needs in standard-length pieces, rather than total number of feet. You will be surprised how planning reduces waste.

• Yards generally cut lumber without charge so you can get it into your car (if not, find another yard), but most charge to cut to dimension.

• Buy dimension lumber in as long a piece as you can handle. Long pieces tend to have less warp than short pieces—don't ask me why.

• Buy A-C EXT fir plywood in preference to A-D INT even for interior jobs. The better-quality back and core plys are worth the small extra cost, unless you are using whole plywood panels.

• For furniture making, you can generally get ¾-inch pine or birch veneer plywood at lumberyards for $12 to $15 more per panel than A/C Exterior and it can be finished without the surface preparation necessary with fir plywood.

• You have the right to expect that each piece of lumber you buy meets the standards for the grade you are being charged for.

• Need top-quality veneer plywood in less than full-panel quantities? Check local cabinet and millwork shops for job leftovers. Also a good source for small quantities of hardwood.

• If you need select-grade pine, but will cut it into small pieces, buy common lumber and cut around knots.

• While hardwood usually comes in random lengths and widths, some retailers also sell it in neatly cut pieces. Unless you can use these pieces with zero waste, you save money buying random-size pieces and paying by the board-foot—*Thomas H. Jones.*

TABLE IV. Dry softwood lumber dimensions

BOARDS					DIMENSION & TIMBER	
Thickness (except Redwood)*		Width			Thickness & Width	
Nominal	Actual	Nominal	Actual		Nominal	Actual
4/4 1"	¾"	2"	1½"		2"	1½"
5/4 1¼"	1⁵/₃₂"	3"	2½"		3"	2½"
6/4 1½"	1¹³/₃₂"	4"	3½"		4"	3½"
7/4 1¾"	1¹⁹/₃₂"	5"	4½"		5"	4½"
8/4 2"	1¹³/₁₆"	6"	5½"		6"	5½"
9/4 2¼"	2³/₃₂"	7"	6½"		7"	6½"
10/4 2½"	2⅜"	8" and wider			8" and wider ¾" off nominal	
11/4 2¾"	2⁹/₁₆"	¾" off nominal				
12/4 3"	2¾"					
16/4 4"	3¾"					
*Redwood is often sold in ¹¹/₁₆" thickness rather than ¾".						

wall accents with wood moldings

Look around the room you're sitting in. What hides the seams where walls meet ceiling and floors? If your house was built before World War II, chances are these areas are covered by handsome wood moldings. But this richly carved decoration could be invisible for all the attention we generally give it.

There are other uses, too, for molding strips. They can revive a dull wall, give a custom-designed look to an ordinary room, and even create unique built-ins such as room dividers and canopy beds.

If you live in a modern, post-war house, moldings can create the bold graphics or classic carved paneling that will distinguish your unadorned walls from all the look-alikes in the area. And if you have been wanting an elegant carved wall or wainscoting, you'll find that the look you're af-

Airy-looking lattice (right) creates a custom bed canopy for this striking room. Painted lattice strips also form the dramatic wall graphics and window frame. Diagram above shows (top row) how to assemble strips for wall frames and canopy lattice. Quarter rounds flank edge casing to form the chair rail (bottom, left). Two sizes of s4s (sanded four sides) molding strips, plus lattice (right), are used.

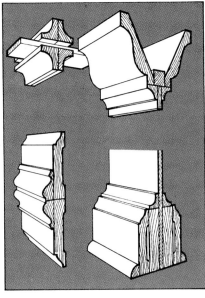

Paneled room divider (right) echoes this room's elegant wainscoting. Four cove moldings sandwich lattice (above, top) to form divider posts. Cove moldings also frame the plywood panels. Center rosettes are made by mounting base caps atop base moldings (bottom, left) and mitering into four wedges. Crowns and coves nailed to square make divider top; coves and bases nailed to s4s, bottom.

Mirror-backed lattice on one side of corner produces intriguing light-and-shadow pattern. Each grid is best laid out on floor—half the lattice strips trimmed and laid parallel to form the rear diagonal, the other half laid atop, at right angles. Cove strips form frame. Glue and brads hold assembly together as it's raised in front of wall mirrored with mounted sheets or peel-and-stick squares.

The rich look of carved paneling is achieved by nailing s4s molding and base caps to plywood paneling. No solid lumber sold today is wide enough to carve out paneling in one piece as craftsmen once did, so molding is today's means to get this effect. Actual molding type used depends on the effect wanted. Quarter rounds or coves could substitute for the base caps shown here.

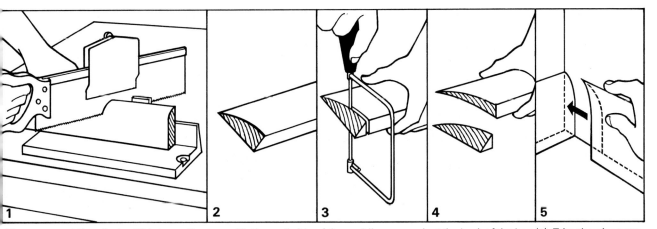

To cope a molding, first set it into a miter box with the wall side of the molding up against the back of the box (1). Trim the piece at a 45-degree angle to expose the exact profile of the molding face (2). Use this as a guide line for the coping saw (3), slicing away excess molding while keeping blade at a 90-degree angle to the molding face. This cut duplicates the curve of the molding (4) so it butts snugly against the face of an adjoining piece (5) to turn a corner.

ter may be possible only by using moldings.

"In the old days, they handcrafted the molding on the spot," Neal Heflin of the Wood Moulding and Millwork Producers told me. "They used wider lumber, and a lot more of it. If you did a room that way today, it would cost thousands of dollars."

Today's wood molding is factory-milled and finished—and a lot cheaper. A major woodworker's catalog (Woodworkers' Store) lists a 1-inch astragal (scalloped shape) molding at 54¢ a foot in pine, and a half-round rope-twist molding (½-inch-wide poplar) at $1.50 for 4 feet. Lumberyard prices vary widely, of course, but most should be in the 50¢- to $2.50-a-foot range, depending on the molding's width and intricacy. That's well under the cost of wall coverings such as fabric, custom wallpapers, and prefinished paneling.

And though most molding projects require careful planning and installation, they are not as tricky as you might expect. Most wall designs can be glued instead of nailed in place, for example. "If you're making a supergraphic, or a wall frame, you can use adhesive," Heflin said. "It's fine in any application that doesn't get stress. For a door casing or a heavy ceiling cornice, you'd want nails," he added.

Designing with moldings

The first step is to become familiar with the varied molding shapes and sizes. A good way to start is by browsing through brochures from manufacturers' associations (see list previous page). There are three basic types of wood moldings. The first, and cheapest, are unfinished strips of milled wood. These give you the greatest design latitude, but you do have the extra work involved in finishing the wood.

Next there are "toned" wood moldings, prefinished with a stain. Finally, there are wood moldings covered with a wood-grain-printed vinyl. These prefinished types are more expensive, but if their colors match your planned decor they can save you time. (The smaller molding designs also come in unfinished or vinyl-clad plastic. These are lighter than wood equivalents, less subject to warp, and can be cut without splintering. Vinyl moldings are often color-matched to a particular line of prefinished paneling.)

Your local home center or lumberyard should have some examples of each of these types. But it's unlikely you'll find a full selection of all possible shapes (or profiles, as the industry calls them). So it's best to plan carefully. Know the effect you want to get and what different molding profiles will give you that effect.

Precise measurements are another timesaver. Moldings come in 2- to 11-foot lengths. The shorter lengths are much easier to work with—and most projects will use lengths under 8 feet. When planning your purchase, list the specific lengths you'll need, then round each measurement to the next largest foot to allow for cutting and trimming. If your project requires mitering, allow for the width of the cut by adding in the width of the mitered pieces. (For an inside dimension of 30 inches, a 3-inch-wide piece mitered on both ends will require 36 inches, for example.)

There's one timesaver you shouldn't use: Don't just hand your list of molding profiles to the lumberyard clerk. Insist on picking out the lengths yourself.

Finish first

It sounds obvious, but in the excitement of creation, you may forget: Staining or painting moldings once they're wall-mounted is a mean job. It's usually best to apply your finish *before* putting it up. Where possible, it's also smart to assemble your molding project on the floor before fixing it in place. For supergraphics, paneling squares, and even some room dividers, you might consider making a jig to ease assembly. Nail a scrap-lumber frame on a panel of plywood so that its inside dimensions equal the outside ones of your graphic.

Not for walls only

Think about ceilings. Moldings can make a modern rosette to highlight a handsome chandelier. They can also turn a plain fireplace wall into a classic showpiece. Dull doors and cabinets can be pepped up with a few well-chosen pieces of molding. They can even give plain unfinished furniture a custom-made look. And moldings can be used structurally to create grilles and railings. Once you get hooked on the possibilities, you'll never lack for home-improvement projects—*Susan Renner-Smith.*

calculating angles
for compound miters

Recently I helped my son figure out how to calculate the cutting angles to make a planter with tapered sides. Deriving the two formulas was tough, but you'll find *using* them (with a calculator equipped for trig functions) makes it easy to calculate saw angles for cutting the sides of any structure with identical, sloping sides—picture frames, for example.

Don't let the mention of trigonometry scare you off. You don't have to be a whiz at trig to use this method. And you don't need a fancy, expensive calculator. Any low-cost model with preprogrammed trig functions (including inverse or arc functions) will do the job. A table with selected settings is provided here for those who don't have access to a suitable calculator.

To calculate saw-angle settings, you have to know the number of sides and the slope angle between any side and the vertical of the structure you're building. The number of sides determines the value of an interior angle—called angle A in the hexagonal planter illustrated. This value will be needed in the formulas that follow. The interior-angle figures below give angle-A values for regular structures with three to fifteen sides. You can

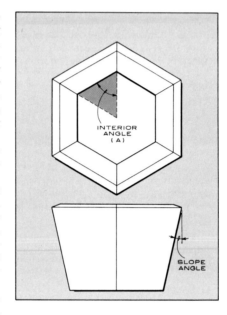

confirm these values using this formula:

$$\text{angle } A = 90° - \frac{180°}{\text{no. of sides}}$$

Practical slope

The slope angle may be anything between zero and 90 degrees, but the practical range is from about 5 to 70 degrees. Once you know the slope angle and angle A, you can calculate the arm angle and blade-tilt angle for your radial-arm saw, or the miter and tilt angles for your table saw.

Here are the two formulas used to calculate saw angles (the abbreviated forms of trig functions, such as tan for tangent, are used):

$$\tan(\text{arm angle}) = \cot(A) \times \sin(\text{slope}), \text{ and}$$
$$\sin(\text{blade-tilt angle}) = \cos(A) \times \cos(\text{slope})$$

The first equation shows that the tangent of the arm angle is equal to the cotangent of angle A times the sine of the slope angle. (Most calculators don't have a direct cotangent function, so you'll use the 1/x function on your calculator to find the reciprocal of the tangent, which is the cotangent.) The second equation says the sine of the blade-tilt angle is equal to the cosine of angle A times the cosine of the slope angle.

To calculate the saw angles, you simply plug the values of angle A and the slope angle into the right side of these equations, and solve for the arm angle and blade-tilt angle. The calculator makes this very easy. Note

	3 sides		4 sides		5 sides		6 sides		8 sides	
Slope angle	Tilt angle	Arm angle	Tilt angle	Arm angle	Tilt angle	Arm angle	Tilt angle	Arm angle	Tilt angle	Arm angle
5	59.6	8.6	44.8	5.0	35.8	3.6	29.9	2.9	22.4	2.1
10	58.5	16.7	44.1	9.9	35.4	7.2	29.5	5.7	22.1	4.1
15	56.8	24.1	43.1	14.5	34.6	10.7	28.9	8.5	21.7	6.1
20	54.5	30.6	41.6	18.9	33.5	14.0	28.0	11.2	21.1	8.1
25	51.7	36.2	39.9	22.9	32.2	17.1	26.9	13.7	20.3	9.9
30	48.6	40.9	37.8	26.6	30.6	20.0	25.7	16.1	19.4	11.7
35	45.2	44.8	35.4	29.8	28.8	22.6	24.2	18.3	18.3	13.4
40	41.6	48.1	32.8	32.7	26.8	25.0	22.5	20.4	17.1	14.9
45	37.8	50.8	30.0	35.3	24.6	27.2	20.7	22.2	15.7	16.3
50	33.8	53.0	27.0	37.5	22.2	29.1	18.8	23.9	14.2	17.6
55	29.8	54.8	23.9	39.3	19.7	30.8	16.7	25.3	12.7	18.7
60	25.7	56.3	20.7	40.9	17.1	32.2	14.5	26.6	11.0	19.7
65	21.5	57.5	17.4	42.2	14.4	33.4	12.2	27.6	9.3	20.6
70	17.2	58.4	14.0	43.2	11.6	34.3	9.9	28.5	7.5	21.3

Notes: All angles in degrees. Slope angle measured from the vertical. For table saw, substitute miter angle for arm angle.

that if you're using a table saw, you simply substitute the miter angle for the radial-arm saw's arm angle. The blade-tilt angle is the same in either case.

Before we try a sample calculation, a word is necessary about the differences in calculator models. Some use the algebraic entry system, in which operation keys ($\times$, $-$, $+$, etc.) are generally used just as they're encountered in equations. Other models, such as the Novus 4520 I used, have an entry system in which the operation key is used last. Another difference between calculator types involves the key for arc or inverse functions: Mine has an ARC key; yours may have an INV key. Both do the same thing. In the following example, the keystrokes given are those for my model, but the sequence should be easy to translate into one your calculator understands.

Now let's try a design example—the hexagonal planter box—to demonstrate the ease of calculation. From the listing of interior-angle figures that follow, you find that angle A is 60 degrees for a six-sided structure. Next, let's choose 10 degrees for the side slope. Plugging these numbers into the two formulas, we get:

$$\tan(\text{arm angle}) = \cot 60° \times \sin 10°,$$
$$\text{and}$$
$$\sin(\text{blade-tilt angle}) =$$
$$\cos 60° \times \cos 10°$$

The keystroke sequence for the arm angle is:

Key step	Result
Press *6*, then *0*	Enters 60 (angle A)
Press *tan*	Calculates tan 60°
Press *1/x*	Converts tan A to cot A
Press *1*, then *0*	Enters 10 (slope angle)
Press *sin*	Calculates sin 10°
Press *x*	Multiplies prior results
Press *ARC*, then *tan*	Calculates arm angle (5.7° in this example)

For the blade-tilt angle, the sequence is:

Key step	Result
Press *6*, then *0*	Enters 60 (angle A)
Press *cos*	Calculates cos 60°
Press *1*, then *0*	Enters 10 (slope angle)
Press *cos*	Calculates cos 10°
Press *x*	Multiplies prior results
Press *ARC*, then *sin*	Calculates tilt angle (29.5° in this example)

To cut the first edge, set the arm 5.7 degrees to the right, and tilt the blade 29.5 degrees (down to the right) as shown in the series of photos. You won't be able to set tenth-of-a-degree angles, but set your saw angles as accurately as possible: Errors tend to be multiplied by the number of cuts you make. As a general rule, it is better to err on the side of larger angles, because then any gaps will show up on the inside of the piece.

Use a blade that provides a good finish cut, such as a hollow-ground combination or a crosscut blade. It is also important to cut all sides exactly the same width; the photo sequence illustrates how.

The large table provides saw angles for fourteen slope angles and five types of structures for those without calculators. But for that custom-designed planter box, hopper, or pyramid, a calculator and the formulas presented can give you the exact angles you want—*R. Joseph Ransil.*

Set and check angle settings, then make first cut (top). Flip board over, measure desired width, and mark rail (center) or set stop to assure equal widths for all cuts. Continue flipping board and aligning it on mark (bottom) till all sides are cut.

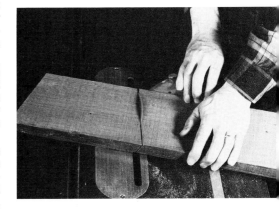

Table-saw cuts are similar. Use masking-tape marker or gauge block to assure uniform size. Press board against miter.

concealing plywood edges

Plywood panels are a boon to the woodworker, but they have unattractive edges that can't always be concealed by joint design. Exposure occurs at front edges of case goods and shelves, and at the perimeter of tabletop sections, trays, and the like.

Some of the more traditional ways to cover edges:

● Heavy wood strips, glued and nailed in place. Standard moldings that cover both single edges and corners are available in various styles.

● A raised lip can sometimes be used. A straight strip conceals the edge; triangular strips or molding blends the lip with the slab. If you cut a rabbet in the strip you intend to use to cover the edge, one piece does the work of two.

● Edges can be concealed during construction by using solid stock inserted at corners where pieces meet (glue blocks behind corners give support). However, this requires preplanning, as inserts take up space and may change a project's dimensions.

A relatively new and easy way to conceal edges is with wood-tape products. They are suitable for use on all natural finishes.

The wood tapes come in rolls and are actually flexible bands of veneer. More and more types have come on the market, so today you can find a match for just about any species of wood used as a surface veneer on plywood. The tapes are thin enough so you can cut them with a knife, yet strong enough so you don't have to worry about breaking them.

Different types are available. Some are self-adhesive, others are applied with a white glue or contact cement. If you work with a white glue, it is best to apply thin coatings to both surfaces and wait for the glue to become tacky before placing the tape. If you work with contact cement, follow instructions on the container. You must be sure the initial placement is correct because the cement bonds immediately.

One exceptional product, so far as application is concerned, is simply called Woodtape®. It has a 1/48-inch thick veneer and a factory-applied thermo-setting adhesive. Don't let the "thermo-setting" worry you, because heat for the application is available from an ordinary electric household iron. Tapes come with a paper backing you peel off before use. They are sticky enough so the tape holds, but the bond will not be effective or permanent un-

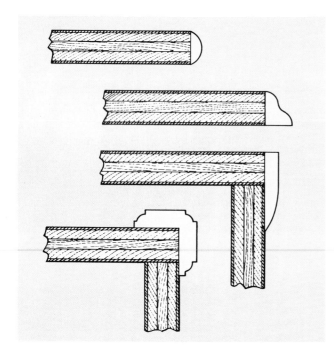

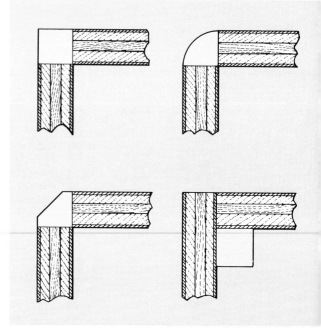

Standard moldings, such as those shown in the drawing above, left, can be used to hide single edges, as stops, or as outside corner guards. To cover the edges of plywood at the corners, you can use solid-stock inserts, as shown above, right. The inserts can be square, quarter-round, or triangular, and they can be reinforced with glue blocks.

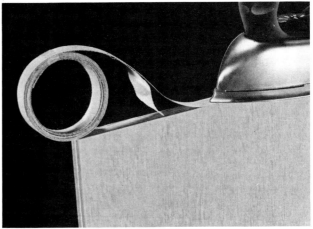

Both edges of plywood are concealed by wood strips as shown in the photos. Example on the left side of the photo requires two rabbet cuts on the wood strip and a groove in the plywood. Thermo-setting Woodtape®, which is shown in the photo directly above, is pressed on with ordinary household iron, set at 400 degrees F. Don't strip off long pieces of the paper backing in advance—remove it piecemeal as you go.

til you run over it with an iron set at 400 degrees F—about the correct setting for cotton.

Be sure the panel edges are square, smooth, and free of sawdust no matter what tape you apply. It is not necessary to fill the edges, but you should plug any large cavity that might cause a hollow to form in the tape.

Thermo-setting tape can be worked on as soon as it has cooled— contact-cement applications are ready to go right away—glue jobs require the cor-rect amount of set time. Sand the tapes as you would any veneer—being aware of their thinness. All are quite smooth, so minimum sandpaper work is needed.

Incidentally, the tapes may be used as inlay strips and, because they cut so easily with a knife or shears, for marquetry—*R. J. DeCristoforo.*

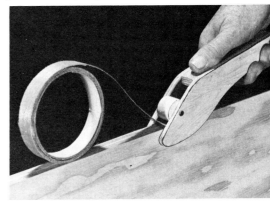

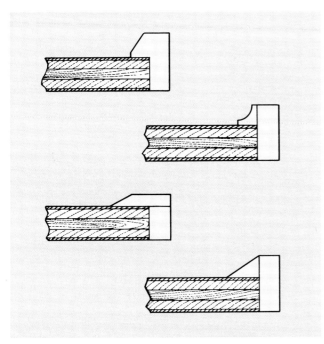

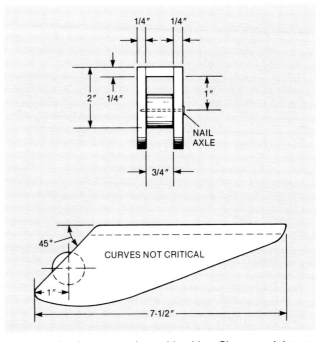

Raised lip (left, above) can be made with a triangular strip, molding two wood strips or one piece with rabbet. Shown at right are a picture of (top), and plans for (bottom) an edge-guide you can make from ¼-inch plywood to help you align wood tapes and apply pressure during gluing. The roller—it rides a nail axle—is cut from a 1-inch hardwood dowel.

making tenons with a plug-cutter

When you're repairing or building chairs, tables, and other pieces of furniture, one of your hardest jobs usually is the cutting and fitting of tenon ends on rungs, back spindles, and side members. Square tenons require carefully chiseled square mortises, while dowels require holes that are accurately drilled into the end grain of the wood.

It's much easier and faster to form tenons on the workpiece itself, using a plug cutter. The plug cutter is mounted in either a lathe headstock or a drill press chuck.

With the lathe, the cutter is fixed and the workpiece is advanced into it with a milling vise and feed screw. To use a drill press, you lock the work in a drill-press vise clamped and aligned on the table and feed the cutter into the wood. While either method works well, the lathe system is easier to align because of the screw adjustments on the milling vise. Both give you accurate, round tenons quickly in any quantity you need.

After cutting the tenon to the desired depth, the waste wood is readily snicked away with a knife, or, in the case of multiple tenons on one piece, sawed free with a fine coping saw blade. If the tenon is smaller in diameter than the thickness of the wood, as is usually the case, it is easier to cut the shoulders first on a table saw. Set up the crosscut gauge and make a cut on each of the four sides.

Tenons cut in this way will fit precisely into holes drilled with a router bit. Since plug cutters come in ⅜-inch and ½-inch diameters, they match equivalent diameter router bits.

Don't forget to file or sand a flat on the tenon for glue relief. If you fail to do this, you will be trying to compress glue between the tenon end and the bottom of the hole—*E. F. Lindsley.*

Tenons made with plug cutter are shown at top of page: Left, as formed before trimming and, next to it, trimmed and glue relief added. Others are single and double tenons formed after cutting shoulders on table saw. Plug cutter in lathe headstock rounds off ½-inch-square chair rung and leaves only slivers on corners to be cleaned up. Lower left: Same operation can be performed in a drill press, but you have to slide drill press vise around to locate it, then clamp. Lower right: Flat for glue clearance helps assembly. File or sand back almost to shoulder. Tenon holes are drilled with router bit.

how to drill big holes

Drilling holes up to ⅜ inch in diameter is usually simple enough—most of the time you can do it with twist drills. If you're working with masonry, you substitute a carbide masonry bit. But that's where the simplicity ends. Larger holes require more specialized bits.

Twist drills that you can chuck in a home-shop tool are limited in size, and their cost rises as the diameter increases. When holes get bigger than ⅜ inch, it may pay to use a bit made for the particular application. The payoff is lower cost; easier, faster drilling; and cleaner holes.

You can drill clean, accurate holes in wood using twist drills (which are designed for drilling metal)—*if* the drill is sharp, *if* you start the hole with a countersink to guide the drill, and *if* you feed the drill slowly (so hard-soft variations in the grain structure won't lure the drill off at an angle). And you must be careful to clamp the work, because a twist drill has a strong tendency to pull itself into the wood with sometimes messy results.

There's no need to risk that trouble, however. For just about every large-bore drilling application (wood, metal, or plastic), there's a specialty bit that does the job better than a twist drill, and often for less cost. Here's how to use them:

Spade bits. Chuck these bits in a portable electric drill to chew holes fast in studs and joists. The holes are rough, but it matters little in studs. In a drill press, use them to make clean-through holes—or bottomed holes, if you can tolerate the deep penetration of the point. They're virtually uncontrollable in end grain, which makes them a poor choice for drilling dowel holes, no matter how well hidden.

Auger bits. Although auger bits are usually seen with square, tapered tangs for use in a bit brace, they are also made with round shanks for chucking in a power drill. Auger bits are sized in sixteenths of an inch: a No. 8 bit is 8/16, or ½, inch in diameter. The feed screw of an auger bit accurately locates the hole and helps pull the spurs into the work, but once the point breaks through, it's usually muscle power that completes the hole. Using a straight-shank auger bit on a

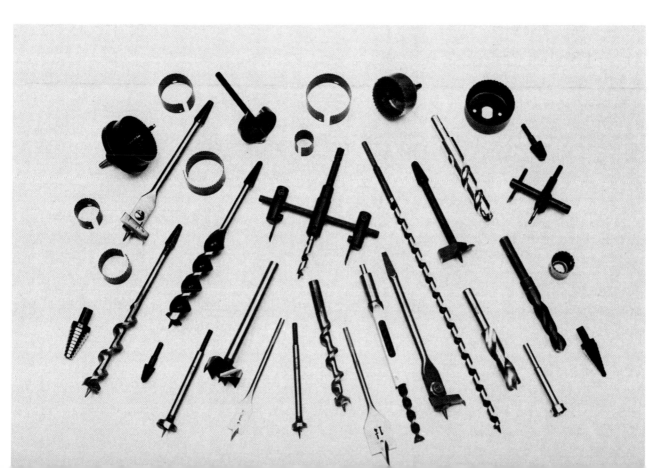

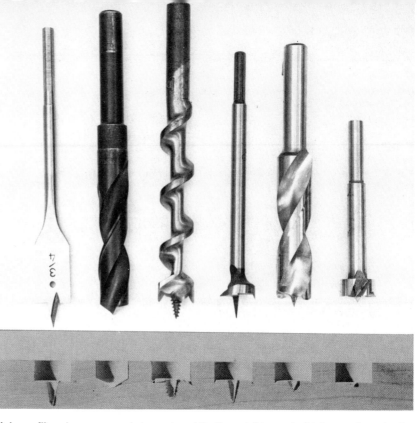

drill press or electric hand drill requires care because the feed screw can abruptly pull the bit out of control and into the work. To lessen the problem, partially file away the threads on the tapered feed screw.

Auger bits are made in several patterns. The solid-center bit is forged from bar stock. It's the strongest and least expensive. The Russell Jennings type is twisted from strip steel; it produces cleaner, more accurate holes and has better chip removal. Use long ship auger bits for boring deep, clean holes.

Power-bore bits. These bits drill clean, accurate holes in wood. They are roughly equivalent in performance to brad-point drills (below), except for the longer tip, which in many applications can be as objectionable as that on a spade bit.

Brad-point drills. The small tip (only 3/16 inch long) on this bit starts the hole accurately and keeps it going straight. The two spurs slice through the wood, keeping the sides of the hole clean as the flutes shave out the wood. The brad-point drill is the best all-around choice for making clean holes in wood. It's best used on a drill press, but can also be used in a portable electric drill.

Forstner bits. Use these relatively expensive bits when you want to drill an especially clean hole partway through the wood without the risk of the spurs or feed screw of an auger bit (or the tip of a brad-point bit or twist drill) going deeper and possibly breaking through. The hole made by a Forstner bit is exceptionally clean

Hole profiles above are made by various bits (from left): spade, high-speed-steel twist, solid-center auger, Stanley Power Bore, brad-point, and Forstner.

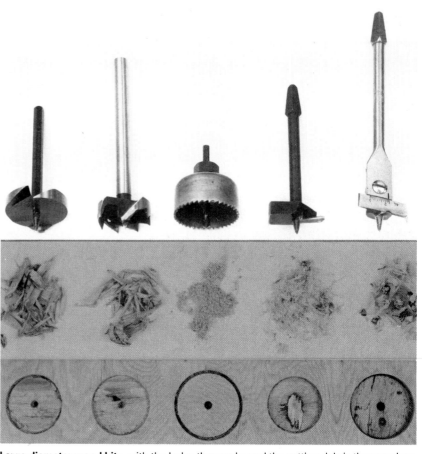

Forstner bit chucked in a drill press can drill large holes with flat bottoms diagonally in work pieces. Bit won't deflect as it enters wood.

Large-diameter wood bits, with the holes they make and the cutting debris they produce, are (from left) Stanley lock-set bit, multispur bit, hole saw and mandrel, door-lock bit, expansive bit. Holes are cut in fir plywood. Regardless of debris, all bits cut clean hole.

and has a flat bottom. Its brad point is typically only ³⁄₃₂ inch long. Flat-bottom hole drilling is important when drilling holes for dowels in thin boards. A Forstner bit can also drill partial-diameter holes—holes slanted into the side of a board, as for screws holding a table top to an apron. The Forstner bit is for wood only; you must use a drill press; and the work, except for full-diameter straight drilling, must be firmly clamped.

Multidiameter bits. Having on hand a set of twist drills to handle all possible drilling needs in metal, plastic, and thin wood between ³⁄₈ inch and 1 inch would be expensive. A plumber's tapered burring reamer is one solution to the problem, if you have a bit brace. However, maintaining accurate hole location and diameter is difficult because the tool is very fast-cutting in soft or thin materials. Arco's multidrills are single-flute tapered reamers. They are more controllable, and maintaining accurate hole location is easier. When you use the bit in a drill press, hole diameter can be accurately controlled with the depth stop.

A Unibit is the best approach to a multidiameter bit. It's a step drill with diameters in ¹⁄₁₆-inch increments. If you can work from both sides of the material, straightsided (not tapered) holes can be drilled in material up to ¼ inch thick. Working from one side only, the limit is ⅛ inch. Even when drilling with an electric hand drill you can count steps for repetitive drilling of the same-size holes.

Expansive bits. Bits for braces are made up to No. 24 (1½ inches), and the bigger ones are expensive. A pair of expansive bits can take the place of a set of auger bits when you need holes over ⅝ inch in diameter, and can be used to bore holes up to 3 inches. When setting an expansive bit, always check the hole size in scrap first. Don't trust the calibration. And always be sure the cutter locking screw is as tight as you can get it.

Hole saws. There are two kinds. The inexpensive type comes with a single mandrel and a set of seven blades. The blades resemble pieces of wide hacksaw-blade stock formed into circles. The advantage of low initial cost is offset by not being able to replace worn blades individually.

In the better type of hole saw, the blade is in the form of an inverted cup with teeth around the rim. The cup mounts on a mandrel. Blades and mandrels are purchased separately, although they are sometimes available in kits. Use high-speed steel blades on wood, machinable steel, iron, brass, copper, aluminum, and most plastics (except fiberglass-reinforced and thermo-plastic). Carbide-tipped hole-saw blades cut all of the above materials, plus fiber glass-reinforced plastic, gypsum board, and plaster (but not masonry).

Both types of hole saws have twist-drill pilot drills. Use either of them in a drill press or portable electric drill. When drilling deep holes it's a good idea to back out the drill occasionally and chisel out the scrap material. The saw runs cooler with less chip clogging, and you won't have the time-consuming problem of getting the plug out of the saw cup when you're finished.

Lock-set bits. The most common need for a large-diameter wood bit around the house is for installing a new lock set on a door. You can make the large hole in the side of a door in a number of ways: You can use a hole saw; if you have a bit brace, you can use an expansive bit; if you have a lot of doors to do, you might use a special door-lock bit or a lock-set bit. If you have a drill press, you can use a hole saw, lock-set bit, or multispur bit. (Multispur bits can drill semicircular holes, just as the Forstner bit can.)

Circle cutters. Also known as fly cutters, circle cutters are used in a drill press for making large-diameter holes in metals, plastic (except fiber-glass-reinforced), and wood. Work

Auger bits, from top, are double-spiral Russell Jennings, solid-center auger, solid-center auger with straight shank for drill presses, ship auger (for a flat-bottom hole).

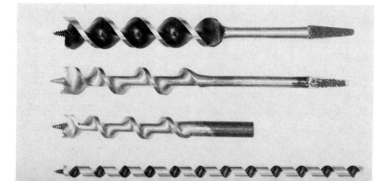

Circle cutter from Brookstone (top) cuts a ⅛-inch kerf, good for thick material; general's cutter (center) works best with thin material. Compass Cutter (bottom) from Hit Products works with a portable drill; its bit acts as a saw.

Multispur bit is used to drill exactly located holes in clamped wood. Performance is comparable with that of Forstner bit, except for the larger point. Bits range from ½- to 2⅛-inch diameter.

Unibit step drill bores clean holes in thin material easily. Tubing can be drilled without clamping—the bit has no tendency to walk.

Mortising bit for drill press bores a round hole, and the chisel squares it. Considerable downward force is required for chisel to cut.

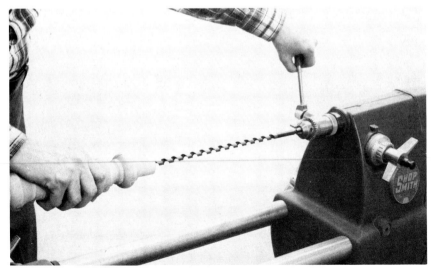

Ship auger is used for boring deep holes, such as a run for an electrical wire in a wooden lamp, above. The bit shown has a tapered feed screw, and the length of the twist section is 12 inches.

should be clamped and backed with scrap plywood. For a clean hole, cut partway from one side and finish from the other. Your drill-press speed should be slow, and the feed should be extremely slow.

A variation of the fly cutter is Hit Products' Compass Cutter, which chucks into an electric hand drill. It can cut circles up to 18 inches in diameter using a special cutter bit. The bit travels a line set by an adjustable arm tethered in the center of the cut. Use the tool for either cutting a large circle in plywood, plastic, and other similar material, or for cutting out a disc. It will cut through a 2 × 4.

Deep-drilling bits. Extra-long twist drills, brad-point drills, and auger bits are for boring very deep holes, such as in turned lamp parts. Of the three, the brad-point drill is the most accurate with the auger second. Use a slow drill speed and slow feed. For drilling holes in several diameters, do initial boring with a brad-point drill for accuracy, then ream with twist drills for larger diameters to save the cost of buying several expensive bits.

Mortising bits. A mortising bit drills a square hole. Use these to make mortises for tenons. You make rectangular holes by drilling overlapping square holes. The mortising bit consists of an end-cutting drill rotating inside a hollow square chisel. A special attachment clamps the chisel to the drill-press quill. The drill is chucked normally. Precise adjustment between the drill and the chisel is essential, and the chisel must be honed razor-sharp for the mortising to work at all. To drill the square hole, you have to bear down; the drill cuts a round hole and the chisel squares it. A hold-down restrains the work as you bear down and release. The advantage? You can make a lot of mortises fast, once the machinery is set up.

Drilling a big hole doesn't have to be a big project. If you have any doubt about how the hole will turn out, practice on a scrap piece of material similar to that of the project— *Thomas H. Jones.*

SOME SPECIALTY-BIT SOURCES
Brookstone Co., 127 Vose Farm Road, Peterborough Road, NH 03458; **Constantine's,** 2050 Eastchester Road, Bronx, NY 10461; **Craftsman Wood Service Co.,** 1735 W. Cortland Court, Addison, IL 60101; **The Fine Tool Shops, Inc.,** 20-28 Backus Avenue, Danbury, CT 06810; **Frog Tool Co., Ltd.,** 700 W. Jackson Boulevard, Chicago, IL 60606; **Garrett Wade Co.,** 161 Avenue of the Americas, New York, NY 10013; **Hit Products, Inc.,** Box 6906, Hollywood, FL 33021; **Leichtung,** 4944 Commerce Parkway, Cleveland, OH 44128; **Sears, Roebuck & Co.** (any catalog store); **Shopsmith, Inc.,** 750 Center Drive, Vandalia, OH 45377; **Woodcraft,** 313 Montvale Avenue, Woburn, MA 01801; **The Woodworkers' Store,** 21801 Industrial Boulevard, Rogers, NM 55374.

master drill-press jig

A drill press can be your most versatile wood-shop power tool. But for each job you need a special setup. This master jig—actually a basic table and eight accessories—will outfit your drill press for drilling, drum sanding, routing, shaping, and other woodworking chores. All will be done more easily and accurately since you won't have to improvise setups. Furthermore, you'll be able to use your drill press in otherwise-impossible ways: for drilling and sanding pivot-guided circles, for example, and for pin routing, routing grooves parallel to a curve, and V-block work. Some of these jobs can't be done any other way.

Though you'll probably have little reason to remove the basic table from your machine, it takes only seconds to do so. The table sits solidly on the tool's own table and gets ample anchorage from a C-clamp or two.

Here, the jig is shown mounted on a 15-inch drill press with a fairly average-size (11 by 14 inches) table. A smaller or larger table won't affect how the jig is built, but a few areas—

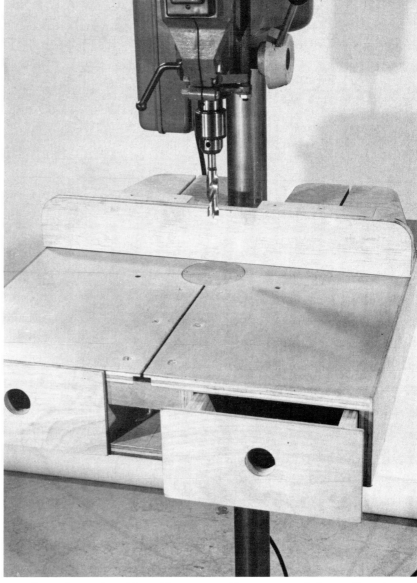

Main table for the master drill-press jig rests on the tool's regular table and is secured with one or two C-clamps. Two drawers provide storage for accessories you build. Here jig is equipped with the straight fence, which makes it easy to drill holes equidistant from the stock's edge, as shown in left photo. Other uses for the fence are shown on following pages.

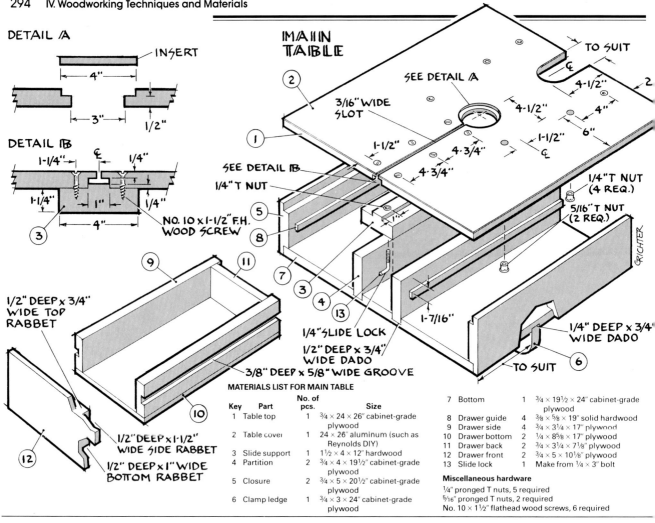

DETAIL A

INSERT

4"

3"   1/2"

DETAIL B

1-1/4"   1/4"

1-1/4"   1"   1/4"

4"

NO. 10 x 1-1/2" F.H.
WOOD SCREW

MAIN TABLE

SEE DETAIL A

3/16" WIDE
SLOT

TO SUIT

4-1/2"   2

4-1/2"   4"

1-1/2"   6"

1-1/2"

4-3/4"

4-3/4"

1/4" T NUT

1/4" T NUT
(4 REQ.)

5/16" T NUT
(2 REQ.)

SEE DETAIL B

1"

1/2" DEEP x 3/4"
WIDE TOP
RABBET

1/4" SLIDE LOCK

1/2" DEEP x 3/4"
WIDE DADO

3/8" DEEP x 5/8" WIDE GROOVE

1-7/16"

1/4" DEEP x 3/4"
WIDE DADO

TO SUIT

1/2" DEEP x 1-1/2"
WIDE SIDE RABBET

1/2" DEEP x 1" WIDE
BOTTOM RABBET

GRICHTER

MATERIALS LIST FOR MAIN TABLE

Key	Part	No. of pcs.	Size
1	Table top	1	3/4 × 24 × 26" cabinet-grade plywood
2	Table cover	1	24 × 26" aluminum (such as Reynolds DIY)
3	Slide support	1	1 1/2 × 4 × 12" hardwood
4	Partition	2	3/4 × 4 × 19 1/2" cabinet-grade plywood
5	Closure	2	3/4 × 5 × 20 1/2" cabinet-grade plywood
6	Clamp ledge	1	3/4 × 3 × 24" cabinet-grade plywood
7	Bottom	1	3/4 × 19 1/2 × 24" cabinet-grade plywood
8	Drawer guide	4	3/8 × 5/8 × 19" solid hardwood
9	Drawer side	4	3/4 × 3 1/4 × 17" plywood
10	Drawer bottom	2	1/4 × 8 5/8 × 17" plywood
11	Drawer back	2	3/4 × 3 1/4 × 7 1/8" plywood
12	Drawer front	2	3/4 × 5 × 10 1/8" plywood
13	Slide lock	1	Make from 1/4 × 3" bolt

Miscellaneous hardware
1/4" pronged T nuts, 5 required
5/16" pronged T nuts, 2 required
No. 10 × 1 1/2" flathead wood screws, 6 required

INSERTS

1/4"

DRILL AND COUN-
TERSINK FOR NO.
4 x 3/4" F.H.
SCREWS

4"
DIAMETER

SOLID

DIAMETER
OF GUIDE
TO SUIT
DRUM

SPECIAL INSERT FOR
PATTERN SANDING

FOR DRUM SANDING
(INSIDE DIAMETER TO
SUIT DRUM)

Inserts fit four-in. hole in main table; they're used for drum sanding and other operations. Make them from 1/4-in. tempered hardboard (diagrams above). And make plenty—the more you use them, the more jobs you'll discover for them. Cut holes in some inserts to accommodate sanding drums of various sizes, rotary files, and burrs.

Inserts with holes let you use the full width of the sanding drum. Move the work against drum's direction of rotation, and keep it moving slowly but steadily to prevent indentations. (For inside curves, put work in place before lowering and locking drum.)

For pattern sanding, attach a disc the diameter of the sanding drum to an insert and align it perfectly with the drum (center). Tack the pattern under rough-cut work and sand (right). Pattern will ride against the disc, which will serve as a guide.

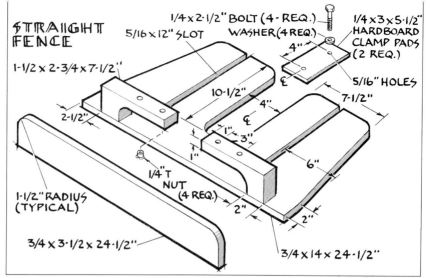

1/4 x 2-1/2" BOLT (4-REQ.)
WASHER (4 REQ.)
1/4 x 3 x 5-1/2" HARDBOARD CLAMP PADS (2 REQ.)
5/16 x 12" SLOT
4"
5/16" HOLES
1-1/2 x 2-3/4 x 7-1/2"
10-1/2"
7-1/2"
2-1/2"
4"
1"
3"
1"
6"
1/4" T NUT (4 REQ.)
1-1/2" RADIUS (TYPICAL)
2"
2"
3/4 x 3-1/2 x 24-1/2"
3/4 x 14 x 24-1/2"

Surface or edge sanding with a sanding drum is done by passing work between straight fence (sketch, right) and drum. Slots on base of fence let you locate it to fit work. Make light cuts and keep work moving. Feed against drum's rotation.

Straight fence keeps you accurate on drilling, routing, sanding jobs. First make base and fence. Attach fence with glue and nails; be sure it's vertical. Make brackets and, after installing the four T nuts, attach each bracket with glue and a two-in. flathead screw (up through base). Bolts through clamp pads fit T nuts in main table.

Straight-line routing can be done against fence. (But be sure to substitute a router chuck for the standard chuck.) Make the pass so the cutting action will tend to force the work against fence. Feed from left to right. Use highest speed and feed slowly.

Mortising can be done against the straight fence if you equip your drill press with standard mortising bits, chisels, and adapter. Use a slim piece of wood and C-clamps as a hold-down to keep the work from pulling up when you retract the chisel.

the opening for the column, the placement of the clamp ledge, and the hole for the circular inserts—must be tailored specifically for your machine.

Making the Basic Table

Cut the plywood top and aluminum cover to size (see diagram), and bond them together with contact cement. Mark the long dimension with an accurate center line. Precisely on the line, cut the opening for the drill-press column, using a saber saw. The width of the opening and the radius of the arc must suit the diameter of your tool's column.

Put the top in position on your drill-press table, and use the drill to make a small hole on the center line. This will mark the exact center of the circular cutout that receives the inserts used with sanding drums. Use a fly cutter or a hole saw (or a saber saw) to form a three-inch-diameter hole. Then, working with a portable router equipped with a template guide, form a four-inch-diameter, 1/4-inch-deep concentric recess (see diagram) around the perimeter of the three-inch hole.

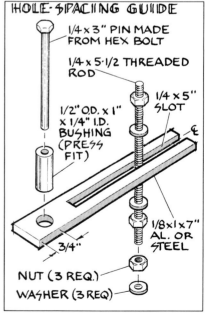

HOLE-SPACING GUIDE
1/4 x 3" PIN MADE FROM HEX BOLT
1/4 x 5-1/2 THREADED ROD
1/2" O.D. x 1" x 1/4" I.D. BUSHING (PRESS FIT)
1/4 x 5" SLOT
1/8 x 1 x 7" AL. OR STEEL
3/4"
NUT (3 REQ.)
WASHER (3 REQ)

Hole-spacing guide lets you automatically and accurately set distance between holes. Author used 1/4-in. guide pin, so all starter holes must be 1/4 in. (They can be enlarged later.) You could use smaller pin and bushing or prepare an assortment. To use guide, drill first hole, then set gauge and pin to spacing needed. Thereafter, inserting pin in drilled hole will automatically position work for next hole. Guide adjusts vertically and laterally, and it can be put in any of the T nuts on the straight fence's brackets.

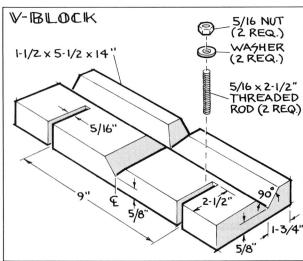

V-BLOCK

1-1/2 x 5-1/2 x 14"

5/16 NUT (2 REQ.)

WASHER (2 REQ.)

5/16 x 2-1/2" THREADED ROD (2 REQ.)

5/16"

9"

5/8"

2-1/2"

90°

1-3/4"

5/8"

Drill accurate holes through rods and tubes by placing them on this V-block, which attaches to the main table of your master jig. This one has enough built-in adjustments so you can be precise in aligning the drill bit with the center of the V. The V-block is secured with threaded rods that fit T nuts in the main table.

This forms a lip to hold the inserts. Or you can outline the four-inch recess with a fly cutter and remove the waste with a chisel. If you do it the latter way, outline the recess before you make the three-inch hole.

Providing for Add-ons

Carefully locate and drill the holes for the four ¼-inch and two ⁵⁄₁₆-inch T nuts. (Bolting on various accessories.) In each case, first drill a ¹⁄₁₆-inch pilot hole all the way through. Enlarge this from the top to the bolt size that will be used and from the bottom to accommodate the outside diameter of the T nuts. These T nuts do not have to be installed flush, but be sure to use the pronged type.

Next, use a table saw to form the slot in the table top and the groove below (see diagram detail). A very useful slide rides in this groove. Be sure the saw is aligned so you will cut exactly on the center line. First form the ³⁄₁₆-inch-wide slot by making repeat passes. Then, with the blade projecting ½ inch above the table, shape the one-inch-wide groove—again with repeat passes.

Shape the slide support as diagrammed, and after flush-installing the T nuts for the slide lock, attach the support beneath the table with glue and six No. 10 by ½-inch flathead wood screws. Be precise when countersinking the screws; they must not project above the table surface.

Cut the partitions, closures, and bottom to size. Assemble the parts on the drill-press table so you can mark the exact locations of the dadoes in the bottom for the partitions and for the clamp ledge. Attach the drawer guides with glue and brads, then assemble all

parts with glue and finishing nails. Follow this sequence: First install the clamp ledge on the bottom, then attach the partitions by gluing and nailing into the sides of the support. Finally, add the bottom and closures.

A point about the clamp ledge: On

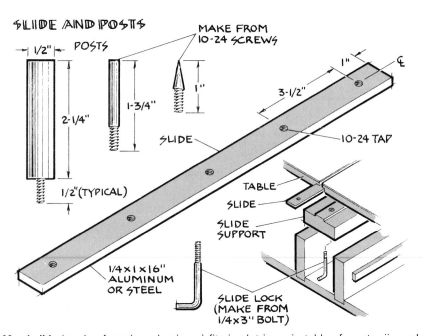

SLIDE AND POSTS

1/2"

POSTS

MAKE FROM 10-24 SCREWS

2-1/4"

1-3/4"

1"

1/2"(TYPICAL)

SLIDE

3-1/2"

1"

10-24 TAP

TABLE

SLIDE

SLIDE SUPPORT

1/4 x 1 x 16" ALUMINUM OR STEEL

SLIDE LOCK (MAKE FROM 1/4 x 3" BOLT)

Metal slide (made of steel or aluminum) fits in slot in main table of master jig and accommodates posts that guide work for various jobs. Smaller posts are made from 10-24 screws; the ½-in. post can be made on a metal-turning lathe, or you can cut a ½-in. steel rod to length, mount it in a drill press, file one end, and use a die to form the threads. The slide is held in position by an L-shape slide lock.

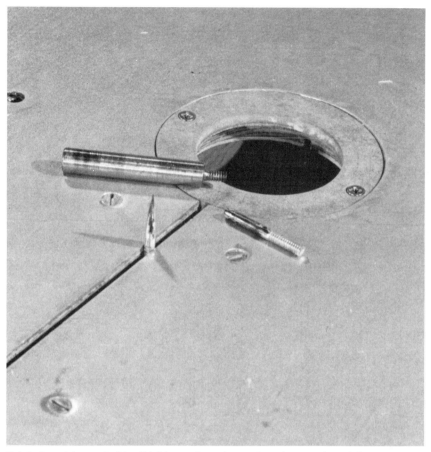

Pointed post (mounted in slide) is used as pivot point when work can't have a center hole. Use the straight post when it can; ½-in. post is shown in use on next page.

Drilling holes around a circumference is easy when you mount the work on a post on the slide. Just center the drill bit on the line, lock the slide in position, and drill.

some drill-press tables, the front edge is not 90 degrees to the table's surface. In such a case, use the clamp ledge only as a positioning guide; use a C-clamp or two at the back edge of the table to provide anchorage for the jig.

The drawers hold the accessories and necessary hardware. Their design is pretty basic—not the kind of thing you'll find on heirlooms—but adequate. Be sure that the drawers will slide easily. Bore 1½-inch fingerholes through the drawer fronts. (Knobs or pulls might snag clothing.)

Workmanship Is Critical

Be persnickety when constructing the master jig. With careful layout work and construction, you'll produce a long-lived and accurate piece of workshop equipment. Carefully sand all parts before and after assembly. Set finishing nails slightly below the surface of the wood, and fill the holes with wood dough. Treat all surfaces with a couple of coats of sealer. Polish the aluminum cover with very, very fine steel wool, then frequently apply paste wax, rubbing it to a polish. Also, wax all wood surfaces against which work must bear or move.

The photos show some uses for the master jig and its accessories. The diagrams tell you how to make all the parts.

In general, follow the standard rule: When your cut must be deep, take the time to achieve full depth by making repeat passes. Remember that sanding should be part of a *finishing* operation—don't attempt to sand when you should use the saw.

When using your drill press for routing or shaping, use chucks that are specifically designed for those operations. A three-jaw chuck, for example, is not designed to take the side thrust that routing produces.

Keep your hands away from cutting areas regardless of the operation. Even a drum sander can do damage. Always wear safety goggles and, when needed, a mask.

Master Drill-Press Jig Accessories

The diagrams shown here include two guards for the jig (page 147). Make and use them. But remember that they can't think for you. Keep your hands away from cutting areas, wear safety goggles, and, when needed, wear a mask—*By R. J. De Cristoforo. Illustrations by Gerhard Richter.*

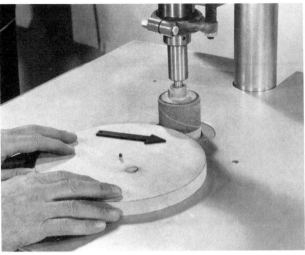
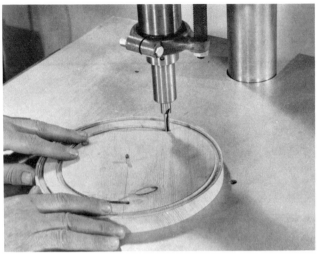

For pivot sanding, lock the slide so work just contacts the sanding drum and rotate it clockwise. A circular table insert is cut to fit the diameter of the sanding drum. Use the same technique to cut circular grooves or rabbets in a disc.

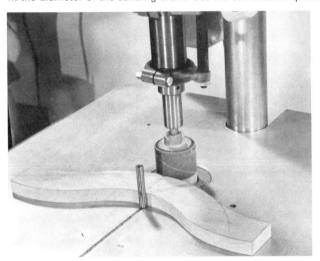

Use the ½-in. guide post to sand parallel curves. First sand (freehand) the edge that rides the post, then sand the second edge by moving the work between the post and drum. Routing a groove parallel to a curved edge is also done with this post.

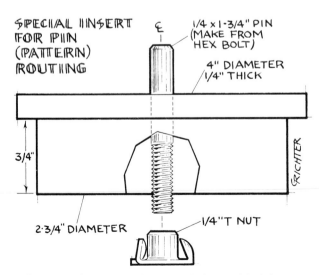

SPECIAL INSERT FOR PIN (PATTERN) ROUTING

1/4 x 1-3/4" PIN (MAKE FROM HEX BOLT)

4" DIAMETER 1/4" THICK

3/4"

2-3/4" DIAMETER

1/4" T NUT

RICHTER

Pin (or pattern) routing guide is made from a blank insert—a four-in. disc cut to fit the hole in the main table of the jig. You lock the blank insert in the hole and use the drill to form the center hole. A T nut holds the pin in the insert, as diagramed.

Pattern for pin routing duplicates what you want to rout in the work. It is tack-nailed, as shown, to the bottom of the work. Then the work is flipped and moved so that the pattern rides against the guide pin. You can incise designs or raise a panel..

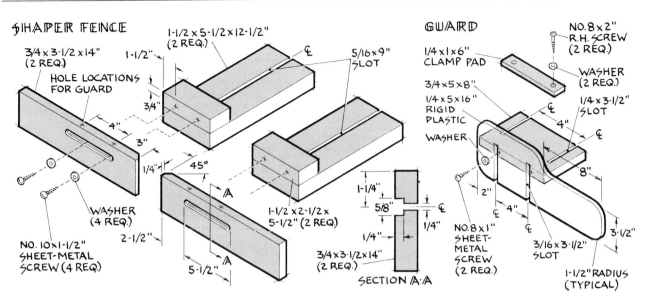

SHAPER FENCE

3/4 x 3-1/2 x 14" (2 REQ.)

1-1/2"

HOLE LOCATIONS FOR GUARD

3/4"

4"

3"

1/4"

45°

WASHER (4 REQ.)

2-1/2"

NO. 10 x 1-1/2" SHEET-METAL SCREW (4 REQ.)

5-1/2"

1-1/2 x 5-1/2 x 12-1/2" (2 REQ.)

₵

5/16 x 9" SLOT

1-1/2 x 2-1/2 x 5-1/2" (2 REQ.)

A

A

3/4 x 3-1/2 x 14" (2 REQ.)

1-1/4"

5/8"

1/4"

1/4"

₵

SECTION A·A

GUARD

NO. 8 x 2" R.H. SCREW (2 REQ.)

1/4 x 1 x 6" CLAMP PAD

3/4 x 5 x 8"

1/4 x 5 x 16" RIGID PLASTIC

WASHER

WASHER (2 REQ.)

1/4 x 3-1/2" SLOT

4"

₵

2"

₵

4"

8"

NO. 8 x 1" SHEET-METAL SCREW (2 REQ.)

3/16 x 3-1/2" SLOT

3-1/2"

1-1/2" RADIUS (TYPICAL)

Shaper fence works like commercial units: Each half is adjustable to control depth of cut. Each can be moved laterally to minimize the opening around the cutter. Slots in fences and lips around them can be cut either with a router or by drilling overlapping holes. (Use a ⅝-in. bit set to cut ¼ in. deep. Chisel out the slot; on its center line, drill overlapping holes with a ¼-in. bit.) Acrylic guard, an essential safety feature, mounts on the in-feed fence and moves in and out to accommodate different work thicknesses.

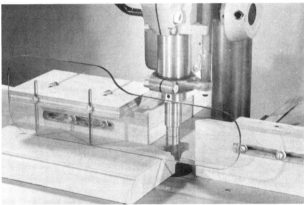

When entire edge of stock is removed (left), out-feed fence is moved forward to equal depth of cut. Thus, work is supported before and after it passes the cutter. In-feed and out-feed fences are in line (right) when the cutter is removing part of the edge.

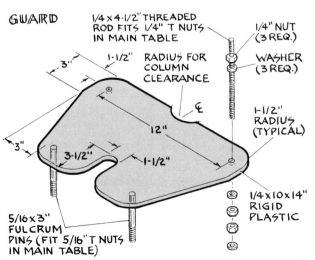

GUARD

1/4 x 4-1/2" THREADED ROD FITS 1/4" T NUTS IN MAIN TABLE

1/4" NUT (3 REQ.)

WASHER (3 REQ.)

3"

1-1/2" RADIUS FOR COLUMN CLEARANCE

₵

12"

3"

3-1/2"

1-1/2"

1-1/2" RADIUS (TYPICAL)

1/4 x 10 x 14" RIGID PLASTIC

5/16 x 3" FULCRUM PINS (FIT 5/16" T NUTS IN MAIN TABLE)

Freehand shaping is done when straight fences can't be used. Fulcrum pins, made from 5/16-in. bolts, fit in T nuts in the table and provide support for the work. Depth of cut is controlled by collars that mount on the shaper adapter along with the cutter. To start the cut, brace the work against the left-hand pin and advance it carefully into the cutter until the edge rests against the depth collar. At this point you can swing the work clear of the pin or continue to use it for support. Make—and use—the guard.

table-saw master jig

Ever wish you could make your table saw do more? With a master jig, you can. The multipurpose jig shown here turns your saw into a versatile yet precise tool. In fact, once you use it for a while, you'll wonder how you managed without it.

Its secret? Since the work and jig table move together, sawing is easier and more accurate. And attachments for mitering, feathering, splining, tenoning, slotting, and many other standard—and not so standard—operations make it one of the most useful accessories going.

The jig is shown on a Rockwell 10-inch Unisaw, which has a 27 × 36-inch table. Many other 9- and 10-inch machines (the most popular sizes) are similar, so the dimensions in the drawings are generally applicable. The only tailoring you need to do is on the dimensions of the bars and their placement on the main table. The bars slide in the table slots, and their positions vary from saw to saw.

The thickness of the sliding table reduces the maximum blade projection, but since projection is normally 2¾ to 3½ inches, reducing it by ½ inch isn't critical; it'll still cut most standard stock.

Accurate construction of the jig is important, although some tolerances are built in. For example, the fastening holes in the attachments are 5⁄16 inch in diameter, even though they are secured with ¼-inch locking hardware threaded into ¼-inch T nuts. This permits 1⁄16-inch adjustments.

Use a good grade of maple or birch plywood. After each part has been sized and the corners rounded, use fine sandpaper to smooth surfaces and edges. For the table top, cut a sheet of aluminum to size and bond it to the table using contact cement.

Next, shape the bars to fit your table slots. Sand the bars so that they slide easily in the table slots without wobble. Put the bars in position, then place the sliding table so it's centered over the saw blade. Make sure its edges are parallel to the table slots. Use C-clamps to hold the bars to the sliding table, and drive a short brad to keep them in place. Repeat this procedure at the opposite ends of the bars, and permanently attach them with ¾-inch #8 flathead wood screws. Be sure to drill shank holes for the screws; if you don't, driving the screws may spread the bars and cause them to fit too tightly in the table slots.

Next, form the saw kerf. Work with a good saw blade,

Table-saw master jig consists of an aluminum-veneered sliding table with attachments for a variety of shop jobs. Shown crosscut fence, adjustable stop, vertical work support, vertical miter guides, hold-down, and right-angle guide (mounted on table).

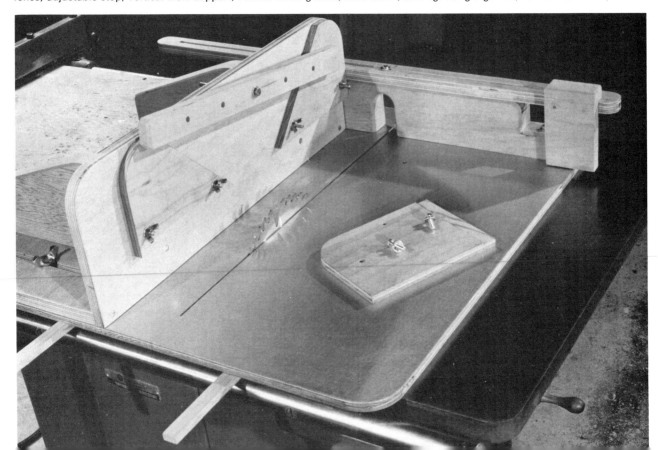

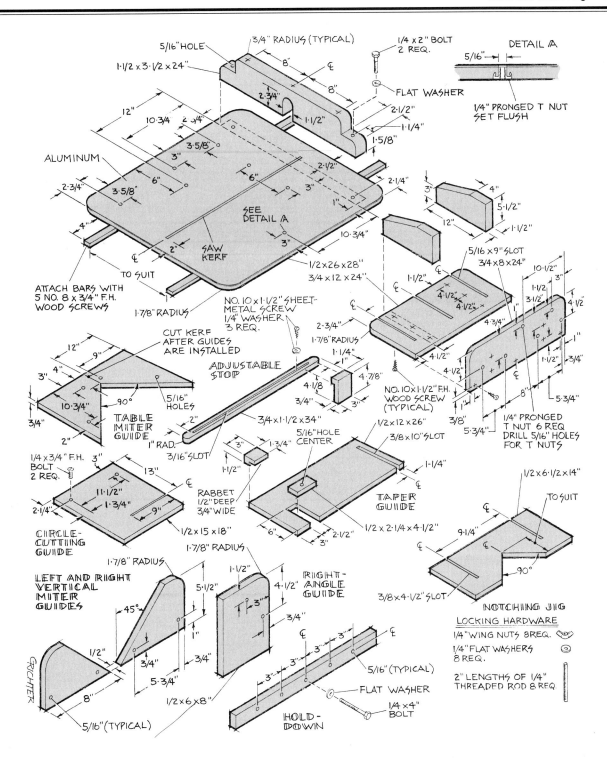

one that you will always use with the master jig. Don't use a conventional hollow-ground blade—the best kind to use is a carbide-tipped combination blade.

With the machine off, set the blade to its lowest point and put the sliding table in place. Turn on the machine and slowly raise the blade until it cuts through the sliding table, then move the table to lengthen the kerf.

Carefully mark the locations for all the T nuts needed for the table. Work with a scriber, but mark lightly so you don't mar the aluminum. Mark the hole locations with a prick punch and then drill a ¹⁄₁₆-inch hole at each mark. Use a ¾-inch brad-point bit on the underside to form a ¹⁄₁₆-

inch-deep counterbore and then, from the top side, open up each of the holes to ⁵⁄₁₆ inch.

Install the ¼-inch T nuts by tapping them into place with a hammer. They must be flush with, or slightly below, the surface of the plywood.

Shape the crosscut fence, and then drill the ⁵⁄₁₆-inch holes for the bolts used to secure the fence to the table. The three hole locations on top of the fence are for the screws that hold the adjustable stop when it's in use.

Rather than being a one-piece V-block, the miter guides are made in two pieces. You can use both pieces when mitering parts that have been precut to length or just one

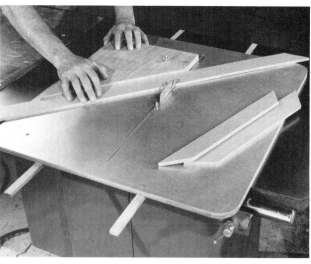

Use a square to set crosscut fence 90 degrees to the blade before tightening fence bolts. Difference between ¼-inch locking bolt and ⁵⁄₁₆-inch holes in fence allows for minor adjustment.

To make consecutive cuts along a single length of stock, remove the crosscut fence and work with one guide. If stock can't be turned over, you can alternate left- and right-hand guides.

Use the adjustable stop to saw multiple pieces to the same length. This attachment permits cuts up to 28 inches long. Hold work firmly and return to starting position before removing.

Use table miter guides to cut slots in rounds. To mark center of round or square stock, lower blade to minimum and make two cuts at right angles; center is where the kerfs intersect.

With table miter guides in place you can form accurate miters on precut stock—even molding, since you can cut on either side of blade. Check position with triangle before locking.

Vertical right-angle guide is used for end cuts such as slots and tenons. Before securing in position, check with a square to be sure guide's bearing edge is 90 degrees to the table.

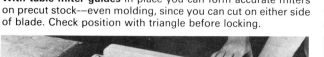

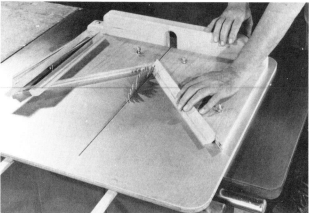

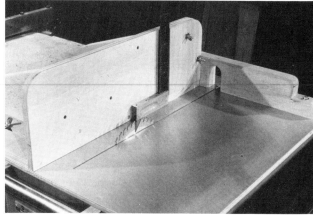

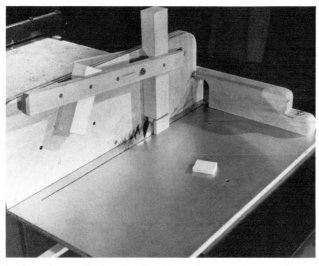

To form tenon, first make shoulder cuts and set up as shown for cheek cuts. For second cuts on each you just reverse stock's position. Use same-size scrap under free end of hold-down.

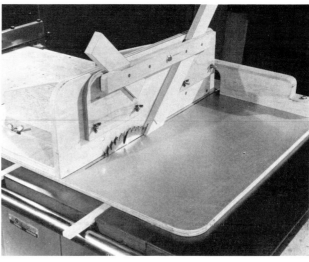

For centered spline groove, reverse stock for second cut. For off-center groove, use both guides. Face matching surfaces toward guide, cut both pieces, reset guide, and pass again.

To form a slot in narrow work, set the vertical work support to the width you want the shoulder of the slot to be. Make a pass, reverse stock, and make another—the slot will be centered.

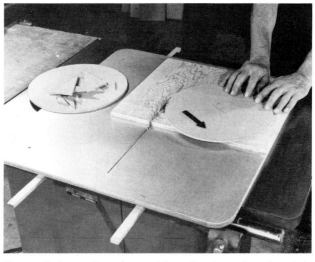

To cut circles, nail stock to guide and make series of straight cuts, rotating work 10 degrees with each pass. Then align nail with blade front and rotate work in direction shown.

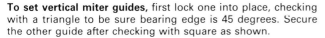

To set vertical miter guides, first lock one into place, checking with a triangle to be sure bearing edge is 45 degrees. Secure the other guide after checking with square as shown.

Notching jig can be used to make odd-shaped pieces that would be difficult to form with standard tools. Shape of jig varies according to what you need to make with it.

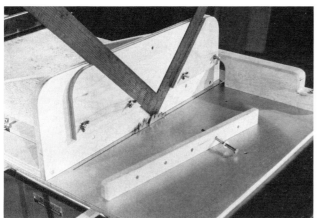

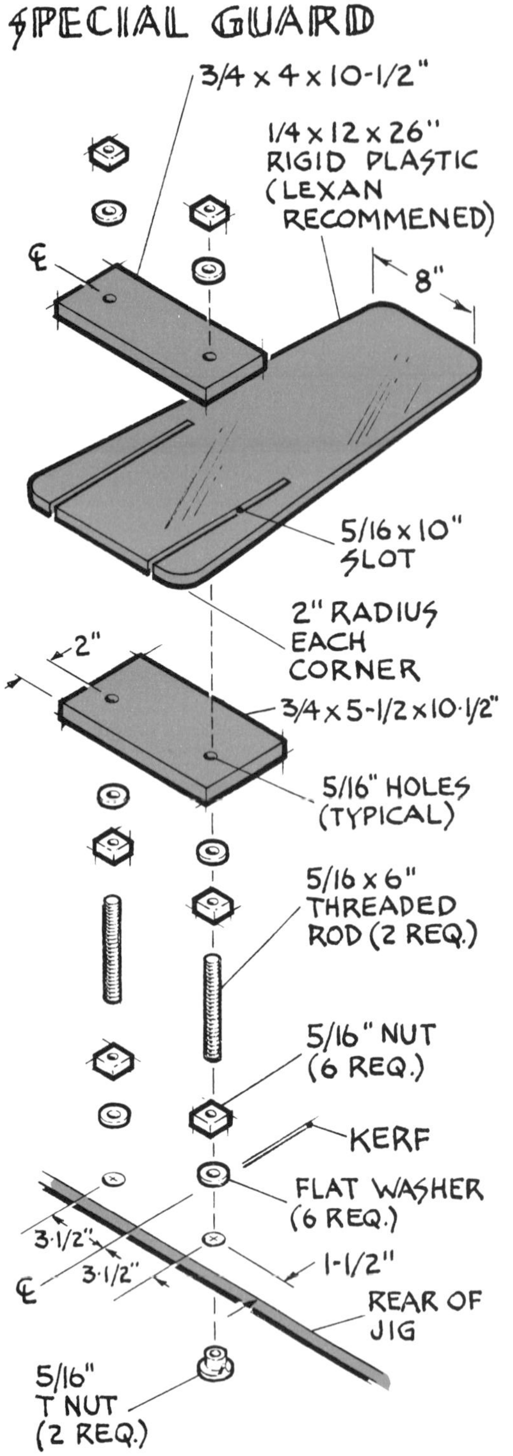
SPECIAL GUARD
3/4 x 4 x 10-1/2"
1/4 x 12 x 26" RIGID PLASTIC (LEXAN RECOMMENED)
8"
5/16 x 10" SLOT
2" RADIUS EACH CORNER
2"
3/4 x 5-1/2 x 10-1/2"
5/16" HOLES (TYPICAL)
5/16 x 6" THREADED ROD (2 REQ.)
5/16" NUT (6 REQ.)
KERF
FLAT WASHER (6 REQ.)
3-1/2"
3-1/2"
1-1/2"
REAR OF JIG
5/16" T NUT (2 REQ.)

A special guard. The only required modification of the jig is the addition of the two holes for the 5/16-inch Tee-Nuts. The posts (5/16-inch threaded rod) thread into the Tee-Nuts and are secured with a washer and nut. The guard parts mate as shown in the drawing.

The guard is adjustable vertically and longitudinally so the blade and the cut being made will always be covered by the plastic shield. Adjust the height of the guard so it is between 1/4 inch and 1/2 inch above the blade. The width of the shield keeps your hands away from the cutting area.

The guard is used for all operations done with the sliding table. It is not used with the vertical work support. But with this accessory, hands don't have to be placed in a hazardous position.

when cutting to size. You can remove the crosscut fence and use either the left- or right-hand guide when making consecutive miter cuts on a single length of stock.

Mark the 45-degree angle on each guide by using a combination square. Saw approximately to the mark and finish by sanding exactly to it. Lock the guides on the table so that the short edges abut and the joint is centered over the kerf. Then move the table so the saw blade spreads them apart. When the guides are mounted, use a triangle to be sure they are in correct alignment with the saw kerf.

To make the vertical work support, first make the base—the slots can be formed by making repeated passes with the saw blade—and then add the braces. Check with a square to be sure the front edges of the braces are 90 degrees to the base.

Shape the face and carefully lay out locations for the T nuts. Here, the T nuts do not have to be set flush. All you need to do is drill a 1/16-inch pilot hole and then enlarge it to 5/16 inch.

Mark the 45-degree angle on the vertical miter guides by using a combination square as shown in the illustration.

To form the long slot in the adjustable stop, first drill 3/16-inch end holes and then cut between them with a coping saw or jigsaw. The slots in the other attachments can be formed by repositioning the parts and repeating passes on the table saw.

Sand all parts before assembly. Apply two to three coats of sealer, sanding between coats and after the final one. Apply paste wax to the saw table and to the bars and underside of the sliding table, then rub to a high polish—*R. J. Cristoforo.*

Materials list
Sliding table
Main table: One 1/2 × 26 × 28-inch cabinet-grade plywood
Table cover: One 26 × 28-inch aluminum sheet
Bars: Two 3/8 × 3/4 × 36-inch hardwood
Crosscut fence: One 1 1/2 × 3 1/2 × 24-inch hardwood; nine 1/4-inch pronged T nuts; ten 3/4-inch #8 flathead wood screws; two 1/4 × 2-inch bolts; two 1/4-inch flat washers
Vertical work support
Base: One 3/4 × 12 × 24-inch cabinet-grade plywood
Face: One 3/4 × 8 × 24-inch cabinet-grade plywood
Brace: Two 1 1/2 × 5 1/2 × 12-inch hardwood; six 1/4-inch pronged T nuts; thirteen 1 1/2-inch #10 flathead wood screws
Table miter guides
Guide: Two 3/4 × 12 × 16-inch cabinet-grade plywood
Adjustable stop
Bar: One 3/4 × 1 1/2 × 34-inch cabinet-grade plywood or hardwood
Stop: One 1 1/4 × 3 × 4 7/8-inch hardwood; three 1 1/2-inch #10 sheet-metal screws; three 1/4-inch flat washers
Circle-cutting guide
Platform: One 1/2 × 15 × 18-inch cabinet-grade plywood; two 1/4 × 3/4-inch flathead bolts
Taper guide
Platform: One 1/2 × 12 × 26-inch cabinet-grade plywood
Stop: One 1 1/2 × 1 3/4 × 3-inch hardwood
Clamp pad: One 1/2 × 2 1/4 × 4 1/2-inch hardwood or plywood
Vertical miter guides
Guides: Two 1/2 × 5 1/2 × 8-inch cabinet-grade plywood
Right-angle guide
Guide: One 1/2 × 6 × 8-inch cabinet-grade plywood
Hold down
Bar: One 5/8 × 1 1/2 × 18-inch hardwood; one 1/4 × 4-inch bolt; one 1/4-inch flat washer
Example notching jig
Guide: One 1/2 × 6 1/2 × 14-inch cabinet-grade plywood
Locking hardware
General-use pieces: Eight 1/4-inch wing nuts; eight 1/4-inch flat washers; eight 1/4 × 2-inch lengths of threaded rod

router gauge for dadoes

Tack the gauge to the jig and it becomes a lot easier to cut slots in the gauge.

If laying out dadoes and cutting them with a router have always been tedious projects for you, this gauge—made of ⅛-inch hardboard—will be a handy addition to your shop. It takes just a few minutes to make, but will save you hours of figuring and improve your dadoing accuracy.

To make the gauge, you need a jig. It consists of an about 18-inch-square piece of plywood or particleboard, with a straightedge of ¼-inch stock nailed about 10 inches in from one edge (see sketch). Dimensions are not critical.

Now cut a piece of ⅛-inch hardboard 8 inches square. Measure and mark stop lines 2 inches in from each edge, as shown in the accompanying sketch. Place one side of the hardboard square firmly against your jig's straightedge and secure it with brads tacked through the outside corners. Put a ¼-inch bit in your router and set it to cut through the hardboard. Using the straightedge as a guide, cut a slot in the hardboard up to the stop line. Turning the board, repeat this process using a ⅜-inch bit, a ½-inch bit, and a ¾-inch bit, so your gauge resembles the illustration.

To use the gauge, lay out the outlines of the dadoes on the workpiece. Then at either end of the proposed cut, carefully straddle the outline with the proper slot in the gauge and mark a line at the corresponding edge of the gauge. Mark the other end of the cut in the same way and tack a straightedge on these marks. Using the straightedge to guide your router, proceed to make your cuts—*Frank H. Day.*

Using the gauge to lay out guide lines (near right) ensures accuracy of dadoes. Cutting dado with straightedge tacked to workpiece is fine for most projects (right), but with fine woods, use padded C-clamps to secure straightedge.

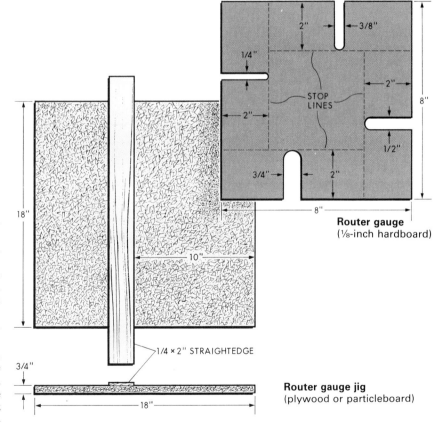

Router gauge
(⅛-inch hardboard)

Router gauge jig
(plywood or particleboard)

sharpening shop tools

Yes, razor sharp tools are dangerous—if you handle them carelessly or keep them where the young or unknowing can get at them. But many tools must be keen to do the job, and if they aren't, they'll be dangerous because you'll force them. Less than keen shop tools also increase the risk of ruining a workpiece.

Ten basics

Here are ten basics designed to guide you toward keeping your shop tools in cutting shape.
● Sharpen often. The moment a tool starts to get dull, stop and hone it, or use another until you can. It will only get duller—maybe to the point where it can't be resharpened.
● Recognize that there are some tools that it is not practical, or even reasonably possible, to resharpen. The list includes jig-saw blades, band saw blades, hacksaw blades. Simply replace them when they get dull. Some new circular saw blades are also intended to be "throwaways." Usually these are marked to that effect.
● Be aware that there are some tools you may not be able to sharpen very well—specifically, carbide-tipped tools. Many new circular saw blades have brazed-on silicon carbide tips that require grinding with a silicon carbide grinding wheel on a special grinding machine. Carbide-tipped masonry bits can be ground on a bench grinder if it has a silicon carbide wheel. A normal grinding wheel won't touch carbide.
● Consider buying simple sharpening aids. Some of the accompanying photos show relatively inexpensive ones. They pay for themselves in no time, even if you use them only once in a while. Depending on your tool collection, you may not need all those shown, but at least consider those you can use. They make tool sharpening easier and much more accurate.

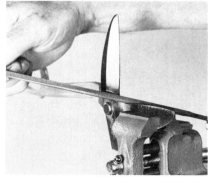
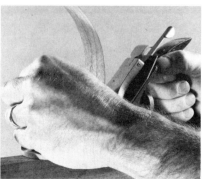

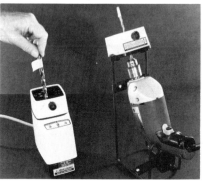

Sharp, clean-cutting tools are not only a joy to use, but they are safer and reduce chance of error and ruining work. Blades for planes (top, right) are just one of tools covered here. Many tools—such as snips at top, left—are easily sharpened by filing cutting edge carefully; rule of thumb is to duplicate maker's angle. Twist drills are among toughest tools to sharpen properly. Task is made simple with a sharpening aid. Two versions of "pencil sharpener" grinder are shown at center, right—self- and drill-powered. Little "Eclipse" sharpening aid (center, left) works well if drills are not badly worn or damaged. Sharpening is done by rolling back and forth on sheet of abrasive paper. With chisels, punches, and the like (bottom, right), chamfering the striking end to remove flare—it can chip off and hurt you—is just as important as sharpening (note two chisels at top, right in the photo, shown before head grinding). Bench grinder is a good buy. One with simple notch or angle mark on tool rest aids in hand drill grinding. At bottom, left, carbide tipped masonry drill is being sharpened with a carbide wheel.

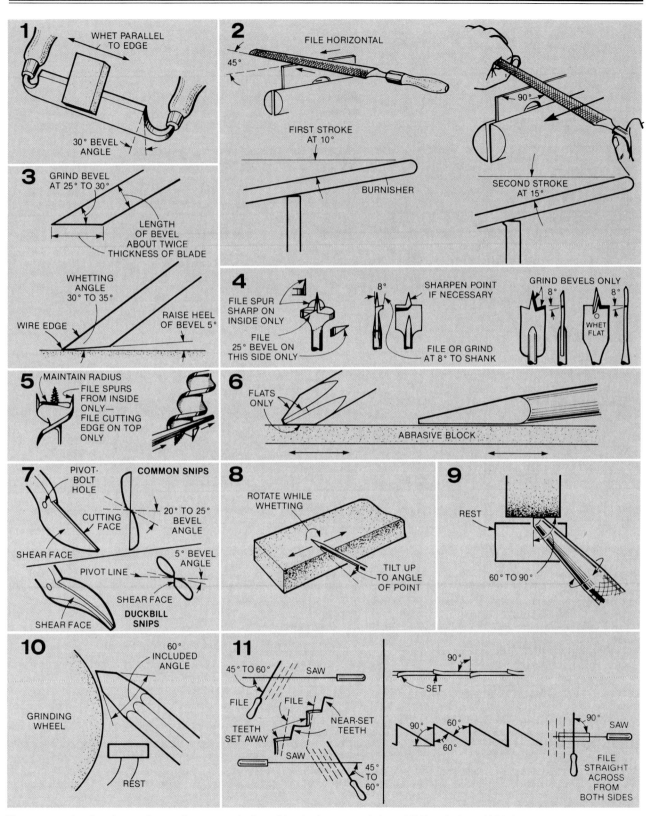

Here, some tips for sharpening tools commonly found in the home workshop. **(1)** Drawknives: With hone stone, whet edge as shown; if nicked, dress with file first. **(2)** Cabinet scrapers: With file flat (A), draw it as in (B); roll over a sharp edge with 10- and 15-degree strokes with burnisher or steel bar. **(3)** Wood chisels and plane blades: Power-grind or hand-sharpen on abrasive block as in (A); whet fine secondary edge with fine abrasive block as in (B). **(4)** Spade boring bits: Pick type you have, file as shown. **(5)** Auger bits: Sharpen with file as shown. **(6)** Screwdriver blades: Hand-hone as shown. Regular screwdrivers can also be hollow ground on bench grinder. **(7)** Metal cutting snips: File bevel angle of blades as shown (normally not necessary to take snips apart). Don't file shear face or cutting face. **(8)** Awls, scribes, picks: Whet on abrasive block as shown. **(9)** Centerpunches: Maintain angle shown for job intended; rotate punch while grinding. **(10)** Cold chisels: Grind both cutting edges evenly on bench grinder. **(11)** Crosscut saws are alternately filed as in (A). Rip saw blades are filed successively, right down the blade (B).

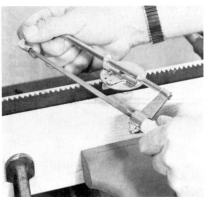

Auger bits and spade drills can be sharpened with file (top, left) small enough to clear skirt of augers. (See previous page for data on filing wood bits of different types.) Aid is important in sharpening router cutters; one shown top, center, fits on router base. Both Sears and Stanley have bench grinder attachments that fit many grinders (above right) to traverse clamped work in front of wheel. Simple, inexpensive filing aids like one shown far left, are available for both hand saw and circular saw blades. The sharpening aid shown near left positions plane blades, chisels, screwdrivers, and the like to the angle desired for honing.

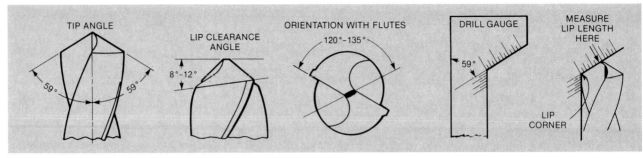

Drawings, above and right, show twist drill appearance and relationships that must be maintained. Of particular importance is orientation of grind with flutes. An inexpensive drill gauge is helpful in keeping the grind equal.

● Use a sharpening service when you need to. While you can, for example, sharpen either a hand-saw or circular-saw blade by hand with a file (and quite accurately with a sharpening aid), you probably have a local sharpening service that can do the job by machine much better and at a price you can't touch if you value your time at even a very low rate. The secret here is to keep spares so you won't be out of business when some of your cutting tools are being renewed. Professional sharpening is almost a must if the blade is to be reset or "gummed" (gashed deeper).

● Consider the purchase of at least an inexpensive bench grinder—or a wheel grinder accessory for another stationary tool, if you don't already own one.

● Nearly all cutting tools are made of special steels that are heat-treated and then tempered (carefully reheated to less than the hardening temperature) to give the tool edge just the right degree of hardness and toughness to do their intended jobs. Any grinding must be done very slowly, with frequent stops to allow the steel to cool. Overheating, which destroys the temper, is to be avoided. In nearly every case, when the edge is hot enough to reach a straw color, the damage has been done. Unless the edge is retempered properly, it will never perform as well as it should.

● Get the basic equipment you need. Besides the bench grinder and perhaps some sharpening aids, needs are minimal: a good flat file; a small triangular file; perhaps a small round file; a fine/coarse abrasive block (see photo with the blade sharpening aid); a small hand abrasive stick; and a fine hone, such as an Arkansas stone.

● Know your angles. Determining the angles to which various tools must be sharpened may be a problem if you're inexperienced. A good rule of thumb: If in doubt, duplicate the angles the maker put on the tool.

● Get magnification. Unless your eyes are super good, investment in a small magnifying glass can be a big help in doing good sharpening. Why? So you can have a good look at the cutting edge. Then you can quickly detect off-angles, nicks, flat spots, roughness, and burrs—all of which you can and should fix before the tool can be said to be really sharp.

Drill bits

Discounting the "throwaway" saw blades, chances are you use twist drill bits more than any other cutting tool. Bits are also more difficult to sharpen than other tools.

If a drill is not sharpened just right, it won't cut at all, or if it does cut it will overheat, wander off, or cut crooked. The relationship that must be maintained if the drill is to perform well is shown in one of the drawings. Your best bet is to purchase a sharpening aid for drills.

Drills can, of course, be sharpened by hand on a bench grinder without an aid. If you choose to do it that way, study the drawing to see how the point must look. Inspecting the tips of small drills is a good place to use a magnifier —*Phil McCafferty.*

cleaning a drill chuck

Nothing is handier than the Jacobs chuck on your electric drill—until it gets sticky from dust, dirt, and drill lubricant. Then it's twist, twist with the chuck key, over and over, just to open or close the jaws. But a thorough and complete cleanup doesn't take more than thirty minutes and, unless you've abused your chuck badly, it will work as smoothly as when it was new.

Such chucks are threaded—right-hand thread—onto or into the drill output shaft; to remove them from the drill, simply insert the key shank in a hole and whack it smartly with a hammer. There's a joker in this if your drill is the reversible type: Here, the chuck is locked by an inner screw so that it won't unscrew when the drill is running in reverse. Before removing the chuck you have to open the jaws and go in with a narrow screwdriver to remove the lock screw, which has a left-hand thread.

With the chuck off the drill, all that's necessary is to force the press-fitted outer sleeve off the central member. You can use a piece of pipe, a socket wrench, or even a hole drilled in a piece of hard wood to support the outer sleeve while you press or drive the center out. For my 1/4-inch drill, a 15/16-inch socket just fits the sleeve, but allows the inner member to pass inside. A vise or arbor press can be used to force the sleeve off, but if the chuck is small, a few taps with a hammer does the trick.

With the sleeve off, you can see the three sliding jaws and the split ring around them. The threads on the inner diameter of the ring mate with those in the jaws. Lift out the two halves of the ring carefully and place them in solvent (e.g., lacquer thinner), and clean, perhaps using an old toothbrush. Keep track of the top and bottom as you work, and don't turn one upside down against the other—a little care that helps avoid confusion on reassembly.

The jaws are not identical. Each is threaded a little differently so that, when acted upon by the ring threads, it moves evenly in proper relationship to the others. Should you drop the jaws on the floor, you can probably figure out how they go together by studying the threads, but for cleaning, it's a lot easier to remove one jaw at a time and then replace it exactly where it came from.

You can push the jaws out from the top with a small stick, though they might be hard to remove if the chuck is badly fouled. Wash the jaw, and especially the threads, until all surfaces are bright. Use a small, round brush to clean the hole in the chuck body. Clean each jaw and each hole, in turn, until you can slide the jaw back and forth freely in the hole over its full travel.

Here's where a bit of experience pays off. While it took just a washing out to put the jaws back into one of my chucks in free sliding condition, on another, the jaws wouldn't slide freely no matter what I did. Examination with a magnifying glass revealed minute burrs and turned edges at the end of the central member, where the jaws came out. Such burrs may be caused by using an oversize drill, loose drills that wallow and batter the chuck, and from running the chuck hard and flush against a surface. In any case, it took nothing more than some careful cleaning up of the burrs with a small hone to cure the sticking problem on my chuck.

To reassemble your chuck, slide all three jaws down until the outer ends are even in the full closed position. The two rings should drop neatly into the threads in the upper parts of the jaws. Slip the outer sleeve over the inner parts and drive or press it solidly home in the reverse of the disassembly process. Squirt a little light oil into the jaws and threaded areas and your chuck will work like new—*E. F. Lindsley.*

Reversing drills have an additional screw with left-hand thread inside chuck. Dirt may obscure screw slot until you dig it out. Chuck key keeps chuck from turning while you remove screw.

Sharp hammer blow loosens chuck from standard drill and, after screw is removed, from reversing drill, too. If it doesn't, have drill serviced. Excessive hammering may damage gear drive.

Large socket wrench supports outer sleeve, smaller one protects upper end. Hammer blow forces inner member through and out of sleeve, so inner wrench must clear OD of inner member.

Shown at bottom, are the outer sleeve, split, threaded ring, and one jaw of a chuck soaking in a solvent-filled tray. The other two jaws of the chuck are still in place—this to avoid mixing jaws up, since each is different. The hole in the inner member is brushed clean with solvent.

care and refinishing of wood floors

It's true that professional floor finishers know what they're doing; they also make short work of emptying your pocketbook for their services. Do you need to hire a pro to do the job? Not if you're able-bodied, have plenty of spare time, and are bent on saving money. But prepare yourself—refinishing a floor is a tough number.

To sand and refinish a floor, you need a drum sander, disc-edge sander, and hand scraper; sandpaper (grades 3½, 1½, and 2/0); stain (optional); filler (paste or liquid); varnish, shellac, or penetrating finish; paint brushes; and clean cloths.

You can rent drum and disc-edge sanders at rental service stores or large hardware stores. Be sure to ask how to attach sandpaper to both before you leave the shop. The drum sander does the basic sanding job; the disc-edge sander is used along baseboards and other less accessible areas. For little nooks and crannies, you need a hand scraper, available at hardware stores.

First, put on old clothes, empty the room, and open the windows. (If you use flammable solvents, don't smoke or light a fire during application and drying.) Remove shoe moldings, registers, and electric plates. Try to loosen radiators so you can at least move them out of the way enough to sand under them. Nail down any loose, protruding, or creaking floorboards.

Sanding

A major sanding job is done in three steps, with three grades of sandpaper. The first sanding removes the old finish down to bare wood, takes out deep scratches, and removes high spots. For this, use coarse, open-coat No. 3½ (20 grit) sandpaper.

Move the drum sander lengthwise over the floor, along the grain of the

wood. Don't push it—it may take you right into a wall! Just guide it as it moves slowly, under its own power. Start at one wall and move straight to the opposite wall, then walk backwards, pulling the sander back along the same path. Overlap each previous pass by about 3 inches, but be careful—if the sander rubs one place for long, it'll cut through the wood. The cost of repairing that mistake will

cancel out anything you saved by doing the job yourself.

To sand close to walls, use the disc-edge sander with No. 3½ paper. Move the sander constantly, and don't tilt it or you'll carve deep circles in the floor.

Use the hand scraper, with the same grade sandpaper, for corners. Keep the blade sharp by turning it upside down and running a fine-tooth file over it lengthwise. Bear down on the scraper; pull it toward you with one hand, while pushing down on the head with the other. Always scrape with the grain. Vacuum the floor thoroughly after the first sanding.

Now change to a medium-grade, No. 1½ (40-grit) sandpaper to remove the rough surface left by the coarse paper. Sand the floor, using the same technique as before. Use the same paper to edge and scrape, then vacuum the floor well.

Change to fine-grade, No. 2/0 (100 grit) sandpaper and sand as before. Work in socks so you don't leave shoeprints after this final sanding, which produces a smooth surface suitable for the finish. Touch up any rough spots by hand-sanding with medium-grade sandpaper.

Metal key turns mechanism that opens and closes drum on sander (below). Sandpaper is wrapped around drum, and ends inserted in the open slot (bottom). Hold paper in place as you close drum with key. You need a three-prong plug adapter for the drum sander. In using the machine (facing page), get a firm grip on it and, moving slowly (guide it, don't push it), follow the grain of the wood.

Follow the final sanding with a good vacuuming for the entire room (floor, walls, windows, doors, woodwork) and a bath for yourself. You'll need it.

Fillers

The pros mix stain and the fine dust stirred up during sanding to fill imperfections in the wood as they stain. However, that requires a special machine and you're using your own two hands. So make do with paste or liquid fillers.

Disc-edge sander uses a circular sanding disc. Use a wrench to remove the center nut; place sandpaper over the opening, and replace the nut.

Wrap sandpaper around the blade of the hand scraper to sand corners. As you work, use your hand to maintain a constant, even pressure on the scraper.

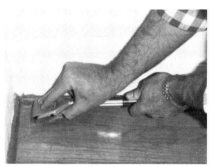

Filler should be thinned with paint thinner and applied with a good-quality brush. You can color filler by mixing in enough oil stain to get desired tone.

If your floor is open-grain wood (walnut, ash, mahogany, oak), close the cells and tiny crevices with a paste filler, thinned with turpentine. You can color the filler by mixing in a little oil stain. Let the filler set twenty to thirty minutes, then rub it into the pores of the wood. Wipe away any surplus (shows up as blotches or smears) when the filler dries. Remove any smears that persist by wiping carefully with a cloth moistened with thinner or pure turpentine. Be thorough. Any filler you leave on the sur-

Apply equal pressure with both arms to keep the disc sander level. Any tilting of the machine may carve deep, impossible-to-repair circles in your floor.

You will need to use a metal file to keep the blade of the hand scraper sharp. Rub the file evenly over the blade of the scraper to sharpen it.

Sanding sealer is used on unstained floor after sanding. Brush sealer on and let it dry two or three hours. Then sand lightly, vacuum, and apply a finish.

face will cloud after you apply the finish. And there's no way to fix that.

Open-grain wood floors need filler. Without it, the finish sinks into the wood, giving the surface a rippled look.

Staining

Staining your floor gives it color and enhances the grain of the wood. It's an extra step, but it's probably worth the trouble. If you want to stain your floor, this is the time to do it.

Before you start, vacuum or sweep all dust from the floor. If you don't, you'll end up with a sealed layer of dust hiding the grain you've worked so hard to show off. And be sure to check the label of the finish you plan to use to be sure it's made for use over the stain you've chosen.

Floor-care experts recommend three types of stain:

1. *Nongrain-raising stain* (also called "fast-to-light" or "nonsand" stain). This type of stain is made to be dissolved in a solvent that does not raise the grain of the wood. As a result, it does not require sanding before finish is applied. It can be used under any type of finish coat and can be mixed in a wide range of colors. But it's expensive, and you're trying to economize. So read on.

2. *Penetrating oil stain.* This is used by most professionals. It, too, is nongrain-raising, but it tends to bleed or dissolve and mix with later filler coats, varnish, and/or lacquer. To prevent bleeding, seal the stain with a wash coat of shellac.

3. *Pigment oil stain* (also called "wood stain," "pigment wiping stain," or "uniforming stain"). Actually a thin paint, this does not fade or bleed and is easy to apply, but it tends to cover the grain pattern more than other stains. If your floor has an open grain, use a filler before staining with pigment oil stain, or the stain will clog the pores of the wood and make it look muddy.

It's wise to test the color of an oil stain by brushing a little on the floor of a well-lighted closet. Let it stand five minutes, then wipe off the excess. If it's too light, brush on another coat for two minutes. Continue until you know how long the stain should stand for the right color, and follow that timing for the floor. Apply the stain with a wide brush in an even coat, with straight edges to minimize overlap. After it penetrates the wood, wipe up the excess with clean, dry rags. Let the floor dry for 24 hours before applying a finish.

Finishing

The final step in refinishing your floor is applying a finishing coat. Floor finishes protect the work you've already done by putting a protective seal on it. There are three main classes of finishes:

1. *Shellac.* Shellac is economical, flexible, quick-drying, and durable. And you can add toner to it to change the color.

The main varieties are orange, white, and dewaxed. Orange darkens wood; white (clear) does not; and dewaxed is transparent. White shellac is best for most floors. Avoid shellac substitutes; they scratch and mark easily and do not withstand heavy traffic.

Shellac is brushed on the floor and sanded between coats. Never apply it on a warm, muggy day or over a damp surface or it will cloud.

2. *Varnish.* An excellent, transparent finish, varnish outdoes the others in depth and build. Good varnish is extremely hard and durable. Don't economize here; cheap grades become brittle and show scars.

Make sure the surface is completely dry, sanded, and dust-free when you apply varnish. Do the dusting (tacking) with a rag moistened with varnish; the tack rag picks up small particles that no amount of dry dusting could remove.

Abrasion-resistance is high in varnishes, especially those containing urethane. Varnish is more water-resistant than shellac, but it is susceptible to scratching and becomes darker with age.

"Quick-dry" varnishes are usually less durable than the slow-drying ones. Many professionals use *spar varnish,* a dark, slow-drying, moderate-gloss type that is tough, elastic, and durable. (Don't use filler under spar varnish; temperature extremes and the sun decompose it.) *Floor varnish* is harder and faster drying. It is quite elastic and tough enough to withstand grinding heels and scraping furniture.

All varnishes are difficult to patch. No matter how careful you are about it, the patches will always show.

3. *Penetrating sealer.* This type of finish puts tough resins *in,* rather than on the wood. It seals the wood against dirt and stains and makes it very wear resistant. Some sealers (like Wood Finish by Minwax) are colored, so staining, sealing, and finishing can be done in one operation. You also can add some color to any commercial sealing product you use.

Penetrating finishes are the easiest of all to apply. Just brush or wipe the finish on, let it sink in five to fifteen minutes, then wipe away the excess. Your floor probably will need two or three coats, applied at twelve-hour intervals. Wait twenty-four hours after the last application before waxing. Later, you can repair worn spots by applying some of the sealer to the area; unlike varnish patches, sealer patches never show.

Application of wax

Most paste waxes are rubbed onto a clean floor with a soft cloth or extra-fine (00 grade) steel wool. Be sparing; you can't get the wax too thin. Let the coat dry for about five minutes, then polish it with a weighted brush or an electric floor polisher. If the floor is slippery, it needs more buffing.

Self-polishing waxes are less desirable, but if that's what you choose, apply a thin coat with a dry wax applicator. The wax dries to a shine in thirty to forty minutes. Porous floors may need a second coat.

Apply buffable liquid wax in the same way. Then, before it dries completely, buff the coated floor by hand or with a dry wax applicator. If you're using an electric floor polisher, wait twenty to thirty minutes before buffing the dried wax.

Maintenance

If you wax and buff your floor properly to begin with, it won't take a lot of time or effort to keep it in good shape. Unless your floor is exposed to hard wear or excessive moisture, it should need only routine dusting, occasional buffing, and a wax job a couple of times each year.

Use a dust mop or a vacuum cleaner to remove grit and dust from the floor. A little Endust or a similar product will help make dusting go more quickly. For most homes, a once-a-week vacuuming or dusting will do the trick. Use a brush attachment on your vacuum cleaner and be sure to lock it in place, so the brush, rather than the metal, hits the floor.

Since wax doesn't penetrate wood, rebuffing the floor rids it of surface scuffs and will restore the sheen of the wood. Wax two or three times a year with a cleaning wax, a buffable liquid wax, or a paste wax. All must be buffed.

If the floor is old, watch for loose and creaking boards. Keep them nailed down tight. If the old nails don't hold well, drill a very small hole at an angle through the loose board and drive in 4-inch, cement-coated finishing nails. Countersink nail heads and cover the holes with plastic wood.

Or, if your floor is well-sealed, try applying a bit of lubricating oil along the cracks between planks. Be sure to wipe off surplus oil. If there are wide cracks between boards, fill them with wood putty.

If wood pegs in a pegged, wide-board floor come loose, reset them with white wood glue.

Glue splinters down with white glue as soon as you notice them.

Stripping

If your floors are not overwaxed, there never should be a buildup that requires complete removal (unless you use self-polishing liquid wax). However, when scuffs become hard to buff out, it's a sign that your floor should be stripped of old wax.

Don't use water or water-base stripping compounds like those used on resilient floors. (The water damages wood.) Instead, use a waterless floor cleaner. Be careful if you use naphtha; it is highly flammable.

Bad spots

Deep scratches require a thorough sanding of the surrounding area to level the surface of the wood. Some scratches on a floor with a shellac finish can be filled with a melted shellac stick of the proper color. And deep scratches in a stained floor can be stained to match surrounding wood.

Surface scuffs often can be rubbed out with paste wax and steel wool. Or, on floors with a shellac finish, use alcohol. Scratches in painted floors can be sanded, spackled, resanded, and repainted.

Or try Varsol, a petroleum product that takes up heel marks, cleans tar off your car, kills weeds, and maybe even cures sinus trouble. (It's sold at Exxon stations in 2-gallon containers. Or you can bring your own container and buy smaller portions.) Use a rag moistened with Varsol to rub the mark away. A warning though: Varsol also takes the wax off your floor; the spot must be rewaxed.

To remove dents, try this: Turn a bottle cap upside down over the dent and heat the cap for brief periods with a warm iron to raise wood.

For treating special problems—burns, paint spills, and the like—see "Special problems" above—*Denise Allen Zwicker.*

Special problems

Wood floors are just as susceptible as any others to spilled drinks, cigarette burns, water damage, and other such catastrophes. Repairing the damage is just a matter of learning the proper strategy:

● Fresh paint: Use the appropriate paint solvent.

●Dry paint: Rub with a rag that has been dipped in a mix of rottenstone (a cleaning powder you can buy at hardware stores) and salad oil.

●Rust: Mix one part sodium citrate with six parts water and seven parts glycerine. Add whiting and stir to a thick paste. Spread on stains and let it dry two or three days, then scrape it off. If stains remain, repeat the process.

●Cigarette burns: Scrape blackened area *carefully* along wood grain, until you reach brown wood. Wipe out color with benzine, paint thinner, or bleach; smooth with sandpaper or steel wool; apply stain; finish to match surrounding wood.

Filling in with plastic wood sounds easier, but it's hard to find any to match the floor color. You can, however, mix ordinary plastic wood with an alcohol stain that matches the floor.

●Crayon and lipstick: Use liquid cleaning wax.

●Oil and grease: Try wiping with paint thinner or benzine, but don't rub the oil further into the wood. Or place cotton saturated with hydrogen peroxide over the stains; then soak another piece of cotton in ammonia and spread it on top until the cotton dries. Repeat the process until the stain disappears.

●Alcohol: If you break a bottle of wine on the floor, use a dampened cloth or mop, but be sure to dry the floor thoroughly; if you don't, the water will penetrate the wax and turn it white. The only solution, then, is to rewax.

Wipe alcohol stains with a rag dipped in salad oil and rottenstone, rinse with benzine, and apply wax. Really old stains will require a little extra work with the same treatment, unless the floor has a shellac finish. In that case, rub out the stain with 00-grade steel wool; brush on new shellac, diluted fifty-fifty with denatured alcohol; rub well with steel wool; reapply shellac, and rub down again.

●Chewing gum: Chill the gum with an ice cube until it's brittle. Then scrape it off with a dull knife. Remove any residue with trichloroethylene.

●White water marks: Rub with cigarette ashes and salad oil. Or daub spots with spirits of camphor. Let the camphor dry for half an hour; then rub with a rag dipped in oil and rottenstone, clean off residue with benzine, and apply wax.

Water allowed to stand for long periods (e.g., under planters) eventually will stain wood almost black. There are three things you can try on these marks: (1) Rub with coarse steel wool and a good floor cleaner or paint thinner. (2) Sand, first with medium, then with fine sandpaper. (3) Bleach with three applications of oxalic acid. If one of these suggestions works, even out the finish around the marks with fine sandpaper, apply new finish, and wax. The only other alternative is deep sanding and refinishing.

●Candle wax: Scrape as much as you can away with a dull knife, then use naptha or trichloroethylene to clean the rest.

●Mildew: For this, you must use water. First, scrub with a rag dipped in a strong solution of chlorine bleach and wrung out. Then rinse with a rag dipped in water and wrung out. Dry thoroughly.

●Food: Most foods are neutral and will not affect the floor finish. Use water to remove any food residue, then dry thoroughly.

Rottenstone and salad oil can be used to atone for a number of sins (left); the mixture even will remove dried paint and old alcohol stains. Be careful when scraping a burned spot (top, right). A sharp knife blade or too much pressure can seriously damage the floor. Scrape carefully along the wood grain. With dark water stains, sanding is imperative (bottom, right). Use medium sandpaper to remove the damaged wood; switch to fine paper to smooth the finish.

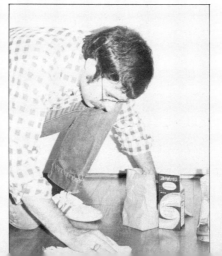

furniture repairs

The accompanying photos illustrate a typical furniture repair—one that includes all the structural elements you're likely to encounter in working on your own furniture. Except for very expensive pieces, where you might find difficult-to-repair mortise and tenon or dovetail joints, furniture today is almost always put together with dowels, screws, and glues. With the glues that are now available, you can forget about sending your broken pieces to a specialist for expensive repair. With a little care (put down newspapers to catch the drips), you can rebuild most joints right in your living room.

Not too long ago, the only way to repair the living room chair shown here would have been to make a new cross member (the piece that split). Today, with epoxy, split pieces can be made as good as new. Used correctly, epoxy makes virtually foolproof repairs. And, for joints, the new wood glues are far superior to anything the old cabinetmaker used to mix up.

Breaks occur gradually—in time, dowels and screws work out of a piece of furniture until they are too weak to hold. If you're alert, you can catch such potential breaks and repair them before they give way. Repair procedure is simple, but allow two or three days for a job, as the glue should set thoroughly between each step.

To repair an actual break: Mix a generous batch of epoxy. Spread it carefully on both sides of the break, then clamp the pieces together, using wood blocks on either side to protect the furniture from clamp marks. Near the edges of the break, apply the epoxy very thinly, or it will ooze out and permanently fasten the clamp blocks in place. (A piece of aluminum foil or waxed paper between the blocks and the break will prevent this.)

Next, thoroughly clean out—but don't enlarge—any dowel holes. Broken dowels may have to be carefully scraped, whittled, or even drilled out.

Remove any screws. Refill screw

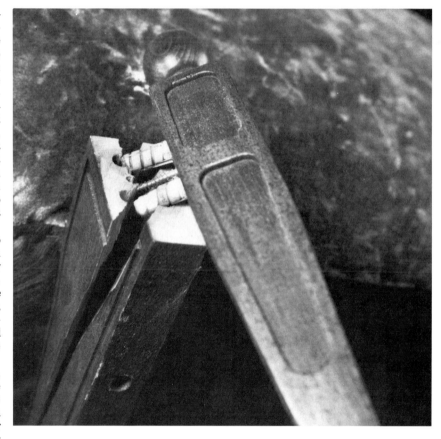

holes either with glue and splinters, driving them in, or some other hard-setting material that will create a holding surface for screw threads.

If you plan to countersink a screw and cover the head with a hardwood plug, as in the photos, remove the plug prior to backing out the screw. This is likely to require both a small drill and a sturdy knife blade, as the plugs are well glued when inserted, and sanded, stained, and varnished with the rest of the piece. Plug holes, too, must be carefully cleaned out without enlarging them.

If necessary, get suitable replacement dowels (or make them from doweling) and plugs. Make sure plugs fit the openings tightly; if they're too large, sand them down a little.

Using a good wood glue (don't forget the dowels and holes), reassemble the pieces and clamp if necessary. Replace screws and tighten well to hold the pieces together until the glue sets. Plugs may be glued in after other glue has set.

Unless scars are massive and the piece requires refinishing, just go over the finish with brown shoe polish. Well rubbed in, this works about as well as anything for covering scars in dark-stained wood, especially when scars are in the lower part of a piece where they will not be inspected too closely.

The technique described above will enable you to repair 90 percent or more of the furniture breaks that occur in a home—*John Robinson.*

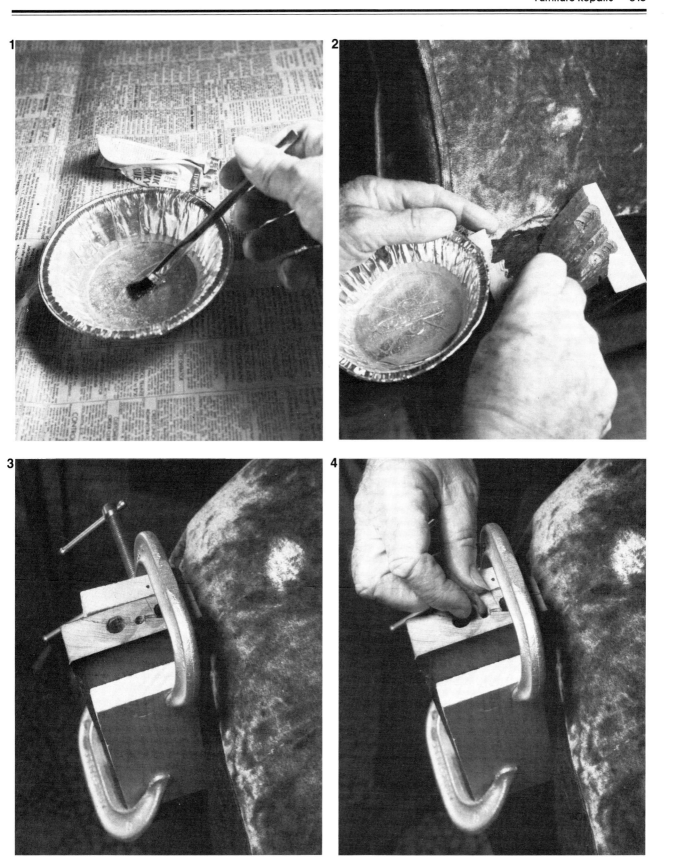

Steps in repair of typical furniture break—split hardwood, broken dowels, loose screw: **(1)** Use epoxy to fuse break in crosspiece. (Avoid the fast-acting kind; it sets up too quickly for this use.) Small brushes, such as the one shown, are inexpensive and disposable. Spread paper to catch drips. **(2)** Spread break apart and apply epoxy generously to both surfaces. **(3)** Tightly clamp split pieces, using wood blocks on both sides to protect furniture. Aluminum foil or waxed paper prevents blocks from sticking. **(4)** To provide new purchase for screw threads, work mixture of powdered wood, sawdust, and glue or some other hard filler into the screw hole.

7

8

1

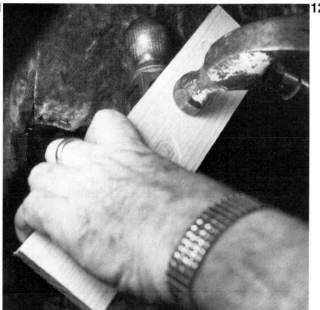

12

15

For the kind of joint in the chair being repaired, a screw and two dowels are usual elements. **(5)** Note that one dowel is broken. Most well-made furniture has countersunk screwheads **(6)**, covered with hardwood plugs. If possible, remove plug with a knife, or drill carefully. A support makes the job easier. **(7)** Back out the screw and **(8)** remove broken dowel stub remaining in the hole, using either a sharp knife or a drill. **(9)** If you can't find the right size dowel, very carefully sandpaper around a slightly too large one to take off a little. **(10)** Here, a snug-fitting, homemade dowel has been glued in place. Note that the tip has been slightly rounded with sandpaper. **(11)** Use wood glue on dowels and faces of joint, carefully tapping in for tight joint. **(12)** Immediately after joining, put screw in place and tighten thoroughly. For some repairs, you may need a cord tourniquet to keep parts tightly in position, but here the screw is adequate. **(13)** Hardwood plugs are available in hardware stores in various sizes; they're usually displayed near ready-made dowels. **(14)** Very carefully check the plug in the hole and, if necessary, sand it down a little, all the way around. The fit should be slightly snug. Tap the plug into position carefully. **(15)** Here, repairs are completed, but no attempt has been made to refinish the parts. Rubbing brown shoe polish into the scars will make them invisible to all but the most careful inspection. And that's all there is to repairing breaks in most furniture around your home.

secrets of drywall taping

Taping drywall is one of the toughest do-it-yourself jobs. Few homeowners have the proper tools and materials to do the job right, to say nothing of know-how or experience. And the best place to experiment is not on your living-room walls, where every crack, blister, nail hole, and tape line becomes a daily source of regret and irritation. That's why most homeowners turn to drywall professionals to do the job.

That's fine for big projects, but you may not want to call in a pro for small jobs—finishing a basement, remodeling a bath, or just repairing a damaged wall. I believe it is possible for first-time tapers to get good results using a type of drywall cement that shrinks very little and dries quickly to a hard, durable finish. Used with some other drywall-finishing products that may be unknown to non-professionals—fiberglass-mesh adhesive tape and screen-type backless sandpaper—the fast-setting compounds enable the average home handyman to finish drywall without any noticeable imperfections.

The cements I'm referring to, polyindurate compounds, aren't all that new, but manufacturers have finally overcome the lumpiness and other inconsistencies that plagued

Array of taping knives, mud pan, adhesive mesh tape, and sanding screen surrounds sacks of twenty- and ninety-minute hot mud.

past formulations. In the trade we call these compounds hot muds, because they give off mild, chemically generated heat when they are mixed. For pros, their main advantage over vinyl-type cements is that they set quickly, which means that jobs requiring two, three, or more coats can be completed in one day instead of three. That may also be an advantage for do-it-yourselfers, but hot mud's low-shrink quality is even more important. With vinyl, it is necessary to overfill drywall joints and to feather out the edges to allow for shrinkage. This is where most people go wrong, leaving too much or too little mud and slopping up the joint. You don't overfill with hot mud.

Because they have been used almost exclusively by professionals until now, hot muds have generally been available only in 25-pound bags from building-supply stores. Now some makers are packaging the powder in 4 or 5 pound packages in consumer outlets. There are many brands, including Fast Set, Quick Set, Rapid Bond, Durabond, Sudden Bond, and Sta Smooth. These are made in a variety of setup times, ranging from fifteen minutes to four hours; the most common are ninety-minute muds. There are also exterior types. Pros may use different types of mud for first-coat and finish work, but a handyman can get by perfectly well with a single mud (ninety minute or slower) mixed to differing consistencies.

The art of mixing

Proper mixing is crucial. Otherwise, you get a lumpy mud and disastrous results. Here's the right way: Put clean water in a clean bucket and pour in the powdered mud, mixing as you pour and not allowing the powder to sink to the bottom. Mix quickly to a stiff consistency, let the batch sit for a few minutes, and then remix and add water to reach the final consistency.

Different jobs require muds of different consistencies. For metal corner bead and on flat joints (both tapered board edges and full-thickness butts), you need a thick mix that clings to your taping knife. For the second coat, the mix should be softer, but not so it falls off the knife. For flattening uneven areas, taping angles (inside corners), or spotting (filling) nail holes, use a soft mix that drops off the blade. As little as one-quarter cup of water will change a bucketful of mud from one purpose to the next.

The reason a softer mix is needed for finish, spotting, and angle work is that mud stiffens considerably when worked. Those jobs involve more knife work than first-coating, in which you get rid of the mud in a single pass. When doing these jobs, make sure the mud doesn't start setting up in the pan. If a batch does begin to set prematurely, it can at first be washed away with spray from a garden hose. Later on, it will have to be chipped and scraped clean.

As important as having the proper mix is using the proper tools. Most do-it-yourselfers err by using the 6- or 8-inch knives they happen to have around. A 10-incher is the only knife to use for flat joints and spotting. For angles, you need a 6-inch knife; for feathering out on butt joints, a 14-inch may be needed. Use only straight knives, not the offset-handle contraptions with concave blades.

One other ingredient goes into a quality taping job: proper technique. That includes everything from how the knife is held to how much mud is removed from the pan to the strokes used to apply it to the wall. Journeyman tapers take months perfecting the special shoulder, back, arm, wrist, and finger motions needed to do the job effortlessly and quickly. But since do-it-yourselfers don't need a pro's speed, they can pick up sufficient skills with just a little practice.

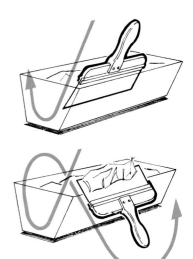

To draw mud from pan, put knife point between mud and metal (inserting whole edge risks nicked blade), dig across and up, then wipe back against pan's lip.

The first and most important motion to learn is the correct way to draw mud from the pan—what I call the figure 8. The idea is to pack the mud on the one side of your knife and leave the other side clean. Study the drawing above, and practice the repeated process of digging in, pulling up, and wiping back until it becomes second nature.

Now that your knife is loaded, you are ready to begin running angles and flats, spotting, and touching up. Each of these procedures calls for different strokes, but the knife is always held the same way: with the middle, fourth, and little fingers wrapped around the handle and the thumb and forefinger pushing on the blade itself, not the rib. (Some tapers put the middle finger on the blade, as well.) In this position you are ready to exert either thumb or finger pressure as the task requires.

Everything I've said about technique applies equally to hot mud and vinyl. But there's one important difference. When applying vinyl cement, the knife is held at a low angle to the wallboard to allow the blade to bow and overfill the joint. With low-shrink hot mud, hold the blade so it's more nearly perpendicular to the wall, to avoid humped joints.

Now let's run through a few typical procedures. Usually, the first job you'll do on fresh drywall is taping the flats with self-sticking fiberglass mesh. This tape is superior to paper because it is thinner and doesn't require an embedding layer of mud. When taping boards that were cut to size, be sure to pound in (with the knife handle) any ragged edges that may have been left. It's crucial that the tape lie absolutely flat.

Now, using either thumb pressure and pulling up or finger pressure and pulling down (but not both), apply a layer of mud over the tape with your 10-inch knife. Then, on a second pass, scrape off the excess, leaving just enough mud to fill the holes in the mesh but with the tape visible.

On angles, conventional creased paper tape must still be used. Using a 6-inch knife, first run a thin undercoat of mud along both sides of the corner. Then cut pieces of tape to length, fold them on the crease, and press them into place. Or you can use a banjo taping machine to perform all operations at once.

After taping, you're ready for spotting—filling the small nail or screw holes created when the wall was hung. The

To begin, top center photo, string mesh tape with the thumb-to-thumb method on all flats, but don't overlap at the joint intersections. Above left, there's no pressure exchange when coating on flats; forefinger is held straight out. Above right, spotting requires a swirling motion. Here taper is finishing stroke with finger pressure after starting with thumb. Below left, use two-finger pressure for first-coating butts, leaving as little mud as possible. Below right, use 6-inch knife in angles only—for bedding, scraping, and smoothing (shown).

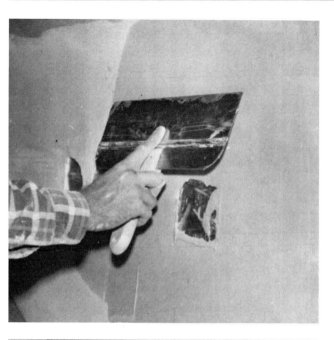

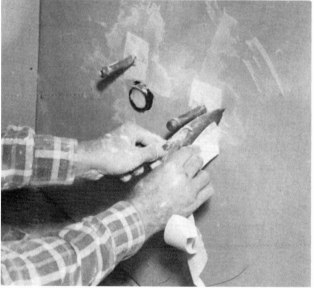

Above top, tape around electrical boxes; then coat over with mud. Above, don't use tape scraps around pipes; tear semicircles out of folded paper tape in paper-doll fashion. Below, knife blade should spring when touching up blemishes.

basic motion is to apply cement and wipe it clean with a single swirling motion. A pressure exchange occurs between the thumb and forefinger. If you hold the knife with your elbow turned in, then the pressure begins with the forefinger and ends with the thumb. If you begin with the elbow turned out, then the thumb pressure comes first. As you work—generally from bottom to top and from left to right (it's right to left for lefties)—look out for mud sagging in the holes. If the mixture is even slightly too thin, you must remove the mud twice from the hole, or you'll end up with hardened domes all over your walls.

Finishing for smooth walls

Once your first coat of mud is complete and fully set, the next thing to do is scrape. Anywhere the compound is not perfectly smooth—at tape edges or where the knife has left chatter or stop marks—you simply scrape lightly; the finish becomes smooth as glass. No sanding is necessary. Tape that has beaded up can be simply sliced off; its mesh network is unaffected by the loss of a piece here and there.

Now comes the finish coat. Covering the tape line on angles is easy when working with soft hot mud. Coat both sides with a 6-inch knife, then scrape off, working up from the bottom and down from the top.

Finishing butt joints requires great care to avoid leaving a noticeable hump. If the butt does not meet properly, it may have to be feathered out over a distance of 2 feet or more. After the first coat and a good scraping, slide the edge of a broad knife along the joint to locate the more severely sloped and hollow side. Fill this side slightly with your 10-inch knife. Later you'll come back for third and fourth treatments. For these, use a 14-inch knife and spread the joint out over a 28-to-30-inch width, being careful not to build up over the joint itself.

When all joints, nails, plumbing runs, and electrical boxes (see photos) have been fully smoothed out, there is one more step before you're ready to coat the wall (unnecessary if you plan to use a textured finish). Using a 14-inch knife, apply a skin coat of mud to the entire wall surface, then remove it. This leaves a frost over everything that highlights any slight imperfections that would show up when the wall is painted.

The blemishes that appear are touched up using a technique called the one-shot coat-and-clean. It's a special movement pros use to work at great speed with a minimum of return strokes to the mud pan. Although you may not need to perform with the same efficiency pros do, it may still be useful to know the proper method. The key to the technique is getting a shot of mud properly centered on the blade edge. This is done by loading the knife in the usual way, then cutting off one corner and shaking the rest down to the center. The one-shot uses the natural spring of the blade to cover a blemish and scrape the tool clean all in one motion. With finger pressure applied, push down on the blade and make it bend back, then as you pull away, elevate the handle until the blade springs back. I've seen skilled journeymen do touch-ups with this technique for several minutes without once hitting knife to pan and without leaving any chaff behind.

When the touch-up is complete, remove the skin coat. This is the only time I ever sand, using 150 paper to lightly brush down the entire surface (the backless-type sandpaper pictured on the opening page is a great boon because it never clogs). Then sweep off the dust with a soft broom and the wall is ready to be primed and painted. My favorite paint treatment for a smooth wall is two coats of semigloss latex enamel over a thinned primer coat —*Mark Lee Due.*

installing a deadbolt lock

The first step in securing your home from burglars is to make sure all entrance doors are solid and reinforced with secure locks. Of course, nothing is 100 percent secure—an intruder may smash a window, cut around a lock, or pry a door away from a jamb. In such instances, neither the finest lock, nor the most carefully selected door is any help. Still you can make it as difficult as possible for an intruder to enter. Installing deadbolt locks on doors that now have only key-in-knob locks will be a step in the right direction.

The accompanying photos and captions show how to install a mortised cylinder deadbolt lock. The lock used in this installation (The Barrier by Lori) has a 1-inch throw of hardened steel to prevent saw-through. The lock is built around a solid cast cylinder that threads into a housing, so installation varies slightly from the method used for deadbolt locks held in place by screws. (It requires one extra step and an Allen wrench—generally supplied with hardware—to join the bolt block with the cylinder housing.)

Standard tools needed for installing deadbolt locks mortised into a door are: hole saw, electric drill, ¼- and 1-inch drill bits, chisel, and punch. Before installing any lock, open the package and check that all parts have been included—*E. D. Cormier.*

Steps in installing deadbolt lock: (1) Measure your door—this is important because door thickness (1⅜ or 1¾ inches) determines center location and "backset" position of lock. **(2)** Using template supplied with lock (template must have same backset as lock you purchased), position and mark center of holes to be drilled. Center location can be marked with pencil, but hole made with punch serves as better guide for pilot drill. To insure accuracy, use small, adjustable carpenter's square. **(3)** Drill small pilot hole with 1¼-inch bit—hole must be at 90-degree angle with door and parallel to floor. Then, depending on the lock, use a 2 or 2⅛-inch diameter hole saw to drill about half way through door. Stop as often as necessary to remove wood chips. **(4)** Do not attempt to saw all the way through from one side of the door, or the hole won't be straight and will have ragged edges. After pilot bit penetrates the back side of door, drill from opposite side of door, as shown, until you have a large hole that goes completely through the door. Caution: Installation instructions vary between models and makes. Be sure to check the guidelines provided here against the instructions that were supplied with your lock. **(5)** A 1-inch flatbit, or smaller hole saw can be used to drill the second hole in the edge of the door for the deadbolt. This will penetrate through to the main hole. Chisel is then used to smooth off the excess wood, including any that protrudes in the middle of the cylinder hole and that could impair a smooth

fit. **(6)** Insert the bolt assembly with the front through the 1-inch diameter hole; mark outline as shown. **(7)** Use sharp chisel to cut the outline to the proper depth. Remove the wood in thin, lean chips, working from the hole to the top and bottom with alternate cuts. For a neat job, end with a clean break at the cut line. **(8)** Insert the cylinder housing assembly into the large hole. Then insert the bolt housing into the 1-inch hole and push it into cylinder housing. **(9)** Insert and tighten the two cylinder housing screws. **(10)** Slip the key into the cylinder. Pull it out one notch as shown in the photo; then screw cylinder into housing in door until it stops (this step varies from lock to lock; in this case, since you are using the key almost like a wrench, you must be very careful not to damage it.) Now line up the cylinder with the door—

(Continued)

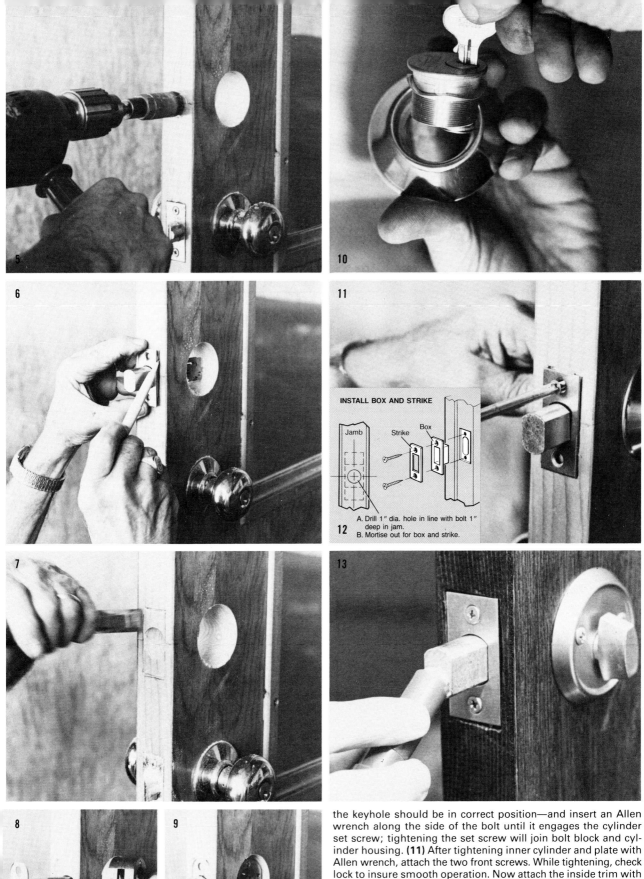

INSTALL BOX AND STRIKE

Jamb   Strike   Box

A. Drill 1″ dia. hole in line with bolt 1″ deep in jam.
B. Mortise out for box and strike.

the keyhole should be in correct position—and insert an Allen wrench along the side of the bolt until it engages the cylinder set screw; tightening the set screw will join bolt block and cylinder housing. **(11)** After tightening inner cylinder and plate with Allen wrench, attach the two front screws. While tightening, check lock to insure smooth operation. Now attach the inside trim with the supplied machine screws. If your door has glass panels, you may want to install a second cylinder, rather than a turn knob. **(12)** Once the box and the strike are installed, the job is complete. Drill a 1-inch diameter hole, 1-inch deep, into door jamb and mortise out for box and strike, as shown. **(13)** Easy way to determine the location of hole for deadbolt is to coat the end of the bolt with lipstick or stamp-pad ink. With the bolt in, close the door and turn the key to throw the bolt against the jamb to mark the location of the strike.

preframed window replacement

According to the Architectural Aluminum Manufacturers Assn., there are more than three-quarters of a billion windows in U.S. homes. So how come you got the ones that leak air? Well, you're not alone.

Most homes still have single-pane windows that cost, it's estimated, from $20 to $100 a year in heat loss through conduction and drafts. But you can cut that loss in your home by 50 percent or more, claims the AAMA, with new double- or triple-glazed windows. And window replacement can be simplified.

Preframed aluminum windows are available in a variety of sizes and styles through local lumberyards or home-improvement centers. Basically, you measure the frame, carefully remove the old window, and install a replacement window system of matching size. There are no structural changes, so no carpentry is needed; you may not even need to repaint. And since the new window is installed from inside the house, you won't need scaffolding and the job can be done at any time.

These photos show the simple procedure. The only tools you'll need are hammer, screwdriver, broad chisel, ⅜-inch drill, square, plumb, light hacksaw, and caulking gun. Result: easy-to-operate airtight windows that save money and add to the value of your home.

Remove molding and inside stops with a chisel and save for reuse. Remove spring balances, pull out bottom sash (above), and cut weight cords. Pry out parting stops at top and each side of the window frame, as shown above. This will allow you to slip out the top sash.

After removing the new sash for easier handling, place the header expander on top of the frame. Or if the windows have fins, then trim the fin at the proper serration.

After a trial fit, remove the frame and caulk against the blind stop at both top and sides.

Push the window frame against the caulked blind stops, and drive the first screw. Be sure you have the proper screwdriver at hand.

If the frame has alignment screws, adjust them until both sides are plumb. If not, add shims at the center of both jambs until square.

Once the frame is square, complete the installation with additional mounting screws. Then you place both sashes in their tracks.

Apply caulking all around the window framing as an inside seal. This, along with the blind-stop caulking, will prevent any air leaks.

If an expander header is used, lift it to the top of the opening. Drill mounting holes, and insert wood screws to anchor the header.

Replace the inside stops and molding, which were previously removed. Use care with the hammer—or you may not yet be finished.

renewing a pool deck

When this 40-foot pool was installed on the steep slope behind Ken Herrington's home in California, a plywood apron was suspended around it. For a cool, neat-looking walking surface, Herrington covered the plywood with outdoor carpet. The very month his five-year warranty expired, Herrington tells us, the carpet deteriorated rapidly: "So I ripped it up and let the exposed plywood dry completely."

A still older deck, stretching 62 feet across the back of his house, had been connected to the pool area by steps and smaller deck sections. This was all of redwood, now badly in need of refinishing. Herrington considered the major chore of sanding off the weathered surface—difficult because of all the surface nailing.

He then decided to tackle the renewal of all his deck areas as a single project. First he covered the plywood

pool deck with 30-pound building felt. Then he nailed 1×2 cedar sleepers every six inches over the felt, at right angles to the pool edges.

When planks are nailed on top of these slats, there's a space beneath for drainage. At the sides and far end, the pitch of the apron encourages rainwater to run off the outside of the deck, instead of into the pool.

Before nailing the planks across the sleepers, however, Herrington painted the bottoms, edges, and ends with a polymer wood stabilizer made by the Flecto Company (Box 12955, Oakland, Calif. 94604) called Varapel (any good quality deck paint will work).

Some of the advantages of Varapel are that you apply it as it comes from the can (you don't thin it or use paint thinners to clean up your brushes); and that special resins penetrate deep into wood-cell walls and fibers and, on subsequent curing, reinforce the nat-

ural wood structure, increasing its water resistance.

After finishing off his pool deck by brushing two top coats on the face of the new planks, Herrington decided to coat all the old weathered decks with Varapel, as well. His only preparation was to reset all popped nailheads. Where nails weren't holding planks flat, he drove in new spiral nails.

Herrington offers two tips for working with Varapel: "Sometimes, when lumber goes through a planer, the resins become burnished and slick in spots. Roller coating such new wood won't make the paint adhere as well as brushing. If you see any slick spots, it's best to sand them rougher before you paint.

"When you come to clean your brushes, first try warm water and soap. But if the paint is stubborn, switch to lacquer thinner—*By Al Lees. Photos by K. L. Herrington.*

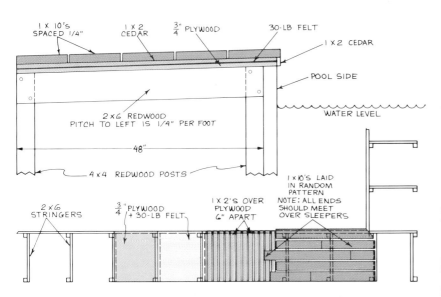

1 X 10'S SPACED 1/4"
1 X 2 CEDAR
3/4" PLYWOOD
30-LB FELT
1 X 2 CEDAR
POOL SIDE
WATER LEVEL
2 X 6 REDWOOD
PITCH TO LEFT IS 1/4" PER FOOT
48"
4 X 4 REDWOOD POSTS
2 X 6 STRINGERS
3/4" PLYWOOD + 30-LB FELT
1 X 2'S OVER PLYWOOD 6" APART
1 X 10'S LAID IN RANDOM PATTERN
NOTE: ALL ENDS SHOULD MEET OVER SLEEPERS

Pool apron stands on 4 × 4 posts, since pool extends above ground. Stringers between posts pitch the deck away from the pool to avoid drainage of rainwater into pool. Gaps between planks let water run down between sleepers.

Edge strip is nailed to ends of sleepers, flush with their tops. First plank is then laid over strip as shown in sketch.

Three spiral nails used in project (l-r): paint-dipped stainless (because of higher cost, on four rows nearest pool only), galvanized, and aluminum. All hold well.

Brushed on weathered, unpainted wood, Varapel can cover in one coat, for effect seen at left where previous day's coat has cured. We topped this with second coat.

Cedar planks (1 × 10) are laid on sleepers with 1/4-in. gaps. After trial positioning, lift and paint planks before nailing.

Stepped decks were sound, so were just painted to match new pool apron. Roller speeds application on weathered wood.

tuning up your mower

All the spring mower-tuneup instructions you've ever read probably say the same old things:

- Change the oil.
- Put in fresh gasoline.
- Install a new spark plug.
- Clean the air filter.

After that, if you trust what you read, you just sharpen the blade, oil the wheels, and away you go—maybe.

What if the engine refuses to cooperate? There's nothing more frustrating than spending hours trying to start a balky mower. To avoid such a hassle, here's a quick series of steps that'll get your mower going again, or at least prove that a trip to the local repair shop is really necessary—*E. F. Lindsley.*

1. Whether your mower is a two- or four-cycle model, it has to have ignition, fuel, and compression to run. First check for ignition by removing spark plug, shielding it from bright light, and pulling starter rope with throttle in the "run position. Look for strong, hot spark. The clothespin shown is one way to hold a plug wire to avoid a high-voltage jolt. If you have no spark, consult your service manual for repair or take the mower into a shop. If you see a good spark, go to the next step.

2. Remove the air cleaner and test the governor and throttle linkage for free movement. Open and close the throttle to make certain the spring pulls the throttle wide open in the "start" position. Check the connecting wire and choke action if manually linked. If the choke is automatic (as shown here), put your finger in the carburetor throat to test for free movement of the plate. A gummed-up choke plate may stick (and indicates that the carburetor should probably be cleaned).

3. Spray a small amount of starting fluid into the carburetor throat and immediately pull the starter rope. The engine may now start. A burst of full-speed operation can clear a slightly gummed carburetor; if it does, you can start your work. But if the engine repeatedly starts and runs only a few seconds, the carburetor might be clogged, and it may have to be cleaned in a professional shop. But before you resort to that, check for other causes—proceed to the next step.

4. If the carburetor seems clogged, inspect the needle valve for gum (your carburetor may have more than one needle valve). Before removing a needle valve first screw it down gently and count the number of turns (and fractions of turns) it takes to seat, so you'll know where to reset it later. Remove the valve and look it over closely. Brown or gummy deposits on the tip may be a sign that a complete carburetor cleaning is needed. Clean the *valve,* then go on to the next step.

5. Squirt the carburetor cleaner directly into the needle jet. Let the cleaner soak for a minute and follow with a flushing shot. Replace the needle valve(s) at the original setting(s), squirt a small amount of starting fluid into the carburetor throat again, and try to start the engine once more. Usually it will clear its throat, cough a bit, then run—and you can get on with mowing. But if the machine refuses to crank up now, you may have some other problems. Proceed to the next step.

6. Erratic starting or stuttering while running may be a sign that this tiny magneto ground wire on the stop switch (part of throttle bracket) is grounding out. Dirt, grease, or moisture can do it. Slip the wire out of its clip and push it free of contact with all metal. (Disconnecting this wire deactivates all interlocks; if you start your engine with it out, you must short the plug with a screwdriver to stop.) If you get spark after freeing the wire, clean and check the sliding parts of the switch.

7. A leaking head gasket reduces compression, a common reason for hard starting. One method of checking is to apply gentle pressure against the head bolts. They should feel tight. If you find two or three that seem loose compared with others, especially in the exhaust-port area, it's almost certain your head gasket is leaking. It's not a good idea to rely on a compression gauge because you can get a false impression of what the true compression is—it may vary with each tug on the rope.

8. A typical bad gasket from a small mower engine shows dark areas (center, top) where gases were leaking. Matching area is visible on the head. Tightening the head down onto a gasket in this condition may get you going, but a new gasket, properly torqued, is the only real fix. If you have the tools and a reasonable amount of skill, you can replace the gasket yourself. In any case, do not overtighten any of the bolts; doing so will distort the head and cylinder.

9. A two-stroke engine must have compression in both its crankcase and its combustion chamber. The collection of oily dust on this air cleaner, plus other deposits around the carburetor, indicates that the crankshaft seals are leaking. Seals, which are vital to compression, are replaceable, but that's a shop job. Another problem in two-stroke engines is that the oil-and-gasoline mix tends to foul spark plugs easily. A plug that has its gap bridged with carbon cannot start an engine.

10. In a typical two-stroke engine, these six thin, flat reed valves admit fuel and air from the carburetor to the crankcase. Even fragments of grass holding one or two open will prevent the engine from starting. It always pays to check for fouled reed valves if you have the tools and experience to remove the carburetor for access. Valves shown are beginning to corrode. If there are other problems in the engine, such as bad bearings and seals (photo 9), it's probably not worth repairing.

shopping for plastic plumbing

Sorting carefully through the bins of plastic pipes and fittings in the plumbing section of a large department store near Detroit, I selected these items to put into my shopping cart: a short-shot pipe plug with half its threads unformed; a toilet flange flashed so badly that it wouldn't sit level on a floor; two drainage elbows with internal ridges that could stop up wastes; and a Y with internal recesses.

I felt sure the checkout clerk would reject the short-shot. It was so obviously unusable that anyone would have noticed it. But if she did, she said nothing. The short-shot was rung up on the cash register with all the rest of my faulty fittings.

I can't really blame the clerk, though. The bad parts should have been tossed out by the manufacturer, the distributor, or the store's buyer. But no one cared enough. If I hadn't known better, I might have used them in my home's plumbing system, later wondering what I did wrong.

This experiment confirmed my suspicions: Shopping for plastic plumbing products is like buying fruits and vegetables in a produce market. *You* must be the inspector. It is you who must reject the bananas with the soft spots, the broccoli with the too-large stems. If you pick and choose, you can end up with quality. Otherwise, you may end up with a mess.

Plastics, properly used, are great plumbing materials. They are easy to install. They don't corrode, as metal pipes do. And no flame is needed to join them.

But it isn't quite as easy as it sounds. There's a huge variety of types and materials of plastic plumbing, and choosing the proper one for a particular use can be tricky. A table gives the vital statistics for each material.

Water-supply piping can be divided into two groups: pipes able to handle hot water under pressure and cold-water-only pipes. Chlorinated poly-

vinyl chloride (CPVC) and polybutylene (PB) are the only plastics suitable for hot-water supply tubing. CPVC is a rigid plastic; PB is flexible. PB is sometimes promoted as a universal water-supply tubing, but it is at a great disadvantage where many fittings are needed. Use CPVC in applications where the lines run straight and PB where you need to run a line around corners without fittings (see table). To couple the two types of supply pipes, you'll need a brand of fittings that offers CPVC-PB adapters.

Polyvinyl chloride (PVC) and polyethylene (PE) are made as pressure lines, too, but neither material will

take hot water under pressure. Don't use them in the house. Rigid PVC and flexible PE are most useful for underground plumbing, in irrigation and sprinkler systems. PE pipe is also good in well casings.

The same two plastics are among several others used for less-demanding sewer, drainage, and drain-waste-vent piping. PVC and acrylonitrile butadiene styrene (ABS) are the most common drain-waste-vent and sewer-pipe plastics—ABS chiefly on the West Coast, PVC everywhere else. PVC drain-waste-vent and sewer pipe is made in Schedule 30 and 40 ratings. They are the same size inside, but

A gallery of faulty fittings

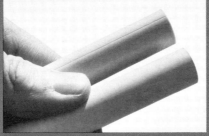

Upper CPVC water-supply pipe is marred by a full-length extrusion line. Solvent-welded joint made with it might leak.

Which spigot fitting would you choose? You'd have to fully remove price sticker off weld surface or risk bad seal.

Exterior flash harms only fitting's appearance, but it should tip you off to manufacturer's poor quality control.

Waste and drain pipes must be installed at exact slope. Badly curved pipe would create low spot, impede flow.

Close look at inside of PVC Y shows deep recesses caused by worn-out mold. This weakens fitting wall, could trap wastes.

Scuffed and flattened pipe end, caused by dragging on ground, will prevent good seal. Always inspect pipe ends.

Schedule 30 has thinner walls so it is smaller outside. It is sometimes referred to as "in-wall" pipe because a 3-inch Schedule 30 pipe (the only diameter manufactured) with its fitting hubs will slip into a standard 2 × 4 wall. To accommodate same-size Schedule 40 fitting hubs, the house wall would have to be furred out.

PE is also used for sewer and drainage pipe, or as a combination. The combination pipe may carry wastes, but not inside the house. Rubber styrene (RS) is another material often used for subsoil drainage piping.

The plastic plumbing material with the greatest heat and chemical resistance is polypropylene (PP). This plastic takes heat so well that it is used to line the insides of dishwashers. That's why it is also the material of choice for the most vulnerable part of your home plumbing system: the sink trap.

PLASTIC-PLUMBING MATERIALS

Material	Its uses	Color	Joining method
Polyethylene (PE)	Flexible cold-water pressure lines, buried or in well casings; made in various strengths; not for hot-water or indoor use; made in iron-pipe sizes	Black	Barbed clamp couplings
Polyvinyl chloride (PVC)	Rigid cold-water pressure lines buried in ground; not for hot-water use; also used for rigid drain-waste-vent, sub-soil sewer and drainage piping, and fixture traps; water tube comes in iron-pipe sizes; DWV and sewer pipes come in Schedules 30 and 40; drainage pipe comes in Schedule 30	Beige; also made in many other colors	Two-step solvent welding
Chlorinated polyvinyl chloride (CPVC)	Rigid hot- and cold-water pressure lines indoors and buried; comes in copper-tube sizes	Beige; sometimes colored black or gray	Two-step solvent welding
Polybutylene (PB)	Flexible hot- and cold-water pressure lines indoors and buried; comes in copper-tube sizes	Beige; sometimes colored black or gray	Mechanical couplings
Polypropylene (PP)	Tubular drainage products for fixtures—traps, etc.; most resistant to heat and chemicals of all plastic-pipe materials	Beige	Slip-jam-nut couplings
Acrylonitrile butadiene styrene (ABS)	Rigid drain-waste-vent and sewer piping, chiefly on West Coast; also, fixture traps and slip-jam nuts	Black	One-step solvent welding
Rubber styrene (RS)	Rigid subsoil drainage piping	White, milky, or black	One-step solvent welding

Feel around insides of fitting sockets to ensure that solvent welding surfaces are smooth. Inspect threaded fittings, too.

Test-fit pipe and fitting before buying. Pipe should fit snugly so that it doesn't bottom out or fall off when it's inverted.

You will find traps made from other materials, too, including PVC and ABS. ABS suffers from intergranular stress cracking, in which contact with animal fats or vegetable oil can suddenly relieve molecular stresses created in the molding process. It happens like an earthquake on a molecular scale. PVC and PP traps are resistant to stress cracking.

If all of this doesn't have you confused already, then consider the variety of colors, sizes, and joining techniques available. Pipes and fittings may be black, beige, white, milky, or other colors. Some materials use a two-step solvent-welding process, some a one-step. Others require mechanical couplings, barbed clamps, or slip-jam nuts. Sizes are derived from the conventions used for metal pipes. Thus PE and PVC are designated like iron pipes, by their inside diameters, and PB and CPVC lines are usually measured by their outside di-

ameters, as is copper tubing. Just make sure that the pipe and fitting sizes you buy are compatible.

Now that you know the apples from oranges, keep remembering bananas when you go to the store. Be suspicious of every part you see; any of them may be defective.

Here are some of the common problems you're likely to encounter. Flash—ragged webs of superfluous plastic—is characteristic of all injection-molded plastic parts. The tiny spaces between parts of the mold fill with molten resin, which solidifies when cooled. Flash on the solvent-welding surfaces of a fitting can affect the joint. Flash on the insides of a fitting can impede flow. Quality fittings have the flash trimmed off.

The same is true for sprues, solidified fill holes where the raw plastic entered the mold. Most sprues are located on the outside of the fitting, where a small projection hurts nothing

but the appearance. Some manufacturers use inside sprues, however—a bad practice. If not ground off flush, an inside sprue forms a waste catch.

With threaded fittings, look out for poorly formed or shortened threads. Avoid using female plastic fittings with metal pipe. Plastic expands at a faster rate than the metal it's threaded onto; since it expands away from the metal, leaks are bound to result.

Beware of color variations between fittings of the same brand. These warn that the manufacturer's resin-mix control was haphazard. Be especially careful when buying white CPVC or PVC, whose natural color is beige. Manufacturers sometimes add chalk to extend the resin, but this weakens the plastic. Burned spots, dirt showing in the material, and surface roughness are other indicators of poor procedures at the factory.

Many do-it-yourselfers will still feel overwhelmed when confronted by plastic pipe in the store. Home plumbers need all the help they can get in selecting pipes, fittings, and solvent cements, but too few stores offer it. In that Detroit-area store, for example, I found pipes and fittings in white, black, gray, and beige, but no signs identified the plastics. Also, the store featured an extensive line of solvent cements varying considerably in price, but no information directed me to the proper cement for the job. If I had been a price-shopper, I might have chosen the cheapest cement and taken home a material that wouldn't work on my piping.

That's one extreme. At the other is the store with displays that clearly identify pipes and fittings and explain how they are used. The solvent cements to use with each are indicated. If you are really lucky, a clerk who understands plastic plumbing materials is available to advise.

Once you select a brand of materials, stick with it. Buying a pipe by one manufacturer, a fitting by another, and a solvent cement by a third is no route to quality plumbing. When all parts are made by the same firm you know that they were made to fit together and the solvent cement was formulated to work with them.

Don't just rely on a familiar name, though. Check for an ASTM number on each pipe and fitting. That means the part conforms to the standards established by the American Society for Testing and Materials. In water-supply piping, also look for the National Sanitation Foundation's "NSF-pw" approval, meaning parts are suitable for potable water—*Richard Day.*

PIPE OF CHOICE FOR HOT-COLD WATER SUPPLY

Use	Rigid CPVC	Flexible PB
Fixture drops (air chambers, etc.)	Best	Too many costly fittings
Fixture branches (off mains)	Best	Many costly fittings
Hot-cold mains, outdoor hose bibbs	Best for shorter runs	Best for long, fitting-free runs
Exposed in basements, utility rooms	Best	May look unworkmanlike
Service entrance, between-floor risers, garage branch	Too many fittings	Best; done with few fittings
Plumbing remodeling work behind existing walls	Difficult to run	Best; may be threaded behind walls
Around obstacles	Too many fittings	Best; done without fittings
Shower riser pipe	Best	Offers no support for shower arm
Bath/faucet pipe to spout	Not enough support; use a metal pipe	No support; use a metal pipe
At water heaters, softeners	Excellent (use proper transition fittings)	Excellent (use proper transition fittings)

how to solvent-weld plastic pipe

Plastic pipe has become the universal problem solver for the do-it-yourself plumber. With most code restrictions toppling, you can plumb water-supply, drain-waste-vent, sewer-septic, or irrigation systems with easily cut, lightweight thermoplastic pipes and fittings. Best of all, most plastic components can be speedily joined with solvent cement.

Solvent welding is just about foolproof. There's no flame to start a fire while the water pressure is off. A saw, knife, and brush are the only tools needed.

Plastic pipe used for cold-water supply or drainage, including PVC, ABS, and polystyrene (often just called styrene) can be solvent welded. So can CPVC (chlorinated PVC), used in hot-water systems. A few plastic-pipe materials—notably polyethylene, polybutylene, and polypropylene, used for chemical-resistant fixture traps—are so resistant to solvent attack that they must be joined mechanically.

Solvent-welding cement consists of plastic filler (of the same material as the pipe to be joined) dissolved in a mixture of active solvents. The mix can be clear or pigmented. The handiest cements come with daubers or brushes for easy application.

To make a solvent-welded joint, cement is applied to the pipe end and fitting socket, which are immediately pushed together. The resulting joint can be handled gently within a minute, take water flow within a half hour, and handle full water pressure in two hours. A full cure takes about twenty-four hours. These time periods vary somewhat, depending on temperature, humidity, and solvent used.

During a complete cure, the solvents evaporate, leaving only pure plastic resin, which becomes one with pipe and fitting. The joint is actually

Solvent welding plastic pipes is easier and safer than sweat soldering copper pipes—especially when plumbing is overhead. Eye protection guards against solvent drip. Good ventilation is essential when working with strong solvent chemicals.

welded with plastic, hence the term solvent welding. A solvent-welded plastic piping system is joined into one continuous fitting from beginning to end. No weak spots are left for corrosive attack.

Solvent-welding tips

For advice on good do-it-yourself solvent welding, I talked to Ken Pepper of Genova, Inc. (Davison, Mich.), maker of vinyl (thermoplastic) plumbing products. Pepper, an authority on solvent cements, outlined three basic steps that will ensure success for the home plumber. "First, make sure the parts to be joined fit properly; next, clean the mating surfaces thoroughly; and finally, use ample amounts of a quality cement," he advised.

Plastic plumbing parts are designed with an interference fit. This provides space for the solvent cement, yet leaves no voids when the solvents evaporate. Unfortunately, a poor fit may be the rule rather than the exception. Pipe and fitting dimensions are specified by the American Society for Testing Materials. Often, the pipe-only manufacturer reduces the outside diameter and wall thickness of his pipe to the smallest prescribed ASTM tolerance to ensure that his pipe will fit into every manufacturer's fittings. The fitting-only maker expands his fitting sockets to the larger ASTM tolerance so they'll fit over every pipemaker's pipe. The result is a sloppy fit between the two. And if the additional ASTM out-of-round tolerances in pipe and fitting don't happen to coincide during as-

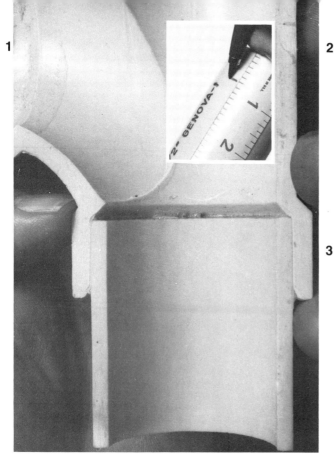

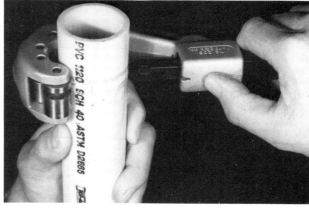

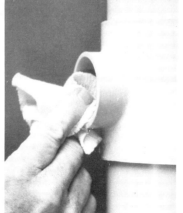

1. Cross section of watertight joint shows how solvent cements pipe and fitting into one continuous part that's literally welded together by the plastic filler in the cement. As the fingertip at left of picture indicates, the pipe has bottomed out inside the fitting and has come to rest squarely on the flange. This is crucial for a watertight seal. To make sure it happens, mark the fitting socket's depth on pipe end (inset), and check for proper fit. Pipe should be tight enough to stay in fitting when turned upside down. To make sure system fits into alloted space, dry-assemble all cut pipes with fittings.

2. Cutting pipe perfectly straight and scraping off plastic curls stuck to pipe end are essential steps for a good solvent-welded joint. For the best bond, the entire inner surface of the socket must contact the pipe. An off-square pipe end can reduce this vital contact by as much as 20 percent. Using a special plastic-cutting wheel attached to a good pipe cutter as shown will ensure straight cuts without a miter box. A hacksaw is easier—but only if you have a good eye and a light touch. Be sure to inspect pipe closely for gouges and cracks; cut pipe end if necessary.

3. Apply an etching primer-cleaner to both fitting socket and pipe ends to remove joint-spoiling dirt and grease. Etching also readies mating surfaces for full solvent attack. When cleaning, be sure to avoid rubbing off the socket-depth mark on pipe end. Piping must be kept dry: Water would mix with solvent cements, displacing plastic-attacking solvents and creating leak-prone unwelded spots in the joint. Once a joint is welded, water and dirt can't hurt it.

4. Telltale bead of solvent circling assembled joint shows that enough solvent cement has been applied for a secure joint. For best results, apply cement liberally to pipe end, to fitting socket, and *again* to pipe end. This sequence ensures that excess cement is squeezed out of the joint, where it can be wiped off, and not forced down into the pipe bore or fitting, where it would impede water flow. After applying solvent, join pipe and fitting as quickly as possible. Push them together with a slight twist to bring the fitting to correct alignment and break up any areas where cement is thin. Make sure that pipe bottoms out. Hold for 20 to 30 seconds.

sembly, the joint may be far too loose for successful solvent welding.

The only cure for too loose a joint is to find another pipe and fitting with an acceptable fit. The best way to do that is to buy pipes and fittings of the same brand. A sloppy fit is almost unheard of between parts of the same brand. Even so, it's good solvent-welding practice to test-fit each joint.

The second essential step is to clean the mating parts of the joint. Some instructions call for the use of sandpaper or steel wool for this. Ken Pepper frowns on this advice.

"That's what you do in sweat soldering," he says. "Solvent welding is very different." Pepper fears that sanding might remove too much material from the parts, leaving the joint loose or with flat spots. Instead, he recommends a two-step welding process using a cleaner-primer before solvent cement.

Pepper also notes that the biggest single cause of joint failure is inadequate coating of the joining surfaces with cement. That's why he advises coating the pipe end *twice* with cement. "It's tough to use too much cement," says Pepper. "Only when solvent cement runs down the inside of the pipe have you used too much."

What about mistakes?

Warnings to the contrary, you may get away with pulling apart a pipe-fitting assembly after the joint has been doped and assembled. But you'd better be quick. In just seconds it will be held so tightly that a weight lifter couldn't get it out. (You should only try a separation on piping used in nonpressurized systems.) If you're successful, both the pulled-out pipe and its fitting may be used again. But if you fail to pull the joint apart, you'll have ruined it in the process. You must then cut out the fitting and replace it with another one. Two pipe couplings will enable you to install the new fitting.

Suppose you put solvent cement on a pipe and fitting, but discover an error before joining them? You needn't throw them away. They're still fully usable. Just keep them clean until the next use.

In all cases, be sure to give the used pipe a double application of cement to get full softening through the aborted doping.

Choosing and using cement

A solvent-cemented pipe joint is tested at conditions that are more severe than any of those that will be encountered in normal use. The basic ASTM test for a solvent-welded CPVC joint, for example, calls for the twenty-four-hour-cured joint to be immersed in 180°F water for thirty minutes, then pressurized to 521 psi with the same hot water. The heat and pressure are held for at least six minutes to simulate 11.2 years of usage at 100 psi and 180°F.

A properly welded joint is grossly overdesigned. It will stand up to hot-water pressures that can burst the fittings. The joint works continuously and indefinitely. Even so, you should use a quality solvent cement as insurance against problems. Trouble is, you can't tell a good cement from a poor one by looking, smelling, or shaking.

A quality cement contains plenty of highly active plastic-attacking solvents that soften piping walls. These work with sufficient depth and speed for good welding. A good cement is not oversaturated .vith plastic filler. It needs unattached solvents to work. But it contains enough plastic filler to bridge any reasonable gap. A quality cement also sets quickly enough to be efficient to use.

Finally, a quality solvent cement contains enough spare dissolving power to permit its continued use after some of the solvents have evaporated.

The most active attack solvent in a good cement is tetrahydrofuran (THF). THF is quite costly, so cheaper solvents contain less of it and more of such lower-cost solvents as methyl ethyl ketone and cyclohexanone.

Most solvent cements contain all three of these solvents in varying degrees.

Because cost can be so affected by the generous use of THF, quality can sometimes be judged by price. But you can be assured of quality if you buy the whole system—pipes, fittings, and solvent cements—from the same firm. Besides using materials designed to work together, you'll have one responsible organization to deal with should you have complaints. Otherwise, one manufacturer may blame another's product.

Another caution: Keep the cement can capped as much as practical. Screw the cap down snugly or at least enough to mesh the threads. The solvents in all cements evaporate quickly when exposed to air. That's one of the criteria for a good cement. But if too much solvent evaporates, there may not be enough left to soften a joint's mating surfaces properly.

Evaporation also makes a cement thicken in the can. If a solvent cement thickens so it will not pour, get a fresh can. Don't try to thin it, even with a cleaner-primer; these have different formulations. And never mix an old, thickened cement with a fresh, properly constituted one. Ordinarily, a solvent cement will keep for a number of years if evaporation is prevented.

Yellowing of solvent cement in the can indicates aging. CPVC cements are especially affected. There's no problem as long as the solvent will pour readily. But if a solvent cement turns rusty or dark brown, it's useless.

Temperature also affects solvent cements. Most are formulated to work best at, or near, room temperature. In really hot weather, they tend to dry too quickly; in icy temperatures they may set too slowly. There are special hot- and cold-weather cements, with high-temperature limits of about 90° F and low-temperature limits of 40. Even a normal solvent cement may be used beyond these limits if conditions are allowed for. In hot weather, work more quickly. In cold weather, allow for more holding and curing times.

When you've finished the last joint on a solvent-welded pressurized-water-supply system, wait a half hour or longer if possible. Then flush water through the system without pressurizing it. To do this, make sure that all outlets, such as faucets, are fully open. Open the main valve slightly to let water flow slowly into the new system. As water reaches the lowest outlet, it will begin flowing out there. Adjust this faucet to a steady trickle. Move through the house, adjusting each flowing outlet in turn. The trickles of water will dissolve and carry away any solvent vapors left within the piping system. This trick also expedites curing of the cement and helps purge the system of tastes and odors.

After ten minutes of trickling, shut the main valve completely for a half hour. Reopen it a crack for another ten minutes of trickling, then repeat once again.

Finally, pressurize the system by fully turning on the main valve. Flush out any debris from each faucet by opening it fully, then closing it. Don't forget to flush toilets, too.

If you've followed Ken Pepper's simple solvent-welding tips, you need never worry about leaks—even if you've been less than perfect at it. As Pepper says, "A good solvent cement is very forgiving"—*Richard Day*.

Matching plastic plumbing with cement

Material	ABS cement	Styrene cement	PVC cement	CPVC cement	All-purpose cement
ABS					
Styrene					
PVC					
CPVC					

How much cement you'll need

Pipe size (in.)	Approx.* no. of joints per pint of cement
1/2	255
3/4	170
1 1/2	68
2	38
3	30
4	21

*Varies with user and cement type

There's a cement for almost every kind of plastic pipe, and some are versatile enough to work with most plastics (see chart, above left). But these are often more expensive. Consider two factors when picking a solvent: attacking power and duty (temperature resistance). A cement designed to work with ABS—a plastic with low resistance to solvent attack—won't be able to handle PVC pipe. Nor will that cement be able to withstand the high temperatures and pressures that a CVPC pipe may be subjected to. But a CVPC cement could certainly weld ABS. If your project uses two kinds of piping, you might find it simpler to use a higher-rated cement, despite the added expense. Use the table above (right) to estimate how much cement to buy. Remember that applicators can't be used interchangeably with different-size pipes.

kit for emergency plumbing repairs

The temperature kept dropping. By morning it had sunk to 22 below, colder than it had been in years. The Lloyds awoke, ready to spend a quiet Sunday buttoned in the bosom of their suburban home. But Cindy Lloyd soon discovered there was no water pressure anywhere in the house.

"Must be a frozen pipe," George said as he bundled up to go out and check. He was back shortly, stomping snow off his feet. "Someone unplugged my heat tape," he accused. "Pipes in the crawl space are probably frozen solid. They should be thawed soon, though."

Soon, however, they heard a disheartening sound coming from the crawl space: the steady trickle of running water. "Blasted pipe's split, I'll bet. Gotta turn off the water," George muttered as he hurried outside.

"Shall I call a plumber?" Cindy shouted.

"Guess you'd better," he yelled back.

But the only plumber she could reach was on his way out to a long list of emergency calls. The other plumbers were already gone. The Lloyds weren't the only ones with frozen pipes that morning.

George Lloyd ended up taking his family to a motel, where they spent two nights before the pipes were repaired. The repairs, at overtime rates, plus the motel bill and meals cost the family well over $300.

You can keep this from being your story by putting together an emergency plumbing-repair kit. I've designed one that's so simple to use you won't mind doing the repairs yourself (see table). The kits contain CPVC-plastic adapters, tubes, and couplings. These can be used to replace sections of ½- and ¾-inch house piping. The parts are assembled with solvent-welding cement, which you also include in your emergency kit.

Why CPVC? First, this tough, heat-resistant thermoplastic is rated to withstand a pressure of 100 psi at 180 degrees F. Second, solvent welding is super-simple; no pipe threading or sweat soldering is required. Another advantage is that CPVC will halt the electrolytic action that transfers metals within a plumbing system, especially in hard-water areas. (Spots from which metal is transferred can get thin and leak.) Your system will be even better after the repairs than it was before.

You'll need two sizes of repair kits—½- and ¾-inch—because most houses have both sizes of water-supply pipes. Choose either the kit for copper or CPVC pipes or the one for threaded-metal pipes, depending on the kind of plumbing your house has. Parts for both types are shown in the drawing as well as listed in the table. The tubes and fittings can be purchased at a good hardware store or home center. The kits will cost very little to put together. (A service call from a plumber will cost you far more.)

I show parts made by Genova. If you use another brand, be sure it offers

EMERGENCY PLUMBING-REPAIR KITS

Pipe Type (House)	Pipe Size	Parts	Fits Pipe Removed (Min.-Max.)	Tools Needed
Threaded galvanized-steel or brass	½-in.	1 ½-in. by 10 ft. tube* 2 ½-in. CPVC couplings 2 ½-in. transition unions Solvent-welding kit	4¾-in.–10 ft. 4 in.	Pipe wrench, hacksaw, and pliers or open-end wrench
	¾-in.	1 ¾-in.-by-10 ft. CPVC tube* 2 ¾-in. CPVC couplings 2 ¾-in. CPVC transition unions	5½ in.–10 ft. 4¾ in.	
Sweat-type copper or solvent-welded CPVC	½ in.	1 ½-in.-by-10 ft. CPVC tube* 2 ½-in. Genogrip adapters (or equivalents) 4 ½-in. CPVC couplings Solvent-welding kit	1⅜ in.–1½ in. (using just adapters and couplings) 2⅝ in.–10 ft. 1½ in.	Hacksaw or tubing cutter
	¾ in.	1 ¾-in.-by-10 ft. CPVC tube* 2 ¾-in. Genogrip adapters (or equivalent) 4 ¾-in. CPVC couplings	1⅞ in.–2 in. (using just adapters and couplings) 3½ in.–10 ft. 2 in.	

*Cut to convenient storage length—couplings included for 40-in. lengths

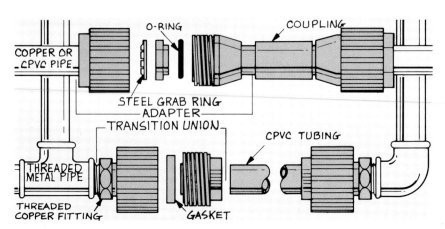

To repair copper or CPVC pipe (top) you need adapters and coupling. For longer repairs you need CPVC tubing. Transition unions for threaded pipe accept CPVC tubing directly.

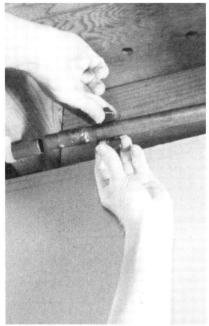

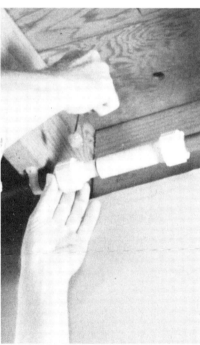

To repair a leaking copper or CPVC tube, cut out the defective portion with a hacksaw or tubing cutter (top). Next, slide an adapter onto each tube end and tighten, following package directions. Slip a coupling onto each adapter, then cut CPVC tubing to bridge the gap. Slip it into the couplings, then solvent-weld all the CPVC slip joints as shown above.

transition unions to go between the plastic and metal piping and take up differential thermal movements. Tape or wire the parts of the kit together and put them in a handy place. The kit is for repair of pipes and tubes only. If there's a faulty fitting, it will have

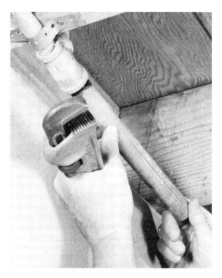

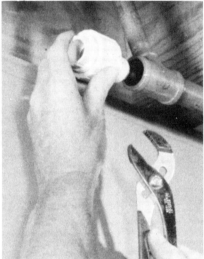

To repair a leaking threaded-metal pipe, saw through the defective pipe, then remove both ends with a pipe wrench (left). Next, thread on the transition unions, using one at each end of the remaining metal pipe (center). Tighten with pliers or an open-end wrench. Use pipe dope or TFE tape on the male threads. Now measure the distance between the gaskets inside the two transition unions and deduct one inch. Cut the CPVC repair tube to that length, and solvent-weld it into the transition unions (right). Let the welds cure two hours.

to be replaced, of course.

The parts of the emergency kit you should use depend on the required length of your repair. A short repair in copper or CPVC—up to 1½ inches long in a ½-inch tube and up to two inches in a ¾-inch tube—can be done with just the two adapters and one CPVC coupling between them. An adapter is pushed onto each cutoff end of tubing (see photos) and tightened a bit beyond hand-tight. It helps if you coat the tube ends with petroleum jelly or silicone lubricant for easier sliding. Each adapter comes with a plastic grab ring inside and a stainless-steel version on the blister card. Discard the plastic ring (it's meant for flexible tubes), and insert the steel one.

With ½-inch copper or CPVC tubing, repairs of lengths between 1½ and 2⅝ inches cannot be made: They fall between lengths that the parts will fit. With ¾-inch tubing, you can't make a repair between two and 3½ inches. Make your cutouts short or long enough to avoid these "blind spots." There are also minimum repair lengths for both sizes of tubing. They're listed in the table. Beyond these lengths, two CPVC couplings are used, one at each adapter. A length of CPVC tubing cut to the proper length slips into the couplings to bridge the gap (see illustrations).

A look at the table shows that the shortest repair you can make in ½-inch threaded-metal pipe is 4¾ inches; in ¾-inch threaded pipe it's 5½ inches. You make the repairs by threading a transition union onto each end of the good pipe and connecting them together with a length cut from the CPVC tubing. Longer repairs simply call for a longer connecting tube.

The table also lists the sizes of repairs the kits will handle. The maximum length with each kit is just over 10 feet. By adding more CPVC tubing and couplings to link the tubes, longer repairs can be made. Because 10-foot CPVC tubes are too long for convenient storage, you'll probably want to cut them into shorter lengths. I've listed the parts in the table assuming you'll cut the tubing to 40-inch lengths. If you want shorter lengths, add more couplings—one for each saw cut you make—and you'll still be able to make a 10-foot-long repair.

By keeping the parts of the kits together where you can find them, you'll be able to fix a leaky pipe at any time. The repair should last as long as your house plumbing does. And if you make a copy of this article to put with your emergency kits, it will remind you how to use them.—*By Richard Day.*

tapping into water pipes

It's often necessary to tap into a pipe: to install a bar sink, for example. Or maybe to add an extra outlet for your garden hose. There are many useful adapters, tap-tees, and special unions available from your hardware/home-center dealer. Knowing what connectors are available and how to use them can spell the difference between a job that's done right and one that leaks.

The accompanying photos show the more important fittings and a few of their applications. And here are spe-

cific do's and don'ts about putting some of them to work for you:

PVC slip-coupling tee. This popular tee should never be connected to a hot-water-supply pipe. Polyvinyl chloride (PVC) is suited for drainage and cold pressurized water, but not for hot pressurized water. Hot water can soften PVC enough to cause a leak.

Also, plastic expands faster than metal. As soon as hot water flows, the female threads on the fitting's branch tapping expand away from a metal pipe that's threaded into them. This

alone can open the joint to leaking. No plumbing code allows PVC for hot water.

Female plastic threads on a threaded metal pipe are not the best idea for cold water under pressure, either. This setup works well only with drainage fittings.

Celcon plastic fitting. To use this one, you simply push the chlorinated polyvinyl chloride (CPVC) or polybutylene (PB) water-supply pipe in. The fitting holds it. No tightening is needed—or possible. It's a great idea, except that this unique fitting material cannot stand up to the chlorine almost always present in municipal water. Celcon has a weakness Cl– ions that could result in failure. Nevertheless, this fitting is widely sold for both hot- and cold-water use.

Dielectric union. When piping systems of differing metals such as galvanized steel and copper are joined, don't just use a male or female adapter. Use a dielectric union, instead.

Pipe adapters, mostly for water-supply systems: (1) Male adapter connects female pipe threads to polyethylene cold-water pipe; (2) male sweat adapter connects female pipe threads to sweat-soldered copper pipe; (3) female flare coupling connects male pipe threads to flared copper or plastic; (4) hose nipple connects female pipe threads to rubber or vinyl tubing; (5) hose-to-pipe swivel connector joins male pipe threads to male hose threads; (6) dielectric union connects male pipe threads and sweat-soldered copper; (7) Genogrip push-on adapter connects polybutylene or copper pipe to a CPVC fitting; (8) transition union adapts thermoplastic pipe to metal pipe, absorbing thermal movements (prevents leaks that would otherwise occur when two different types of pipe are heated and expand at different rates); (9) one type of quick-connector that connects washing-machine- or dishwasher-hose female threads to faucet aerator; (10) tapped bushing fits female pipe threads, presents the same, and permits a ⅛-inch pipe-thread tapping for filtered drinking fountain, etc; (11) hose nipple connects female pipe threads to female hose threads; (12) saddle-tee clamps around a drilled hole in pipe and presents female pipe threads; (13) slip-coupling tee connects sawed-off pipe ends, branches to reduced-size male pipe threads; (14) dishwasher-disposer coupling clamps over various waste pipes; (15) tailpiece for kitchen sink allows the dishwasher to drain through a common pipe.

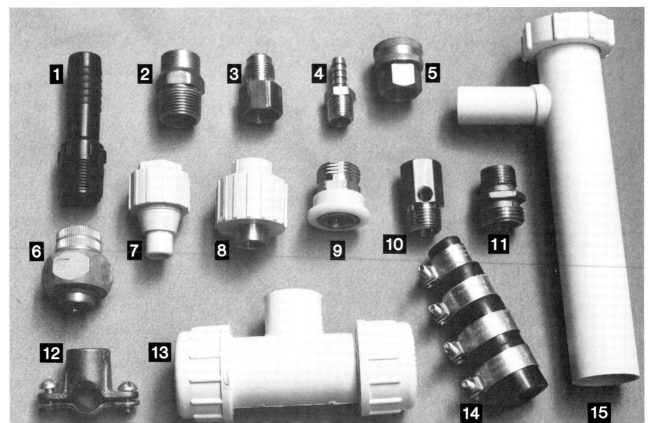

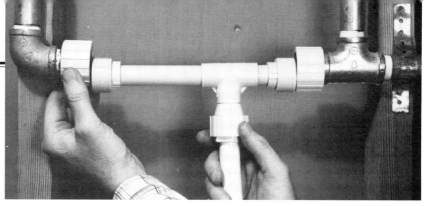

This puts an elastomeric rubber gasket between the dissimilar metals. Moreover, a plastic washer behind the union's clamping collar further breaks any electrical continuity between the two systems, greatly reducing electrolytic corrosion. The problem is especially severe with highly ionized hard water. Whether or not your plumbing code requires a dielectric union, it's a good idea to use one between dissimilar metals.

Transition union. This is another type of pipe-protecting device. It gets its name from the job it does—making the transition between metal and plastic piping systems. Every time a pressurized plastic hot-cold water-supply pipe is joined to a metal one, a transition union is necessary to prevent cracks and leaks. These are caused by the previously described differing expansion-contraction rates between metal and plastic.

One type of transition union faces off the metal and plastic across a mediating elastomeric gasket, similar to a dielectric union. However, the purpose is not to break up electrical continuity but to allow for differential thermal expansion and contraction without strain or leaking.

Transition unions are mandatory in hot-water supply systems. And they're advisable in cold-water systems. They are not needed with polyethylene (PE) pipe used outdoors and in wells. Nor are they necessary for nonpressurized applications. Simpler male adapters may be installed in these cases.

Special push-on, hand-tightened Genogrip adapters, the kind that work with copper pipe as well as plastic, are also effective transition fittings. These patented fittings are designed for PB water-supply systems, enabling adaptation between flexible PB and rigid pipes. Rubber O-rings which do the water-sealing chores, also allow for differential movement between copper and plastic.

Flare and compression fittings serve as transitions, too. They are best for small piping, such as that for humidifiers, water coolers, drinking fountains, and the like. In larger water-supply sizes they become costly. Flare and compression adapters, male or female, connect into the water-supply system. A saddle tee often has a reduced size compression fitting for copper or vinyl tubing, along with a shut-off valve. Don't expect a small saddle tee to supply water for a garden hose, though. If you want big flow, use a slip-coupling tee (for cold water) or build a no-threading, no-soldering CPVC tap-off such as that shown in

No-threading thermoplastic branch in threaded hot- or cold-water system is added by cutting and removing a length of pipe, replacing it with a pair of transition unions and a tee-containing length of CPVC pipe. Here rigid CPVC has been further adapted to flexible PB.

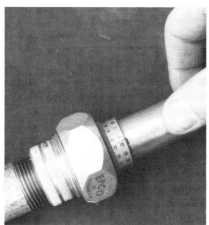

A dielectric union should be used when connecting two pipe systems made of different materials. This will prevent corrosive pipe electrolysis. The insulated jam nut joins the two systems across a non-conductive rubber-gasketed union.

No-soldering branch can be made from a copper hot- or cold-water main with a pair of push-on, hand-tightened Genogrip adapters in the copper-pipe size. Be sure they're right for copper pipe. The adapters solvent-weld to a CPVC tee.

the accompanying photos. Which one you use depends on whether your house has threaded pipes or sweat-soldered copper plumbing.

Garden-hose connectors. A wide variety of adapters and quick-couplers is available. Basic, of course, is the threaded hose bibb, but where this is not available or desired, male or female hose adapters may be used. In case you haven't tried it, a garden hose connects poorly to similar-sized ¾-inch threaded pipe, both because of the tapered pipe threads and the lack of a good gasket seal on the pipe end. Hose adapters that solve this problem are made to fit either ½-inch or ¾-inch pipes and fittings. Adapters for 1-inch hose are available, too.

From there, you can install quick-couplers for complete ease in moving hoses from one set to another. If your local plumbing-supplies dealer or hardware store doesn't have what you need, try a farm or irrigation-supplies dealer. Once every hose outlet, hose, sprinkler, and so on is fitted with a male or a female quick-connector, coupling and uncoupling take only a second. It's worthwhile where many changes are necessary.

Male and female adapters. The simplest of all, these cost little and work well where no bimetal or metal-vs.-plastic connection calls for something else. One end fits threaded pipes; the other fits sweat-soldered copper, nonpressurized plastic, rubber tube, or vinyl tube.

For use with polyethylene pipe, adapters threaded at one end and barbed at the other are available in either galvanized metal or plastic. The metal tends to corrode and the plastic may break under strain. Which to use depends on conditions. If the adapter is subject to vibration or strain, it's probably best to use galvanized. But if not, the plastic may outlast metal. You may have to shop around to find the type you want.

If you adapt to water-supply pipes correctly, the built-in, leak-free life of your home plumbing system will be kept intact. For that, it's well worth searching out the correct fitting.

If you encounter a problem not mentioned here, ask at your local home-care center for information or locate a plumbing-supply house and ask about the appropriate fittings to use—*Richard Day.*

plumb in an automatic washer

If you live in an older house without provision for an automatic washing machine, you can add it. The job couldn't be easier than with Genova PVC drain-waste-vent pipe and CPVC or PB hot/cold water supply tubing.

Select a washer location convenient to a vent stack or building drain where you can pipe the waste water from the washer. Give second consideration to nearness to a point where you can tap a hot and cold water supply. You must also consider what floor space is available. An upstairs location may prove step-saving and it has the advantage that water can drain away by gravity. On the other hand, a basement location often is selected because the space is there.

In a basement laundry, unless your sewer runs below the basement floor level, waste water must be pumped out. Not many public health codes will permit the use of a sump pump for this, even though that's the way it's often done. While an ordinary sump pump system will handle laundry wastes all right, bacterial action takes place in the sump pit, sometimes making for a smelly basement. Moreover, a periodic sump cleaning becomes a nasty job. The proper way to pump out laundry wastes from a basement is with a sealed sewage-ejector.

Connecting a Drain

Since an automatic washer's drain pipe is least flexible, make that run first. You may wish to add a laundry tub at the same time you plumb in the washer. It must be connected to a drain and vented the same as a kitchen sink. Use a 1½-inch PVC waste pipe and vent. A laundry tub permits the use of a suds-saving automatic washer. In any case, the washer empties into the tub.

The products listed here are by Genova, Inc. Comparable products by other manufacturers may be available, as well.

You can also drain a washer directly into what is called a standpipe, a 1½- or 2-inch PVC pipe reaching about 36 inches above the floor and located behind or beside the washer. A P-trap below the floor seals off the DWV system's gases from the house. With a standpipe, a suds-saving washer cannot be used effectively because there is nowhere to store the suds.

If the distance from the trap to the nearest vent is more than 2½ feet (1½-inch pipe) or 3½ feet (2-inch pipe), the trap must be revented, according to most plumbing codes.

The washer's drain pipe can tie into a vent stack using a tee. Tie into a horizontal drain by dropping in from above via a 45-degree elbow and a wye inserted in the horizontal pipe. One drawing shows the use of a Part No. 61231 saddle tee. If your vent stack is a 3-inch Genova in-Wall Schedule 30 one, this easy method may be employed. In any case, the fittings you use to make the connection depend on

what kind of pipes you are connecting to.

Water supply. A pair of ½-inch CPVC or PB hot and cold water pipes are run to the wall behind the washer. This is probably an ideal use for PB's flexibility. Either way, the system should end in a pair of threaded hose bibbs. Ahead of them you'll need two extra-large air chambers made of ¾-inch CPVC tubes 18 inches long and capped at the top. These oversized chambers prevent damage to the water supply system when fast-acting washer solenoid valves snap shut after a fill cycle. A water-hammer arrester will also do the job.

The drawings show the components of a CPVC and a PB system with two types of drain hookups. They are guides to the parts you will need for your hookup. A basement system would be most similar to the attic-type hookup, which is supplied with water from above—*Richard Day. Art courtesy of Genova, Inc.*

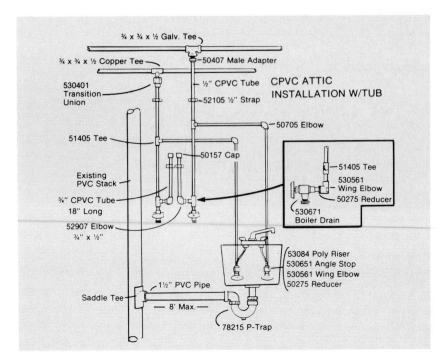

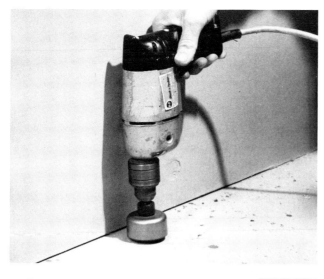

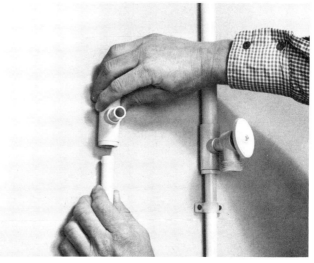

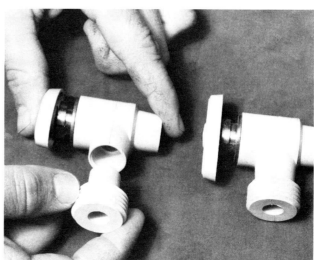

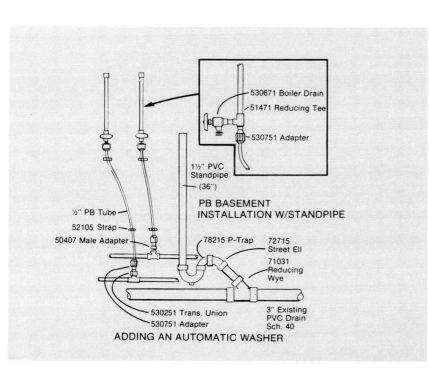

PB BASEMENT INSTALLATION W/STANDPIPE

530671 Boiler Drain
51471 Reducing Tee
530751 Adapter

1½" PVC Standpipe (36")

½" PB Tube
52105 Strap
50407 Male Adapter

78215 P-Trap
72715 Street Ell
71031 Reducing Wye

530251 Trans. Union
530751 Adapter

3" Existing PVC Drain Sch. 40

ADDING AN AUTOMATIC WASHER

1. The neatest, fastest way to make a hole in the floor for the washer's standpipe is with a hole saw. Chucked in an electric drill, this one cuts a 2" hole, clean as you please. (Other sizes are available.)

2. Drain hose from the washer slips inside the PVC standpipe and discharges waste washer water to the house drainage system. To keep system gases from escaping, a P-trap is installed below the floor.

3. Behind-the-washer supplies for hot and cold water are solvent welded of CPVC tube and fittings. A pair of $3/4'' \times 3/4'' \times 1/2''$ reducing tees with reducing bushings permit ½" supply tubes, ¾" air chambers.

4. Lacking Genova Part No. 530671 washer hose valves for washer supply hose attachment, you can make them from Part No. 530661 ½" angle stop valves and Part No. 53128 male hose adapters solvent welded in.

how the modern home plumbing system works

Where does the water come from; where does it go? Your home plumbing system is two separate systems, really—water supply and water disposal. Both are made up of several hundred feet of pipes and fittings that join them. Water in the water supply system is under pressure—some 50 pounds per square inch (psi). Thus, water supply pipes can be fairly small in diameter, yet still carry enough water. Water in the disposal, also called the drain-waste-vent (DWV) system, always flows by gravity. For this reason its pipes and fittings must be larger in diameter to carry the required flow without clogging or backing up. Both systems are designed to operate safely and quietly.

The systems, water supply and DWV, never are connected to each other. If contaminated water got into the drinking water, it could sicken or kill. Water from the water supply system flows into the drain-waste-vent system, never the other way around— *Richard Day. Art courtesy of Genova, Inc.*

This illustration shows a typical plumbing system for a two-story home with a basement. Adjustments for a one-story home, or a house without a basement, are easy to make. In any layout, it is critical to keep the water supply and DWV systems separate.

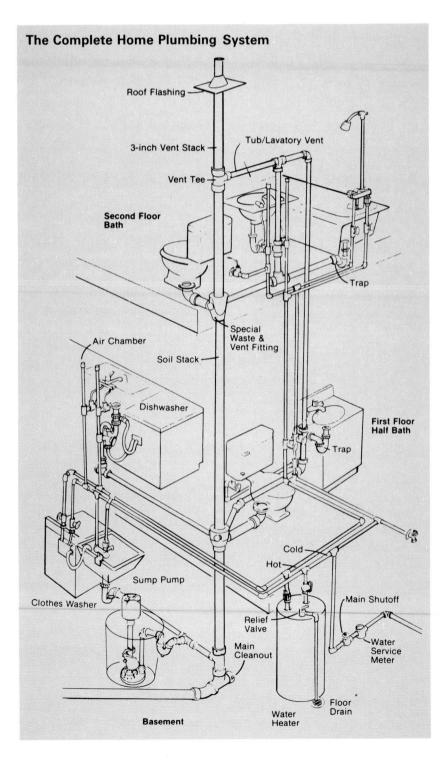

The Complete Home Plumbing System

Roof Flashing

3-inch Vent Stack

Vent Tee

Tub/Lavatory Vent

Second Floor Bath

Trap

Air Chamber

Special Waste & Vent Fitting

Soil Stack

Dishwasher

First Floor Half Bath

Trap

Cold

Hot

Clothes Washer

Sump Pump

Relief Valve

Main Shutoff

Main Cleanout

Water Service Meter

Basement

Water Heater

Floor Drain

how to wire a post lamp

I f you've been wanting an outdoor post lamp for both its practical and decorative attributes, want no more. You can install one, just by following the directions below.

First, decide where you'll locate your post lamp and its switch. The lamp can be placed almost anywhere, but not so close to the driveway or sidewalk that car doors may open into it or vehicles backing into the drive could inadvertently knock it over. Also, avoid property easements or installation over a septic tank or any other buried utility that may, in the future, need uncovering. The switch

would probably be most convenient at the entrance door nearest the post lamp and there is probably a switch box already there.

Before dismantling the switch box, turn off the power at the main panel box. Then take off the switch plate and carefully pull out the switch or switches. Leave them connected; at present, you just want to find out if there is a feed or source of electricity in the box.

To do this, look at the back of each switch: If there are two wires connected to a switch, it is a single-pole (S/P) switch. If there are three wire

connections, it is a three-way switch. If the box contains only one switch and there are four wires connected to it, close it up; another means of switching will be needed.

S/P switch

If there is an S/P switch in the box with two black wires connected to it, and there are two or more white or "neutral" wires spliced together in the back of the box, you have a feed. To determine which black wire is HOT, turn the switch *OFF*, uncap the white wires but leave them twisted together. Make sure the white and the black are

Floodlight assembly is installed as easily as post lamp. Use rework box in eave, push wire out from attic recess.

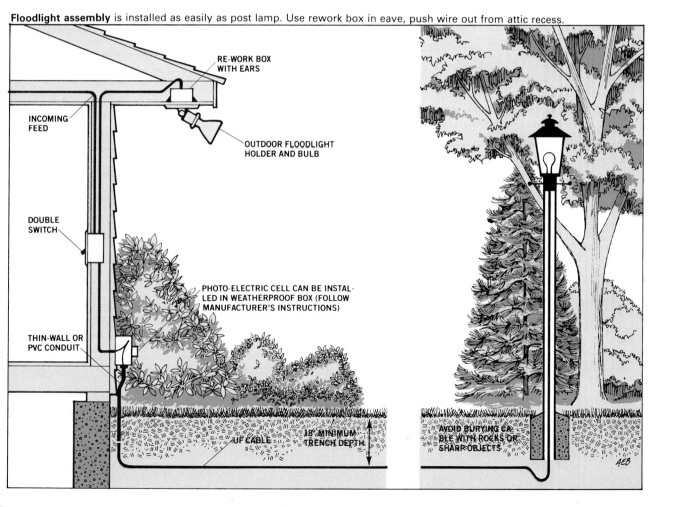

RE-WORK BOX WITH EARS

OUTDOOR FLOODLIGHT HOLDER AND BULB

INCOMING FEED

DOUBLE SWITCH

PHOTO-ELECTRIC CELL CAN BE INSTAL-LED IN WEATHERPROOF BOX (FOLLOW MANUFACTURER'S INSTRUCTIONS)

THIN-WALL OR PVC CONDUIT

UF CABLE   18" MINIMUM TRENCH DEPTH

AVOID BURYING CA-BLE WITH ROCKS OR SHARP OBJECTS

AEB

not touching and turn the power back on. Using your voltage tester, touch one probe to the white wires, and one to a terminal on the switch. Only the HOT terminal will light up the tester. Tag that wire for later reference.

Three-way switch

If there is only a three-way switch in the box, and there are two or more white wires spliced together in the back, follow the same procedure as above. This time, however, if a feed is present, the voltage tester will light up in *both* switch positions when touched between the white wires and the common terminal of the switch. If the "common" wire is HOT, tag it for later reference.

In the unlikely event there is no feed in your entrance-door switch box, and there is no other convenient place from which to switch a post lamp, you will have to use a cut-in or rework box, and add a new switch to the wall. It will then be necessary to pull a cable from a box that does have a feed—like a receptacle or another switch box—to the new box. This will require fishing the cable through the voids within the walls. You will probably need to drill holes in the basement or attic to get to wall interiors.

Buying material

After determining the location for your switch and post lamp, purchase the materials for the job. You will be using "Romex" cable or nonmetallic sheathed cable, Type N.M. for any indoor wiring. The underground stretch will have to be Type U.F., suitable for direct burial. To determine the size to buy, inspect the fuse or circuit breaker that controls the circuit you will be utilizing. If it is a 20 amp circuit, buy #12/2 with ground; for a 15 amp circuit, buy #14/2 with ground.

You will also need a weatherproof (W/P) box, preferably with side mounting ears and a W/P blank cover; a Romex connector to fit the ½-inch hole in the back of the box; about six wire nuts; and, for use as a sleeve, a short piece of conduit and a ½-inch W/P conduit connector.

If you're adding a separate switch box, buy a regular S/P switch and switch plate. If you are going to utilize an existing switch box, buy a stack switch. In such case you will need a switch plate to accommodate the new configuration of switches installed.

Starting the job

Again, shut off the power to the switch box that you will be working with.

Remove all the switches in it to allow yourself enough room to work, but take care to mark which wires go where so you'll be able to replace them properly. Clear the bottom of the box by pushing aside the remaining wires, and knock out one of the prepunched holes in the bottom (this is where the post lamp wire will enter).

On the outside of the wall directly in line with the switch, but closer to the ground, drill a hole through to the interior. Make the hole about 1½ inches in diameter (use a hammer and chisel if necessary). The main idea is to be able to fish a wire through the wall, and still be able to cover up the hole with the W/P box. In a frame house, there will be a clear channel between the interior switch box and the exterior hole, with the exception of the insulation. In a masonry house, there will be a hollow core inside the cement blocks; it will run from the interior switch box to the exterior hole, if the two have been properly aligned, and no insulation will interfere.

Getting wire through wall

The challenge comes in getting the wire through the cavity in the wall, from the outside to the inside. In the case of the frame house, a stiff wire or

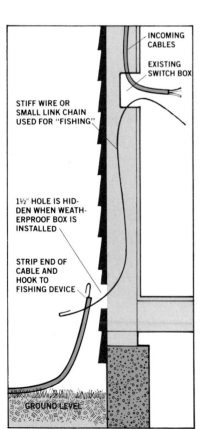
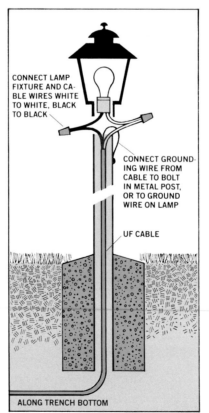
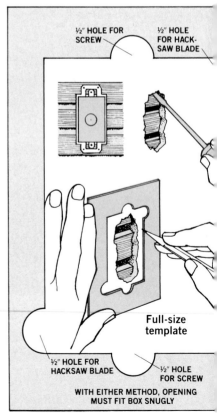

How cable is fished through wall is shown left; about a foot of cable should hang out either end. Above center: lamp wiring. Right: Two ways to install rework box. Next page: To make box with ears (No. 1) snug, simply tighten screws. Box without ears (No. 2) is retained with "Hold it" clips; they slide in next to box, tabs are bent inside. Next page, right: Typical stack switch connection

electrician's fish tape can be pushed through the knock-out hole in the switch box and forced down through the insulation to the hole on the outside of the wall. It will then be necessary to use a shorter piece of wire, and insert it in the outside hole, hook the first piece of wire and bring it to the outside, where the electric cable can then be attached and drawn up through the wall and into the switch box. In a masonry house, the same method may be tried, or a small link chain can be dropped through the knock-out hole in the switch box to the exterior hole and retrieved in the same manner as above. Attach the cable and carefully pull it up to the switch box.

Once the switch wire for the post light is inside and there is a good length hanging out of the switch box, you can cut it off on the outside of the wall, leaving about a foot exposed. Insert a Romex connector in the back of the W/P box and slide it over the exposed wire. Secure it to the wall with suitable screws.

Install a ½-inch W/P conduit connector into the threaded hole on the bottom of the W/P box and snug it up. Place the U.F. cable into a 24-inch deep trench from the W/P box to the location of the post lamp, making sure

to keep it free of kinks or sharp bends and objects. Leave enough cable at each end to make your connections. Slide a short piece of conduit over the cable to cover it from the W/P box to a point a few inches below the finish grade of the soil. Secure the conduit in the connector at the bottom of the box, and attach it to the wall using a conduit strap. Leave about a foot hanging out of the box. Cover up the cable to within a foot of the post lamp location. Slide the post over the cable, leaving about a foot hanging out of the top.

The post will probably have to be buried about 2 feet into the ground (follow the manufacturer's suggestions). Take care not to set the sharp edge of the post directly on the wire when filling in the hole with soil. Plumb the post with your level and press the soil down firmly around it.

Wire connections

When splicing household wires, simply strip the insulation back about ¾ of an inch; twist the bare ends together; snip off the very end of the twist, leaving a nice clean spiral; twist on a wire nut, and you're in business. Be sure the wire nut covers the entire bare portion of the wire.

Connecting post head

In connecting the post head to the post, connect white to white, black to black, and ground wire to ground wire. The same applies for the junction in the W/P box. As for the connection in the switch box, the white wire will splice together with the rest of the white wires. The black wire will connect to one pole on the switch, and the black wire that feeds the box will connect to the other pole on the switch. If you're using a stack switch, the feed wire connects to the side of the switch marked "Line"; the black wire from the post light connects to one of the terminals on the opposite side of the switch; and the black wire that was on the previous switch connects to the terminal right next to the post light terminal. Before you close the box, turn the power back on and carefully try each switch to see that it functions properly.

Once you have the switches working properly, turn off the power, secure the switches in the box, replace the switch cover, and turn the power back on. Enjoy your new post lamp and delight in the fact that you have just saved between $80 and $200—*Lloyd Lemons, Jr.*

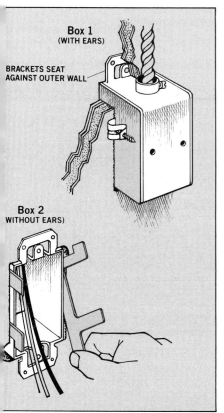

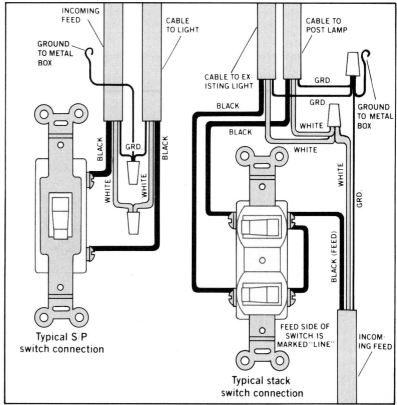

is shown at bottom; using stack switch, it's possible to have two switches occupy same space as one switch. Stack switches are available S/P over S/P or any other combination needed. Drawing at left shows typical S/P switch connection. With switch in OFF position, touch voltage tester probes from uncapped white wires to black wire. Only feed will light up tester.

how to wire a home workshop

If your workshop is a maze of extension cords and you're always blowing fuses or tripping breakers, you're flirting with disaster. Don't chance it. Wire that workshop to handle the load you're likely to impose on it, and enjoy the safety, convenience, and peace of mind it will bring.

Table saws, radial-arm saws, large drill presses, and other power tools with a ½-hp rating or more should have an individual circuit. The surge of power in the line the moment the motor is started up requires it. So does underload power consumption—a table saw, for example, may draw two or three times as much power when a board is being cut than when idling.

Many of these motors can be operated on either 120 or 240 volts. Given the option, utilize the 240-volt operation—it's better for the motor in the long run. To convert a motor from one voltage to the other, remove the small end plate and arrange the wires on the terminal board inside to correspond with the wiring diagram or manufacturer's instructions for the voltage desired. A 240-volt motor must have a 240-volt receptacle and plug. This prevents plugging a 120-volt tool into a high-voltage outlet.

If you have more than one heavy-duty power tool, one circuit can handle all of them, *if* they all operate on the same voltage and *if* you never run more than one tool at a time. The instruction manual that came with the power tool will give you the electrical data needed to wire for it adequately.

Other circuits

A separate 120-volt circuit will be needed to operate any other small tools you use. Install receptacles in strategic locations to operate tools like grinders, hand drills, sanders, or extra drop lights for close work. This circuit should be run with #12 copper wire and fused with a 20-amp fuse or circuit breaker. (For brevity, any fuse assembly or circuit breaker will hereafter be referred to as an "overcurrent device.")

A 15-amp lighting circuit may be needed if you plan to install a lot of lights, or if you plan to use many high-wattage bulbs. In the average workshop, however, the lighting needs can be supplied by an existing circuit that supplies some other part of the house. Remember, the 20-amp circuit mentioned above can also be used for extra lighting. A reflector flood lamp with a clamp-on assembly works well for lighting up specific work areas.

The type of general illumination used is a matter of preference. Fluorescent fixtures produce an even, diffused

Drawing below shows the wiring for a typical home workshop. Note special provision for tools operating on 240 volts.

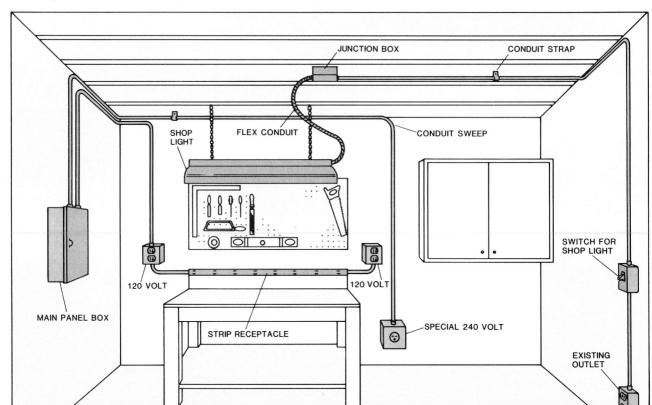

light that generally works out well. But if you're one of those who finds the stroboscopic effect irritating or that it tends to make moving tools appear stopped, incandescent lighting is your choice. Incandescent light glares more than fluorescent, making certain kinds of work hard to focus on, and it's slightly more expensive to operate, requiring more fixtures to get ample light.

Materials

The workshop circuits will be run in type NM (nonmetallic) sheathed cable, commonly called Romex. In the event that any cable needs to be buried in the earth, type UF or a type suitable for direct burial will need to be used. When purchasing cable for a specific power tool, be sure to buy the correct wire gauge (see chart, next page). Thin-wall aluminum conduit (½ inch) will be needed to encase wires running on the surface of a wall or flat finished ceiling.

Also needed: metal outlet boxes with covers; conduit connectors and conduit straps for holding conduit snugly in place; couplings for connecting two lengths of conduit; and receptacles and overcurrent devices rated at the proper voltage and amperage for the wire used (see chart).

Running circuits

Running the circuits for a workshop is nothing more than running the cable from the circuit or panel box to the location of the power tools. Ca-

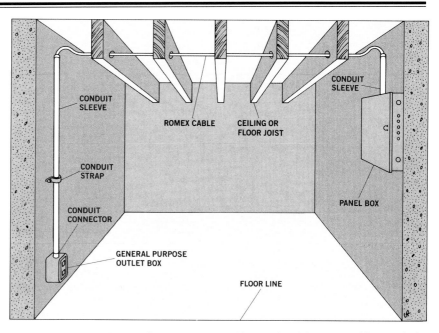

If your plans are to finish off the ceiling on which you're doing your wiring work, be careful not to drill holes too close to the edge of the beam. That way, you'll avoid having the cable penetrated by a nail when the ceiling work is done.

This main circuit panel, below, shows a 240-volt connection for large motors and a 120-volt connection for small motors.

Below is a neat mini-panel. If a panel has a main circuit breaker like this one, the two hot leads connect to the breaker. If there's no breaker, the hot leads connect directly to the buss bar lugs.

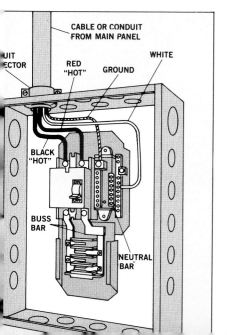

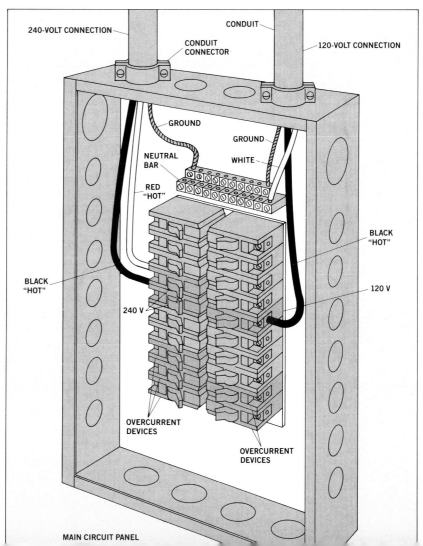

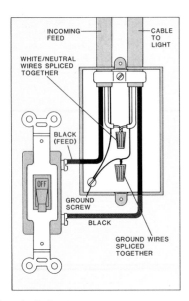

Receptacle configurations for various equipment

| 15 amp. 120 v. Standard outlet. | 15 amp. 250 v. Power saws, drill presses, etc. | 20 amp. 250 v. Power saws, sanders, etc. | 30 amp. 250 v. Sometimes used for welders. | 50 amp. 250 v. Sometimes used for welders. |

A typical single-pole switch connection. Note: All metal boxes must be grounded.

ble consisting of two insulated conductors and one ground conductor is suitable for both the 240-volt circuits and the 120-volt circuits.

In basement installations where there are overhead wood beams, holes should be drilled through the beams. The cable can then be drawn through the holes to the receptacle location. Sleeve the cable running down the wall in conduit. Connect the conduit to an outlet box, and install the receptacle and cover. (Use bushing on conduit sleeve to protect cable.)

Garage installations may be similar, or if an attic is available, the cables can be run up the wall from the panel, through the attic, and then down the wall to the location of the receptacles. Again, sleeve any cable running on the surface of the walls.

If your workshop is located in a place that has no attic access, and does have a finished ceiling, the circuit can be run entirely in thin-wall conduit. Run it up the wall from the panel box, across the ceiling, and down the wall to the location of the receptacle. Use a conduit bender to get around corners, or purchase ready-made Sweep Ell's. Strap the conduit to the ceiling and wall surfaces as necessary to provide for a firm installation.

In the latter case, the use of Romex

isn't necessary. The completed conduit run serves as the ground connection, and two individual conductors (Type TW) can be drawn through the conduit to provide the necessary voltage.

After the cable or conduit assembly has been run, the receptacles can be connected by attaching the white wire to the white terminals, the black wire to the dark terminal, and the ground wire to the green terminal.

Panel box

The connection for the 120-volt circuit requires a single pole (S/P) overcurrent device; the connection for the 240-volt circuit, a double pole (D/P) overcurrent device. Before making the connection, shut down the main switch that controls the entire house. All lights will go out, so have a flashlight ready. Work cautiously, because the main lead-in wires may still be energized.

Secure the overcurrent devices in place. On the 120-volt circuit, the ground wire connects to the multiple terminal where the other ground wires are; the white wire connects to the multiple terminal where the other white wires are and the black wire, to the new overcurrent device. On the 240-volt circuit, the ground wire connects to the ground bar; the red and black wires connect to the two terminals on the new (D/P) overcurrent device.

Turn the power back on and you should be in business. Before plugging in any power tools, check the receptacles with a voltage tester.

If an extra 15-amp circuit is needed for lighting, use the same method of connection as above for 120-volt operation. The only difference is the HOT cable, coming from the panel, should feed a switch first and then run to the light.

When taking a feed off of another source in the house, the connection is white to white, black to black, and ground to ground; just be sure you have a continuous HOT, and not something that is controlled by another switch.

Adding a subpanel

If your workshop is a great distance from the main panel box, it might be best to install a subpanel, or minipanel box directly in the workshop. This is a small circuit box of perhaps 30- to 50-amp capacity, and is wired from the main panel box by a single cable with four conductors (three insulated and one ground) large enough to handle the entire workshop load (see chart). The workshop circuits could then be wired from the subpanel, saving on wire, conduit, and voltage drop.

In the main panel box, the ground wire and the white wire connect to the ground terminal and the white terminal respectively. The black wire and the red wire connect to the overcurrent device, supplying the subpanel with 240 volts. If there are no spaces left in the main panel box to install another circuit breaker, the subpanel may have to be fed from the main lugs supplying the entire house. That is a job for an electrician. The subpanel connection is white to white, ground to ground, black wire to buss bar, and red to opposite buss bar.

Once the subpanel is wired, the individual workshop circuits can be wired from it. If there is any doubt about working inside the main panel box, wire everything up to the point of the main connection, and leave the final connection to a pro. You will have already saved a great deal of money—*Lloyd Lemons, Jr.*

Right wire for the tool

240 volt		120 volt	
Motor size	Wire size	Motor size	Wire size
½ hp—370 watt	#14 cu.*	¼ hp—180 watt	#14 cu.
¾ hp—550 watt	#14 cu.	⅓ hp—240 watt	#14 cu.
1 hp—746 watt	#14 cu.	½ hp—370 watt	#12 cu.
		¾ hp—550 watt	#12 cu.
		1 hp—746 watt	#12 cu.**

* cu. is the abbreviation for copper
** A 1 hp—120 volt motor with a wire run over 75 feet should utilize #10 cu. wire.

Right wire for the circuit

Romex cable size copper conductor	Current capacity
#14 AWG*	15 amps
#12 AWG	20 amps
#10 AWG	30 amps
#8 AWG	40 amps
#6 AWG	55 amps

*American Wire Gauge

mounting wall and ceiling fixtures

You will seldom encounter complications in mounting wall or ceiling fixtures as most of them are designed to fit standard outlet boxes. In general, both wall and ceiling fixtures may be mounted either by means of a threaded "fixture stud" attached to the center of the box, or by a mounting strap with boxes that lack the stud. The stud is favored for heavier fixtures.

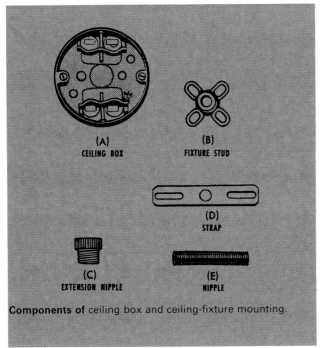

Components of ceiling box and ceiling-fixture mounting.

(A) CEILING BOX

(B) FIXTURE STUD

(C) EXTENSION NIPPLE

(D) STRAP

(E) NIPPLE

Fixtures in New Work. In new work (home construction) the boxes are mounted in the framing before the walls and ceilings are covered. Standard metal hangers are then used to secure the boxes to studding or joists. A wide variety of these hangers is available at hardware and electrical supply dealers. Some are designed to hold the box firmly to a single stud; others are adjustable to permit spacing the box at any desired distance between studs or joists. As the house framing is exposed, installation of the boxes is very simple.

Fixtures in Old Work. In old work a number of different methods and devices are used to simplify installation. Switch and outlet boxes, for example, can be mounted without fastening to the wall framing at all. The plaster or wallboard is used as support. One type of box used in this way is fitted with a folding clamp on each side. It is inserted in the hole cut to fit it and pushed in so that the front brackets seat firmly against the outside of the wall.

The side clamps, flat against the box, slide into the hole easily. To lock the box in place, the screws that open the clamps are turned in, spreading the clamps and drawing them snug against the inner surface of the wall.

Another device that can be used on standard boxes is made of thin sheet metal and sold under such trade names as "Hold-It." In form it might be compared to a T with two vertical legs instead of one. The box is pushed into the hole made for it and brought up snug against the outer wall surface (stopped there by the brackets or ears at the ends). Then the sheet-metal fasteners are slipped in on each side of the box, tipped at an angle with the cross of the T inside the wall. Next, they are set straight (so the T cross is vertical inside the wall if the box is set vertically) and pulled outward by the legs until the cross member is seated firmly against the inner surface of the wall. Then the protruding legs are bent over the edges of the box to lock it in place. From there on the box is handled in the usual manner.

Ceiling Boxes. To mount a ceiling box an "old-work hanger" is used. This is simply a metal bar or heavy strap with a sliding stud on it. As a first step, cut a hole in the ceiling to match the size and shape of the box to be installed. The cable may then be snaked through the hole and connected to the box. (The box must be a type with a knockout or hole for stud-mounting.) Next, slip the bar or strap of the hanger up through the hole and slide the stud so that half the hanger extends to each side of the hole.

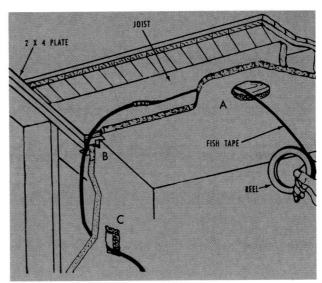

To lead new wiring from ceiling (A) to wall (C), it is necessary to remove small section of plaster at B where wall and ceiling meet so 2-by-4 plate can be notched to pass cable. After cable has been led through, plaster can be patched to conceal hole.

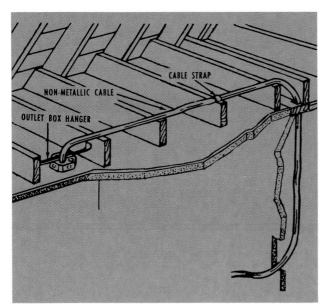

NON-METALLIC CABLE

CABLE STRAP

OUTLET BOX HANGER

If attic is unfinished, wall-to-ceiling wiring is easier. Hole can be bored from attic into wall; outlet box and hanger are easily mounted from above. Use plywood panel for working platform in unfloored attic. Nonmetallic cable is shown here, but BX or conduit may be used, depending on local requirements.

The stud should be centered in the hole. Then push the box up into the hole so that the stud extends downward through the stud hole in the center of it, and turn the nut loosely onto the stud. Make sure the cable is not cramped against the inner ceiling surface, then tighten the stud, and the job's done. The bar should run crosswise of laths in plaster ceilings.

If the ceiling box is to be mounted in a ceiling with an unfinished attic above it the job can often be done simply by using a new-work hanger. Cut the hole in the ceiling first, then mount the hanger to hold the box in the hole, working from above in the unfinished attic. A few boards or half a sheet of plywood can provide a working platform across the ceiling joists if there is no flooring in the attic.

Mounting a New Fixture in an Old Box. If you are simply mounting a new fixture on an old box, the work is much simpler. An examination of the existing fixture will quickly tell you whether it is mounted with screws or a stud. If you can arrange to have a helper in removing or mounting fixtures, the job will be easier and faster. If not, have some heavy but soft iron wire on hand, like that used in coat hangers. This can be bent to form a double-ended hook to hold the fixture while you disconnect the wiring.

All such work, of course, must be done with the current definitely off. You can turn it off at the main switch or unscrew the fuse that supplies that particular circuit—if shutting off power throughout the house would involve serious inconvenience. But do not merely shut off the wall switch supplying the fixture. There is too much danger of someone inadvertantly turning it on again while you're working on the wiring.

Form one end of the wire hook before you remove the stud nut or screws holding the fixture in place. If you have a helper, of course, he can hold the fixture while you disconnect it, eliminating the need for the hook. Once the fixture nut or screws have been removed, lower the fixture carefully to provide room to disconnect the wiring. Almost always you will find a hole or clamp in the box over which the hook can be anchored. Do not anchor it over the wires.

The lower end can be slipped through the stud hole or the screw holes of the fixture canopy and bent upward for a firm hold. This prevents the fixture from slipping or dangling in such a way as to place a strain on the wires before you can disconnect them.

If the wires are connected with solderless connectors, the job is fast and easy. If the wires are spliced, soldered, and taped, clip them close to the splice on the fixture side of the splice, leaving just enough fixture wire to grip with pliers. With the fixture disconnected and out of the way, you can use a soldering iron to melt the solder on the splice while you pull off the remaining fixture wire with pliers. As the fixture wire is usually the flexible multi-strand type, the solid wire from the box may have little or no distortion in the bared end-portion, making it usable again without clipping. Try to save as much of its length as possible for ease of work when you resplice.

Wiring the Fixture. Merely connect the white wire to the white, black to black, as in regular outlet wiring. In connecting the new fixture use solderless connectors if you want to speed the job and simplify any future changes.

Because of the wide difference in fixture design, you may need a different length nipple for the new one if the mounting is by means of stud and nipple. Often, however, you will find that the "hickey" which joins the nipple to the fixture stud in the box will provide enough adjustment.

Fixture Repairs. If a fixture fails to light when switched on, the trouble may be either in the fixture or the switch. Often a defective switch can be spotted by the sound it makes. The click (if it's a snap switch) may sound dead. If the switch controls more than one fixture, however, and the others light, the trouble is in the individual fixture. If in doubt, try replacing the switch first. It's an easier job than removing a fixture that may not be in need of repair.

The commonest causes of fixture troubles are in switches mounted on the fixtures themselves, and in the bulb sockets. Naturally, if one or more bulbs fail to light in a multi-bulb unit, check the bulbs first, trying them in another lamp or fixture. Next, *with current off* at the fuse or main switch, check the center contact at the base of the socket, using a flashlight. If the contact is blackened, scrape it clean with a sharp-tipped screwdriver. Then try a new bulb in it. Often corrosion at this point is the cause of the trouble. With current on again, the bulb should light if the contact was at fault.

If the bulb still does not light, the trouble is either a broken wire or a loose connection at the socket terminal screws, or possibly a defect in the socket itself. With current off, you can remove the socket from its base (if standard) by pressing it at the point indicated by the word "press" stamped on the shell of many popular brands. If the terminals are tight, disconnect them and substitute another socket as a test.

With current on, if a bulb lights in this socket you have located the trouble and can then buy a new socket to match the fixture, if the test socket was borrowed from a lamp or from the workshop gadget box. If the test socket bulb does not light, the trouble is in the fixture's wiring. (Neon-glow test lights are sometimes used to check the various parts of fixture wiring, but socket substitution is safer as no live terminals are exposed when the current is on.)

If wiring must be replaced, particularly through curved ornamental tubing (as in many chandeliers) it is best done by firmly twisting the bared ends of the new wiring to those of the old, so the old wiring pulls the new wiring through. As you pull the old wiring out of one end of the tube, you pull the new wiring in the other end, and finally all the way through.

Fixture Mounting

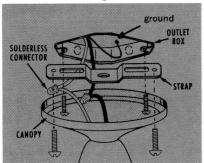

If there is no stud in box, strap is fastened to threaded ears, and fixture is then fastened to strap.

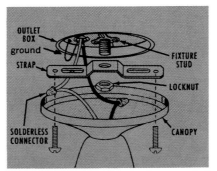

If box has stud, strap may be mounted with threaded nipple and locknut. Fixture is mounted on strap in usual way.

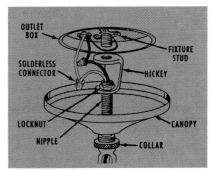

Ceiling drop fixtures are usually mounted from stud, using two nipples joined by "hickey." Both hickey and collar can be adjusted to draw fixture canopy snugly against ceiling.

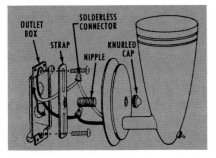

Wall fixture is attached to rectangular box by means of strap and nipple.

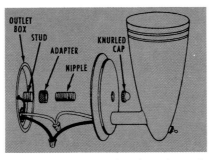

Outlet box with central stud requires only adapter and nipple to attach wall fixture.

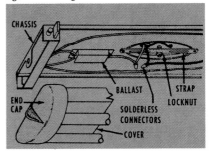

Fluorescent fixture can be ceiling-mounted with stud, nipple, and strap.

Soldering Electrical Work. If a splice must be soldered or heated with a soldering iron to separate it, you can use an old-style soldering iron heated by a blow torch. Naturally, the current to the wiring being repaired must be off. Certain types of electric soldering irons which have no electrical contact between current supply and heated tip can be used with an extension cord to another circuit in the house that has not been shut off. Before doing any electric soldering by this method, however, *be sure* to check with the manufacturer of the soldering iron as to its safety in this type of use. The reason: when a fuse is unscrewed to shut off current to a house circuit only the hot wire (black) is "broken." The white ground wire is still connected to the power source. Any contact between the white wire of the fuse-out circuit and the black (hot) wire of any other circuit would cause a direct short.

Facts About Lighting

For general overall lighting in a room, the ceiling fixture can provide shadowless light in working areas such as kitchen or workshop. This is achieved by using several fixtures spaced apart to flood a given area with light from a variety of angles. The principle is simple: a shadow cast by light coming from one direction is illuminated by light coming from the opposite direction. The effect is especially easy to achieve with several large fluorescent fixtures. Other fixture types with various additional features such as dimmer switches offer a light range from a mere candle glow to full illumination. Others have a three-way switch, enabling you to have focal downlight, candlelight, or a combination of both. Some models have a concealed spotlight to dramatize a centerpiece on a formal dining table. With all these features to choose from, providing good lighting is easier than ever.

Since the ceilings in today's homes are considerably lower than those in older ones, many people think that chandeliers are out of the question, except perhaps over a dining table where there would be no danger of bumping your head. Such is not the case. The new fixtures have been designed with this in mind, and modified versions that still retain traditional design (where it is desired) are available. Some new designs are conceived so that they fit snugly against the ceiling, and proper proportions in the scaled-to-fit models make their use practical in the smallest homes.

Other types are mounted on ceiling tracks. This allows you to have the overhead light at more than one location, according to your needs.

The Science of Lighting. Good lighting does not mean just enough light. It means also control of glare, which can make reading, sewing or other tasks difficult, and irritate the eyes. Proper distribution of the illumination is also important. Unshaped lamps do not produce good lighting by any means. Use lamp bulbs of ample wattage with a proper shade to focus the light without allowing direct light to assail your eyes.

When your lighting, by experimenting with various lamp wattages and shades, seems comfortable, and your eyes do not tire after extended use with the lamp, take a reading with a photo light meter, and make a note of that reading. Make the reading on a piece of ordinary gray cardboard. Then when you want to duplicate your successful formula in another part of the house, all you have to do is try different bulbs until the meter reading is the same as before. The reason for using the gray cardboard is that different colors on walls and ceilings have different reflective factors, but the neutral gray assures you of getting the same effect each time. This is an especially good procedure for desk and reading lamps, but is not as important in over-all illumination.—*By George Daniels.*

pour yourself a parking pad

A driveway is a little like a clothes closet—no matter how big it is, there's never enough room. Solution: for your shirts, add another shelf; for your car, try a parking pad. It's an additional parking spot for company or your own cars, and it's also a perfect work area.

The parking pad I constructed is 18 feet square and six inches thick. I found that I could save a considerable amount of money by doing the preparation myself, as shown in the accompanying photos (next page).

On a project this size, however, it is best to buy premixed concrete from the pros. They'll know the right mix and aggregate size for the compressive strength you'll need—at least 3,500 psi.

On the finished pad (below) I used crusher-run gravel as fill between the drive and slab. The fence is not just a finishing touch—it's also a necessary marker during the snow season—*By Ray Hill.*

Preparation is as important as using the right concrete. Begin by leveling ground (1) with a shovel and rake. Then tamp soil with tamper. Spread two to three inches of crusher-run gravel (2) and tamp down again. (Moisten the earth slightly before tamping; it helps compact the gravel and earth more solidly.) After ground is prepared, set up 2 × 6 form boards (3). Stakes hold boards in place. Author used a mason's line to place the first form board in position. The other three boards were positioned using a square and level. Reinforcing wire (4) is cut with bolt cutters and should cover entire pad area. Weight the wire down with heavy rocks as shown. Wear gloves to protect your hands. Just before concrete is poured, wet the area thoroughly (5). Start pouring concrete in one corner (6) and spread it evenly. Routinely raise the reinforcing wire up as you work (7)—the weight of the concrete tends to push it against the ground. The idea, of course, is to keep the wire centered within the pad for strength. After concrete is poured, use a bull float to level it (8). Push the float forward, with the leading edge raised slightly, as is being done here. Then pull it back toward you, again with the leading edge raised. Repeat the passes with the bull float until the pad is smooth. No other floating is necessary. Before concrete hardens, use a trowel to cut the concrete away from the form boards (inset). Then round off the sharp edges with an edging trowel. Finally, spray curing compound over the still-damp concrete, and let dry.

index